THE FOOTBALL GROUNDS OF GREAT BRITAIN

SIMON INGLIS

CollinsWillow
An Imprint of HarperCollins*Publishers*

THE AUTHOR

Simon Inglis is a freelance writer and Aston Villa supporter. Born in Birmingham near St Andrew's, he graduated from University College London before teaching history at a school near Brisbane Road, East London. After six months in Latin America he lived near Maine Road, Manchester and concentrated on journalism, including reporting football for *The Guardian*. His first book, *The Usborne Guide to Soccer*, is in its third edition and in 1983 he wrote *The Football Grounds of England and Wales*. He followed this with *Soccer in the Dock*, a history of British football scandals 1900–1965, and in 1988 wrote *League Football and the Men Who Made It*, the official centenary history of the Football League.

The events following the Bradford fire in 1985 confirmed Simon Inglis as the country's leading expert on football grounds and led to the publication of this second edition. In researching the subject he has now travelled some 9000 miles and visited 150 grounds all over Britain.

In 1987 he broadened his horizons by embarking upon a 51,000-mile journey around Europe, resulting in the publication of *The Football Grounds of Europe* in 1990.

He lives near Hendon FC in North West London and is married to TV presenter Jackie Spreckley.

COVER ACKNOWLEDGEMENTS

Front Everton *Allsport/Dave Cannon*; Aberdeen *Taylor Industrial Photography*; Aston Villa *Colorsport*; Plymouth Argyle *Sporting Pictures(UK)Ltd*; Chelsea *Sporting Pictures(UK)Ltd.*

Back Ground alterations at Aston Villa *c.* 1910 *Colorsport*

First published by Willow Books

First published in hardback in 1983
Reprinted 1984 (twice)
First published in paperback in 1985
This second edition published in 1987
Reprinted 1987, 1988 (twice), 1990, 1991
Last reprinted in 1993 by
CollinsWillow
an imprint of HarperCollins*Publishers*
London
© Simon Inglis 1987
All rights reserved

A CIP catalogue record for this book
is available from the British Library

ISBN 0 00 218249 1

Set in Linotron Century by Rowland Phototypesetting Ltd,
Bury St Edmunds, Suffolk
Printed and bound in Great Britain by Butler & Tanner Ltd,
Frome, Somerset

CONTENTS

INTRODUCTION

From being the preserve of a few, travel happy enthusiasts who might have been regarded as slightly eccentric, the subject of football grounds was elevated to that of a national issue in 1985.

Three events in one month, at Bradford, Birmingham and Brussels changed everyone's perception. For a few traumatic weeks a confused and worried public became familiar with such previously obscure matters as the Safety of Sports Grounds Act, the Green Code, perimeter fencing and pre-match drinks in executive boxes.

This second edition is the result of a whole series of changes at British football grounds since 1983. Of course the situation is ever-changing (see Postscript), but 1985 brought great change, not merely to the fabric of grounds but to our whole thinking about their form and purpose.

Observers like myself who spoke fondly of that quaint old stand at Bradford were suddenly shaken out of their nostalgic reveries. Suddenly those Liverpool fans on the Kop were not so amusing or sportsmanlike as we had wanted to believe they were.

Football grounds were being scrutinized from all sides. By government ministers who preferred rugby or opera. By investigative journalists who were often astonished by the neglect and mismanagement they encountered. And by the fans themselves, many of whom decided enough was enough. But a significant minority were determined that football was worth defending.

The inclusion in this edition of every Scottish League venue will, I hope, be welcomed. Scotland is rich in fascinating grounds, some of them basic by English standards but, on the whole, well kept, bursting with character, and above all wonderfully hospitable.

Every other entry has been checked, updated and where necessary, corrected. The historical background on Ipswich, Coventry and Huddersfield has been improved, largely thanks to new club histories. Countless other minor details and additions have been suggested by readers, and I have been happy to make appropriate changes.

Hardly any ground in Britain has not been touched by the events of 1985. Some dear old stands have gone – at Hartlepool, Doncaster and Bury. Some interesting new stands have gone up, at Brentford, Watford and Old Trafford. Manchester United's new soccer museum is a long-awaited pleasure.

For the first edition I was able to poke and pick at so many squalid parts of football grounds around England and Wales. I hope my critical faculties have survived, but most clubs really have made tremendous efforts since then. I was hard on Reading, Chester and Crewe, and indefensibly soft on Bradford, whose Main Stand I described as being 'worthy of preservation'.

So many different approaches, so many different shapes and sizes. No wonder that so many football fans tremble with anticipation when a new ground appears on the horizon. That feeling of excitement as one approaches a ground for the first time, walking calmly at first, but quickening as the turnstiles beckon.

And once up those stairs or through that corridor, there is always that wonderful elation at seeing the pitch, the stands and the faces spread out before one's eyes.

The experience of visiting a football ground is inseparable from the game itself. Every ground provides a different atmosphere which colours one's entire appreciation of a match.

Even when deprived of a game, the football grounds enthusiast will strain for a glimpse of floodlights from the window of his car or railway carriage. A glimpse of a pitch or a stand is even more tantalizing.

I cannot explain this mania. I can, I am afraid, only fuel it with this second edition.

It is a celebration of the variety of British football grounds. Thousands attend them every week and despite falling gates, football grounds are still better used than many other local places of entertainment, or even worship.

And though architectural books might be full of the dullest churches and faceless office blocks, none of them consider football grounds. Even Nikolaus Pevsner, author of the many-volumed *Buildings of England*, the most comprehensive survey of British architecture ever accomplished, mentions only two grounds in passing – Wembley and Hillsborough.

He describes a perambulation of Everton, its parks, churches and public buildings, but ignores the solid mass of Goodison. Similarly in Highbury, there is no indication that Pevsner was even aware of Arsenal's existence, despite the 1930's grandeur of the façade.

I do not pretend that all our grounds have architectural merit. Only a few have features worthy of preservation – the frontages at Arsenal, Ibrox and Villa Park for example. But to ignore them completely is surely a slight to the millions who have passed through their doors.

I hope this revised appreciation will redress the balance.

Simon Inglis
August 1987

1993 POSTSCRIPT

So rapid has been the pace of change during the five years since this edition was published in 1987 that it is hard to imagine how apparently changeless British football grounds were for so long before the 1980s.

And yet change there had to be, and in large measure. As mentioned in the preceding Introduction, following the Bradford fire of 1985 the majority of improvements which took place were essentially to the existing fabric of stands and terraces. The Popplewell Report patched up and poked around the problem, but it turned out only to be a prelude. Four years later, the Hillsborough disaster and the subsequent Taylor Report, published in January 1990, demanded an even more radical reappraisal of football grounds: their design, construction, management, ambiance, even their location.

To ignore the lessons of Hillsborough, however tough and unpalatable they were, would have been an unforgivable act for a nation cursed with the worst record of crowd accidents in international sport.

That is why, since that fateful day in April 1989 when 95 Liverpool supporters died, football grounds in this country could never be the same again.

At one point in 1991, 48 Football League clubs were said to be considering relocating to new sites, and although the majority of these plans soon faltered in the face of funding and planning obstacles, by early 1993 major redevelopments were taking place or were planned to take place at no less than 63 Premier League or Football League grounds.

Four of the grounds included in this edition no longer exist. Chester City ended two years of exile at Macclesfield by taking possession of the small, uniform Deva Stadium in 1992. This joined the recently completed grounds belonging to Scunthorpe (Glanford Park, opened in 1988), St Johnstone (McDiarmid Park, 1989) and Walsall (Bescot Stadium, 1990) as pioneers of the new era. Of course not everyone, least of all this observer, liked everything they saw. Some of the designs have been castigated for their utilitarian appearance and, compared with their fondly-remembered predecessors, their lack of character.

Many grounds have been transformed since 1987, for example Newcastle (whose familiar battleship main stand was demolished in 1987), Notts County, (where incredibly three new stands were erected during the summer of 1992) and Port Vale (redeveloped at both ends, including a stand bought from Chester's old ground). In Scotland, Montrose and Brechin boast spanking new all-seated stands. Ibrox's famous South Stand has been extended with a third tier and distinctive corner stairway blocks.

There are as many exciting (and controversial) prospects for the coming decade, including Millwall's new stadium at Senegal Fields (opening in 1993), Arsenal's new North Bank Stand at Highbury and the ambitious redevelopment of Stamford Bridge, Ewood Park and the Racecourse Ground. Molineux is in the process of being reborn, while if planning and funding obstacles can be overcome, new stadia for Blackpool, Bristol Rovers, Clyde (though situated at Cumbernauld), Huddersfield, Portsmouth, Shrewsbury, Southampton and Sutherland promise to make the 1990s as busy a decade for ground developers as were the 1890s.

Two old friends featured in this edition are no longer host to senior football: Newport County and Aldershot have slipped into non-League circles, while Colchester, Darlington and Lincoln have all bounced back after losing their League status. Three new clubs have joined them since 1987 (and thus are not featured in this edition): Scarborough, Barnet, and poor Maidstone United, who found fleeting fame while members of the Fourth Division from 1989-92, but were forced to base themselves in Dartford. Rejection of their plans for a new stadium and sports complex back in Maidstone proved to be their final undoing. Painful as this was, the rejection was only one of many. The ground plans of at least eleven other clubs fell foul of their local planners during the period from 1989-1993.

Amid this concern, one event has caused great cheer to all football ground enthusiasts – the dramatic return of Charlton Athletic to the Valley. After seven years in exile at Selhurst Park then Upton Park, a wave of public enthusiasm, commitment and sheer hard work (entailing a remarkable political campaign *en route*) carried the club back to its spiritual home on December 5th 1992.

Never mind that the Valley remains until now only three-sided or that its main stand is an ugly, temporary affair. The triumphant return of the Robins has acted as an inspiration to beleaguered supporters all over Britain, particularly in West London, where there is renewed hope that Craven Cottage might yet be saved for Fulham. Nearby, the collapse of the property market has also given Chelsea another lease of life – twenty years at least – at Stamford Bridge.

Of course major worries remain, the most serious of which is the potential effects of Premier League and First Division clubs having to convert their grounds to seating-only by August 1994.

Under the watchful eye of the Football Licensing Authority, a body set up on the recommendation of Lord Justice Taylor, clubs must not simply bolt seats onto existing terraces and thereby create as many problems as they were meant to solve. The seats have to offer decent sightlines, unrestricted views, and be provided with reasonable cover.

Research and advice on these matters was provided by the Football Stadia Advisory Council, another body set up after the Hillsborough disaster. Ominously, however, this organisation had its funding withdrawn by the Football League and Football Association in March 1993, leaving the clubs to fend for themselves when it came to professional advice. The revolution had suffered its first casualty.

But a revolution it remains. At the time of writing only 21 grounds still had any perimeter fencing, and all but three clubs had appointed ground safety officers. The number of police at matches continued to drop, to be replaced by a growing band of properly trained club stewards. Ipswich Town became the first all-seated ground in August 1992, and to the surprise of many, supporters all over the Premier Division seemed to adapt to the newly seated areas with remarkable ease.

Despite this, clubs in the Second and Third Division were made exempt from Taylor's all-seater ruling in May 1992, and while this was a relief to many, early indications show that ambitious clubs continue the conversion of their grounds neverthe-less. At the same time, the Government and the FLA made it clear that any terracing which does survive will have to meet stringent standards, a requirement given extra significance when crushing on a terrace at Burnley led to injuries in January 1993.

Undoubtedly the major worry for terrace regulars is the price to be paid for this new post-Taylor era. Significantly, at grounds where admission prices have been kept low, the new seats have been a great success. Worries too that the atmosphere at grounds will become too placid once everyone is seated have also proved groundless – it is fans who make noise, not steel crush barriers.

But what of the traditions? Can the new concrete and steel stands and stadia of the 1990s really evoke the same emotional responses as the old wood and brick structures of the Victorian and Edwardian era? Efforts have been made, such as the replacement of roof gables at Hillsborough and Meadow Lane, but there remains, acutely as ever, the need for colour and character to make supporters feel they belong.

For those fans, this 1987 edition must now serve as the record of a completed chapter in the history of British football grounds. A new chapter is in the making, with new ground rules in place and new ground stories to tell. We await its contents with anticipation, hope, and it has to be said, with not a little trepidation.

Simon Inglis
January 1993

·1·
HISTORY

Early Stadiums

Apart from the ancient Greeks and Romans very few civilizations have built stadiums. In fact, between the fall of Rome and the rise of Roker (which falls somewhere between the fall of Athens and the rise of Aldershot) not one stadium was constructed in Britain.

No permanent sports arenas were built in Europe during the Middle Ages; the only spectator sports being belligerent activities like jousting, or cockfighting, neither of which inspired any lasting architecture. The only major examples of purpose-built arenas for open air events are found in Latin countries, where the bull ring developed, more as a theatre of ritual than a sports stadium.

So when the likes of Everton and Celtic wanted to build football grounds in the 1890s their only historical models were Greek hippodromes – U-shaped and primarily designed as race-tracks, and Roman examples such as the Circus Maximus – an arena built in Rome and reputed to have held 255 000 in three tiers. Initially these ancient arenas were for the performing of religious rites and worship only. Competitions and races came later as an accompaniment to the celebrations. The most famous arena however was the Colosseum in Rome, completed in 80 AD, which could hold about 50 000 spectators, and even had a canvas cover which could be drawn across the stadium as a roof. The Colosseum was very adaptable, for it could be flooded in order to stage mock naval battles. The word 'arena' is Latin for sand which was used to absorb all the blood left behind by gladiators, man-eating lions and other sadistic displays. From Latin we also get the word 'vomitory', referring to the access points within a grandstand.

The Mexican Aztecs built stadiums of sorts. There is one at Chichen-Itsa in the Yucatan peninsula, where a strange kind of ball game was played in a long court with high stone walls, with protruding rings acting as goals.

The nearest our English ancestors came to a fully enclosed football ground was the university quadrangle, where undergraduates sometimes used to have a kick around between tutorials. Not until the nineteenth century do we find anything remotely akin to a football ground.

Development

Cricket clubs were the first to establish properly enclosed grounds, and inevitably some of them decided to form their own football teams, or rent the facilities to an outside club. Cricket grounds were not in use during winter, often had a pavilion of sorts, and certainly had the best pitches, so they were perfect for staging football. Grounds like Bramall Lane, the Oval, Trent Bridge and the Racecourse Ground, Derby, were among the first multi-purpose grounds in this country. Other early football clubs played on fields near a public house (although at Gainsborough, Trinity players had to walk 150 yards along busy streets in order to reach the pitch!). The public house provided changing rooms, a place for an after-match meal and also for the committee to meet in during the week. In return for their generosity the public houses enjoyed increased custom from among the club's followers.

Certain clubs soon found that people were turning up in such numbers that it was worth hiring a separate field and even passing a collecting box around to help pay expenses.

More spectators meant more thirsts to quench, votes to attract, loyalties to win, and sixpences to be earned, and within two decades of the FA being formed, football was already on the way to becoming a business.

The first step was to fence in the field, with gates where spectators could be charged. The fence also established a club identity. Before long the fence began to carry advertisements, an additional source of revenue. In order for more people to have a better view, the next stage was to build sloping banks around the pitch. Local coal-mines were able to sup-

The original Goodison Road Stand at the turn of the century

ply ash and cinders, and several clubs invited the public to come and dump their rubbish at the ground. Fulham used street-sweepings for their viewing slopes. Once the rubble and muck had settled, the club could cut steps, or terraces, into the compacted material.

Meanwhile, the owners of the breweries and businesses which had invested in the clubs wanted somewhere for themselves and their visiting committee members to sit under cover, so small wooden grandstands were built on the half-way lines. The players were usually kept separate in a dressing tent or hut in a corner of the ground. But not all stands were covered. Wooden constructions for standing spectators were also put up, and were especially useful as temporary accommodation at cricket grounds.

But real progress did not begin until after 1888, when the Football League was formed and crowds increased. Of the 12 original member clubs, only three still use the same grounds they occupied then – Stoke (since 1878), Preston (since 1881) and Burnley (since 1883). The plan of Deepdale shows that it was perhaps one of the most developed at this time (although it had been used as a sports ground since 1875).

Of the nine other clubs, three played at rented cricket grounds (Accrington, Derby and Notts County) while six were using grounds they would vacate within 12 years. Everton were based at Anfield which, like most of the grounds, was barely developed.

In Scotland, of the current 38 League clubs, 9 had moved to their present homes by 1888, and of those 9 Dumbarton have been in the longest continuous occupation, having been at Boghead since 1879.

The first major developments took place during the 1890s, not only in Britain but in Greece, where an almost exact copy of an ancient hippodrome was built

in Athens for the first modern revival of the Olympic Games in 1896.

In Britain Goodison Park and Celtic Park were built in 1892 (for a detailed description of these grounds see both club entries). These were followed by redevelopments at Ewood Park (opened 1890), Molineux (where Wolves had played since 1889), and the opening of several major grounds. Easter Road (1893), Burnden Park (1895), Villa Park (1897), Roker Park and The Dell (both 1898), Hillsborough (then called Owlerton), Ibrox Park, Rugby Park, Pittodrie, Dens Park and Fratton Park (all 1899).

Between 1889–1910, 58 clubs belonging to the current League moved into the grounds they now occupy. Eight were already in occupation before then, and the remaining 26 moved between 1912–55.

In Scotland, 19 of the 38 League clubs moved into their present grounds between 1889–1910. The remaining 10 settled between 1917 and 1974 (Meadowbank being the last).

At least 35 of the current League grounds were recreational or sporting grounds in some form before the clubs moved in. Villa Park and Molineux were, for example, well-established amusement areas in regular use for major sporting events, while several clubs simply took over the grounds of failing clubs.

In Yorkshire, Valley Parade and Elland Road were rugby grounds, Bootham Crescent a cricket ground. In London, Loftus Road and Brisbane Road belonged to struggling amateur soccer clubs, while Stamford Bridge was an athletics ground.

Other sporting venues taken over were Derby's Baseball Ground (baseball was a popular sport in the late Victorian era) and Wrexham's Racecourse Ground. Venues like Gay Meadow and the Old Show Ground were also popular open areas used for a variety of events, until football clubs took them over.

In short, so powerful and popular was the game of

Stamford Bridge in 1945; the beginning of the attendance boom which was to test the capacity of every ground in the country

football in the first three decades of the League that in many towns and cities it was able to monopolize some of the prime open land which might otherwise have remained or become public property. In several cases, if the clubs themselves could not afford to purchase, breweries or businessmen were willing to help in return for control of the clubs. In other cases favourable rental arrangements were agreed.

But the majority of clubs took on sites that were far from ready for immediate use. For example, St Andrew's, Ninian Park, Maine Road, Burnden Park and The Valley were originally rubbish dumps, disused quarries or pits. Craven Cottage and White Hart Lane were overgrown wildernesses, and Owlerton (Hillsborough) an outlying rural region far from the city centre.

Whatever their beginnings, there is no doubt that the existence of a football ground was considered to be highly prestigious, not merely for clubs but for the local municipality. These lines are from the *Chatham and Rochester News* in 1893:

> 'The "colony" of New Brompton is laudably ambitious and kingly desirous to at least keep abreast of its neighbours . . . it possesses a Technical Institute which 'ere long will be open to students: it has a safe dock . . . the foundation work for a new pier goes on slowly, but surely to crown it all a football ground has been purchased and laid out . . .'

The ground in question was Gordon Road (now the 'Priestfield Stadium').

The openings of grounds were often occasions of ceremonial pomp and splendour. Roker Park enjoyed a particular spectacular opening, with pipe bands marching through the town, two steamboats on the river, and Lord Londonderry officially opening the pitch's entrance gate with a golden key.

A football ground was in many ways as much part of a burgeoning corporation as a public library, town hall or law courts, and was certainly used by more people. Furthermore, a football ground was often the only place in a town outsiders would visit.

In order that away spectators would have easy access to the new grounds, proximity to railway stations was vital. This is one of the reasons why so many grounds are now in hemmed-in locations, too near town centres. But the grounds also had to be convenient for local inhabitants, which meant they had to be within easy access of public transport.

In Scotland, railways seemed to attract football grounds like a magnet. No fewer than 20 of the current 37 grounds were originally built within 100 yards of a railway line.

Inevitably there were many mistakes in choices of location. For example, Newton Heath found their Clayton ground too distant from the major centres of population, while Woolwich Arsenal saw their only salvation as being a long-distance move to another part of the city altogether. York City's ground was too far from the supporters' homes and the railway station, so the club canvassed supporters for their views and moved to Bootham Crescent. In 1910 Torquay moved from a central ground by the railway station out to the suburbs, in the hope of winning more support. Arguably this was not a good move. Nevertheless, very few clubs have moved very far from their original sites. Moving too far away carries the risk of losing loyalties and perhaps, as Arsenal discovered, of trespassing on other clubs' territory. Dundee United surely took the biggest risk however. They moved to a ground not 200 yards from Dens Park, their biggest potential rivals.

Elsewhere in Scotland there are confusing cases of clubs moving their pitches by just a few yards and reopening the ground with the prefix 'Greater', or 'New' attached. There have also been three Hampden Parks and two each with the following titles: Ibrox Park, Celtic Park, Rugby Park, Cathkin Park (one of which was actually Second Hampden), Gayfield, Shielfied Park, Easter Road and Tynecastle. Either the Scots had no imagination or were remarkably loyal to a name.

Two grounds that did have great potential but for various reasons were abandoned were West Ham's Memorial Recreation Ground and Queen's Park Rangers' Park Royal. The former was reputed to have a capacity of 120 000, the latter 60 000. Had either survived until each club reached the League they might well have become major football and sporting venues.

In 1923 Charlton's directors made the apparently

The second Goodison Road Stand, the first double-decker to be built

ridiculous decision to forsake The Valley, having invested large sums on it a year before, for another ground which needed yet more money spent on it to make it only half-usable. They were back at The Valley within a few months. QPR tried leaving Loftus Road twice, each time for the wide open spaces of neighbouring White City. Each time the club lost a great deal of money and games.

Becoming a Business

Every League club is a limited liability company. In the majority of cases the change from being a committee-run club to a joint stock company, issuing shares and being run by a board of directors, was the result of the rise of professionalism and the desire to purchase or rent and develop better football grounds. The second factor was often the more important.

For example, Everton turned professional in 1885, but did not become a limited company until 1892, when they were forced by a greedy landlord to seek another ground. In order to raise the £8000 necessary to buy and develop Goodison Park they had to issue

What football maketh the developers soon swallow up – the remains of terracing at Arsenal's Invicta ground, now in a back garden in Hector Street, Plumstead

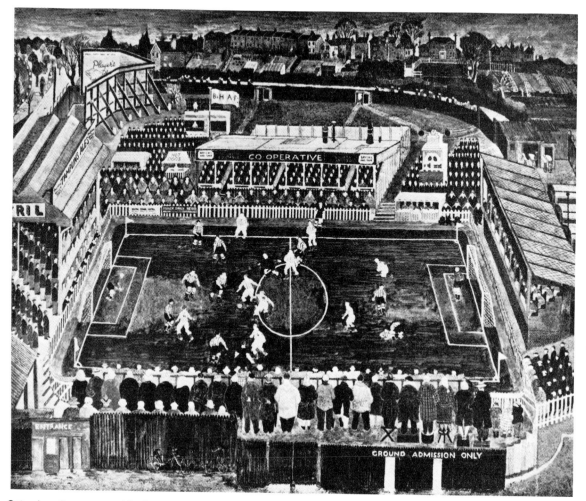

Saturday afternoon: an idealised view of the typical, small-town ground, cramped but cosy

shares to the public. A year later Woolwich Arsenal, who became professional in 1891, did the same so that they could purchase the Manor Ground.

This also occurred with Aston Villa, Reading and Bolton in 1895, Luton Town in 1897, Tottenham in 1898 and The Wednesday and QPR in 1899.

In several other cases clubs were formed, turned professional, became limited companies and adopted their new grounds all in one move. Liverpool were the first such 'instant' club, moving into Anfield a short time after Everton departed.

Two clubs came into being because there existed a ground for them to occupy – amateurs Plymouth Argyle turning professional and becoming a limited company when they moved into Home Park in 1903, and Chelsea, whose birth in 1905 was due only to the fact that no existing club wanted to use Stamford Bridge.

In the beginning, many of these limited companies were not only interested in staging football. Their homes were called 'Athletic Grounds' and were used for exactly that purpose, for although attendances were rising rapidly, they were still well below the peak averages reached in the 1930s and 1940s. By the turn of the century crowds of 20 000 were still considered high. In addition, the idea of mass spectator sports was still relatively new, and the public thirsted for almost any kind of spectacle – sporting or otherwise. Floodlit games were just one example of early attempts by promoters to find money-spinning attractions (see Floodlights). Goodison, Burnden, Celtic, Villa and Molineux each had cycling and running tracks. They staged parades, pageants, and even rugby games until just before the First World War. There was also a thriving but short-lived baseball league involving several League clubs.

But football crowds continued to grow, and by 1914 most of the cycle and athletic tracks had gone, swallowed up by the need for extra terracing. Multipurpose stadiums had come and gone in the space of

13

only 25 years, and from then on, a football ground was a football ground, and nothing more.

Those grounds which retained their elliptical shape were able to stage either or both of the new popular sports, speedway and greyhound racing. Wembley and White City helped start the ball rolling, followed by Eastville and Somerton Park in 1931, Shawfield in 1932, Stamford Bridge in 1933 and Vicarage Road a year later. Field Mill and The Shay also staged racing. At the same time, there were League clubs renting facilities at greyhound stadiums, including Southend (from 1934–55), Clapton Orient (1930–37) and the short-lived East London club, Thames (1930–32).

After the First World War attendances reached unprecedented levels, and it is interesting to note that only one club's attendance record dates back to before 1914 – that of Bradford City in 1911. The 1920s and 1930s saw 36 grounds enjoy their largest ever attendances, most of them the older, established First Division clubs.

A direct result of these larger attendances was that football grounds changed dramatically in order to cope (see Design and Safety). With greater size came greater prestige. Goodison Park was again at the forefront of these developments, followed by such grounds as Villa Park, Highbury, White Hart Lane, Ibrox and Hillsborough. Grounds became symbols of grandeur; outward expressions of power and success.

Stadiums also reflected national pride, such as Wembley, or the Olympic Stadium in Berlin. Indeed, every Olympic games seemed to give birth to yet another bigger and better stadium, as each country tried to outdo the previous hosts.

But whereas in several countries the existence of such magnificent new stadiums prompted a number of neighbouring football clubs to share the facilities, in Britain the growing prestige of clubs and the expanding football industry had the effect of entrenching 'ground identity' even further. Directors and supporters alike saw no reason to share grounds while the going was good.

By 1939 the establishment of football grounds was complete, both physically and in terms of tradition, and once the latter had set in, it became even harder to contemplate radical change.

In fact football grounds spent the next 30 years blissfully content with their pre-war designs, ideals and standards. If not for the disaster at Bolton in 1946 (see Safety) there might have been even fewer changes than there were before the 1960s. Most of those that did occur were quantitative rather than qualitative, except at grounds recovering from war damage, or those of smaller clubs on their way up, such as Peterborough and Ipswich.

Four other exceptions were Hull, Port Vale, Stirling and Southend, where completely new grounds were built between 1945–55. Also, the 1950s did witness one major innovation, the development of floodlighting (see Floodlights).

Kenilworth Road; gardens lie behind the Oak Road End

In fairness to the clubs, two additional obstacles were placed in the way of further developments: the introduction of entertainment tax and the restrictions on building materials after the War. The former was particularly burdensome. Entertainment tax (revived now in the form of Value Added Tax) took one penny in 1s 6d and 3½d in 1s 9d. Crystal Palace, for example, paid £3000 tax in the 1952–53 season.

The greatest single boon to development occurred in the late 1950s, with legislation allowing clubs to run their own pools. All over the country, supporters began raising vital extra funds by this means and thus were able to contribute to new building projects, especially the provision of floodlights. Pools revenue alone has been the biggest single factor in ground development since the War. Ibrox Park is the best example (see Rangers).

The 1960s were boom years, with a succession of large stands being built and grounds being improved. But, as discussed in the chapter on Design, not all the work was successful or well thought out. There was too much piece-meal patching up and not enough long-term planning.

Today, crowds are back to their pre-First World War level (and falling), and clubs are gradually realizing the need to use their grounds for more than just football.

The football grounds of today are uncomfortably situated in the locations of yesterday, in a world in which motorways are more important than railways and luxury boxes attract a new class of spectator.

Today's football grounds are seldom packed to capacity and are expensive in rates and maintenance. Yesterday's prestige is today's burden.

This book is in parts a catalogue of dreams. As property developers hover over suitable sites for supermarkets and hyperstores, club chairmen wax lyrical about that wonderful new all-seated stadium they are going to build, usually out on the ring road, with artificial turf and artificial food served to a docile family audience.

If previous history is anything to go by, few of these plans will reach fruition. However, there is a very real possibility that Luton, Northampton, Scunthorpe and Oxford will have moved grounds by 1990.

After years of debate, ground-sharing finally became a reality in 1985, though sadly, not under ideal conditions. Charlton left under duress for Selhurst Park. A year later in similar circumstances, Clyde moved to Partick and Bristol Rovers to Bath. Both left grounds they had sold to greyhound companies in times of stress. The means of their survival thus became the cause of their departure.

We face the possibility therefore of The Valley and Shawfield being swallowed up like Gateshead or Third Lanark's grounds, by nature or by bulldozer. It is a reminder to us all how ephemeral a football ground can be in the overall scheme of cities. In a few hundred years our stadiums could be as much a curiosity as the Colosseum is today.

If future generations do study our contemporary sporting foibles, let us hope they will at least have a few surviving relics of football grounds to study at first hand.

·2· DESIGN

The First Steps

The history of football ground design in Britain is hardly noted for great names or achievements recognized outside the narrow circles of football. There is, however, one man whose name appears time and time again and to whom in many ways we are indebted for the shape and form of all our major grounds. Thousands have sat in his grandstands and stood on his terraces without ever knowing his name – Archibald Leitch. He was a Scottish engineer and architect and very little is known about his life.

Here, in rough chronological order, are the grounds which Leitch certainly either designed, improved and/or built grandstands for: Parkhead, Ibrox Park, Hampden Park, Bramall Lane, Stamford Bridge, Craven Cottage, Ewood Park, White Hart Lane, Goodison Park, Leeds Road, Valley Parade, Park Avenue, Old Trafford, The Den, Hillsborough, Highbury, Filbert Street, Tynecastle Park, Douglas Park, Cardiff Arms Park, Dens Park, Fratton Park, Villa Park, Roker Park and Selhurst Park. Several more grounds bear his stamp, even in work completed after his death in 1939.

Archibald Leitch was born in Glasgow in 1866 and attended Hutcheson's Grammar School and Andersonian College, before being apprenticed to the engineering works of Messrs Duncan Stewart and Company Limited, Glasgow, at the age of 16. After five years there, plus six months as a draughtsman, Leitch spent three years at sea as an engineer. In 1890 he obtained a Board of Trade certificate and returned to Duncan Stewart, where he became superintendent draughtsman in its Marine Department. Eight months later he resigned, and in 1897 set up his own company.

In 1902, his business reasonably established, Leitch was elected a full member of the Institute of Mechanical Engineers, and was appointed consulting mechanical engineer to a number of county councils and public bodies in Scotland. He was also known for his activities as a lecturer. But this emphasis on his engineering capabilities is important, for he was principally a technician.

It was around the beginning of this century that Leitch's association with football grounds began,

Archibald Leitch c. 1930

probably at Ibrox and Parkhead and then for the construction of Hampden Park in 1903. It is just possible that his first work at Ibrox came as a result of the 1902 disaster, which established the need for proper engineering. At these grounds the Leitch formula was laid down – a formula that he was to repeat at every other ground he worked on. This was simply the provision of a full-length, two-tier grandstand on one side of the pitch and three open sides of terracing.

The first evidence of contact with a club south of the border appears to be in late 1900, when Messrs Leitch and Davies of Glasgow are reported to have worked on a stand at Bramall Lane.

16

The East Stand, White Hart Lane, under construction

In 1905 Leitch was responsible for the design of Stamford Bridge, Ewood Park, Craven Cottage and the beginnings of White Hart Lane's redevelopment. Soon after he began work at Huddersfield and Goodison Park. Many of his two-tier stands were identical, his trademark being a pedimented centre gable on the roof, as at Chelsea, Fulham, Spurs and Huddersfield. The only known survivors are at Craven Cottage, where the gable is still prominent, and Hillsborough. At Fulham and Blackburn he designed ornamented brick frontages, each still in existence. (In 1914 Leitch also did drawings for Aston Villa's projected Trinity Road Stand, although when finally built in 1922 ornate staircases were added which may have been the work of another architect.)

During the first decade of this century Leitch moved to offices at 66 Victoria Street, London, SW1, although he retained an office in Liverpool and another at 30 Buchanan Street, Glasgow. Certainly the biggest concentration of his work was in London, culminating just before the First World War in the lay-out of Arsenal's new ground in Highbury.

After the War his style changed, and it may be significant that in 1925 he was admitted to the Incorporated Association of Architects and Surveyors. He did not, however, join the senior body of architects, RIBA, which suggests that he remained essentially a technician.

His post-war stands differed from his earlier work in two respects. Firstly, they were not all main stands. He designed both end stands at White Hart Lane and Goodison Park for example. Secondly, his major works were double-decker stands. All of these were unmistakably Leitch, with the now familiar white balcony, criss-crossed with steel framing. There are surviving examples of this at Ibrox, Goodison Park, Roker Park and Fratton Park. Only once did he return to his pre-war style, and that at Selhurst Park was probably because the club had less money to spend.

A report of the luncheon to celebrate Selhurst Park's opening in August 1924 provides us with a tantalizing hint of Leitch's character. In his speech he described the business of building new grounds as, quoting from Macbeth, 'a sanguinary business', perhaps a reference to the labour problems which delayed the opening. He predicted that Selhurst would be the biggest ground in London – a false prophecy as it transpired – and remarked 'I am not a speaker but a Scotsman!'

17

Leitch's career reached its peak on 1 January 1929, when his largest stand, seating 10 000, was opened at Ibrox Park. The criss-cross balcony was there, and also a castellated press-box high up on the roof, such as he had designed at Hampden. This stand survives today, and is still the club's proud centre-piece, despite their £10 million redevelopment of the rest of the ground. A few months later he designed a smaller version of the same stand for Sunderland.

His final work for football grounds was at Hampden Park, Roker Park and White Hart Lane in 1936–37, by which time he was 70 years old. The East Stand at Tottenham will perhaps always be his most dramatic work; certainly it was his most expensive – Everton's Bullens Road Stand, built by Leitch in 1926, had cost £30 000 whereas ten years later Spurs paid £60 000 for their East Stand.

There was nothing new about the design, although the criss-cross balcony wall had become simpler and lighter, but the stand was built on a shelf of terracing which made it much higher and more imposing, with the press-box towering above his West Stand, built opposite before the First World War. The East Stand was the last of the truly great inter-war stands. Significantly only a few miles away at Highbury, an acclaimed architect was already surpassing Leitch's work. Artistry and contemporary design had easily eclipsed Leitch's more mechanical approach.

He died on 25 April 1939 virtually unrecognized by the press and the world of architecture. However his designs did not die with him. For example, when Plymouth Argyle rebuilt their bombstruck ground in the 1950s, the new main stand was virtually a carbon copy of one of Leitch's double-deckers.

Demands and Restrictions

Designing a football ground in Leitch's time was basically a question of filling the space left available once the pitch had been marked out. With the money available one had to try and fit in as many spectators as possible.

Open terracing was the cheapest and most spacious solution but those who wanted and could afford to sit also had to be provided for. Seats took up a lot of space, as did changing rooms, tearooms, board rooms and such like, so putting all these facilities under one roof was the wisest plan. In Scotland however the favoured lay-out was to build a pavilion housing all the club facilities in one corner, with a stand alongside (Broomfield Park and Craven Cottage are the only survivors of this format).

The grandstand was in fact an enlarged version of the pavilion, beginning as a wooden and iron structure on the half-way line until it gradually stretched along the length of the pitch.

In England the first major grandstands were at Goodison (1892, replaced in 1909), Anfield (1895, replaced 1973) and Villa Park (1897, redeveloped 1964). There then followed a spurt of building activity between 1904–14, in which major stands at at

least 19 grounds were completed. It is significant that building costs during this period were no higher than they had been 30 years previously, but were to shoot up by over 50 per cent in the 1920s.

Having spent most of the money on the main stand, the rest was open to adaptation. Terracing could be built in two ways: either in three rectangular blocks or in an unbroken U-shape with the main stand forming the fourth side. An elliptically-shaped ground allowed more terracing and the installation of a track, which could be used for staging other events such as cycling and athletics.

Once the basic shape was established, how could the grounds then expand? In Scotland, where an elliptical shape was favoured at grounds such as Hampden, Ibrox and Celtic, the answer was to raise the terracing. Rangers tried to do this by erecting a massive wooden structure, with disastrous consequences in 1902 (see Safety). Earth banking was obviously a much safer method, although just before the First World War Sunderland and Bradford City showed how concrete could be used to construct a solid platform for tall terracing. (In practice however concrete was rarely used until after the 1940s because it was more expensive. Wembley was an exception.)

But in England stadium design took a different turn. Grounds were changed from elliptical to rectangular shapes, with terracing coming within yards of each goal-line. Examples of this transformation were at Burnden Park, Goodison Park and Villa Park. In each case the running and cycle tracks were removed to allow for the expansion.

Leitch's plans at Goodison and Hillsborough show that the most efficient use of the rectangular space was to have four curved corner sections linking each side. Though each site placed different demands, from 1900 onwards it is true to say that most clubs wanted this shape of ground, with only a few exceptions. Southampton for example did not have enough space at The Dell for high banking, so they built two grandstands on either side and small open terraces at each end. The Dell was, in 1898, possibly unique in having seats on both sides of the pitch.

Visitors to Leitch's grounds before the First World War would have noticed very few differences between them apart from the relative heights of the terracing. One suspects that he hardly changed his plans at all.

The next stage in design was to improve the lot of the standing spectators, firstly by providing a roof and secondly by concreting the terracing. A correspondent signed A.H.M., summed up the necessity for this in a letter to the *Birmingham Mail* in 1905: 'Why not covered accommodation for spectators, dry ground to stand on, and a reduced admission if possible,' he wrote. 'The profits will stand it. Many a wreath has been purchased by standing on wet grounds on Saturday afternoons.'

Events on the pitch suggest that this was by no means an over-dramatic statement. One example will suffice: when Villa played Sheffield United in November 1894, it is reported that the weather was so cold that several players collapsed during the interval (which was always spent on the pitch) and that some wore great-coats in the second half. One Villa man was even said to have used an umbrella! It was quite common for players to have to retire early because of cold and exhaustion, so imagine how much more uncomfortable it must have been for the standing spectators.

But the covering and concreting of terraces took some while. Indeed some of Leitch's grounds had no standing cover for years. Stamford Bridge had a token cover (The Shed) in the 1930s, but Craven Cottage had none until 1961 and Selhurst Park none until 1969. Probably the first ground to have some cover on all four sides was Goodison Park in 1909.

The principle of two-tier stands – a stand with seats at the back, and a small standing enclosure in front – was already well established by that time. But in 1909 Leitch designed the country's first double-decker, in which the seating tier was actually above part of the terrace. This was a major advance because it enabled more spectators to be accommodated in less space.

The most characteristic elements of a grandstand were its size, its facings (balcony wall, gable, fencing) and its roof. There were three different styles of roof used for grandstands built before the Second World War. The most popular, as used by Leitch, was a pitched roof. Cheaper than this was the barrel roof, as at Villa Park, St James' Park and Rugby Park. To provide extra cover it could be doubled with two barrels, as at Anfield and Elland Road. The third type, found only at five grounds, was the multi-span roof – which from the front resembled a series of pedimented gables. Old Trafford's original main stand had such a roof, as did Highbury, before 1936. There were other examples at Molineux, Clapton's Homerton Ground and The Valley. None survive.

If Leitch's work at the beginning of the century was one landmark in ground design, the next came in the 1930s at Highbury, with the building of the West, then East Stands in 1932 and 1936.

It was not the first time a recognized architect (as opposed to an engineer) had been commissioned to design a grandstand. At the Boleyn Ground, Sir E. O. Williams had designed West Ham's East Stand (repeated at Filbert Street) and Wembley was the work of architects John Simpson and Maxwell Ayrton.

But the Highbury stands by Claude Waterlow Ferrier and Major W. B. Binnie were in many ways the first attempts to translate contemporary forms and style into football ground design. They were, in that case, outside the main stream of such design, for until the 'cantilever era' began in 1958 football grounds were always some way behind trends in architecture.

Arsenal were able to make this break because they had the funds. But perhaps more importantly, they had imagination also. Until then stadium design had

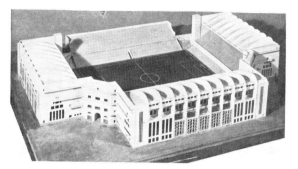

Maxwell Ayrton's futuristic 1945 scheme for Derby

been largely concerned with technical, rather than aesthetic requirements. For example, Edward Bill, writing on the design of football grounds in *Architects Journal* (24 February 1926) considered it purely functional. 'The entrances to the higher priced seats should be kept away from the entrance to the open stands and if possible, on a different side of the ground.'

With this kind of progressive thinking it was no wonder British grounds were even then well below the standard of many foreign contemporaries. For example, cantilevered roofs were already in existence in Rio de Janeiro and Florence while the Municipal Stadium, Cleveland and the Los Angeles Colosseum, among several in the United States, were far in advance of even Wembley and Hampden Park.

Most British football clubs lacked both imagination and money. If a new stand was to be built, directors invariably opted for the familiar, asking for something similar to one belonging to another club. For example, the architect of Firhill's redevelopment in 1927 provided Partick with a typical Leitch stand, pointed gable and all. He also copied Leitch at Celtic Park. Had the grounds been municipally owned and community based there is no doubt that progress in

A rare architectural indulgence: Filbert Street's classical players' entrance, now sadly almost hidden by the addition of extra seats

design would have been much quicker – albeit not necessarily the right sort of developments – but two pilot schemes at Derby and Wolverhampton after the Second World War showed just what could be done.

For Derby in 1945, Maxwell Ayrton designed a 78 604 capacity stadium which could be used as a health centre during the week (see illustration). Reviewing the plan in *Art and Industry*, August 1945, the editor commented: 'Without enlarging his stands, or increasing the cost of the football ground as such, he [Ayrton] has converted mere platforms for sight-seers, used on comparatively few occasions, into a composite building for many activities, functioning every day of the year, for the benefit of each section of the community, and continuously earning revenue to make it self-supporting.'

The scheme was never carried out. Clubs buried their heads in the sand and maintained their grounds as outdated temples of under-use.

As the editor concluded in his appreciation of Ayrton's plan: '. . . it is a new conception of the development of the social usefulness of a football stand that has never before been attempted,' and was not going to be attempted for another three decades at least. It is interesting to compare Ayrton's design with that of modern-day Ibrox. There are many similarities.

Post-War Design

After the War no-one had the money to emulate Highbury (see History) and few had the will, even though attendances were at their highest.

Stand design did at least take a major step forward in the 1950s. At St Andrew's and Elland Road the first of a new generation of stands were built – propped cantilevers, in which the number of supporting uprights was reduced dramatically and all-round vision improved. Then in 1958 came a breakthrough, at a most unexpected venue.

Jack Arlidge of the *Brighton Evening News* wrote: 'It was at Scunthorpe that I saw a new cantilever stand, a very modern looking affair and the sort we can expect to see more of in the future.' This was the country's first cantilever stand at a football ground; quick to build, perfect for viewing, and attractive in appearance.

But the new era really caught the nation's imagination at Hillsborough in 1961, with the completion of Wednesday's full-length cantilever North Stand. Not since the redevelopment of Highbury between 1932–36 had such an exciting and bold initiative been taken. The architectural press took notice, and even Pevsner saw fit to mention it in passing – the only time a League ground is mentioned in his guides to the *Buildings of England*.

The Hillsborough stand was revolutionary in three ways. It utilized new building techniques and materials, especially aluminium roof sheeting. It was an all-seater with no standing paddock in front. It also looked modern; even today it retains a streamlined quality rarely matched by recent stands.

Hillsborough's pride, the cantilever

A third, less dramatic cantilever stand was opened at Tannadice Park in 1962. Being L-shaped it was, and still is, unique in Britain.

From 1961 the trend, at top grounds at least, was to increase seating capacities, and to make those seated areas more comfortable. Elsewhere, the design of stands carried on apparently oblivious to change, as smaller clubs did what they could to improve their grounds on the slimmest of budgets. Yet new building methods were available to help them build more quickly and cheaply. For example, in 1957 Portsmouth redeveloped the Fratton End of their ground with prefabricated concrete units for only £10 000. Coventry also used prefabrication to build the Sky Blue Stand in stages during 1963–64. Blackburn covered one end of Ewood Park with a massive concrete cantilever cover in 1960–61.

Manchester United took the cantilever theme one step further in 1964. Like Wednesday's new stand, the United Road Stand sat 10 000, but also had a paddock in front. But its most significant feature was the addition of private boxes, the first to be installed at any football ground in Europe. This was indeed an indication of how football audiences were changing.

The executive customer was asked to invest large sums in the club over the space of two or three seasons, in return for luxury accommodation. Chelsea followed suit, and by 1986, 34 British clubs had private boxes in one form or another. With 103 boxes Old Trafford has the most.

A new form of executive box appeared in 1986, at Luton and Watford, two grounds which suffer from cramped surroundings but which lead the way in customer-relations. The boxes, copied from cricket, allow users to step onto a private seated balcony, thereby providing a choice of watching indoors or outdoors. Manchester United provide their box-holders with speakers to relay the sound of the crowd, adjustable with a volume switch!

Still at Manchester United, another important feature of the new cantilever stand was that it was designed as part of an overall development scheme. Until then every stand had been seen as a separate entity, with no particular long-term plans in mind. So that where United were able to add to the new stand by continuing it along the Scoreboard End, clubs like Aston Villa and Liverpool built stands which fitted into no overall plan. Lack of planning, allied to a lack of money and an impatience to build, meant that in later years clubs would regret their earlier investment and be unable to add the kind of structures they would have wished.

For this reason, only a few British grounds have any structural unity; Old Trafford (since 1964), Goodison Park (since 1938), Loftus Road (since 1982), Ibrox Park and Elland Road (since the 1970s). Apart from Highbury, which will always be a special case, the vast majority have at least one stand which was built to solve only short-term demands. Between 1958–68 it is estimated that League clubs spent £11 million on ground improvements, £6 million of which was by First Division clubs. But during that period building costs had risen by nearly 30 per cent. Building new stands was becoming the prerogative of the rich and for the rest it was mostly a case of maintaining what they already possessed.

The new generation of stands began, as mentioned above, at Hillsborough in 1961 where completion costs amounted to £150 000 (compare this with the £130 000 Arsenal spent on their East Stand in 1936). Old Trafford's United Road Stand cost £350 000 in 1964, but could yield a higher income. In 1970 Bristol City found a cheaper method of building a column-free stand by suspending the roof from a huge goal-post structure, in which the vertical supports were outside the stand. This cost £235 000, but it did include a lucrative indoor bowling club underneath, worth around £20 000 a year in rental today. Villa Park, Celtic Park, Ibrox and Carrow Road all have stands built on the goal-post principle.

In 1971 Everton built the then largest stand in Britain – a triple-decker main stand – which cost £1 million, and just as transfer fees were rising to equally dizzy proportions, Chelsea spent twice as much on

only a slightly bigger stand in 1974. The 1970s and early 1980s saw major stand construction at no fewer than 27 League grounds, with smaller stands being built at another 13 grounds at least. Prices never ceased to rise. For example, Chester's new stand cost £556 000 in 1979. Three years later the same stand was quoted to another club at £1 million. Three stands represented another landmark in ground design, beginning at Molineux in 1978–79 and followed at the City Ground and White Hart Lane.

For Wolves and Spurs the architects were Mather and Nutter (now Atherden and Nutter), who had also designed Old Trafford's cantilever stands. At Nottingham, the Sheffield company of Husbands (designers of Wednesday's cantilever) built an almost identical stand for Forest.

These three are advanced in two ways. Firstly, they are just one phase of an overall development (though it seems unlikely that further work will be carried out for some time yet), and secondly, they set a standard for future generations. For example, the private boxes (42 at Molineux and 72 at White Hart Lane) were placed between two tiers of seats, unlike Manchester United's which are at the back of the stands.

But perhaps more importantly, they catered for the need to earn additional income other than on match days. Molineux's stand has office accommodation, White Hart Lane's has two large reception areas. The ideas of Maxwell Ayrton for Derby in 1945 were at last beginning to take effect. The trend continued with the total redevelopment of Ibrox Park, to include two stands with office and exhibition space (see club sections).

At the other end of the scale there were few developments. Many grounds gathered dust and weeds, while only a handful had facelifts. As gates declined from 1976 onwards it became apparent that pre-war design had become obsolete and was sometimes not even worth keeping in repair. For example, after the Safety of Sports Grounds Act 1975 (see Safety) Orient found it cheaper to install seats than restore the terracing. It hardly mattered that the seats did not yield much more revenue than standing spectators – demand for the terraces was not high anyway. Other clubs simply fenced off terracing rather than spend large sums on repair. This raises the question of all-seater stadiums. What do the spectators feel about them?

This is an incident told by an official of Coventry City, the first English club to make its ground all-seated. He was discussing the development with an extremely disgruntled Sky Blue supporter who had stood on the terraces all his life but would never consider sitting at Highfield Road, not even to see Manchester United.

'That's a shame,' the official replied, 'because I was going to offer you a free seat ticket for the match against United next week.'

'Ah well, that's different,' said the man, taking the

Clashing styles and unconventional angles at Anfield

ticket, 'Thanks very much.' And of course he did carry on watching his favourite team. Coventry have suffered from their decision, in that the conversion of the ground coincided with the recession, which hit Coventry harder than most cities. Despite the team's encouraging performances, gates were among the lowest in Division One. There are two other all-seater stadiums in Britain. Pittodrie was the first, converted in 1978. Clydebank's ground followed. In England, QPR made a move towards all-seating, but in 1982 took out some seats under pressure from their followers, who still wanted some standing space.

Coventry gave way by allowing 2000 to stand in 1983, followed two years later by the restoration of a whole side to standing, also after pressure from supporters. A study by Leicester University's Department of Sociology (see Bibliography) of Coventry's two year all-seater experiment found that it had failed for several reasons, not least the manner in which the policy had been introduced without consultation and the method of ticketing employed to prevent sales of tickets on match days.

Nor did the experiment prevent hooliganism or vandalism, as had been its main aim. Indeed after

riotous outbreaks, perimeter fencing was re-installed in 1983. The report called all-seating 'an expensive mistake', and yet, as the chapter on Aberdeen shows, all-seated grounds can be popular.

It is my contention that Coventry's biggest mistake was to install plastic tip-up seats in the so-called 'popular' areas. Bench seating has proved far more acceptable at Aberdeen and Clydebank.

The best solution, one which QPR and Coventry seem to have realized, is to offer a mixture. Old Trafford and Goodison Park are the only examples of grounds with both seated and standing provision on all four sides (White Hart Lane and the Baseball Ground were until recently). In order to increase their seating capacities, however, some clubs have made rather too hasty attempts to convert terracing to seated areas, by simply bolting seats onto old steps which do not have the correct rake for adequate viewing. Examples of such conversions which are not conducive to easy viewing are Maine Road, Tynecastle and Burnden Park (where the seats are comfortable but the sight lines are very poor). There are excellent conversions at Carrow Road and the Goldstone Ground.

Seating is one way of improving an outdated ground. But it is only one way, and depending on the club's circumstances and support may not always be the means of salvation. As Watford have demonstrated, the relationship between the club and its followers is just as vital as the improvement of facilities. Several clubs have consciously decided against installing private boxes, preferring instead to update their general accommodation. As the experience of Spurs has proved, installing boxes can have the effect of vastly increasing building costs and reducing the number of other seats available.

Perhaps the best example of a ground rescued from pre-war decay is Loftus Road. In 14 years, QPR rebuilt all four sides, quickly, cheaply and efficiently and with the minimum of fuss and disruption. They now have three double-decker stands, 17 500 seats out of a total capacity of 23 000, and above all, have retained the ground's famed and cherished intimate atmosphere. This is no small achievement on a budget of around £1 million, because development can either ruin or enhance a ground's atmosphere. In all too many cases, the former has resulted.

Since the introduction of the Safety of Sports Grounds Act in 1975 (see Safety) and the rise in building costs, the need for careful planning has become more important than ever. Football creates its own requirements for spectators. A cricket ground, for example, needs space for crowds to circulate behind the stands. Football grounds are for viewing only. The majority of spectators go straight to their positions, and apart from brief sorties to toilets and refreshment stalls, stay there. Once the game is over they leave as soon as possible, many before the final whistle.

Viewing requirements are also different. Spectators at rugby and athletics matches prefer to watch from the side. But in football the tradition of 'ends' is still strong. Very few grounds see the younger, more vocal elements congregate on the sides, unless absolutely necessary, as at Maine Road for example, where both ends are seated, or if the ends are uncovered. The notion of being on the side is still regarded by many as being somehow non-commital. An 'end' stands for identity, and generally the further one is to the back of the terrace, the more vocal and partisan the crowd seems to become.

There is a danger that new and bigger stands have the effect of alienating support. I was told, for example, at Tranmere and Chester that the most ardent supporters complained for years how cramped and inadequate the old main stands were, but once these were replaced by efficient, but soulless concrete and steel structures fans pined for the old wooden stand. The success of Loftus Road's redevelopment was that it kept the new stands within the size and shape of the ground. Similarly, West Bromwich Albion's new main stand crept into The Hawthorns almost imperceptibly, without affecting the atmosphere at all. Another problem is that some clubs have tended to

build big on their way up, and then suffered as a result. The history of ground design is full of clubs who declined rapidly after building a major stand. To name just a few: Sheffield United, who completed a £750 000 cantilever stand in 1975, but seven years later were in Division Four for the first time in their history; Bristol City, who built a stand in 1970 when they were doing well and then found they had the best ground ever to grace the bottom of the Fourth Division; Burnley, who also redeveloped their ground but dropped into Division Four. The most extreme example in another respect is Chelsea, who began building their enormous East Stand in 1972. Soon after it was finished two years later the club was relegated and in deep financial trouble. Large stands have caused similar financial problems for Wolves and Spurs.

The lengthy redevelopment at Chelsea also affected the atmosphere of the ground. Their decline coincided exactly with the building of the East Stand, when one side of Stamford Bridge was completely out of use, with an inevitable loss of revenue (from seats) and atmosphere. On the other hand, while the same occurred at White Hart Lane for one year, the club still managed to win one major trophy.

An admirable compromise has been reached by several clubs, among them Ipswich and WBA, whereby stand redevelopment during the season is done in such a way to allow a certain section of seating along that side to be used continually. Similarly, Peterborough, Swindon and Chester built their main stands behind the existing stands, with the minimum of disruption to atmosphere. And once again I must cite the case of Loftus Road, where virtually all the work on three sides took place during successive close seasons, thereby allowing both players and supporters to adjust to the changed circumstances gradually.

A further point, as several experts both in design and administration have stressed for some years, is the crucial need to design stadiums as a means of regaining support. Few extra spectators are going to be lured to a ground to sit in a more expensive seat if they are already tired of the product on view. They have to become accustomed to going to the ground for other purposes. In other words, a football ground has to be more than a football ground. By turning the football ground into a community area in daily use, for whatever purposes, the public would establish a closer relationship to the club, and in that way attendances might rise.

Already several clubs have training pitches, artificial and all-weather, which they share with the community as part of a Sports Council scheme. But there are still grounds with excellent facilities that lie dormant for most of the week.

Harry Faulkner-Brown, who leads the team of architects in the north east who were responsible for the redevelopment of St James' Park, has made a study of spectator accommodation at football grounds. He emphasized that football grounds, like theatres, need to bring the crowd reasonably close to the players. Spectators want to be able to see their heroes' faces, expressions and movements.

Taking his calculations from a number of stadiums, Faulkner-Brown has determined that the ideal limit for viewing football is roughly 90 metres from the centre circle, or 150 metres to the furthest corner flag. The maximum distance should be 190 metres. The plans below (taken from *The Architects' Journal*, January 1979) show how these calculations relate to some contemporary football grounds.

(Dark circle line is 90 metres radius from centre spot, or 150 metres from furthest corner – the optimum viewing distance. Broken line is 190 metres from furthest corner – maximum viewing distance.)

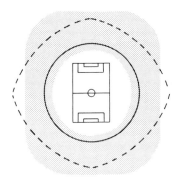

The Aztec Stadium was built especially for football, yet still suffers from too many spectators too far from the action. It is built in the quadric plan, whereby each side is not parallel to the touchline, but curved slightly to allow better sight-lines. The Greeks curved the seats of the arena with a chord of 3 metres in a 200-metre arc, a calculation also used at the Aztec Stadium

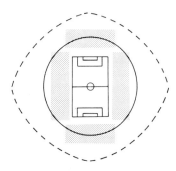

The traditional football ground with four rectangular stands, parallel to the touchlines, but without using the corners for viewing. Although most of the ground comes within the optimum viewing circle, the number of columns and barriers obstructing the view has to be taken into account

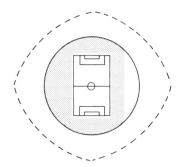

The ideal football ground follows the quadric plan but keeps all the stands within the optimum viewing circle. If space is limited the West Side should be larger, so that more view the game with the sun behind them

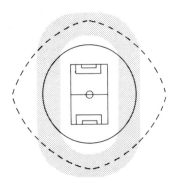

Elliptical grounds such as Wembley show that the majority of spectators are outside the optimum viewing circle, and maybe one-fifth (20 000) are beyond the maximum viewing circle. Wembley also suffers from being a one-deck stadium (ie not double-deck) and having a wide perimeter track

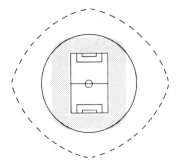

To fit a rectangular-shaped piece of land the stands can be made parallel to the touchlines and outer limits (roads, houses etc) but with curved corners. This plan is followed at Old Trafford, and is the basis for St James' Park's redevelopment

In order to fit more people into a ground, but at the same time bring them closer to the play, added tiers are the best solution, though costly. The diagrams below show how four different stands distance the spectators from the pitch.

At Coventry, two tiers are sufficient to hold a moderate number of spectators near to the pitch

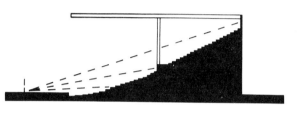

At Wembley, where the numbers are greater, two tiers are too shallow and make the back rows too far from the pitch, a situation exaggerated by the extra width of the perimeter track

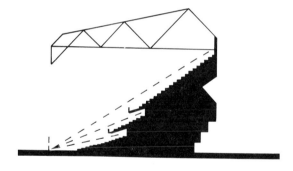

At Chelsea the distances are relatively small, but the three decks are very expensive to build and make the top, back rows very high up

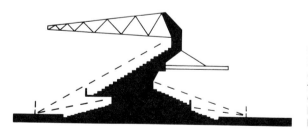

Cardiff Arms Park (designed by Osborne, V. Webb and Partners) has a unique set-up, in which overlapping decks are used, the upper with a steep rake, but behind the stand is built another stand for the Cardiff Rugby Club. If some major cities were to have football stands like this, the top clubs could use the main stand, and lesser clubs the rear stand

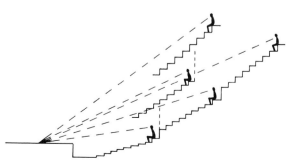

Three straight tiers of seating are cheaper to build but take up more room. By separating and overlapping the tiers the spectators are closer to the pitch with better sight-lines. The angle of rake should not be steeper than 35 degrees, for safety reasons

Finally, a brief look at some of the long-term requirements of football ground design.

The axis of a ground is important, in terms of wind and sun. The best orientation is a long axis of north to south (that is, the ends are north and south), with the main stand on the west, so that the afternoon sun is behind the stand.

In order that the pitch is exposed to natural ventilation, for drying, it is also important to have one end open, or at least with a low roof. Those grounds which have all-round cover, such as Old Trafford and the Baseball Ground, certainly suffer from more pitch problems (see Pitches), especially if the sun is unable to penetrate. Lack of sun means slower drying and slower growth.

Car-parking is a further bugbear. In the United States several stadiums are completely surrounded by open parking areas, as at the Houston Astrodome. At Cincinnati a stadium has been built over a huge underground car-park. The West Germans plan their new stadiums on the basis of one parking space per four spectators. Hardly a ground in Britain enjoys such an advantage, although Plymouth's Home Park and Doncaster's Belle Vue ground are well blessed for parking space in proportion to their number of spectators.

The ideal ground would satisfy the following requirements: safety, compactness (a good pitch/stands relationship), variety (seats/standing), comfort, flexibility (for ground sharing with other sports), economy (to maintain), continuity (minimum disruption of existing facilities if extra development undertaken), identity, attractiveness, and finally sympathy with its surrounding environment (no huge stands in low rise areas, sensitive landscaping and so on).

If it were possible, the ideal ground would be quadric in plan and with three sides covered, two of them double-decker stands, and be surrounded by parking space for at least a few thousand vehicles, preferably with easy access to the main routes. There is, after all, little point in building a wonderful new 50 000 stadium in the midst of small streets.

Those large-scale redevelopment plans which do exist, such as at Molineux and White Hart Lane, even if completed would still suffer from access problems. If the sites were sold, however, would the profits be sufficient to rebuild adequately? Southampton considered this possibility and stayed at The Dell.

But in defence of the bad old British ground, it is true to say that the traditional atmosphere is still highly regarded. Would we really want to see our local teams perform in soulless concrete bowls that look much like any other concrete bowl?

Isn't the essence of British football grounds the tremendous variety and idiosyncratic qualities of each – however uncomfortable and ramshackle some of them may be?

I believe that the present generation of football enthusiasts may feel this deeply and this book is in many ways a celebration of our eccentricities. But what about the future footballing generation, if indeed there is to be one?

Wherever possible, clubs should always seek to improve grounds along the lines that men like Harry Faulkner-Brown have suggested, and in that way preserve the closeness always demanded between the spectators, and the players, who, like actors, need a good audience at every performance. Maybe Wembley does provide the best atmosphere for a football match we could ever aspire to in this country. But modern football ground design can do a lot better than they even knew was possible in 1923. New grounds will bring new traditions, however much traditionalists will claim otherwise. Every ground has to start somewhere.

Over the Top

Before leaving the subject of design, a quick look at what is happening to stadium design elsewhere in the world and what might happen in the future.

If you do not relish the idea of multi-purpose stadiums this may be because the British are not used to watching football across an athletics track. But instead of giving up the idea of multi-purpose grounds, the stands could be moved to fit the event. This is not as ridiculous as it sounds. The Houston Astrodome can change the seats around within hours for soccer, baseball or whatever. In Denver, the Mile High Stadium has grandstands which move on water. In Hawaii, the Aloha Stadium needs one man to move each of the four grandstands, in 25 minutes. They change positions by using air cushion lift pads.

We can put a roof over our ground of the future. A sliding roof even, so that during the week the pitch is protected, but on Saturday afternoon it opens. Or we can have a permanent roof. Light plastic covers, supported by air, make such roofs a very real possibility, albeit at great expense.

If we can move stands and cover pitches, we can theoretically combine our three most beloved spectator sports – football, rugby and cricket, just as in the late Victorian era.

For decades football clubs have been notoriously inexperienced clients for architects, lacking foresight, imagination and often good business sense. Thankfully that is now changing.

The Bradford fire in 1985 signalled the end of some of England's most-loved, but also most potentially dangerous stands. Several clubs now plan to build new stadiums in better locations and with more modern facilities. Whether they will be able to avoid the mistakes of their predecessors largely depends on good planning, good taste and good architects.

Spiralling costs may determine that most modern stands will be relatively plain constructions, although technological advances in cladding material at least allow for some bright colouring. But a club still faces the age-old choice of what to concentrate their resources on – a bold, dramatic roof or

Modern prefabrication has allowed clubs like Hartlepool to build basic cantilever stands. Providing facilities in the space below is, however, an expensive business

plush facilities underneath; a higher standard of seating overall or bench seats in front and expensive executive boxes behind.

Above all, it may no longer be worthwhile to hire an architect with no previous experience in the field, as has happened so often in the past. Which brings us back to the pioneer and past master.

One day there will be no trace of Archibald Leitch's work – of his fine pedimented gables, his sweeping banks of open terracing and his towering, precarious press-boxes high up on pitched roofs, and however exciting the challenges and possibilities of modern design outlined in this chapter, when that day comes we will have lost one of the most important, though barely recognized parts of our footballing heritage.

·3·
SAFETY

History and Background

On 11 May 1985 the entire football world was shaken by the death of 56 spectators at Bradford City's Valley Parade. In terms of human life it was not the worst disaster to befall British football, nor was it the only one in recent years. On the same day a young man died under a collapsing wall at Birmingham; there had been several deaths that same month at a match in Mexico City, and more than 20 deaths at the Lenin Stadium in Moscow a few years earlier. In 1982 the collapse of a stand in Algiers cost another ten lives. Two weeks after the fire at Valley Parade, 39 fans died at the Heysel Stadium when a wall collapsed, like Birmingham, in the wake of a senseless riot.

What made the events at Brussels and Bradford all the more shocking was that both were captured by television cameras. Ibrox in 1971 was shown only in black and white, after-the-event news reports. Bradford burned before a nation in full colour.

City's tragedy was the first time football spectators had been killed in a fire. Millions of television viewers saw how antiquated was the stand and how quickly it was destroyed. They saw how people hesitated for a few vital seconds before realizing the gravity of the situation.

They saw how several brave individuals made gallant attempts to rescue those caught in the conflagration, but did not see how many others also risked their lives behind the palls of smoke and the chaos of terror. They saw and heard the tactless antics of several young fans, chanting on the pitch, but did not see the so-called hooligans in tears. And nor did they see, until later, the kind of obstacles which had met those fleeing for their lives at the rear of the stand.

The Bradford fire was in many ways a turning point in the history of British football grounds, but, as this chapter explains, it was only one turning point. Furthermore, it was an avoidable incident, as indeed every British soccer disaster has been.

A century ago clubs did virtually nothing to protect spectators. Thousands were packed onto badly constructed slopes with hardly a wooden barrier in sight. About the best that can be said of the early grounds is

1902 disaster at Ibrox, as portrayed in the *Graphic*

that with only ropes around the pitches there was little to stop a build up of pressure sending hundreds pouring onto the pitch. On the other hand, as incidents at Fallowfield showed in 1893, there was also little to stop many non-paying customers from gate crashing (see Cup Final venues).

Yet apart from regular problems of overcrowding, accidents were rare until clubs started developing their grounds; then one starts reading of collapsing terracing and broken fences. At Blackburn in 1896 part of a stand caved in and five people were injured.

Rovers were found to have been negligent and had to pay one spectator £25 compensation. At Newcastle shortly afterwards a railing collapsed and one boy lost his foot in the crush.

Pitch invasions and unruliness were far more commonplace than today, as fans assaulted players, referees and even their own club's property. Nevertheless there were still surprisingly few casualties.

The first major tragedy was at Ibrox Park, Glasgow on 5 April 1902, during an international between Scotland and England. At the time both Rangers and Celtic regularly competed for the right to stage big matches, which might earn up to £1000 in extra revenue.

To improve their chances Rangers erected a 50-foot high bank of open terracing behind the west goal, constructed out of wooden planks on an iron framework. Even by standards of the day it was regarded as being suspect. One man wrote to a newspaper about vibrations he had felt standing on the terrace, and a journalist suggested that most regulars 'in the know' avoided this end.

Shortly after kick-off the crowds strained, apparently to see a Scottish move down the wing. Suddenly the terracing in one rear section 'collapsed like a trap door'. According to one survivor, a gulf 20-yards square appeared without warning, without noise. The 26 victims fell almost silently to their deaths, 50 feet below. Some 500 more were injured.

And yet after a stoppage caused by fans trying to move away from the hole, the game went on, with most of the 75 000 crowd barely aware of what had happened. Indeed the broken terrace was quickly reoccupied once the game restarted, despite the obvious risks or the gory scenes below. As one observer wrote: 'Not even the cries of dying sufferers nor the sight of broken limbs could attract this football maddened crowd from gazing upon their beloved sport.'

The players realized the enormity of the tragedy at half-time, when they found the dressing rooms full of the dead and injured. Small wonder the second half was 'a mechanical charade' which finished in a draw.

The disaster proved conclusively that the days of wooden terracing were over. Solid banking or, a decade later, reinforced concrete, were the only safe ways of constructing high terraces.

Less serious accidents continued however – the collapse of a wall at Hillsborough in 1914, causing injuries to 80 people, a man's death in a crush at Burnley in 1924.

It is interesting to note, however, that at the first Wembley Cup Final, when 200 000 were said to have packed into the new stadium, there was not one recorded incident of violent behaviour. People were crushed, shunted about, by one another and the police, and yet by all accounts the afternoon passed off relatively peacefully. After these chaotic scenes, a report on the problem of: 'abnormally large attendances on special occasions' was ordered by the country's first Labour Government.

A Departmental Committee on Crowds was set up, with representatives from Wembley Stadium, the Rugby Football Union, Aston Villa, Manchester United and Queen's Park, together with the Chief Constables of Doncaster, Liverpool, Birmingham, Glasgow and the Metropolitan Police, and the chiefs of various transport companies. (The FA in its infinite wisdom refused to comply with a request for information, while Chelsea also declined to give evidence, even though they had staged three Cup Finals at Stamford Bridge only a few years previously.)

The committee undertook tours of Roker Park, Hampden and Ibrox, Villa Park and St Andrews, and attended an RAF pageant at Hendon and a race meeting at Doncaster, before delivering the report to the Home Secretary, Arthur Henderson, on 13 March 1924 (Command Paper 2088).

This was the first serious attempt at understanding the nature of safety at large grounds, and however unscientific many of the methods, some of the conclusions were very similar to those reached by studies conducted 50 years later.

The committee stressed the desirability of using mounted police where possible, no doubt in reaction to the efficacy of horses at Wembley, and these became a common sight at most major grounds thereafter. Not only are horses a daunting and persuasive form of crowd control but from the higher vantage point officers have a clearer view of crowd flow and possible areas of difficulty.

Another suggestion was that Chief Officers, rather than ground officials, should determine how many policemen are necessary, and that the clubs would have to pay for that number, or incur a heavy responsibility in the event of trouble or accidents. This rule is still in force.

To co-ordinate policing and stewarding the report also recommended that telephone links be placed around the ground (this was before the days of personal two-way radios).

Advanced booking was to be encouraged wherever possible and certainly for Wembley Cup Finals. (Wembley, said the report, was a special case not only because of the large crowds but because the majority of spectators were unfamiliar with the stadium and its locality.) This suggestion was adopted immediately, so that the events of 1923 were never repeated.

On the construction and design of grounds, the 1924 report made several proposals. Smaller sections, or pens, on the terracing were suggested as a means of dividing crowds and lessening movement. This was one far-sighted idea not fully implemented until the 1970s, since when most large grounds have fenced off larger areas of terracing.

The approaches to grounds were also to be divided by barriers, to channel spectators towards clearly designated turnstiles, of which there should be at least one per 1250 people. Groups of turnstiles were to be under the supervision of one man who could

Burnden Park 1946. The shoeless body of a woman attending only her second football match lies near her dead brother. Most of the crowd thought the victims had fainted and roared for the game to restart

open and shut gates as and when necessary. This supervisor, said the report rather optimistically, should: 'keep an approximate count of the numbers who have come through the turnstiles'. But until the introduction of electric automatic counters on each turnstile, the task of counting was far beyond the capacity of one individual.

On the evidence of Hector McKenzie of Queen's Park, the committee recommended the use of crush barriers with a wire rope slung between the verticals, as at Hampden Park. These, he believed, were safer because they yielded to pressure. Rigid barriers were nevertheless installed almost universally, and wire ropes soon passed out of use.

Perhaps one of the most telling points made by the 1924 report concerned the placing of barriers. They should be staggered, it advised, to prevent the existence of vertical gangways on the terracing, and where terracing was curved or angled, the barriers should be continuous. Again, these findings were exactly those enforced 50 years later, and the failure to apply them contributed a great deal to the Bolton disaster in 1946.

One practice the report disfavoured was having

lines of seats inside the perimeter fence. This was quite common at many grounds, the seats being offered on a first come, first served basis at the same price as a place on the terracing. But the occupants could easily mount a pitch invasion, as at White Hart Lane in 1904. So the only people allowed to sit inside the perimeter fence were to be officials and first-aid personnel. The report added that it did not wish to stop the practice of allowing disabled men to be wheeled into favourable positions near the touchline.

The report concluded that licensing of grounds might be a good idea, although it added that without licensing there had actually been very little trouble. But if licences were to be introduced, the authorizing body should be the local authority, in conjunction with the police. There might be three categories of grounds; those with a capacity of under 3000, under 10000 and over 10000. This last point is the essence of the 1975 legislation on ground safety, and it took two major accidents for its value to be recognized.

The first of these occurred at Burnden Park on 9 March 1946, but it might have happened almost anywhere else. Bolton were in many ways unlucky to have been caught out by a series of unfortunate circumstances on the day, and were no more to blame than dozens of other clubs who had not fully implemented the 1924 recommendations.

The fault arose in the north west corner of the ground, where a section of turnstiles was overrun by part of an unexpectedly large crowd of 85 000. Inside the ground, the corner terracing became so over-crowded that 33 people died and 400 were injured in a quite horrific crush. (For a full account of the disaster, see Appendix.)

Immediately after the event, the Labour Home Secretary, Chuter Ede, appointed R. Moelwyn Hughes KC to set up an enquiry, and yet again another set of conclusions and recommendations was proferred to the authorities.

'How easy it is for a dangerous situation to arise in a crowded enclosure,' wrote Hughes. 'It happens again and again without fatal, or even injurious consequences. But its danger is that it requires so little influence – an involuntary sway, an exciting moment, a comparatively small addition to the crowd, the failure of one part of one barrier – to translate the danger in terms of death and injuries.'

It was reckoned that a total of 28 137 people had paid to enter the section of terracing in question, the Railway End. This was not the largest number ever recorded. There had, for example, been 28 435 at that end in 1929. Since then extra terracing had added 300 places. But on 9 March between 1000 and 1500 people had gained unauthorized entry, mainly by climbing over gates and through an emergency gate, so that at the time of the disaster there were probably 29 000 to 30 000 people in the Railway End.

How could it be known what the true capacity of such a terrace really was? And how could the club know when that capacity was reached, especially since the counters on the turnstiles were not looked at until the end of the game. The report embarked on some calculations of its own:

If each person filled a space of 1½ square feet, the Railway End's capacity would be 28 600. Alternatively, if each person had a width of 15 inches and there were two people per step of terracing, by measuring the total length of terracing, plus a few areas not terraced but with a view of the pitch, the capacity came to 26 350.

The situation of the Railway End at Bolton is complicated, however, by the existence of turnstiles on one side of the terrace only. In view of this the 1946 report considered a maximum capacity of 25 000 to 26 000 to be safe.

Therefore, if there were 28 137 paying customers, plus 1500 gatecrashers, but 2500 to 3000 of them were removed from the Railway End to the Burnden Stand, the final total was probably about 26 500; more or less a reasonably safe number.

So if numbers were not the problem, how did the accident occur? The report blames three factors. Firstly, it took too long, about 15 minutes, to close all the turnstiles, by which time it was too late. Second-

Safety officers test crush barriers at Highfield Road

ly, there had been a large scale illegal entry over the turnstiles and fences and through one door. Thirdly, there was evidence that one of the barriers which collapsed had a rusty upright.

Surprisingly, especially in view of the 1924 report's findings, the lack of continuous barriers in the corner section of curved terracing, where the fatalities occurred, was not blamed. Even though there was a barrier-free pathway down to the front, the 1946 report claimed that downward pressure was filtered 'round the ends of the barrier'.

Finally, Hughes concluded that Bolton were not to blame. There were sufficient police – 103 for this game, compared with 60 for a previous game attended by 43 000 – but the ground officials had placed too great a burden on them. Co-operation between the police inside and outside the ground had also been defective, and the reserve call-up had been haphazard.

So Hughes made his recommendations. Some of them had been made before and some would be made again. He called for closer examinations of grounds, for licences to be issued and for a more scientific method of calculating a ground's capacity. The only work on the subject Hughes was able to find came from what he described as 'crowd-fond Germany'.

Knowing the true capacity is only worthwhile, however, if it is known when that point is reached, so Hughes suggested an electrical means of counting be found, adding up at a central point. This last idea was adopted once the technology became affordable, and by the mid-1960s all large grounds had some central-ized method. (Nowadays several large grounds have computerized systems which can automatically close turnstiles.)

As a result of Hughes' enquiry, in 1948 the FA began a system of voluntary licensing for all grounds holding 10 000 or more. But the system was still inadequate, because all it depended on was proof that an inspection had taken place. It did not lay down specific standards, gave no guidelines, and the FA accepted each report without question. Furthermore, the FA did not specify what it meant by 'qualified personnel' to carry out the inspections. It could have been the club chairman.

Clearly there had to be more than general advice, for although many clubs did their utmost to improve ground safety factors, in the absence of any real standards it was too easy for the FA to be lenient towards those clubs it knew could not afford to make improvements.

But as the 1950s wore on it became apparent that the post-war boom in attendances had been a flash in the pan, and that in future crowds would not be so great. People were still packed in, but clubs at least knew when to close the gates.

Nevertheless, there were still accidents. At Shawfield in Glasgow a boy was killed and 50 were hurt when a barrier collapsed in 1957. At Ibrox Park in 1961 two people died when a wooden barrier on the infamous stairway 13 collapsed. Eighty people were injured in a crush at Roker Park three years later. In 1968 a fire in the main stand at the City Ground, during a match, highlighted the need for quick evacuation procedures.

The 1969 report by Sir John Lang was not so much the result of these events as the rise of football hooliganism. This was the beginning of the era of 'bovver boys'. After 16 months of investigation, Lang came up with yet more recommendations, some of them affecting football grounds.

He considered the existing system of voluntary licensing to be sufficient, but thought that if more seats were installed, less hooliganism would occur. The police said that having seating behind standing areas was a significant aid to their own abilities. It enabled officers to look down on the terraces from the seats, and reduced the potential areas of trouble, although they recognized that many standing spectators did not want to see their favourite end chopped in two.

Countering Lang's theory was a report by the Sports Council and the Social Sciences Research Council which stated that: 'it should not be assumed that seating will necessarily limit unruly behaviour'.

In view of subsequent events it would seem that both reports contained a measure of truth. Extra seats do not stop violence breaking out, but they do make it easier to stop. Lang also found that the majority of arrests and ejections took place in the hour before kick-off and in the first 15 minutes of the game, when, as any terrace regular will confirm, bad tempers often arise from cramped conditions and boredom. If more people were seated, or at least in their seats only shortly before kick-off, much of the frustration would be relieved.

Lang's report was an interesting document but it had little effect. It needed another major accident to bring about definitive recommendations, and eventually legislation.

The second Ibrox disaster, on 2 January 1971, was

Behind bars

the most serious ever to occur in Britain, and like the Bradford fire in 1985 it had been avoidable.

Before 1971 Ibrox's Stairway 13 had been the scene of three major incidents. Apart from the death of 2 people in 1961, there had been 8 further injuries in 1967 and 24 people hurt on 2 January 1969. After the first incident Rangers installed steel barriers on this long, steep stairway in the Cairnlea Drive corner.

But new barriers could still not prevent large numbers pouring onto the stairway, and at the end of the match v. Celtic in 1971, according to one eye-witness, the crowd just 'caved in like a pack of cards. It was as if all of them were falling into a huge hole'.

Some reports suggested that the disaster had occurred when fans already leaving heard roars behind them when Colin Stein scored a last minute equalizer for Rangers. In an attempt to see what had happened the fans turned back on the stairway, only to meet many more coming down.

The subsequent enquiry found no truth in this theory. Eye witness accounts suggested that the crowd had stayed on to the very end and was heading in the same direction when the fatal crush occurred, halfway down the stairs. The disaster may well have been precipitated by two boys bending down to pick up items thrown into the air with jubilation because of Rangers' late escape.

As more people pushed their way down onto the staircase, the steel barriers gave way and 66 people were asphyxiated, or suffocated in the ensuing crush. Several died upright, many were literally squeezed out of their shoes and socks.

Yet it had not been an ill-tempered afternoon. The police reported only two arrests and said it had been the best behaved Old Firm meeting for years. Perhaps the late goal had made the crowd more excitable. Certainly the attendance was not unusually large. A limit of 80 000 had been set for a game which might otherwise have drawn a capacity crowd of 118 000.

The enquiry into the disaster itself did not apportion blame – that would be decided, as at Bradford, by the courts – but it did find the Rangers administration complacent in their attitude to previous problems on the stairway. Although Ibrox was one of the best grounds in Britain, and Rangers had spent £150 000 on improvements in the previous decade, the disaster highlighted the fact that first, clubs still had no established standards to adhere to, and second, the police and local council had no powers to order a club to make improvements.

It was just too easy to dismiss the incident as a freak accident, as some attempted to do. What was really needed was a modern, scientifically conducted report into the whole subject of safety at British football grounds. Called the Wheatley Report (Command Paper 4952) it was the first stage in the process which led to the Safety of Sports Grounds Act of 1975.

Wheatley referred to previous guides on safety and also the Lang Report on crowd behaviour and the Chester Report on the state of football, completed in 1968. It began by stating that the system of voluntary licensing was inadequate, that it was not sufficient for a qualified person to make an annual inspection of grounds holding 10 000 or more, be he architect, consulting engineer, the chairman or secretary of the club. Instead, the report considered other methods of inspection.

The first was a regional panel of experts to cover all the grounds in its area under the jurisdiction of the FA. This, it was concluded, would involve the football authorities in too much work and expense in bringing members of the panel together.

A second suggestion was that grounds be brought within existing legislation, and therefore not issued with insurance certificates if found to be unsafe. Insurance inspectors would at least have the qualifications to pass judgement. This too was deemed unsuitable, because it exposed clubs to possible commercial exploitation. The best solution seemed to be a licensing system operated by local authorites, an idea mooted in the 1924 report.

The reasoning behind this recommendation was that a sports ground depended on the paying public, so its owners had a duty to make it safe, as did proprietors of other public buildings. A local authority could call on a variety of sources: building inspectors, engineers, sanitary inspectors, surveyors, architects, the police and the fire brigades, all accustomed to this type of inspection work in their other duties for the authority. A football ground would be treated in the same way as a cinema, a library or a restaurant. There was, however, a danger that the inspectors would be too zealous, led perhaps by personal or local considerations and that there might be inequality of application throughout the country.

Despite this danger, it was felt that any form of governmental supervision would be too expensive and that local authorities were best equipped to deal with licensing.

But it was no use delaying any further, stated Wheatley. The idea of licensing had been around a

long time, and as the Ibrox disaster showed, a club could have spent, as Rangers did, a great deal on ground improvements but still have faulty or inadequate design and construction. There was a need for standard guidelines and legislation to enforce their implementation.

The Wheatley Report was the first stage. The second was the setting up of a working party by the Minister of Sport, Denis Howell, to produce a set of guidelines, called the *Guide to Safety At Sports Grounds*, published in 1973. It is otherwise known as the Green Code. Then in August 1975, 51 years after the first investigation into safety, the Safety of Sports Grounds Act was passed. This was at a time when clubs were being caught in the whirlwind of falling attendances and rising costs. Suddenly they were confronted with yet another burden on their dwindling resources.

The Safety of Sports Grounds Act 1975

When the *Guide to Safety at Sports Grounds* was published shortly after the Wheatley Report, many clubs voluntarily acted on its recommendations. The 1975 Act introduced the system of compulsory licensing and thereby made adherence to the guidelines a matter of priority. Either a club conformed or it would not get its licence.

Briefly, the Act specifies:

Grounds which, in the opinion of the Secretary of State, hold more than 10 000 spectators may be 'designated'. A designated ground must have a safety certificate issued by the local authority, specifying the ground's capacity, the activities for which the ground is used, and for how long the certificate applies. (A special safety certificate may also be granted for specific events – perhaps concerts, prayer meetings or other sporting events not mentioned on the general safety certificate.)

The safety certificate not only specifies the ground's total capacity, but how many each section might hold, and the number, size and situation of all the entrances and exits (including emergency and fire exits). These should all be maintained and kept free of obstruction. The certificate also states how many crush barriers are necessary, and their strength and situation.

Once designated, a club is given reasonable time to effect the improvements, up to about twelve months, depending on the circumstances. However, if a stand or section of terracing is beyond repair, or if the club has insufficient money to repair it, then it must be closed immediately.

Even after improvements have been made, the ground is still subject to regular checks. If found wanting, the Act provides for fines of up to £2000, or a period of imprisonment, to the person found responsible. Examples of this occurring are rare, nevertheless. Bristol Rovers were fined £200 for making unauthorized changes. Aston Villa were fined £500 for leaving an exit door locked and West Ham were fined

£1750 after stewarding faults were found. In general, however, clubs have done everything demanded of them in a spirit of co-operation with their local authorities.

If the club still feels a local authority has been too demanding, they can appeal to the Secretary of State. St Mirren did this and the Scottish Secretary of State overruled the local authority's decisions.

Yet even after a certificate has been granted, there can still be problems. A newly appointed fire officer may be stricter than his predecessor, or may have different theories. To aid this, the Government has, since 1975, asked local authorities to be 'reasonable' in their interpretation of the Green Code.

Here are some fairly typical problems raised by the Act. One designated club found that all its crush barriers were 2 centimetres lower than the minimum height recommended by the Green Code. The authority did not order replacement. Barnsley discovered that it would cost £80 000 to add a further 2000 to their capacity which was hardly worthwhile. Preston ran out of steel for new barriers so accepted a lower capacity. Several clubs, such as Chelsea, Brentford, Bury and York fenced off sections of their terracing, rather than have to pay large sums to maintain their capacities. Falling attendances have meant that capacities have not had to remain so large.

The Green Code
The advisory document is not light reading. For example, the Code advises on terraces and viewing slopes:

> 15.4.1 The capacity of a terrace or viewing slope should be assessed from the area available for standing (that area of the terrace or viewing slope from which the whole of the playing area can be seen, excluding gangways) by allowing a packing density of between 54 and 27 persons per 10 square metres, depending on the condition of the terrace or slope. For this purpose the extreme allowances are:
> a. 54 persons per 10 square metres when the terrace or viewing slope is in good condition (as defined in paragraph 7); and
> b. 27 persons per 10 square metres when it materially deviates from the recommended guidelines, so as to constitute a possible hazard to individuals closely packed.
>
> It may be necessary to interpolate between these figures where conditions fall between the two extremes. When the positioning and width of gangways do not meet with the recommendations of paragraph 7.5.1, an appropriate reduction should be made in the area available for standing.
>
> 15.4.2 When crush barriers conform to the

Putting across the message . . . at Gigg Lane

. . . at The Den

. . . at Home Park

recommended guidelines on spacing (see paragraph 12) the capacity of the terrace is calculated by multiplying the area available for standing by the appropriate packing density. The following formula may be used:

$$\text{Capacity (no. of persons)} = \frac{A}{10} \times 27 \text{ or } 54$$

Where A is the area available for standing in square metres.

Compare this with the calculation made in the 1947 Report on the Burnden Park disaster. Ground safety nowadays is no longer a matter of simple arithmetic.

The Green Code outlines three basic problems: firstly, hazards to individuals which might cause tripping, slipping and falling are to be avoided by the general construction of the ground. For example, there must be sufficient lighting, strong walls, well maintained gangways and railings, and precautions to stop people climbing structures like floodlight pylons.

Secondly, crowd pressures must be controlled, especially on the terraces and exit routes, by the provision of adequate crush barriers, gates, and stairways.

Thirdly, the ground must be able to handle quick evacuations arising from fires, hooliganism, or any emergency situation. One very obvious recommendation is that all exit doors must be capable of opening outwards. If a stand is made of non-combustible material it should have sufficient gangways and exits to allow for a complete evacuation within eight minutes. If the stand is wooden or otherwise a greater fire risk, that limit is two and a half minutes.

And the best place to evacuate everyone to is the pitch, so there should be no security fences in front of seats.

In addition to some very technical points concerning terracing, gangways, seats, fencing, lighting, flow rates and such like, the Green Code has some advice on crowd control.

Terraces, it recommends, should ideally be divided into self-contained sections, home and away fans should be segregated, as now happens everywhere, and it should no longer be possible to transfer within the ground.

Security fencing should divide standing spectators from the pitch, but allow for the police or first-aid personnel to enter and leave the terracing at certain points.

The Bradford Fire

Had the Safety of Sports Grounds Act applied to Valley Parade it is almost certain the fire would not have taken place. Either the stand would have been closed or its construction so modified that litter would not have been able to accumulate under its flooring (see Bradford City and Appendix).

But if a fire had broken out in the stand after designation, it is equally certain that casualties would have been far fewer.

Almost every deficiency that particular stand suffered from is covered by the Green Code. The rear exit doors would have been unlocked and properly manned by trained stewards. Access to the pitch would have been clear. If the stand had been allowed to remain at all, fewer spectators would have been allowed to sit in it. And most crucially of all, as determined in Section 8.12 of the Code, the gaps between the flooring, where litter was dropped, would have been sealed. About the only hazard not covered by the Code was the design and materials used for the roof.

One serious objection to the Green Code's recommendations did come to light. Had Valley Parade been designated, the Main Stand, by virtue of the standing area at the front, might have had a security fence to stop pitch invasions (although this was by no means obligatory). Had such a fence been up at the time of the fire the death toll would have been perhaps ten times greater.

Otherwise, it was almost as if the stand had been a model specially created to show safety officers all the worst possible problems they might have to encounter. Its design was unique, its combination of hazardous features unrivalled. Other stands in Britain had safety problems, but none had so many in such a concentrated area.

So why was Valley Parade not subject to the control of the Safety of Sports Grounds Act?

When the Safety of Sports Grounds Act became law in 1975 it was recognized that the cost to clubs would be high, so initially only clubs in the First Division and Scottish Premier Division were designated, in 1976, together with Cardiff Arms Park, Twickenham and Murrayfield. In 1979 Second Division clubs were also brought under the Act.

From then until 1985 the situation was such that once a ground became designated it remained so, whatever its team's subsequent status. By 1983 therefore a total of 50 Football League grounds had safety certificates. These consisted of the 44 in Divisions One and Two, plus those 6 clubs which had since been relegated.

The size of a ground was irrelevant. Small grounds like Cambridge or Shrewsbury were designated, while a large ground like Bramall Lane was not, simply because Sheffield United had slipped into the Third Division in 1979.

Inconsistencies in the application of the Green Code meant that promotion to Division Two (and therefore designation) was actually feared by certain clubs because of the poor state of their grounds. Furthermore, once promoted, one club might have found its local authority willing to wait a bit longer before work was carried out, whereas another club might have been ordered to complete the improvements immediately. The difference in costs could have been the equivalent of buying an extra player and maybe even retaining Second Division status.

Smaller clubs were therefore quite happy there should be no great movement towards extending the Act below the Second Division, even though, had the legislation's earlier momentum been continued, the remaining League grounds would have been designated by 1982. As it was, perhaps influenced by powerful lobbying from club chairmen who saw designation as a path to ruin, when the fire broke out in Bradford's stand the matter was still in discussion.

Blackpool's all-wooden stand survived safety checks in 1985 but many like it did not

This delay cost 56 lives.

Immediately after the fire the Government launched into action, as governments do. Not only had they to consider a set of safety problems not raised by the Ibrox disaster, but also the issue of hooliganism, which on the same afternoon as the fire had caused one death and over 200 injuries at St Andrew's.

(The collapse of a wall at Birmingham was similar to an incident at Middlesbrough in 1981, when two people died after a gate had been forced down.)

In fact a so-called 'war cabinet' to fight hooliganism had already been formed by the Prime Minister Mrs Thatcher the previous March, after a serious riot at Luton. Significantly, the politicians had drawn up a six point plant to clean up football's tarnished image.

One of those recommendations was the designation of the 36 League grounds still without safety certificates. Valley Parade was one of them (although in any case, having won promotion to Division Two the ground would have been designated that summer).

Never had football been at such a low ebb. While the charred remains of Bradford's stand were picked over by forensic experts, the Chelsea chairman erected an electric fence to keep supporters off the pitch and the people of Liverpool wondered how their supporters could have behaved so appallingly at Brussels.

In Westminster, the most immediate consequence of the fire was the setting up of a Committee of Inquiry into Crowd Safety and Control at Sports Grounds, chaired by Mr Justice Popplewell. Meanwhile, on 9 August 1985 the Safety of Sports Grounds Act was extended to the 36 Third and Fourth Division grounds still undesignated, plus 22 Rugby League grounds.

The effect on the smaller clubs was quite devastating. All over England and Wales stands and parts of terracing were closed or condemned. Down came Hartlepool's rickety Main Stand. Away went small but lovable wooden stands at Bury and Doncaster. Off went the roof of Northampton's Main Stand. Three sides of Sincil Bank and one side at Stockport were closed. Almost every single dark and gloomy stand, every little squalid corner or crumbling terrace was checked.

Designated grounds also had stringent checks made by local councils, all of whom were anxious not to fall into the same difficulties then facing the West Yorkshire authority over Bradford. Wimbledon's South Stand and Swansea's West Stand were closed, while Wolves lost two stands. Virtually every club, even the likes of Liverpool and Manchester United, faced superficial repairs which seemed cosmetic to the fans but cost a great deal in reality. Barriers, exits, gates, handrails, lighting, gangways, fire-proofing – it all added up.

In total 27 League clubs plus 3 in Scotland kicked off the 1985–86 season with stands or terraces either closed or severely reduced. Capacities had been slashed, some grounds to as few as 3000, and at least 15 grounds played for most of the season with at least one side of their ground closed, with all the loss of atmosphere that entails.

But few clubs complained, at least in public. Several realized that their conditions were no better than Bradford and commented on the lines of 'There but for the grace of god, go I'.

Fans arrived at grounds to find they could not smoke in their usual spot, and could not buy an alcoholic drink at half-time. The banning of alcohol was perhaps the only measure seriously challenged, mainly because although magistrates did, in time, allow bars under stands and terraces to reopen, executive boxes and lounges overlooking the pitch remained dry all season. Curtains were drawn, some windows were boarded up. At Old Trafford anyone wanting a drink with their meal before a match had to sit behind a screen. It was a ridiculous situation brought about by hasty legislation. Popplewell advised that the measure be reconsidered, since it was clearly obvious that hooligans (of the football variety at least) did not sit in executive boxes.

For most clubs sales of alcohol represent a major source of income. At least two, Tottenham and Watford, announced that because of the drinks ban they would shelve plans for new stands. Manchester United estimated a loss of £500 000, but went ahead with their new stand anyway. Meanwhile at Northampton directors shivered in front of a temporary stand with half-time cups of tea, their former haunt having been declared unsafe.

Within a few short months of the Bradford fire, football and football grounds had become a major issue. Whatever one felt about the Government's policies or attitudes, no previous government had intervened with such force. Not everyone agreed with Mrs Thatcher's dictates, but no one could ignore them.

The Popplewell Report

Appointed only two days after the Bradford fire and Birmingham riot, Justice Popplewell's brief was to investigate each incident, to study the operation of the 1975 Act and to recommend what further steps should be taken to improve both crowd safety and crowd control at sports grounds. Just as his work was getting under way the Heysel Stadium disaster occurred and this too became part of his investigations.

Popplewell and his committee visited 31 British grounds, plus other sporting venues for rugby, tennis, cricket, horse-racing, athletics and so on.

His final report, delivered in January 1986 (Command Paper 9710) covered many different aspects of

Terracing like this at Hampden Park, pictured in 1982, largely disappeared with stricter codes of safety

the game. On the Safety of Sports Grounds Act, Popplewell called for its wider application, to include rugby and cricket, although curiously not athletics – the 17 000 capacity Crystal Palace stadium remains undesignated (Popplewell originally considered designating any ground holding over 5000 spectators, but modified his views in the final report).

In August 1986, 52 more venues were designated. They were: Berwick Rangers, members of the Scottish League but playing in England; 19 Rugby grounds (3 RL, 16 Union); 7 cricket grounds; and 25 non-League football grounds (including Bath, who were about to share with Bristol Rovers, Barnet, Boston, Kettering, Telford, Chelmsford, Worcester, Southport, Workington and Gateshead). In Scotland further designation orders in October 1986 took in 15 more League clubs.

By the end of 1986, therefore, among senior clubs only Torquay, Clydebank, Montrose, Forfar, Brechin and Stranraer remained undesignated, because all had capacities under 10 000.

The Popplewell Report also recommended that any sports ground with a stand holding over 500 should be subject to the 1971 Fire Precautions Act. If passed, this regulation would affect dozens more undesignated grounds.

His other recommendations which affect football grounds were, briefly:

Annual renewal of safety certificates, after an inspection. This would force clubs to complete improvement work quicker than was the case.

No new stands to be built of combustible materials, and no smoking to be allowed in any combustible stands. This was especially important since it had been established that discarded smoking material had caused the Bradford fire (not a smoke bomb, as was originally suggested by the *Star* newspaper).

Installation of closed-circuit television. Evidence from Manchester and Huddersfield suggested its benefits not only for spotting offenders but helping to monitor crowd movements.

A review of the ban on alcohol in areas within view of the pitch. It was seen, rightly or wrongly, that a measure aimed at improving behaviour at football matches also indirectly hindered ground improvements by reducing revenue.

Club membership schemes. The original Government demand for a national scheme was recognized as being difficult to implement, but partial schemes were to be encouraged. Reports suggested that several clubs already operated such schemes (season ticket sales amounted to the same thing), but Luton went one stage further and made their whole ground members only. By even restricting one or two sections to members, clubs found their policing bills reduced and more family groups attending.

(The concept of family entertainment became a catchword for 1986, but it was a misleading concept, since no amount of window dressing can disguise boring football. In addition, all fans should be well treated by clubs, not just those who take children.)

Perimeter fencing. This was a thorny issue, more so after the Bradford fire, when it was realized that a perimeter fence would have reduced most survivors' chances of escape. Popplewell called for the design of a standard, efficient fence with proper exits. He noted, 'It would be splendid if perimeter fencing and segregation barriers could be removed . . . in the past we looked with superior amusement at countries elsewhere where it was thought necessary to introduce them,' and added that in Scotland such fences are almost non-existent. In calling for a standard design he also mentioned that good design included allowing spectators a decent view (perhaps he had been to Oxford's ground) and that other methods existed to stop pitch invasions, such as dry moats and double fencing, found on the Continent.

Eminently sensible though all these recommendations were, the cost was likely to be enormous, particularly to the smaller clubs recently designated. So fine was the detail now demanded by safety authorities that one Fourth Division match was nearly called off minutes before kick-off because a senior police officer found the bulbs in an exit corridor had broken. Staff were sent to a corner shop for replacements and the game was saved.

The cost of all these changes is astronomical, which raises the question of who pays.

Football Grounds Improvement Trust (FGIT)

Had there been no outside help given to football clubs after the passing of the Safety of Sports Grounds Act most would not have coped, so in 1975 the Football Grounds Improvement Trust was set up.

Its role is to give financial aid to clubs who have to carry out safety improvements, but certain conditions were introduced in June 1982 to avoid abuse.

Firstly, the club must notify FGIT what work is to be carried out. FGIT then sends its own appointed surveyors to assess these plans and decide whether they are necessary for 'spectator safety'. Anything beyond the players' tunnel is not eligible – that is improvements to dressing rooms, directors' lounges, or anything merely concerned with comfort or cosmetic appearance, though naturally a club will often try to convince the surveyors that their plans are of course essential to safety.

If approved by FGIT the work must then be put out to commercial tender. Once completed the work is then inspected by the surveyors, and if in order, FGIT pays the grant. Each designated ground is allowed a total of 75 per cent of the cost, up to a maximum expenditure of £700 000. So that if a club has spent £700 000 it will receive back £525 000. If it has to spend above that amount FGIT will not provide further assistance.

In 1975 the limit was £200 000, since when it has risen progressively to the present amount, so that for example, Blackburn Rovers reached their limit in 1981, but the amount was raised and they were able to spend more thereafter. By February 1986 only two clubs had not received grants from FGIT; Clyde and Meadowbank, neither of whom owned their prospective grounds (Clyde moved to Partick's ground shortly after). Only one club, Celtic, had reached its grant limit, with Manchester City, Sunderland and Queen's Park close behind.

In addition to helping designated grounds, the Trust also paid grants to Irish clubs, non-League clubs and local community schemes. Together with the Football Trust, which has a wider brief for football, a total of £40 million has been paid out in the first ten years.

The Football Trust, which has contributed towards improvements at Wembley, Hampden and Windsor Park, and has funded CCTV installations at most major grounds, is funded entirely by a donation from the Pools Promoters Association's Spotting-the-Ball competition at the rate of 20 per cent of turnover. In 1985 this represented about £7 million a year.

Of that amount, 54 per cent is passed on to finance FGIT, approximately £3.75 million per year. But to help overcome the extra strain placed on FGIT in 1985–86, an extra £1 million was made available by the Football Trust.

There are seven members of FGIT, all appointed by the Football League. Members in 1986 included League secretary, Graham Kelly, former secretary of the PFA, Cliff Lloyd, and the ex-England and Preston winger Tom Finney.

After Ibrox and Bradford it may be thought that every eventuality at a football ground had been considered. Indeed grounds in 1986 are safer than they ever have been before. Awareness of potential dangers is also much greater, although one sees the occasional, though understandable example of over-zealous caution – for example, at one Second Division match a steward sitting completely alone on a huge, empty concrete terrace, nursing a fire-extinguisher.

Fifty-six died when Valley Parade's Main Stand went up in flames, bringing to an end an era of complacency and negligence

There are still wide variations between how each local authority applies the recommendations of the Green Code. So, a wooden stand survives in Blackpool, but not in Doncaster. A terrace is closed at Tranmere but not at Colchester. Every decision has its reasons, but they are not always apparent to the fans (or to the clubs).

No one has yet devised a totally hooligan proof ground, and it is depressing to consider how much money football clubs will have to spend in future just to contain this small unruly element. Luton's members-only policy, however controversial, will be watched closely by other clubs of a similar size.

Could a disaster like Bradford's happen again? I think not. But if sufficient numbers of people, hooligans or otherwise, were to crowd a small area there is no guarantee that accidents might not occur again. However fortress-like one builds a ground, it only needs a sudden panic to create mayhem.

Football's biggest priority for the future, therefore, is to make sure the grounds are habitable, comfortable and well-designed, in the hope that the fan of the future will live up to the fabric. Poor conditions will encourage poor behaviour. And poor football will drive everyone away, in which case every ground will be perfectly safe.

·4·
FLOODLIGHTS

An early floodlit game at The Oval, November 1878. Clapham Rovers v. the Wanderers

Two of the most significant developments affecting modern football have been the growth of international air transport and the use of floodlights. Without the former there would be no European Championships, no European club competitions, and considerably smaller World Cup competitions. With floodlights all these extra games have been made possible, and in Britain they have allowed the creation of a host of new competitions, notably the League Cups, now called the Skol Cup in Scotland and the Littlewoods Cup in England and Wales.

Floodlights have brought to an end the long practice of staging mid-week replays in the afternoon, causing thousands of fans to leave their workplaces, officially or on false pretences and whole towns and factories to grind to a halt.

Floodlights meant that Saturday afternoon fixtures could all have the uniform kick-off time of three o'clock, instead of some time between one and two o'clock, depending on when it became dark. No longer would games have to finish in the evening gloom; the ball barely visible against the darkening background.

To the present generation, which knows no other way, it is hard to believe how anyone could possibly object to the introduction of floodlighting. Like goalnets, the idea seems so obvious and simple. But the idea was vehemently opposed for years, and while some parts of the world became quite accustomed to watching floodlit sport, Britain lagged behind. For instance, Wembley was built at the same time as the Los Angeles Coliseum in 1923 and yet the Coliseum had floodlighting from the very beginning and Wembley not until 1955.

Yet England was probably the first country in the world to have used floodlights for a sporting event. The venue was Bramall Lane, Sheffield, on Monday 14 October 1878. Here is how the *Sheffield Independent*'s reporter described the scene:

'Those who have seen the enclosure under a blaze of a sun, with thousands of excited spectators witnessing the performances of Yorkshire's favourite cricketers, can hardly possess a complete idea of the black wilderness it presents by night when there is no moon or the heavens are overcast. To walk there is literally like wandering about a bleak moor, for look which way you will scarcely a light can be seen except it may be from the bedroom windows of an adjoining row of houses.'

Two Sheffield representative teams were billed to play, but the public came to see the spectacle rather than the game. Altogether around 20 000 packed into Bramall Lane for the scheduled 7.00 p.m. kick-off but although the organizers, Messrs Tasker, had lit the pitch, the gates and fences were not illuminated, and only 12 000 people paid to enter, the rest sneaking in under cover of darkness!

Mounted on four wooden towers, one at each corner, the electric floodlights were powered by Siemens dynamos; driven by two 8-horsepower engines behind each goal. By 7.30 p.m. they were working, and with their reflectors the lights were hauled up the towers to a height of 30 feet above the ground (the average floodlight pylon nowadays is 100 feet), where they were described as giving out 'a soft blue light . . . under which players could not only play the game but the points were distinctly visible.' It was, said the *Sheffield Independent*, 'a scene of great animation'.

The lights, according to *The Guardian* correspondent, were equal to 8000 standard candles, and cost under 4d an hour to operate. Another correspondent from Manchester noted how 'additional fun was now and then caused when a charge was made in the face of the lights and they (the players) became dazzled'. The only real criticisms were that at first the lights were too bright (Mr Tasker solved this before kick-

off) and that perhaps the towers were too close to the pitch. Otherwise the experiment was a great success. The crowd had been four times larger than that of the 1878 Cup Final (attendance 4500) and was the first gate higher than 10 000 recorded for a match outside of Glasgow.

Eleven days later there were two more attempts. At Chorley, Lancashire, 8000 people waited two hours in torrential rain before the electrician gave up trying to switch on the lights, while up in Glasgow at Cathkin Park, the lights did work with great success.

But the next game, at the Aston Lower Grounds, Birmingham (now Villa Park) was another flop. This time there were 12 lights spaced evenly around the pitch, but wind and rain led to several of them failing and the game took some time to complete. Two more attempts took place a week later on 4 November, at Accrington and at the Oval where Clapham Rovers played the Wanderers. As in Birmingham the event was not a great success, and significantly there were the first recorded signs of an attitude which the FA was to assume towards floodlighting for the next 80 years. For example, one observer wrote in *Illustrated Sporting and Dramatic News*:

'. . . remembering that the attempt was of necessity an experiment, its comparative failure is no very important matter. Besides who wants to play football by artificial light? As a novelty now and then, or to attract wandering shillings after dark, it may be all very well, but for the real purpose of the game daylight is quite good enough and long enough.'

In the following weeks a Mr Paterson of London demonstrated electric floodlighting for games at Crewe, Nottingham, Chorley, Edinburgh, Ipswich, Glasgow and Kilmarnock. At the latter venue one of the three lights failed and in the shadows two players were so badly injured they never played again.

Meanwhile on 25 and 26 November Messrs Mootham and Barnes held bicycle races and football under lights in Dean Park, Bournemouth (next to the present ground). On 27 November the show moved to Southampton's Antelope Ground, but heavy rain forced postponement until the following night, when a rugby match was played.

After this series of matches either the novelty wore off or promoters felt they were not reaping sufficient profits to carry on. Certainly we read very little of floodlit games until 1887 when the FA gave permission for two floodlit games to be held in Sheffield. Note that the FA by then deemed this a matter for its control. There followed another spate of demonstrations, at venues including Lincoln in 1888 and Forest's Gregory Ground in 1889. Then on 26 February 1889, the two leading Manchester clubs, Newton Heath and Ardwick (later Manchester United and City respectively) played a floodlit match at Belle

Vue, thereby raising £140 for the Hyde Colliery Explosion Fund.

What is interesting about this match was that instead of using electric light, illumination was provided by Wells' lights, a system which was to prove popular over the next decade of floodlit football. For example, eight Wells' lights were used at Clee Park in April 1889 for exhibition matches between Grimsby and Boston. As one advertisement for a match in Glasgow said: 'This light has the reputation of being possessed of the finest illuminating properties,' and is 'excellently adapted . . . for the purposes of out-door recreation.'

Light was produced by pumping inflammable oil under high air pressure to a burner, creating a flare. But it needed a great deal of attention and much oil. One match at Turf Moor in 1891 was lit by 16 Wells' lights, which used up 140 gallons of creosote oil, and one can readily imagine the acrid smells that must have drifted across the pitch. The barrels of oil were also a fire risk.

One other method suggested was to follow the ball with a spotlight, and on Christmas Day 1893 Celtic unveiled yet another system. Sixteen arc lamps were hung from high poles around the Parkhead, with an extra row being suspended across the middle of the pitch. A crowd of 5000 saw a 1–1 draw v. Clyde on a foggy night, but the lights were not used again and it can only be presumed the ball kept hitting the suspended lamps.

Spotting the ball was a major problem, for although the players could wear bright colours, leather in those days was leather; dark and brown, especially in wet weather. One way to solve this was to have a number of balls on hand and keep dipping them in whitewash. As the white wore off, another ball would be thrown on! This was the method used at a testimonial match played under Wells' lights for Blackburn's forward Jack Southworth, at Ewood Park on 31 October 1892, watched by 8000.

Floodlights continued to be something of a curiosity in this country until after the First World War, with the FA definitely opposed to clubs using them for anything but friendlies or charity games. But abroad, and especially in the Americas floodlighting was becoming a regular feature, for baseball, gridiron football, and in South America for soccer. Advances in technology made powerful and more reliable electric lighting possible, and of course in hot climates it was preferable to play matches at night when the air was cooler. So while in Britain the only floodlit games were exhibition events, for example a ladies' match at Turf Moor in 1924, elsewhere they were being taken very seriously indeed.

The FA's response to the growing demand for action was quite simple – in August 1930 it placed a complete ban on any member clubs taking part in a floodlit match. (It was not just floodlights of which they disapproved. Other innovations such as the numbering of players or entering the World Cup were

Going through the roof at Burnden Park

equally scorned.) Not everyone was happy to let the matter rest however. Herbert Chapman, the Arsenal manager argued (among several of his progressive ideas) for the introduction of modern floodlighting to Britain.

After visiting Belgium in 1930 he wrote:

> 'The field was illuminated by lights fixed to five standards running down one side behind the spectators. From each standard the rays of 20 powerful lamps were thrown across the pitch at different angles, and as they intersected and spread they did not leave a dark or even a dull patch . . . I wished that the public at home could always have such a good view.'

In Austria Chapman saw another floodlit game, played under the lights of car headlamps, and decided on his return to install some lights on Arsenal's training pitch behind Highbury. A railway company provided the equipment, and Chapman was so sure that the idea would catch on that he invited the press to come and see his 'lanterns'. The reporters were cool about the idea, saying it was too cold at night to expect the public to attend. But Chapman believed that night matches would attract more people away from the growing popularity of greyhound racing, which swept London in the late 1920s and early 1930s. He even went as far as putting lights on the stands for training purposes, but again the FA banned its use for official matches. (I am indebted for this information to Stephen Studd, author of Chapman's biography.)

Tottenham were also pressing for the FA to lift its ban. They called a meeting of every London club, with the result that the FA permitted a floodlit match to take place at White City, by then the top greyhound stadium in London and also being used by QPR. The match was played on 4 January 1933 between two representative teams from London clubs in front of a very disappointing crowd of 12 000. The old bucket of whitewash trick was still in use even then (strangely enough Chapman had tried white balls and dismissed them as a gimmick!).

After this relatively unsuccessful trial the idea lay dormant once more. Chapman died in 1934, and as Britain was hit by the Depression it was felt that most clubs would not be able to afford lights anyway. Typical of the official view was the opinion of Sir Frederick Wall of the FA. He wrote in 1935:

> 'Clubs cannot do just as they like – even if they desire floodlight football. That may be in the future. I cannot easily predict an era when the sorcerers of science may easily turn night into day as they now talk to a man on the other side of the world.'

Immediately after the Second World War, however, the argument for floodlights began to gather momentum. Attendances were reaching an all time high, and industry could ill afford to have its workforce taking afternoons off to watch football. But even if the FA had given its approval it is doubtful whether many clubs could have obtained the necessary material until rationing and austerity measures eased.

One advocate of floodlights was Liverpool, who went on a summer tour of the United States in 1946 and on their return suggested setting up a mid-week floodlit league. A few years later Southampton, Hibernian and Arsenal also undertook foreign tours and reached similar conclusions. Eventually the FA withdrew the ban in December 1950.

Small semi-professional teams led the way. In 1949 South Liverpool played a floodlit friendly v. a Nigerian XI in front of 13 000 spectators at their Holly Park ground. Of the present Football League clubs, the first was Headington United, who played Banbury Spencer under floodlights on 18 December 1950, in aid of a local children's charity. Mounted on individual wooden poles around the pitch were 36 lamps, borrowed from various buildings in Oxford which had their walls lit up at night for effect. Only 2603 attended the game, but other clubs soon heard about Headington's trial installation and there started a steady stream of League clubs, large and small, asking to play matches at the Manor Ground and ask advice from the Headington directors.

Among the visitors were Brentford, Cardiff, Tottenham, Charlton, Fulham, Northampton, QPR, Millwall, Colchester, Leyton Orient, Watford and Wolves. But the first club to act on what they had seen at Oxford was Swindon Town, then in Division Three South. Town were the first League club to install lights, eight behind each goal, first used on 2 April 1951 for an exhibition match v. Bristol City.

In January 1951 the FA had added a qualifying clause to its original lifting of the ban. This stated that no competitive matches were to be played under floodlights without permission from the FA or the County FA and the organizers of the competition concerned.

Not surprisingly Arsenal was the next club to install lights, and at Highbury, with two stands of the same design and height on either side of the pitch, installation was relatively simple. The first game was a friendly v. Hapoel Tel Aviv in September 1951.

But the first test of the new FA ruling came weeks later when Southampton asked the Football Combination for permission to stage a reserve match at The Dell under their £600 lights, installed a few months before but used only for training. The Combination gave their approval, and on Monday, 1 October 1951 the first competitive football match under floodlights was played in Britain. An enthusiastic crowd of 13 654 attended the match, and as the Southampton manager, Sid Cann remarked the following day, 'Floodlit soccer has come to stay'.

On 17 October Highbury staged their second exhibition match, this time the annual challenge match v. Glasgow Rangers, watched by a huge crowd of 62 500.

At the end of the month The Dell staged another competitive game, a Hampshire Combination Cup tie between Southampton and Portsmouth, watched by 22 697. Then in Scotland, in the apparently unlikely surroundings of Ochilview Park, Stenhousemuir staged the first Scottish floodlit match in modern times, a friendly v. Hibernian on 7 November 1951.

After 1951, the next major development was the staging of floodlit games against European opposition, an important factor in the subsequent organization of the European Cup in 1955. Wolves were the best known of the floodlight pioneers. After switching on their lights in September 1953, they played famous games against Honved of Hungary (December 1954), Moscow Spartak and Moscow Dynamo. Tottenham Hotspur switched on their lights with a friendly v. Racing Club de Paris, also in September 1953. And significantly in Scotland, Hibernian were the first British team to enter the European Cup, having switched on their lights in October 1954.

Not only had the floodlit era begun, but so had a whole new era of international club football.

The next stage was for the FA to allow FA Cup matches to be held under lights. Permission had already been refused Headington, who wanted to stage their replay v. Millwall in 1953–54 under lights, a decision which drew national attention (see Oxford), but eventually in February 1955 it was decided that the following season floodlights could be used for replays up to and including the Second Round. The first was Kidderminster Harriers v. Brierley Hill Alliance in a Preliminary Round on 14 September 1955.

The first such match to involve two League clubs was Carlisle v. Darlington, a First Round replay played at St James' Park, Newcastle on 28 November 1955. Two days later Wembley had its first taste of international floodlit action when the lights were switched on for the last 15 minutes of the England v. Spain match because of fog (although England had already played one complete game under lights, v. USA in New York on 8 June 1953).

Then in December 1955 the FA relaxed its rules even further by stating that Third Round ties played on 7 January could be played all or in part under lights, which is what happened at Highbury, Fratton Park, Hillsborough, White Hart Lane and the Boleyn Ground.

Meanwhile, the Football League had been having its own discussions on the matter. At the annual meeting in June 1955 Sunderland proposed that postponed League matches be played under floodlights if both clubs agreed. This was adopted, although at the time only 36 League clubs actually had lights.

In Scotland the first competitive games under lights were on 8 February 1956, both Scottish Cup ties – Hibernian v. Raith and East Fife v. Stenhousemuir. The first floodlit Scottish League match was four weeks later when Rangers beat Queen of the South 8–0 at Ibrox on 7 March (the Ibrox lights were actually used once before during a League match, v. St Mirren in December 1952, but the referee ordered Rangers to switch them off immediately).

The Football League's big night came on Wednesday, 22 February 1956, at Fratton Park, with Portsmouth scheduled to play their postponed Division One match v. Newcastle. The whole country had been submerged in snow, Fratton Park's pitch was rock hard, and it was a bitterly cold night. Nevertheless, the evening represented a significant breakthrough, and was greeted enthusiastically by almost everyone. *The Times* correspondent, for example, seemed particularly inspired:

> '. . . there arose a vision of the future. In 20, even 10 years time, will all football be played under the stars and moon? There is much to recommend it. There is a dramatic, theatrical quality about it. The pace of the game seems accentuated, flowering patterns of approach play take on sharper, more colourful outlines. In the background of the night the dark, surrounding crowd, half shadow, yet flesh and blood, can produce the effect of a thousand fire-flies as cigarette lights spurt forth.'

A bulbous cluster at Selhurst Park

And it was true. Floodlit football did have a different edge to it.

But the players themselves were not so keen, or at least that was the impression they gave. For them, floodlit football meant working nights, travelling at more unsociable hours, and adjusting to a new set of conditions. They were earning little enough as it was, in their view if not their employers', so after the Fratton Park game the Players Union banned its members from playing in floodlit games from 13 March onwards. Just two days before that date, however, the League agreed to consider their extra wage demands, and in June the players were told that an extra £2 to £3 would be paid for every player taking part in a floodlit game.

At the same time the Football League relaxed its rules by allowing any League match to be played under lights, as long as both clubs agreed. Yet still only 38 of the 92 League clubs had floodlights.

Two years later, at the annual meeting in June 1958, the final restriction on League games was lifted – that is, it would no longer be necessary to obtain the agreement of the other club for staging a floodlit game – but the League did state that clubs' lights would have to be of a sufficiently high standard for League fixtures, and several installations were obviously not.

Indeed the standards varied enormously. Some clubs still had individual lights on wooden poles around the ground, while more were replacing their original systems with four corner pylons. Costs were naturally rising all the time. Sunderland's four 75-feet pylons with a total power of 72 kilowatts cost £7000 in 1952, but by 1956 Stockport were paying £17 000 for only a slightly more powerful set of lights.

Not everyone was convinced about floodlights, and there were still several teething problems to overcome. Many club chairmen saw lights as a passing fad and would not invest funds to buy them, leaving in most cases the supporters' clubs to raise the money. The view of Gillingham's Vice-Chairman was quite typical. 'I don't think there is any future in it at all,' he said, 'the novelty will wear off soon.' In one sense he was right, the public soon became accustomed to floodlit games, and attendances gradually reduced.

The difficulty of spotting the ball was less acute by this time, because developments in the treating of leather soon made orange and white balls quite commonplace. But floodlights did present a problem concerning kit. Clubs found they had to use lighter shirts to be visible to the crowd and to their own players. Glossy, new, synthetic shirts appeared as a result.

But what about the match officials, still in their all-black strips? They were the least visible against dark backgrounds. For one match, Tommy Lawton's testimonial at Goodison Park, the referee and linesmen wore specially made fluorescent shirts, but the idea was never taken further.

Another problem was reliability and design. All kinds of technical problems arose during the first decade of floodlit football. Lights failed, or were misdirected by the wind. Some lights were too low and dazzled the crowd and the players. Doncaster's, for example, had to be low in order to avoid glare for pilots landing at the adjacent airfield. Clubs found that as technology advanced they were having to replace their installations every few years to maintain standards.

And finally, floodlit football created one difficulty for journalists. Afternoon games presented no deadline problems, but a game finishing at 9.00 p.m. or later, demanded a whole new school of reporting, concentrating on the first half's action with a hastily added final score at the end. Never had there been such a scramble for the telephones.

As the 1950s wore on and more clubs had lights, there were suggestions for new competitions to be played solely on mid-week evenings, for example, a Southern Floodlit Cup and an Anglo-Scottish Floodlight League, neither of which materialized. One suggestion did find root however. The proposed Football League Floodlight Cup was adopted in 1960, but under the name of the Football League Cup. All its games were played mid-week, and most therefore under floodlights, and it was only from 1966 onwards that the final was switched to Wembley.

When the League Cup began, 68 League clubs had floodlights and only two in the First Division were without – Forest and Fulham.

But the existence of this potential money spinner inspired a rush of clubs to get lights installed. Seven clubs had them put in by October 1960, and by the end of 1961 only a handful of clubs were still without. The last two clubs in the League to install lights were Hartlepool in 1965 and Chesterfield in October 1967. In Scotland, 18 of the 37 League clubs had lights by late 1959. The last clubs to switch on were Alloa in August 1979 and Stranraer in August 1981.

Floodlighting involves several factors which may seem surprising to the average spectator. For example, the way the pitch has been rolled can actually affect the illumination as can the turf's moisture content, colour and condition. The placement of stands is important, explaining why some clubs have light pylons tucked into the corner of the pitch while others have them high up on roofs or embankments. Luton Town wanted to have corner pylons but had so little room that each pylon would have had to be ridiculously tall, so they had to opt for shorter ones along each side. Some grounds now have lights along the eaves of the stands, or hung underneath them, as at Goodison Park, The Dell, Anfield, Arsenal and Ibrox. This is cheaper to install and easier to maintain, but can cause glare to spectators opposite, and to television cameras. But worst of all they make it very hard to find the grounds! There is no better homing guide for any traveller than the sight of distant floodlight pylons.

The demands of colour television, accompanied by significant advances in lighting technology have meant that several top grounds now have lights up to four times more powerful than before. Measurement is now in lux, a term for lumens per square foot. This indicates how much light is available on the working plain, but because we look at the players and the ball, the measurement usually taken is one or one and a half metres above pitch level. Television needs a level of about 800 lux for adequate colour coverage, though for long lens close-ups they prefer up to 1400 lux. The minimum UEFA requirement for their matches is 750 lux. Modern lamps last much longer than the older types (about 1000 hours compared with 200 hours), cost less to run, but are very expensive to replace. A Thorn CSI sealed beam lamp, as used at grounds as varied as Hampden and Berwick, Tottenham and QPR, costs about £122 to replace.

Despite the advances, there is still a wide disparity between some League grounds, from the tallest pylons at Elland Road to the simple poles at Exeter.

It has taken almost a century to get this far, but despite the earlier misgivings there is no doubt that floodlighting has contributed a great deal to football in Britain and world-wide. It remains to be seen whether other ideas such as artificial turf and covered stadiums will take another hundred years to gain acceptance. The experience of floodlighting suggests that sooner rather than later would be to everyone's advantage.

·5·
PITCHES AND POSTS

Groundstaff at Tottenham laying down 3000 bales of straw to combat frost in 1925

The development of grounds' fixtures and fittings has been mainly a matter of experimentation and luck, shaped along the way by a series of random decisions.

Today, over a century after the birth of the FA, it is hard to see how the basic concept of pitch, goals and nets might be changed. Technological advance may allow the use of new materials, but the shape and form seem almost sacrosanct. For this reason, while all around, grandstands, players' kit, spectators, tactics and customs change with every season, the fixtures and fittings needed for a game of football are the most dependable constant we have.

Pitches

In common with cricket, rugby and hockey, football pitches can vary greatly in size, as long as the so called 'appurtenances' are of the required dimensions; that is the penalty area, goal area and centre circle.

When the first sets of laws were drawn up, each group of rule-makers deliberated according to the facilities they had available, so that Harrow School stipulated a maximum length of 150 yards and a maximum width of 110 yards, while Winchester's rules stated a pitch measurement of 80 × 27 yards. They also required that 'the ground is to be of good level turf'. Eton's early footballers had no such luxuries. Their eighteenth-century wall game was played on a patch 120 yards long but only 6 yards wide.

The first set of FA rules, drawn up in December 1863, stated that the playing surface should be a maximum of 200 × 100 yards, to be marked off with flag-poles (rather than pitch markings).

As the game became more organized and the crowds bigger, pitch markings were introduced in 1882, but only to mark the four boundaries. A half-way line was then added, not only for kick-offs but also to mark the extent to which a goalkeeper could handle the ball! Incredibly the goalkeeper was confined to handling the ball only within the penalty area as late as 1912.

By 1887 there was a centre circle, and two 6-yard semi-circles in front of each goal from which goal-kicks could be taken. A line 12 yards from the goal-line was added for penalty kicks, introduced after a suggestion from the Irish FA in 1890, and behind this was a shorter 18-yard line behind which players had to stand when the kicks were taken. Originally the penalty kick was taken from any point on the 12-yard line and the goalkeeper could advance 6 yards from the goal-line. The minimum distance an opponent could stand from a free-kick was 6 yards.

Finally in 1902 the more familiar markings of today were adopted, and have remained the same with just one addition – the penalty arc, brought to this country from the continent in 1937, when the minimum distance from free-kicks was raised to 10 yards.

At this stage of the pitch's evolution, only one feature had survived from the earliest laws, the corner flag, and only one change to the present pitch markings has been seriously suggested since. This was the addition of offside lines 35 yards from each goal-line. The idea originated in the United States, where soccer often had to take place on the narrower grid-iron pitches, and it was felt that by reducing the area in which a player could be offside would improve tactics and create more goals. It does have some advantages, in that play is less concentrated in the middle third of the pitch, but FIFA has essentially been unimpressed by the US innovation.

The current rules concerning pitch dimensions date back to 1887 and apply to all League clubs. They state that the length of the pitch should be a minimum of 100 yards (90 metres), a maximum of 130 yards (120 metres) in length, and a minimum of 50 yards (45 metres), a maximum of 100 yards (90 metres) in width, as long as the pitch is rectangular (that is, not 100 × 100 yards (90 × 90 metres)).

For international matches, however, a slightly narrower margin is required: between 110 and 120 yards (100 and 110 metres) length and 70 and 80 yards (64 and 75 metres) width. In fact, every one of the 91 Football League grounds and all but 10 in Scotland come within those narrower margins, albeit some only just.

The exact half-way points of both national and international sets of measurements represent a pitch 115 × 75 yards (105 × 69.5 metres), and it is no surprise to find that this is the most popular dimension found at top-class football grounds. Apart from Wembley and Hampden Park, 13 grounds are this

size, including all three Birmingham clubs, Ibrox Park, St James' Park and Hillsborough.

The League's biggest pitch used to be at Belle Vue, Doncaster, until the manager decided to lop off 8 yards, so now Maine Road is the largest, measuring 119 × 79 yards, or 9401 square yards in area. But Maine Road is neither the longest nor the widest pitch. The County Ground, Northampton is the longest, 120 yards, while Hartlepool and Orient are the widest, 80 yards. Generally, pitches are now much smaller than they were before the First World War, when, for example, the City Ground and the Priestfield Stadium had playing surfaces measuring 120 × 80 yards. The extra yards were used for expanding terraces and also the increasing number of running tracks laid down for training. But some grounds were big enough for large pitches and tracks. The Hawthorns originally had a pitch 127 × 87 yards, with a 9-foot wide cinder track.

The smallest pitch in the Football League is at The Shay, measuring 110 × 70 yards, or 7700 square yards in area. Imagine therefore the physical and psychological differences between playing at Halifax and at Maine Road, which is 1701 square yards larger, or the equivalent of a stretch of turf 120 feet square. When you are fighting for breath it is an appreciable amount.

It might be concluded, therefore, that the proportions of a pitch have a marked effect on the style a team might adopt, but this does not seem to be the case. For example, the flying wingers of the Wolves in the 1950s had a field only 72 yards wide, exactly the same as that of the Boleyn Ground, and yet West Ham's ground is generally thought to be narrow and cramped. Nor have Manchester City or Orient with their wide pitches been renowned for consistently producing first-class wingers.

The design of the ground is far more important to one's perception of pitch size than its dimensions. One would never have thought Highbury's pitch to be small – it is such an uncluttered, grand stadium – and yet the pitch is actually a fraction smaller than those at West Ham, Luton and Southampton, and is the smallest League pitch in London! Similarly we talk of the wide open spaces of Wembley, but never of York, Rotherham or Arbroath, even though the playing surfaces are of equal size.

In Scotland pitches are generally smaller. The largest is Ochilview, measuring 112 × 78 yards. The smallest is Brockville Park, 100 × 70 yards. So the difference between playing at Stenhousemuir and Falkirk is 1736 square yards, the equivalent of a patch of turf 125 feet square. Ochilview is also Scotland's widest pitch, with Airdrie, Brechin and Raith being the narrowest at 67 yards. There is, therefore, a considerable variety of shapes and sizes. However, there are very few instances of clubs who have failed to meet the requirements set down by the FA concerning pitches, the prime examples being Exeter between 1908–11 and Clapton Orient in 1930, when

Waterlogged pitch at Tottenham in 1937

their pitches were either too short or too narrow.

The most important factor is quality rather than quantity; I mention the statistics in this section mainly to emphasize the importance of architecture and design to one's image of a football ground. The numbers game can otherwise be a misleading diversion. (In addition, pitch measurements can change annually. My comments are based on figures listed in *Rothmans Football Yearbook* and *Clydesdale's Scottish Review*.)

Turf Technology

Having decided the dimensions of the pitch, how can the actual playing surface be improved? In the early years teams were quite happy to find a reasonable patch of grass in a public park, but once they asked spectators to pay to watch, it was only right that they should provide the best possible surface on which to display their talents.

Yet even today some top clubs are guilty of concentrating a disproportionate amount of funds on transfer fees and executive boxes, to the detriment of the turf, and to the ridiculous extent that once, a leading First Division club, having spent a few million pounds to assemble a team, would not spend £3500 on a new lawnmower. In other cases clubs have spent large sums on sophisticated new pitches but then only the bare minimum on vital maintenance. Much

depends on the circumstances of the club and the ground. To sustain a good playing surface needs money, but more than that it needs expertise and dedication.

The location of a ground is also crucial. A groundsman in an area of high rainfall has a much harder job than his counterpart in a drier region with a milder climate: so between Lancashire and Suffolk there is a significant difference. The height of the ground and its proximity to rivers can also have a marked effect on the quality of the pitch and the level of maintenance needed.

Stadium design is important. Every pitch needs natural ventilation and sunlight, but tall stands and completely enclosed grounds hinder both. The shadows from a stand can make one side of the pitch hard and threadbare while the other side is perfect.

But perhaps the most significant feature of a pitch lies underground, in the sub-structure and drainage, and when the Sports Turf Research Institute in Bingley, Yorkshire, conducted a survey of League grounds in 1982, 50 per cent only of the clubs replying could give any details of their drainage system. And yet the most common cause of postponed matches is a waterlogged pitch.

In the early days of League football, conditions were quite different. There are reports of steeply sloping pitches, as at WBA, surfaces as hard as pavements, as at Newton Heath, and methods of maintenance which seem positively ridiculous by today's standards. A favourite remedy for waterlogged pitches was to smother the surface with straw. In 1893 New Brompton bought 2 tons of coconut fibre to solve their watery problems, while Newcastle once tried to melt frost by laying down straw and setting fire to it. Once the fires got going, rain started falling and left the pitch a glutinous morass. United therefore covered the whole lot in sand!

To make matters worse, in many cases football pitches were used for a variety of other events – fêtes, parades, athletics, and most common of all, for grazing animals. A player launching himself into a sliding tackle had no guarantee of what he might land in! Grazing was encouraged because it brought in much needed revenue, and saved on cutting the grass.

There was also much greater access to the pitch from the terracing, so that before and after matches it was quite easy for hundreds of people to wander across the turf. Then during the week the pitch became the team's training ground. (Nowadays even the humblest clubs can find somewhere else to train for at least a couple of days a week, while those with their own training grounds need never set foot on the pitch at all between home games.) In the early years, therefore, the standard of playing surfaces was well below that to which we are accustomed now.

So many clubs had had to construct pitches on what had been a waste ground or refuse tip that it was often a mammoth task just to level the surface. The most effective sub-layer for drainage was clinker – the burnt ash residue from coal. Tons of this dirty, black substance were dumped on grounds all over the country, not only on the pitch but on the running tracks and to cover the terracing. In only a very few cases was the natural soil suitable for drainage, and even when it was the ground had still to be levelled, so that no pitch is truly 'natural'.

The value of a cambered surface was also realized, one of the first being at Burnden Park in 1895. Gibson and Pickford commented that the pitch had: 'a curious whale-back surface so that those sitting at one side of the ground only have the upper half of the players on the opposite wing in their vision'. They go on to state rather dubiously that this must be something to do with the drainage.

In fact Burnden Park's camber is still very pronounced, but the usual crown is about a foot higher in the centre circle than on the wings, and is often most noticeable along the bye-line where the turf rises up towards each goal post.

Installing proper drains underneath the pitch was another new idea, although the drains themselves were useless if the sub-soil was impervious or the top surface compacted. Often the drains would collapse or crack in extreme winter conditions, leaving puddles and damp patches. Very few clubs enjoyed the services of a full-time, trained groundsman. It was often left up to the trainer or a few unemployed labourers on a Saturday morning to give the pitch a

quick forking over. In return, the men would be given free admission in the afternoon. During the Second World War it was quite common for prisoners of war to be commandeered in the event of snow. Just before the Second World War the Wolves' manager Major Buckley tried to gain an advantage for his players by watering the Molineux pitch during the winter, because he felt they were at their best on heavy grounds, and that the ball was too lively on hard pitches. The FA did not approve, and allowed watering between March and October only.

Another short-lived idea in the 1930s was a spray which melted frost. Herbert Chapman went especially to Derby during the hard winter of 1933 to see the spray in use, but found that the frost soon returned within an hour.

In the 1950s Arsenal tried undersoil heating using electric wires, while both Liverpool clubs abandoned early attempts at heating and had to reconstruct their pitches. Nowadays most undersoil systems are oil powered, with hot-water pipes to melt the frost and drain pipes to carry off the excess water. In the winter of 1982 it was noticeable that Maine Road's pitch was in regular use, while Old Trafford suffered postponements. City had undersoil heating, United did not.

But the system is expensive. In 1982 the undersoil heating at Maine Road cost £4500 to operate during the season. Oldham Athletic paid £8000 (although Boundary Park is on high ground and suffers more from the cold). By 1986 costs had risen to approximately £1000 per match and the system itself cost between £60–100 000 to install. Yet there is no point in heating a pitch if the terraces and approaches to the ground are still ice-bound and too dangerous to use, and the public is unlikely to want to spend an afternoon or evening in the freezing cold.

Another idea was to protect pitches from above, by enormous plastic sheets draped over the turf. Leicester City installed a 'tent' which covered 90 000 square feet and was raised by means of blowers. These not only melted the frost but also allowed the players to train underneath, albeit in rather claustrophobic circumstances. Nottingham Forest and Aston Villa also installed plastic pitch covers. But none of these systems achieved what was hoped of them. The plastic tears easily and if the covers stay on too long there is a danger of fungus growing on the actual turf. They are mainly useful for protecting the pitch against rain for a few hours before kick-off, and after a heavy snowfall are quicker to clear than grass. But the cold air can still penetrate and allow frost to set in, so they are only about 40 per cent effective.

The pitch of today gets very little use. In the First Division typical usage is four hours a week, and even in the lower divisions the average is only five to seven hours. If it was not for bad weather, therefore, all the grounds would have almost perfect playing surfaces.

So how has turf technology developed to cope with the British climate? The Sports Turf Research Insti-

Polythene balloon, supported by a cushion of hot air, hovers above Filbert Street's pitch – a miracle cure which did not catch on

tute (STRI) is the main centre of research in this country, and was set up in 1929 to help not only football but much tougher customers like crown green bowling, cricket, lawn tennis and golf. It is a non-profit making body funded by a grant from the Sports Council, with research commissioned by the Department of the Environment. It gives advice to local parks and professional clubs, from Hackney Marshes to Wembley Stadium.

In May 1982 the FA and the Football Trust helped the STRI set up a laboratory to research the particular needs of football, the results of which will have a significant effect on football grounds in the future. The Institute studies types of grass, methods of irrigation, fertilization and drainage. It even tests turf for ball bounce. (There is as yet no standard factor of 'ball bounce', but the usual is about 30 to 35 per cent, meaning that a ball dropped from a height of 10 metres will bounce to a height of 3 to 3.5 metres.)

The researchers also have a machine to test wear and tear with different types of stud. It measures the vertical forces which produce compaction of the turf, and horizontal forces which tear the surface as, for example, would a sliding tackle.

There are three different types of pitch. The simplest, which has the minimum amount of drainage, is sufficient for perhaps local authority usage of up to three hours play a week. A better pitch with sand-slitted drainage could withstand up to nine hours a week. Sand-slitting is a system whereby every 2 feet a slit 2 inches wide is cut into the turf, filled with sand which carries the excess water down through a gravel channel to the sub-layer of slightly coarser gravel underneath. The advantages of the system are that it is cheaper and involves less reconstruction, but it can if badly installed create small dips in the surface. Also, if the turf is torn, or sheared, the sand-slit will be covered, or capped, and therefore make the drainage inoperative.

The Rolls-Royce of pitches is a sand-ameliorated construction, which has an 80 per cent base of sand on a gravel carpet. This costs about £75 000 to install, but can be used up to 20 hours a week. Portman Road

and Ewood Park both have such a pitch, and it is no coincidence that both are highly commended by players. There is one at the FA coaching centre in Lilleshall which supports 40 hours a week.

But no matter how well a pitch is constructed, if not tended properly it will spoil rapidly. Elland Road's pitch, for example, was described in 1971 as the best in the country, but when the team hit a bad patch there were fewer resources to maintain the turf's high standard. Less sand could be purchased to help break up the top surface and thereby improve drainage, and to raise income the club staged a rock concert. The effect of so many people standing on the grass, as Wembley discovered after the Pope's visit, was to compact the turf.

Elland Road then saw the introduction of Rugby League, putting further strain on the pitch. And so the recession had set up a vicious circle.

Leeds are by no means the only club to have suffered in this way. The trend suggests that more and more clubs are cutting back on turf maintenance as one of their first economizing measures.

Which is why artificial turf is so tempting a prospect. Consider the facts: the maximum reasonable usage of a high quality natural surface is perhaps 20 hours a week. A synthetic surface has unlimited use, not merely for sport but for exhibitions, concerts, and even markets. It allows a football ground to be used every day of the week, and therefore offers a hard-pressed club (and every club is hard-pressed) a chance to make some money.

If only it was that simple.

Artificial surfaces are not new. In 1906 a man called E. Cleary drew up a scheme to play indoor football matches at Olympia in London, under electric light and on a synthetic grass mat, reputed to have cost £5000. The FA naturally disapproved most strongly, but it need not have worried because the scheme was a complete flop. Indoor football itself was not uncommon; for example the two Nottingham clubs played each other annually in a large indoor hall for many years before the First World War. But unnatural surfaces were anathema.

The modern generation of synthetic turfs began with an embarrassing mistake in Houston. The Houston Astrodome, which Texans call the eighth wonder of the world, was the first and largest indoor stadium built for major sport. It was opened in 1965, with a natural grass surface. Unfortunately, the glass skylight panels in the domed roof had to be painted in order to reduce the glare of sunlight on the field, and as a result the grass could not prosper, and the pitch soon became a dusty, dry and hard surface.

Fortunately for the owners, the Chemstrand Company was able to develop a new artificial grass, which on installation in March 1966 became known as 'Astroturf'. So was launched 'a new and wondrous era in recreational engineering', in the words of Houston Judge Roy Hofheinz, whose idea the Astrodome was. A year later Astroturf was developed for use out-

Ground sharing at Elland Road. Notice the fine old stand of the greyhound stadium in the distance, sadly now demolished

doors, and all over the United States stadium authorities began to rip up their turf and lay down the revolutionary plastic grass. By 1970 there were 27 Astroturf pitches, and by 1975 it was widespread for baseball, grid-iron football and soccer.

Other chemical companies took up the idea, and a decade later Astroturf was already obsolete. It had a reputation for causing burns, for putting players' joints at risk, and above all for taking the element of unpredictability out of the game – whatever the game. Also after ten years' use it needed replacement, by which time the newer types of synthetic surface had ironed out some of the problems.

But not all, which leads us to Loftus Road, the first League ground to have installed an artificial surface. QPR chose a £350 000 system called Omniturf, already popular around the world and even used for a tennis court at Wimbledon. Omniturf is a sand-filled surface with grass made out of polypropylene fibre. Rangers wanted it to be strong enough to withstand not just regular sporting activity but also rock concerts and even performing circus elephants. But with the technology advancing so rapidly, it was in many ways a calculated risk, because Omniturf had not been tested in this country for football. Its main success had been in the United States.

Firstly, although the Football League gave its approval for an initial three-year period (1981–84), the FA was far from happy (shades of 1906), and there was a possibility that it would not permit Cup matches to be played on the new surface. Eventually permission was granted, although UEFA has yet to concede fully.

At first Loftus Road buzzed with activity. On one day alone three football games were held: a youth match, and two senior non-League fixtures. There was a four-nation hockey festival (artificial grass is particularly well suited to hockey), a London rugby Sevens' competition, and plans galore for pop concerts, US football and baseball matches. But the dream did not come true. Loftus Road was not in use every day of the week, and the rest of the footballing

fraternity did not seem particularly amused by the thought of Rangers bringing their Omniturf with them into the First Division in 1983–84.

QPR wanted their surface to withstand the heaviest use, but in providing for this they had to alter the base recommended by the manufacturers. Hence the pitch was harder and bouncier than is generally acceptable for football. Eventually the club had to bow to criticism by softening the bounce with extra quantities of sand. This has improved the pitch, but has hardly placated the critics.

Throughout this book there are examples of clubs and the authorities being afraid of innovation and new developments, so it would be rather unfair to criticize QPR. True, they might have waited for further developments and more research but someone had to do it sooner or later, and Loftus Road was one of the most suitably designed stadiums to cope with a wider range of events, having a large proportion of seats and almost total cover on four sides.

QPR, I believe, are to be saluted, in exactly the same way that Herbert Chapman deserved praise for trying to get approval for floodlighting. The FA did not like that idea either, but 30 years later almost every club in the League had floodlights.

No one would claim, least of all the various suppliers and manufacturers, that synthetic grass will solve every club's problems. Clearly it would be inappropriate at grounds like Anfield, Highbury or Old Trafford. But since QPR's much-maligned efforts, a further four clubs (Luton, Preston, Oldham and in Scotland, Stirling Albion) have installed much superior artificial pitches.

For some years the debate suffered from a lack of any serious study. This was remedied by the publication in 1986 of a Sports Council report on artificial grass. The report was the work of a committee, chaired by the former England manager Sir Walter Winterbottom, comprising representatives of football's senior bodies, including the Professional Footballers' Association, together with the Sports Council, the Rubber and Plastics Research Association and the Sports Turf Research Institute.

Published by the Sports Council, the report noted that apart from North America, artificial surfaces were being used in Sweden, Finland and the Middle East (since publication, eight UEFA nations have approved synthetic surfaces). It then set out to discover how the new turf measured up to the real thing and which standard tests should be applied to measure a product's suitability for the level of football for which it was intended.

Three levels were set: internationals, national league and cup competitions, county and regional competitions, and local football, recreational and training usage.

Three performance characteristics were examined: the reaction between ball and surface (for example, ball bounce), individual players' movements (twisting, turning and tackling) and the impact between

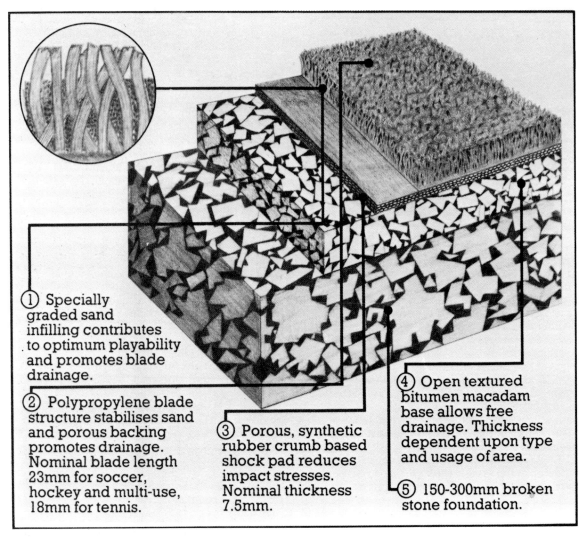

1 Specially graded sand infilling contributes to optimum playability and promotes blade drainage.

2 Polypropylene blade structure stabilises sand and porous backing promotes drainage. Nominal blade length 23mm for soccer, hockey and multi-use, 18mm for tennis.

3 Porous, synthetic rubber crumb based shock pad reduces impact stresses. Nominal thickness 7.5mm.

4 Open textured bitumen macadam base allows free drainage. Thickness dependent upon type and usage of area.

5 150-300mm broken stone foundation.

En-tout-cas, one of several types of artificial pitch construction

the player and the surface (how did it feel to run or fall on the surface?). Some of the tests were performed by machines similar to those used at Bingley, but players' reactions were also closely evaluated.

The committee then took their tests to eight League venues and Wembley, before testing thirteen brands of synthetic pitches in use around the country.

The report also considered research carried out at Newcastle and Leeds into the causes and effects of football injuries. Of particular interest was a survey conducted in Leeds by Dr Ian Adams of 1174 games played on natural surfaces and 1042 games on a local artificial pitch. It represented the most comprehensive study of the subject ever undertaken. Until then, all the critics of plastic grass had to go on was evidence concerning grid-iron football in the United States.

Having studied the evidence, Winterbottom's

report concluded that at amateur level and below artificial pitches resulted in fewer injuries. At professional level only the club physiotherapists at QPR and Luton were able to offer evidence.

Luton Town had followed Rangers' example in 1985, by which time the technology had advanced way beyond Omniturf's original specifications. The club's interest arose initially because of the possibility of a move to an indoor stadium in Milton Keynes (see Luton). After opting to stay at Kenilworth Road Luton then decided to install their own artificial surface. They chose a brand called Sporturf Professional, made by a Leicestershire company En-tout-cas.

At a symposium organized at Kenilworth Road in May 1986, the Luton club doctor reported on the past season's injuries among his 27 players plus those of visiting players, and found that the new pitch resulted in 18 per cent fewer injuries (measured in terms of missing games). The problem of burns was also found to be less than feared with this new type of pitch – it was always recognized that earlier versions did induce more burns – and Luton claimed that the number of burns reduced considerably once their pitch bedded down later in the season.

Luton's physio also stated that because of the pitch's all-weather availability, Luton's players benefitted by being able to train normally throughout the year and by avoiding the usual fixture pile-up which inevitably followed a harsh winter.

Other observations are worth noting. First, not every player disliked the pitch. Indeed some were complimentary and three managers, Brian Clough included, professed themselves to be quite happy with it. Other endorsements came from Ron Greenwood and Mike England.

Secondly, Luton did not appear to gain a major advantage. In that first season their home record was no better than seven of the previous nineteen seasons (QPR's home record since 1981 was hardly impressive either). Luton players said that the pitch gave them added confidence, made shooting easier, especially on the half-volley, and reduced the spoiling abilities of less talented opponents. Indeed Town's own central defenders enjoyed their best ever disciplinary record in their first season on the new turf.

Thirdly, and perhaps most importantly to those clubs considering artificial turf, Luton's new surface earned them an extra £100 000 in that first season. In just seven months it was estimated that 7000 players used Kenilworth Road for over 200 matches and various coaching sessions. Other activities included lacrosse, netball, rugby, American football and a concert. The actual pitch itself cost £350 000 to install, five times as much as a high quality grass pitch, but was less costly to maintain.

Few of these facts managed to persuade some League chairmen – if indeed they ever studied the Winterbottom report or Luton's evidence. Until 1985 League clubs had needed a vote of approval from fellow members before putting down a plastic pitch. Tranmere Rovers were, for example, turned down in 1983, and comments such as Terry Cooper's that he would resign if an artificial pitch was laid at Ashton Gate, were frequently made, if not always heard.

By 1986, however, the attitude had softened, and in May Preston became the third club to install a new pitch. They also chose an En-tout-cas product, as did Oldham shortly after. But just as these pitches were about to go down the voice of obscurantism raised its hoary head within football circles, just as it had during the debate on floodlighting.

In February 1986, at a time when matches were being called off with depressing regularity and players were risking injury on frost-bound pitches, the players' union announced that a ballot of their members had shown an overwhelming majority against synthetic surfaces.

Then in May the FA banned the playing of FA Cup matches on any artificial surface installed after 1985, which meant that Luton and QPR could use their grounds in the event of a home tie, but Preston could not.

In a statement of bewildering illogicality the FA explained that they had nothing against artificial pitches but wanted every club to have an equal chance in the Cup. They did not, however, order Ipswich or Blackburn to tear up their excellent pitches, or tell Yeovil to level their notorious slope.

Unreason followed unreason. Within the League, opposition was marshalled by Leicester City (ironically so, since En-tout-cas are based nearby). Their chairman told television viewers that 'spectators did not get the same value for their money watching a game on plastic as they do on grass'.

This was perhaps the most crass generalization made during the entire debate, but Leicester persisted and at the League's Annual General Meeting on 23 May 1986 proposed a change of Rule 68 so that 'No match in the First or Second Division of the League be played on an artificial surface after 31 July 1988 except in exceptional circumstances . . .' Everton seconded the motion, and after speeches for and against – some of which betrayed little or no recognition of the Winterbottom report's findings – the proposal was defeated.

Artificial surfaces had survived, and immediately Oldham went ahead with their installation. Six other clubs received permission from the League, although few of them were in a position to afford actual installation at the time.

Then in October 1986 the FA relented and allowed Preston and Oldham's pitches to be used for FA Cup ties, only to reimpose a blanket prohibition the following March. The situation as of 1987–88 was therefore that no synthetic surface could be used in the FA Cup, the affected clubs being Queen's Park Rangers, Luton, Preston, Oldham and non-Leaguers Hyde United and Feltham. In 1987 QPR's new chairman, David Bulstrode, decided that Rangers would return to grass in 1988, so the experiment at Loftus Road at least was over. But Luton remained committed to the cause and were due to challenge the FA's ban in the courts in late 1987.

Meanwhile, other research suggested a different approach to turf technology. This was for a pitch made up of a subtle mixture of natural and synthetic elements.

Called Cell System by its Swiss developers, such a pitch was installed by Fulham in 1983 to replace their overused, diseased and commonly waterlogged surface at Craven Cottage.

Cell System is a natural surface built on a sand-based sub-layer which is lined underneath by polythene, therefore creating a controllable environment for growth and maintenance. The pipe system can hold or release water as required, and has the capacity to drain up to an inch of water an hour. In comparison a sand-ameliorated pitch can cope with 2 to 4 inches a day. But because the Cell System pitch drains so well, it also means that the vital nutrients wash through the sub-layer much quicker, so extra fertilization is necessary – up to twice as much as a conventional pitch.

So the pitch needs more attention, though maintenance is comparatively simple, and also costs more to install – about £160000. In return, however, it will theoretically be playable for more hours and in worse conditions (see Fulham).

It has certainly been a success in places like the Greek National Stadium in Athens, in Vancouver and various stadiums in the Middle East, but in the British climate? Results at a trial pitch in Southwark, London and at Craven Cottage indicate that the Cell System has an excellent chance of success in League football.

For roughly the same cost as this system a club could also install an artificial surface with a natural base. The system employs a similar top surface to the Omniturf variety, but rests on a nylon filament mat on top of the existing surface (if the drainage is sufficient). This provides extra 'give', absorbing shock and allowing a ball bounce equivalent to that of a normal turf pitch – about 30 to 35 per cent. Because it can be laid without extensive excavations it costs around £180000 to £200000.

Other developments include the possibility of natural grass grown on a plastic mesh, a combination of real and artificial turf able to withstand harder wear and last longer through a process of regeneration.

Although the En-tout-cas system and its sisters will hardly take over League football, it will undoubtedly become the accepted surface for local authority sports centres, where 60 to 80 hours a week is the normal playing requirement. Already clubs including Manchester United, Manchester City, Barnsley, Arsenal, Tottenham and Wigan have installed and share with the community artificial surfaces for training purposes, either indoors or outdoors.

The debate will run and run for sure, and the outcome is impossible to predict accurately, given the speed with which new developments are being made. With the state of affairs as it stood in 1986 it seemed most clubs would not turn to wholly synthetic surfaces but would lean more towards the Cell System and other improved types of natural pitch construction. Artificial turf will be found more on training pitches, which the clubs will share with their local communities, and in indoor arenas for six-a-side soccer, hockey and tennis.

If every surface was perfect, football would become soft and too clinical. And surely, no amount of technological advance would be able to reproduce the smell, the lush swath of a freshly mown pitch. No plastic could change with the season, or remind you that this is Burnley on a wet, winter's evening, or Blackburn on a sunny afternoon. There has to be variety.

A hundred years ago players were lumbering about sodden, bumpy pitches, kicking a ball so heavy with water that some actually died from heading it. Matches finished with greatly reduced teams because players had had to go off from exhaustion. The standard of football pitches has still to improve, and if artificial turf stimulates that process it is decidedly a good thing. More important is the need for all parties concerned to be cognizant of the facts. Synthetic pitches alone are far less damaging to football than the brand of ill-informed argument which has dogged the debate so far.

Goals

It has taken a long time for the present style of goals to evolve, through a process of trial and error combined with a large measure of arbitrary judgement. Early forms of the game did not always require goals; the 'goal' was often simply to get the ball across a distant line, or hit a certain wall. For example the Eton wall game, dating from 1717, used a garden door for a goal at one end, and an elm tree marked in white at the other. At Winchester there were no specific goals, although it is recorded that on one occasion a boy acted as a goal by standing with his legs apart, potentially a very painful role. Westminster School used two trees, 20 yards apart as their goal.

In 1720 Matthew Concanen described the goals at a match in Ireland as being, 'form'd by sticking two willow twigs in the ground, at a small distance, and twisting the tops, so that they seem like a gate'. Joseph Strutt's account of football in 1801 refers to the goals as 'two sticks driven into the ground about two or three feet apart'.

The poles rather than the Irish arch caught on during the nineteenth century, and Eton's rules between 1800–63 stated that goals should be formed by two 7-feet poles placed 11 feet apart. Harrow School had a quite extraordinary rule: if the first day's play should result in a draw, the space between the poles was to be doubled from 12 to 24 feet. How different the game would have been had this rule been adopted more widely. Harrow called their goals 'bases'.

A most influential set of rules came from Cambridge in 1863, and these allowed for two poles of indeterminate height to be placed 15 feet apart. A goal was scored if the ball passed between them, but at any height, so it was as well that most of the participants were sporting gentlemen who would not see fit to dispute an umpire's decision. The FA, formed in October 1863, stated in its rules that goals were to consist of poles set 8 yards apart, and this apparently random choice has persisted ever since.

About three years later the Sheffield Association started using crossbars, although this was possible because their goals were 9 feet high but only 4 feet wide. The expertise for having longer crossbars did not exist. But the FA did decide to place a tape across their goals on the suggestion of the Chairman, who had seen a goal scored at Reigate from a kick which sent the ball between the posts but 'quite 90 feet in the air'. There was also pressure from Sheffield to adopt the use of a crossbar, but the FA would not permit this until 1875. Finally the crossbar became obligatory after a conference in Manchester in 1882. The 8-foot high, 8-yard wide goal had arrived to stay.

From then on, it was a question of what shape and size the actual posts and bar should be, and in 1895 the final ruling was that the width and depth of posts should not exceed 5 inches (12 centimetres). One club, Turton FC near Bolton, had used telegraph poles for their goals, sunk half their length into the ground. But even the much thinner posts, now obligatory, had to be sunk into the earth and supported from behind either with guy ropes or stanchions. It was nevertheless quite common for goalposts to collapse in the course of a game. The shape could be round, half-round or rectangular, but was usually square.

Then in 1920 a new company in Nottingham called Standard Goals developed an entirely different type of goalpost and crossbar, shaped elliptically. A set of these goals was presented to Nottingham Forest in 1922, and although the FA did not give its official approval until just after the Second World War, every League club in England adopted the elliptical posts. This led to one legalistic problem. Should the 8 yards be measured from the innermost plane of the posts, or the front edge? The FA ruled in 1938 that it should be the inside measurement, and for several years the City Ground's goals were about 2 inches narrower than all other clubs'.

The elliptical posts were different in two ways. Firstly the shape made a rebound more unpredictable than the square posts, and secondly they were stronger. The modern crossbar is reinforced with a metal rod to give it greater suppleness without breaking, and can be deflected up to a foot up or down. Previously crossbars were prone to sagging, so the new reinforced bars are actually manufactured in a banana shape, so that when hung between posts the curve is straightened up by the force of gravity.

Most goals are made out of hardwearing Douglas Fir, and if looked after by a conscientious groundsman can last up to 15 years of League football. But it needs only one pitch invasion to permanently damage a set, or as used to occur but is now banned, for a goalkeeper to swing on the bar. This happened once at Prenton Park when Rochdale's keeper managed to snap the bar.

A set of wooden elliptical posts, with ground sockets, costs about £350, or a crossbar alone about £100, and even though they are supposed to last a while, many clubs choose to replace them at the end of each season.

Instead of wooden goals, several clubs have started to use aluminium sets, imported from Sweden, which cost almost twice as much but are lighter and need less maintenance. On the other hand they are more brittle in collision. Wembley has a set of aluminium

Portman Road's clever aid to grass cutting

goals, and they are round rather than elliptical in shape.

The shape can make a difference to a game, if one compares the rebound of shots against a square post and an elliptical post. Several Scottish grounds have the square post, largely for traditional reasons.

There have been many suggestions made over recent decades to enlarge goals in order to increase the chances of scoring, but there has never been any attempt to change the colour of the posts. White may seem the most obvious choice, but with new developments in luminous paints and plastics there is no reason why bright green or orange goals could not be used. Outside Britain it is quite common to see black and white striped posts, so there is no hard and fast rule.

One day perhaps we may even see electrically lit goals, the posts and bars having fluorescent tubes inside. These would look marvellous at night matches. Another development might be electric eyes to determine whether a ball has gone over the line.

Traditionalists may scoff, but without innovation or evolution we would still be playing with two poles and a tape.

Nets

Anyone who has played football without nets will know how difficult it can be to assess whether or not a goal has been scored. Yet it was not until 1892 that the idea was finally approved by the FA. Until then a shot on target could quite happily sail into the crowd, or even bounce back off spectators behind the goal.

The apparently obvious, but simple idea of nets is attributed to J. A. Brodie, a Football League referee and the City Engineer of Liverpool, although there is a suggestion that they may have been tried in Birmingham as early as 1885. It apparently took Brodie 20 minutes to work out his design in 1889, but he then put it away and forgot the plans until reminded a year later by a letter in the press, suggesting the introduction of nets. Brodie had his design made up and tried out at a game on the Old Etonians' ground in Liverpool, situated almost exactly where the present entrance to Anfield now stands.

The League sanctioned the use of Brodie nets

almost immediately, and for once the FA also acted quickly. In 1890 they told members that they could use nets if desired.

A further trial took place in January 1891 at a North v. South game at Forest's Town Ground, and also for a League match between Bolton Wanderers and Forest, when nets were used in only one goal.

Scotland's first official view of nets was on 1 January 1892 for a friendly between Celtic and Dumbarton.

The FA gave its final approval in February 1892, when it was agreed with the patentee what price clubs should pay for the nets. Brodie then went on to engineer the country's first dual carriageway, the Queen's Drive in Liverpool, and later assisted in the designs for New Delhi, India. Yet it is for his nets that he became famous; such is the power of football.

In March 1892 goal nets made their first appearance at the Cup Final, between WBA and Aston Villa at the Oval, and have been a compulsory feature at grounds ever since – although the FA rules still say that nets 'may' be attached. But as Raith discovered to their cost in 1894, it was even then generally accepted that all clubs should have nets. Rovers had to replay a Scottish Cup tie v. 5th Kings Rifle Volunteers because they failed to supply any nets for the original tie.

Having established the principle, it then became necessary to perfect the arrangement. For example, in 1908–09 WBA scored a goal v. Blackpool, but the nets were so tightly drawn that the ball bounced back into play. Although it came straight to the feet of an Albion forward who could have simply tapped it back

in, the players all trotted back for the restart. But the referee waved play on, thinking the ball had hit the bar.

Albion scored another two goals, both rebounding out, but both allowed. The cancellation of the first goal proved to be very costly, since Albion missed promotion to Division One by 0.0196 of a goal. Who said goal nets were uncontroversial?

In more recent years at Filbert Street, in 1970, Aston Villa scored, but the ball hit the back stanchion and rebounded out. Even though Leicester's goalkeeper said it was a goal, the referee waved play on. That disallowed effort eventually meant Villa were relegated to Division Three. As a result of this and similar incidents, goal nets have been adjusted to hang in front of stanchions, at least where the stanchions are very close to the posts.

The introduction of modern materials has meant that goal nets can be any colour, even striped as at Blundell Park, and will last much longer. Most clubs change the nets every season, but they should have a total life-span of up to ten years. There are two types; the conventional 2-inch square mesh, usually made of polythene, which cost about £90 for a pair, and a new type of anti-vandal nylon nets, with a closer mesh, more expensive at about £220 a set.

Even though the new generation of nets are weather resistant, they still have to be taken down for pitch maintenance, except at Portman Road, where the groundsman has devised a simple system for lifting the nets clear off the pitch without unhooking them (see Ipswich Town). Another apparently obvious, but remarkably simple idea.

·6·
NORTH WEST

MANCHESTER
·UNITED·

Previous Grounds

Manchester United's first home was at North Road, just north east of the city centre. The club formed as the L & Y Railway FC and in 1878 became Newton Heath, named after the company's main Manchester depot. Described as 'a mud-heap' at one end and 'hard as flint' at the other, North Road was often submerged in smoke from nearby locomotives and chimneys. The players changed at the Three Crowns pub on Oldham Road and had to walk a few hundred yards to the ground, which is now covered by Moston Brook School, on the corner of Northampton Road and Church Lane (the location should not be confused with North Road, Clayton, near United's second home).

Newton Heath joined the League in 1892 and in 1893 moved a short distance to Bank Street, Clayton. Gibson and Pickford were highly complimentary in 1906 when they noted that, 'today at Clayton one sees palatial stands, 20th Century appointments everywhere'. In fact the ground stood in the shadows of a chemical works and was little better than North Road, as *The Guardian* correspondent wrote of a match against Portsmouth in 1907: 'All the time the struggle was waging the 30 Clayton chimneys smoked and gave forth their pungent odours, and the boilers behind goal poured mists of steam over the ground.' A further disincentive to the fans was the ground's distance from the road. So badly off were the club that for offices they borrowed a wooden hut erected by the *Manchester Evening News* for their football correspondent's telephone. On one occasion bailiffs waited at the turnstiles to impound the gate money, and the gas supply was cut off. The club went into liquidation in 1902 after the team finished near the foot of Division Two. But they were rescued, and transformed into Manchester United by a local brewer, J. H. Davies, who invested £500 and paid for a small stand. Bank Street was even the venue for an inter-League game between Scotland and England.

After Cup Final victory in 1909 Mr Davies gave the colossal sum of £60 000 to purchase a site several miles away to the south west of the city centre, adjacent to the headquarters of Lancashire County Cricket Club. United played their last game at Clayton on 22 January 1910, beating Spurs 5–0. Shortly after one of the stands collapsed in a storm. The ground's exact location was opposite Ravensbury Street, between Bank Street and the Ashton Canal. Still open land, the only surviving element of the ground is a 10-foot stretch of wall.

Old Trafford

Bobby Charlton called Old Trafford 'a theatre of dreams'. It is the best attended stadium in Britain and one of the most popular among visiting players.

When the Stretford End roars the noise is equivalent to a modern jet airliner taking off. United fanatics from all over the world come to tour Old Trafford with all the reverence and awe normally reserved for stately homes or cathedrals.

An early sketch of the ground shows Old Trafford was the identical shape it is today, but in 1909 there was only one stand with a multi-span roof on the railway side where the main stand is now. Messrs Brameld and Smith of Manchester were responsible for the building, under the supervision of Archibald Leitch. The official opening was on 19 February 1910 when a 50 000 crowd saw Liverpool win 4–3.

It was at this time that the FA held an enquiry into the club's affairs and found it 'extravagantly run'. Davies was receiving £740 rent for 14 acres of land which the club did not even use. United were called 'Moneybags United' and stigmatized for being a 'private monopoly'. Much of the criticism was justified, but the element of jealousy was equally strong, for Old Trafford was, in one writer's words, 'a wonder to behold'. It had a billiard room, massage room, a gymnasium, a plunge-bath, a capacity of 80 000 and attendants to lead patrons to their five shilling tip-up seats from the tea-rooms.

Soon after the War, Old Trafford witnessed two very different record attendances. On 27 December 1920 United's largest ever League attendance,

Old Trafford between the wars. Notice the multi-span Main Stand roof

70 504, watched a League match v. Aston Villa. In May the following year, only 13 people bothered to pay for a Second Division fixture between Stockport County and Leicester City. Edgeley Park had been closed following crowd disturbances, County were also doomed to relegation, so the fans decided to boycott proceedings. In fact there were about 2000 at Old Trafford to see the game, but the majority had stayed on after United's afternoon match v. Derby County to see two games for the price of one!

By the late 1920s Old Trafford had become rather outdated as other clubs developed their own grounds along modern lines. The multi-span roof was then extended at each end with corner roofs (one of which essentially survives today) – an indication that even then United had a long term strategy for the ground's development. On the United Road side was an 80-yard long pitched roof standing cover. Even so, compared with grounds such as Highbury, Goodison, White Hart Lane and Villa Park, Old Trafford remained fairly basic.

Old Trafford is very close to the Manchester Ship Canal and the important Trafford Park industrial estate. During the War German bombers spent many nights trying to cripple key installations, but they also dropped two bombs on United's home on the night of 11 March 1941, one virtually destroying the

Main Stand, another hitting the United Road terracing and cover. The pitch was also scorched.

To rebuild the stadium required determination enough, but to develop a comprehensive rather than piecemeal restructuring demanded admirable foresight and confidence. Indeed it was United's ability to survive and conquer after 1941, just as much as after Munich in 1958, which has won the club its magical aura. When Jimmy Murphy joined United in 1946, the task of rebuilding was formidable. He recalled: 'The ground was a bombed out shell; we had no money; there was some sort of pokey little dive of an office where Walter Crickmer as Club Secretary operated; then Matt (Busby) got hold of a nissen hut which the lads used for changing. The practice pitch was a mile or so away, while the business of the directors was carried on largely at Mr Gibson's, the Chairman's office at his storage firm in Cornbrook.'

United were by no means the only club to suffer war damage, but they were certainly the worst hit. In August 1945 the War Damage Commission granted the club £4800 to clear the debris, with a further £17 478 to rebuild the stands. A keen United supporter at this time was the Stoke MP, Ellis-Smith, who lived in nearby Eccles. He tried hard on the club's behalf to increase the Ministry of Work's aid, especially after the Chancellor of the Exchequer said in the House of Commons in February 1948 that his Labour Government 'desired to encourage all forms of entertainment'. United planned a stadium to hold 120 000, but in the end settled for a simple stand to replace the old one, built of tubular steel and scrap metal. United were then £15 000 in debt, and were paying out large sums to Manchester City to use Maine Road until Old Trafford was rebuilt. City fared well from their neighbour's inconvenience since United were having a good Cup run and attracted huge attendances. For the 1947–48 season alone United paid City £5000 plus a share of the gate receipts. Eventually, after eight years at Maine Road, City asked United to leave, so the Ministry of Works stepped up the repairs and on 24 August 1949 the Reds went home to beat Bolton 3–0.

At that stage the Main Stand was seated but not roofed, and the two corner sections which had survived the War provided the only cover. The United Road terracing opposite and both the Stretford and Scoreboard Ends were open. In 1951, as materials became available, the Main Stand roof was completed.

Although their training ground at The Cliff had been floodlit a few years before, Old Trafford's lights were not switched on until 1957, first used for a League game on 20 March, v. Bolton Wanderers. Until then United had played their mid-week European games under Maine Road's floodlights.

After Munich, and as United built the famous team of the 1960s, Old Trafford began to assume the form it takes today. The Stretford End was covered in 1959, then in 1962 the club were asked to prepare for the 1966 World Cup. With a grant of £40 000 the United Road cover came down in 1964 to make way for a magnificent cantilever.

Taking responsibility for this was a Manchester firm of architects called Mather and Nutter which later went on to design stands at Molineux and White Hart Lane. If the Hillsborough cantilevered stand can be regarded as the first large-scale modern stand of the post-war period, the United Road Stand at Old Trafford must be seen as the actual trendsetter.

Firstly, it allowed for expansion at either end. Secondly, it recognized the spectators' preference for both standing and seated accommodation, but thirdly, and most important of all, it incorporated the first private boxes ever seen at a British football ground. To persuade the United directors, Mather and Nutter took them to see private boxes installed in their new grandstand at the Manchester racecourse, but with little effect. Who would want to watch football behind glass? Soccer fans were surely a breed apart from the racing fraternity. But the architects persisted, and as the new stand progressed they sat the directors in seats placed at the back of the stand and asked them to visualize the possible lay-out. Immediately their clients saw the advantages, and the boxes were installed.

When completed the United Road Stand had accommodation for 10 000, with a covered paddock in front. Its total cost was £350 000, and it quite transformed the ground. Old Trafford had built a team for the 1960s, and now they had the beginnings of a super stadium to match. The sleek cantilever reflected well the popular image created by the likes of George Best and Denis Law, so that Old Trafford was in many ways as much part of the period as were the Beatles and swinging London. All over the world people wanted to support Manchester United, to an extent which even more successful clubs, like Liverpool, have never quite enjoyed.

After the United Road Stand, a further £76 000 was spent on ground improvements for the 1966 World Cup, in which Old Trafford hosted three games in Group Three. Two years later United reached their peak, winning the European Cup.

The last section of the ground to be covered was the Scoreboard End, a name retained after the cantilever stand was carried round to that end to meet up with the old corner roof in 1973. An additional 5500 seats were installed and the number of private boxes totalled 80. In place of the old manual scoreboard, an electronic system was introduced in the corner.

Now that Old Trafford was fully covered, the next stage was to replace the older elements with cantilevered roofs, in line with the United Road side and Scoreboard End. United started with the Main Stand roof, replaced in three sections, starting at the centre in 1978. This phase, costing £1.5 million, ended in December 1984 with the opening of new offices and executive suites behind the Main Stand. What had been an open driveway between the main entrance and a railway line was now almost entirely covered by multi-storey buildings, partly on stilts.

Once the new offices were ready this paved the way for the old office and boardroom block, behind the Warwick Road corner terrace, to be replaced. United had to cut away the old terracing and roof like removing a slice from a cake. All that survived was the corner section of terracing in the front paddock. Work began in late 1984 and was completed, at a cost of £1.5 million, in August 1985. The cantilever roof thus swept round 75 per cent of Old Trafford, leaving only one corner and the Stretford End unmodernized. The new section also brought the total number of private boxes up to 103 (Spurs, with 72 boxes, own the second highest number).

Thus, as Old Trafford nears completion it represents the nearest Britain has come to one of the more modern Continental stadiums, and is certainly far in advance of other British grounds, with the exception only of Ibrox Park, which is based on an entirely different concept.

Like Rangers, however, United have proved that money alone is not enough; other clubs have spent as much over the years and achieved much less. The crucial factor at Old Trafford has been adherence to a sensible, long-term plan which avoided prolonged disruption and linked stands of the same design yet

Old Trafford in 1986 looking towards the Stretford End

built twenty years apart. Old Trafford's current capacity is 56 500, of which 25 693 are seated (only a handful less than Maine Road).

One other development at Old Trafford is worthy of note. When the most recent corner was built the architects – the same firm as in 1964, although now called Atherden and Nutter – suggested that apart from creating the Sir Matt Busby Suite, United might like to fill the remaining space with a Manchester United museum. This had long been the ambition of the late Denzil Haroun, a Manchester United director. Haroun was well respected as a champion of the ordinary fans, but sadly never lived to see the museum and visitors centre open in May 1986.

The museum is believed to be the first of its kind at any club ground in the world, and provides an entertaining, if inevitably superficial, glimpse of United's eventful history. Of particular interest in the present context are photographs and plans of United's previous grounds, plus a pictorial record of Old Trafford's development, although the most poignant exhibit is a telegram sent by the late Duncan Edwards to inform his landlady that United's flight from Munich had been delayed.

The museum is open six days a week with invited parties only on match days, and forms part of a tour of the ground.

Old Trafford's future is clearly mapped out. In 1986 new lights were installed on gantries around the roof so that the original floodlight pylons can be dismantled in 1987. When sufficient funds are available the surviving corner and Stretford End roof will be replaced and the cantilever continued from the Main Stand to the United Road side, without gaps. The Stretford End will, however, be all standing. The estimated cost of this work, at 1986 prices, is £3 million.

How soon the work is done depends largely on ambitious plans outside the ground. On what is now number one car park, United plan to build a 10 000-seater indoor sports arena for basketball, rock concerts and other major indoor events. Also to be designed by Atherden and Nutter and estimated to cost £3 million, this arena would make Old Trafford the most advanced sporting complex in Britain – a veritable Wembley of the North. And since it would have the potential earning power of £20 000 per day, it would seem likely that this project will be built first, in order to help finance the completion of the stadium.

Ground Description

Old Trafford is on the border between Manchester

and Salford, which to visitors seem like one entity, but to locals are definitely separate. If taken on its own, Salford is the largest town in England without a League club. Behind the ground runs the country's oldest canal, the Bridgewater Canal, and a few hundred yards north are Manchester's docks, connected to the sea by the Manchester Ship Canal – hence the apparently incongruous sight of dockside cranes on the skyline around inland Old Trafford. To the east is the massive industrial estate, Trafford Park, and to the south the more famous Old Trafford Cricket Ground. Also nearby is the now disused White City Greyhound track.

The ground is best approached from Warwick Road North, past numerous fast-food take-aways, over the railway bridge, to the forecourt where in 1958 Manchester United fans gathered in reverent silence to pay tribute to the dead after the Munich aircrash. A clock over the offices is dedicated to their memory, and further along on the back of the Scoreboard End Stand is a plaque recalling those players and officials who died.

The stadium (the term 'ground' becomes inappropriate once inside) is like a huge red cavern, with the dramatic sweep of the cantilever roof covering three sides. Yet there is not total uniformity. The base of the Main Stand, for example, is in essence part of the original stand built in 1909, although one has to look closely for details. From ground floor level upwards it becomes the post-war stand, and from the seating tier above, where restaurants and lounges look down onto the pitch, all is post-1973.

From here to the immediate right is the newly cantilevered corner stand, exclusively reserved for family use – that is, no adult is admitted without a child. Underneath are televisions, special refreshment bars and an area where players meet the fans before and after games. This corner also incorporates the museum, the Sir Matt Busby Suite and a computerized ticket office.

Because the new corner followed the lines of the Scoreboard End cantilever, when it met up with the Main Stand the rake of seating was found to differ by about 6 feet. There is therefore a slightly awkward join in the corner.

To the left is the Stretford End, named after the district. Most popular ends are all standing but there is a small section of 1500 seats at the back of the stand, barely visible from the front. You can see quite clearly from the colour of the roof where the 1959 Stretford End roof was built onto the pre-war corner section of the Main Stand. Now that three quarters of Old Trafford has been updated, the Stretford End seems positively archaic in comparison. The seats are wooden benches, the view is restricted by roof supports (as at most other grounds) and in the corner between here and the Main Stand the rear section of terracing is wooden, built up on a web of steel. Walking around the base of this end provides a clear illustration of how the ground was originally banked up in 1909.

Opposite is the United Road Stand, running the length of the pitch and curving round the corner along the Scoreboard End. The roof seems quite small from here, but it does in fact span some 100 feet. The fascia is plain, and the paddock rear wall is bare concrete, but to compensate all the seats are red.

The boxes at the back barely intrude at all, unlike the black fronted boxes in more modern stands. These boxes were used for a scene in Albert Finney's film, *Charlie Bubbles* (1968), which showed the disappointment of a child taken to Old Trafford but separated from his heroes by the sheet of glass, a poignant indication of how removed the supporter could be from the essential experience of live football.

United have to an extent solved this problem by providing each box with loudspeakers which can relay the noise from inside the stadium. Patrons even have a switch to vary the level according to their mood! (Luton and Watford have adopted another solution, by installing a private seated balcony in front of glass sliding doors, thereby allowing boxholders to 'sit out' if they so desire.)

Incidentally, Old Trafford has appeared in more feature films than any other British ground. Apart from *Charlie Bubbles*, other credits include *Hell is a City*, with Stanley Baker and Donald Pleasance (1960), *Billy Liar*, starring Tom Courtenay and Julie Christie (1963), and *The Lovers*, with Richard Beckinsale and Paula Wilcox (1972).

An all-enclosed stadium is all very well in a hot country, but in rainy Manchester it has presented problems for the Old Trafford pitch, which does not get enough natural ventilation. Undersoil heating was installed in 1984 but after embarrassing failures during the following season the system was overhauled and the pitch resurfaced in 1986.

But Old Trafford is more than just a football stadium. During the week it thrives with activity in its various lounges and suites, while the car parks are fully used for major cricket matches down the road (United's car parks have room for over 2000 cars).

United still, therefore, live up to their old nickname of 'Moneybags United', even though Old Trafford is one of the cheapest venues in the First Division. You could buy two of Manchester United's best season tickets, plus a season ticket for the car park, all for less than the price of just one season ticket at White Hart Lane.

Old Trafford is not as apparently impregnable as Anfield, or as grand as Villa Park or Highbury, yet its more uniform design and three covered corners make it a sound trap of red and white aggression. Since United are so well supported, I would add that for sheer partisan noise and atmosphere, there is not a ground in England to match Old Trafford.

Nor is there a ground to which so many visitors flock, just for a look around; a fact illustrated by the sign which requests visitors not to walk on the pitch. It is written in five different languages.

◆ MANCHESTER CITY ◆

Previous Grounds

Manchester City were originally called Ardwick FC, a club formed in 1887 by the amalgamation of two teams, West Gorton St Mark's and Gorton Athletic. The former had begun playing in 1880 at a rough cricket ground on Clowes Street, just off Hyde Road. A season later they moved to Kirkmanshulme Cricket Club, on the corner of Kirkmanshulme Lane and Pink Bank Lane. But the cricketers objected to the damage to the turf so Gorton switched to a field on Queens Road, called 'Donkey Common'. This ground was next to a very noticeable spice mill. From 1884–87 the club played on another field off Pink Bank Lane, until one day when taking a short cut to his work in a timber yard, the Gorton captain, K. McKenzie, climbed over some hoardings in Bennett Street and discovered a perfect patch of waste ground. It turned out to be the property of the Manchester, Sheffield and Lincolnshire Railway Company, which agreed to let the land at £10 for seven months from August 1887. This was the club's first properly enclosed ground, and became known as Hyde Road, the nearby main road running from Manchester to Hyde, Glossop and Sheffield.

It was here that the name Ardwick FC was adopted, and in 1892 the club joined local rivals Newton Heath as members of the Football League, although Ardwick were elected to the Second Division, and Newton Heath went straight into the First. Some would say it has been a bit like that ever since (although Newton Heath soon joined Ardwick in the lower division after two disastrous seasons).

Hyde Road was a fairly large ground, but hemmed in by the railway to the west and sidings to the north, and railway drivers would often slow down as they went past for a quick view of the game, as happened at Burnden Park and The Den. According to one observer Hyde Road was characterized as being surrounded by subterranean passages and railway arches. There were two stands, and an estimated capacity of about 40 000.

Hyde Road was visited by King Edward VII, an occasion very nearly ruined when a small fire broke out in the Main Stand, and also by the Prime Minister, A. J. Balfour.

By the beginning of the First World War, when Hyde Road was taken over as stabling for 300 horses, it was becoming apparent that the ground was no longer adequate for the growing number of supporters. The decision to move was given greater urgency when, on the night of 6 November 1920, the Main Stand burnt down. The cause was not, as might be thought, a stray firework but a cigarette end.

All the club's records perished in the fire, as did their faithful watchdog 'Nell', an Airedale terrier.

The stand was all wooden and held 4000 people, but the ground had another stand opposite and this had to suffice until other arrangements were made. Meanwhile, 50 men were hired to clear up Hyde Road, and it was reported that they must have been City devotees because they finished the work at a speed which would have shocked other contractors!

For a time it had been planned for City to move to nearby Belle Vue, a large pleasure park where they had played before in an early floodlit game v. Newton Heath, and where the existing speedway and greyhound stadiums still stand. But the site available was only eight acres, and City wanted somewhere larger. (Belle Vue became in 1926 the site of the first formal greyhound stadium in Britain.)

The club soldiered on at Hyde Road until the summer of 1923, by which time their new stadium at Moss Side was ready. The last game at the ground, whose lease was up in any case, was a public practice match on 18 August 1923. City left straight after, taking with them just a few turnstiles and the goalposts. The remaining stand was sold to Halifax Town for just under £1000, and is still at The Shay.

Hyde Road today is the site of a bus depot, the actual pitch being covered with a skid pad for training in Bennett Street. All the previous grounds have been built over, except Queens Road, which now forms part of Gorton Park, on Hyde Road.

Maine Road

In moving to Moss Side, City were moving closer to Manchester United. The new site at Maine Road was two miles west of Hyde Road, and about three miles east of Old Trafford. There seemed to be two advantages. Firstly, Moss Side was a densely populated suburb close to a vast new council housing development, with easy access from all South Manchester and the city centre, but secondly and more important, the site offered the chance to build the biggest stadium in England apart from Wembley, which had just been completed.

An architect called C. Swain was assigned the task of designing the new stadium, and the first job was to drain and level the site, until then used as a claypit for brick making. Only one stand was built, but it was huge, seating just under 10 000 on a single tier, even though it did not run the complete length of the touchline. The rest of the ground was open terracing, a total of 20 miles of concrete steps. In plan it was identical to Old Trafford, a rectangle with slightly rounded corners, but it was bigger. Estimates of its capacity ranged from 80 000 to 100 000, and the total cost of building came to nearly £200 000, a vast sum in those days.

One week after City's last game at Hyde Road on 25 August 1923, a crowd of 60 000 saw Lord Mayor W. Cundiff pronounce Maine Road open, before City's opening First Division fixture v. Sheffield United.

The ground soon proved its capabilities. For example, a crowd of 76 000 saw City v. Cardiff in the FA

Maine Road in its early days. Notice the slight curved gable on the roof. The base of this stand still exists

Cup quarter-final later that season. On route to their second FA Cup triumph City played Stoke City in the 6th Round, on 3 March 1934. The attendance of 84 569 was the highest for any English club match apart from a Cup Final, and the first of several attendance records Maine Road was to notch up.

But before these, there was another development at the ground. Just before the war the Main Stand roof was carried round the corner and extended over the Platt Lane End.

After the war Maine Road became the busiest ground in the country, for Old Trafford was unusable after extensive bomb damage (see Manchester United) and City played host to their neighbours. They could not have picked a better time to share the ground, because United were in top form in both League and Cup. This, allied to the spectacular rise in attendances following the war, meant that Maine Road was regularly packed to capacity.

The attendance of 80 407, for a Cup semi-final replay between Derby and Birmingham in 1946, was the highest ever recorded for a mid-week game, at a time when these were played in the afternoons. The following season City won the Second Division Championship, United were runners-up in the First Division, two representative matches were held at Maine Road, plus the Cup semi-final between Burnley and Liverpool, and finally the ground also staged the Northern Rugby League Final. Altogether some 2 250 000 spectators had attended Maine Road in just one season, a record for any League ground.

The following season saw United runners-up again in the League and winners of the Cup. By now attendances of over 70 000 were commonplace at Maine Road, and in a short space of time in 1948 United attracted 82 950 for a match v. Arsenal – the highest ever League match attendance – then 81 000 for their Fifth Round Cup tie v. non-League Yeovil (won 8–0).

Maine Road therefore held the record attendances for both League and Cup matches. But even though City were charging United up to £5000 a season (as in 1947–48) plus a share of gate receipts, in 1949 they asked United to leave. Old Trafford was restored for

the beginning of the 1949–50 season, and City now had their ground all to themselves again. It did them no good, however, for in 1950 they were relegated.

Those post-war years brought in large profits, and part of these were spent on an unusual development, the installation of seats on the Platt Lane terracing. Nowadays this is a common occurrence, but it was quite novel then. It took Maine Road's seating capacity to about 18 500, more than any other club ground in Britain.

City were once more back in Division One, and on 14 October 1953 they switched on their floodlights for a friendly v. Hearts. This innovation brought Manchester United back to Maine Road for a series of vital mid-week matches in various competitions, until Old Trafford had its own lights in 1957.

In 1956 City won their third FA Cup, and a huge roof was built over the Kippax Street banking opposite the Main Stand. This left only the North or Scoreboard End uncovered, and meant that Maine Road was almost identical to Old Trafford for a spell during the 1960s. But there were small changes. The Main Stand had a very slight semi-circular gable in the centre of the roof, with decorative moulded fascia. In the 1960s this was replaced with a new roof which had a raised section in the centre, allowing an unhindered view for at least the two middle blocks of seating, but at the same time robbing the stand of any dignity. It now looked larger but very plain.

In 1963–64 the floodlighting system was sold to non-League Leamington, and replaced with four very tall pylons visible from miles around, plus another smaller gantry on the Kippax Street roof. During a run of successes in the 1960s the Scoreboard End was rebuilt and covered by an impressive cantilever stand. Unlike Old Trafford's Scoreboard End cantilever, this one was all-seated and could not link up with its neighbours. Called the North Stand, it holds 8100 seats.

The most recent development has been the replacement yet again of the Main Stand roof in the summer of 1982. Ostensibly the first phase of a £6 million redevelopment scheme – at a time when the club was heavily in debt – the new roof cost £1 million to erect and was paid for by the Supporters' Development Association. Work began on the last day of the season, and the builders promised City £50 000 compensation for every game played with the roof incomplete. After a difficult summer's work, the stand was finished on time, and both parties were happy.

Recent safety adjustments have only slightly reduced Maine Road's capacity from 52 500 to 49 500, but the total number of seats, 25 700, is still marginally the highest at any English club ground (Old Trafford is just behind).

In view of this, Maine Road would seem a perfect venue for major games, yet apart from the 1984 Milk Cup Final replay between Liverpool and Everton, it is often overlooked. As described below, quantity does not necessarily mean quality, while the ground's design, which makes segregating rival fans a problem, is a further obstacle.

Ground Description

Maine Road is approached from any of several back alleys or small streets, some of them named after famous City players, like Frank Swift (who died at Munich) and Sam Cowan.

The main entrance on Maine Road is very simple; the façade is large, but without distinction.

Inside the ground the most immediate focal point is the new roof, a huge white canopy resting rather awkwardly above the old stand. This canopy is composed of 16 barrel-vaulted sections of glass-reinforced plastic panels, joined together to resemble a huge piece of corrugated iron. Each panel can bear the weight of 7½ feet of snow and had to be tested to withstand the heat given off by the floodlights above.

Supporting this structure is a huge steel cross-beam, itself supported at each end by 3 feet thick steel uprights. The roof is therefore not a cantilever.

From other parts of the ground the roof looks totally out of place, and even rather awkward, especially at the North End where it overhangs the original stand but does not quite link up with the North Stand cantilever roof, several feet lower. But the Main Stand's old roof made it quite the gloomiest, most miserable stand imaginable, whereas now it is transformed into a light and pleasant seated area. The white panels and steel work contrast well with the new blue seating, but make the few surviving old wooden bench seats with their curled iron armrests seem wholly incongruous. Along the cross beam new executive boxes are planned, though the position seems uncomfortably high over the near touchline.

From here, to the right is the Platt Lane Stand, curving round from the Main Stand to the far open corner, in a style similar to that of the old corners at Old Trafford. The roof is wooden, with advertisements painted onto the wooden fascia. The stand has bench seats bolted onto the old terracing, and has been built up at the back on wooden terracing. The rake is therefore unchanged, and with a line of uprights along the front, viewing is not always ideal. Compared with the North Stand opposite the arrangement is positively archaic, and is no doubt part of the reason for Maine Road not being able to attract semi-finals. But possibly the most telling weakness of the ground is on the east or Kippax Street Side, now the only part of the ground left for standing spectators. Controlling rival supporters, who must stand on either half of the Kippax Street bank, demands considerable effort. Once inside the ground they are barely separated by a thin gangway.

The Kippax roof is vast, dark and low, so that when standing under it, even the sunniest day seems quite cold and gloomy. In the centre of the roof is a sign welcoming you to Maine Road.

The North Stand is the neatest and most complete part of Maine Road, and until the erection of the new

Maine Road's all-white new Main Stand roof

Main Stand roof it would have seemed logical to continue the cantilever roof round that side of the ground. This was technically impossible, but the cantilever might still be extended towards Kippax Street (it is one of Maine Road's peculiarities that Kippax Street is actually behind the North Stand, while Platt Lane is several streets away).

The North Stand lacks colour, being essentially grey and light blue, but offers a superb view. At the back is an electronic scoreboard.

If this early account of Maine Road's development seems taken up with statistics, I fear I must now introduce one more, for here is the largest pitch of any British football ground (see Pitches). This size is most evident by the Kippax Street touchline, where instead of high security fencing, there is room for an additional fence beyond the perimeter wall, and even then there is a wide running track and spare turf. City have installed undersoil heating.

Nowadays size is not the most crucial factor at a modern football ground. Villa Park is smaller in capacity than Maine Road but can still attract big games, even though Maine Road has more seats. The ground is a frustrating mixture of the very best and the very worst, from the spacious North Stand to the confined Kippax Street enclosure. It lacks stylistic unity and identifiable character because it has not had a feasible development plan. For this reason Maine Road will always seem second best to Old Trafford. On the other hand, bricks and mortar are not everything, and sheltered within Maine Road is one of the friendliest clubs in the League.

This is not merely a platitude. While 35 000 packed the ground for a rock concert at Maine Road in 1986, over at the club's training ground on Platt Lane, a new sports centre financed jointly by club and an urban aid programme attracts over 60 000 people every year, from 7-year-old footballers to senior citizens. City have invested £210 000 in the project, which has two artificial surfaces (one sometimes used for flat green bowling) and one full size grass pitch with a synthetic running track open to the public. No other League club has shown such a commitment to its local community.

STOCKPORT ·COUNTY·

Edgeley Park before the distant Cheadle End Stand was demolished and the timber terracing concreted over

Previous Grounds

County started life in 1883 as Heaton Norris Rovers, playing at the Heaton Norris Recreation Ground. The following season they moved to the Heaton Norris Wanderers Cricket Ground on Brinksway. In 1885 Rovers moved to Chorlton's Farm, off Didsbury Road, then amalgamated with rivals Heaton Norris and played at the Ash Inn Grounds on Manchester Road. 1887 saw them at Wilkes Field, Belmont Street, until 1889 when they found their first enclosed ground at the Nursery Inn, Green Lane. They changed their name to Stockport County, and the players built a wooden stand which held 4000 but had no roof. After 12 years they moved to Edgeley Park. Since it was at the time also the home of Stockport Rugby Club, County continued to play some first team and most reserve games at Green Lane.

Edgeley Park

When County joined the rugby club at Edgeley Park they had been in Division Two for two years. In 1921 they were relegated and the ground was closed following crowd disturbances.

The 1930s saw a revival. County scored a record number of goals, including a 13–0 win over Halifax, but were plunged into despondency on 22 July 1936 when the first wooden stand was burned down. In the blaze the club records were lost, though one player, Billy Bocking, heroically managed at least to save his beloved boots. The present main stand was built soon after.

Whereas the Army had used the ground during the First World War, the Second World War saw the return of rugby with Broughton Park RFC, whose own ground was used for military purposes.

The post-war boom in attendances brought Edgeley Park's largest crowd on 11 February 1950, for the visit of Liverpool in the FA Cup 5th Round. A crowd of 27 833 saw County lose 2–1.

Floodlights were first used on 16 October 1956 for a friendly game versus the Dutch team Fortuna '54 Geleen.

When Edgeley Park became designated in 1985 safety inspectors ordered the demolition of the mainly wooden Cheadle End stand, built in the 1920s. The old timber terracing on the Railway End and parts of the Popular Side also had to be concreted over and a 9-foot wide perimeter path laid.

In the Main Stand the small paddock area at the front was closed and wider gangways created between seats. Whilst this work was done, at a cost of approximately £150 000, the capacity was reduced massively from 16 000 to 6000. A final capacity of 8000 was the aim, to include 1500 seats.

Ground Description

However distinct Stockport's identity as a town may be, as for Bury, Oldham and even nearby non-League Altrincham, there can be no escaping the fact that both Manchester clubs are within an easy few miles.

Yet as one approaches the main entrance from Hardcastle Road the small town feel of the ground makes Old Trafford seem like another world.

The simple unadorned Main Stand seats 1500 and once accommodated Queen Elizabeth when she visited Stockport for a display by schoolchildren during her Jubilee year; 9000 attended, which suggests County might be wise to offer Her Majesty a season ticket. The ground also staged the World Lacrosse Championships in 1978.

From this Main Stand, which has bench seating at either end and a neat, striped perimeter fence, you can see the Railway End to the left. Now concreted over, its most distinguishing feature is the remains of a tall old scoreboard, now an advertisement, clearly visible to passengers who travel within yards of this end on the main London–Manchester railway.

Opposite the Main Stand is the Popular Side which originally held 16 000 standing but was cut in half in 1979 to provide space for an all-weather five-a-side pitch behind. This explains why the roof appears awkwardly high over the terracing.

To the right is the Cheadle End, where formerly stood a low, but cosy, all-seated stand with a faded advertisement along the roof. The chimney of a bleach works is prominent behind.

The stand once helped to tie each side of the ground together and give Edgeley Park a modest unity. Now that it is gone, a rather bare, flat terrace occupies the spot and the ground suffers accordingly, one example of how the sudden designation of Third and Fourth Division clubs improved safety but harmed the appearance and atmosphere of small provincial grounds such as this.

·BURY·

Gigg Lane

Bury have played at Gigg Lane since their formation in April 1885. The club immediately secured a tenancy of the land, which formed part of the Earl of Derby's estate. If the ground seems larger and more imposing than one might expect of a club in the lower divisions, remember that Bury have spent most of their existence in Divisions One and Two, and were twice winners of the FA Cup in 1900 and 1903.

The first stand was built in November 1887 on the South side for £50 11s 8d, followed by a Members Stand on the North side two years later. By 1895 Bury had joined the League, replaced the original stand and expanded Gigg Lane to hold 20000. But as we learn from Peter Cullen's centenary history of Bury – to which I am indebted – gates were so low, even in the First Division, that it was once suggested the club relocate to Rochdale. A cover at the Gigg End (or Cemetery End) was built after the first Cup Final win and in 1906 the current South Stand was built, originally for standing only.

Money was a constant problem for Bury – one valuable source of income was a 'smoking cafe' at the ground – so when the Earl of Derby and a certain John Brandwood presented the ground to Bury as a gift in June 1922 it was like manna from heaven. The new owners enhanced their property by rebuilding the ends parallel to each goal-line, thus losing the ground's former elliptical shape.

Promotion to Division One in 1924 brought considerable changes to Gigg Lane, costing £12000 and raising the capacity to 41600. The current Main Stand was built around the base of the former Members Stand, 2000 seats were installed in the South Stand and a 500-capacity Boys Stand with bench seats built next to it, although a roof was not added until two years later. Other improvements included the conversion of the field behind the Main Stand into a car park and the erection of turnstiles along Gigg Lane. In common with Aston Villa and Hibernian, Bury suffered from strikes in the building industry during this period, but they overcame this by simply agreeing with the unions to hire the men directly under the club manager's supervision.

Bury must have felt proud when a record gate of over 33000 came to witness the reopening of Gigg Lane by League President John McKenna on 30 August 1924. And although the club was soon back in the Second Division, after a public appeal in 1938 the Manchester Road End stand was built at a cost of £3440, thus giving Gigg Lane cover on all four sides.

After the war Bury terraced the South Paddock, and in 1952 saw the roof of the Cemetery End stand torn off by a gale. But the winds of change really blew the following year, because Bury were the first club in the North West to have floodlights.

These were inaugurated on 6 October 1953 against Wolves, whose own lights had been switched on only a week before. Like Wolves, Bury then played a series of floodlit friendlies against top clubs, including Admira Vienna, Hadjuk Split and both Manchester clubs, although the Shakers received little of the acclaim heaped upon Wolves for their pioneering efforts. Gigg Lane also staged the first floodlit cricket match, played over two nights between England and a Commonwealth XI. Unlike the football, these matches failed miserably. Only 1782 people attended and the experiment was not repeated until Chelsea tried it in 1981.

Gigg Lane's record gate came in January 1960, when 35000 attended a Cup-tie v. neighbours Bolton and two years later, after ten years of fund-raising by the supporters' club, a new £9000 roof was built over the Cemetery End (notice how in so many cases, the clubs have paid for stands with seats while supporters have had to raise money to keep themselves dry on the terraces).

Gigg Lane has been considerably affected by safety regulations. From a capacity of approximately 35000 including 7500 seats, the figure was first reduced to 22500. Then in 1985 following the Bradford fire, the all-wooden Boys Stand was removed and the predominantly wooden Main Stand, whose paddock had been closed in 1982, had 4000 (or 71 per cent) of its seats debarred from use. Extra safety work cost the club nearly £100000 and left Gigg Lane with a much reduced capacity of only 8000, of which approximately 3500 were seated.

Ground Description

For a crash course on the state of modern football, Gigg Lane would make a perfect starting point. In a small town which, courtesy of the motorways, is now within easy reach of Old Trafford, Gigg Lane is a pre-war ground cut down to size but accustomed to crowds even smaller than the new limit.

Yet it remains the most attractive enclosure in the

Gigg Lane's South Stand

North West. Tucked away behind the Manchester Road, amid narrow streets and trees, its stands reflect a bygone era of optimism while its short, squat floodlights are modest, toy-like and barely intrusive.

The large Main Stand, whose rear blue frontage backs onto a car park as big as a football pitch, once held 5600 and now holds only 1500. Its glass screen ends are chequered with blue squares and its deep blue balcony wall juts in and out along the now disused paddock. This wall used to be delightfully striped blue and white but now has a more serious aspect, as if to confirm that the good old days are over.

To the left is the more modern Cemetery End terrace, with a plain sloping roof and modern housing units behind. By the south east corner, where once stood the tiny wooden Boys Stand, is now a flat no-man's-land used to segregate rival supporters. Boys are different now, it would seem.

Opposite is the South Stand, over 80 years old, an exquisite relic of an age of innocence. Lined by trees at the back and with access only from the front, this long, low wooden stand has wavering benches and narrow iron pillars. Its high rear terrace wall mirrors that of the Main Stand and there is a wide paddock in front. Fortunately it has survived recent safety checks and, with Preston's Grand Stand, is one of the oldest structures at a League ground.

To the right is the covered Manchester Road terrace. Manchester's northern suburbs are only three miles south of the ground. The rear section of this gently sloping end is fenced off with the wood which used to form its terracing.

Despite the changes, Gigg Lane retains much of its appeal, for in the centre of all that blue paint and pre-war design lies a pitch still reckoned to be among the best in Britain. There is no track, the grass grows right up to the perimeter. One observer at the turn of the century noted, 'its turf is reputedly unsurpassed', and the same might still apply. Between 1919 and 1981 Gigg Lane was tenderly groomed by just two groundsmen, Jim Savery and Tommy Marshall, and their legacy lives on. Gigg Lane may have been hurt, but it is homely still.

◆ OLDHAM ATHLETIC ◆

Previous Grounds

Although Lancashire is regarded as the birthplace of the Football League and of those teams who prospered in it during the early years, not all Lancashire clubs predate 1888. Oldham Athletic's history, as told by Stewart Beckett in *The Team from a Town of Chimneys*, began in 1897 in the form of Pine Villa, a pub team playing on a pitch near Pine Mill. When the town's professional soccer team, Oldham County, went into liquidation two years later, Pine Villa moved to their home at the Athletic Grounds, on Sheepfoot Lane. Now called Oldham Athletic they turned professional, but after only a few months had a rent dispute with the landlord and had to move to a pitch by Westhulme Hospital, at Hudson Fold. During the summer of 1906 they moved back to Sheepfoot Lane, to their present ground.

Boundary Park

Boundary Park was the property of J. W. Lees Brewery, a family firm which has had close dealings with the club since. Originally the home of Oldham County, the first sod had been ceremonially cut in July 1896 with a silver spade now kept in Oldham's VIP suite. The first match should have been on 19 September 1896, when Robert Ascroft MP kicked off a friendly v. Chorley, but the weather was so appalling that both he and the teams sought refuge in the dressing rooms and the game was abandoned. When Athletic returned to the ground a second time (see above) their inaugural match was on 1 September 1906 v. Colne, watched by 3454 spectators.

Boundary Park had two stands in its early days. On the site of the present Main Stand stood a quite substantial pitch-roofed stand with covered seats and an open paddock. Its most distinctive feature was a central raised gable for viewing, similar to that of Bramall Lane.

Opposite was the Flat or Broadway Stand, built hastily when Oldham were elected to the League in 1907. A long and low stand with a flat roof, it too had a distinctive central gable, almost a mirror image of the one opposite but less enclosed, rather like a log-cabin on stilts.

While early photographs show how spectators stood on top of the flat roof, Oldham's manager, the bowler-hatted David Ashworth, went further by running along the roof in order to follow play. On one occasion, against Leeds in 1908, he almost ran off the end, leaving himself in a most undignified position.

The present Main Stand was begun in 1913 but not completed until 1920, although it was intended to add wings as finances allowed. One of the highest attendances at the ground was not for football but for the Prince of Wales's visit in 1921.

Boundary Park's Main Stand

Oldham were already an average Second Division team when in October 1927 the Chadderton Road Stand, a covered terrace, was opened. But not for long. A winter's gale blew it down again soon after. When reconstructed, openings were put along the back wall to let the wind blow through the stand, and the roof has been secure since.

Boundary Park's highest ever attendance, 47 671, came to watch Athletic's 4th Round FA Cup tie v. Sheffield Wednesday, the First Division Champions on 25 January 1930.

Three decades later the club had to seek re-election and was near to closing down completely, but a year later Oldham installed new floodlights, first switched on for a friendly v. Burnley on 3 October 1961. Athletic were the last League Club in Lancashire to have lights.

Years of optimism followed, with the club in Division Three and plans were prepared to transform Boundary Park into a super stadium. By the end of the decade the plans were forgotten as Athletic slipped back into the Fourth Division. But when they made a quick recovery in 1971, a new stand was indeed built, for Oldham had not only won promotion, but also a short-lived competition known as the Ford Sporting League.

Held for one season only, Ford gave points for goals, but deducted them for bad behaviour on the pitch, and they stipulated that Oldham had to spend their £70 000 prize money on ground improvements, even though at the time the club were receiving aid from the local council just to stay in business. The result was a quickly-built new stand named after the sponsor, in place of the old Broadway Stand. This brought the seating total to 2939, but after the introduction of the Safety of Sports Grounds Act, as a Second Division club Oldham had to spend £250 000

to keep all those seats in use. The overall capacity was nevertheless reduced by some 8000, and now numbers 26 300.

Being one of the highest grounds in Britain, Oldham's pitch was prone to freezing, so in 1980 some 16 miles of undersoil pipes were laid at a cost of £60 000. This meant the pitch was usable when most of Oldham's neighbours were out of action. For example, Boundary Park once staged an Oldham RLFC match and on Boxing Day 1981, when Oldham were due to play at Ewood Park, for the first time in League history the authorities allowed the venue to be switched.

The chances of Oldham staging more matches in all weathers was increased in 1986 when Boundary Park became the fourth League ground to install artificial turf. Like Luton and Preston before them, Oldham chose En-tout-cas, but Boundary Park's 6-foot slope had to be levelled first.

Ground Description

The name is apt. From the new roads linking Oldham with the motorway, Boundary Park appears to stand quite on its own, unchallenged on the skyline except by the large Monarch Mill to the north west.

The Main Stand is a short, blue-painted stand, oddly angled to the west as if it were meant to continue to the goal-line but could not quite reach. The roof appears to have bowed with the effort. In front of the high paddock rear wall is now a line of modest private boxes.

From here, to the left, is the covered Chadderton Road End, a simple pitched roof over a dark interior. The blue barriers cease where there are wooden terraces at the rear. It is said the stand is haunted by the ghost of 'Fred', a man who stood at the same spot on these terraces for many a year, until his death during a match in the early 1960s.

Opposite is the Ford Stand, also not running the full length of the pitch. The stand is a very simple modern version of the traditional post and beam construction, a necessary choice because in 1971 £70 000 did not go far. In fact, it seems hardly different from the previous Broadway Stand. It seats only 1406, with an uncovered paddock in front.

To the right is the open Rochdale Road End. Spotland is six miles to the north. The banking has been cut down in recent years, but the predominant image is that of the Monarch Mill, looming up behind the bank, a chimney pointing up between the floodlight pylons.

First with its undersoil heating and now with its shining new synthetic surface and private boxes, Boundary Park is no longer the archetypal Northern ground coated in grime. The mills and chimneys are still there, just, and while the silver spade which cut the first turf in 1896 might not be joined by the spade which cut the last grass in 1986, not far away at a local hospital a newly laid lawn is much admired. The old turf gives pleasure still.

·ROCHDALE·

Spotland

Spotland was originally called St Clements playing field. The first football club to play there was Rochdale AFC in 1900, followed in 1903 by another team, Rochdale Town. Both clubs disbanded after only one season at the ground, which was then used for rugby. In 1907 the present Rochdale club was formed and has played at Spotland ever since.

Rochdale bought the ground for £1700 in 1914, and joined the League in 1921. In their first season occurred the first of three mishaps to befall the Main Stand, which has survived until the present day. In December 1921 a gale blew down the roof, causing £500 damage. The club also finished bottom of the League, a position it has occupied four times since.

The Pearl Street roof dates from this period, and in 1927 the Willbutts Lane Side was also covered.

The Spotland pitch had a notorious 5-foot slope from west to east, until the summer of 1948 when the excess earth was dumped onto a corner of terracing, forming a miniature Spion Kop. Crush barriers were put up on this new mound for the visit of Notts County in the FA Cup in December 1949, which attracted Spotland's record crowd of 24 231.

Floodlights were used in February 1954 for a friendly v. St Mirren, but although Rochdale was only the third club in the north west to have lights, in his history of the club, Brian Clough (not the manager!) reports that manager Harry Catterick described the 7000 gate as 'the lowest so far for the opening of any floodlight installation in the country'.

Fate dealt the Main Stand a second blow in August of that year, when a fire caused £350 damage. From that figure one can guess the size and structure of the stand in question.

A new cover over the Sandy Lane End was built in 1961, with £6000 raised by the supporters. Five years later, as if it had not suffered enough, the roof of the Main Stand collapsed once more, this time under the weight of a heavy snow fall.

Spotland was in the news again for the wrong reasons in 1970, when Coventry City refused to play a postponed FA Cup match under Rochdale's by now outdated floodlights. To add insult to injury, their manager Noel Cantwell added the gamesman's retort, 'Where's Rochdale?' He soon found out, for 13 011 people turned out on a Monday afternoon to see Rochdale beat the First Division team 2–1.

However, in August 1971, the lights were replaced with the present set for the cost of £18 000, and were officially switched on by Sir Matt Busby.

In 1980 Rochdale sold Spotland for £175 000 but three years later, with help from a £60 000 loan from Rochdale Council, the ground was repurchased for a similar sum.

The present capacity has been reduced from 20 000 to 12 000, with only 730 seats.

Ground Description

The Main Stand is situated well back from the touchline, behind a wide track and a flat path that runs round three sides of the ground. This distance, and low terracing and seating, make viewing far from ideal. The stand's front wall shows the effects of the 1954 fire, for it is wood on one side, concrete on the other. Behind the stand is the very heart of Rochdale, the supporters' social club, without which survival would be even more difficult than it is.

From the seats you can see Knowl Hill straight ahead on the left, and Rooley Moor on the right, both over 1300 feet high.

To the left is the Sandy Lane End, a covered terrace, ahead is the Willbutts Lane cover, much improved in 1982, and to the right is the Pearl Street End. All three terraces have only a shallow rise, and until 1984, when concrete resurfacing was begun, the timber and cinder terracing at the Pearl Street End was the last of that type surviving in the League. A new roof completes the end's refurbished look. Behind rises the steeple of St Clement's church.

The highest ground is the south east corner, the Kop, or 'the hill'. Otherwise even the neighbouring terraced houses are as tall as the stands.

The overall combination of a wide pitch, a wide perimeter track, low stands and distant hills give Spotland a distinctly dated appearance – too open to be cosy, too underdeveloped to have much distinction. This is of course exactly what the condescending 'Where's Rochdale?' brigade would expect: stone walls, open moors and cobbled streets. And yes, they are all there around Spotland, but those who know this part of Lancashire appreciate that the scale and spirit of Rochdale will long survive, even though three miles away a motorway entices people to Old Trafford and other more glamorous neighbours.

Spotland's highest spot is the Kop in the corner

· BOLTON · WANDERERS

Previous Grounds

Bolton adopted the title 'Wanderers' for the obvious reason, that they had no particular home to call their own. The club formed in 1874 as Christ Church FC but disagreement with the vicar forced it to break away three years later. Among many early grounds used were the Park Recreation Ground and Cockle's Field, until Wanderers finally struck roots at Pikes Lane in March 1881. Dr P. M. Young's history of the club tells us much about Bolton's grounds.

Pikes Lane, a notoriously muddy ground, also suffered from being situated at the foot of a hill, from where an excellent free view was to be had. *Athletic News* reported in February 1884 that between 4000 and 5000 spectators had assembled on the slopes during Bolton's Cup replay v. Notts County, and an enterprising farmer charged them half the Pikes Lane entrance fee.

Annual rent for the ground was £35 in 1881, but by 1893, with Bolton now in the Football League and enjoying higher gates, this rose to £175. All around, building speculators were closing in, so the club began to look for a more suitable site. Bolton Corporation owned some land on the Manchester Road, bought with the intention of expanding the gasworks, but when these plans fell through Wanderers made enquiries to the local Gas Committee, in August 1893. Soon after losing their first FA Cup Final, at Goodison Park in 1894, Bolton were told they could have a 14-year lease on the 5-acre plot, at an annual rent of £130. Two small roads would have to be closed, which meant seeking permission from the Tar Distillery Company and Bleachworks, and in order to gain more influence, Wanderers became a limited company. Pikes Lane was last used at the end of the 1894–95 season.

Burnden Park

In 1895 the site of Burnden Park was miserable; one end bound by a railway, and the land a stagnant mess of dumped refuse and chemicals from nearby works. This was a frequent sight in Victorian industrial cities, yet time and again football clubs were able to transform such wilful neglect into order.

It was said that the pitch was built up on old barrels and cotton bales, but whatever its foundation, this was the most cambered surface ever seen in the League (see Pitches).

A Scarborough contractor was called in to lay out the new ground, under instructions from John Norris, who specifically requested a cycling track round the pitch, just like the one laid for the King of Italy. A firm called Coopers of Bolton built the Darcy Lever

Grand Stand, opposite where the present Main Stand is situated. Apart from an old house abutting on the north west corner, the front courtyard was entirely clear up to the Manchester Road. (This house survived until 1946.)

As at Goodison Park three years earlier, Burnden Park was opened on 17 August 1895 with an athletics meeting, the town's 9th Annual Athletics Festival, attended by an impressive crowd of 15000. Bolton played their first game at Burnden Park on 11 September, a benefit match v. Preston North End.

However fluctuating the team's performance in the next few years, Burnden Park was a successful stadium, and in 1901 was chosen as the venue for the Cup Final replay between Tottenham and Sheffield United. In eager anticipation of a bumper crowd – the first game was watched by 114815 at Crystal Palace, England's first six-figure attendance – the town's tradesmen brought in massive stocks of pies and souvenirs. But the day turned into a disaster, for Bolton Railway Station was in the process of being rebuilt and the railway company refused to offer cheap-day excursion tickets. A lot of merchandise went to waste that day, known for years afterwards in Bolton as 'Pie Saturday'. There were undoubtedly more than the official gate of 20740 present, perhaps up to 30000, but still this represents the lowest crowd at an FA Cup Final in this century.

But it was a mystery why the FA chose Burnden Park in the first place. Goodison Park was objected to as a venue by neighbours, Liverpool, who had a home game on the same day, but what was wrong with Villa Park, or the Victoria Ground, Stoke?

Poor Bolton were never honoured again. While neighbours Blackburn, Burnley and the two Manchester clubs were all chosen to host England international matches until the Second World War, Burnden Park was overlooked.

If 1901 was disappointing, the club won back its pride in 1904 by reaching its second Final, this time at Crystal Palace. Although they lost, the extra revenue enabled Bolton to start building the first section of the existing Main Stand, on Manchester Road, for a cost of about £3500. That season Wanderers returned to Division One, and Bolton Corporation extended their lease by ten years on the original terms. Also that year, in order to accommodate the growing crowds, Burnden Park's cycle track was taken out.

During the following season, with Bolton back in Division One, the Great Lever End was terraced and covered. In 1915 the Main Stand had an extra wing added at the Southern End, so that the stand resembled Ewood Park's Main Stand, with a cranked end section. (Both grounds in fact developed in a similar pattern, though Rovers were slightly more lavish.)

After a period of considerable success, Bolton began in 1928 to build a new structure seating 2750 in place of the original Darcy Lever Stand. But just before its completion controversy struck. The Burnden Stand cost £20000 to erect, not a vast amount

Burnden Park in 1952. Is that Arthur Askey on the footplate?

when compared with the £30000 Everton had spent on their new Bullens Road Stand two years earlier, and surely not beyond the means of a successful club with two packed Wembley finals recently under its belt. So imagine the uproar in Bolton when their Cup-winning hero David Jack was transferred to Arsenal in October 1928 for the then record fee of £10340. As *Athletic News'* correspondent remarked, 'Bolton's choice: new stand but no new players'.

Burnden Park's official highest crowd was 69912, for the visit of Manchester City in the FA Cup in February 1933. During the Second World War the ground was taken over, the pitch for use by the Education Authorities, the stands by the Ministry of Supply. The Burnden Stand was still full of food supplies when the event which was to stand out in the history of all football grounds occurred on 9 March 1946. (For a full description of the disaster, see Appendix.)

The match was unusual in itself, for that season immediately after the War it had been decided that every Cup-tie up to the semi-finals should be two-legged. These extra games would help to compensate for the fact that League Football did not resume on a proper basis until September 1946. Bolton had won the first leg of this quarter-final tie at Stoke 2–0, and an estimated 85000 squeezed into Burnden Park in the afternoon, most of whom knew little about the tragic events at the Railway End.

In the depressing aftermath, questions were raised which were to bring about lower capacities at every ground. Bolton felt a great deal of remorse although the report did not blame the club specifically. After the government report, in 1947 the club spent £5500 modernizing the Railway End, improving the turnstiles and gates, adding barriers and fencing off the railway line (see Safety).

On 14 October 1957, Bolton's new floodlights were switched on for a friendly v. Hearts. It was claimed that they possessed sufficient power to light the streets from Burnden to Blackpool.

During the summer of 1979, 4342 seats were put on the Great Lever End terrace and, the pitch, a poor drainer despite its camber, was dug up. All manner of compressed, rotting matter was found underneath. Undersoil heating and sprinklers were installed and, though the pitch was vastly improved, in 1986 Bolton sought permission to install an artificial pitch, which may go down in 1987 if funds are available.

But the greatest change took place in late 1986 when the 16000-capacity Railway End terrace was cut in half and a superstore built on the land flattened behind (as at Crystal Palace). Thus the famous embankment, with its haunting memories and railway at the back, was gone forever.

On the other hand, access to the Burnden Stand and the rear of the truncated terrace was vastly improved by the building of a road, car park and new turnstiles along the route of the former railway.

Despite these developments the capacity of Burnden Park remains a healthy 33000, including 11000 seats (reduced from 41646).

Ground Description

Approaching the ground from Bolton station, the Manchester Road Stand is almost hidden behind a complex of offices, social clubs and executive facilities. The car park and back of the Main Stand was the backdrop for L. S. Lowry's painting *Going to the Match*. Inside the stand is the predictable, wooden stand of the early 1900s. The later right wing is angled towards the pitch. There are 4644 seats, surprisingly many considering the low roof makes the stand seem small. On the roof is a prominent television gantry, which does not enhance the stand's appearance either. Yet jumbled though it seems, Burnden Park's age gives it a definite sense of tradition.

To the right is the covered Great Lever Stand, named after the district nearby. Apart from the huge, bright advertisement on the black roof its most prominent feature is the floodlight pylon on the far side. All the terraces have now been covered with seats, a rather careless conversion it has to be said, effected when the club were briefly back in Division One. Plastic bucket seats have been bolted into the original terraces, and therefore the rake is too shallow to provide a good all-round view, especially as the high security fences still line the front. The same firm which put up this cover, John Booth of Bolton, also built the Manchester Road Stand and erected much of the steelwork at Wembley Stadium in 1923. A luminescent sign with their name adorns the top of the Great Lever Stand.

Opposite the Manchester Road Stand is the Burnden Stand, a simple 1920s' design with a large paddock in front of a covered seating area accommodating 2460. White roof fascia and terrace facings emphasize its simplicity. Note how the uprights seem to branch out at the tops and how the entire back row is well lit by a line of windows.

Behind the stand is a modern sports hall and a floodlit artificial playing surface used for training and by the local community. Opened in October 1986 the pitch cost £150 000.

To the left is the now truncated Railway End. The north west gangway where the disaster brewed is exactly in the corner between the Manchester Road Stand and the end terracing, just behind the corner flag. It was from this terrace that Burnden Park played a small part in Arthur Askey's film, *Love Match* (1954), in which a train-driver pulled up on the tracks behind the Railway End to watch a stirring match played in front of a packed crowd, all wearing cloth caps and smoking Woodbines. The same spot today will allow you to buy filter-tips without so much as a glimpse of the football.

Finally, Burnden Park's pitch deserves attention. The camber, as noticeable as in 1906, is all the more pronounced because in places the turf is actually 3 feet higher than the perimeter track. Plastic grass, when installed, will no doubt need less of a camber.

Burnden Park shares many physical similarities with nearby Ewood Park, but somehow fails to display a similar spruceness. Having grown up on large crowds, its three solid but dated stands appear wholly anachronistic, although even if they were given the capital it seems unlikely Bolton would again opt for a new stand in preference to new players. The real clue to Bolton's dilemma, and that of every other club in the area, is that more customers are flocking to places like the superstore behind the Railway End. A modern Lowry would have a very different picture to paint.

BLACKBURN
·ROVERS·

Previous Grounds

Blackburn spent much of their first season without a home but still managed to win every 'away' game. When in 1875 they did find a pitch, on a farm by Preston New Road, it was barely adequate, for in the middle was the farm's drainage pool or 'cow-pit'. The father of Duckworth, one of the Rovers team, was a timber merchant and so the club was able to cover the pool with planks and disguise it with turf. In 1876 they moved to Alexandra Meadows, the East Lancashire cricket ground, where they attracted a record gate of 5000 for a game v. Partick Thistle. In 1881 the club switched to Leamington Road where a grandstand seating 700 was built. The move obviously suited Rovers, who immediately enjoyed a run of 35 successive games unbeaten. Having just won the FA Cup for the fourth time the club moved to their present ground, Ewood Park in 1890.

Ewood Park

In common with much urban development in industrial Lancashire, Ewood Park was built in the late Victorian period and has suffered from being outdated ever since. The first match there was v. Accrington in September 1890, but the following Christmas brought crowd trouble. Darwen were the visitors, and so incensed were their supporters when Rovers saw fit to field only three first team players they pulled up and broke the goalposts, smashed dressing room windows and tore up carpets in the reserved seating section.

An early attempt at floodlit football was made at Ewood Park in October 1892, also for a game v. Darwen (see Floodlights), then in 1895 Rovers bought the ground for £2500. At the same time the club's headquarters were moved from the Bay Horse Hotel to Ewood Park.

Further crowd problems during Everton's visit in January 1896 arose when part of a stand collapsed among a 20 000 crowd. Five people were injured and one of them won £25 compensation for his injuries, the club being found negligent. Possibly in reaction to this court case Rovers became a limited liability company soon after.

A photograph of Ewood Park taken before 1906 shows a small hut in one corner, presumably the changing rooms, a wooden railing round the pitch, which had no track, and wooden barriers dug into grass banking. The Darwen End of the ground had been covered in 1905 at a cost of £1680 and held 12 000 spectators.

1906 was a year of major improvements, all still visible. The main Nuttall Street Stand, designed by

Tramlines, terraced houses, a mill and a brook give Ewood Park an archetypal Northern setting

Archibald Leitch, was built at a cost of £24 000, a considerable outlay even then, and opened on New Year's Day 1907 for a match v. Preston. Though only mildly impressive from without, the Nuttall Street Stand was very good within and has, in part, been lovingly preserved by the club. In between two Championship wins in 1912 and 1914 the club built another stand, the double-decker Riverside Stand, and in 1915 reported the capacity of Ewood Park to be a massive 70 886, including 7000 seats. In 1928 the wooden perimeter railing was replaced by the present concrete wall, the Blackburn End was terraced and the Riverside Stand reroofed for a total outlay of £1550. A year later Ewood Park saw its largest crowd, 61 783, for a Cup tie v. Bolton on 2 March.

In 1958 the club installed floodlights, first used on 10 November during a friendly v. Werder Bremen. A Cup Final appearance in 1960 provided funds for erecting a concrete cantilever roof over the Blackburn End terrace, an early example of cantilever construction and its first use for an end terrace.

Ewood Park has had to adapt more than most grounds to the requirements of the 1975 Safety of Sports Grounds Act, having spent nearly all their grant from FGIT (see Safety). Without this work it is likely that more damage would have been done by a fire which broke out at the Blackburn end of the Nuttall Street Stand in July 1984. Rovers chose a novel way of restoring the damage by building into the stand's existing structure a new block of executive boxes and a glass fronted lounge overlooking the ground. The development, which cost about £250 000, was named the John Lewis Complex in honour of the club's founder.

In 1985, following the Bradford fire, safety checks revealed structural problems in the Riverside Stand and the upper seating section was closed as a result. The loss of capacity was not great, but even so the present capacity of 21 100 (including 2209 seats) is way below the 1915 figure of 70 886, even though the ground remains essentially the same size.

Ground Description

As you leave the main road and walk past rows of terraced houses to Ewood Park, you can see how the club has actually grown into its surroundings. There is, for example, a programme seller's window in one house's backyard wall. The club's offices are in a small block on one street corner and two terraced houses, 110–112 Nuttall Street, belong to Rovers.

The redbrick Nuttall Street frontage reminds one of the stand's exact contemporary at Craven Cottage, also the work of Leitch (see Design). Having already passed down either Tweed Street or Velvet Street it should come as no surprise to find at the Darwen End, the cobbled entrance to Fernhurst Mill.

To the Blackburn End of Nuttall Street is Kidder Street, also cobbled and with a line of particularly well kept houses. And just in case any southerner is still not convinced of Ewood Park's solidly northern credentials, he should also notice the old tramlines in the street.

The turnstiles in this corner of the ground were used in a television commercial for Hovis, with the predictable accompaniment of brass band music.

Before we enter the ground proper, two further points are worth noting. Firstly, the graphics which adorn every part of Ewood Park, inside and out, are a commendable feature of the club's policy of both informing the public and maintaining a high standard of appearance at the ground. Watford have used a similarly uniform system of lettering and colours to create such a corporate image, which other clubs might do well to imitate. Secondly, although few visitors can gain access, the oak-panelled boardroom in the Nuttall Street Stand is quite magnificent, and by no means a dusty inner sanctum (see colour section).

The Nuttall Street Stand is cranked and some distance from the touchline. Like the rest of the ground it is brightly painted in blue and white. Red fences and barriers, a cream-coloured perimeter wall and a neat terracotta track add to the ground's spruce appearance. The players' tunnel is covered by a clear perspex barrelled canopy, with the club's crest on a sign above the entrance. White moulded fibre-glass dug-out covers flank the tunnel and give it prominence. Because the stand is basically wooden throughout, stringent fire precautions have been taken, especially underneath where there is often a chaotic bottleneck at half-times. My advice is to stay in your seat if you can hold out!

To the right is the Darwen End. Darwen is a small town four miles from Blackburn and had its own League club for eight years in the 1890s. This covered terrace is slightly cranked, with a line of 13 pillars along the front and many signs warning against the fragile roof.

To the left, beyond the John Lewis Complex is the more modern Blackburn End, its cantilever roof angled at several points. The slabs of grey concrete of this bus shelter-like roof are in dull contrast with their freshly coloured surrounds. Opposite is the Riverside Stand, now partially closed, tall and narrow with red concrete facings and a steep uncovered terrace in front. It is less impressive from the back where it is clad in weathered sheets of corrugated iron. The stand is so-called because behind runs the narrow River Darwen. There is a grass-covered pathway, between the riverbank and the foot of the stand.

Note especially two gateways in the perimeter wall in front of Blackburn's Riverside Stand, with stone ornamental spheres on top of each gate-post, picked out in blue to contrast with the cream wall. Such attention to detail, in what is an undeniably dated ground, prevents Ewood Park from appearing dowdy and the pitch, laid down by the Sports Turf Institute, is one of the best in the country. From the panelled boardroom to the new executive complex, Ewood Park is proof of how conscientious maintenance and a touch of elbow grease and imagination can bring back life to the worn and weary.

◆ BURNLEY ◆

Turf Moor

Burnley Rovers played rugby at Calder Vale, and their players had to bathe in the river after each game. In May 1882 they formed a soccer club and dropped the name Rovers soon after. The club made their first appearance at nearby Turf Moor on 17 February 1883, for a local match v. Rawtenstall. Only Preston, Dumbarton, Falkirk and Stoke have been in longer continuous residence than Burnley at their grounds.

Turf Moor is as it sounds, a patch of turf amid moors, but it is also a well-developed ground, suitably modified to the needs of a small town. Burnley is the smallest town to have sustained a First Division club for any length of time, with a population of about 75000. (In League history Glossop, in Derbyshire, was the smallest town to have a First Division club. More recently, Carlisle, slightly smaller than Burnley, enjoyed just one season at the top.)

The ground's early history is recorded in David Wiseman's history of the club (*Up the Clarets*, 1973) which begins with a description of Turf Moor from the magazine *Football Field*, in September 1884. Burnley had built a grandstand seating 800 and 'added to and rearranged a natural earth work making standing room for 2000 more'. An uncovered stand, along two sides of the field and accommodating over 5000 was also in the process of being erected. We presume the work was completed, for in March 1884 12000 people came for a match v. locals rivals Padiham, in those early days an enormous crowd indeed. Only 4000 attended that same year's Cup Final.

Turf Moor is believed to be the first football ground ever visited by a member of the Royal family, when in October 1886, having just opened the nearby Victoria hospital, the Queen's son Prince Albert watched Burnley v. Bolton in the company of 9000 others, some of them paying a guinea just to sit near the Royal party. Afterwards Burnley were nicknamed the Royalites, and appropriately it was Burnley who played in the first FA Cup Final to be watched by a reigning monarch, at Crystal Palace in 1914.

By 1908 the two sides were covered; the Main Stand on Brunshaw Road and opposite, the stand known as the Star Stand. When more room was needed for an FA Cup match v. Manchester United this stand was moved backwards to make an enclosure in front, and £600 was spent on extra banking and barriers. Considerable improvements were necessary in the summer of 1913 because gates were rising every year, up to 49734 for one match in 1914, roughly as many as lived in the town itself! The record gate was in February 1924 when Huddersfield Town were the visitors in the FA Cup; 54775 attended, but one man died in the crush. Three months later a First Division game at the ground attracted only 3685.

In 1954 a new roof costing £20 000 was built over the terracing on the Long Side, opposite the main stand, and the floodlights were switched on in December 1957 for a friendly v. Blackburn Rovers.

In 1967 work began on a new stand at the Cricket Field End. Finished in 1969 at a cost of £180 000 it housed all the players' facilities, and was the first stand in Britain to incorporate underfloor heating for the 4500 seated spectators. The system was powered by an oil-fired air heater, but was used only for two seasons before being pronounced uneconomical. The stand was given official blessing by the Prime Minister Edward Heath, a personal friend of Burnley's Chairman Bob Lord, on 23 November 1973.

For a while the Cricket Field Stand became the Main Stand, while the original Main Stand was taken down and replaced by the new Bob Lord Stand. Some locals called it the Martin Dobson Stand, after the Burnley player whose £300 000 transfer to Everton in August 1974 was said to have paid for the construction.

Edward Heath also opened this stand, on 14 September 1974. It seats 2500 people. Unfortunately the club slipped out of the First Division two years later and by 1985 were in Division Four, having two modern stands but having sold most of their valued players.

An indication of how up-to-date Turf Moor had become was that while most small clubs had their capacities drastically cut by safety restrictions, Burnley were one of the few clubs anywhere to raise theirs, from 21 000 to 25 000, including 7000 seats, after expenditure on safety work between 1977 and 1985 of over £300 000.

Ground Description

Turf Moor is one of several grounds to use a combination of cream and green to good effect, and the green particularly stands out. This may be to reflect the

Turf Moor before modernization and the Fourth Division

image of 'turf', or could be a throwback from the days when the team played in green.

The Bob Lord Stand stretches along Brunshaw Road, next to the club offices. The design is very simple; a plain flat roof, steeply raked seating leading down to the front cream-coloured wall. Notice in the centre a wooden gate with steps and the club crest. There is a large proportion of executive seating in the centre, and you can see rolled up covers at the front, used to protect the carpets.

To its left is the Cricket Field Stand, named after the sponsors, 'National and Provincial Building Society Stand'. Behind it is the cricket field belonging to Burnley Cricket Club. The stand is quite unusual for an end stand, firstly because it houses the players' tunnel, to the right of the goal – as found only at Bloomfield Road, The Den and Meadow Lane – but is a long way from the offices, and secondly because it looks like a box made out of children's building bricks. The screen ends have distinctive square panels of glass, the stone walls are cream and the seats green. Though it has aged, its size commands attention.

The rest of the ground is standing only. Opposite the Bob Lord Stand is the Long Side cover, a large structure of exactly the same design as at Leeds Road. From here you can see the moors rising up beyond the stand opposite. Along the front perimeter wall notice the old dug-outs, used when the Main Stand was being rebuilt.

The Long Side roof dominates Turf Moor and is only partially lightened by an advertisement which, coincidentally, is for a paint and varnish company. To the right is the open bank called the Bee Hole End, after a colliery which once stood nearby. The bank is a maze of barriers running in every direction. The floodlight pylons, one of which stands outside the ground behind this end, are of the same design and manufacture as those at Burnden Park. From the top of this terrace one gains the best view of Turf Moor. It seems from here as if the ground has been denied any bright colours, and even the club colours, claret and blue are absent. The pitch once sloped quite badly, as one can see from the height it has been raised above the cinder track behind the Bee Hole End goal.

For a small town, Turf Moor is indeed a finely equipped ground, much of which is due to the effort and energy of the late Bob Lord. But it has to be repeated that the improvements cost Burnley nearly £1·5 million, and coincided with the team's decline. Had the club waited a few years, no doubt the rise in prices would have made such developments less likely, though they might have received aid from the Football Grounds Improvement Trust. Modern stands or not, the ground even now barely stands out from the East Lancashire landscape of rolling hills and decaying mills. Turf Moor is in name and appearance a down-to-earth venue, a compromise between the demands of the new generation and the traditions of the old.

·PRESTON· NORTH END

Deepdale

Preston began playing football in 1881, but had existed for many years before as a cricket, rugby and athletics club. When they moved to Deepdale in 1875, as Preston Nelson, the ground was part of Deepdale Farm. Opposite was the recently opened Moor Park, where the club played in their early days.

Preston North End, as they became, soon found soccer to be their forte, and crowds gathered in increasing numbers as the club took on famous teams such as Queens Park, and Old Carthusians. Banking and fences were gradually constructed around the pitch, though sheep were still allowed to graze there, and the club even had to abandon their policy of allowing in ladies free of charge, so many turned up to see this new attraction.

In Berry and Allman's *Centenary History* of the club is a sketch map of Deepdale in November 1890, showing two stands, 'Large' and 'Small' on the west side, with a press-box in between, and uncovered stands on the north and east sides. Along the east touchline were to be 3 feet 6 inch high railings and a new stand, not roofed, was proposed for the South End. A covered stand was also planned alongside the 'Small Stand' on the west. In the north west corner, at an angle, was the Dress Tent, a hut containing changing rooms. The club's chairman, William Sudell, a pioneer in the fight to establish professional football, was said to have had his own entrance to the ground. Reports from *Athletics News* suggest the Large Stand dated from 1883 and held 600, and that the uncovered stands gave the place 'the appearance of a huge amphitheatre'.

In 1893 a magnificent new stadium was planned for Preston's all-conquering 'invincibles', next door to Deepdale. It was to have a large Main Stand and a cycle-track, as grand as Molineux (opened 1889) and Goodison Park (1892), if not quite so big. But nothing ever came of the plan, and Deepdale changed little until the turn of the century, by which time it was quite primitive compared with the likes of Villa Park, Burnden Park and Ewood Park.

Preston fought their way back into Division One in 1904 and in January 1906 a new stand was built to replace the three older buildings on the west side. The Grand Stand housed dressing rooms and offices, and although modest in comparison with contemporary designs such as those of Leitch at nearby Ewood Park, it did provide Deepdale with a memorable feature that still survives today and remains one of the finest relics at any British football ground.

In January 1921 the club extended and covered the North End of Deepdale at a cost of £19 000. Preston were back in Division Two four years later, but definitely on the way up when the next major development was undertaken in 1934. This was the construction of the Pavilion, opposite the Grand Stand. In order to raise the necessary capital, the club's chairman, J. R. Taylor, set up a separate Preston North End Pavilion Company with 9999 shares issued at £1 each. The actual building cost a little over £9000 and when completed in February 1934 added another distinctive piece of architecture.

It was only 50 yards long, built on the half-way line, and had new offices, dressing rooms, an elegant boardroom and guest rooms on three floors, with an electric lift to the top storey. At the same time, a new stand was built on the Town End for standing spectators, as modern as the Pavilion was sumptuous, and the Grand Stand quaint.

In 1936 another stand was completed, called the South Pavilion (although on the east side it was south of the original Pavilion). It was in effect an extension of the Pavilion, though a little less luxurious. Also in 1936 the firm of Abbotts in Lancaster installed specially-designed stained glass windows in the boardroom, and not even Highbury had those. Deepdale's highest crowd of 42 684 saw Preston v. Arsenal, a clash between two Championship contenders.

The ground was taken over by the Army in May 1941, in return for £250 a year compensation; then in March 1943, they commandeered the club's car park for a mere £5 a year. Prisoners of war were also held at Deepdale, and for two war-time seasons Preston played at the ground of Leyland Motors.

Since the War, Deepdale has changed little in outward appearance, but substantially in other ways. In October 1953 the floodlights were first switched on, for a Lancashire Senior Cup match v. Bolton. On promotion from the Third Division in 1978, the club found Deepdale far below the standards required by the Safety of Sports Grounds Act. A total of £500 000 has since been spent on the ground, much of it on barriers, fencing and access points. But it was money well spent, because when further checks were made after the Bradford fire in 1985 few changes had to be made, although the capacity dropped from 25 000 to 19 500, including 4100 seats.

In March 1986 new floodlights, costing £60 000 were switched on for the first time and the following summer Deepdale became the third League ground to install an artificial pitch. Preston chose the En-tout-cas type found at Luton, and paid £300 000.

It is appropriate that the community should have a wider use of the ground since Deepdale is now owned entirely by the local council, the club having sold the last patch of land they owned, on which stands the pavilion and car park, for £220 000.

Ground Description

That Deepdale has not seen much glory in recent years is plain to see. Not because the ground is in a state of disrepair. On the contrary, it is spick and

Deepdale's pride, the immaculate West Stand built in 1906. It now looks down on the modern marvel of synthetic grass

span throughout. Not because the stands are aged. The Baseball Ground, even Highbury, are no more modern. There is a peaceful, untroubled air at Deepdale and one could no more imagine a club winning the European Cup there than one could think of Anfield hosting a Fourth Division match.

The sense of composure begins on Lowthorpe Road, where the back of the Pavilion is clothed in ivy, and the top windows are stained glass. Inside the stand, across the Korkroyd floors, up in the lift to the Directors' Box, it is like Highbury built in miniature and on a lower budget.

The original Pavilion, that is the section over the half-way line, seems like any ordinary stand but its seats are spaciously arranged, gangways wide, and best of all, the roof is concealed by a low, white wooden ceiling, creating a most exclusive environment. J. R. Taylor obviously knew how to obtain the maximum luxury with the minimum outlay.

To the left is the less commodious South Pavilion. Looking at both stands from the ground, the join is in the middle, where Preston's crest appears on the blue roof fascia. This long blue board along the gutter is the only modern addition, and ties the two pavilions together neatly. But then everything at Deepdale is neat. In front of the stand is a line of private boxes, a rare reminder of modern times.

Again from the Pavilion, the remaining 20 yards of this touchline towards the North End, is open terracing, which bends round the north east corner to the North End. This is covered only at the very back,

by a plain, gently sloping roof.

On the west side, its roof touching part of the North End roof, is the quite exquisite West or Grand Stand, probably the best preserved stand of its age. In design it could not be more basic: a barrel 'Belfast' roof made of wood is supported at the front by a line of very thin, round iron poles, spaced only 10 or 12 feet apart. The seating tier is composed entirely of benches, brightly painted in a shadowy interior. The facings are blue, the ironwork white. (Notice the mouldings along the guttering, at the top of each column.) All is in perfect harmony and proportion, and Preston have tended it with care and sensitivity.

To the left is the Town End, at first glance a modern construction like a propped cantilever, with a flat roof pitching steeply upwards, but in reality over 50 years old.

Finally, Deepdale's new pitch. The former grass surface was always wide, at 78 yards from side to side; perfect for the likes of Finney. But the new pitch dispenses with the cinder track and runs right up to the perimeter fencing, giving the ground even greater apparent width.

As tidy and rich in hue as the surrounding stands, this new pitch may have ended the possibility of sheep ever grazing at Deepdale again, but who knows how many budding Finneys will win the chance of playing here as part of the wider community use? Preston may never emulate their 'invincible' forerunners, but as Deepdale confirms, the club remains as proud as ever.

·WIGAN ATHLETIC·

Springfield Park

Football is only one of an unusual variety of sports played at Springfield Park since at least 1897. In the 1920s, for example, horse-trotting was very popular at the ground. There was a half-mile track for the horse-and-traps to negotiate, and stables on the town side of the ground. There was also a cement cycle track around the pitch, some of which is still evident. In addition, Springfield Park was used for rugby and by the local police for their athletics meetings.

The ground has been the home of no less than five clubs bearing the title Wigan. From 1912–21 teams called Wigan County, Wigan Town and Wigan United had brief spells here, followed by Wigan Borough, a club that joined the newly formed League Division Three North in 1921, but had to resign because of insolvency on 26 October 1931. The following year Wigan Athletic formed and bought Springfield Park from the liquidators. During the Borough years, the existing standing covers were erected, the first in the early 1920s at the Shevington End, the second on the Popular Side in the late 1920s. The original Main Stand dated back to this era also, but was gutted by fire in May 1953. The present Main Stand was built the following year.

Wigan Athletic established themselves as one of the top non-League clubs in the country, and despite having to contend with their famous Rugby League neighbours at Central Park, Wigan regularly commanded gates envied by many League clubs. When the Springfield Park capacity stood at 35 000, a non-League encounter v. Hereford United (then in the Southern League) attracted their highest attendance, 27 500, in December 1953.

The floodlights were first switched on in October 1965, for a Northern Floodlit League match v. Crewe Alexandra (Central Park did not have their lights until 1978).

Athletic joined Division Four in 1978, in place of Southport, and have since spent £100 000 on ground improvements at Springfield Park.

Since the ground became designated in 1985 capacity has been reduced from 20 000 to 10 800, with 1000 seats.

Ground Description

Visitors to Wigan beware! The most prominent set of floodlights in the town belong to the rugby club, Wigan Athletic's ground is further from the centre and has smaller lights.

Once you find Springfield Park, through a network of narrow streets, the first sensation is of breezy openness as you emerge onto the ground's large exposed car park.

Because this side of the ground stands high above the town, the Main Stand seems particularly tall and

Springfield Park

vulnerable to the elements. It is about 50 yards long and straddles the half-way line; a solid, box-like post and beam construction with a gently sloping roof. Wigan is one of the very few clubs in the lower divisions to have installed private boxes. In front is a seated family enclosure created in 1986. The rest of the ground is relatively undeveloped.

At either end the terraces are shaped around the compressed oval-shape of the turf, a reminder that it was once surrounded by a track. Indeed the actual terrace steps at the Shevington End, to the left of the Main Stand, were visibly constructed on the old track. They rise up in shallow fashion a couple of yards, behind which a grass slope leads to a very basic and hardly used cover at the back. The club did try to erect a proper roof over the actual terracing in 1972, but this was taken down four years later, because it was too close to the pitch and reduced the numbers who could see from that end. The story had a happy ending though. Wigan sold the steelwork to an engineering firm for more than it cost them to build the cover in the first place.

Opposite the Main Stand is the Popular Side, on St Andrew's Drive, half covered along its length. The roof was built in two sections and is slightly angled at one end.

To the right is the open Town End, also curved round the pitch, with a mixture of blue and white barriers. Behind it is an all-weather floodlit pitch which the club shares with the community. The best overall view of the ground is from here and also of the flat landscape of housing, fields and industry, beyond the Main Stand.

If the club could afford it, or the local council were willing, Springfield Park would make a perfect site for a modern multi-sports stadium. The ground occupies a 14-acre site, much of it flat and unused except for parking. But while the town's main sporting focus is Central Park it seems unlikely that Springfield Park will be much developed, however well the football team performs, and the most logical step – sharing facilities with the Rugby League club – remains only a dim and distant possibility.

·BLACKPOOL·

Previous Grounds

Blackpool formed in 1887 and first played at Raikes Hall Gardens, a venue made famous since by its Crown Green bowling tournaments. In 1897 the club moved to the Athletics Grounds, next to the cricket ground in Stanley Park, but had to move back to Raikes Hall in January 1899. After three seasons in the League, Blackpool amalgamated with another local team, South Shore, whose ground in Bloomfield Road became the new club's headquarters in December 1899.

Bloomfield Road

There is always an irresistible urge to associate Blackpool with the great days of Matthews, Mortensen *et al* in the early 1950s, but Bloomfield Road itself, though improved during this period of success, nowadays appears much as it did before the Second World War.

Before explaining this, we must go back to the beginning of the century, when the all-wooden West Stand was built. It is a miracle that it has survived until now, for directly behind used to run a railway line, so close that passing locomotives would shower the back wall with sparks. Apart from structural repairs, and the addition of safety exits leading to the paddock, the West Stand is unchanged. In 1925, as part of a general scheme of improvement, the existing South Stand was built behind the goal, with new offices and players' facilities, for the cost of £13146, a good price even then. Between the South and West Stands a tiny corner stand was built at an angle to the pitch.

The North End at this time housed a small wooden seated stand, called the Motor Stand, as behind it was a small car park. On promotion to Division One in 1930 this structure was moved to the north west corner where it linked up with the end of the West Stand, and the Kop banking was hurriedly raised. When the club returned to the First Division in the late 1930s the present East Paddock roof was erected. When War broke out the RAF immediately requisitioned the ground and used it as a training centre.

The club's golden era came soon after 1945 and the Kop was covered at the turn of the decade. Bloomfield Road was therefore covered on all four sides, and though somewhat unusually balanced, with two tall ends and two low sides, it was a happy home that would no doubt adapt to modern demands.

As a further sign of success, a record gate of 38098 attended a League fixture v. Wolves in September 1955, then on 13 October 1958 the first floodlit game was staged, v. Hearts.

There have been two alterations to the ground since then, both regrettable. Seats which had been installed in the East Paddock – a forward thinking move – were removed after a short period to compensate for the results of the second change, the removal of the Kop roof in the late 1970s.

The supporters are still bitter about this measure, which it is thought was effected in a state of panic, when following the introduction of the Safety of Sports Grounds Act surveyors deemed the roof to be unsafe, despite the fact that it was barely 30 years old. It cost £40000 to demolish, but a new one would have cost at least five times that amount. If, as has been said, it could have been easily strengthened, the hasty decision to remove it was even more unfortunate. The standing spectators sought cover thereafter in the East Paddock, hence the withdrawal of the seats.

Although the wooden stands passed safety inspections following the Bradford fire, Bloomfield Road's capacity has been much reduced for such a large ground from 18000 to 12700, including 3200 seats.

Ground Description

Thousands of holiday-makers see the ground without visiting it, from the observation platform of nearby Blackpool Tower. At street level you cannot miss Bloomfield Road (though beware of confusing its floodlights with those of the neighbouring rugby league and greyhound stadium), for the back of the South Stand is a garish wall of bright orange, white and blue, lined with advertisements.

Though behind the goal, this stand is the administrative centre of club and also houses the players' tunnel, an arrangement found elsewhere only at Turf Moor, The Den and Meadow Lane.

The South Stand has been completely refurbished inside, but still looks remarkably young for its age, with the minimum of pillars and a tall roof. Unfortunately its new red seats clash painfully with the green woodwork and orange uprights. The small box to the left is the South West Stand, now accommodating schoolchildren. It closes off the corner quite neatly, and provides an excellent view.

From this end you can see the Blackpool Tower behind the Kop. The Kop still keeps the back wall and the remains of the roof supports, and although not an eyesore, for those who knew it when covered it now seems somehow naked and inadequate. The two side stands needed the end roof to disguise their lowliness.

To the right of the South Stand is the covered East Paddock, known more familiarly as the 'Scratching Shed'. Along its low black roof is a marvellous fading advertisement which recalls Blackpool not only as the home of stylish football but as a popular resort with exotic fantasies: Ismail and Company, Tea and Coffee Merchants.

One observer described Bloomfield Road as the most uncomfortable ground in the League. He probably had the West Stand in mind. What the Roker End at Sunderland was to labyrinthine concrete, the West Stand is to wood. Behind and underneath it resembles a timber merchant's yard, made more hos-

Bloomfield Road in the mid-1930s. The roof advertisements have changed and the railway lines replaced by a road and more car-parks, making Bloomfield Road one of the most accessible grounds in the country

pitable but more cramped by a line of small offices, refreshment huts and all the paraphernalia of ground maintenance equipment (see page 36).

The stand has a seating tier with narrow terraces in front, covered by a low sloping roof adorned with more large advertisements. Roof advertising is something of a mania all over Blackpool, and when you are at the top of the Tower you can understand why.

At the northern end of the West Stand is the also wooden but very short North West Stand, with a few more wooden seats overlooking that corner of the pitch.

It has needed considerable attention to keep the West Stand safe after 80 years of use, but since every attempt by the club and developers to rebuild on that side and on the disused railway line behind have all failed at the planning stage, this effort has been worthwhile.

However, Bloomfield Road may well be transformed beyond recognition in the near future. A massive indoor stadium costing between £10–12 million is planned, to enable Blackpool to stage not only football, on an artificial pitch of course, but also concerts and various other sporting events. If built – and this could only happen with outside commercial involvement – it would be the biggest of its kind in Britain since the Wembley Pool was built in the 1930s.

In the meantime there ought to be tours from the Promenade taking visitors to Bloomfield Road, if only to see the West Stand. It is the quintessential British football grandstand, impossible to recreate in concrete and steel. How long it will survive perhaps only Blackpool's famous fortune tellers can say.

·CARLISLE UNITED·

Previous Grounds

Carlisle had two grounds before Brunton Park. Their first was at Milholme Bank, used for two years after the club formed in 1903. The site is now built over, but their second home at Devonshire Park is now playing fields for Trinity School. Carlisle played there until 1909.

Brunton Park

There have been three League clubs in the Cumbria area, but only Carlisle remain, since both Barrow and Workington failed re-election in 1972 and 1977 respectively. A local derby for Carlisle now means a 58-mile trip to Newcastle, although Berwick or Stranraer are not much further away. This distance has always marked Carlisle apart from other League clubs. Norwich are also some distance from their nearest club Ipswich but have a neighbourly affinity with them, 43 miles away. Carlisle, however, is separated from the pack by long stretches of mountainous, open countryside.

Sometimes unfair words have been written about Brunton Park. When Bill Shankly joined the club in 1949 he called the ground, 'a hencoop, a glorified hencoop. The stand and terraces and everything about the ground were in terrible condition, except for the pitch, and that was always a good one.' It has never been an easy life at the outpost of the League.

Carlisle played their first game at Brunton Park on 2 September 1909, a friendly v. 'nearby' Newcastle. But it was not until the club joined the League in 1928 in place of Durham City that the ground was properly developed. First the small wooden stand was extended and turnstiles built. The club bought the site for £2000, and in 1929 relaid the pitch with Solway turf, the type favoured for bowling greens (Solway Firth is about ten miles west of Carlisle). As Shankly commented, the pitch was indeed one of the finest in the country. In the early 1930s United sold their promising young winger Jackie Cape to Newcastle for £1500, and were thus able to build the 'Scratching Shed', a cover over part of the terracing opposite the Main Stand.

Soon after the Second World War, Ivor Broadis joined Carlisle from Tottenham Hotspur. Now a local journalist, he wrote that it 'was like stepping down from the Savoy Hotel into the Jungle Cafe. The Spurs cockerel with its dazzling plumage, or a worn-out, tired looking Cumberland fox ... conditions were a bit primitive, the old wooden stand looked to be reeling drunkenly under the weight of its years, the sleepers providing the terraces where ashes weren't banked, resembled a switchback, and I imagine that fans leaned on the post and rail fence surrounding the pitch at their own peril.'

When Pat Waters came to Brunton Park from Deepdale in 1950 he called the Main Stand, a 'big wooden rabbit hutch'. Nevertheless, Carlisle were the first English League club north of London to install floodlights. These were switched on first for a friendly v. Blackburn Rovers on 25 February 1952.

It was after another floodlit game, in March 1953 v. East Fife that the 'rabbit hutch' burned to the ground. For a while the club was in difficulties, having to borrow kit from Newcastle and using James' Street swimming baths as changing rooms for the players. A temporary stand was erected at the Warwick Road End. But the following year, helped by the transfer of Geoff Twentyman to Liverpool in December 1953 and the formation of a supporters' club, a new Main Stand was built. Ronald Cowing wrote in his history of the club, from which much of this information derives, that the fire formed a turning point in the club's history.

In 1957, a full house of 27500 was recorded for the first time, for a Cup tie v. Birmingham on 5 January. On promotion to Division Two in 1965 the present Warwick Road End was covered.

The 1970s were an eventful decade for Carlisle, beginning with another full house in February 1970 for a 5th Round Cup match v. Middlesbrough. But the greatest event came in 1974, when Carlisle finished third in Division Two, and so won promotion to the First Division. The summer was spent building extra wings onto the Main Stand, erecting impressive new pylons, and of course constructing a television camera gantry onto the Main Stand roof.

But though their success was short-lived, that season had the all-important effect of giving the club and its supporters expectations. Several developments occurred during those five years which were to make Brunton Park a much more viable ground. One of the greatest problems over the years had been flooding from the nearby River Petteril, so badly that once in the 1970s one of the crossbars was just under water, but the other stayed above. From this the groundsman, in a boat of course, was able to determine that the pitch sloped 3 feet! He had also to rescue several wooden floating sleepers that had become dislodged from the terracing. After this flood the club concreted over part of the terraces. The Water Board has since built a bank to prevent the worst of the flooding, but water can still rise up from under the pitch.

In 1981 Brunton Park's other sporting facilities were opened, comprising squash and tennis courts, an all-weather floodlit pitch and an indoor gym. The club even own their own guest house at the ground, Brunton House. Executive boxes were built at the back of the Main Stand, and a Rugby League team formed at the ground. The aim has been to make Brunton Park in use all-year round, every day of the week. Carlisle were lucky to have space to develop – they own 18 acres in total – but there is no doubt that their self-confidence arose largely from the realization that even though they might not be able to

Brunton Park, an outpost of the League

sustain a First Division club, sound planning and sensible management would ensure that never again would Brunton Park be spoken of with derision, least of all among the community in which they are now playing such a part.

The current capacity has been reduced from 25 000 to 18 200, including 2172 seats.

Ground Description

Approaching from the M6 Motorway, Brunton Park stands out as almost Carlisle's first landmark in an otherwise rural landscape, with the extremely tall and thin floodlights especially prominent. Whenever television cameras come to Brunton Park they usually open with a wide angle shot of the fields beyond the Popular Side. The setting invites such an angle.

The main gate is adorned with the metal silhouette of a player kicking a ball, rather akin to those pictures so often seen on club programmes in the 1950s. There is a sizeable car park with room for 1500 vehicles – an asset many clubs would envy. At the back of the Main Stand is an excellent new entrance hall, tastefully designed in almost high-tec decor, with rubberized floors, tinted glass and potted plants; a welcome and encouraging relief from all those football ground entrances decked in formica, garish carpets and simulated wood.

Unfortunately, inside the ground the Main Stand is somewhat less appealing. You can see clearly where the wings have been added to the original 1954 central section, which resembles in many ways a section of Birmingham's Main Stand – plain brick, blue steel, utilitarian and uninspiring. As the rest of the ground is comparatively low this Main Stand seems tall. From the back seats can be seen the view already described, of unbound countryside stretching beyond the opposite stand.

To the right is the Warwick Road End covered terrace, with a multi-span roof similar to one at Prenton Park, but slightly larger. The crush barriers at this end are of curious design, similar to walking frames used by the aged and infirm, but sturdy no doubt.

To the left is the open Petteril or Waterworks End, an exposed bank behind which runs the River Petteril, on its way to link up with the River Eden and so into the sea at Solway Firth. Also behind the terracing is the new sports centre, such a vital element of the ground's new role. At the back of the bank stands a scoreboard and flagpoles, constantly buffeted in the stiff breezes which add to your sense of being out in the wilds. Notice how large the playing surface is at Carlisle. Since the introduction of Rugby League, extra turf behind the touchlines has been added, and the overall length and width makes this pitch second only to Maine Road in area.

Opposite the Main Stand is the Popular Side, covered in the centre. With some justification this used to be known as the Scratching Shed. In recent years however the old timber terracing has been concreted over and the wooden crush barriers, which looked like sawn-up telegraph poles, replaced by new steel barriers.

No doubt it was the view from the Main Stand which prompted the lyrical words of the *Daily Mail*'s football writer Brian James in *Journey to Wembley* (Marshall Cavendish, 1977). He called Brunton Park, quite rightly, 'a frontier post of football indeed, guarded only by sheep. Nothing moves out there. And the notion that a ball kicked over the wall would go bouncing until it dropped off the end of the world is hard to shake off.' One comment among many about a ground that despite many failings is actually better prepared for the needs of its patrons than some of the grander stadiums which seem so splendid on Saturdays but lie idle the rest of the week. Carlisle, population 70 000, cannot expect much better, and at last the Cumberland Fox looks a lot more spritely.

·7·
NORTH EAST

· MIDDLESBROUGH ·

Previous Grounds

The club was formed in February 1876 but did not apparently play its first proper game until a year later, at the Old Archery Ground, Albert Park. As attendances grew the Parks Committee decided the turf had suffered enough, and in March 1879 Middlesbrough moved to Breckon Hill Road, where they rented a field from a Mr Kemp. The following summer they moved again, to Linthorpe Road, the home of Middlesbrough Cricket Club, conveniently placed next to the Empire Hotel, which belonged to the club chairman. In 1885 some members of the club decided they would like to turn professional. They left Linthorpe Road, rented the nearby Paradise Ground on Milton Street (Paradise Found?) and as Middlesbrough Ironopolis joined the Football League in 1893. Amateurs Middlesbrough were in danger of being completely upstaged as Ironopolis attracted better gates. But football plays some funny tricks on public expectations, and despite finishing their first season in eleventh place Ironopolis slipped out of the League.

The last game at Linthorpe Road was in April 1903. Since then the site has been covered by buildings, between Princess Street and Clifton Street, although the Empire Hotel still stands. Breckon Hill Road Ground is part of Longlands College, and the Old Archery Ground is still in Albert Park, behind the groundsman's cottage. The Paradise Ground has been lost to developers.

Ayresome Park

Middlesbrough was already a First Division club when Ayresome Park was opened on 9 September 1903, for a League match v. local rivals Sunderland. Performing the ceremony was James Clifton Robinson, the Managing Director of the local Tram Company, who, according to Arthur Appleton's book, *Hotbed of Soccer*, not only devoted his life to tramcars but died in one in New York seven years later.

The new ground was quite magnificent for its time, having cost £11 000 to buy, with a capacity of 40 000 and two stands. The one on the South Side was about 50 yards long and had come from Linthorpe Road. The North Stand, which still exists, was an impressive full-length structure built at a cost of £1250 (the highest transfer fee of this period was £1000, paid by Middlesbrough for Alf Common from Sunderland). It had a barrel roof with a small, semi-circular gable, topped by an ornate wrought-iron flourish.

To honour Middlesbrough the FA chose to stage an international v. Ireland at Ayresome Park on 25 February 1905, the first of three full internationals played at the ground. But it is really as a venue for amateur games that Ayresome Park was most favoured, staging three amateur internationals and nine Amateur Cup Finals.

The next development followed during the club's spell in Division One between 1929–54. The South Stand was demolished and the existing construction built in 1936. The terraced banks at either end were also rebuilt, the rear sections being on concrete frames similar, though far less intricate, to those at Roker Park. The West End cover was also erected.

These improvements gave Ayresome Park a capacity of 54 000, a total almost reached in December 1949 when 53 596 saw Middlesbrough play Newcastle United in the First Division. This is the ground's record gate, but it was only one of several occasions when the ground's gates were locked.

It was reported that for one 6th Round FA Cup game v. Burnley in 1947 the thousands locked outside were given a running commentary of the action by the Chief Constable of Middlesbrough, A. E. Edwards, himself once an officer in Burnley, who stood on a wall surrounding the ground.

The ground's floodlights were first switched on for a friendly v. Sunderland on 16 October 1957, when Middlesbrough were in the Second Division, and ironically the ground's greatest honour came when the club was at its lowest ebb in the Third Division. Ayresome Park staged three World Cup matches in 1966, having been chosen as a venue relatively late, in April 1964, in place of St James' Park.

To prepare hurriedly for the tournament a new

Ayresome Park's North Stand. The 'dashboard' gable was once crowned with ornate ironwork

East Stand roof was built and 4000 seats installed on the terracing. An extra 3600 seats were put on the North and South Stand paddocks, reducing the ground's overall capacity to 40000.

Middlesbrough hosted three games in Group Four, including the unforgettable heroics of North Korea, but the total attendances at the games amounted only to a disappointing 57200.

The World Cup brought Ayresome Park right up to contemporary standards, and when the ground became designated a healthy capacity of 42000 was set. Since then, however, stricter safety regulations have led to a further restriction on the terracing and the limit is now 30000, including 9500 seats. (Ayresome Park was the scene of an appalling accident in January 1981 when fans leaving the ground after a game against Manchester United caused a gate to collapse, killing a middle-aged couple on the other side.)

But perhaps the biggest development was the opening in March 1986 of a sports hall next to the ground. Originally built in 1981 the hall stood incomplete for five years; firstly because, according to the local council, planning permission had not been obtained, and secondly because despite grants of some £325000 the club could not afford to finish it. They offered, unsuccessfully, to sell it to the council until finally the club put in one last great effort to finish the £1.2 million complex. It is now completely owned by Middlesbrough but brings in revenue from public use. Accepted wisdom has it that clubs should put more into their communities, but as Middlesbrough found to their cost, it is no simple matter.

Meanwhile back in the ground the club had to spend a further £100000 on fireproofing the stands, and so after years without success on the pitch it was no surprise that up to and particularly during 1986, the club's survival became a constant source of speculation.

Ground Description

The usual trick for finding previously unvisited football grounds is to look for floodlight pylons. At Middlesbrough this is like looking for a needle in a haystack, for there appear to be floodlight pylons strewn across the Teesside horizon, and Ayresome Park's are not easily distinguished.

The North Stand is of considerable interest to the connoisseur of football ground architecture. It has a large barrel roof whose supports have been adapted from their original form to having a pillar at each end, plus two extra pillars halfway back in the middle. The most prominent feature is the central gable, its round clock flanked by two roundels, part of an advertisement on the gable front.

On the upper tier are red- and ochre-coloured seats, on the front tier white seats. A splash of colourful advertisements and two early-style electric scoreboards make this a very busy interior. It is the second oldest stand (after Grimsby's) still in use as a main stand in the League, yet still looks fresh.

To the left is the East End with ochre seats at the back and a standing enclosure at the front, under what appears to be a typical pitched roof, such as is found over many a terraced bank. The seating is flanked on both sides by two open corners of terracing curving round to meet each side stand, with barriers, but no screens, dividing the seats from the terraces.

The South Stand would be a fairly straightforward design were it not for its deep overhanging pitched roof. Two white poles in front of this support not the roof but the extra weight of the television camera gantry. The platform itself has two covered pigeon loft covers on either side, as if it were an army gunpost.

To the right is the West Stand, almost identical to the East but for standing only, and with two uncovered corners. The chimney behind is part of a hospital complex.

In plan Ayresome Park resembles Maine Road or Old Trafford – a rectangle with neatly curved corners, and plenty of space between touchline and perimeter fence, especially on the sides, where there are wide cinder tracks.

Here are old fashioned stands and old fashioned proportions, all looked after with pride.

Indeed, throughout their long, lean years, Middlesbrough continue to have the aura of a big club. Part of this can be ascribed to the size and substance of Ayresome Park which, despite its mid-1960s refit and new sports hall, is one of the last really large grounds to have remained largely untouched by the modern era of stadium design.

◆ DARLINGTON ◆

Feethams

Football has been played at Feethams since at least 1866, when a group of enthusiasts hired the land next to the cricket pitch from John Beaumont Pease, and laid it with turf taken from another cricket pitch in Old Park Street. A football club was formed in 1883, but by the beginning of the First World War it was in dire financial straits. An up and coming local team, Darlington Forge Albion offered to amalgamate in 1917, and immediately fortunes rose. In 1919 the club finished building the East Stand, begun in 1914, joined the League in 1921 and there followed a spell of success which saw Darlington into the Second Division and the building of the West Stand.

Feethams was also host to several amateur semi-finals and finals, in a period when north eastern clubs dominated the competition. A crowd of 20 000 attended a Final replay at Feethams in 1933.

The ground changed little until 1960. In the summer a simple cantilever cover was put over the shallow Cricket Field End terrace. Then on 19 September, Darlington's floodlights were first used for a 4th Division game v. Millwall. Later that night the West Stand burned down, though there was apparently no connection between the events. Shortly after, in November 1960, Feethams had its highest attendance of 21 023 for the visit of Bolton in the League Cup.

Of course the supporters expected to see a bright new stand in place of the West Stand, and were amazed to see an exact replica of the old one being built instead in 1961.

Another fire, this time in Bradford in 1985, had a much more devastating effect on Feethams. Following safety checks the capacity was reduced from 15 000 to 8400, which included only 320 seats. In effect the East Stand became confined to directors, visitors and staff, while the West Stand's capacity was halved. In both cases structural improvements and fireproofing were completed in 1986, and together with refurbishing the South Terrace this cost Darlington over £80 000 but increased the capacity to 10 400, including 1200 seats.

Ground Description

The ground and its environs are unashamedly charming and belong to a middle-class Edwardian world.

You must approach the ground from Victoria Road, where you see first a solid redbrick wall with an ornamental gateway, and the words Darlington Cricket and Football Club written between two decorative towers. As Frank Tweddle, the club historian remarks wryly, they are the only twin towers Darlington are ever likely to see!

Through these gates you come to the cricket pitch, around whose boundaries you must pass to reach the football ground on the furthest side of the pitch, a reminder of how these English sports once coexisted so closely. The cricket club own all the land, charging the football club a nominal rent.

The East Stand adds to one's sense of nostalgia. It runs two-thirds of the length of the pitch, with six floodlight gantries on a barrel roof – a sort of Newcastle in half-scale. Along the front is a line of white steel pillars, formed into distinctive arches under the eaves. Frank Tweddle observes that, coincidentally, there are the same number of arches as there are letters in the name Darlington. Behind the stand is the River Skerne, across which is a tree-lined avenue of Victorian villas.

To the left is South or Polam Lane terrace, recently resurfaced and with new barriers. There is a small brick cottage next to the terracing, and more football pitches beyond. From here the handsome town clock tower is visible straight ahead.

Opposite is the West Stand, in fading blue, looking every bit a 1920s' wooden box stand, sitting on the half-way line. Only a plaque on the side confirms that it was built in 1961. To its left is a fenced-off terrace where a sports hall has been built with grants from the Playing Fields Association.

Behind the stand there used to be a tall wooden barn which formed an entrance to the ground. Sadly that had to come down. On the right, on a rise behind the ground are the huge northern works of the National Bus Company.

Finally, to the north is the cricket pitch, blocked from view by the cantilevered covered terrace, which hardly protects anyone from the weather but does stop wilder shots going onto the cricket field.

Feethams is the sort of ground where one sees the odd squirrel scooting across the terraces, evoking memories of how football and football grounds once were – not an imposition upon the landscape, but simply an open space where sporting young men turned out for the love of the game.

It is a relief that, despite all the safety work done at Feethams, this atmosphere still prevails.

Feethams: football and cricket living side by side

HARTLEPOOL
·UNITED·

Hartlepool's temporary Main Stand survived wind and rain for sixty-five years until swept away by events at Bradford. All that remains now are the sawn-off wooden stumps of the pillars

The Victoria Ground

A rubbish tip opposite the Hartlepool docks was made into a sports ground in 1886, and named after the Queen, who celebrated her Golden Jubilee in the following year. In those early days, the Victoria Ground and the adjacent Hartlepool Stadium were linked, and used mainly by the West Hartlepool Rugby Club. Association football was played there from 1890, and in 1908 it became the home of the newly formed professional club, Hartlepools United. The rugby and soccer pitches were divided and the one ground became two separate entities.

The Victoria Ground does not occupy much space in the annals of great soccer, but it did witness an unusual event during the First World War. On the night of 27 November 1916 two German Zeppelins were attempting to raid the town when they were caught in the searchlights, and hit by guns of the Royal Flying Corps. The airships jettisoned their load of 100 bombs, then burst into flames and crashed into the North Sea. The *Daily Mirror* described the raid as 'a complete fiasco' in which the only casualty was a woman who died of shock, but they did not mention that two of the German bombs had fallen on the wooden grandstand at the Victoria Ground.

For several years after the War, United conducted a lengthy correspondence with the German Government, demanding compensation of £2500. (Their pleas went unanswered, and during the Second World War German bombers returned over Hartlepool, but just missed the football ground.)

Although they joined the League in 1921, United decided to build only a temporary replacement to the Main Stand. This was especially sensible because the council had plans to widen Clarence Road, behind the stand, which would mean shifting the pitch several yards to the west. But the club was not the only body short of funds, and as the years went by although the traffic grew heavier the road stayed as it was.

So to 1957, and the visit of the Busby Babes, Manchester United, in the 3rd Round of the FA Cup, on 5 January 1957. A record gate of 17 426 squeezed into the Victoria Ground as Hartlepools were squeezed out of the competition. Manchester United went on to the Final, but Hartlepools earned sufficient funds to extend their north and south terracing and prepare for the eventual moving of the pitch. But the years went by and the road stayed as it was.

In 1965 a young Brian Clough became manager of the club and noticed immediately that the Victoria Ground had no floodlights. By the end of that year lights had been installed and first switched on for a game v. Southend. For the first time in their history,

United won promotion in 1968. Down came the old cover over the terracing opposite the Main Stand, and up went a splendid new full-length cantilever stand, at a cost of £40 000 (see page 27).

Quite sensibly, this new stand was erected some distance from the touchline, to allow room for when the pitch was inevitably moved. Also in 1968 the club changed its name to plain Hartlepool, but in 1977 changed again to Hartlepool United. By 1982 the capacity of the Victoria Ground was 18 000, including 2320 seats, but this figure was reduced drastically in 1985 when the ground became designated. The Main Stand was a perfect example of the kind of antiquated accommodation the Safety of Sports Grounds Act aimed to eliminate; rickety though quaint, potentially dangerous though cosy (the stand was once apparently a favourite haunt for canoodling couples from the nearby skating rink).

To enter it from the road one passed through a narrow door in an unsteady fence. Inside was a gloomy alley with wooden doors and patched-up walls, supported by cross-beams at all angles. The stand resembled a decaying timber yard, with telegraph poles holding up the roof at the front and roof struts flapping loosely in the sea-breeze.

Although it extended only a third of the touchline and was barely 20 feet deep, the old stand somehow squeezed in 620 seats, dressing rooms, a tiny office and a club room. When the wind was high the roof swayed, and some matches were postponed.

Even without the Popplewell Report the Main Stand was bound to come down and so, rather than spend a large amount on fireproofing, Hartlepool decided to dismantle it entirely. In its place portable buildings bought from the fire brigade were installed.

Inevitable though this was, in March 1986 the club suffered a further blow when they were ordered to dismantle the terrace covers at each end of the ground. Neither was substantial, resembling at best a narrow bicycle shed, but their removal meant there was no longer any cover for standing spectators.

By the summer of 1986 the Victoria Ground was reduced to a capacity of only 3300, including 1600 seats, although with new barriers it was hoped to raise the limit to 14 000. Future developments hinged entirely on whether the club would be able to purchase the ground back from the council. If this happened Hartlepool would build new facilities under the Mill House cantilever stand.

In the meantime, the club were still unable to plan any developments on the site of the old stand, because it was still not decided whether a certain road plan would go ahead . . .

Ground Description

United's ground is in location similar to Blundell Park, Grimsby, a short distance from the sea with a railway line in between. But the Victoria Ground is more open and windswept and therefore more a part of the seaboard landscape, an impression heightened by the changes made during the 1985–86 season. With no Main Stand to dominate the Clarence Road side and no covers at either end, the ground is especially bare. Apart from the Mill House Stand it is certainly not an obvious venue for League football. From the line of portable buildings along the touchline, where once stood the Main Stand, to the left is the Town End terrace, behind which is the Hartlepool Stadium, used for greyhound racing. To the right, or north, is the Rink End terrace, named because there was once a popular roller skating rink behind.

Across the pitch, one of the widest in the country and with yards of turf to spare because of the road plan, is one of the finest stands in the lower divisions. The Mill House Stand, named after a nearby pub, seats 1600 quite comfortably and is a copy-book prefabricated structure, built behind a line of terracing.

From here one has an excellent view, over Clarence Road to the railway line which runs from Sunderland to Newcastle, beyond which are the docks. The fresh sea-air is more noticeable up in the stand, blustering across the ground into the spectators' faces. To the right, over the Town End, you can also see the stands of the Hartlepool Stadium. It is typical of the haphazard development of English sport that two such grounds should be so separate.

Underneath the Mill House Stand, between the already rusting steel supports, is a great deal of room; surely enough to house all the facilities once crammed into the stand opposite. Hartlepool could only proceed with this if they received grants from the Sports Council, who in turn would only help if the club owned the ground. Meanwhile, behind the Mill House Stand a beautiful new sports centre has been built. A new entrance to the Victoria Ground on this side, sharing the centre's car park, would give Hartlepool a whole new lease of life. The potential is there but, as we gather from the road-widening saga, development in Hartlepool is no speedy affair.

·SUNDERLAND·

Previous Grounds

No other Football League club has had the history of its grounds better chronicled than Sunderland, thanks to the research of Arthur Appleton. His *Centenary History of Sunderland*, written in 1979, leaves hardly a question unanswered. Sunderland's first home in 1879 was the Blue House Field, Hendon, not far from the Board School where the idea for a club originated with one of the teachers, James Allan. The ground lay next to the original Blue House public house. But Sunderland and District Teachers AFC found the annual rent of £10 too high, so in 1882 after trying various pitches they moved to Groves Field, Ashbrooke, probably on the site of the Ashbrooke Ground, formally laid out in 1887. Sunderland moved to Horatio Street, Roker in 1883. This was their first ground north of the River Wear, the others being on the south side close to the seafront and docks.

Horatio Street itself was then built up, but on the other side of the pitch was a claypit and brickworks. The pitch had a heavy surface and was sometimes called 'a clay-dolly field'. The ground is now covered by Givens Street and Appley Terrace. After only one season there, Sunderland moved to Abbs Field, Fulwell Road, their first properly enclosed ground. Rent was a paltry £2 10s to begin with, but as the club attracted more support and a better reputation, it rose to £15 in the second season. The ground was near where the Central Laundry now stands, opposite Cliff Road.

Sunderland had already played some games at the neighbourhood's best ground on Newcastle Road, owned by two sisters called Thompson, and in early 1886 the club succeeded in procuring a year's lease for the ground, at a rent of £15. The ground already had walls round three sides, so Sunderland had only to board up the Newcastle Road Side, at the east end of the pitch. Two players were each paid five shillings for tarring the new fence, and a clubhouse was bought for £2 10s.

On the north side was built a small wooden grandstand on the half-way line, seating 1000 spectators, the work carried out mainly by supporters from Thompsons North Sands shipyard.

Sunderland's first game at Newcastle Road was on 3 April 1886 v. Darlington, and the ground obviously met with approval for attendances rose rapidly. But the club was still technically amateur, and although turnover was high, it still felt the need to rent the ground for grazing in return for 30 shillings a year – cheaper than a lawnmower. The Thompsons also helped out by handing back the first season's rent to Sunderland.

The issue of professionalism was almost the ruin of Sunderland, beginning with their expulsion from the

Roker in readiness for the World Cup. Note the Fulwell End is seated for that event

FA Cup after a tie v. Middlesbrough at Linthorpe Road. A disgruntled Jimmy Allan, the club's founder, decided to break away and form a proper professional outfit called Sunderland Albion. Taking seven of Sunderland's Scottish players with him, he set up on Sunderland's original ground, the Blue House Field. Money was poured into Albion, who would have comfortably surpassed Sunderland and become the town's premier club had intense local rivalry and bitterness about Allan's actions made Sunderland determined not to play second fiddle.

In the summer of 1889 Newcastle Road was downcast, overshadowed by events across the Wear, until the shrewd appointment of Tom Watson. Backed by shipbuilding money, he rejuvenated the club and ensured its ascendancy. Newcastle Road was improved with a new clubhouse and an enlarged stand. Capacity rose to 15000, making it the biggest and best ground in the north east (St James' Park was not improved until 1898). A cabin for reporters was placed in the stand.

Also in 1889, Watson assembled the famous 'Team of All Talents' at Newcastle Road, whose highest attendance, 21000, saw a Cup tie v. Everton in January 1891. Two months later the ground was chosen for an international v. Wales.

Despite having laid the only cinder cycling track in Sunderland and built 'substantial' stands at the Blue House Field, interest in Sunderland Albion waned so drastically once Sunderland became a major national force, that Albion went into voluntary liquidation in August 1892.

Meanwhile to cope with Sunderland's growing support, Newcastle Road was again extended, to a capacity of 18000, although not everyone had a good view and the stand roof was often covered with spectators. Rent in 1896 was up to £100 a year and a limited liability company was formed in July of that year, because although the previous seasons were remarkably successful, very little capital had been amassed. Issue of shares helped of course, but the club could not really develop Newcastle Road as long as it had an annual lease. If Sunderland could have bought the freehold, a cycle and athletics track might have been laid, new stands built and the capacity enlarged. But gates were down to a few thousand, Watson had been lured to Anfield, and they probably could not have afforded to buy the ground anyway.

There then appears to have been a disagreement with the Thompson sisters; perhaps over rent, perhaps because the ladies wished to sell the site for development. Whatever the reason, chairman Henderson and his brother started looking for an alternative site in 1897, and found Roker Park. Sunderland played their last game at Newcastle Road on 23 April 1898 v. Nottingham Forest.

There is one famous picture of Newcastle Road still in existence, on view in the main foyer at Roker Park. It is an oil painting by Thomas M. Henry, depicting an extremely crowded goal-mouth incident during an imaginary match v. Aston Villa in the 1894–95 season. The North Stand is just visible on the left of the canvas. Behind the goal is a steep, probably exaggerated representation of the sloping terraces.

The actual pitch was built over by Netherburn Road and Newington Court. Ellerslie Terrace, where the club's headquarters were, was demolished in the mid-1960s and became a car lot.

Roker Park

Since moving north of the Wear, all Sunderland's grounds had been within a couple of hundred yards of each other. The site picked by chairman Henderson was farmland belonging to a Mr Tennant, who leased the site only on the condition that the football club's activities would not prevent the building of houses on the remainder of the site up to Fulwell Road. Henderson had to agree to pay the ground rents until the sites were sold.

The grandstand was a single-deck having 3000 seats with a small paddock in front. Opposite was the original Clock Stand, for standing only, with 32 wooden steps each rising 9 inches (228 millimetres, compared with the current recommended height of between 75 mm and 180 mm). The open ends of the grounds were called North and South, as they were before the present names, Roker End and Fulwell End were adopted. Finally, fine quality Irish turf was imported, a perfect camber created, and drainage installed.

Roker Park was opened with much pomp on 10 September 1898, in front of 30 000 spectators, when Liverpool were the visitors. Sunderland's President, Lord Londonderry, opened the small gate leading from the dressing rooms onto the field with a golden key, photographs were posed for, and Lord Londonderry praised the Henderson brothers for their efforts in delivering Sunderland 'from the misfortune of being without a football ground'.

Events at St James' Park on Good Friday 1901 (see Newcastle) had shown quite vividly how fanatical north east football followers could be, and how a minority of Sunderland's supporters proved themselves to be especially unruly, committing offences which make the present day hooliganism seem almost tame.

One referee had to escape from Roker Park disguised as a policeman, as angry men waited for him outside after the match. In 1903, The Wednesday team were stoned by Sunderland fans as they drove away from the ground along Roker Baths Road, and in punishment Roker Park was closed for one match, which Sunderland played at Newcastle.

There were more pitch invasions during games v. Newcastle – often owing to overcrowding rather than malice – but in September 1909, a police horse was stabbed as police cleared the pitch at the Fulwell End. There was another invasion when West Bromwich were the visitors in February 1912, hardly surprising since the attendance of 43 383 was some 13 000 above the ground's capacity. Later that year, as more people struggled to see Sunderland v. Manchester City in the Cup (the match had been switched to Roker Park after a pitch invasion at Hyde Road in the first meeting), a crowd watched from the roof of the nearby Roker Coal Depot. This gave way under the weight and 20 people were hospitalized.

Naturally, success brought security and improvements at Roker Park. The ground was bought in 1908, for £10 000, and in 1913 the Roker End was enlarged at a cost of £20 000. Instead of being built up on earth banking, as was common practice, the terracing was built on a huge, labyrinthine base of concrete supports, like a complex M. C. Escher fantasy framework. It was an early example of the art of on-site concrete building, which was to develop to the level of sophistication seen at Wembley Stadium in 1923. The structure also provided the players with a covered, if rather gloomy area under which to train during wet weather. Roker Park's capacity was now 50 000.

At the opposite end of the ground the Fulwell End was re-terraced in 1925. Meanwhile the Main Stand was distinctly primitive for such a successful club. One reporter described Sunderland's press facilities as the worst in the country.

By 1929–30, the ground had grown to hold 60 000, after extensive improvements in the summer. Most important was the erection of the present Grand Stand, in place of the original wooden stand. Archibald Leitch was the designer, and although built on a slightly less grand scale than contemporary Leitch stands at Goodison and Ibrox Parks, it has stood the test of time as well as any other. At Roker, Leitch's criss-cross steelwork balcony – his trademark – was painted red, whereas the other clubs he designed for used blue, so this one was unique at least for that.

Opened on 7 September 1929, the new stand cost £25 000 (compared with Everton's expenditure of £30 000 in 1926 for their Bullens Road Stand) and at the same time the Clock Stand was extended.

Attendances still grew, reaching a climax on 8 March 1933, when on a Wednesday afternoon 75 118 saw Sunderland lose in extra time to Derby County in a Cup 6th Round replay. Arthur Appleton was in the packed crowd, unable to raise his arms in the crush or prevent himself being carried from the back to the front of the Roker End. The rest of town seemed to shut down just for that afternoon.

Yet just one month later only 4000 turned up to see Sunderland's final home game v. Portsmouth, because most people were pressed up against a wireless set listening to the live broadcast of the FA Cup Final at Wembley. Armchair football was then a novelty, and not until after the Second World War were Finals played after the last Saturday of League football.

In the midst of a successful run in Division One, the Clock Stand was rebuilt in the summer of 1936. Archibald Leitch was again the designer, and it was one of his last major works at a football ground before his death in 1939 (see Design). The new Clock Stand ran the full length of the pitch and held 15 500, in two sections of terracing; the rear half being wooden terracing, the front paddock having ash and concrete terracing. Lady Reine opened the stand in September 1936.

Roker Park was unaffected by the war until March 1943, when bombs fell on the pitch and just outside the ground, killing a policeman. In May, more bombs damaged the car park and the clubhouse, then at the corner of Roker Baths Road.

After the war, the upper section of the Grand Stand paddock was converted into a seating tier in 1950, making a total of 5400 seats at the ground (Everton did the same to their Bullens Road Stand).

In December 1952 Roker Park became the second First Division ground to have floodlights (Highbury was the first), switched on for a friendly v. Dundee, that year's Scottish Cup runners-up. The lights were updated in 1973 for £22 000.

The next major developments came with the World Cup in 1966. Roker Park and Ayresome Park were chosen to stage matches in Group Four, with Sunderland also hosting the quarter-final between the USSR and Hungary. The Roker pitch had to be extended by 3 yards, permanent seats installed at the rear of the Clock Stand, and temporary seats added to both paddocks and the Fulwell End. This end was also covered for the first time. Altogether there were an extra 9000 seats. A television camera gantry was built on the Clock Stand roof. But perhaps the most substantial improvement was behind the Grand Stand, where new offices and executive facilities were built on stilts. Much of the outlay was provided by a government grant and a loan from the FA.

During the 1970s, less noticeable but no less important innovations were private boxes in 1973, an underground sprinkler system for the pitch in 1974, and then to conform to the Safety of Sports Grounds Act, over £250 000 had to be spent on new barriers, access points, lighting and refreshment bars.

Sadly, in the summer of 1982, safety requirements dictated the demolition of most of the Roker End's maze of concrete supports, so that the capacity of the terrace was reduced from 17 150 to 8000.

Roker Park's current capacity is 37 603, of which 8753 are seated.

Ground Description

Once you have become immersed in the built-up streets of Roker, having crossed the big red bridge across the Wear, it is almost impossible to realize how close Roker Park is to the sea.

Before 1983 it would have been worth taking a walk around the back of the Roker End before gaining admission, just to see the concrete struts holding up the terracing. It is hardly surprising they had to come down; they were like a concrete version of Ibrox's wooden terracing in 1902, like grey logs bolted together. And yet they withstood so many huge crowds for so long. Rising 50 feet above the street, the Roker End was like an unfinished tower block, its guts exposed to the passer-by, who could see deep into a dark cavernous web of beams. Truly there

was never terracing like it, nor ever will be again.

But all that is no more, and we must return to the Grand Stand, to the dark passages underneath the executive suites and social clubs. Inside the foyer is Henry's painting of Newcastle Road.

The Grand Stand is typical Leitch, but with a distinctive character of its own. Some of the balcony wall has been obscured by advertising, but enough remains to mark it clearly as Leitch's work. Underneath the balcony is a line of private boxes, more like commentary boxes than executive ones, but no doubt much warmer than the very exposed seats in the rear paddock. Every seat on this side is scarlet, which adds neatness and shows how uniform colours can create style, even in the oldest stand.

The roof and sides have also been refurbished, a process which sadly disposed of the distinctive chequered pattern of red and glass panels at each screen end. Nevertheless the red details are a welcome contrast to the predominantly blue and white examples of Leitch's other stands of this type.

From here the open Roker End is to the left, now in its truncated form, half the original size. The floodlight pylons are almost on the lower corners, and thus parts of the terrace have an obscured view, especially the corner meeting up with the Grand Stand.

Opposite is the Clock Stand, with of course a clock on the centre of the roof. But such a small clock, dwarfed on either side by the cumbersome camera gantries! Presumably this clock predates the other one placed above the players' tunnel. The stand is low, with a pitched roof, and half-time scoreboards at each end, one of them, now disused, tucked inside the screen wall so that it is barely visible from beyond the shadows. There is a paddock in front of the seating tier, but it was once all standing and therefore a very unusual sort of standing cover for the side of a ground. Perhaps Leitch had always intended it to be converted into seating.

To the right is the covered North, or Fulwell End, named after the nearby district. This holds 12 500 standing, and has a high roof, almost higher than would appear necessary, in gun metal grey. Next to such a modern, plain roof, the presence of a wooden fence around the back of the terracing seems wholly anachronistic. In fact the fence was there to stop people falling over the side of the tall banking before the roof was put up, and has never been removed simply because if hooligans wish to bang their fists and feet against something they can do less damage to a solid wooden fence than to thin metal sheeting.

Despite the modernization of both ends, Roker Park is still an essentially pre-war ground with new trimmings, as for example the Baseball Ground or Burnden Park. It falls between the major stadiums and those archetypal Second Division grounds. But the feature which elevates Roker Park to the ranks of 'special' is the people who fill it and the Roker Roar which when caught in the sea breeze, is sent swirling across the ground and over the rooftops.

NEWCASTLE ·UNITED·

St James' Park

United began life as Newcastle East End in 1882, playing on a ground at Chillingham Road, Heaton. To the west on Town Moor, played their greatest rivals, Newcastle West End. West End had taken over the ground from a team called Newcastle Rangers, and had a 14-year lease. The pitch had the slight disadvantage of an 18-foot slope from north to south, but was perfectly located for the city centre and public transport. The club allowed butchers to graze their sheep on the pitch to fatten them up before slaughter.

In 1892 Newcastle West End amalgamated with East End, changed their name to Newcastle United and moved into the Town Moor ground, which became known as St James' Park. Facilities were negligible, the home players having to change at the Lord Hill pub on Barrack Road, the visitors at other local hostelries. West End had put down wooden boards in 1889 to prevent spectators getting wet feet on the rough banks, and a press-box stood on the Leazes Terrace Side. Leazes Terrace, still partly visible from the ground today, was part of a larger Georgian development for the gentry built in 1829, on the pattern of Eldon Square, Newcastle, or Regents Park, London. Leazes Park, to the north of the ground was laid out on part of the Town Moor.

United negotiated a lease for St James' Park in 1892, but could not purchase the freehold because all the land occupied originally by Town Moor had been granted by Newcastle to the Freemen of the city. This is how the situation remains today, the club having two landlords, the city council and the Freemen, who are entitled by law to all the 'eatage and herbage' of St James' Park.

United joined the League in 1893 but it was not until 1898 when they were promoted to Division One, that a dressing room was erected, and this was for the home team only. The visitors changed in the County Hotel and were ferried to the ground in landaus. As more and more people packed into the ground, its capacity was stretched to the limit, once with terrible consequences. In a First Division match v. Blackburn Rovers some railings collapsed, one youth had his foot torn off, another suffered a broken leg and there were many minor injuries.

A complete restructuring was imperative. During the following summer of 1899, an extra 4 acres of land were leased, and by moving the pitch and shifting tons of soil, United were able to reduce the slope to about 4 feet from north to south. Terracing was cut into the banks on the Leazes Park End and the Leazes Terrace Side, increasing the ground's capacity to 28 000. 'Immense structures of corrugated iron' surrounded the ground, giving it the enclosed impression of a hippodrome, wrote Gibson and Pickford in 1906.

Still the ground was not large enough to cope, nor the pitch quite up to standard requirements. A report in February 1901 tells how in an attempt to melt the frost-bound pitch, straw was laid down on the turf and then set alight. But rain started to fall, the straw stuck in the mud, and sand had to be laid over the whole glutinous mess!

But worse was to follow on Good Friday, 5 April 1901. Sunderland were the visitors, and they were a few points above their north east rivals in strong

St James' Park; the old West Stand entrance before demolition in August 1987

contention for the Championship. An estimated 35 000 crowd tried to squeeze into St James' Park, with as many more outside desperate to gain admission. Fences were trampled down, and before long the pitch became a battleground between rival supporters. *Athletic News*'s correspondent reported that the: 'club flag was torn from its staff and riven into shreds; the goal nets at one end shared a like fate'. He went on to note, 'we are delighted to hear that the cross-bar in falling fetched one or two of the rioters a reverberating "sock" on the headache department'. It took until 5 o'clock for the police to clear the ground, using truncheons in a less than restrained fashion, and the match had to be abandoned.

Incredibly only nine people were sent to hospital, including one reported to have fallen out of the grandstand, which nearly collapsed. One Sunderland supporter sued Newcastle for his money back, lost his case and had to pay expenses of around £70 (it was not until a riot occurred at Goodison Park a few years later that League clubs began posting up signs warning that in no circumstances would money be refunded).

Although they lost for the second successive year, in the Cup Final of 1906, United undertook further improvements at St James' Park using their profits. The club built a new West Stand seating 4680 and costing £8082 14s 11d, and at the same time increased the banking on all three open sides, to double the ground's capacity to 60 000.

The new stand was similar to one at Anfield, built a few years earlier, in that it had a distinctive curved gable in the centre of the roof. Underneath the stand was a small swimming pool for the players. The West Stand still exists, although the pool has since been covered over and is now used as a reservoir for the pitch's sprinkler system.

The ground remained unaltered until the summer of 1930 when the Leazes Park End was covered. The roof carried some 20 yards round the north east corner along the Leazes Terrace Side, and remained in its truncated L-shape form until 1978. No sooner had the roof gone up, than St James' Park saw its highest ever gate of 68 386, for the visit of newly promoted Chelsea on 3 September 1930.

In 1948, the open Leazes Terrace Side and the Gallowgate End were laid with concrete terracing, and in 1953 St James' Park became only the third First Division ground to have floodlights, switched on for a friendly v. Celtic on 25 February. These first lights were mounted on telegraph poles and were used for the first ever floodlit FA Cup match between two League clubs, Carlisle and Darlington, in a 1st Round replay on 28 November 1955. An improved system on four pylons was installed in 1958, and were switched on for a Football League v. Scottish League representative game in March.

The 1950s were prosperous years at St James' Park, United winning three Wembley Cup Finals between 1951–55. Reflecting this success was the West Stand's new Director's Suite, added in 1957, and giving the club a grander entrance and foyer in typically 1950s' style; ivory terrazzo floors and mahogany clad walls, the polished utilitarian style.

In 1967 the city council asked a firm of architects to investigate ways of making St James' Park the centre of a multi-purpose sports complex. A plan was drawn up showing the ground as an elliptical-shaped stadium with a sports centre under a new West Stand for use by the community and Newcastle University. The East Stand would be solely for United's purposes. Overall there were to be 31 000 seats and room for 32 000 standing (at a time when St James' Park still only had 4680 seats) and the ground would have a practice pitch and car parks, also for sharing with the University. To tempt United with the proposals, the council offered the club the security of a long lease (for a detailed study of the plan, see *Architectural Review*, May 1968).

United's willingness to enter such a scheme was not the major barrier. Money was. The scheme never left the drawing board, and so United have had to pay for the redevelopment of St James' Park without the council's aid. But they did negotiate a 99-year lease with their landlords before commencing work.

The club's plans centred on the Leazes Terrace Side, where for years they had considered building a double-decker stand, but had never had sufficient capital or security to go further. The long lease helped, but as important was the revenue earned during three consecutive seasons competing in the European Fairs Cup from 1968–71, the first of which saw United winning the trophy.

Building began in 1972 and finished in March 1973, later than planned because of a building workers' strike. Thanks to the keen interest in stand design shown by the architects, there is a detailed account of which factors they considered important (see Design). The factors which related specifically to St James' Park were that the stand had to offer standing room, for traditional reasons, had to be part of an overall development plan, and most importantly, had to respect the architectural integrity of the Georgian Leazes Terrace. How this was accomplished is described below, but such constraints added to the cost, finally agreed at £420 000. The East Stand had seats for 3400.

The capacity of St James' Park was then set at 55 000, but when the Safety of Sports Grounds Act was introduced, United suddenly faced a bill of £150 000, to comply with its recommendations. Again the ground's consultant architects outlined the specific problems facing League clubs under the new Act (see Safety) and the one which affected Newcastle most was that although the crush barriers themselves were strong enough, their foundations were not. When the terracing had been concreted over in the late 1940s, the barriers' original foundations were simply covered over, but had since become insecure. The base of each barrier was attached to the

St James' Park; the old West Stand with its curving lines and brooding presence will be sadly missed

old timber 'stringer' which used to form the stepping of the terracing. So that whereas the Leazes End had once held a capacity of 17 000, under the new standards it had to be reduced to 7000. For this reason the club decided that since the cost of replacing every barrier was enormous, they might as well continue the ground's redevelopment at that end rather than anywhere else.

Much to the regret of every Newcastle fan, the roof at the Leazes Park End was taken down in 1978, the same year as United went down to the Second Division – an ill omen for the future.

It cost Newcastle £500 000 just to remove the banking, build new foundations and take down two floodlight pylons. This was before any extension of the East Stand could occur. But now, as at Elland Road, the foundations are all there is to show for the work. The Leazes Park End terrace now holds only 5000 standing spectators, all without cover. In fact the only cover for standing spectators was for those in the paddock in front of the new East Stand, and that didn't last long either. Part of the terrace was taken up by the construction of 23 executive boxes along the rear. Then, after insisting originally that standing on that side should be preserved, the club had to install bench seats in an attempt to prevent crowd trouble, a blight which St James' Park has never quite shaken off since Good Friday, 1901.

There were serious pitch invasions in 1974, when United's Cup quarter-final v. Nottingham Forest had to be replayed at Goodison Park, and again in 1977 during United's 4th Round Cup tie v. Manchester City. The latter came in spite of the most stringent efforts to prevent encroachment of the pitch by building special security barriers around the perimeter.

There have been occasions, however, when United have been delighted to see crowds on the pitch, for St James' Park has become in recent years one of the

foremost rock concert venues in the North. It began in June 1982 when 35 000 – 10 000 of them on the pitch – attended a Rolling Stones concert. Since then Newcastle have staged concerts by some of modern music's legendary figures. To the list of heroes who have graced the St James' Park turf – Hughie Gallacher, Jackie Milburn, Malcolm MacDonald and Kevin Keegan – must now be added Mick Jagger, Queen, Status Quo, Bruce Springsteen and perhaps the greatest of all, Bob Dylan. No other football ground in Britain, with the exception of Wembley, can claim such a distinction.

Greater safety measures in 1985 led to substantial changes at St James' Park. First the West Stand paddock had to be completely remodelled to allow for easier access from the seats to the pitch – a major feat of engineering because of the way the pitch slopes and the terracing dips below the perimeter. Then the much-loved press box in the West Stand gable had to be closed because access to it was so limited (via a narrow spiral staircase). Finally in May 1987 the local authority condemned the West Stand completely, and rather than modify it further the club felt it more cost-effective to start again. Despite the fact that a new season had only just begun, down it came in August 1987, one of the longest surviving main stands in the country.

But instead of building in its place a copy of the East Stand, so that the whole ground could eventually be linked up, as was the intention certainly at the Leazes Park End, another set of architects was commissioned and they opted to build a pre-cast concrete stand based on Watford's new Sir Stanley Rous Stand (see page 231). Estimated to cost £4 million, Newcastle's new West Stand will hold 6300 seats and have 39 executive boxes, giving St James' Park an approximate total of 11 300 seats in a 35 000 capacity.

Ground Description

St James' Park sits on a rise above the city, perhaps not as splendid as the Parthenon, but in Newcastle at least as revered. It is even visible from the opposite bank of the Tyne, from Gateshead, where League football is now only a memory.

From the city centre we climb up to Strawberry Place, where a new Metro station is built, and St James' Park suddenly takes on a gargantuan scale. Sadly, the huge battle-grey frontage with the words NEWCASTLE UNITED in letters 50 feet high has gone – a landmark in the city and the idea originally of Harry Faulkner Brown, architect of the East Stand.

Until the new West Stand is complete, it is hard to assess whether it too will have such an impact. There is no doubt however that the new stand is an excellent design, as has already been seen at Watford. Light, airy and, in current jargon, user-friendly, the new West Stand should stand proud on the Newcastle skyline. But one cannot help wondering why no attempt was made to integrate the design into the plans – if any still survive – for the rest of the ground. Is this another example of piecemeal ground development? (The demolition angered some season-ticket holders who had paid up to £170 thinking they were going to be in the centre stand only to find themselves at the Leazes End sitting on plastic seats with no roof over their heads. The majority were however re-housed in the East Stand.)

From here, to the left is the now open Leazes Park End, another concrete mass of barriers. Newcastle was the first club to study segregation of rival fans, after the 1974 incidents, so they know all about fences and barriers here. They use not a tall security fence at the perimeter wall, but a couple of low walls divided by a shallow moat – a system borrowed by Crystal Palace and one which inhibits no-one's view of the pitch. Behind the terrace you can see the green, tall wall which once formed the rear of the original terrace. It is plain to see how the East Stand was intended eventually to curl round the corner and fill this space.

Between here and the East Stand the row of houses called Leazes Terrace is visible. The East Stand has had to fit in as much as possible with its neighbours. Accordingly, the external facings have been textured and coloured to harmonize with the ageing stone of the terrace. St James' Terrace, also behind the East Stand, has had to change as well. Old houses have come down and a pedestrian courtyard created. You cannot prevent a stand like this overpowering everything in sight, but at least care has been taken to preserve some of the street level's qualities.

The East Stand itself is a tall, exposed cantilever, without screen walls and therefore forming a dark silhouette of angled concrete standing out against the sky. Nowhere else is the wonder of cantilever technology more stunning than here. The roof has no right to defy gravity and stay up, but it does. It is composed of corrugated aluminium barrel vaults, tied along the front to seem flat. As on the West Stand there are floodlight gantries along the roof. There is a paddock in front, now covered with simple bench seats. The people's desire to stand has given way to the club's desire for peace.

At the rear of the paddock are glass-fronted executive boxes, faced in grey. For years St James' Park was a no-frills ground for the hardy Northern soul. Such is progress.

To the right from the West Stand is the Gallowgate End, named after the main thoroughfare behind, leading to the city centre. As the name suggests, it is a dour terrace indeed, bordered by thick concrete walls like a huge open bunker, overlooking the town. From the top, the city lies behind to the south, falling down the valley into the Tyne. Directly behind the terracing is a neatly laid out slope covered in shrubs.

A small building behind the terrace is the club's former offices, built in 1904 and now used as a police station on match days. The police also operate, with closed-circuit television, from portakabins stacked behind the Leazes Park End.

At the top of the Gallowgate End is a new and dominant electric scoreboard. Directly behind it is Wellbar House, home of the Newcastle Weather Centre. The building to the right of this block is the headquarters of Newcastle Breweries – a temple to so many – but also a source of some fairly acrid odours.

Newcastle have conscientiously tried to solve the problem of hooliganism at St James' Park – it is hoped that shrub gardens might soothe many an angered brow and promote some pride in the place – and have gone some way to satisfying the demands of local conservationists, but they have not been able to solve that slope whereupon lies the 'eatage and herbage'. Even when the East Stand was built the design had to slope with the land, otherwise all the sight lines of the West Stand would have been disrupted. As the stands' facings show, the drop is still 4 feet from north to south. But that is perhaps the least of the problems facing United. There are foundations to be built on, stands to be completed.

Of course money is the key to this and, as Jagger sang, 'You can't always get what you want.' To which no doubt the Newcastle faithful would hope to be able to reply with Dylan's words, 'The times they are a-changing.' They certainly are at St James' Park, which will never be the same again without the dark brooding presence of the old West Stand. We can only hope that its replacement won't mess up the acoustics . . .

◆ SHEFFIELD ◆ WEDNESDAY

Previous Grounds

Although Wednesday are the fifth oldest club in the League, having formed in 1867, a Wednesday cricket club had existed since 1816. It was so-called because its members played on their half-day holiday, Wednesday. The football club played their first games on a field now occupied by Highfields Library. In 1869 they moved to Myrtle Road, Heeley, and went on to use Sheaf House, Hunter's Bar and Endcliffe until 1887, when they moved to their first substantial enclosure, Olive Grove. Even then, some important games were staged at Bramall Lane until 1895.

Olive Grove was situated off Queen's Road, between Sheffield and Heeley railway stations, and like Bramall Lane was owned by the Duke of Norfolk. Wednesday secured a seven-year lease, but had to spend some £5000 to prepare the field, across which ran a brook. Olive Grove was proudly opened on 12 September 1887 with a 4–4 draw v. mighty Blackburn Rovers.

The most bizarre match at Olive Grove was in the 1898–99 season. Wednesday's November home game v. Aston Villa had been abandoned after 79 minutes because of bad light, with the score at 3–1. The infamous remaining 11 minutes were played at Olive Grove in March, Wednesday adding one more goal. The ground thereby staged the shortest encounter in League history.

The end of that season saw Wednesday relegated and also the last match at Olive Grove, which had been bought for development by the Midland Railway Company, owners of the adjoining line. The ground was then in a sorry state, only 4000 attended, and spirits were low indeed.

Olive Grove had been, in Richard Sparling's words, 'a most comfortable little ground. It was a place to foster friendships and it appeared to encourage that feeling in the spectators "The Wednesday are part of us."'

It was suggested that Wednesday share Bramall Lane with United and use Sheaf House for reserve games, but talks broke down. The supporters were asked to vote on their preferred new site: 4767 opted for one at Carbrook, 4115 for another at Owlerton, 124 were neutral in the matter, and only 16 fancied a return to Sheaf House. Meanwhile someone else bought the Carbrook land, and the Owlerton site proved to be impracticable, so with only a few weeks before the next season, another site was found at Owlerton. Perhaps only Arsenal's crossing of the Thames 14 years later was to be such a daring and speculative move.

Hillsborough

Owlerton in 1899 was not even in Sheffield, but in the unspoilt hills on the other side of the city to Olive Grove. The 10 acres Wednesday had bought were meadowland in need of at least £5000 worth of preparation. With only £2000 in the bank the club decided to form itself into a limited liability company.

So began the task of building, 'out in the wilds'. The old stand at Olive Grove was re-erected at Owlerton, rubbish was tipped at either end to form banking. But even then, why should the fans come all that way to see Second Division Wednesday when First Division United were so close at hand? The Wednesday directors had made a shrewd prediction. The new electric trams ferried support from town at 1d a ride, and Owlerton was soon absorbed by Sheffield's expanding suburbs.

The ground was opened for Wednesday's first game in Division Two, v. Chesterfield on 2 September 1899, by the Lord Mayor, Alderman W. E. Clegg, one of two Clegg brothers who had dominated Sheffield football in its early days.

In 1914 Owlerton became part of the new parliamentary constituency of Hillsborough, and the ground changed its name accordingly, although Wednesday are still nicknamed the Owls.

Hillsborough in the 1930s

The existing South Stand was opened in January of 1914, in place of the old Olive Grove Stand, for a cost of £10 000. Archibald Leitch was responsible, and it may be considered among his best designs, as I shall describe below.

The record crowd at the ground was 72 841 for Manchester City's visit in the FA Cup in February 1934. At that time there was, opposite the South Stand, a double-roofed stand with 2000 seats (which survived a bomb blast and was only replaced in 1961), next to which stood a funny little short cover over the terracing in the north west corner. The West End terrace was half covered by a low roof at the back. The Kop was uncovered and unterraced at the very rear.

Hillsborough's first floodlit game was played between a Sheffield XI and an International XI in aid of Derek Dooley's trust fund on 9 March 1955. Dooley had tragically lost a leg after a playing accident. A crowd of 55 000 came to pay tribute to the man, and to see the new lights; the best in Britain it was claimed.

The next development at Hillsborough really deserves a chapter of its own, but since space is limited, suffice to say here that the new North Stand was, at the time of its opening by Sir Stanley Rous on 23 August 1961, the most advanced football grandstand ever built at a British football ground. It not only raised spectators' expectations, but proved to architects and directors alike that football architecture need not be dull or merely utilitarian, a point Leitch and Ferrier (at Highbury) had tried to show before the War. (For a detailed appraisal of the North Stand, see *The Structural Engineer*, November 1962.) It took 11 months to build the stand, which cost £150 000 and was the second cantilever stand in Britain, after Scunthorpe, but the first one to run the full length of a pitch. The roof is 45 000 square feet, weighs 17 tons and was made possible by the architect's (Husband and Company of Sheffield) use of aluminium sheets hung under a steel frame, supported at the back by three miles of prestressed, precast concrete units. The aluminium was of course lighter than the commonly used asbestos or corrugated iron sheeting. All 9882 seats are well protected from the weather.

The North Stand attracted more architectural interest than any other football stand since Wembley and even merits inclusion in Pevsner's mammoth work on the *Buildings of England*. No other League ground is mentioned.

We move on to the inevitable consequence of the North Stand's construction, the decision to stage four World Cup games at Hillsborough in 1966. For the occasion, the new West Stand was built in 1965 at a cost of £110 000, and extra seating put in the South Stand's paddock, lowering the ground capacity to 60 000, but giving Hillsborough more seats than any other ground at the time. A new tavern was also built behind the South Stand, on stilts, and a large sports hall erected behind the North Stand, for use during the World Cup as a press centre. Three Group Two matches were played here, plus a quarter-final between West Germany and Uruguay. With a grant from the Government, Wednesday had spent £200 000 on preparing Hillsborough for the event.

Apart from football, the ground has also staged world-class tennis in 1938, boxing in the 1950s, a schools display for the Queen in 1954 and a Harlem Globetrotters basketball display in the 1960s.

Hillsborough is the only major ground in England to have increased its capacity by any margin since 1975. The cause of this was the erection, in 1986, of a £1 million cover over the Kop. Rather than cut down the oddly shaped terrace to conform with the demands of a roof, as so many other clubs have done, Wednesday squared off the rear of the Kop by adding almost a further 5000 places on new terracing raised on a steel framework in the north east corner. This was not just an extravagant gesture towards the standing spectator; Wednesday calculated it would have been costlier to reduce the terrace than expand it. When complete the new Kop gave Hillsborough a capacity raised from 50 142 to 55 000, including 23 224 seats.

Ground Description

Hillsborough is a stadium, with all the grand connotations the term implies.

An unusually square set of six floodlight pylons rising above trees and factory roofs signal your approach to the stadium. Enter if you can at the South West End, across a bridge over the tree-lined River Don, which flows behind the South Stand from the Pennines to the Humber, via (of course) Doncaster. The West Stand proclaims Sheffield Wednesday along its back.

For an old stand, the South Stand is surprisingly roomy. Leitch obviously enjoyed the lack of restrictions, for inside there is a sense of spacious cleanliness and light, as is the case at Leitch's Main Stand at Ibrox. A better perspective however is to be had from opposite the stand.

Notice especially the Leitch trade-mark, the pointed central gable, with a clock and a copper ball on its pinnacle, reminiscent of White Hart Lane's West Stand, sadly no more. A television gantry on the front of the roof does its usual spoiling job.

To the right is the newly covered Kop, which with a capacity of 22 000 is marginally smaller than the biggest in the League, at Aston Villa. The roof has changed Hillsborough completely, depriving it of that once rather wild hill which opened out the ground to the sky. But it fits in remarkably well with

Hillsborough before the Kop cover

its surrounds, is pleasingly clad in blue and provides long awaited cover for Wednesday's faithful terrace support.

To the left is the West Stand, with 4465 seats in an upper tier, and open terraces in front. Next to the other two stands it looks rather ordinary, but the view it provides is excellent, as are its facilities, and it does close off the ground effectively without cramping the style of either of its neighbours. The pitch slopes from this end down to the Kop by 2½ feet.

But the focus is all on the North Stand ahead. There is not a misplaced line in this remarkable stand. The roof is a clean sweep, from the concrete back to the ribbed blue roof fascia hanging 16 feet in front of the first row. A clock in the centre is flanked along the rooftop by a line of flagpoles, put up for the World Cup but now as much part of the stand as the central floodlight pylon protruding from the roof. Glass screen ends, like those of the South Stand, tie the flowing roof lines to the end walls, linked by a 362-feet long white perimeter wall.

From any angle the North Stand is quite breathtaking. It is like an architect's model of the dream stand of the future, a space age stand. Yet it still retains its fresh and modern appearance as if it had risen above the ravages of building fashion.

This bright spectacular stand, the vernacular charm of the South Stand and the now sharp lines of the Kop make Hillsborough more than just a ground. They lend dignity to any game played there, give heart to Wednesday's followers who may just feel that 'the Wednesday fellows are part of us'. Hillsborough has proved that a club can provide all the facilities a supporter wants, without robbing the surroundings of their intrinsic character. It is surely no coincidence that Wednesday men are always ready to talk about the club and Hillsborough, and about the city of Sheffield that everyone seems to love. This is still a place to buy boiled sweets at the corner shop, wear a rosette with pride but then go and watch in comfort. Indeed a visit to Hillsborough on a crisp, autumn afternoon remains one of the quintessential joys of English sport.

⋅SHEFFIELD UNITED⋅

Bramall Lane

Sheffield United share with Chelsea and Plymouth Argyle the distinction of having been formed in order to make better use of an existing sports ground. A Sheffield Cricket Club was formed in 1854, and secured a 99-year lease for the Bramall Lane grounds from the Duke of Norfolk, who stipulated that matches 'be conducted in a respectable manner' and that there should be no 'pigeon shooting, rabbit coursing nor any race-running for money'. The first Yorkshire CC match was in August 1855, but no football took place until December 1862, when Sheffield FC (the oldest club in the world, formed in 1857) played Hallam. The Wednesday subsequently played a few games at Bramall Lane after 1867. Teams had to give the Bramall Lane Ground Company 25 per cent of their gross match receipts, 33 per cent after 1883.

Athletic News described the ground in March 1877 thus:

> 'At the top or pavilion end there is a wooden stand that would seat . . . about 1500 spectators, whilst the side next to the lane is the place for the 6d "pit", safely and securely railed off and made in a succession of terraces so giving everybody an opportunity of seeing what is going on . . . the proprietors have been recently levelling one end of the ground, and I don't know how many thousand cartloads of earth have been put down to remove a dip which occurred at the bottom end of it.'

On 14 October 1878 Bramall Lane won a permanent place in the annals of football when it staged the first recorded floodlit match ever played (for a description, see Floodlights). The first football international at the ground was in March 1883, but it took until 1889 for the cricket club to form their own

Bramall Lane football and cricket ground shortly after the Second World War

resident football team. The decision was made soon after they hosted an FA Cup semi-final between Preston and West Bromwich on 16 March. Gate receipts amounted to a handsome £574, more than enough to persuade the club that football was big business. So in 1889 Sheffield United came into being, and three years later gained admission to the newly formed League Division Two (Wednesday were elected to Division One in the same year). They were promoted within a year, and in 1898 won their first and only League Championship. As a result, in March 1899 they formed a limited liability company, Sheffield United Cricket and Football Club, and bought Bramall Lane from the Duke of Norfolk for £10 134, announcing plans for concerts, dancing and other theatrical events, but still no 'pigeon shooting, rabbit coursing, nor any race-running for money'.

At exactly the same time Wednesday were being forced to leave Olive Grove, having been relegated, whereas United were FA Cup winners and full of confidence, a disparity which might well have prevented negotiations to share Bramall Lane with Wednesday from succeeding.

Before 1899 United's footballers had changed in the cricket pavilion, but now the John Street Side opposite was developed as the football club's headquarters. The Main Stand, built at the turn of the century by Archibald Leitch (probably his first commission outside Scotland), was considerably distinguished by a tall, mock-Tudor gable in the centre of the roof. It had a gallery with five openings, like a small house, and later became the press-box, but at the time it was undoubtedly also used by the growing number of cricket spectators. As well as hosting the occasional football international, Bramall Lane was also a venue for Test matches. By the 1930s, the football pitch was covered on its three sides. The John Street Stand had an angled corner at its West End, which joined up with a lower roof covering the Bramall Lane End terraces as far as the corner flag. From this point round to the Pavilion, and round further to the high banking of the Kop opposite, the terraces were open. The Kop had a roof at the back. United's record crowd of 68 287 came in February 1936 for an FA Cup 5th Round tie v. Leeds, when many of the fans would have watched from the cricket side some distance away. For the 6th Round match v. Tottenham, the club built a temporary wooden stand along the open fourth touchline, actually over the sacred cricket wicket. This happened only once.

The War brought devastation to Bramall Lane. Ten bombs hit the ground in December 1940, destroying half the John Street Stand (and its marvellous gable), the Kop roof and badly cratering the pitch. By 1953 most of the Main Stand had been repaired, although the new gable was but a shadow of its predecessor. A new double-roof was erected over the restored Kop.

Floodlights came back to Bramall Lane, permanently this time, in March 1955, a week before

Concrete and steel now at Bramall Lane's square-leg boundary, which was on the left

Hillsborough's. The opening game was v. neighbours Rotherham.

Although cricket was still played regularly, and the players certainly enjoyed the lively atmosphere at Bramall Lane, especially the noisy but witty comments they heard from the so-called 'Grinders Stand' on the Bramall Lane Side, there was no denying that the football club wanted rid of the cricketers so they could build on that open side.

In a series called 'Homes of Sport', Norman Yardley and J. M. Kilburn wrote in 1952 that Bramall Lane, from a cricket lover's point of view, had 'scarcely anything to commend it'. Their further comments are ironic in light of the boast of the Duke of Norfolk's agent that Bramall Lane had 'the advantage of being free from smoke'.

> '... there is not a tree to be seen, and both sight and sound reflect encircling industry. The clatter of tramcars and the scream of a saw-mill and factory hooters make a background of noise to the cricket, and a brewery chimney periodically pours smoke and soot into the air.'

They add the suggestion that the brewery would deliberately emit its foul fumes only when Yorkshire's opponents were at the crease! The cricket and football pitches actually overlapped only by about 20 yards, an area making a rough outfield, awkward for fielders and slow for batsmen expecting boundaries. Furthermore, the view was never quite right. The Pavilion was too far from the soccer pitch, the John Street Stand too far from the wicket. Since the perimeter was fenced off by a low wall and railings, fielders had to retrieve every boundary, whereas at other grounds they might leave the task to willing spectators. The spectators themselves had in many parts of the ground to sit on the concrete terraces, amid the crush barriers, and it was apparently quite common to see hundreds of people rise each time a wicket fell, stretch their limbs and rub their aching buttocks! As cricket audiences declined, the football side developed further when a new 3000-seater stand, with room for 7000 standing below, was opened in 1967 on the Bramall Lane End.

But the sad financial truth had already become apparent. The club's 1962 accounts showed that revenue from football amounted to £127 802, but from cricket a mere £2927. In the club's own words, it was 'absurd' that they should 'have to suffer such a freak as a three sided ground'. That Northampton had managed, and even made a brief sortie into the First Division, mattered not one jot. Having visited Bramall Lane only a few times when it was three-sided, I can only say that the sensation was not so much freakish as different, like watching a drive-in movie or an open air concert. One soon became accustomed to the vast expanse of green beyond the opposite touchline. But no one can criticize United for wanting to be like the rest. Indeed it is likely that had they made their decision ten years earlier, the subsequent financial burden would have been considerably lighter.

The inevitable axe fell in 1971. United were punch drunk with the success of their first season back in Division One since 1968 and plucked up sufficient courage to give the cricket club two years' notice to quit Bramall Lane.

Some felt that this was akin to a son evicting his mother, to whom he owed both life and home, and that while United might gain a smart new grandstand, the city of Sheffield would lose for ever its ability to stage first-class cricket.

The final County match was on 7 August 1973, the end of 150 years of cricket at Bramall Lane.

I will leave the final judgement to the people of Sheffield, except to add that no sooner had the £750 000 new cantilever stand gone up over the old pitch than United began a six-year slide which eventually dumped them unceremoniously into the Fourth Division for the first time in their 90 years' membership of the League. Was this a judgement on the ungrateful child?

Ground Description

The new main entrance to the ground is in Cherry Street, where you see a large car park in front of the imposing cantilever stand, with its striking façade. By the gates stood the Pavilion, finally demolished in 1982. The car park covers what used to be the cricket pitch. How quickly, how comprehensively, the new obliterates all trace of the old. The new South Stand is a full length cantilever, designed by the same architects as Wednesday's North Stand, although inflated building costs and the need for extra facilities have dictated that this one is less pleasing to the eye from inside the ground. But the frontage is undoubtedly the most impressive of any post-war stand in the country, helped because there is space to stand back and admire the red, black and white trimming.

It seats 7949 and was opened for a First Division match on 16 August 1975. Along the roof are 18 flag-poles, and suspended beneath it is a large television gantry with an electric winch to haul up the heavy cameras (most grounds need the crew to do this by hand).

The near touchline is some yards from the front row, to allow room should the club ever afford to redevelop the opposite side. You can see the four gothic pinnacles of St Mary's church tower, built in 1850, clearly above the John Street Stand roof straight ahead.

The John Street Stand, a conventional pitched roof stand with seating behind a paddock, is the oldest construction at Bramall Lane. Its former dressing rooms and offices have been unused since 1975, and in 1984 the stand was further depleted when the ground became designated after United's promotion to Division Two. (One of the Safety of Sports Grounds Act's anomalies was that Bramall Lane, despite its size, remained undesignated for so long because United were relegated just as Second Division grounds were brought under the Act in 1979.) The stand's seating capacity was reduced from 4262 to 2690, and its weathered roof and convoluted steelwork stood in some contrast to the clean, metallic lines of the South Stand. In the east corner is a pen for juniors and the disabled.

To the right is the covered Kop, which used to hold 22 000 standing. Behind is open ground along Shoreham Street, where once were the cricketers' practice pitches. United hope to develop this land with a small hotel and shops.

To the left is the Bramall Lane Stand, a rather drab, tall construction in grey, brown concrete. The seats offer an excellent view, but the terraces immediately below are dark and cramped. An electronic scoreboard now adorns the front of the stand, where formerly there was a clock, donated by the supporters' club to replace the once familiar cricket pavilion clock.

The old clock had looked across a ground that was 8½ acres of grass, the size and shape of two football pitches side by side, with room for some 60 000 spectators. The capacity now is a still healthy 39 000, mostly under cover, with 13 473 seats.

In 1982 United escaped from the trauma of Fourth Division football, where they had certainly the best ground and facilities ever seen but found themselves in serious financial difficulty. This was mainly owing to falling gates, but the cost of the South Stand was a factor.

By 1984 United were back in the Second Division and although Yorkshire County Cricket lovers had problems enough without continuing to lament the loss of Bramall Lane, there still remained a lingering sense of affront among Sheffield's cricketing stalwarts, which even the promise of First Division football at the ground could only partly alleviate. Bramall Lane may yet see footballing glory return, but if the Almighty wears white flannels . . .

ROTHERHAM ·UNITED·

Previous Grounds

A club called Rotherham Town played from 1880 at Clifton Lane cricket ground, which still exists, before moving to Clifton Lane, which was between Clifton Grove and Lister Street (now built over). From 1893–96 Town were members of the Second Division. Meanwhile in 1884 another team called Thornhill United formed and played at the Red House Ground. The pitch was so small and uneven that United were prohibited from entering the FA Cup, so in 1907, having changed the name to Rotherham County in 1905, the club moved to Millmoor. In 1919 they joined League Division Two, and in 1925 amalgamated with Rotherham Town to form Rotherham United.

Millmoor

I shall deal quite concisely with the developments at Millmoor, because a description of the ground tells more than dates can. The first occurred not long after Town and County joined forces, with the building of the Main Stand, now considerably modified. About the same time a small cover was put up over the terracing opposite along Millmoor Lane.

It was during a run of success that Millmoor experienced its highest ever gate of 25 000, twice in 1955; first v. neighbours Sheffield Wednesday in January, then v. Sheffield United the following December, both in Division Two.

In 1957 the Railway End terracing was covered, and in November 1960 the floodlights were first used for a League Cup tie v. Bristol Rovers. In the mid-1960s an extended roof was erected over the Main Stand, and a gymnasium built adjacent to the stand. In 1968 a roof over the Tivoli End terrace was constructed.

Since then seating has been added to the Millmoor Lane Side, firstly under the old roof, then at the southern end over which a new roof was built in 1982, next to the old.

This brought the seating total to 3407, a figure unaffected by further safety checks in recent years, although the overall capacity has been reduced from 21 000 to 18 000.

Ground Description

However idyllic the name may sound, the reality at Rotherham is quite different. Millmoor stands in the three-sided grip of a collection of scrap yards, whose walls on two sides form the back of the stands. There is literally no room to manoeuvre, as cranes swing back and forward almost over the ground itself.

But we start on Masborough Street, the main access point to the ground. Entrance to the main stand

Millmoor, looking towards the Main Stand, with the inevitable crane in the background. The old Tivoli cinema is just visible above the far roof (right)

is under the raised offices, along the side of a wall at an angle to the pitch, and from there into a cavernous underground corridor. Even the players must take this route to reach the changing rooms, and must therefore be exposed to crowds on the terrace to the left of the Main Stand. A unique, but hardly satisfactory arrangement, though the reason is self-evident. Directly behind the wall and the back of the stand you can see the cranes and piled up debris of the scrapyard. As you pass along the wall, notice the press-box, a wooden hut perched above the terracing. Again, a unique arrangement.

The Main Stand itself is unusual. It starts just before the half-way line, and there is a wooden gate leading to the changing rooms and other facilities at the far end. Underneath it is like a dusty car park. You can see the old, original roof peaking out above the newer roof, which as at Scunthorpe and Doncaster extends to the terracing in front but at Millmoor is actually cantilevered from the original pillars frontwards. It looks from one side as if the roof is balanced delicately on these old white uprights. The sloping roof fascia point down like a bird's beak. It's an all-red, dark wooden stand, denied any prominence by the adjacent drab, brick gymnasium and the scrapyard buildings beyond. From here you can see, ahead to the right, Boston Castle on a tree-lined rise in the distance.

The Millmoor Lane Side opposite is in three parts; on the left, open terrace, in the centre the old cover now seated, with four front pillars unusually rooted on the pitch-side of the perimeter wall, and on the right another seated section whose roof is on stilts, with no screens or a back wall behind the top row. Millmoor Lane behind here is a thin narrow alley leading down the enormous yards of C. F. Booth.

You can see these yards quite clearly behind the Railway End, to your right from the Main Stand. The end itself is a good bank of terracing, but with a low roof and high security fences. Behind it are all manner of doomed items. When at Millmoor I could see quite clearly, beyond the entrances at the back of the end, two silvery London Underground trains ready to be chewed up. When United were up for sale in recent years C. F. Booth apparently wanted to make a bid for control, but having seen what his machines can do to rolling stock I would not have given frail Millmoor much of a chance.

To the left of the Main Stand is the Tivoli End, so called because behind on Masborough Street is the now dilapidated Tivoli Cinema, a magnificent but now forlorn example of early cinema architecture. Built just before the First World War, you can just see the upper storeys over the stand roof. From here the pitch slopes nearly 3 feet down to the Railway End.

Altogether Millmoor is quite a mixture of oddities in odd surroundings, but as the result of good maintenance and lots of red paint, is actually a compact, cosy and cheerful island in the midst of a clanking and rather noisome sea of debris.

·BARNSLEY·

Oakwell

Oakwell has been the home of Barnsley since the Reverend Tiverton Preedy formed the club as Barnsley St Peter's in 1887, but as Grenville Firth noted in his club history, their first pitch was just behind the present Brewery Stand. The landowner, Arthur Senior allowed the Reverend's boys to use the ground saying, 'You can have it so long as you behave yourselves'.

They turned professional a year later and moved to the present pitch by 1895 when the first stand, 20 yards long was built. Shortly afterwards it was blown onto the pitch in a gale.

In 1898 Barnsley joined Division Two and had to shift 3000 cubic feet of soil from one end to the other to level the pitch. The slope of several feet from side to side, apparent today, was obviously a lesser evil.

A Pontefract Road End Stand was opened in 1900, followed four years later by the central section of the present Main Stand. The Mayor, Alderman Bray, did the honours, and the stand cost £600, with 1200 seats. Since then wings have been added to give Oakwell a seating capacity of 2154, the lowest of any club in the top two divisions (in 1986–87). Modernization has been a considerable undertaking, for in anticipation of promotion in 1980 the club had to spend £250 000 on ground improvements alone.

Andrew Ward and Ian Alister recalled much of Oakwell's life during the 1950s, when for example, the Main Stand had swing doors. It was one professional's jocular habit to enter them head first, until a mean joker reversed the hinges and the unfortunate player knocked himself out. In the same era, another Barnsley player tumbled over the perimeter wall and broke both collar and shoulder bones, but gallantly played on. The pitch was narrowed to its present width thereafter.

The first floodlit game was a friendly v. Bolton in February 1962.

Undeveloped though Oakwell may seem, it occupies a massive 22-acre site (compared with Highbury's 10 acres), bought for a mere £1376 in 1911. In 1986 the club were even considering buying a few more acres to increase their already considerable assets. Where there's muck in those surrounding car parks there is also plenty of potential brass, which will no doubt secure Barnsley's future for some time to come. But the extra land is not all undeveloped. Behind the ground is a valuable training area with two artificial five-a-side floodlit pitches which Barnsley share with the local community.

Inside the ground, new barriers and resurfacing work in 1986 increased the capacity from 35 554 to 36 864, a figure not so far short of Oakwell's record gate of 40 255 for a Cup tie v. Stoke in February 1936.

Oakwell from the Kop

Ground Description

The Main Stand is set high behind the open paddock, and is remarkable for its lack of pretension, as is the Directors' entrance on Grove Street, a gate in a long red wall. But the stand's centre gable, which once announced the club's name, is now horribly obscured by an ugly television gantry.

Opposite, to the east, is the Brewery Stand, a cosy standing enclosure extended in 1954 when the wooden boards at the back were added for £6000. To the right, or south, is another covered standing area, the Pontefract Road End, whose cover dates back to the late 1940s. To the left is the Spion Kop, from whose blustery heights you can see the training ground and a bowling green behind, the huge brewery advertisements on the stand roofs below, with the town centre ahead. To the north east is a sprawling landscape of scrubland and factories, coal mines and glass-works, Barnsley's industrial backbone, both represented on the club crest. A low white perimeter wall and bright terracotta track links all together; the red, grey and green of Oakwell knitting comfortably with the surrounding terraced houses, chimneys and hills. To complete the scene simply add a Michael Parkinson football tale, narrated with brass band accompaniment.

For the time being at least Oakwell fans say Pah! to your executive boxes. Two new portable buildings behind the Main Stand are about as fancy a hospitality suite as you can expect for the time being. The real warm welcome is on the terraces, where Barnsley fans prefer to stand and mingle, not sit and stew.

DONCASTER
·ROVERS·

Previous Grounds

Doncaster are the second oldest League club in Yorkshire. They formed in 1879 and played at the Intake Ground until 1916, in which time they were elected then voted out of the League twice within four years!

A new limited company was set up in 1920, and for two years Rovers played at Bennetthorpe, now submerged by the Great North Road, half a mile from their present ground, on Low Pasture, now called Belle Vue, where they have played since 1922.

Belle Vue

Just after moving to Belle Vue, Rovers were re-elected to the League for the third time. Their supporters completed most of the work of preparing the new ground, namely shifting large amounts of ash from nearby coal tips to form banking and a foundation for the pitch. They also jacked up the Main Stand at Bennetthorpe, wheeled it down the road and resited it on the northern terrace. A new Main Stand was built on the East Side, but has been extended since, and in 1938 the Popular Side was covered.

The highest gate was 37 149, for a Third Division North derby v. Hull in October 1948.

Doncaster were the second club in the north of England to install floodlights, in February 1953, first used in a reserve game v. Lincoln. They were also credited with the largest pitch in the League, until manager Billy Bremner decided to cut off eight yards from the length. It now measures 110 × 77 yards. The surface has always been admired, and in the early 1970s Wembley Stadium's owners offered Rovers over £10 000 for the Belle Vue turf. Rovers refused. They knew that the top surface was only good because of the drainage below, where the ash lay.

In 1985 Belle Vue was designated under the Safety of Sports Grounds Act. The capacity was virtually halved from 21 150 to 10 500, including 1050 seats and Rovers were forced to spend £140 000 on safety work. Regrettably this included the demolition of the quaint 700-seater former Bennetthorpe Stand, which sat behind the North Terrace and in recent years served as a family enclosure. Neatly turned out in red and white, with advertisements and a clock capping the roof, it was just one of several homely little stands up and down the country condemned in 1985.

But neighbouring developments promised to humble Belle Vue even more. Alongside the ground is the 300-acre former RAF base, lately Doncaster Airport, which in September 1986 was largely taken over by work on a £22 million sports and leisure centre. Destined to be the most advanced in Britain, the council-built centre is planned to comprise, *inter alia*,

Belle Vue's now departed North Stand

swimming pools, ice rinks, squash courts, a sports hall, a social club and a running track.

Rovers, council tenants themselves, would have wished the last facility to have been built at a revamped football ground. But it was not to be, so now Doncaster must watch as its neighbouring giant, scheduled to open in 1989, threatens to overshadow Belle Vue's more modest assets.

Ground Description

The overwhelming sensation at Belle Vue is one of spaciousness. On the east side is Bawtry Road, and the famous Doncaster Racecourse, and it is worth crossing the road to see one magnificent old grandstand which dates back to the late eighteenth century in parts, and an equally impressive 1960s' stand.

Rovers rent Belle Vue from the council for £1500 a year, which includes use of the vast car park behind the Main Stand. If a race meeting clashes with a match, the former has priority use of the car park. But except on St Leger day, the footballers usually attract a larger crowd than the horses. Traffic can be a problem, however, especially as it must come to a complete halt to allow the horses to cross Bawtry Road from the stables to the racecourse.

The Main Stand is essentially in two parts; the back, tall thin section for seating being the original, the front terraces being covered by a later flat roof. Similar roof extensions have been put up at nearby Scunthorpe and Rotherham. Notice there are two players' tunnels, one for each team.

To the right is the open North Terrace, now bereft of its lovable wooden stand.

Opposite is the Popular Stand, a covered terrace where the 'pigeon box' hangs from the roof. An owl used to nest in it, and fans would say that if the owl came out during a game, Rovers would win. A video camera now lives there.

To the left is the high, open South Bank. From here one may appreciate how, from Rovers standpoint, Belle Vue's vue might not seem so belle after all. With the racecourse to the right and the new leisure centre to the left, the club has every justification for feeling in danger of being left behind at the last furlong marker.

SCUNTHORPE ·UNITED·

The Old Show Ground

As the name suggests Scunthorpe's home was once the venue for various popular events in the town, especially the Scunthorpe Show. One photograph taken at the turn of the century shows horse jumping at the ground. There was a club called Scunthorpe United who played there from their formation in 1899, then amalgamated with North Lindsey United in 1910. The new club chose the Old Show Ground as their headquarters and adopted the somewhat unwieldly title of Scunthorpe and Lindsey United Football Club. The date of formation was not, as is often quoted, 1904. Most dates are taken indeed from 1912, when the club turned professional and joined the Midland League. For this and much of the following information I thank the club historian John Staff.

United purchased the Old Show Ground from the Parkinson family for £2700 in 1924, a year which also saw the Main Stand destroyed by fire. In an effort to raise funds for rebuilding, the club organized a raffle for a pig, which then broke loose on the pitch as the draw was made. A new Main Stand was built in 1925, and survives in modified form.

During the Second World War the Old Show Ground played host to Grimsby Town, who were in 1939 a First Division Club. (Blundell Park was too exposed to enemy action to risk large crowds.)

Scunthorpe and Lindsey United were elected to the League in 1950 (they dropped Lindsey from the title in 1955) and for the next ten years the Old Show Ground changed considerably. The Doncaster Road End was covered in 1954, no doubt helped by the receipts from Scunthorpe's record gate of 23 935 for a Cup match v. Portsmouth in January. (Before then, as a non-League club their highest attendance had been 13 775.) The floodlights were first switched on for a game v. Rochdale in October 1957, but later that season the old wooden cover over the East Side burned down. It was replaced in 1958 with a stand that gives the Old Show Ground pride of place in the annals of football ground development. For here, on the East Side of the Old Show Ground, was built the very first cantilever stand at a British football ground.

You ask, quite naturally, why not at Old Trafford or Highbury or Villa Park? The answer is simple. The United Steel Structural Company Limited, with a base in Scunthorpe built the stand on generous terms, fully hoping that it would carve a place for them in the annals of football ground development. It did not, and thereafter everyone assumed the first cantilever stand was built at Hillsborough. But here the record has at last been set straight.

The cantilever stand at the Old Show Ground, the first in Britain

The new East Stand was opened on 23 August 1958 by Lieutenant Commander G. W. Wells RN, having taken just the close season to erect; a fitting and proud way to begin the club's first season in Division Two. And to confirm that this was indeed the modern era the second half of that opening match v. Ipswich was broadcast live on BBC Radio. The transformation of the ground continued the following year, when the Fox Street cover, first put up in 1938, was replaced by the present more substantial roof.

In 1985 the Old Show Ground became designated under the Safety of Sports Grounds Act and found its capacity reduced from 25 000 to a mere 5000. Initially the club had to spend £45 000 on safety, then a further £40 000 to raise the limit marginally to 6096, of which 2396 are seated.

Drastic though the safety measures were, with the Official Receiver on their doorstep, Scunthorpe had little scope to invest the estimated £200 000 the ground needed to have a decent capacity level. But in August 1986, in the words of one club official, 'a dream came true' when planning permission was received for a supermarket developer (who else?) to take over the Old Show Ground, while at the same time helping Scunthorpe build a new stadium somewhere out on the ring road.

Building was due to begin in the autumn of 1987 on this new ground, an 11–12 000 capacity stadium at Gunness Strait, a mile from Scunthorpe's present home. Costing in the region of £2.5 million it was expected to be ready by the beginning of the 1988–89 season. After that, the Old Show Ground would make way for a Safeway supermarket. Such is progress.

Ground Description

If you can catch it before the bull-dozers move in, from the outside the Old Show Ground looks remarkably untouched by the glamour of League football.

Inside, the West Stand is a hodgepodge, a stand disunited. The original stand is evidently the seating section with its old sloping roof at the back, accommodating 600 in the vicinity of the half-way line. In front of this and to a few yards either side are portions of terracing, but only as far as each 18-yard line. These areas are covered by a flat extension roof from the seats to the terracing, a later addition and an awkward one at that. Strangely enough this use of the extended roof from an old Main Stand to cover terracing is also found at Scunthorpe's neighbours, Doncaster and Rotherham, although with rather less clumsiness. Then along the touchline to the left is a separate section of terracing and to the right more terracing, covered with its own lower and older roof up to the corner flag.

This convoluted West Side of the ground does not, however, spoil the ground's overall appearance. To the left is the Fox Street End covered terrace, to the right the Doncaster Road terrace. Both roofs are similar, box-like with supports along the front. Opposite the West Stand is that prized possession, the East Stand. It covers half the pitch on either side of the half-way line and is made prominent by having the letters SUFC picked out in the coloured seats. Although now somewhat weathered and scarred by vandals, the stand still has an air of self-importance. Its structure shows quite clearly how cantilever stands are built, because the base of the rear steel supports are open to view. The front wall where there is a narrow terrace, is in untreated brick, which does reduce the stand's overall impact, and the screen ends are glass. The designers and builders were obviously quite confident, for the roof is particularly deep and, for an original, the design in little apparent need of change. The curious thing is that copies did not spring up all over British football grounds. Without the East Stand, the Old Show Ground would be ordinary and uninspiring, but its presence, far from casting aspersions on its neighbours, gives the ground added unity. It ties the rest together and provides an attractive focus which, from outside, one would never have expected. Such surprise is surely one of the most alluring assets of our British grounds.

The East Stand might well prove one of the shortest-lived post-war stands built in Britain, because when Scunthorpe move the stand will not go with them. Perhaps another club may wish to buy the steelwork and resurrect it. If not, it will be a sad loss to football, as will the Old Show Ground, where once a pig roamed the pitch, and where in future the new show will be bacon rashers.

·GRIMSBY TOWN·

Previous Grounds

The club was formed in 1878 as Grimsby Pelham FC, playing at Clee Park in Cleethorpes (except during the 1880–81 season when a ground on the site of Lovet Street was used). The players had to change in bathing huts brought up from the sea shore. One of the earliest signings came in 1883, while the club were having a 500-seater wooden stand erected at Clee Park. One of the joiners employed turned out to be a member of the Spilsby team, the best side in South Lincolnshire at the time, so Grimsby persuaded him to join them instead! Clee Park was the scene of two early floodlit games using Wells lights, v. Boston and Rotherham Town in April 1889. Shortly after Grimsby had to leave the ground, which belonged to the Earl of Yarborough, who wanted to develop the site more profitably. There had been plans to build a proper sports stadium there, but Clee Park now is the home of a pub of the same name. Appropriately, its sign depicts a Victorian footballer.

Grimsby's second ground was near the Top Town area of Grimsby at a field on the south side of Welholme Road. The club brought over the stand from Clee Park and spent £300 preparing a ground capable of holding 10 000 spectators, many of them on a large bank at one end. *The Eastern Daily Telegraph* even built its own exclusive press-box by the pitch.

Abbey Park was opened in August 1889 with a match v. West Bromwich, the previous year's Cup holders. In 1892 Grimsby joined the newly formed League Division Two, and although they built another stand at the ground, always knew that Abbey Park would only be a temporary home. Initially the club had negotiated a seven-year lease with the landowner, Edward Heneage MP, who intended to build houses on the land. When the seven-year period expired, he did grant a further three years, but at the end of this Grimsby had to move. Abbey Park was between the park and Farebrother Street, on Welholme Road.

Blundell Park

Blundell Park was close to Grimsby's first ground at Clee Park, and formed part of the land which Lord Torrington had described in 1791 as 'three miles of boggy turf' on the coastal approach to Grimsby. Nowadays we call it Cleethorpes. Since the ground is not technically in Grimsby (just as the City ground is not technically in Nottingham) a favourite question at sport quizzes has been: 'which team plays all its home games away?'

The land had been part of the manor of Itterby, purchased by Sidney Sussex College, Cambridge in 1616, with money left to it by a Peter Blundell. There are also nearby recreation grounds called Sidney and Sussex Parks.

From research by Les Triggs and Patrick Conway, we know that Grimsby took with them to Blundell Park the two stands from Abbey Park. One went on

Blundell Park showing the Findus Stand

the south west side, where the new Findus Stand now is, the other, called the Hazel Grove Stand, was placed behind the goal where the Osmond Stand is now situated. Originally, the south west side was to be the ground's focal point and administrative centre. Grimsby's first game at Blundell Park was a Division Two match v. Luton in 1899, by which time a cover had also been erected over the Pontoon End banking. The players changed at the nearby Imperial Hotel, which still exists.

In 1901 a new wooden Main Stand was built on the sea-board side of the pitch, the central section of which is still the Main Stand. It is therefore the oldest surviving structure at a League ground. The sea air must have been kind to its ageing timbers.

Even at this stage, Grimsby were still unsure if Blundell Park would become their permanent home. Having lost their previous grounds to development, they had to have more security before the ground could be properly improved. *Athletic News* reported in 1909, 'the district is being rapidly built up and in the near future there is the probability that the site may be too valuable to be retained for purely athletic purposes'.

In 1925 a Ground Committee was formed at Blundell Park, resulting in considerable improvements all round. The old Abbey Park Stand was replaced by a cover on the half-way line named the Barrett Stand, after Alderman Frank Barrett, a patron of the club. Wooden terracing was laid on either side of the stand. In July 1927, thanks again to financial support from Barrett, Grimsby were able to purchase the ground.

During their spell in Division One, from 1929–32, Grimsby extended the Main Stand down to the east corner, then followed their most successful period in the years up to the Second World War. They reached the 5th Round in 1937, drawing Wolves at Blundell Park on 20 February. The ground's highest attendance of 31 657 saw Town held to a draw before losing the replay. The semi-final was reached in 1939, and with the revenue Grimsby replaced the old Hazel Grove Stand and built the Osmond Stand, a small 700-seater in the middle of the rear terracing. Like the Barrett Stand, it was named after one of a family of benefactors. Also during summer 1939 a cover over the corner terrace was built between the Main Stand and the Osmond Stand.

Floodlights were installed and first used on 9 March 1953, when the visitors were Lincolnshire neighbours, Gainsborough Trinity, for a Midland League fixture. Curiously, the lights were mounted not on conventional steel gantries or pylons, but on short concrete towers. They were, however, deemed inadequate for Football League games, so in 1960 new pylons were mounted on the concrete bases and with new lights Grimsby were able to stage their first floodlit League match in September of that year v. Newport. A year later the old Pontoon cover was replaced by the existing Pontoon Stand, paid for by the supporters. There was even talk of moving the club to a new ground on Cambridge Road.

Promotion to Division Two in 1980 cost Grimsby £280 000 in ground improvements, of which £160 000 was a grant from the Football Grounds Improvement Trust (FGIT). But the club also decided to invest further money in building a dazzling new stand in place of the Barrett Stand, which was no longer safe.

One of the local frozen fish companies, Findus, provided £200 000 towards the total cost of £425 000, and the television companies chipped in to provide a camera gantry. The new so-called Findus Stand was intended to take all the offices and players' facilities away from the old stands opposite, and to provide Blundell Park at last with seating and executive accommodation which would reflect the team's ambitions of First Division football. But building took a long time. Every bore hole drilled for the foundations would fill up with water, the ground being only a few hundred yards from the sea. And the club had insufficient capital to put in the offices or to open up the executive boxes straight away. So the stand was not quite complete when it was first used on 28 August 1982 for a game v. Leeds United. Some of the Leeds fans were so overcome with excitement at seeing the Findus Stand that they kicked out the back of the Osmond Stand, tore out seats and, unable to contain themselves, urinated into the gardens behind.

In addition, the stand was so tall in comparison with surrounding buildings, that the club had to pay for installing cable television to nearby houses whose roof aerials had been rendered useless. But Grimsby being the generous club that it is went further, by giving out 65 free season tickets to the neighbours, by way of compensating them for all the disruption caused during building work, and throwing a Christmas party for local children and old age pensioners. There is a lesson to be learned here.

At the same time the Findus Stand was built, Grimsby put in seats where once had been a paddock at the front of the Main Stand. During these alterations it was discovered that the oldest section of the Main Stand, built in 1901, had simply been plonked onto the ground, without foundations. Its survival was even more remarkable for that. These extra seats, plus those in the Findus Stand, make the seating total 6000 in an overall capacity of 20 402.

Ground Description

If you are travelling to the ground from the south, you need not enter Grimsby, which would be a shame. To fully appreciate the warmth of this club and its environs one really should wander round the town and docks beforehand.

Blundell Park is situated in a long, thin built-up area between the main road to Grimsby and the Humber Estuary. Beyond the Main Stand is open land leading down to the water, broken by the railway line from Cleethorpes to Doncaster and Lincoln. In some ways, the situation is similar to that of the Victoria Ground, Hartlepool.

Rather than begin with the Main Stand, we will start in the new Findus Stand, destined to take over in the coming years. Behind is a small car park hemmed in by the neighbouring houses. The façade is small when compared with new stands at bigger clubs, but cleanly faced and styled, like a small hotel. Grimsby have negotiated the establishment of a community centre in one half of the stand, with their own facilities in the other half.

From inside the Findus Stand is one of the finest views in football. Ahead, over the Main Stand roof, stretches the Humber Estuary, with the North Humberside peninsular (formerly North Yorkshire) visible in the distance. Over to the right is the furthest tip of the Estuary, Spurn Head, and to the left is Kingston-upon-Hull, across the water, but too far to be visible in any weather.

Turning to the land, to the right is the centre of Cleethorpes, and to the left Grimsby docks and the many warehouses of various frozen food companies. But most prominent of all is the Grimsby Dock Tower. Built in 1852, this landmark is the tallest brick building in Lincolnshire, and a replica of the Sienna Town Hall clock tower in Italy.

To concentrate on the ground itself, the Findus Stand does not run quite the length of the pitch, and is flanked by two sections of open terracing. In construction it is a propped cantilever, with angled uprights. There are 2400 seats, with the name Findus picked out among them in letters so high that on a clear day they can be seen by passengers on the ferry out in the Estuary.

Separating the upper tier from the paddock in front are 14 executive boxes opened in 1984. As the other stands are much lower, the Findus Stand towers over Blundell Park. But like Scunthorpe's cantilever stand or Wigan's Main Stand, it gives the ground that vital focal point which holds the rest together.

From here, to the left is the plain, flat roof of the Pontoon End, named after the fish docks in Grimsby. To the right is the Osmond Stand, an unusual arrangement comprising an ordinary terrace end, covered only from the near edge of the penalty area, but with a small island of seating directly behind the goal. The roof continues round the far corner to link up with the more recent section of the Main Stand.

With pillars and barriers in so many places a clear view of the pitch is difficult, and to compound one's irritation, the roof is so low and the corner so dark that one feels almost trapped.

Next we come to the Main Stand, which is in two sections, the older, all-wooden half being that nearer the Pontoon End. On the right, the 1931 section is fairly typical of the period, with a light brown roof, steel uprights and wooden floors. But the older half is a miracle. Notice how the roof seems to waver unevenly along the gutter, and how the wooden roof supports branch out into different directions at the top, like a tree. Look closer at these uprights and you will find them worn thin and smooth by time, gnarled

by repairs but still quite reassuringly solid. The roof overhangs to the touchline, and the glass panelled screen stops level with where the paddock used to begin. From the back rows of the Main Stand the roof is so low you can barely see a foot of turf beyond the far touchline, let alone the base of the Findus Stand. Even on a good day.

But perhaps the most remarkable feature of the Main Stand is how little work it needed after the more stringent checks made on all stands after the Bradford fire, even though it is the oldest main stand still in use. Having been updated internally in 1980 when the ground was first designated, the only modifications needed were two extra inspection hatches. Indeed local safety officers regard Blundell Park as a model of safety.

The Main Stand comes to a halt level with the penalty area, where open terracing begins towards the Pontoon End. Behind the stand is the old entrance way, where a series of gates and turnstiles, small out-buildings and offices lead onto Harrington Street. There is nothing on the other side of the street except scrubland, a railway line, and a few hundred yards away, the water.

The floodlights are unusually mounted on thick concrete frames, the remains of the first set of towers. Notice that the lamps are mounted on open-ended bars, not a boxed-in frame, as usually seen on pylons (Chester and Brighton's are similar). Note also the distinctive black and white striped goal-nets, a present to the club from a local fishing net company when Grimsby won the Fourth Division Championship in 1972. The netting, made from nylon and polythene, is very strong. Finally, all credit to Grimsby for keeping their wooden fence around the pitch, pointed stakes and all, like every ground used to have. Only Blundell Park and Bootham Crescent have retained them. Sadly, the demands of commercialism have meant that Grimsby's fence is now largely obscured by advertisement hoardings.

Despite this, and apart from one awkward corner, Blundell Park is a most appealing and likeable ground. So many grounds could be anywhere. They don't inspire you to explore, ask questions or care about the surrounds. Not so Blundell Park. You don't go there just for football, you go there for Grimsby; the town, the people, the smell of fish and the sea.

· HULL CITY ·

Previous Grounds

Having formed as a professional club in 1904, City entered a three year agreement to use Hull RLFC's Boulevard Ground, their fixtures to alternate with the rugby club's. Problems arose before the first season was over when, following crowd disturbances at a rugby game, the Rugby League closed the Boulevard for a short period. Perhaps worried by competition, they also ordered Hull not to allow any soccer to be played at the ground during the suspension period (they subsequently instructed members not to share their grounds unless admission charges were dropped for soccer matches – an intentionally punitive limitation designed to deter sharing). After this hitch City's footballers started using the Circle, Hull Cricket Club's ground on Anlaby Road, with occasional matches played at Dairycoates, a ground used until 1903 by an amateur club also called Hull City.

About six months after joining the League in 1905, City moved from the Circle to an adjacent pitch on Anlaby Road, their home until the Second World War, although during 1906–07 they played a few games at the Boulevard, where the sharing agreement had yet to expire. Their last League match at the Boulevard was in February 1907.

By the 1930s Anlaby Road was covered on three sides, with about 4000 seats in the main West Stand (nearest the Circle). This stand replaced one destroyed by fire in 1914. Anlaby Road's record attendance was just under 33 000 for a 6th Round Cup replay v. Newcastle, which saw City reach the semifinal for the first and only time in their history.

Perhaps from the profits of this Cup run, in 1930 Hull purchased land a few hundred yards south with a view to building a new ground, since at that time Anlaby Road was due to be requisitioned for railway developments.

However work at the new ground, to be called Boothferry Park, was so slow that Hull were based at Anlaby Road until 1943, when their lease ran out. Several reports suggest that Anlaby Road was destroyed in the war, but as Hull expert Chris Elton – to whom I am much indebted – points out, various matches were played on the ground during the war and Hull's Junior and 'A' teams continued using it until the early 1960s, when the long-delayed railway development finally swallowed up the land.

The ground was situated north of Arnold Lane, next to the Circle, which is still used for cricket and rugby. Dairycoates is now an industrial estate of the same name, off Hessle Road. The Boulevard, which did receive a direct hit during the war and to which City returned briefly during the 1944–45 season, is still home to Hull RLFC and Hull's speedway team (Hull Kingston Rovers play across the city at Craven Park, used also for greyhound racing).

Boothferry Park

When City bought the land in 1930 it had last been used by the Hull Golf Club, but despite piecemeal work during the 1930s, and the offer in 1939 of a £6000 development loan by the FA – who were obviously keen that soccer kept a strong foothold in this bastion of rugby – Boothferry Park was not ready for use until 1946. In 1986 it was the third youngest ground in use by a League club. But Hull, with a population of about 280 000, is still the largest urban area in England never to have had a First Division soccer club.

City were in Division Three when their new ground was opened. The Main or West Stand was complete, with an entrance on North Road, and the North Stand, behind which was a large car park by Boothferry Road, was one-third complete in the centre. By 1950, the North Stand was complete, giving the ground a total of 6000 seats, a respectable number for a club just promoted to Division Two, and more than many First Division clubs at the time. And the ground had already proved its overall capacity, when a record 55 019 attended City's 6th Round Cup tie v. Manchester United on 26 February 1949.

As war-time restrictions eased, more building was carried out. On 6 January 1951, the first British Railway's train pulled into Boothferry Park Halt, the ground's very own railway station behind the East Side, with 595 passengers aboard. They could enter the ground directly through turnstiles on the station platform, which backed onto the terracing; a unique arrangement of which Hull was justifiably proud.

The following April, the cover on the East Side terracing was completed, so three sides were now sheltered. The first floodlit match took place on 19 January 1953 v. Dundee, with lights on gantries along each side roof.

As steady members of Division Three, Hull's prospects were made much healthier when in May 1963 Harold Needler made the club a substantial gift of £200 000. A large gymnasium took £50 000 of this. It was built south of the ground and opened on 21 January 1964. The existing floodlight system of six tall pylons was installed in 1964, and early in 1966, during Hull's promotion season, the South Stand seating 3000 was completed at a cost of £130 000. Boothferry Park was now a ground of First Division standard, with 9000 seats and a large car park. Surely greater success on the field would soon follow.

Sadly for Hull it was a case of so near and yet so far. Everyone expected the team to rise to Division One and yet they slipped down into the Fourth Division, before a change of management reversed the decline.

Boothferry Park suffered with the team. During 1981–82 the average gate was just under 4000, in a ground that held 42 000. So in 1982 it was decided to demolish the North Stand to make way for a supermarket. It was a similar deal to one completed by Crystal Palace, by which the club lease the land on a long-term basis, but keep a smaller section of open

Hull's well-proportioned North Stand before it made way for a supermarket. Note the unusual screen-end on the Main Stand (left)

terracing in front of the supermarket.

The super-stadium was further cut to size when it became designated under the Safety of Sports Grounds Act in 1985. The entire East Side was closed because of inadequate barriers and terracing, thus reducing Boothferry Park's capacity from 33 000 to 15 000.

Improvements costing £500 000 enabled the centre of the East Side to reopen in 1986, when the capacity stood at 20 000, including 5600 seats. It was hoped to reopen the remaining parts of the terrace to provide a final capacity of 28 000.

Ground Description

Although a well-appointed ground in many ways, Boothferry Park is also rather soulless, like the sprawl of semi-detached houses lining Boothferry Road from the Humber Bridge to the town centre.

Where the North Stand once stood is now the supermarket, with a large car park in front. City's swish new ticket office block, built in 1966, was used as the builder's site office during construction, before being demolished also.

The West Stand, sometimes called the 'Best Stand', is the original construction, refurbished inside. It is fairly typical of early post-war stands, built on the same principle employed in the 1930s but with squarer lines and more use of brick and steel. A plain wall lines the back of a narrow paddock in front, the two screen ends are solid (as opposed to glass panelled) and the roof fascia is white and plain. In the centre is a television camera gantry and above the players' tunnel is the 'Hull City' sign donated to the club by British Railways, when the locomotive of that name was scrapped. In 1985 the sign made one further unscheduled journey before being recovered by the police six weeks later.

If the stand seems undistinguished from without, inside it is comfortable enough. The press-box is particularly well equipped, another improvement of

the mid-1960s. Surprisingly, the dug-outs on either side of the tunnel are painted bright red.

From here, to the left is the now open, truncated North Terrace, in front of the new supermarket. This used to be the paddock in front of the North Stand, which had 3000 seats. City have done well to preserve this terrace, but for those who knew Boothferry Park before 1982, the absence of a stand is sorely felt. There are plans to construct a concrete shell on the supermarket roof to enable Boothferry Park to stage concerts.

Opposite the West Stand is the large East Side, in 1986 in a state of transition. It is no surprise that the terracing or barriers were found wanting. In the north east corner particularly one could see how old barriers had been submerged under thick layers of concrete and new barriers built above them – the old uprights were still visible but the horizontals had simply been lifted up onto the new supports. Also, the old terracing was unlike that at any other ground, having beaded mouldings along the front of each step. Behind the refurbished terracing is the railway platform, Hull's unique asset.

To the right is the more modern South Stand, beyond which you can just see the grey walls of the gymnasium. The stand sits behind a large paddock, and resembles in many ways the Sky Blue Stand at Highfield Road, built two years earlier at a similar cost. Hull's stand is extremely light, with glass screen ends, transparent panels in the roof, and a line of windows along the back, so that the roof almost seems to be suspended on glass.

In its day it was no doubt the height of fashion, with its clean lines, plain white fascia, polished wooden seats and boarding. Nowadays it enjoys a new lease of life, thanks to the addition of bright new yellow seats in 1983, one sign of the club's new-found optimism.

Boothferry Park does have another unique feature apart from the railway station. It is the only ground to have six, free-standing floodlight pylons, three, very tall, on each side. They, the South Stand, the gym and the press-box, were all part of the dream Boothferry Park in the mid-1960s. But they have survived the nightmare years, and the loss of one stand has by no means ruined the ground's potential. Boothferry Park still craves success and large crowds, and before long the dream might well revive even more strongly than before. The ground will be more than ready and able in that event.

·9·

NORTH AND WEST YORKSHIRE

· LEEDS UNITED ·

Elland Road

Although Association football was well established in South Yorkshire by the turn of the century, West Yorkshire remained a solid rugby stronghold without one senior, professional soccer club until Bradford City was formed in 1903, by the members of a rugby club. Leeds City were born the following year, also with a strong rugby connection.

The club bought Elland Road from Holbeck Rugby League Club, and a year later joined Bradford in Division Two. The ground then had a small main stand and three open sides of banking, but with acres of open space all around for expansion. Leeds did not look like winning anything until the arrival of Herbert Chapman as manager in 1912. When League football ceased in 1915, the ground was used for army drilling and shooting practice, Chapman became a manager at a munitions factory, and City's ailing affairs were put into the hands of a receiver, who tried to sell the club to Leeds Northern RFC at Headingley.

A syndicate rallied round to keep City at Elland Road, but after the First World War the League and FA ordered the club to present their accounts for inspection, suspecting there had been illegal payments made to players during the war. Leeds refused to hand over the accounts and were therefore expelled from the League. 'We will have no nonsense,' said the League President John McKenna, 'the football stable must be cleansed.' But it is doubtful whether Leeds were any more guilty than many other clubs.

For a short period Elland Road was used by a top northern club, Yorkshire Amateurs, and in late 1919 it seemed certain that Huddersfield would take over the ground (see Huddersfield). Soon afterwards, however, a new professional club called Leeds United was formed. Within a few months they were voted into the League, no doubt aided by those clubs who had been so glad to escape punishment the previous year.

By 1939 United were a run of the mill First Division outfit and Elland Road a completely different ground to the one we know today. The Main or West Stand, built in the Leeds City era, had a double-barrel roof. The Elland Road terrace cover was a typical 'scratching shed' with a wooden barrel roof almost identical to one at Huddersfield, also built in the 1920s (and still in existence), and on the east side was the Lowfields Road Stand, built on a bank of terracing running the whole length of the ground. The North End was an enormous, open Spion Kop.

Immediately after the Second World War Leeds were relegated, but though in danger of becoming Second Division also-rans, the club made a wise investment by buying the training pitches immediately behind the West Stand. They would have liked to buy all the land from the West Stand to the Leeds–London railway line, but did not have sufficient resources. With more land they could have developed the site profitably without losing any of the training areas.

On 9 November 1953 Elland Road's first floodlights were switched on for a friendly v. Hibernian.

Three years later disaster struck. Just as Leeds were fighting their way back to the top, the West Stand was destroyed by fire caused by an electrical fault. Leeds had to build temporary dressing rooms on the training pitch, until the replacement stand was ready in 1957.

Nowadays the West Stand seems almost quite ordinary but, in the context of stand design, it represented a bridge between the old and the new. It was a propped cantilever and although Birmingham City had built an early version of this type a few years previously, theirs did not extend so far. In addition the Leeds stand had a modern façade; a styled entrance way which gave the ground an added sense of importance. Such conceits are all too rare at football grounds, and before then only the façades of Villa Park, Highbury and, to a lesser extent Molineux and Craven Cottage, had any semblance of architectural dignity. Even in recent years only a few clubs have taken any pains to improve their frontages, the most notable being Sheffield United.

Elland Road in the 1960s before redevelopment

Elland Road's new stand cost the then astronomical sum of £150 000, but it has weathered well and remains a considerable asset. But United's fortunes rose most dramatically when Don Revie arrived at Elland Road in 1958, changed the team colours, changed the staff, changed the whole outlook and eventually helped change the ground, all funded by a string of honours and near misses up to 1975. During this spell Elland Road's highest attendance was recorded, when 57 892 saw Sunderland hold Leeds to a 1–1 draw in a 5th Round FA Cup replay on 15 March 1967.

Huge profits poured in, and were spent largely on Elland Road. In 1968 the Spion Kop was removed, a process which took only six days. The flattened area was then left unused and a new North Stand built behind it, right up to the extremity of United's land. When finished, the front terracing was therefore 60 feet from the nearest goal-line. The flat area where once the Kop had been, was then turfed and the pitch moved 30 feet towards the new stand, so that now both end terraces were 30 feet from the goal-lines. The North Stand was standing only and cost £250 000.

The next development came in 1970, when the North Stand was joined to the West Stand with a covered corner section. As an indication of how building prices had escalated, this small section alone cost £200 000. It had seats at the back, standing in front.

A year later work began on the other side of the North Stand. Another corner section was to be built,

needing the removal of yet more earth banking, and since the plan envisaged continuing the corner along the length of the east side, in place of the Lowfields Road Stand, a gap was left in order to build proper foundations. This cost Leeds another £250 000.

In 1974 the last major change began, at the Elland Road End, when down came the small scratching shed. Since there was already 60 feet of extra turf, the pitch was moved up to the North Stand, and on the space left the new South Stand was erected. This construction cost £400 000.

The next stage would have been to build a corner section linking the South Stand to the east side, and it was here that the Elland Road plan came unstuck. After losing the European Cup Final in Paris in May 1975 Leeds began to slip out of the limelight. Don Revie had taken the England manager's job in 1974, and inflation put paid to Elland Road.

It cost the club £1 million just to demolish half of the Lowfields Road Stand and build foundations for the new corner section. Leeds called it a day and pronounced themselves content with what they had.

Apart from the building programme outlined above, however, there were other changes to the ground. For example, in 1971 the pitch was completely reconstructed and undersoil heating installed with help from the Sports Turf Research Institute at Bingley, Yorkshire (see Pitches) and was generally held to be the best surface in the north. In the summer of 1982 Elland Road staged a rock concert by Queen and several thousand feet plus heavy equipment on the pitch compacted the top surface. Then in 1982–83 Hunslet Rugby League Club began using Elland Road, having lost their own ground, and although rugby does not in itself spoil the turf as much as soccer, the extra usage meant that greater care would be necessary to keep the pitch in order. But Leeds were crippled by debts and could afford only the minimum amount of maintenance, with the inevitable result that the pitch began to suffer.

Another development concerned the floodlights. When the new stands were built taller pylons had to be built outside the ground to provide adequate illumination. Three were erected in 1973, with temporary lighting in the south east corner. Now there are four 250-feet high pylons, the tallest in the Football League.

Finally, as attendances dropped, the club decided to put in extra seats in the west and south paddocks. This took the total number of seats to 19626, in an overall capacity of 43900.

Leeds were now no more than a hopeful Second Division outfit, yet in 1983 they became the first club in Yorkshire to install executive boxes, built at the rear of the South Stand. This, plus the need for wider gangways and improved access points, reduced the seating total to 17243 in a capacity of 39243.

Between 1956 and 1982 Leeds had spent £2·5 million on Elland Road, and it was therefore a poignant moment when in November 1985 the club was forced by its debts to sell the entire 13.5 acre site to Leeds City Council, for ... £2·5 million. Meanwhile the foundations in the north east corner are likely to stand exposed for some time to come, since the cost of developing this section has been estimated at roughly £2 million.

Ground Description

Not only has Elland Road changed beyond recognition in the past two decades, but its surroundings are also totally different, mostly due to the arrival of the motorway linking the M62 with the centre of Leeds. It passes within a hundred yards of the ground and makes Elland Road one of the easiest League venues to reach by road.

Elland Road itself, as the name suggests, takes you west to the town of Elland, near Huddersfield (where Leeds Road takes you back into Leeds).

The main entrance to Elland Road leads into a car park between the West Stand and the training ground, where there are still the dressing rooms erected after the fire.

Like so many 'ultra-modern' stands of the mid-1950s and early 1960s, Elland Road's 1956 façade has a certain clinical style, enhanced by the open space in front and made more impressive by its recent refurbishment. The successful Leeds teams of the late 1960s and early 1970s would pose in front of the main entrance, their white kit standing out against the blue cladding and white lettering.

Inside the stand there is a problem. To illustrate

this, the players' tunnel is now to the right of the half-way line, but when first built it was in the centre. Since the pitch was moved north, the south section of the stand has been rather out on a limb. Anyone sitting at this extremity has a better view of the traffic on Elland Road than of the pitch, and if they look straight ahead see the side of the South Stand. To compensate for this – obviously in 1956 they had not conceived the redevelopment plan – the club have added a curved section of seats linking the West Stand paddock with the South Stand paddock.

From the West Stand, to the right is the South Stand, standing square behind the pitch. It is in the same style as all the new additions, a propped cantilever with deep overhanging roof, plain white fascia and all blue seating. Elland Road runs directly behind, and there are 16 executive boxes along the rear.

In the far corner the paddock curves round, the blue seats giving way to open terracing, at the back of which is a tall wooden fence. Behind are the foundations of the corner which was never built. It is claimed they will not suffer from continued exposure and could be built on at any time. That, now, is up to the council.

The Lowfields Road Stand is the oldest remnant at Elland Road, but fits in remarkably well. The southern half has been chopped off, but as a new glass screen end has been added one could never tell. Originally the stand was for standing only.

Behind is a large open space lying in the shadows of the elevated motorway. Leeds had hoped to buy this land and build a sports complex, linked to the ground by an overhead walkway above Lowfields Road.

Redeveloped Elland Road in 1975, with the Lowfields Road Stand still intact. Notice how the roof of the 1956 West Stand ends level with the goal-line of the old pitch

Apart from the lack of funds, the project was hindered by the local residents who were worried that if the nearby greyhound stadium site was used for light industry *and* United built a leisure centre, the area would lose what residential quality still survived. So many houses have been demolished in the area that those left on the estate behind Elland Road are in danger of being swamped in a sea of development.

To the left of the Lowfields Road Stand is another open space behind the paddock, where further development was also planned. Some 20 yards away begins the corner section of the North Stand.

Both corners of the North Stand have seating at the back and standing below, but the North Stand itself is all standing, still in the same style as the South Stand. At the back of the stand is an electric scoreboard, but for those in the North Stand who cannot see it, the club have installed smaller scoreboards facing inwards under the roof, a refreshing demonstration of concern for a section of fans sadly well known for their unruliness elsewhere.

Standing out on the skyline for miles around are United's four enormous floodlight pylons, distinguished not only by their height but by the diamond-shape lamp holders at the top.

Elland Road is so well equipped, with almost every modern convenience, including executive boxes (in Yorkshire!), that it is surprising how little the ground has been used for major games. The capacity is reasonable, there are enough seats, and access is superb. But the ground lacks character. There are no features to hold one's attention and the colouring is cold; blue seats, grey roofs, white fascia, grey concrete, almost as if all the faults of which Don Revie's team had been accused had been embodied in the steel and cement of Elland Road.

This is not quite the club's fault. No other ground has been so completely redeveloped at such a reasonable cost and in such a short time. Yet the fact that the scheme is unfinished is probably one of the most redeeming features of the ground. The presence of the Lowfields Road Stand at least provides a break from the uniform structures on the other three sides.

If the ground was completed, it would no doubt resemble a smaller version of Old Trafford, but even then there is a nagging suspicion that Elland Road would still lack character. Perhaps it changed too soon, founded on quick success and no long-term tradition. Once inside there is hardly any indication as to whom the ground belongs.

Throughout this book, I have made a plea for clubs to put signs on their roof fascia, or flagpoles or clocks, or even to paint the club colours on a wall or two. Nowhere is this plea more heartfelt than at Elland Road. All-white strips and functional architecture were all very well in the 1960s and 1970s, but now the club should put more of the gold and blue back into the ground to give Elland Road an unmistakable identity to match its excellent facilities.

·YORK CITY·

Previous Grounds
A team called York City played from the turn of the century until the First World War at a ground called Field View, Holgate, only a few hundred yards from the present ground. In 1922 York City were reborn, but on the other side of the city, near the university campus, at Fulfordgate. But Fulfordgate was too far from the railway station and the club's centre of support, so in 1932 the club asked its followers for their views on a move, and in the summer of that year York City took over Bootham Crescent. Fulfordgate stood where Eastward Avenue is now.

Bootham Crescent
Bootham Crescent belonged to York Cricket Club when York City purchased the land and set about converting it into a football ground. A Main Stand, a section of the existing structure, was built and a cover put up over the Popular Side. The ground was opened on 31 August 1932. Although the team hardly caused a ripple in the Third Division North, City did cause a few shocks in the FA Cup, and it was their 6th Round tie v. Huddersfield Town in March 1938 that attracted Bootham Crescent's highest gate of 28 123.

During the Second World War, the ground suffered damage when a bomb fell on the Shipton Street End. Soon after the war the terracing was laid properly with concrete. City's greatest achievement came in 1955, when they just failed to beat Newcastle in an FA Cup semi-final and then lost the replay. United won the Cup, but City spent their profits wisely, building an extension to the Main Stand.

Despite losing to Newcastle, good relations were maintained between the two clubs, and on 28 October 1959 United sent a team to Bootham Crescent to mark the switching on of York's new floodlights, which cost £14 500.

Seats were installed under the Popular Side roof during York's spell in Division Two from 1974–76, and a decade later, just before the ground was designated, the club embarked on a series of improvements costing £300 000. Financed mainly by York's Cup exploits against Arsenal and Liverpool in 1985, the work included building hospitality suites behind the Main Stand, new offices and turnstiles, replacing crush barriers and adding more seats to the Popular Side. This gave Bootham Crescent a seating total of 2883 in a capacity of 13 185.

Ground Description
Compared with the Roman and medieval treasures of the city itself, Bootham Crescent is a mundane sort of pleasure. The Main Stand sits along three-quarters of the pitch nearer to the northern end, a plain box-like construction with seats sandwiched between

Bootham Crescent Main Stand. A white wooden perimeter fence is a rare survivor of a once common feature

HUDDERSFIELD ·TOWN·

Leeds Road

Huddersfield Town was one of several instantly created professional clubs set up in rugby strongholds just after the turn of the century. Formed in 1908, they rented the Leeds Road ground from the Huddersfield Association Ground Company, who had bought the old showground in order to stage important local matches. We learn from George Binns' comprehensive history of the club that Leeds Road's first major soccer match was a district cup final in 1899.

Town's first game at the ground was on 19 August 1908. The pitch then ran parallel to Leeds Road and the dressing rooms were in an old tramcar. The only stand was a set of uncovered wooden bleachers. Leeds Road as we know it today began to take shape in 1910, the design being that of the ubiquitous Archibald Leitch.

Leitch's design gave Huddersfield a 4000-seater main stand virtually identical to the one he had designed at Fulham three years earlier, based on a formula that was to survive well into the 1930s, with an upper tier of seating, paddock in front, sloping roof enhanced by a central pointed gable. The Leeds Road End was covered at the rear with a basic wooden roof, and the two other sides were open banks. (Binns' history includes several photographs of this work in progress.) The new Leeds Road was opened in 1911 by League President John McKenna, but the ground was also honoured by the staging of two amateur internationals in 1910 and 1911.

After the First World War, Town reached the biggest crisis in its history. Gates were so poor that on 6 November 1919 it was announced that Huddersfield, £25 000 in debt (equivalent to £1.25 million today), were leaving for Elland Road, home of Leeds City, who had the previous month been disbanded by order of the FA following investigations into their accounts. (The Leeds manager at the time the irregularities were alleged to have taken place was Herbert Chapman, who became Town's manager in 1920.)

As at Oxford in 1983, there were demonstrations at the ground and a massive fund-raising and propaganda campaign to keep Huddersfield at Leeds Road. One press report suggested that the ground had actually been sold to a manufacturing company. After a few months of desperate bargaining the club was saved from extinction, and even more remarkably the team went on to reach the Cup Final and promotion to Division One. Never has any club turned the corner so dramatically, with gates at Leeds Road going from 3000 to over 40 000 within months.

a line of advertisements along the roof facings, and a plain brick wall behind the narrow front paddock. The newer section can be distinguished only by the colour of the bricks and the fact that it has a glass screen end, whereas the other end is open. The Tunnel is in the centre of the original Main Stand. At the rear are York's new executive facilities, leading straight to the back row of the stands, a sensible arrangement for a club with limited space.

From here to the left is the uncovered Grosvenor Road End terrace. The rear of the bank has been fenced-off, a precaution taken by the club when cracks were found in the rear walls of the banking.

To the right is the Shipton Street terrace, also uncovered, but slightly higher than the opposite bank. At the rear is an old scoreboard, now used as an advertisement hoarding.

It is hoped eventually to cover the Shipton Street End, but until that happens one can just see the fifteenth-century central tower of York Minster above the roof tops.

Opposite is the Popular Side, newly decked with bright red seats. The revival of this side provides a good example of how to convert former standing areas without spoiling the atmosphere. Behind lie the Territorial Army's Duncombe Barracks.

I formerly described York's ground as being, in Oliver Goldsmith's words, 'Dull without a single absurdity'. After Bootham Bar, one of York's medieval gates, and Bootham School, a fine Georgian edifice, Bootham Crescent is still without a great deal of charm, as Arsenal and Liverpool would no doubt agree. But York are a progressive club who have invested well, so that Bootham Crescent is now a tidy and functional enclosure, one of the few to have retained its capacity after the events of 1985. York are also to be praised for preserving on both sides of the ground the last visible wooden perimeter fence in the League. That is one single absurdity we can surely all approve.

Leeds Road in the mid-1930s, the Popular Side in mid-construction. Note the typical Leitch gable on the Main Stand roof

The record gate of 67 037 came for an FA Cup match v. Arsenal on 27 February 1932, by which time Arsenal had inherited not only Herbert Chapman, but also Town's almost overwhelming domination of English football.

Despite Huddersfield's treble of Championships in the 1920s, the only change at the ground was the erection of a Belfast roof at the Leeds Road End, now called the Cowshed. But in the 1930s Huddersfield took the major step of reconstructing all the ground's terracing, and installing such strong crush barriers that when tested by safety inspectors in recent years they were found to be well up to modern standards.

The ground must also have impressed the FA because in the 1930s Leeds Road was a regular venue for FA Cup semi-finals. (The town's first semi-final was in March 1882, but at the Fartown rugby ground. Fartown is still a Rugby League venue, now preposterously renamed Arena '84, with the team being retitled Huddersfield Barracudas. Understandably locals have largely ignored this attempt to Americanize their hallowed sport.)

In November 1946 Leeds Road played host to England's first post-war match against Continental opposition when Holland were the visitors for a midweek afternoon international. (Another highspot was the staging of the Rugby League Championship Final in 1952.)

Disaster struck Huddersfield on 3 April 1950, when fire destroyed Leitch's stand. It took only 15 minutes for the entire stand to be engulfed in flames, but the cause was never established. The replacement stand, built the following summer, had a similar basic pattern, but was a squarer design and without the gable. Photographs suggest that the Cowshed roof was also damaged by the flames and had to be replaced. Town's fortunes began to decline from then, but during a brief return to Division One, the club erected a vast cover over the Popular Side opposite the Main Stand, in the summer of 1955, at a cost of £24 000.

The first set of floodlights was switched on in January 1961 for a Cup replay v. Wolves and paid for from the proceeds of Denis Law's transfer to Manchester City, but in February 1962 two of them blew down onto the pitch in a gale. A new set were promptly installed for the start of the next season.

Town's return to Division One in 1970 prompted the installation of 2000 seats in the Main Stand paddock, giving Leeds Road a capacity of 41 000, including 6000 seats. Designation reduced this in 1983 to 30 000. Although the old barriers were still adequate new ones had to be added, and further capacity was lost, but in an admirable cause, when supporters completed a sponsored walk to Blackburn to raise money for a £20 000 enclosure for the disabled. Leeds Road's current capacity is 32 000, including 5489 seats.

Ground Description

The ground lies at the foot of a line of hills which an enthusiast would do well to ascend for a marvellous panoramic view of the football stadium and its surrounds. But down on street level we find the Main Stand, now quite open at the back because of extensive demolition in the vicinity. As is so often the case, local industry has declined even faster than the club's fortunes. But the club cannot be faulted for keeping a clean, well maintained house. Inside, the Main Stand is very orderly, but like other stands of the 1950s, rather characterless.

A new television camera gantry on the roof, however odd, adds focus. The gantry had originally been suspended from the Popular Side roof, until being moved in 1972, partly for safety reasons but also because the cameras were too often pointing directly into the sun. From the Main Stand you can see the Leeds Road End to the left. This has a wonderful wooden barrel roof, with a blue and white striped back wall. Between each upright is an arch filled with wooden lattice-work. It is predictably called the Cowshed – Elland Road had an almost identical one – but is much finer than the term usually implies. Opposite is the huge Popular Side bank of terracing, covered with a vast roof identical to one at Turf Moor. Notice how sturdy the barriers are, despite their age. To the right is the open Dalton Bank End, topped with an old fashioned half-time scoreboard. In the 1950s this end boasted the first electric scoreboard in the country, a gift to the club from PSV Eindhoven. Unfortunately burnt out by vandals, it proved uneconomic to repair. Although the terracing is open here, the ground seems quite enclosed because, immediately behind, is a steep, grass-covered hillside, rising up to the Dalton Bank housing estate at the top.

During Town's golden era between the Wars, this hillside was often covered by spectators unable either to gain or afford admission.

Huddersfield's pitch, which is the same size as Wembley's, is particularly fine, with lush turf and a perfect crown. The cinder track in front of the Main Stand was popular for sprint races held during the early years at the ground. The other three sides are fenced off by security barriers, the same type incidentally as those at Anfield and Old Trafford. On a summer's day Leeds Road shines with pride. The pitch seems to dazzle the stands and terraces with its glossiness. But in mid-winter it can be a gloomy place. Like The Den or Ninian Park – fairly large grounds of concrete and blue – without sunshine or a big crowd, Leeds Road looks as if it's sulking. But neither of those grounds has witnessed such glory as Huddersfield, which can make Leeds Road doubly poignant when the going is rough.

·BRADFORD CITY·

Valley Parade

On 11 May 1985 Valley Parade was the scene of the worst disaster to befall any English football club. The purpose of this extended chapter is not to evaluate the repercussions (see Safety) or detail the events (see Appendix), but to help explain why Bradford's ground constituted such a risk.

Valley Parade was originally the home of Manningham Rugby Club, who after three years of struggle decided to adopt Association rules in the hope of increasing support and revenue. To everyone's surprise, in 1903 the new club was immediately voted into the Football League in Doncaster's place, because the League wanted to break rugby's hold on West Yorkshire. City's defunct neighbours, Bradford Park Avenue, evolved in a similar fashion four years later (see Lost but Not Forgotten).

On City's promotion to Division One in 1908, Valley Parade was transformed into one of the best grounds in the country, with a capacity of 40 000.

The Main Stand, which was to burn down on that fateful May day, was built in the summer of 1908. Described at the time as 'a mammoth structure', it held 5300 seats with room for 7000 standing in front. It was an unusual stand even for its time, being built into the side of a hill with entrances only at the rear. The roof was a double-pitched, wooden construction, supported at the front by 22 thin verticals, reinforced by cross struts. Part of the paddock was subsequently taken up by an extra tier of seats to raise the seating total to 6000.

Opposite the Main Stand, a second stand on the Midland Road side was built soon after. Holding 8000 standing spectators, it also had to conform with the ground's hillside location.

The rear was built up on sloping ground with a complex web of concrete stilts, such as Roker Park was to have in 1913. Designed by Archibald Leitch (see Design) the stand's base was described by a technical magazine as 'a striking example of open framework construction'. One stepped down into the Main Stand, and climbed up to the Midland Road stand.

From inside the ground the later stand appeared to be smaller, but more elegant, with three ornate gables along the roof, decorated with mock Tudor relief work. On its centre pointed gable was a clock, an unusual if not unique feature in those days. The Kop, large enough by any standards today, was then twice its present size. It was originally called Nunn's Kop, after one of the club's founding fathers.

In this golden era, City's was the first name to be engraved on the new FA Cup, coincidentally designed by a Bradford firm, in 1911. During that cup run, in March 1911, Bradford's largest crowd of 39 146 saw them play Burnley, and so the club can

The Main Stand at Valley Parade, once called a lovable tangle of pillars and struts, later to be condemned as a fire-trap. Millions saw it burn, fifty-six people died in it

claim to have the longest standing attendance record of any League club.

But the glory soon faded, and after 1937 as Valley Parade became increasingly outdated, Bradford slipped into the lower divisions. In the early 1950s, Bradford Corporation ordered the Midland Road stand to be demolished because the foundations were considered unsafe. (The upper metal frame of this stand went by rail to Berwick Rangers, who bought it for their new ground at Shielfield Park in 1952 for just £400. It cost Rangers a further £3000 to rebuild what is still today their main and only stand.) A new stand was built in its place in 1954, but this too proved unsafe and was pulled down six years later. The ground remained three-sided until 1966, when the pitch was moved closer to the Main Stand, and a very narrow, flat area along Midland Road covered for standing spectators.

City's first floodlights were on telegraph poles along each side, switched on for a friendly v. Hull City in December 1954. Replacement pylons were bought second-hand from West Ham in 1960, and two years later the south east corner one was blown over in a gale (as happened at Leeds Road nearby). When Gateshead played here and lost in an FA Cup tie soon after, they complained unsuccessfully about the use of only three pylons.

Three of the current pylons were erected in 1983–84 after another of the older ones had blown down.

In 1962 the club built new offices and dressing rooms in the south west corner of the Main Stand. Until then they had used three houses at the back of the Kop, at the north end of the Main Stand. The players changed in the cellars, which were often flooded and ridden with cockroaches, and entered the pitch along a tunnel under the Kop.

For years the two Bradford clubs resisted amalgamation, to both their costs perhaps, since Park Avenue undoubtedly possessed the finer ground. For one poignant season, 1973–74, Park Avenue, then in the Northern Premier League, played their last games at Valley Parade before liquidation.

Many a British football ground enthusiast, myself included, fondly regarded the ill-fated Main Stand as an inconvenient but cosy sort of place. We forgave its dreadful inadequacies rather like we might a favourite old car, turning a blind eye to its potential dangers and praising its individuality. In an era when concrete and steel seemed to have replaced most of British football's more idiosyncratic stands, this one at Valley Parade seemed to be the essence of down-to-earth Yorkshire grit; no fancy executive boxes, no unnecessary comforts. Even the directors had to reach their lounge by joining the ordinary people on the often crowded rear corridor. No one could claim that the directors were shielded from the inadequacies of the lay-out.

In 1983 I described the stand as a lovable tangle of pillars and struts. Sitting in that stand was, I wrote, 'like watching football from the cockpit of a Sopwith Camel', because of the antiquated web of struts and supports.

The stand was in many respects unique in British football. Firstly, because it was built into the side of a hill, the only entrances were at the rear, at the highest point. One entered from the street through gates in a stone wall, and was faced by a barrier about 8 feet ahead, obscuring your view of the pitch down below. This passageway along the back was dark and gloomy. At half-time it would get packed with people queuing at the small refreshment bar or rushing to the narrow toilets built into the wall. But at Bradford there were plenty of familiar folk and one was as likely to bump into a famous visiting football manager on a scouting trip as an old-age pensioner whom all the locals knew.

Secondly, the main part of the stand flooring was wooden, raised up by wooden supports dug into the sloping ground. The gap between the floor and the earth was hardly more than a couple of feet at most and would not have constituted a hazard had the flooring been completely sealed. The only other stands built into a hillside have solid concrete bases with no gap – for example at the Crystal Palace Athletics Stadium or at Odsal Stadium, also in Bradford (see below).

At Valley Parade the gap was such to allow litter to accumulate under the seats. I wrote in 1983 that 'underneath the seats are flaps which open to reveal piles of litter'. On questioning this at the time I was told by a member of the groundstaff that it was common for litter to be swept under, but that the rubbish was cleared out at the end of each season when repair work was done.

I did not pursue the matter. It was a lovely stand and besides which, one day it would fall down of its own accord anyway. Disasters then meant the type of crushing and overcrowding which killed people at Ibrox and Burnden Park. Or collapsing walls which killed a couple at Middlesbrough.

Fires at football grounds were the sort of thing that happened late at night. No one had ever been killed by fire at a football ground.

Routine repair work on the stand was carried out most seasons. It even involved repairing those flaps and seats in that part of the stand where I had sat in 1983 (and on several other pleasurable visits).

The Bradford chairman Stafford Heginbotham, who rescued the club first in 1965 and again in 1983 (when City went into receivership with debts of over £375 000), had worked on the stand himself, helping to lay six rows of concrete flooring at the front of the seated section.

But because of the club's parlous financial state it was invariably a patching up operation. On one occasion off-cuts from a local television cabinet factory were used to strengthen the seats.

According to evidence given at the enquiry immediately after the fire, the club were first warned about litter accumulating under the stand's wooden floors in September 1980, by the Health and Safety Executive of West Yorkshire County Council. Valley Parade was not covered by the 1975 Safety of Sports Grounds Act (see Safety), because it applied then to only First and Second Division clubs. But the inspector still suggested that the voids under the seats be 'completely blocked off' as recommended under the Act's advisory Green Code (Section 8 Paragraph 11).

There were no repeat checks made to see if the work had been done, and Bradford had, technically, no legal obligation to comply with the inspector's advice, just as the inspector, technically, had no duty to enforce his recommendations.

City were warned a second time in July 1984, ten months before the fire. An engineer from the County Council was invited to Valley Parade because the club wanted to submit claims for ground improvements to the Football Trust.

The County Council wrote two letters within seven days to say that the stand's construction and the build-up of combustible material underneath the seating was potentially hazardous. One letter warned that the problems 'should be rectified as soon as possible'. The second letter stated, 'A carelessly discarded cigarette could give rise to a fire risk.' But once again, no repeat visits were made to enforce this warning. Nor did the fire brigade visit the stand. They had no statutory duty to do so, because Valley Parade was not designated.

But it was alleged that City had received and noted the contents of these letters because they sent copies of them with their application for grants to the Football Trust. As a result, in January 1985 City were told by the Trust that a 60 per cent grant would be made available.

City's chairman later denied that he had seen the two letters. In July 1984, he told the press the club's correspondence was still being handled by the Official Receiver. But the club certainly intended to start repair work on the stand because in March 1985 it took delivery of steel to be used for a new roof.

Amid the grief and anger which followed the fire, the County Council's letters and Bradford's response were examined by the press and the enquiry. It was recognized that while both City's administration and the safety inspectors' pursuit of their recommendations were highly suspect, no personal blame could be attached to any individual or organization. It was, rather, a disaster which anyone might have foreseen but no one took the initiative to prevent.

As *The Guardian*'s Malcolm Pithers commented on the enquiry, 'Such phrases as "not my responsibility", "not my concern", "out of my jurisdiction" and "not within the scope of my authority" were commonplace. Not a single witness out of the 77 who gave evidence ever spoke about his moral responsibility.'

Responsibility may yet be adjudged, for in November 1986 relatives of the victims began legal action against the club and the safety authorities. It is not this book's place to apportion blame. And yet so many of us are to blame.

The football grounds' writer who spotted the litter and took the matter no further. The groundstaff who swept litter under the seats. The people who dropped the litter. The journalists who failed to report the hazards. The public who sat in the stand week after week and said nothing.

What about First and Second Division directors with experience of the Green Code's recommendations, who must also have sat in that stand and had their private thoughts?

Recriminations and guilt apart, there were many lessons to be learnt from the Bradford fire. The roof was all timber, coated in black felt material which proved to be highly inflammatory. Its design had been such to create a wind tunnel, so that the flames, instead of escaping out of the front or sides of the roof were funnelled along its length.

The exits had been locked at the back of the stand, where most of the victims had perished. Stewards should have been manning them. They should have been able to push the doors open from inside the ground, like any fire door at a public place.

Inside the seated sections, dividing walls made it hard for spectators to clamber from the back down to the front. Those in the rear seats who chose not to go for the rear exits had to surmount three different barriers before reaching the pitch.

Had the ground been designated, all of these design faults would have been eradicated, which is where the afternoon's greatest and most heart-rending ironies lay.

The match against Lincoln was to have been a celebration of City's promotion to Division Two. Indeed it was preceded by marvellous, care-free scenes including the presentation of the Third Division Championship trophy. A larger crowd than usual of over 11 000 had gathered, of which about 3000 were in the stand. That morning a souvenir issue of the *Bradford Telegraph and Argus* carried an article entitled 'Spit and Polish for the Parade Ground', detailing all the safety work which promotion would entail. The report frankly conceded that City's ground was 'inadequate in so many ways for modern requirements'. Estimates for repair work were then put at £400 000.

Already the steel work for the new Main Stand roof was at the ground. Demolition of the roof was due to start the very next day.

Stafford Heginbotham later estimated that in the stand's 77-year history perhaps as many as 5·6 million spectators had sat in it. How many of those were smokers it would be impossible to calculate. Another 55 minutes of football and the stand would have done its stint.

There were many who thought City would never return to Valley Parade. There was, surely, too much pain, too many memories. Furthermore, Odsal Stadium provided an obvious choice for a new home.

Odsal Stadium is one of the least known of Britain's major sporting venues. It was first developed in the 1920s by the common method of raising banks with dumped refuse. So vast was this newly enlarged bowl that when first used in 1934 it was estimated to hold 150 000. In fact the record gate there was 102 575 for a Rugby League Cup Final Replay in May

1954 between Halifax and Warrington, although contemporary accounts suggest that as many as 20 000 gained illegal entry.

Bradford Northern Rugby League Club established their headquarters there in 1934 but the massive stadium has seen speedway, stock-car racing, tennis, show-jumping, pony-trotting and basketball. The first football match was a charity game in 1960.

In recent years Odsal has been improved extensively by the local council, who have long seen it as a potential Wembley of the North. The expression is something of a cliché, but no other venue has such perfect credentials or such awesome dimensions. The floodlighting is excellent. There is covered seating for 5500 with more seats awaiting a new roof on the clubhouse side, where dressing rooms have been built under the sloping banks. Having spent about £2·5 million on these improvements the council was understandably keen for City to move there permanently after the fire.

It was improved mainly for the World Speedway Finals in 1985 (a reduced capacity crowd of 40 000 attended this event, which had been staged at Wembley until then but would not return to Bradford until at least 1990). With Bradford Northern attracting gates of only around 4000, the vast open bowl was in danger of becoming a luxury in a city with two football grounds already in disarray (Park Avenue, which continues to decline, was considered for City's new home but it was felt that the costs and site limitations made development unwise).

The arrival of Halifax's speedway team, from The Shay, brought Odsal more into use, but regular League football would have made it a truly multi-purpose stadium such as no other in Britain. City played 'home' games during the 1985–86 season at Elland Road and Leeds Road before settling into Odsal, but the supporters made it clear that what they desired was a return to Valley Parade.

Their emotional attachment was strong enough to surprise even the directors. Just as important, Odsal proved to be an unsuitable venue for football.

The pitch was never up to League standard, while the open terracing was just so huge that a crowd of 10 000 would still seem overawed by the surroundings (if not soaked by any rain). City experienced the same sense of dislocation felt by QPR supporters during their brief sojourns at White City. It was better to be breathing down the players' necks than standing in splendid isolation a hundred or more feet away from the touchlines. This is an essentially British hang-up. Most other nations cope with longer viewing distances quite happily.

Valley Parade was first used for football again in September 1985 when City's reserves played in front of the charred rubble of the old stand. Only officials and journalists were present. But the game was symbolic of hope, and in the ensuing months plans were drawn up for the ground's rebirth, which, it was frequently reiterated, would have been the sincere

The new Valley Parade – the ill-fated Main Stand was on the left

wish of the deceased. No one wanted Valley Parade to be a shrine, but at the same time there was a deep-seated commitment to rebuild.

In charge of the project were local architects T. Waller and Partners. Work started in July 1986 and was more or less completed six months later for an emotional reopening on December 14 with a match against an England XI.

Waller's plans included a new 5000 all-seated Main Stand on the site of the old one, but extended over South Parade, which now became a pedestrian concourse and car park. The stand was, of course, built on a concrete base, with maroon facings and amber steelwork. The existing clubhouse in the south corner remained.

From this new stand, to the right the Bradford End was reroofed and new terracing and barriers installed, to hold 2000 visiting fans. Opposite, the very narrow Midland Road side was tidied up but no more. It is only 12 feet deep and has no terracing because at the back the roof is only just over 6 feet high.

Behind this is a 20-foot slope down to Midland Road, showing where the original foundations of Leitch's stand still survive. New turnstiles and stairs would at least improve access to this, the narrowest side of any League ground, holding only 960 spectators.

To the left a new Kop was planned. A few feet have had to be clipped off the old one to allow a roof and new stairways to be built, and in the corner, where the old players tunnel used to emerge from the cockroach-ridden houses, a wide exit has been created to improve access to all parts of the ground.

The cost of this new Valley Parade, with a capacity of 15 000, was estimated in 1986 at £2·3 million, and Bradford were fortunate in this respect. The fire came at a time when the West Yorkshire Metropolitan Council had just been abolished by the Government. Every abolished County had surplus funds to dispose of, and in Bradford the football club was given the staggering total of £1·4 million.

Fire or no fire, this disbursement naturally caused some resentment among the region's three other League clubs, among whom were Halifax, just facing enormous improvement bills of their own as a result of designation orders placed after the fire.

The remaining cash for the ground came from FGIT and Bradford's own insurance. None of the £4 million raised for families of the victims went to the club, and none of the money received in grants could have been spent on anything other than ground improvements.

City have marked the events of 11 May 1985 with a simple sculpture on the facade of the new stand on South Parade, donated by an anonymous benefactor. There is another moving memorial by a German sculptor in the Cathedral. But the biggest tribute to the dead is the new stadium itself, risen truly from the ashes in a spirit of enthusiasm and optimism which visitors to Bradford often find hard to comprehend. The reason is simple. While the rest of the world may always now associate the name Bradford with disaster, in Bradford itself new images have to replace the old, new thoughts erase the haunting memories.

All over Britain football grounds have changed because of what happened at Valley Parade. It is only fitting, therefore, that Valley Parade should itself be changed so dramatically. The modernized ground now must serve as a permanent reminder to us all of how our fondness for nostalgia and tradition should never again be an excuse for silence or inaction.

·HALIFAX TOWN·

Previous Grounds

Halifax began playing as a professional club in 1911 at Sandhall, where they remained until the First World War when the site was taken over for a munitions factory. For one season Town played at Exley until in 1921, the year they joined the League, the Shay Ground was finally made ready for use.

The Shay

The Shay, like many other football grounds, was originally a council refuse tip, and is still owned by the council. Town's first year's rent was £10, rising to £100 by their third season. No one is quite sure from where the name derives, except that the area was called Shay Syke.

The club spent £1000 on preparing the ground, much of it going towards buying a stand from Manchester City, who were then playing at Hyde Road. The stand still exists, but only just. Next to it is a hut which served as the players' dressing rooms, until moved to their present location on the opposite side of the ground. It is nevertheless still called the Main Stand, but has no extra facilities.

The new administrative centre is behind what is now called the Patrons Stand, but was actually just a Scratching Shed to which seats were added in 1958.

The Shay's highest attendance was 36 885 for the visit of Tottenham Hotspur in the FA Cup 5th Round on 14 February 1953. Floodlights were first used in 1961 and cost £18 000 to install. Real Madrid were invited to provide the opposition for the first game, but Halifax had to be content with Red Star Belgrade from Yugoslavia instead.

Speedway was introduced to The Shay in 1948 until 1951, then brought back in 1965. The Halifax Dukes speedway team eventually left in October 1985 for Odsal Stadium, Bradford. There was also baseball at the ground just after the Second World War, and in the winter of 1962–63 when the pitch iced over, the club opened it up as a skating rink and earned a welcome £100 during the cold spell. There was also an attempt to establish a golf driving range at one end, opened in 1966 by Jack Charlton, but this was short-lived as the stand roofs suffered from too many wild shots.

For some two decades, apart from the addition of a successful social club in the car-park area, The Shay suffered badly from a lack of investment and poor gates.

When Third and Fourth Division grounds were designated under the Safety of Sports Grounds Act in 1985, therefore, it was hardly a surprise that the Shay's capacity was cut more than any other ground apart from Hartlepool's, from 16 500 to only 3000. Ironically, 2018 of that figure is seated, so Halifax can at least claim to have the highest ratio of seats to standing in the League!

Both ends of the ground were debarred from use, because they lacked proper terracing or barriers and, apart from a section of terracing constructed next to the Patrons Stand at a cost of £46 000, only the two seated areas were kept open. Halifax have estimated that it would cost a further £15 000 to raise the capacity to 10 000 and as much as £500 000 to get back to its previous level.

In 1986, failing a home draw against a big club in the FA Cup, neither level looked attainable without a marked rise in the team's fortunes.

The Shay has a further unenviable distinction. On 16 November 1985 the lowest-ever crowd to watch an FA Cup tie between two League clubs, 1501, saw Halifax play Scunthorpe in the First Round (Darlington held the record until then).

Ground Description

It was once said that the Halifax manager liked to sign new players in the nearby railway station, before they had the chance to see the ground.

The approach up Shaw Hill is, however, pleasant, rising through leafy surrounds with a modern and orderly high-rise estate opposite the ground. The car park is spacious and smooth, decorated with old-fashioned lamp posts outside a new single storey night club, next to the club offices. So far all is favourable, tasteful and even apparently prosperous. Inside the ground is quite a contrast.

The Shay looks large, but it is not; the pitch seems big but is in fact the smallest pitch in the League, measuring 110 × 70 yards (only Eastville was as small). The players emerge from the Patrons Stand, which runs along the middle third of the east touchline. It is supposed to seat the executive element, but they will not need reminding that this is an old, simple cover for terracing with seats added.

Until recently the stand was even more basic, with seats simply plonked down on a cinder surface. Thankfully the base is now concrete and the seats are new, but the view remains imperfect because of the old speedway track between here and the touchline. To the immediate left of the stand, which also accommodates the press, directors and Town's 160 Club, is the new away supporters pen.

To the far left is the now disused Tramshed End, a shallow ash bank curving around the track. Behind a new concrete boundary wall at the rear is a line of trees with a bus, rather than tram depot beyond.

To the right is the larger Trinity Garage End, also disused but before 1985 the more popular of the two ends. Only the central section is terraced. From here one has an excellent view to the left of the Pennines with Beacon Hill most prominent. The most noticeable building behind this end of the ground is the headquarters of the building society with which the town is now so readily associated.

Opposite the Patrons Stand is the forlorn old Main

The Shay in better days

Stand, with bench seats in the centre and terraces on either side and in front. At one end is a poignant, faded remnant of an advertisement. Otherwise all is grey and drab. Yet this could be a relatively smart and comfortable stand, far more so than the smaller structure opposite.

To the left of the Main Stand is a flat stretch of earth, formerly the speedway pits and now with just one surviving outbuilding, used by the groundsman.

The Shay is not gloomy; it is a wide open ground, surrounded by trees and hills, and ripe for development – as a multi-purpose stadium. In its present state, however, it is undoubtedly the worst venue in the League in terms of infrastructure and spectator facilities, so bad that should Halifax finish bottom of the Fourth Division and therefore automatically lose League status (as specified in 1986 by a rule change) technically it is possible that the Shay would not even come up to the standards required in the GM Vauxhall Conference (formerly the Gola League). A sobering thought indeed.

Meanwhile in late 1986 the main concern of Halifax supporters was that The Shay should survive at all, as the Official Receiver hovered over the club and property developers eyed the stadium.

Shabby though The Shay may be, I suspect most Town fans would prefer their home discomforts to the disappearance of professional football in Halifax.

· 10 ·
EAST ANGLIA AND ESSEX

PETERBOROUGH
· UNITED ·

London Road

The present club has played at London Road since their formation in 1934, although another team called Peterborough and Fletton United played there from 1923. For many years United drifted along in the Midland League, until in the mid-1950s the club began an almost miraculous run of success which eventually led them into the Football League. Not even Roy of the Rovers could have credibly concocted Peterborough's record between 1955–60, when in 103 games at London Road they lost just one game, scoring 428 goals in the process.

London Road improved with the team. Before 1955 there had been one small grandstand, seating 400 spectators, so during the 1956–57 season work began on building the present Main Stand, behind the old wooden one. Once completed, the original structure

was taken down, and for a while the players entered the pitch across the site on wooden boards. Then the pitch was moved 20 yards towards the new stand, the club laying a new surface on soil bought from a sugar company's beet fields in the nearby Fenland. The space freed on the opposite touchline was banked up and terraced.

At the same time, two identical covers were erected at either terraced end of the ground. To complete the picture we have today, floodlights were installed during the autumn of 1957 and inaugurated with a friendly v. Arsenal. In just three years the ground had been transformed, gates were consistently above 10 000, so it just remained to win sufficient support for election to the League, finally achieved in 1960.

London Road's highest gate of 30 096, came during Peterborough's best Cup run to date, when they met Swansea Town in the 5th Round on 20 February 1965. In 1985 the capacity was cut from 28 000 to only 9000, including 3570 seats, but with safety improvements it is hoped to raise this total.

Ground Description

Born in the 1950s and barely touched since, London Road is the spirit incarnate of British ground design during that unrewarding decade, even more so than Roots Hall. The basic tenet then was to copy everything that had been done in the 1930s, but replace curves with straight lines, wood with brick. Goodbye character, farewell warmth; welcome efficiency, insurability and long life.

There is no better symbol of this era than the huge electronic counter which sits under the stand – one hesitates to call it a computer but in the early 1960s that is what it was called. It was the first installed at any League ground.

More modern is the executive suite behind the Main Stand, opened in 1985. It overlooks a large car park which stages a market every Thursday. Beyond runs the River Nene.

The Main Stand is very plain, with a rather dark interior hardly relieved by a series of square windows along the back row of seats. Glass screen walls would have helped aesthetically, but no doubt detracted structurally, for the stand is solidly built in brick and steel with only two uprights supporting the roof

London Road, a 1950s' transformation

along the front. Like its contemporaries at St Andrew's and Elland Road, the stand was an indication that the age of the cantilever was near. The roof is grey, without any detail to alleviate the monotony. Similarly, the brick paddock rear wall is untouched by colour or embellishment.

From the Main Stand, to the left is the Moys Road End, to the right the London Road End, both covered terraces, each identical. But although the roofs are also dark, at least along the gutters are lines of advertisements. The roofs are quite low, supported by several uprights at the very front.

In the corner between the Main Stand and the London Road End is a small two-storey block originally built by the club as a restaurant, but now rented out to a local branch of the Probation Service, perhaps as a warning to potential recidivists on the terraces.

Opposite the Main Stand is the open Glebe Road terrace, built on the site of the old pitch and backed by a row of houses. An unusual block of four executive boxes is perched over the centre. London Road is one of only three League grounds to have both ends covered and one side terrace open. Ayr and Brighton are similar.

London Road came a long way in such a short time, for which it was no doubt much admired at the time. Now that fashion and style have changed, however, we must pronounce it dull. Yet it only requires a flourish or two; a flag, a signboard, a crest here and there to give it that extra sparkle it so desperately needs.

◆ CAMBRIDGE UNITED ◆

Previous Grounds

There can be few more idyllic places for a football team to play than the expanse of grass in the centre of Cambridge known as Parker's Piece, still used now for public recreation as it was when the club was formed after the First World War. And there can be few more unusual and evocative names than that of the ground they moved to in August 1932, the Celery Trenches, so called because it was in an area of vegetable plots. The land was just off Newmarket Road on virtually the same site as the present ground, and belonged to the Marshalls, who ran a motor and aircraft firm, and gave most of the site to the club as a gift. The club's headquarters were in the Dog and Feathers nearby. Since the ground was in the Abbey district, actually some 300 yards beyond the Cambridge boundary, the club was called Abbey United. They became Cambridge United in 1949.

Abbey Stadium

If the city of Cambridge was destined to have a League club, the chances were that Cambridge City, not United, would be the likely candidates. City was the senior club, with once the better ground, and at one stage in their history they had a very rich and ambitious chairman. But United had determined supporters, and money cannot buy loyalty on a Saturday afternoon. Indicative of the United spirit were the club's first primitive floodlights in the early 1950s. They were paid for mostly by Len Saward (brother of Pat), who contributed £400 from his own testimonial fund. Similarly, the Habbin Stand was built in 1960 by a group of supporters who called themselves the 'Auto Club', a pun on their tendency to spend many an evening telling each other 'you ought to do this, you ought to do that . . .'

As the promise of League status grew stronger, a small Main Stand was built in 1969 (extended since then), and the present floodlights were inaugurated for a friendly v. Chelsea on 1 May 1970. This was also the occasion of United's highest crowd of 14 000, which is nevertheless the lowest record gate of any League club, mainly because the Abbey Stadium is also the smallest ground in the League. Size however means little nowadays. Because United were designated during their spell in the Second Division from 1978–84, they have had their capacity reduced only marginally from 12 500 to 10 150, including 3424 seats, and have been forced to spend only £10 000 on safety work since 1985. In this respect they were among the first clubs to appreciate that in the modern era at least small really is beautiful.

Ground Description

The name is perhaps misleading; there is no abbey any more, and this is not really a stadium. Nor is the

The Abbey Stadium Main Stand

area what a visitor might have expected in this fine old university city. The Newmarket Road is just like any arterial road on the edge of a town, lined with garages, factories and warehouses, such as the one belonging to the Corona soft drinks company next door. Past this we enter the Abbey Stadium with the club offices in temporary buildings to the left, and the supporters' club straight ahead, in front of the standing cover known as the Corona End. The layout is similar to that of Oxford United's Manor Ground.

The Main Stand, though recent, is not especially modern in design, except in its facilities underneath. There are bench seats on either wing and at the front, where they are divided into several small sections which exit onto the perimeter track. At the Corona End of the stand, where a raised police viewing box occupies the last ten yards of the touchline, the screen wall is glass. At the far end it is brick, and thus you can see how the stand was built in two halves on either side of the half-way line. The paintwork is amber, yellow and white with trimmings of black, which helps unify both the Main Stand and the entire ground.

To the left is the Allotment End, home of the Celery Trenches, a narrow open terrace with a brick wall at the back and high-security fences at the front, divided into sections by yet more fences. Unless you stand at the very back you are likely to see as much

metalwork as football. Not a place for claustrophobics. To the right is the aforementioned Corona End, covered along three-quarters of the goal-line with a plain roof put up in the 1950s. Next to it is the supporters' club, overlooking the pitch, with a clock on the roof. In front is a token three wooden steps of terracing. Opposite the Main Stand is the Habbin Stand, named after Harry Habbin, a former president of the supporters' club whose name is commemorated on a plaque over the central entrance to the stand. To the left of the terraces are some yellow bucket seats, installed at an angle so that the spectators may see in spite of the standing people close-by – a system also used at The Dell. Underneath the stand ran a dyke, which the Auto Club had to fill in with scrap. The dyke ran into a water-filled claypit behind the stand, beyond the training area behind.

The view from the ground is of open land, the Ely to Cambridge railway line, a gasometer and a tall chimney. Hardly a spire or tower in sight. But small though it is, and unlovely compared with the nearby splendours of King's College Chapel, the Abbey Stadium is proof of what community effort combined with astute management can achieve. That is why the ground once hosted League Division Two football, while further into town only hundreds turn out to watch Cambridge City in the Southern League.

·IPSWICH TOWN·

Previous Grounds

Ipswich AFC first played at Broom Hill, Norwich Road in October 1878. As we learn from a meticulous and entertaining history, *The Men Who Made The Town*, by John Eastwood and Tony Moyse (Almeida Books, 1986), to which I am indebted for much of this chapter, the ground was adjacent to their second home, from 1883–88, at Brook's Hall (where Mr Paterson popped up again with his electric lights in December 1878). The site is now bordered by Norwich Road, Sherrington Road and Westwood Avenue. The players changed in the Inkerman pub, which still exists and shared this sloping, bumpy ground with the Orwell Works team.

Portman Road

Used for rugby, cricket and important football games such as County finals, Portman Road had long been coveted by Ipswich AFC. In order to lease it from the Corporation they had to amalgamate with the rugby club, adopting the name Ipswich Town in the process (the rugby players eventually left to play at Broom Hill). The pitch in 1888 then ran from east to west on what is now Town's training pitch and the large open ground was dotted with trees (one actually caught fire during a match in 1906!).

Ignoring league competitions until 1899 and remaining steadfastly amateur, Ipswich were unable to afford many ground improvements. Footboards, to keep spectators' feet dry, were laid along the touchlines and the press worked from a pitch-side table until a hut was built in 1897. Portman Road's surface was so highly regarded that the groundsman received a benefit match. He was probably a busy man because twice in two years the pitch's axis had to be changed to avoid damaging the cricket square.

The suggestion that Ipswich lay their own pitch on rough ground next to the cricket pitch was first made in 1900, but when Ipswich approached their landlords with plans for this, plus a running track and a stand on Portman Road, the Corporation gave their blessing but no money. To raise the necessary capital, therefore, an Ipswich Cricket, Football and Athletic Ground Co. Ltd was formed, with the football club signing a 21-year lease in 1905.

A grandstand was built on Portman Road for £230 and the new pitch was eventually inaugurated on 9 January 1907. Town paid £30 a year rent to the ground company, rising within two seasons to £200 before settling at £150. Portman Road thus reached the stage of development most big city grounds had been at fifteen years earlier (and the gap would widen further over the ensuing three decades).

A pavilion costing £280 was also built in 1907 and this served as the dressing rooms until 1965. In 1911

the stand roof was torn off in a gale (this happened again in 1947), but the worst damage was caused by the Army, who took over the ground for training and storage during the First World War. They not only ruined the pitch but refused to leave until 1920, so that no football was played there for six years.

Even in the 1920s the ground was barely developed. Whippet racing began in 1922 and the groundsman, despite orders to the contrary, kept a variety of sheep, goats and chickens in the stand. One game in 1926 had to be halted after rats were found in the stand! To add to the farmyard atmosphere there was a large cattle market across the road.

Ipswich was then the largest town in England not to have a professional team (although they had played at Wembley once – see Wembley) and Town might have been eclipsed when proposals were made to form a full-time club called Ipswich United, to play at the Suffolk Greyhound Stadium. Town still refused to change their status but after consultation they did agree on a good old British compromise. Portman Road would have a professional first team, with an amateur second team in reserve.

So while Arsenal and Tottenham each built dramatic new grandstands costing record amounts, at Portman Road, where on two sides of the ground there were still wooden bleachers, the first iron railings were installed around the pitch and the first banking built up and covered at the North End. And, as Highbury's new stand was opened, Ipswich installed 650 of Arsenal's unwanted tip-up seats (vintage 1913) in the Grandstand and started to build the Churchman's Stand, so-called because the tobacco works of Churchman (a former Town player) stood behind.

Nothing could stop Town now. If a city the size of Bradford could manage two League teams, surely Ipswich could sustain just one. So it was that in 1938, two years after turning professional, Town were elected to the League in place of Gillingham.

More terracing was laid and both the Main and Churchman's Stands were extended. In 1939 the company which had sub-let Portman Road to Ipswich went into liquidation and Town became direct tenants of the Corporation.

On the outbreak of war, Captain Cobbold, one of the family which has guided Ipswich since 1878 with stern but benevolent leadership, closed down the club so that every man might do his duty. The captain was killed by a flying bomb in 1944 and his uncle took over to prepare Portman Road for peacetime and their second League season.

With its friendly atmosphere and superb pitch Portman Road rapidly became one of the League's most popular venues. The 1950s saw American football and rugby at the ground (grid-iron returned in 1986) and yet again a Portman Road groundsman was honoured by the supporters. Is there another club in the League where the groundsman is held in such esteem? In 1952 the West Side, which had formerly been lined by narrow wooden bleachers, was permanently divided from the practice pitch by uncovered concrete terracing, and the covered North End was also re-terraced in 1954.

Plans for a West Stand behind the terracing were also announced in 1954 but delayed when the Supporters' Association (which represented an astonishing 75 per cent of Town's average gate) stated that strengthening the team should come first. Work eventually began after the club, managed by Alf Ramsey, won promotion to Division Two in 1957.

The West Stand, a typical 1950s two-tier contruction with a pitched roof, was opened by League President Joe Richards, and extended to the full length of the pitch the following year.

The bill for £30 500 had been paid by the supporters, who raised a further £15 000 for floodlights, first used for a friendly v. Arsenal on 16 February 1960. Lady Blanche Cobbold, mother of the current chairman, performed the switching on ceremony and a season later Ipswich won promotion to Division One after just eighteen seasons of professionalism. As if that were not enough, a season later they were champions.

Portman Road now developed apace, largely thanks to the Supporters' Association. New turnstiles were built, the North Stand terracing improved and in 1965 the pavilion was finally superseded by a new block of offices and dressing rooms erected in the south west corner of the ground.

The best was yet to come however (although sadly it came after the Supporters' Association had fallen out with the club). Portman Road's lease from the council was renewed in 1968 for a further 99 years on condition that improvements were made within 21 years, and if this was intended to act as a spur it certainly succeeded. From 1972–82 Ipswich emerged under Bobby Robson as one of the country's most consistently successful teams.

The first major change of Robson's era was the dismantling of the East Stand – it was re-erected at Ipswich's Foxhall Speedway stadium – to make way for a propped cantilever construction called the Portman Stand. Holding 3700 seats, the stand's size took up six feet of best Ipswich turf but brought Portman Road well and truly into the modern era. It was opened most appropriately by someone who had put Ipswich on the road to success, Sir Alf Ramsey, on 14 August 1971. So quickly had the stand been built that Messrs Eastwood and Moyse report that the equivalent building rate would have been one three-bedroomed house per week. Over the following years the stand would have wings added, and a restaurant, squash court and club shop built underneath. The final cost was £500 000. On the day the fully extended Portman Stand was first used in March 1975, the ground saw its record attendance of 38 010 for an FA Cup-tie v. Leeds.

Meanwhile the administration block had been expanded in 1973 to include an indoor gym and further facilities on two storeys, and the floodlights were renewed to a standard above that required by UEFA. They were the best in the League at that time.

The Churchman's Stand was rebuilt in 1977 at a cost of £300 000. This involved removing the old timber footings which had once caught fire during a match. Success in their first FA Cup Final in 1978 then helped finance the building of 24 executive boxes in the Portman Stand paddock, to which a further 1800 seats were added. These and other internal modifications alone cost more than the entire cost of the stand, a measure of how building costs had risen.

The most recent improvement occurred in 1982 when £1·4 million was spent on a new West Stand. Ipswich had already spent £400 000 on safety work following the introduction of the Safety of Sports Grounds Act and although the new stand was a gamble it showed how confident the one-time amateurs had become. Named after Ipswich's sponsors

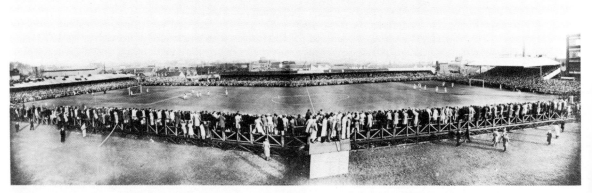

Ipswich v. Colchester, 5 February 1938. It's hard to believe that such an undeveloped ground could hold nearly 24 000 spectators, or that there were wooden bleachers along the west touchline until 1952

Pioneer, the stand was built over the existing West Stand in order to minimize disruption. The old roof was taken off and an extra tier of 4800 seats added above. The Pioneer Stand was opened by Minister for Sport Neil Macfarlane on 5 February 1984.

Every move has been calculated, every detail watched over. In fifty eventful years Portman Road has changed from a rural outpost to one of the most advanced grounds in Britain, with a capacity of 37 000, of which 14 000 are seated. Having progressed so far so quickly it would seem that the story is far from over yet, even though in 1986, as if exhausted from their 18 years in Division One, Town found themselves relegated and heavily in debt.

Ground Description

Portman Road could not be more conveniently located; close to both the railway station and town centre and yet not too confined by its surrounds. Perhaps the best place to start is behind the Pioneer Stand where the training pitch is fenced in. Here it was that Town used to play on the cricket pitch.

The Pioneer Stand has much to commend it. Essentially an old base with a new top, the design is cleverly and neatly unified, with the only trace of awkwardness at the glass screen end, where the lines are somewhat disjointed. The roof, lined with black fascia and the sponsor's name in the centre, is a cantilever. There was a line of narrow wooden bleachers along this touchline until 1952.

From here, the North Bank is to the left, the oldest part of the ground. It has a low, pitched roof over terracing, with an electric scoreboard installed in conjunction with the local newspaper, built into the roof, as at Carrow Road. The gates behind here are all electrically operated, to facilitate a speedy exit in case of emergencies. High walls and high fencing cater for more routine disturbances at this end.

Opposite is the Portman Stand, a dark, sleek stand with not a detail out of place. Grey and orange seats provide contrast, as does the Ipswich Town Football Club sign in white letters set against the matt black fascia. The orange steelwork supporting the cantilever, with rear props exposed at the back, adds a further element of high-tec stylishness. But as at St Andrew's, St James' Park and the Hawthorns, the executive boxes in the rear paddock with their sloping, black roofs, do stand out as late additions.

Although it does not appear to be large, the Portman Stand holds 7000 seated, 500 more than the new West Stand at White Hart Lane, an apparently much larger construction. But whereas the West Stand's roof predominates, at Ipswich the seating tier seems to almost disappear into the shadows.

To the right is the South or Churchman's Stand, another covered terrace, built up on supports behind a small bank. The pitch used to extend as far as the first few rows of terracing.

Here, as everywhere at Portman Road, the barriers, the steps, the paintwork is immaculate, as if Mr Cobbold has personally inspected every nook and cranny.

But the pride of Portman Road is the pitch, acknowledged by most players as one of the finest in the League, if not *the* best. It was reconstructed with the help of the Sports Turf Research Institute in Bingley (see Pitches) and has won awards for the best-kept pitch. It is the only League pitch (apart from QPR's artificial surface) to have staged a hockey international, in 1968.

No doubt the temperate climate in East Anglia has been a factor in the pitch's quality, but it is no coincidence that Ipswich's groundsmen over the years have been repeatedly acclaimed for their diligence. One former incumbent also showed some ingenuity. Stan Prendergast developed a unique system for lifting up the goal nets so he could drive the mower between the posts. Every other club groundsman usually has to tie up the goal-nets for tending the pitch. At Ipswich, the bottom sides and back of the net are attached to bars, which in turn are hinged to the foot of the post. The current groundsman, Winston Chapman, simply has to lift up the bars to raise the net and his path is clear (see illustration in Pitches).

That it was devised at Portman Road is no surprise. The ground and Ipswich Town may have arrived in the big league rather late, but in just a couple of decades they have certainly shown some of the old hands a trick or two. They have also demonstrated, as Leeds did before, that creating a super stadium is often the prelude to a fall. Team building, many would argue, must never take second place to stand building.

⋆NORWICH CITY⋆

Previous Grounds

Norwich City are first recorded playing on a ground at Newmarket Road in June 1902. The original white boarded dressing rooms are still used today by school teams. City turned professional in 1905 but were asked to leave three years later, so on the initiative of chairman John Pyke the stand was transported by horse and cart to a new ground on Rosary Road. It was to become probably the most unusual ground ever to stage League football.

Called The Nest – as might any home of 'the Canaries' – it was in a disused chalk-pit. A large work force had to level the crater with tons of earth and rubble. But the strangest aspect of The Nest was a 50-foot high concrete wall at the north-west corner, barely a yard or so behind the touchline. This wall lined the side of a cliff, at the top of which was a row of houses. There were barriers at the top for spectators to look down on the pitch, making it the oddest Kop ever seen. If a shot went high over the goal, the ball would bounce back; while players might easily run into the wall, if not careful.

The other end was equally cramped. Immediately behind the touchline was a line of back gardens, and it was joked that the goalkeeper had to go into them so many times to retrieve the ball that one day he would marry one of the girls who lived there.

The Nest was opened with a friendly v. Fulham on 1 September 1908, in front of 3300 spectators. Two years later the pitch was relaid with proper drainage, extra terracing was laid on the St Leonard's Road and Rosary Road sides and a cinder track squeezed in for training. It was never ideal, but it was certainly picturesque.

In March 1920 a new Main Stand was built opposite the so-called Chicken Run, but as crowds grew, The Nest's inadequacies became increasingly apparent. In April 1922 barriers on top of the cliff broke and although there were no injuries, it was a lucky escape.

In March 1926, therefore, a plan for a 27 000-capacity ground was drawn up, to be built on a site on Highland Road, off Christchurch Road, at a cost of £20 000. But nothing materialized and Norwich stayed on. The Nest's highest attendance was 25 037 for the visit of Sheffield Wednesday in the 5th Round FA Cup in 1934–35, the last Cup match ever played at the ground. Ostensibly the concrete wall was the main problem, but as Russell Allison (whose son Russell later became groundsman at Carrow Road) recalled, the most important reason for City leaving the ground was the collapse of part of the pitch. Apparently the turf sank up to 30 feet in one corner when the old chalk workings gave way, and Allison had to shore up the chasm with soil and railway sleepers. He also had to warn players to be very careful when taking corners!

Finally, on 15 May 1935, the FA wrote to Norwich saying that The Nest was no longer suitable for large crowds and that measures must be taken. So City said farewell to their charming Nest, and moved about half-a-mile south along the banks of the River Wensum to their new home at Carrow Road.

The site of The Nest and the high wall can still be seen from Rosary Road. According to John Eastwood's and Mike Davage's club history *Canary Citizens* (Almeida Books, 1986), the wall is obscured by the warehouse of Bertram Books. One entrance to the ground was on Malvern Road. It seems incredible that this site was once a football ground filled with 25 000 people.

Carrow Road

As soon as it was realized City must move, the club received the offer of the Boulton Paul Sports Ground on Carrow Road. There were only three months before the start of the next season, a seemingly impossible time in which to build a Second Division ground.

But as Ted Bell in his history of Norwich City records, City put the job out to tender on 1 June 1935, the day they agreed a 20-year lease with Boulton Paul. On 11 June dumping began, with rubble for the River End bank coming from the old Chicken Run at The Nest. By 17 August most of the stands and terraces had been completed, and on 31 August, Carrow Road football ground was opened for the Second Division match v. West Ham United, in front of 29 779 wildly enthusiastic spectators. The miracle had been accomplished in just 82 days!

Carrow Road had a Main Stand, a covered end terrace, and two large open banks, with a potential capacity of about 40 000. It was totally different from The Nest, and so were the surroundings. There were no prim terraced villas and winding lanes here. Boulton Paul's factory surrounded Carrow Road on almost three sides, and on the fourth was the River Wensum and the Colman Mustard works.

Two years later, on 29 October 1938, Carrow Road was honoured by the visit of King George VI, for City's game v. Millwall. He was thus the first ruling monarch to attend a Second Division match.

Carrow Road was an obvious target for German bombers because Boulton Paul was a major arms manufacturer, producing many of the gun turrets for RAF aircraft. To protect the area, two gun emplacements were built in the ground's car park overlooking the Wensum, to be manned by the Home Guard. One of the pair still survives.

The club was in Division Three when floodlights were installed at Carrow Road at a cost of £9000, the first match being a friendly v. Sunderland on 17 October 1956. The ground's record attendance came during one of City's heroic Cup runs for the 6th Round FA Cup tie v. Leicester City, watched by 43 984 on 30 March 1963. Shortly afterwards, the

Carrow Road's Main Stand before the fire. The River End stand is to the left, its roof support doubling as a floodlight pylon

open South Side was covered.

Owing to the introduction of the Safety of Sports Grounds Act, major changes were made at Carrow Road. The South Stand terrace was converted entirely to seating, and at the same time Norwich were told it would cost £400 000 to bring the River End bank up to safety requirements. City decided instead to replace the 15 000 capacity bank with a new River End Stand. It cost £1·7 million to complete and included the club's own public house – the only one built in a stand in the League – appropriately called The Nest. Seating 2350, with standing room for 6900, the new stand was opened in December 1979.

On 25 October 1984 disaster struck Carrow Road. A fire destroyed the central section of the Main Stand and forced its closure for the rest of the season. In 1985 work began on a replacement £1·7 million stand designed appropriately enough by the architects J. Owen Bond of Norwich (another J. Bond had been manager at Carrow Road), and built by R. G. Carter, the firm which also erected the River End Stand. Husband and Co., who designed cantilever stands for Sheffield Wednesday and Nottingham Forest, acted as the club's agents for the project, which was opened at the start of the 1986–87 season. Carrow Road now holds 26 000, of which 10 373 are seated.

Ground Description

One definition of 'carrow' is a wandering Irish gambler, but the road itself takes its name from the twelfth-century Carrow Abbey. Carrow Road now runs from the Wensum to the main railway line from Norwich, bending at a right angle to run along the north and west sides of the ground. On one side of the road is the Boulton Paul factory, on the other is the three-storey façade of the new Main Stand. It all seems very businesslike after finding one's way from the convoluted medieval centre of Norwich.

Named the City Stand, this new construction has one tier of yellow seats (with green seats spelling the club's name) under a propped cantilever roof, with a glass fronted viewing lounge along the rear. Roughly the same height as the old stand it thus fits comfortably with its neighbours, although one cannot deny that its clean lines and plain fascia lack the colour and rather cluttered warmth of its predecessor. The stand is an example of how the trend in stand design has moved away from tall, elaborate double deckers to simpler, single-tier cantilevers with executive facilities at the back. The Hawthorns and Vicarage Road have new stands with similar layouts.

From here to the left is the Barclay Stand, named after an ex-President of the club, Phyliss Barclay, a member of the Barclays Bank family which has strong connections in the area. The stand is a dark, cavernous cover over terracing, tangled with a web of steelwork and security barriers. As at Portman Road, an electric scoreboard is mounted on the roof.

The Barclay Stand is linked to the South Stand by a covered corner section, but with the floodlight pylon in front making the view from here rather awkward. The South Stand has a typical pitched roof, with advertisements lining the gutter. There is no perimeter wall, just a single railing. Unfortunately the yellow and green colour scheme is interrupted on this side by new seats, coloured red and blue, but they are at least mounted on properly rebuilt steps to allow good sight lines down to the pitch.

On the right is the new River End Stand. This resembles the North Stand at Villa Park in design and construction, but the details are quite different. As at Villa, the roof is suspended by a huge goalpost construction, so that although not a cantilever, there are no pillars in the way. The two outside vertical posts are quite thin, and support a bare steel girder across the top, from which the roof hangs. Each vertical, however, continues upwards and holds a floodlight gantry, a very simple but effective arrangement. We are so used to seeing floodlights mounted on pylons, so the Norwich pair on steel poles look most unusual.

The upper tier has yellow seats, with green ones spelling out the word Canaries. Below these is a line of 20 boxes, and in front the paddock is covered entirely by the roof. The River End standing area is much larger than that at Villa Park, with bright yellow barriers standing out against the light grey concrete terraces. It is an attractively balanced piece of design.

Underneath the stand is the club's public house, The Nest, and behind lies the car park, still belonging to Boulton Paul, leading to the River Wensum a hundred yards away. The Carrow Road pitch drains into the river, which flows into the North Sea, 12 miles east near Great Yarmouth.

From the car park the sprawling Carrow Works of Colmans, the mustard and pickle makers, is visible. Their silos are, appropriately for the club, coated in mustard-coloured dust. At the car-park entrance stands one of the surviving Second World War gun turrets, a round brick building which puzzles many visitors.

I have mentioned elsewhere in this book how important the choice of colours and care to detail are to the overall appearance of a football ground, whatever the style or state of its architecture. Carrow Road is a perfect example of a ground that could not possibly belong to any other club. It has yellow and green, canary colours, and reminders of Norwich all round which lend Carrow Road a homely and cheerful identity.

With the completion of the City Stand, Carrow Road is now also one of the best equipped grounds in the country, with a well balanced ratio of seats to standing and cover for almost every spectator – a far cry indeed from the precarious walls and collapsing corners of The Nest.

Norwich's new Main Stand, plain but fireproof

COLCHESTER · UNITED ·

Layer Road

Although United are the youngest club in the League, having formed in 1937, strictly speaking the club was the professional successor to an amateur team called Colchester Town, who had played at Layer Road since 1909. Before then the ground was used by the Army, whose barracks are very close.

The first known development at Layer Road was the building of the present Main Stand in 1933. United were elected to the League in 1950, having won much acclaim for being the only non-League side to have reached the FA Cup 5th Round, in 1948. During the following season's cup run, Colchester enjoyed its largest attendance of 19 072 for the visit of Reading in November 1948. Improvements to the ground followed, and during United's best spell in the League, floodlights were installed. Their first use was for a League match v. Grimsby in August 1959.

In 1985, after the Bradford fire, Layer Road's capacity was cut drastically from 14 000 to only 4000, pending safety work. Most of this involved fireproofing, rewiring and the widening of gangways in the stand, which has 1100 seats.

Ground Description

Like the suburban sprawl of semi-detached houses all around, at first glance the ground is hardly inspiring. The sturdy floodlight pylons are painted green, while the Main Stand is a colourless affair. But it does have an unusual steep sloping roof on the pitch side, with what resembles a tiny airport controllers' tower in the centre but is actually a commentator's booth with room for cameras above. The stand is mostly wood, with basic wooden bench seats along the front. There are seats in the centre section only, the wings being for standing. The Layer Road End's wing roof is a later addition, built in the 1950s, while the other wing is under the same roof as the Main Stand but is separated from the seats by a brick wall topped by iron railings, like those at a primary school.

To the right is the Layer Road End covered terrace, which it is said was constructed by prisoners of war during the 1940s, and moves one to suggest that they appear to have sawn up their beds to provide the materials. The roof is very low, and the terraces are formed out of rickety wooden planks, onto which are bolted wooden crush barriers. There is so little room that the back of the goal cuts into the stand.

Although completely wooden, this terrace was allowed to stay open after stringent safety checks, on condition that any litter was cleared from underneath both before and after each game.

Wooden terracing and barriers at Layer Road

It is worth noting that the goal stanchions are like only those at Bloomfield Road, Blackpool, with two angles on each stanchion. In the right-hand corner of the Layer Road End are the club offices, overlooking the pitch, and in the other corner is the supporters' club. To comply with regulations governing the consumption of alcohol during matches, the windows which overlook the pitch have had to be boarded up.

Opposite the Main Stand is a small cover over terracing, variously known as the Barn, the Shed or just the Popular Side. The old roof was once a source of complaint from those who stood underneath and were showered with rust every time the ball thumped against it. Happily this has not been a problem since a new roof was built in 1983. To the left of this cover, the open terracing, once so dilapidated it resembled the ascents of an Incan fortress, is now resurfaced and has new barriers. Behind this side is a floodlit all-weather pitch.

To the left of the Main Stand is an open bank with no name. It was called the Spion Kop once, of course, then the Clock End, until the clock was removed in the 1970s. This terracing has also been refurbished in recent years after years of neglect. At the back is a blue fence behind which lies a spacious garden.

Layer Road was until recently one of the most hazardous and badly maintained grounds in the League. Its terracing was particularly uneven. Fortunately the club has taken slow, but steady strides towards restoring the ground, although even with its limited capacity it is still, sadly, large enough to cope with United's average crowds. Some small grounds are cosy, some are cute, but the impression at Layer Road is that however much it is improved in substance, it will essentially remain a rather ordinary little ground. Not that many away supporters will have a chance to assess this for themselves, in the near future at least, because in August 1987 Colchester emulated Luton and Torquay by making Layer Road a members-only ground with a capacity of 4900.

·SOUTHEND UNITED·

Previous Grounds

Southend United played their first game on 1 September 1906, on the same ground they now own, but with an important difference; the pitch was then approximately 50 feet higher than it is today! The ground was once the site of a house called Roots Hall, and had been used previously by a team called Southend Athletic. United used it until the First World War, but in 1919 moved to the Kursaal Ground where they began their League career a year later. The Roots Hall site was excavated, as the deposits of sand and gravel were needed for local housing developments. The club stayed at Kursaal, where the record attendance was 17 000, until 1934, when they moved to the Southend Greyhound Stadium, Grainger Road. The highest gate there was in 1936; 22 862 watching Southend v. Spurs. But the club always wanted a ground of their own and in the mid-1950s began looking for a suitable site. By coincidence the best land available was at Roots Hall, their first home. The Kursaal Ground is now covered by housing, next to the Kursaal fairground site, near the seafront. The greyhound stadium has recently been built over by industrial units. Southend have also played at Chelmsford City's ground, when the stadium was used by the Army in 1939–41.

Roots Hall

If there is a monument to the British football supporter, it is Roots Hall, for here is a ground built almost entirely through the efforts of a small, but dedicated group of people.

When the directors chose the Roots Hall site, it was then a rubbish tip, partly owned by the local gas board, and recently levelled to provide extra car-parking space for the annual illuminations traffic. Negotiations began in 1950, the supporters' club provided the £10 000 needed to purchase the land, then financed the setting up of a Trust Fund, which comprised the Mayor, the Chairman of the Football Club and the Chairman of the Supporters' Club. This was almost a return to the pioneering days of football in the late Victorian period, when a football club was seen as vital a necessity for a municipality as a public bath or a statue of the Queen.

Work began at Roots Hall in 1953 and was carried out by just a handful of men, several of the players and even the club manager-cum-secretary Harry Warren. But one man in particular was responsible for building a stadium at Roots Hall, Sidney Broomfield. He was employed to oversee all the work, but inevitably had to do much of it himself. When the site had first been excavated in 1914, diggers had found neolithic and Anglo-Saxon remains, Roman and Viking coins. When Sidney Broomfield started his digging he found only tons of compressed rubbish.

Roots Hall was ready to stage its first match, a Third Division South fixture v. Norwich City, on 20 August 1955. Present on this proud occasion were Sir Stanley Rous, then Secretary of the FA, Arthur Oakley, President of the Football League, and to officiate over the actual opening ceremony, Arthur Drewry, Chairman of the FA. The Southend United Supporters' Club Band (probably the only such band in the country) accompanied community singing and the Mayor received a gift of £1000 for the Trust Fund from the club's President, E. J. Grant. Southend United were thus the last club in the Football League to have moved to their own permanent ground.

However, the ground was still incomplete. The Main East Stand did not run the length of the pitch until 1967. The North Bank cover ran only the width of the penalty area, so had to be extended. The West Side roof covered only the rear section of banking and was later doubled. But the greatest achievement was the terracing of the South Bank.

Because the site had been quarried for so long, the ground was a natural bowl shape on two sides, the highest point being at the top of the South Bank, at the original ground level. In 1955 only a narrow band of concrete terracing encircled the pitch, but in the course of five years, Sid and two other men laid every inch of concreting over the South Bank's 72 steps. 'Some days,' he recalled, 'we would arrive at the ground to discover that heavy overnight rain had swept mud from the top of the banking over the steps we had completed . . . it was a real slog.'

There were many teething problems with the pitch. As it had been laid on compressed rubbish, drainage was very poor. During the first winter, only days before a Cup tie v. Manchester City, the groundstaff had to dig a trench diagonally across the pitch and throw in tons of cockleshells in the hope of improving it. The following year it was decided to start all over again, so the pitch was dug up and replaced, and proper drainage and sub-soil installed, at a cost of £15 000. Floodlights were erected during the summer of 1959.

Roots Hall, before the extension of the Main Stand in 1967

Roots Hall was intended to hold 35 000 spectators, but the highest attendance it has seen was 31 033 in January 1979 when Liverpool were the visitors in the 3rd Round of the FA Cup. Despite the ground's relative modernity, when designated under the Safety of Sports Grounds Act in 1985 the authorities reduced its capacity considerably from 27 000 to 10 753, including 2651 seats. Perhaps the most demoralizing decision, for Sidney Broomfield especially, was the limit of only 1500 placed upon the South Bank, which had formerly held 13 500. To refurbish the terrace with new concrete and stronger barriers would have cost at least £50 000, a sum which the club had already been forced to spend on other safety work.

Roots Hall may well prove to be the shortest-lived ground in modern footballing history. In 1986, 31 years after its opening, Southend made an agreement with a supermarket chain to develop the Roots Hall site. With the proceeds from this United would then develop a £12 million, 25 000-capacity stadium on the south-west corner of Southend airport, on a 40-acre green field site.

If planning permission was given the club expected to leave the ground in 1987, but it would not be the supporters building the new ground, and the pitch would be plastic. In fact the only familiar aspect of the new stadium, if built, would be the weekly market which Southend intend to take with them from Roots Hall.

Ground Description

If you did not know the history of Roots Hall, it would no doubt appear a most ordinary ground. No single part of it is remarkable, nor is the location especially appealing. But when you look at the slopes of the South Bank and think of how just a handful of men constructed the terracing, over the course of five years, then you can begin to appreciate that Roots Hall is rather special.

It is in the parish of Prittlewell, which existed long before the resort. Indeed the town's name derives from the fact that it was built at the south end of Prittlewell. The ground stands well back from Victoria Avenue, with a large car park in between, used twice a week for large markets.

From here we enter the Main or East Stand, the archetypal 1950s' grandstand, as seen at so many other grounds in the country, its design hardly changed from stands built 30 years earlier, its character determined by grey, asbestos roofing, blue steel and wooden seats. Along the gutter a hoarding suggests you try the market at Roots Hall. The screen ends are glass, the narrow paddock's rear wall is blue, with stairs leading to the seats. You can just see where the two wings were added in 1967.

From here the low North Bank is to your right, covered with a plain barrel roof, lined along the front with white hoarding. The pitch is surrounded by a track and low white perimeter wall, which has the effect of tying the ground together neatly. Underneath the roof hangs a sign commemorating the fact that the structure was donated by E. J. Grant.

Opposite the East Stand is the West Side, with a double-barrel roof running almost the whole length of the touchline. This type of construction, though long outdated, did have the advantage of being very economical. Incidentally, the stands were built by a firm called Boulton Paul, once makers of war-planes and guns, and neighbours of Norwich City.

To the left is the tall, open South Bank, once so impressive but now, sadly, deemed to be unsuitable for large numbers. At the top are the floodlight pylons, large advertisement hoardings and a clock. From here the view is disappointing, mainly tower blocks and housing, with no sign of the sea. But the pitch is in excellent shape, thanks to the efforts of groundsman Sidney Broomfield and his long-standing work-mate Joe Auger. Both men were still tending the ground in 1986 and were possibly the longest-serving groundstaff in the League. Roots Hall was the house Sid and friends built for their club, and in 1974, United gave him a testimonial match to thank him for 21 years' service. But would the community spirit which created Roots Hall still be possible today? Probably not. Supermarket owners and property developers are the most likely people to build new grounds nowadays, and while this may be regrettable it has to be said that football's declining audience has been one of the major factors in advancing this trend. In the meantime, Roots Hall stands as a monument to former days, when supporters and players all chipped in to build the ground, never once thinking that in less than forty years their efforts might become bulldozed away.

·11·
SOUTH AND EAST MIDLANDS

·LEICESTER CITY·

Previous Grounds

City were originally called Leicester Fosse when formed in 1884, because they played on a field by Fosse Road South (a 'fosse' is a ditch or moat in front of a fortified place). In 1885 the club moved to Victoria Park, where they were often competing with the more popular Victoria Park Rugby FC for spectators. On 5 November 1887 Fosse switched to their first enclosed ground, Belgrave Road Cycle Track, using the White Hart Hotel as changing rooms. But the rugby club followed their example a year later and made a bid for the stadium higher than Fosse could afford, so the soccer club moved back to Victoria Park. Soon after, however, Leicester turned professional and began playing on a ground at Mill Lane, until the council evicted them and they were forced to make a temporary home at Aylestone Road County Cricket Ground. Finally, after seven years the club made its sixth and final move to the present site at Filbert Street.

Filbert Street

What is today known as Filbert Street or the City Stadium was in 1891 referred to as Walnut Street, then the nearest road actually touching the site. It is thought that the ground was first spotted by a Miss Westland, who considered the 3¾-acre site would make a very nice football ground, which indeed it did. Fosse played their first game there, a friendly v. Nottingham Forest Reserves on 7 November 1891. Three years later they joined the League and in the period before the First World War the ubiquitous Archibald Leitch played some part in the ground's improvement.

In 1919 the club's name was changed to Leicester City, and on 24 November 1921 the present Main Stand was opened.

In 1924–25 City reached the Cup quarter-finals, won the Second Division Championship and thereby began one of the most successful periods in their history. In the summer of 1927 the double-decker South Stand was built, an almost exact copy of West Ham's Main Stand built two years previously. Perhaps inspired by its grandeur the team went on to finish third in the Division in 1928 and on 18 February of that year Filbert Street enjoyed its highest attendance, 47 298 for the visit of Tottenham in the FA Cup 5th Round. Both the Popular Side and the North Terrace were covered around this time.

A wartime fire, caused either by military personnel occupying that section or by a bomb, destroyed a third of the Main Stand and this was not completely repaired until 1949.

The first floodlit match at Filbert Street was on 23 October 1957 v. Borussia Dortmund, that year's West German League Champions. When the club bounced back to Division One in 1971, Filbert Street was extensively redeveloped. Seats were installed first at the North Stand, then along the East Side, and in 1975 a unique arrangement for shelter was provided for the newly seated terracing when the North Stand roof was replaced by a line of 20 private boxes directly above.

Being such a tightly enclosed ground, Filbert Street's pitch had always suffered from a lack of ventilation, and was notoriously muddy in winter. To alleviate this, in 1971 the club installed a huge plastic sheet which could be raised above the pitch with hot-air blowers, so high that players could even train underneath it (although in practice it made for a claustrophobic and uncomfortable environment in which to spend much time). But the cost of running such a system was high, the sheeting was prone to tearing, and since the club improved the drainage the cover has been removed.

City now own Filbert Street, except for the car park and roadway behind the Main Stand (both still belong to the council). The ground's capacity is 31 500, including 15 326 seats.

Filbert Street, the pitch covered by a polythene balloon

Ground Description

An observer once described Filbert Street as a 'shoebox' ground, an impression certainly reinforced by television coverage. But the camera has been known to lie, and in reality the ground seems quite open, two of the stands being low. If there was a sense of confinement, this has been considerably diminished by the demolition of the neighbouring electricity generating station, whose enormous cooling towers used to form a shadow over the south east corner. But the ground is hemmed in quite tightly by the surrounding terraced streets, as for example in Burnmoor Street, where the entrance to the East Stand is, as at Kenilworth Road, actually part of the houses. There are bedrooms above the gateways.

The Main Stand is lower than the end South Stand but has a modest dignity all of its own. Most noticeable is the 'pigeon-loft' box on the roof which houses cameras. It has extra lamps perched along the roof. The most interesting feature is the mock-classical podium built behind the players' tunnel. The tunnel was formerly like a courtyard, extending the full width of the podium (see photo in Design) with two windows on each side of the entrance, until the installation of more seats ruined its grand effect. Otherwise the stand is unremarkable, with solid screen ends, a small front paddock and blue and white paintwork. The seats are a mixture of colours and therefore deny the stand any uniformity.

From here to the right is the South Stand, a copy of one at the Boleyn Ground but not so well preserved. Even though the stand has been there half a century, the standing area is still referred to under its old name of Spion Kop.

The East Stand opposite the Main Stand is low with a shallow rising tier of seats from front to back, obviously a hurried conversion of the old terracing. Its roof is well lit by skylights, but as it reaches the

northern corner it gets messily tangled in a web of steelwork which continues round the corner until meeting the North Stand's private boxes. Underneath this apparently impromptu roof is a section of bucket seats installed in front of a small section of terracing. This is the Filbert Street corner for the supporters' club, where the spectators pay the same and may choose whether to stand or sit.

The North Stand is most curious. The bottom section is covered in bright orange seats and is the usual converted terrace. But above this are executive boxes, forming a roof over the seats. The glass fronts are virtually suspended over the goal-line, and have their own little canopy to keep off the rain. They look like an aquarium at the zoo. It is an unorthodox arrangement, but apparently most successful. Between here and the Main Stand you may notice that behind the odd, white floodlight pylon, is a figure at once familiar but highly unexpected in the depths of Leicester. It is a copy of the Statue of Liberty which dates back to 1920 when the directors of Lennards Shoes, whose premises were on Walnut Street, visited New York and decided they wanted a statue for the roof of their new building. Liberty Shoes, as the company became known, no longer exists but the large stone figure survives. Her hundred-weight torch, which fell onto the pavement below during a frost attack has happily been restored. At the ground entrance in this corner is another quite classical feature, a gateway with a flag on top.

Filbert Street is cramped, with box-like aspects, and certainly there is little room within the stadium. Each goal is narrow, as is the running track. There was a plan to move out and rebuild at Beaumont Leys, on the outskirts of the town, but as so many other clubs have found, by adding seats Leicester have managed to convert their ground into one easily able to cope with the smaller crowds of today.

NORTHAMPTON ·TOWN·

The County Ground

Town share the County Ground with Northampton-shire County Cricket Club and it is therefore the only three-sided football ground in the League (Sheffield United built over the cricket pitch at Bramall Lane in 1974). The 8½-acre site was originally farmland, converted into a cricket field in the 1880s by North-amptonshire County Cricket and Recreation Grounds Limited. The football club formed there in 1897 and initially used the cricket pavilion on con-dition that no football was played before 1 September or after 1 May.

The football side of the ground opposite the pavi-lion was first developed between 1907–12, the years when Herbert Chapman was at Northampton. Im-provements costing £2500 included laying terraces and building a small stand.

Town joined the League in 1920 and opened a full-length Main Stand in 1924. A fire in December 1929 caused £5000 worth of damage, destroying most of the seats and offices, but the stand was quickly restored to its former state.

In the late 1940s the Hotel End was covered, and in the 1960s, the County Ground witnessed the most dramatic rise and fall football had ever known. The story begins in 1960. On 10 October Arsenal visited the ground to inaugurate the new floodlights, and the following May, Town were promoted to Division Three for the first time in their League career. In their second season in the Third Division, they were promoted to the Second and in their second season in the Second Division they were promoted to the First. But despite the rise in gates, the ground's owners would not permit stands to be built on the open side of the pitch, so the club had to be content with a series of small, portable wooden platforms which each held about 20 people.

Town never found life in the First Division easy, and it was for one of their final games at the end of only one season in the First Division that they re-corded their highest attendance. A crowd of 24 523 saw them play fellow strugglers Fulham, on 23 April 1966, just before the World Cup. Four years later, at the end of the decade, Town were back in Division Four. (They even had to apply for re-election in 1972.) To cap the decade, in 1970 the club reached the 5th Round of the FA Cup and were beaten 8-2 by Manchester United.

That game was the only occasion in the ground's history that a full-length stand was put up along the open side of the pitch, which helps to explain why the game attracted Town's record receipts of over £17 000. However, the profits from those heady years

of success from 1960–66 were not used to improve the County Ground.

The reason for Town's lack of investment is bound up in the administration of the County Ground. It is governed by the Cockerill Trust, to which the football club pay rent. But because Town have a minority of members sitting on the Trust board, usually three compared with the cricket club's eight, they have great difficulty in changing the status quo. Their rent effectively goes straight to the cricket club. (The only other member of the Trust represents the bowling club, whose premises are also part of the ground, next to the Spion Kop.) Town also have to play their early and late season games away from home, so as not to clash with Northamptonshire's County cricket matches.

Despite improvements to the Main Stand in 1980, when the façade was refaced in maroon cladding, the roof recovered and new seating installed, when the ground was designated in 1985 after the Bradford fire, the County Ground was found badly wanting.

All the seats were closed off when some of the steel roof girders were declared unsound. Restoring the roof would have been too expensive, so in November 1985 the club had no option but literally to slice off the top half of the stand, leaving only the office and dressing rooms below and the standing paddock, now exposed, in front.

While this work was carried out the club put up a temporary stand near the Kop. Journalists needing a telephone had to watch from the distant cricket pavi-lion while visiting directors experienced a bit of what life is often like on the terraces by having to seek their half-time cuppa in the open air.

Once the roof and seats were gone a new roof, in line with the former rake of the seats, was put over the ground floor facilities, which were in turn com-pletely modernized in 1986. The 400-seater tempor-ary grandstand – called sarcastically the Meccano Stand – was then moved to the centre of the former paddock. It was a makeshift compromise, but North-ampton had no choice. Safety work had lost them

The County Ground in happier days. The roof may have gone but the cars and cricket come back every summer

about £1000 per match and cost them at least £70 000, yet they were still left with only barely adequate seating arrangements.

Meanwhile the rear section of the Kop, raised in the First Division days, was also pronounced unsafe and had to be fenced off. At the opposite end, new barriers, roofing and fencing were erected.

With a capacity of 10 000, the County Ground in 1986 was a ground in transition; pared down to the basics, uncertain as to whether it would rise up once more or simply lie down and die.

Ground Description

The main entrance on Abington Avenue shows only too well how reduced are Northampton's circumstances. The maroon-fronted stand is now half its original height. Two shocks await the unknowing visitor. First the stand has no upper half, secondly the ground is only three-sided.

All that remains of the stand from inside the ground is the maroon and white rear balcony wall and the open paddock. Forlorn though these remains seem, the interior is actually much improved.

To the right is the Hotel End, so-called because in the corner between the two stands is a large public house. Its upper windows overlook the pitch, through the floodlight pylon. The roof and terraces have been much improved in recent years but the front perimeter fence remains a touch primitive. At the end of the terrace one can walk directly onto the cricket pitch, which stretches out in front of the Main Stand. Directly opposite is the pavilion, a building which won much admiration when erected in 1958 for its dainty concrete cantilever canopy.

The football and cricket pitches actually overlap by about 20 yards, but the football area is used as a car park during cricket matches, when a few deck chairs line the boundary and bored children play in the goalmouths.

It is a nightmare for the groundsman trying to prepare for the football season, but since Town share his services with the cricket club he can hardly complain.

The cricket ground itself has about 7500 seats and its highest crowd was for a match against the West Indies in 1950, when 13 200 attended.

To the left of the former Main Stand is the Spion Kop, probably the most curious little appendage at any League ground. When football writers started flocking to Northampton during that one hectic season in Division One, they all found something to say about the County Ground. John Moynihan wrote of his surprise at finding: 'no enormous, ominous overpowering Spion Kop but a small hummock'. Hummock it is, for it does not even extend to the far corner flag. Just as soon as it reaches its peak, behind the goal, it falls away rapidly to nothing, level with the edge of the penalty area. Although relatively modern, the rear section of terracing, on concrete and steel supports, has been fenced off.

From this prehistoric-looking mound, you can see the bowling club to the left, behind the cricket pitch. Notice also the lines along the edge of the pitch, where the football touchline cuts across the smooth arc of the cricket outfield. Northampton's pitch is the longest in the League, measuring 120×75 yards. It is the third largest in area.

In 1986 the County Ground's future hinged entirely on plans to relocate the club to Brackmills, two miles away. Town would lease a 42-acre site from the borough council on a peppercorn rent (reputed to be six pence per year), and build a 15 000-capacity stadium with an artificial surface for soccer, hockey and American football. The £4 million scheme would also include an athletics track and other leisure facilities.

Road access is excellent, the site has no limiting factors, and the current state of the County Ground gives Northampton plenty of incentive to move.

Town feel the difficulties of playing on a three-sided pitch just as greatly as Sheffield United once did, but unlike United they can do nothing about it. Having achieved some success here, the club can hardly claim that it inhibits their progress, and as the only one of its kind in the League, the County Ground, I believe, makes a very welcome change.

But will they stay here? How many times have clubs drawn up such grand designs as the one for Brackmills? Where will the finance come from? It is tempting to be cynical about such matters, so many false hopes having been raised over the years, yet a club which is capable of going from the Fourth to the First Division and back again within a decade is, one suspects, capable of surprising us all.

·DERBY COUNTY·

Previous Grounds

Derby is the youngest of the 12 founder members of the Football League, having been formed four years earlier. The club played at the Racecourse Ground, the home then and now of Derbyshire County Cricket Club. It was chosen by the FA as the setting for the first Cup Final replay, in April 1886, between Blackburn and West Bromwich, attended by 12 000, compared with 15 000 for the first match at The Oval, and it was also the first time a Final had been settled outside London. But County's landlords, the Derby Recreation Company, who themselves leased the ground from the local corporation, did not always give football priority. The last straw came in 1895 when County were refused permission to stage an attractive Easter Monday fixture v. Corinthians, because of horse-racing commitments that week. County's committee called a meeting at the Derwent Hotel to recommend using the Baseball Ground, a mile and a half away, where the club had already played a few fixtures. The County Cricket and Racecourse Ground can be found next to the Pentagon roundabout, near Eastgate.

The Baseball Ground

Had British sporting tastes been different the Baseball Ground may well have been the starting point of a new sporting craze. As we learn from Mike Wilson in *Derby County, A Complete Record* (Breedon Books), the 12-acre ground was first laid out by foundry owner Francis Ley in the 1880s, to serve as a sports ground for his workers. In 1889 he returned from a trip to the United States so full of the joys of baseball that he spent £7000 improving and adapting the ground accordingly.

When Derby County moved in he spent a further £500 on enlarging the pitch and relocating a stand from the Racecourse Ground. Derby's first match as residents was on 14 September 1895 v. Sunderland, watched by 10 000.

Baseball was still played at the ground, however, and for a few years several football clubs, including Aston Villa and Orient, entered baseball teams into a national competition. Derby won this in 1897 with their legendary forward Steve Bloomer playing at second base.

Football continued to be the greater attraction though and by the First World War the Baseball Ground was already too small for County's growing support. In 1923 the club was offered an alternative when plans were drawn up for a municipal sports stadium on Osmaston Park Road. This ground, which County would have rented from the corporation, was to have 4000 seats, modern offices and sport facilities. But sensing that the Baseball Ground could still be

theirs, County opted out of the scheme in March 1924. Four months later they agreed to pay Sir Francis Ley £10 000 for the Baseball Ground and thus lost a rare opportunity to demonstrate that, as on the Continent, a football club can free itself of the burdens of stadium management and maintenance by becoming tenants of the municipality.

Instead they began to invest in their cramped ground. £16 000 was spent on a 3300-seater Main Stand, opened on 4 September 1926. The dressing rooms were moved here from behind one of the goals and the capacity was raised to 30 000.

In 1932 the Popular Side was improved at a cost of £750 (the roof taking on a stepped-up appearance) and a year later a double-decker stand was built at the Osmaston End, part of which had been known as Catcher's Corner during the baseball era. An almost identical stand was built opposite at the Normanton End during 1935. Thus the Baseball Ground was completely rebuilt and covered on all four sides within a decade.

After the Second World War, Derby had another chance to participate in the building of a municipal stadium, designed this time by no less an architect than Maxwell Ayrton, who had worked on Wembley Stadium in the early 1920s. His futuristic scheme, which in several respects predated by 30 years the design of the remodelled Ibrox Park, incorporated offices and a health centre (see Design). It is unfortunate Ayrton's plan was never implemented, for Derby would have taken possession of probably the most advanced concept in stadium design in Europe. Instead, having suffered bomb damage to the Osmaston Stand in 1941, and having won the Cup in 1946, the club stayed put.

The Baseball Ground was reckoned to have been built on the site of an old gypsy encampment, and before that 1946 Final, a journalist visited some local gypsies and asked that they lift their curse – presuming one existed. It must have worked, for County beat Charlton easily. Birmingham City believed they suffered from a similar curse in 1982.

The first floodlights at Derby were mounted on gantries along each roof, and were switched on in March 1953 for a friendly v. Notts County.

Derby were again celebrating promotion back into Division One in 1969 when they built a new stand above the East Side terracing. It was a difficult space to fill, because the terrace is backed by the foundry works of Ley's Maleable Castings Company Limited which owns the land, and therefore to gain the maximum benefit it had to allow standing below, with a tall seating tier above. Access can be gained only from either end of the ground, necessitating gangways over the terracing to the seats. All these problems were solved, however, and the resultant Ley Stand was an attractive addition to an otherwise rather gloomy enclosure. It cost £250 000, and has since had private boxes added at the back.

Thus the Baseball Ground became one of only four

The Baseball Ground before demolition of the surrounding houses. Ley's Foundry is on the right

League grounds to have seating and standing on all four sides, with White Hart Lane, Old Trafford and Goodison Park (Filbert Street and Loftus Road have since developed seating on all four sides). In one of the club's first games back in Division One, the highest crowd at the ground, 41 826 saw Derby v. Tottenham on 20 September 1969.

Since then the Baseball Ground has changed a great deal in substance. The original floodlight gantries were replaced by taller pylons in 1972 to conform with the demands of colour television, and the notoriously muddy pitch was finally dug up in 1965, after Derby's second Championship win, to be replaced by a sand-based pitch costing £40 000. Patches of the old turf were sold as souvenirs. At the same time seats were added to various parts of the ground with the eventual hope of making it all-seated.

First, seats were installed in the middle tier of the Normanton End, then on the Main Stand paddock. Seats were also put on the Osmaston End paddock but in 1983 removed after violence between rival supporters had heightened the need for better segregation on the terraces. By 1986 the ground's capacity was reduced from 33 300 to 26 000, with 10 200 seats.

Ground Description

This used to be one of the most cramped grounds in the League, but considerable slum clearance has created space at least on two sides so that you can now fully appreciate the mouldings around the entrance. The line of terraced houses opposite the entrance at the rear of the Main Stand was demolished to make way for a car park, and the club has created a much improved façade.

The Main Stand is very similar to nearby Chesterfield's, built a decade later, and is typical of its period. The roof however has been replaced and sports a cheaper, modern alternative to a gable. County's 'Ram' logo is on a raised board in the centre, flanked by two boards bearing the name of the stand's sponsor. This detail alone gives the old stand an added sense of dignity, and might well be copied by other clubs having bare expanses of dull roof on view.

Notice at the Osmaston End how the Main Stand roof has been cut away to allow spectators in the top corner of the Osmaston Stand an unimpeded view of the pitch.

From here, to the right is the Normanton Stand, also sponsored. This is taller than the Main Stand and is a double-decker. Both decks are now seated, but as, for example, Everton's Bullens Road Stand, there is still a small terraced enclosure at the front. The Osmaston Stand opposite is identical in design but sits on a slightly higher section of terracing. Both stands are like upright boxes, the sloping roofs barely overhanging the front, and are lined with advertisements along each balcony wall. They touch each end of the Main Stand, so there are no gaps in the corners. The floodlight pylons are therefore behind the stands, peeping over the roofs.

Behind the Normanton End is the narrow Vulcan Street, which comes to an end as it meets the walls of the Ley foundry, running along the entire east side of the ground. Behind the Osmaston Stand the foundry continues and you can see the Ley company's 'Italianate' chimney in the north east corner. Colombo Street, behind the Stand, was also once a dark, narrow street lined with terraced houses, but these have also gone, and on the open ground behind the Baseball Ground is a new community sports centre.

Opposite the Main Stand is the Ley Stand, with its sponsor's name on the white roof fascia. This is taller than either end stand, and is also a double-decker. The upper seating tier is by necessity fairly steep, covered by a plain, flat roof. Of all the stands of the 1960s, it probably has the most attractive lines, with strong emphasis on the horizontal white fascia. A steel gangway to the right links the seating with the Normanton End entrance; its presence suggesting that the foundry behind is beginning to spread into the ground like a steel Triffid. In fact the foundry has been held at bay, as it were, since Derby bought a narrow strip of land behind the stand to improve access.

The Baseball Ground will never be a sunny place, it is too boxed in by tall stands. The pitch is almost as small as it can be, with only a very narrow track round the perimeter, and there is no room to expand in any direction. But the club have developed their older stands well, and with an array of advertising and signs the ground appears much livelier than in previous years. When full there is nowhere for the noise to escape but upwards. Perhaps in the long run, therefore, lack of space has been a blessing in disguise for Derby: they have a compact ground, easily converted with extra seats, but large enough for the likely size of audience attracted to top-class football.

NOTTINGHAM
·FOREST·

Previous Grounds

As the third oldest club in the League, Forest have had more time to change grounds than most, and it is ironic that after so much wandering they should settle on the other side of the Trent from Nottingham, in West Bridgford. Thanks to Arthur Turner's centenary history of the club, there is a detailed record of the club's first five homes, beginning at the ground which gave them their name, the Forest Racecourse. This was a large open space, 'the recreational lung of the town', where the club formed in 1865. Its members had first met to play not the newly formulated Association game, but a North Country variation of hockey known as shinny. The first use of a referee's whistle was recorded at this ground, in a game between Forest and Sheffield Norfolk in 1878. But if large crowds were expected, Forest sometimes played at an enclosed ground in Beeston, as for example when they played Notts County in 1878, in front of 500 people! Today the Forest hosts the annual Nottingham Goose Fair.

In 1879 the club moved to a ground called the Meadows which for several seasons had been the home of Notts County. Forest moved on after only a year, to the most famous sporting venue in the town, Trent Bridge Cricket Ground. They might have stayed here for longer than two years had not rivals County moved in. County's version of the 1883 move suggests that Forest were less desirable tenants of the cricket ground (see Notts County).

From 1882–85 the club played at Parkside, Lenton, at a ground which cost £300 to prepare. The location of this ground is thought to be near Cottesmore School. A further £500 was spent on the Gregory Ground, also in Lenton, where they played until 1890. Apparently, neither of these venues had any proper accommodation for members of the press. 'We hope a desk or table will be supplied as on most grounds in the country,' wrote one disgruntled reporter, adding pointedly, 'Notts have not finished laying out Trent Bridge but it is their intention to erect a covered desk.' But the major problem at Lenton was not the discomfiture of the press so much as the public's apathy, and having turned professional in 1889, the club needed all the support it could muster.

So in 1890 Forest returned to the Trent Bridge area, to a place called Woodward's Field, close to the Towns Arms public house at Trent Bridge on Bunbury Street. This new home, the Town Ground, cost £1000 and required considerable effort to level the pitch, build banking and erect a stand seating 1000 spectators. It was, wrote Turner, a great source of pride that this stand possessed a roof, and that the press had at last been properly accommodated.

The Town Ground was opened on 3 October 1890 in rather awkward circumstances. At Trent Bridge on the same afternoon, Notts County were staging a League match v. Bolton. Forest had invited another League club, Wolves, to play in the first game at their ground, and County naturally objected. So Forest played the Scottish club Queen's Park instead, winning 4-1 in front of around 3000 spectators, while about 6000 saw the League fixture. Since County's use of Trent Bridge was restricted at the beginning and end of each season because cricket always took priority, the Town Ground was often used to stage County's home games, just as Forest had sometimes shared The Meadows with County in the late 1880s.

Continuing in their tradition of pioneering new developments, Forest staged the first official match using goalnets, between representative teams from the north and south, at the Town Ground in January 1891. In 1898, after winning the FA Cup at Crystal Palace, Forest made their final move across the River Trent to their present ground. Thus they left the Town Ground in the city of Nottingham, for the City Ground in West Bridgford. Their old home became a tram depot and is still used by the local transport department.

The City Ground

The City Ground was only a couple of hundred yards across the river from Forest's previous home, and was almost next door to the cricket ground where Notts County had played since 1882. Despite their Cup triumph the club still needed to raise an extra £3000 to prepare the new ground and so they asked supporters and local businessmen to buy bonds worth £5 each. (The club was run by a committee, and did not become a limited company until 1982, the last League club to do so.) They were able to save some money due to the efforts of a committee member, William Bardill, a landscape gardener and nurseryman. He must have been one of the first men (and there are so many 'firsts' in the Forest's history) to appreciate the value of a proper sub-soil for drainage. Accordingly he laid a 2-foot deep layer of clinker, on top of which he put high-quality turf from Radcliffe-on-Trent, brought to the site on river barges.

But if there were no complaints about the pitch, the rest of the ground left much to be desired, if compared for example with Villa Park, opened the year before, or Roker Park, opened in the same month, September 1898. This was partly because there was always a limit on how much money individual committee members could obtain guarantees for from the bank.

Forest spent most of the inter-war years in Division Two, but it must not be forgotten that they were again responsible for introducing a now commonplace feature; elliptical-shaped goalposts, first seen in 1921 at the City Ground. Apart from this innovation, the ground did not alter until the 1950s. The

The two Nottingham grounds: Meadow Lane (above the River Trent) and the City Ground. Notice the old Trent Bridge Stand at the Meadow Lane End and the old East Stand at Forest

West Stand was identical to one built by the same contractors at Meadow Lane in 1910, with a barrel roof. At the Trent End was also a barrel roof and on the East side was a simple flat roof cover.

There were two proposals in the 1930s; that Forest and County should amalgamate, and that the City Ground be used for greyhound racing. The former was scotched when the fans called a protest meeting. The latter, even though supported by the Corporation, Forest's landlords, was disallowed by the FA which did not approve of gambling. So the City Ground and both Nottingham clubs continued to fight for survival.

The War left Forest relatively unscathed, bombs causing £75 worth of damage to the pitch in May 1941. Far worse, however, was in March 1947 when the Trent burst its banks, flooded the ground as high as the crossbars, and so brought about the unusual sight of swans swimming gracefully across the pitch. Forest beat a soggy retreat over the Bridge and sought refuge at Meadow Lane.

Forest began the 1950s by winning the Third Division South (a year after County had achieved the same distinction), and in an optimistic mood drew up plans for redeveloping the City Ground. The initial scheme proposed the erection of a stand at the Trent End, and when this was effected in 1954 with the building of the present standing enclosure, it was hoped to be able to build a new block between the Trent End and the West Stand, comprising offices and dressing rooms. In addition, the Trent End roof

was to be lifted off and a seating tier added above to make it into a double-decker. Quite why this over-elaborate plan was hatched is not clear, since it would have been much simpler to install seating on either of the other two sides. Perhaps the plan also included extra facilities overlooking the River Trent. Of course the Trent End roof has remained undisturbed ever since.

In 1958 a new stand was built on the East Side, providing an extra 2500 seats. Costing only £40 000, it was not a very sophisticated construction – it even lacked toilets – situated at the back of the open terracing, but it at least improved the situation while Forest were back in Division One for the first time since 1925. The open Bridgford End was also improved and extended at this time.

Forest were the second but last First Division club to install floodlights, used first in September 1961 for a League Cup match v. Gillingham. Meanwhile, the old West Stand was reaching the point of collapse – although County's seemed solid enough (but had never been submerged in water) – so between 1962–65 it was reroofed, enlarged and refurbished and new offices were added. The City Ground's highest gate was on 28 October 1967. Forest had finished the previous season in second place behind Manchester United, and when the two clubs met on that day, 49 945 attended. After the floods of 1947 came flames in 1968. On 24 August during a game v. Leeds United, the Main Stand caught fire, the match was abandoned and the spectators and players could only watch from the pitch as the whole building was gutted. But at least everyone escaped from the stand without serious injury, mainly because, unlike the Bradford situation in 1985, there was easy access to the pitch and a modern roof which did not ignite. When the smoke subsided it was found that the columns and girders remained intact, so this time the stand was refitted entirely in concrete and steel, with seats in the paddock.

Forest slipped back into Division Two for a while, but in 1977 returned with a vengeance. A run of success made them League Champions in their first season after promotion, League Cup and European Cup winners twice each in successive seasons, plus runners-up in other years, when they picked up other sundry Cups around the world.

Inevitably, the East Stand was demolished after only 20 years, having proved unsafe under the 1975 Act, and in its place arose a mighty new structure, the new East or 'Executive' Stand costing £2·5 million. Opened in 1980, it closely resembled a stand erected at Molineux – a long, angled cantilever with two tiers of seating divided by a line of executive boxes. The architects were Husband and Company of Sheffield, also responsible for the magnificent cantilever stand at Hillsborough, built 20 years earlier.

The new stand reduced the City Ground's capacity from over 40 000 to 35 507, but raised the number of seats from 6500 to 14 789. No doubt the rates have risen dramatically over the years, but the rent Forest pay to the council is still a peppercorn amount of £750 a year.

Ground Description

Of all the English Football League clubs, Forest and Notts County are closest together, just 400 yards apart with the River Trent between. (In Scotland, Dundee and Dundee United are even closer, and in non-League football, Witton Albion and Northwich Victoria are also near neighbours. Liverpool and Everton's grounds are 800 yards apart.) The City Ground is more prominent than Meadow Lane, by virtue of the height of the Executive Stand, which can be seen almost from the city centre.

The Main or West Stand itself is a simple but unusual construction. In design it is cranked very slightly inwards at each end, barely noticeable except when standing under the roof, which is supported by a prominent and exposed horizontal cross girder, housing the television camera platform and gangway. The stand's colouring is similar to that of Anfield; red seats, metallic grey steelwork, and a low white perimeter wall.

From here to the right is the open Bridgford End, terraced banking over which is a large electric scoreboard which has the irritating ability to spew out continuous advertisements throughout a game, so that one only has to look up from the action for a second to be told where to buy the best fish and chips in Nottingham or the cheapest engagement rings in

Long Eaton. If spectators find it diverting during a tedious game, how much more distracting it must be for the players, if only because at night it flashes on and off repeatedly.

The Executive Stand is practically identical to those at Molineux and White Hart Lane, but with some important differences. At the City Ground the Stand is not cranked, and the cantilever roof girders are exposed beneath the roof panelling, which at the other two grounds is suspended, therefore hiding the steelwork. There is one line of boxes and 'Forest' is written in white seats amid the red seats. If any club can afford the enormous outlay, stands of this design are outstandingly efficient; they will mark the 1980s as effectively as Leitch's work did during the period before the Second World War (see Design).

The Executive Stand, all red and white, streamlined and tall, positively dominates the City Ground. Next to it, the Trent End cover looks quite preposterous, especially from the Bridgford End. It has a conventional sloping roof, pitched low over a fairly small bank of terracing, and on a crowded afternoon, clear vision from here can be quite a strain.

Behind this end, only a few yards away is the River Trent. From the Bridgford End you can see Meadow Lane's floodlight pylons above the Trent End roof, and Trent Bridge cricket ground behind to your left. From the very top of the Executive Stand is an unimpeded view of either, with the town centre clearly visible to the right. The tall, curved block behind the West Stand was once a hotel, and is now the Rushcliffe Civic Centre. Behind the new stand is the club car park.

The pitch is no longer of bowling-green quality, as claimed during its early years, but has been considerably improved recently. Drainage is a serious problem because the pitch and the land on which the ground is built is lower than the level of drains in nearby districts, so that water comes up through the drains after a heavy storm. Forest have tried protecting the turf with a plastic cover raised above the pitch with blowers. You can see the installations behind the Bridgford End goal, along the perimeter fence. As other clubs discovered, this was not the remedy once hoped for (see Pitches) and the cover is now used mainly as protection against rain in the hours before a match.

As the entrance way suggests and the interior confirms, the City Ground is a Second Division ground in new clothes. Seated spectators can have no complaints, but if the club have any available capital they would be wise to concentrate on both ends of the ground and thus give the East and West Stands worthy neighbours. Perhaps then County and Forest might be persuaded to share these excellent facilities for football, while converting the outdated Meadow Lane Ground into a multi-sport complex convenient for either club's training purposes.

⋄NOTTS COUNTY⋄

Previous Grounds

Older than the FA itself, Notts County are the doyens of the Football League. They formed in 1862, and like all sporting clubs of the time were strictly for 'gentlemen only'. The name 'County' signified their genteel leanings. They first played at Park Hollow, part of the private park next to Nottingham Castle. For two years the members played games only among themselves, until in December 1864 County finally turned out against another club, in a 20-a-side game on The Meadows Cricket Ground. This open space became their regular pitch until 1877, although for important matches County hired the Trent Bridge Cricket Ground, then privately owned.

County moved in October 1877, in keeping with their image, to the home of the Gentlemen of Notts Cricket Club, Beeston. If necessary, they still used Trent Bridge, such as when they played Derbyshire on 30 November 1878 in one of the earliest floodlit games. November 1880 saw them at the Castle Cricket Ground, near the town centre, where they played until 1883. Until that time, Forest had been renting Trent Bridge from its new owners, Nottinghamshire County Cricket Club, but they left in 1883 for a new ground in Lenton. Keith Warsop, the Notts County historian, suggests that County's arrival in 1883 at Trent Bridge in place of Forest might have been engineered by the cricket club's secretary, Edwin Browne, who immediately assumed a similar post with Notts County. County's first game as permanent tenants of Trent Bridge was v. Walsall Swifts in September 1883.

At this ground County put aside their former inclinations and turned professional in 1885, becoming founder members of the Football League in 1888. But cricket still took priority at Trent Bridge and each September and April County had to find alternative venues for home fixtures. In the 1880s they used The Meadows and the Castle grounds again, and thereafter until 1908, used whatever ground Forest had at the time. For this reason alone, Trent Bridge was hardly a suitable venue for a League team, although unlike Bramall Lane and the County Ground, Northampton, the ground's owners did at least permit County to rest a portable wooden stand on the open touchline. The club had to move this stand occasionally to prevent wear and tear on the turf.

A more serious handicap was County's lack of support at Trent Bridge. An all-time low attendance for any normal scheduled League match was recorded at the ground when an estimated crowd of 300 saw County v. Crewe Alexandra in Division Two, on 17 February 1894. Such a pitiful turn-out is even more surprising in view of the fact that only a month later County won the FA Cup. No less baffling was one of the lowest attendances ever recorded for a First Division match at Trent Bridge, when 1500 were estimated to have watched County v. Preston North End on 27 March 1901. This was near the close of County's best season in Division One for a decade.

As early as 1905, the Football League had made it clear County should find a home they could use all through the season. Apparently certain clubs threatened by relegation had complained that while some teams had had to play County at 'home' on Forest's ground (when Trent Bridge was being used by the cricketers), they had had to play their fixtures v. County at Trent Bridge. The League agreed this was hardly fair and County began a half-hearted search for new premises.

It was not until 1910 that they moved, the final impetus coming from the cricket club who were anxious to see the footballers leave, even though the football pitch barely enroached on the cricket field – it was on the Fox Road Side of the ground, used mainly as a practice area by the cricketers. Perhaps feeling some pressure, County decided to sell their ground rights in the 1st Round of the FA Cup, when they were drawn to play Bradford City at Trent Bridge.

At last stirred into action, County found their future home across the River Trent, not far from where Forest's old Town Ground had been. Their final match at Trent Bridge was on 16 April 1910 v. Aston Villa.

Meadow Lane

Before County moved to the ground in 1910 as council tenants, Meadow Lane was open ground next to a cattle market. With admirable speed, the contractors managed to erect the steelwork and roof of the new Main Stand in just nine days (and some would say, 70 or more years later, 'it looks like it!') for £3000. Once fitted out, the total cost came to £10 000. The stand was identical to one at the City Ground, built by the same company a few years before.

At the south end of the ground nearest the Trent was placed a small wooden stand, seating 1400, which the club had literally floated across the river from Trent Bridge. It was probably the oldest stand in the League before being torn down in 1978, older

The County Road Stand, Meadow Lane

145

even than the Gordon Road Stand at Priestfield Stadium. It may have been the portable stand mentioned earlier. The other two sides were open terracing, the County Road Side having an open stream, Tinkers Brook, running down to the Trent. A man with a long pole, cane basket on the end, would be stationed by the brook to fish out the ball during games. Naturally, Meadow Lane was opened with a friendly match against Forest, on 3 September 1910.

The Army took over Meadow Lane for much of the First World War, and this gap, together with some unlucky draws in the FA Cup, meant that County did not play a Cup tie at their new ground until January 1920, ten years after moving there. In 1923 the club built a new stand on the County Road Side, actually on top of the banking, over the Tinkers Brook. The terracing under the roof was wooden, and the stand sported a simple triangular gable, a lovable feature of Meadow Lane ever since.

In 1941, despite or because of a machine gun emplacement on the open Kop, bombs destroyed the northern wing of the Main Stand and cratered the pitch so badly County had to withdraw from the wartime League competition. Then during the winter of 1946–47, when prisoners of war were used to clear the pitch of snow, the Trent submerged Meadow Lane only marginally less than the City Ground. Being further from the river banks and slightly higher, Meadow Lane drained more quickly and suffered less than Forest's ground and for a time the clubs again shared their facilities. This happened once more in 1968, when Forest's Main Stand was gutted by fire.

Floodlights were installed at Meadow Lane in 1953, long before Forest's, and first switched on for a friendly v. Derby County on 23 March. How appropriate, for County's opponents in that first ever Nottingham floodlit game in 1878 had been Derbyshire. The lights were too basic for modern usage, however, and in 1962 they were updated.

The occasion of Meadow Lane's highest crowd was not a happy one because 47 310 watched Third Division York City beat Second Division County in the 6th Round of the FA Cup on 12 March 1955. In more recent years the capacity of the ground was reduced to 30 000, until in the late 1970s, both County's improved form and the introduction of the Safety of Sports Grounds Act dictated great changes. Sadly, the old wooden stand on the Meadow Lane End had to be demolished, although many supporters felt it might have gone in a more dignified way – it was after all probably the oldest stand in the League. In its place arose a huge, blank, brick wall, the back of an £800 000 sports complex, the Meadow Club. The complex was built because the club had won promotion to Division One in 1981 but knew that gates were unlikely to average more than 10 000 to 12 000; insufficient to keep County among the top few without extra income. With such low gates they also realized that extra accommodation behind the Meadow Lane goal would not be necessary and so left a void between the goal and the wall. The sports centre also had changing rooms installed, taking them out of the antiquated Main Stand. For a few seasons this blank wall was a real eyesore until, as described below, extra features were added.

Less dramatic was the installation of seats onto the wooden terracing in the centre of the County Road Stand. Even without the sports centre, since 1981 a total of £1·5 million has been spent on improving Meadow Lane just to keep the existing facilities in use. The present capacity is 24 077, of which only 3998 are seats.

Ground Description

Despite its name, Meadow Lane is about as rural as the Boleyn Ground is Tudor. The ground is surrounded on all sides by light industry, Tinkers Brook has been concreted over, and the Trent is hidden from view by factory buildings.

The main entrance is in Meadow Lane, by the new sports centre and offices, behind which runs the Main Stand at a right angle. It has a barrel roof, angled slightly towards the centre. The metal work is black and white, like the rest of the ground, but the seats are for some reason blue. In the centre of the roof a television camera gantry has been built. Notice at the Kop End of the stand, the roof panelling reveals where bomb damage was inflicted during the War. In front is an uncovered paddock. Outdated it most certainly is, but refurbishing can make even the most dilapidated look new.

From here, to the left is the uncovered Spion Kop, topped by a lovely half-time scoreboard with a clock, glass-panelled front, and loudspeaker hailers on each side. New black barriers against the light concrete give this bank a neat appearance. Until being completely renewed in 1981, it was one of the last cinder and timber terraces left in the League. From the summit, Forest's ground is clearly visible straight ahead, but otherwise the view is dominated by industry. Behind are two five-a-side pitches (one covered), and beyond them is Iremonger Road, named after County's long-serving goalkeeper, Albert Iremonger,

Notts County's new sports centre with private boxes before completion

who made a record total of 602 appearances between 1905–26.

Opposite the Main Stand is the County Road Stand, with the familiar pointed gable proudly announcing the club's name, 'established 1862'. Many visitors assume the stand must be as old, but it dates back only to the 1920s. It lies at the back of an uncovered terrace, built up on stilts above what used to be the open brook. All the terracing under the sloping roof is wooden, with an impromptu metal framework in the centre supporting 460 seats. Underneath this charming stand is a small prefab hut used by the supporters' club. From County Road itself, the stand looks remarkably like a chicken house, with wooden shutters along its rear wall. In the Meadow Lane corner, where the scoreboard used to stand, is a tall flagpole.

Finally we come to the solid mass of the Meadow Club sports centre, a few yards behind the Meadow Lane goal. Until recently its blank brick wall quite destroyed the four-sided integrity so vital to any football ground's appearance, but this bleak effect has now happily been alleviated.

At the top are 18 sleek, glass-fronted executive boxes, jutting out of the wall. Higher than Leicester's rather oddly situated boxes, these at County must create in their users feelings of either splendid isolation or lonely disjointedness.

Under the boxes is an 18-foot high patch of brick wall, its bareness now somewhat brightened by advertisements. At the foot of the wall, on the Main Stand side, is a sloping green cover from which the players now emerge. This cover houses not the dressing rooms – they are inside the centre – but the centre's boiler equipment. The cover is sloped so the club have the option to install seating on it.

But the most immediate way to restore the ground's fourth side was to put people behind the goal, and there is now a small terrace in front of the Meadow Club, reserved for juniors and holding 2500. The Meadow Club itself has a sports hall, squash courts and various other facilities and is reckoned to have over 10 000 users a year. Even with its terrace, boxes and boiler it can hardly be described as a pleasing or attractive end to the ground, but its current outlook is at least a vast improvement on the bleak exterior which greeted supporters in its early years.

Although out of the First Division since 1984, County have invested so much in Meadow Lane that plans such as the one in the 1970s for a joint stadium with Forest on Colwick Park Racecourse must now be regarded as dead and buried. As at Liverpool and Dundee, Nottingham's two senior grounds may only be separated by a few hundred yards but in terms of ground sharing they are as far apart as ever.

·MANSFIELD TOWN·

Previous Grounds
Records indicate there was a Mansfield team playing on Parr's cricket field in 1870, and certainly there were several teams in early soccer history with the name Mansfield Town. But the present club's roots date back probably to 1894, to a team known as Mansfield Wesleyans. Their ground was off Newgate Lane, in the area now occupied by Pelham Street and Stanhope Street. This was bought by the local railway company, so the club moved to a ground in Broxtowe Drive, with the dubious title of 'The Prairie'. In 1905 as Mansfield Town they moved to Field Mill, which until then had been the home of Mansfield Mechanics, one of the town's former leading clubs.

Field Mill
Mansfield purchased Field Mill from the Duke of Portland, who issued a covenant stating that the ground must always be used for sporting activities. With the town expanding rapidly, and development swallowing up many open spaces this was a wise precaution. Field Mill was at least a lush patch of green in an increasingly drab town.

Mansfield Town became national news when in January 1929 they went to Molineux in the 3rd Round of the FA Cup and beat Wolves 1-0. Two years later Mansfield were elected to the League. At that time there was one stand at Field Mill, a very low wooden construction on the West Side. Before this the players had changed in the Bull's Head Inn on Portland Street and had to enter the ground along a footpath, which still exists, behind the North Stand. Field Mill was also used for greyhound racing during the 1930s.

Just before the Second World War the existing Bishop Street Stand was built, and this became the main stand, seating 1100. Next to it in the south east corner, were dressing room huts. There is still a gap in the perimeter fence through which the players used to enter the field.

The record crowd of 24 479 was in January 1953, when neighbours Nottingham Forest visited in the FA Cup 3rd Round. Soon after the club built the cover over the North End. It had to be angled to fit the curved terracing which had been shaped round the greyhound track 20 years earlier. Their most important investment was the purchase of the training ground behind the West Stand, which was itself redeveloped completely from 1959. Mansfield bought a complete steel-framed stand from Hurst Park racecourse in South London for £30 000, and erected it behind the original West Stand (a method copied by Swindon and Chester in later years). By the time the framework was filled in with new offices, dressing

The West Stand at Field Mill. The roof is similar in design to one seen at Highbury

rooms and social facilities in 1961, the bill had come to an enormous £200 000. In the same year Sheffield Wednesday opened their new cantilever stand at Hillsborough, and although it did not have any such facilities underneath, was much more sophisticated and £50 000 cheaper. For a Fourth Division club – a not very successful one at that – it was an extremely ambitious, and some might say foolhardy, investment. The wooden stand was demolished and a concrete paddock built in its place, in front of the new stand.

Also in 1961 Field Mill's floodlights were switched on for the first time, by Billy Wright, for Mansfield's League Cup tie v. Cardiff City on 5 October. Field Mill was thus one of the most modern and well-equipped grounds outside the Second Division. Designation under the Safety of Sports Grounds Act in 1985, however, reduced the capacity quite considerably from 23 500 to 8000, including 2200 seats, although this last figure would rise a year later when the Bishop Street Stand was renovated. Overall £200 000 was spent on safety work.

Ground Description

Similar to Elland Road, the main entrance brings you into a car park lying between the stand and the training ground, where there is one full size and two five-a-side floodlit pitches, shared with the local community. From 1984–86 Field Mill was also home to a Rugby League team.

The West Stand facade is less grand than that at Leeds, but for a small club is quietly impressive; although like so many buildings of the 1950s and 1960s it is now quite dated. But the stand itself is a gem. It looks like a plastic kit, like an artist's impression from an old soccer annual of what a modern stand should resemble. In fact, the only stands which

bear any similarity to it in design are the two at Highbury, albeit more luxurious by far. The date of its original construction at Hurst Park racecourse is not certain – it could have been the 1930s or, more probably, a post-war model of streamlined efficiency.

The slightly pitched roof is concealed as at Highbury by a wide, overhanging awning, or 'marquise' with deep ribbed fascia, carrying round each side of the stand. The seating tier, with glass screen ends, protrudes beyond the line of the back wall like a modern cantilever, which indeed the roof would be but for one, very thin supporting pillar in the centre. A high concrete paddock rear wall divides the stand from the uncovered terraces in front. Although the stand has little colour, only steel and concrete, it has far more style and authority than many stands built since in more modern materials and designs. For the lover of football architecture, therefore, it is a rare landmark.

From here, to the right is the open Quarry Lane End, slightly curved because of the old greyhound track, with the supporters' club's headquarters behind. A half-time scoreboard is tucked into the far corner.

Opposite is the Bishop Street Stand, about 50 yards long, on the half-way line. The old dressing rooms were to the right. It is a fairly typical small stand of the lower divisions, with bench seats and glass screens at either end. The stand was closed for one season until safety work could be afforded.

To the left is the covered North Stand. The roof, covering half the terracing, is nicely capped by an advertisement hoarding with a clock in the centre.

Field Mill occupies 9½ acres of land, all owned by the club, full of potential, and the envy of many other clubs. Indeed the West Stand would not look out of place at a First Division ground.

·LINCOLN CITY·

Previous Grounds

A Lincoln FC existed as far back as 1860, but the present club dates from 1883, to a ground off the High Street called John O'Gaunt's. It was also known as the 'Cow Pat' because cows were allowed to graze on the pitch. An early floodlit game was played here in 1888 and Lincoln began their League career at the ground in 1892, as founder members of Division Two. Space was limited, however, and so in 1894 City moved to Sincil Bank. John O'Gaunt's was situated where Abbott and Sibthorp Streets now stand.

Sincil Bank

Lincoln's ground takes its name from Sincil Drain, not an open sewer but a conduit serving as an overflow from the River Witham which flows through the centre of the city. The drain formed the west side of the ground. When Lincoln moved here in 1894 the supporters rallied round to build earth banks, prepare the pitch and erect a small wooden grandstand. A second wooden stand was built behind the south goal, known as the South Park Stand, but both stands were quite small and primitive.

Definitely the lowest attendance for a first-class match at Sincil Bank was during the First World War. Bradford City were to meet Norwich City in a 2nd Round replay in 1915, but the FA ordered that it be played behind closed doors, so as not to interfere with work at the nearby munitions factory. This was in response to a debate in the House of Commons

about the apparent shortage of shells at the battle of Neuve Chapelle in March 1915 and the failure of some to explode. The Government blamed the munitions workers, who were said to be drawing high wages and idling around in public houses. Hence the official attendance of nil at Sincil Bank for that Cup replay – although 200 people were unofficially present. (Far more drastic was the Government's legislation which imposed afternoon closure on every public house, in an attempt to boost munitions' production. The law has remained with us ever since.) The South Park Stand was burnt down in 1924 and replaced with a wood and brick construction a year later. Until then all the club's offices and the dressing rooms had been under the South Park Stand, but these were now moved to the Main or St Andrew's Stand, built soon after the First World War.

During a spell in Division Two, 1948–49, one observer wrote in the *FA Yearbook*: 'Spectators at Lincoln's Sincil Bank ground are well known to visiting sides for their hearty and sustained cheering . . . a Hampden Roar in miniature . . .' The pitch was also described as 'one of the finest stretches of turf in the country'.

City's longest run in Division Two since the War was between 1952–61. At that time there was a very small wooden stand perched upon the top of Sincil Terrace, seating 200. In 1956 the supporters raised money to build a cover in the north east corner, linked to the simple pre-war cover at the North or Railway End.

Lincoln were on their way down to the Fourth Division when their first floodlights were installed.

View from the South Park Stand at Sincil Bank looking over the railway to the Cathedral

The president of the supporters' club officially switched them on for the Third Division game v. Barnsley on 31 January 1962. The lights have been updated since, and the original ones sold to Spalding United.

Lincoln's highest attendance came for a rare clash with a top team in the League Cup in 1967. A crowd of 23 196 saw City go down to Derby in a 4th Round replay on 25 November 1967. In the summer of 1982 the ground was sold to the local council for £225 000, and rented back for £11 000 a year on a 21-year lease, with the option to repurchase it within three years, should Lincoln's finances have improved by then. They did not, and although in the meantime City were rocked by various boardroom struggles these were nothing to the shock Sincil Bank received in 1985 following the Bradford fire.

Firstly, part of the Railway End terrace roof had to be dismantled when the structure was found to be unsafe. Worse, the main St Andrew's Stand was condemned as a fire risk (ironically there is a fire station just a few yards behind the stand). It was allowed to remain in use during the 1985–86 season while the ground's only other seating, in the South Park Stand, was fireproofed at a cost of £20 000, leaving Lincoln with a capacity reduced from 16 225 to 12 167 with 1300 seats. But in the summer of 1986 the Main Stand had to be demolished entirely, giving Sincil Bank a capacity during 1986–87 of only 8968 with 600 seats, all in the South Park Stand.

Work on a replacement 1600-seat Main Stand began during that season at an estimated cost of £1 million, over half of which was put forward by the local council, who were to have a community centre incorporated underneath the stand.

Then on 9 May 1987 disaster struck, not in the stand but on the pitch. Lincoln finished bottom of the Fourth Division and thus became the first League side to be automatically relegated to the Vauxhall Conference. So while Scarborough took their place, Lincoln were left with a half-built, expensive stand and an uncertain future. Spirits remained high however. The council stayed loyal, work continued and the new stand was due to open in September 1987. Nothing limp about these Imps; there is life outside the League after all.

Ground Description

The approach to the ground along Sincil Bank is like a winding country road, barely wide enough for a team coach, with open playing fields on one side and Sincil Drain on the other. Even with the recent changes, the ground retains much of its picturesque qualities. Indeed the old stands' main merit was their ability to display dozens of advertisements on every possible surface. Organized muddle was perhaps the best description. Patrons of the Main Stand would appear to peer through a narrow slit between two levels of hoardings, on the perimeter and the roof.

The new St Andrew's Stand, when completed, will be a straightforward post and beam construction, hardly a break from tradition given Lincoln's limited budget, but from the spectators' point of view a vast improvement. It will have one tier of seating with a plain, sloping roof and of course advertisements along the fascia board.

Like its predecessor it will not fill the whole side. The changing rooms remain in a low block in the south east corner, in a building originally intended as an air-raid shelter.

From here, to the left is an open terrace with the remains of the South Park Stand behind. This too was like an advertising sandwich board with seats tucked in the middle. The surviving section houses Lincoln's social club with bench seats above. The original front paddock was unused after 1975, when a front wall collapsed during a League Cup tie v. Stoke. Behind this end is the undulating green of the South Common.

Opposite the Main Stand is the open Sincil Terrace, which fortunately survived the safety inspectors' scrutiny. Until the South Park Stand is cut down, Sincil Bank is one of the only four British League grounds having two covered ends but one uncovered side (the others are at Brighton, Peterborough and Ayr – The Valley is, alas, no more). The terrace is very attractive, with brown concrete steps, red streamlined barriers, and a clock in the centre, and it is framed by trees which run along the bank of Sincil Drain, behind the terrace. A detention centre is on the far side. Along the perimeter wall the foundations of the old dug-outs are visible. To the right is the Railway End, which now provides the only standing cover at Sincil Bank. The roof at the nearest corner was taken down in 1985, even though it was actually newer than the surviving section behind the goal. Again the roof and perimeter are laden with advertisements, but sadly the railway from which this end took its name is now closed.

When trains did once pass by, they appeared to be gliding along the top of the terrace roof. Beyond the Railway End, you can just make out the towers of Lincoln Cathedral and the Castle.

Sincil Bank's pitch is still a fine stretch of turf, largely due to its natural sand base. Even though Sincil Drain may flood two or three times a year, the pitch, which drains away in the opposite direction to the east, is never affected.

Bruised and bewildered though Sincil Bank undoubtedly was by the events of 1985 and 1987, there can be no doubt that the enforced changes will, eventually, make Sincil Bank a better venue for the spectator. But in common with Hartlepool and Northampton, Lincoln will take years to recover from the aftermath of the Bradford fire. How ironic therefore that Lincoln were Bradford's opponents on that fateful May afternoon, when years of complacency in the matter of ground design came to a sudden and painful end. Valley Parade was only the first casualty.

·CHESTERFIELD·

Previous Grounds

Chesterfield is the fourth oldest club in the League, dating back to 1866. For some years the club played on a site called Spital, near the town centre, until moving to the Recreation Ground on Saltergate in 1884, where football had been played since at least 1870.

The Recreation Ground

For many years the Recreation Ground was little more than an enclosed field, with a small cover on the half-way line along Compton Street. A photograph taken during Chesterfield's first spell of ten years in the League, when for a time the club was called Chesterfield Town, shows a clear view from one side of the ground to the famous crooked spire in the heart of Chesterfield. In 1921 the club bought the site from the corporation and rejoined the League.

On promotion to Division Two in 1936, Chesterfield built the existing Main Stand on the east side along St Margaret's Drive.

The ground's record crowd of 30 968 came just before the War in April 1939, when Newcastle United were the visitors in an end-of-season Second Division match. After a good Cup run at the beginning of the 1950s the Compton Street cover was extended, the playing surface raised to improve drainage, and all the standing areas properly terraced.

In 1961 the Chesterfield and District Sportsman's Association helped erect the cover over the Kop on Saltergate, at a cost of £10 000.

The Recreation Ground holds the unhappy distinction of being the last League ground to have floodlights installed. A £10 000 appeal fund was launched in 1964, in the hope of having a set in time for the club's centenary in 1966, but the ones bought from Sheffield United proved to be totally unsuitable. After erecting only one pylon, which was too short, the bases were found to be insecure, so Chesterfield sold

The Recreation Ground, Chesterfield

the unwanted set to Stafford Rangers and bought new ones. These were switched on in the presence of Sir Stanley Rous, for a friendly v. Sheffield Wednesday on 18 October 1967, more than 16 years after the start of the modern floodlit era. Ironically Chesterfield had been one of the first clubs to have a floodlit training pitch as far back as 1956.

Safety work in 1985–86 costing £150 000 included putting up perimeter fences, rebuilding the entrance to the Main Stand and providing exits from the seating down to pitch level. The current capacity is 11 200 including 2200 seats.

Ground Description

The ground stands on a rise above the town centre and can be easily spotted from a distance. Saltergate itself is a main thoroughfare, but once in St Margaret's Drive all is tranquil suburbia, into which the football club must fit without disturbing the decorum. It succeeds in this assiduously, for the Recreation Ground is a neat, unfussy place.

The Main Stand is a plain, typically 1930s design, adapted for the 1980s by safety exits leading from the upper seating tier to the narrow front paddock, which is now unused. There are 13 new exits, each with 13 steps. An asbestos sheet roof parallels the rake of the seats. The formula is simple, and is executed with the minumum of additional detail.

To the right is the open Cross Street End, a low bank of terracing attractively backed by a castellated wall. Behind is a primary school. From here the famous crooked spire is to your left, now obscured by the Main Stand. In the far corner is a group of turnstiles built by supporters in 1939 after that record attendance.

To the left is the covered Kop, behind which is the social club and Saltergate. Again, the Kop roof demonstrates the timelessness of football ground architecture, for here, put up in the same year as Sheffield Wednesday built their famous cantilever stand, is a cover which might have been a contemporary of the 1936 Main Stand. But having said that, one should add that the design persisted because it was fairly successful, and is improved at Chesterfield by light-coloured paintwork, neat walls and some flagpoles. A plaque over the rear entrance reminds spectators who paid for it, which might account for its pristine condition. Not a barrier or step is out of place.

Opposite the Main Stand is the narrow and low Compton Street Stand, sometimes called the Popular Side. It is distinguished by a line of deep advertising hoardings across the roof, interrupted only in the centre by a wooden box protruding above the roof, as high as the stand itself. This is used by television cameras. The brightest feature of the ground is the orange running track. Otherwise all is quiet and orderly; the small town Third Division spirit perfectly encapsulated.

· 12 ·
CENTRAL, SOUTH AND SOUTH COAST

· OXFORD UNITED ·

Manor Ground

Oxford may have had only a short League career but their history goes back to 1896. Originally called Headington United, they played on a ground next to the Britannia Inn. Shortly before the First World War United moved to Manor Park, a large sports ground used by several amateur organizations. In 1921 the Headington Sports Ground Company Limited formed and bought the ground, then sub-let to United, as well as to cricket, bowls and tennis clubs. There was a small pavilion on the south side, where the Main Stand is now, and sheep and horses used to graze on the pitch during the week. The slope was so severe that whenever a batsman aimed towards the bottom corner he was sure of a rapid boundary.

The situation in Oxford was very similar to Cambridge in that there were two clubs – City and United – and either could have become the senior one. It was Headington who turned professional, leaving the Spartan League to join the Southern League in 1949.

At that point the other sporting clubs vacated the Manor Ground and left United as sole tenants. One of the first things the club did was to build a small stand in the south west corner, seating 180, with dressing rooms underneath. This was opened in October 1949.

A year later an event occurred at the Manor Ground which gives Headington a hallowed place in the annals of football ground history. Headington United were the first professional club in Britain to install floodlighting at their ground. They were only temporary lights, borrowed from those Oxford Colleges which lit up their façades at night, mounted on 36 wooden poles, but they were the first! (See Floodlights) The first recorded match under lights at the Manor Ground took place on 18 December 1950, when Headington played a friendly v. Banbury Spencer (now Banbury United) in aid of local hospitals.

Then in 1953–54, Headington met Millwall in the FA Cup at The Den and managed a draw. They approached the FA and asked to stage the replay under floodlights. Predictably, permission was refused (the first FA Cup match under lights was not until September 1955), but the story received national press coverage and Bill Shankly was quoted as saying, 'Good luck to little Headington for having the pluck to ask a very, very important question, and arouse interest which could be a portent for the future.'

In 1953 Headington won their first Southern League Championship and purchased the ground from the owners, who were close to liquidation, for the sum of £10 000. In 1957 the supporters' club presented United with £33 000 to pay for the new Main Stand built in place of the old pavilion, and the dressing rooms were transferred there from the corner stand. There were 1600 seats and the stand was opened on 24 August 1957 by Denis Follows of the FA. At the same time, the 36 wooden poles were taken down and four pylons erected for the floodlights. Headington were on their way up.

In 1960 the club changed their name to Oxford United and proceeded to win the Southern League in 1961 and 1962, before replacing Accrington Stanley (who resigned from the League in March 1962).

During the summer of 1962 the London Road Terrace was covered, again with money raised by the supporters' club. Also built that year was a tiny stand next to the corner stand, seating just 100 people but reserved for employees of the club, apprentice players, stewards and programme sellers. This Staff (now Juniors) Stand was quite unique, and a symbol of the close relationship between the club and those who helped it attain League status.

The largest crowd to squeeze into the ground was 22 730 v. Preston on 29 February 1964 when United became the first Fourth Division club ever to reach the FA Cup quarter finals.

Much has happened to Oxford since then. In April 1983 club chairman Robert Maxwell proposed a merger between Oxford and Reading to play under the title of Thames Valley Royals at a new stadium midway between the two towns. The scheme provoked sit-ins at the Manor Ground and a mixture of anger, astonishment and derision elsewhere. By mid-May, however, the merger idea was ditched when a

The Manor Ground's trio of stands

new chairman took over Reading.

Then, as if to prove they could go it alone, Oxford rose from the Third to the First Division in two seasons while Reading went from the Fourth to the Second.

The prospect of First Division football raised a host of doubts about the Manor Ground. In March 1984 Oxford City Council offered the club £250 000 towards ground improvements, on condition that United relocate to a site at Blackbird Leys, East Oxford. This would have placed United in the centre of the largest housing estate in Europe, where a sizeable proportion of their fans lived. The club rejected the offer, presumably because they felt the area lacked commercial appeal. But to put pressure on the council to come up with an alternative site Mr Maxwell announced the Manor Ground would have to close unless £1 million was spent on improvements.

Oxford had an undeniable dilemma. Blackbird Leys was the second site they had turned down. In their Southern League days the council had also offered them land at Brasenose Driftway. Under Robert Maxwell, however, United were no longer content to build merely a football ground. Oxford may have excellent sporting facilities but they all belong to the University. The general public have few sporting amenities.

Were United to plough vast sums into the Manor Ground, therefore, they would need both reassurances and aid from the council, both in the short- and long-term. On the night Oxford won promotion to Division One the chairman announced that the Manor Ground would not stage First Division football unless the council contributed £250 000 towards the total improvement costs of £1 million. At the same time he demanded a new site. The result was

that the council gave the grant, but on condition that United participate in various community schemes and offer 400 low-cost season tickets to the unemployed.

The summer of 1985 saw hasty preparations at the ground. To add to the five separate covered sections around the pitch, another small cover was built opposite the Main Stand and the Osler Road terrace was reroofed. At the same time the Manor Ground had to be brought up to the standard required by the Safety of Sports Grounds Act. In such cramped conditions it was a tall order.

A year later more seats were installed under the two Osler Road covers to increase the seating total to 2450 in a total capacity of 14 000. So great was demand that every seat was sold for every home match in 1985–86 and the Manor Ground became the most expensive venue in the League, charging in 1986–87 a set rate of £8.00 for seats and £4.50 for the terraces (compared with, for example, a minimum of £3.40 and £2.60 at Old Trafford). Despite the costs, however, demand has remained high.

Short-term plans for the ground included the building of 10 executive boxes next to the Main Stand, these boxes to form a roof over the now open patch of terracing.

But no amount of piecemeal development could ever disguise the ground's inadequacies, and in August 1986, in conjunction with a property developer, United applied for planning permission to build an ambitious leisure complex with a 25 000-capacity stadium on 81 acres of farmland by the Peartree Roundabout in North Oxford. The plan was rejected and yet again United were left to ponder their future – unwanted in Headington and turned down everywhere else.

If the club should slip back into the lower divisions

perhaps the idea of relocation would be shelved once again. Otherwise a solution has to be found.

In the meantime the Manor Ground must suffice. As Oxford's classic scholars might put it, *Ne sutor ultra crepidam*. To which the chap on the terrace might respond with feeling, *Dum spiro, spero*!

Ground Description

Like the Abbey Stadium, Oxford's ground is far from the hallowed spires of the University, although it is in a pleasant, leafy suburb possessing much of the calm and stone-walled dignity of Oxford itself. One could imagine dons strolling up Headington Road, but massed ranks of supporters from Manchester and Liverpool seem most out of place.

Leafy suburbs do have their drawbacks when you are trying to stage major League and Cup matches. Entrance to the Main Stand, for example, is up a quiet, narrow road one might normally expect to lead to a tennis or bowls club.

The Main Stand is about 50 yards long on the half-way line and is a simple, 1950s' design with a simple brick front wall and a slightly pitched dark roof. On the left side in the corner of the pitch at an angle, like Craven Cottage, is the Manor Club. This was the original stand, and is like a toy-town stand, neatly filling the corner. Immediately next to it on the goal-line is the even smaller Juniors Stand.

The rest of this end is taken up by the Cuckoo Lane Terrace, the tallest section of banking at the ground, rising up to a hump in the far corner. The crush barriers are blue and yellow, set against the brown steps, and with dense green foliage lining the back, it presents a rich and colourful background to the turf. Behind is the John Radcliffe Hospital, set in spacious grounds. At the top of the open terrace is a police surveillance unit. Such are the trappings of success.

Opposite the Main Stand is the narrow Osler Road side, in three sections. On the left is a small covered seating area with a plain roof for visiting supporters. After a short gap there is another small section of seats for home supporters, under the same roof as terracing, to the right.

This links up to the boxed-in London Road End, with its higher, flat roof whose accoustics are perfectly attuned for United's more vociferous supporters. From this end you can see how the pitch slopes some 5 or 6 feet diagonally from the north west down to the south east corner.

The Manor Ground has been teased into the modern era, not by sweeping architectural gestures but by adding a detail here, a detail there. Yet none of this detracts from the Manor Ground's essential homeliness or its ability, when packed, to provide the best of opponents with a heated reception. Of course it is not perfect, but then Oxford is full of unsuitable buildings, and maybe, just maybe, United would lose their heart and soul if they left this cloistered quadrangle for some brave new world out on the ring road.

✦ READING ✦

Previous Grounds

Reading formed in 1871 and are thus the oldest League club south of the Trent. They began at the Reading Recreation Ground, then played at Reading Cricket Ground until 1882. Seven years each at Coley Park and Caversham Cricket Ground followed, until their first game at Elm Park on 5 September 1896. All their previous grounds still exist as open spaces.

Elm Park

A photograph of Elm Park in 1906 shows a stand along the Norfolk Road Side, going round the ground to cover half the Town End. A gale blew this down in 1925, five years after Reading had joined the Football League. A year later the club celebrated promotion to Division Two and built the present Main Stand. The season it was opened also brought Elm Park's highest attendance, 33 042, for an FA Cup match v. Brentford on 19 February 1927.

During the War an enemy bomb destroyed the club offices, which were then in the town centre. After the war, a cover was erected over the centre section of the Tilehurst Road terraces, wings being added in the early 1950s. With the addition of floodlights, first used v. Carlisle on 27 February 1956 and updated three years later, Elm Park assumed the state it is today.

There was an attempt to move from the ground to Smallmead, a stadium only recently established on a council tip near the M4, where greyhound and speedway racing now take place. The costs however were prohibitive.

Elm Park, looking towards the Town End

When designated in 1985 safety inspectors enforced a limit of only 6000 at Elm Park, a massive reduction from its previous capacity of 27 200, and particularly irksome in view of Reading's remarkable start to the 1985–86 season when they were unbeaten for 13 games. Repair work raised the capacity to 13 500 by October, and by August 1986 Elm Park was restored to a more reasonable figure of 20 000, including 2300 seats. Crush barriers and terracing had to be refurbished, fire exits added and the offices completely renovated and fireproofed, at a total cost of £160 000.

Reading's pre-season preparations in August 1986 were marred somewhat when the groundsman, a former player who had tended Elm Park for twenty years, mistakenly sprayed the pitch with neat weedkiller instead of diluting it first. The embarrassing result was a very brown, very dead expanse of turf.

Ground Description

It is remarkable the effect a change of administration can have on a club. Elm Park in the early 1980s was one of the most depressed grounds in the country; ill-attended, decaying, without an ounce of spirit or verve.

But a new staff brought success on the pitch – including promotion to Division Two in 1986 – and a face-lift for Elm Park, which may remain rather ordinary in aesthetic terms but at least no longer looks sorry for itself.

The single-tier Main Stand on Norfolk Road, once rotting and rusting, now has 12 executive boxes at the rear and repainted blue screen ends. Since the ground is built into the side of a hill, the pitch is actually some 6 feet higher than Norfolk Road and there are steps up from the dressing rooms onto the pitch. The dug-outs are particularly low.

From here to the left is the open Reading, or Town End, behind which were the old timbers supporting the roof which blew down. This terrace, and the facing Tilehurst End, also open, have both been extensively redeveloped.

Opposite is the sizeable Tilehurst Terrace, cut into the hillside. Its different roof levels show clearly how it was built in different stages. A clock adorns the centre. Behind here is an all-weather pitch which Reading built with Sports Council aid but no longer use. The club have plans for a supporters' club on the site.

I once called Elm Park the least interesting ground in the League. Its rejuvenation is proof how a tired venue can soon be transformed. A successful team helps, of course, but imagination off the pitch is important too.

·ALDERSHOT·

Recreation Ground

Aldershot are the second youngest club in the League, formed in December 1926. For months the club had no home, but the council-owned Recreation Ground was an obvious choice. As Jack Rollin relates in his club history, Aldershot Borough Council (now called Rushmoor) did not have statutory power to close the park for more than 12 times a year, so to circumvent this they invoked the 1925 Public Health Act which allowed local authorities to lease a ground for organized football, provided they bought land of equivalent value for public use. The council therefore purchased 40 acres of land at Aldershot Park and have leased the Recreation Ground to Aldershot FC ever since. The first game was on 27 August 1927 attended by 3500.

There was a plan for a stand with winter gardens on the roof, but the South Stand was the first to be built in 1929. Three years later Aldershot entered the League in place of the East London club Thames. In the late 1930s the North Stand was built, followed after the War by the East Bank terrace roof.

The first floodlit game was a trial match between Scottish and English born players at the club, in May 1953. In 1954 the ground was host to an early BBC televised game when Aldershot played the Army, to celebrate a hundred years of the Aldershot garrison. The lights were renewed at a cost of £10 000 in 1962.

The ground's highest attendance of 19 138 saw a Cup-tie v. Carlisle in January 1970. Ten years later, new offices and dressing rooms were built behind the North Stand, and with added seats this took over from the South Stand as the main stand. The capacity was 16 000, with 1885 seats, and a very high proportion of this total, 14 000 approximately, under cover. Current restrictions limit the capacity to 8000.

Ground Description

This is the only League ground situated in a public park and access is almost unrestricted during the week. The park gates are shut on match days, when what appear to be ordinary municipal park shelters become turnstiles. From these you pass by clipped lawns and flower beds up to the High Street End, which is just a tarmac path behind the goal, the narrowest end of any League ground, with a high net to stop the ball going into the park or street (often unsuccessfully). A more pleasant approach is down through the eastern heights of the park along twisted, cobbled paths, through thickly wooded gardens past the tennis courts, from where the ground can be seen nestling cosily at the foot of the slope.

Behind the East Bank Terrace, which has a leaking barrel roof and a haphazard array of crush barriers, is a floodlit training area. The Main Stand, once

Genteel turnstiles and prim lawns lead up to the Recreation Ground, the only Football League ground set in a public park. On the right, note how deeply the South Stand roof overhangs without support. Though its lines are modern the stand was built in 1929

all-standing, now has a central section with alternate rows of red and blue seats, with a new Directors' Box in the middle and a compact, well-designed new administrative block behind. Along the front of the stand is an unusual stone perimeter wall with buttresses, formerly draped with ivy. Less picturesque is the tall British Telecom office block at the rear. The small South Stand, straddling the half-way line opposite, looks more modern than it is, with a substantial, almost cantilevered overhanging wooden roof. Behind are the old wooden dressing rooms, now a multi-

gym and supporters' club backing onto the Guildford to Aldershot railway line. Whenever trains pass the South Stand vibrates like a bus in low gear. Because of the narrow, open West End the ground looks a shade incomplete, although there is at least 20 feet of spare turf beyond each goal-line to develop it further.

The Recreation Ground is like part of an arboretum, with the nicely mildewed air of its surrounds.

As the *Athletic News* put it in 1927, it is 'one of the prettiest football enclosures in the South'.

·AFC BOURNEMOUTH·

Previous Grounds

In 1891 AFC Bournemouth were known as Boscombe St John's and played on King's Park, next to the present ground. They moved east to Castlemain Road, Pokesdown in 1899 as Boscombe FC, paying £5 10s a season rent. When J. E. Cooper Dean became involved with the club they moved back to Boscombe, a suburb of Bournemouth.

Dean Court

Dean Court, like Fellows Park and Ninian Park, was named after the club's benefactor, who became Club President. When Cooper Dean let the wasteland to Boscombe FC at a peppercorn rent in 1910, voluntary labour prepared a pitch and built a stand for 300 spectators. Two years later the club turned professional, and in 1923 joined the League as Bournemouth and Boscombe Athletic.

The present Main Stand has a pedigree. Its framework came from the British Empire Exhibition at Wembley where it was built in 1923 as a restaurant. Athletic bought it for £12 000 and the League's Vice-President C. E. Sutcliffe declared it open on 27 August 1927 for a game v. Swindon.

The South End covered terrace was also opened before a Swindon match, in September 1936, by club director and Mayor, Alderman H. G. Harris. In 1957, following the club's most successful FA Cup run, in which they reached the 6th Round and recorded their highest gate of 28 799 v. Manchester United, the New Stand was built. It was refurbished in 1964. Floodlit football had a tenuous start at Dean Court in 1961 v. Northampton, when the new lights failed 15 minutes before kick-off and delayed the match nearly an hour.

The early 1970s promised great changes, as John Bond rescued the club from the Fourth and almost lifted them to the Second Division. To put them at least at the top of an alphabetical list, a new name, AFC Bournemouth, was sneakily adopted in 1971 but editors and compilers seem to have ignored the hint. Meanwhile the club purchased about 20 acres of land from the Cooper Dean estate, and ambitious plans for a new stand and sports centre behind the open end began. The foundations and superstructure went up quickly, like the cost, which rose from an estimated £250 000 to nearer £700 000. With the ground lying deep within suburbia, planning permission was an obstacle, and finally the project was abandoned.

After years of trying to sell the site a housing developer finally took it over and the bare concrete skeleton which once cast a shadow over one end of the ground was demolished. Dean Court's current capacity is reduced from 19 175 to 12 130, including 4130 seats.

Ground Description

The Main Stand, despite its origins, is rather dull, although ironically it shares with Wembley Stadium clear sheeting along the roof front. This was added to give extra cover when the stand was made all seated. An improvement though this was, it sadly meant the removal of the red and white striped balcony wall which had done so much to liven up Dean Court.

The New Stand opposite is a long, low and narrow cover over terracing, lined with advertisements. The South End is half-covered, but also half-boarded off where the back wooden terracing is deemed unsafe. The stands seem painted in a crust of moss, weatherworn but immovable, like park benches in autumn.

To the right is an open terrace, sarcastically called the Brighton Beach End because it used to be a stony bank! Behind are the new houses built on the site which Bournemouth had hoped would be a lucrative sports centre.

All around are tall trees, with King's Park and a large car park behind the Main Stand – no narrow streets here – and a line of prim semis pushing up against the New Stand. A football ground amid the lace curtains, prams and poodles seems about as inappropriate as a beer glass at a cocktail party, and yet Dean Court blends in remarkably well with its surroundings and makes one rather wish there were more grounds like this, tucked in among the lobelias and leaf-strewn paths.

Dean Court in the 1930s

·SOUTHAMPTON·

Previous Grounds

Southampton formed in November 1885 as St Mary's YMCA, playing at the Antelope Ground, now the site of Southampton's County Bowling Club. After turning professional and joining the Southern League in 1894, the club, now called Southampton St Mary's, moved a few hundred yards to the County Cricket Ground on Northlands Road, and in their first season there won the Championship of 1896–97. They then became a limited company, thereby relinquishing their church origins, and were known thereafter as Southampton, although the nickname 'Saints' has persisted to this day.

As crowds grew to 12 000 at the County Ground, Southampton decided to look for a new ground. They found a site nearby, although it was an unlikely spot for a football ground.

The Dell

A painting of The Dell in 1889 shows a tranquil pond in sunshine, surrounded by trees, with two small ducks gently gliding over the water. As Peter East in his history of the club points out, it was exactly on this quiet pond that less than a decade later a football ground would be built.

It cost one George Thomas £10 000 to develop the site, his first task being to reduce the pond to a series of underground streams. He then built two fairly sophisticated stands on either side, providing seats for 4000 spectators, with open terracing for a further 20 000. The 'charming' Dell was by no means a rustic enclosure, for its facilities were among the best in the country. In the Main or West Stand were 6-feet deep plunge baths for the players, two showers plus ordinary baths. Around the terracing were very solid iron railings, and there was even a special enclosure for supporters to store their bicycles during games, at a penny a time. The press were not content, however, because they had no writing tables – a common complaint at the time.

Thomas leased the ground to Southampton for £250 a year, and it was proudly opened on 3 September 1898, for a Southern League game v. Brighton United. Not only was The Dell the best non-League ground of the day – and a good deal better than many grounds in the League – the team was by far the most successful professional outfit south of Birmingham.

However, the club started to decline after 1904, and by 1906 had an overdraft of £3000. George Thomas raised the rent to £500, less £100 if certain repairs were carried out, and for a short time there was even the possibility of the club moving to another ground.

Eventually, Southampton joined the League in 1920, as part of the mass exodus from the Southern League to the Football League, and it soon became apparent that some of The Dell's facilities were not quite up to standard. For example, a house still stood at the north end of the West Stand, its rear wall almost bordering on the touchline. It was demolished in 1922 when Southampton won quick promotion to Division Two.

In 1925–26, with the team settling comfortably into the Second Division, the club purchased the ground, including some neighbouring property, but at the sacrifice of selling some of the star players. Money was raised through various schemes to improve The Dell, including a £20 000 loan from an insurance company, and a newly-formed supporters' club began fund-raising. The existing West Stand double-decker was built with these extra funds, amid arguments that the team should be put before the ground.

Nevertheless the team did well, and finished the 1928–29 season in their best position yet of fourth in Division Two. Unfortunately only hours after the last home game, the East Stand burnt down, the flames spreading rapidly through the structure, fanned by a strong breeze.

Feverish work during the summer saw the new two-tiered East Stand ready for the start of the next season, and now The Dell had two almost identical stands providing a total of 6600 seats in a claimed overall capacity of 35 000, although the figure was never tested.

The 1930s were less successful at The Dell, and when the Second World War broke out Southampton were among the bottom clubs of the Second Division. Being only a mile from the main Southampton docks, the ground's neighbourhood suffered heavily during the Blitz, and in November 1940 a bomb struck the pitch at the Milton Road End, causing one of the underground water culverts to break and flood the pitch under a couple of feet of water.

To worsen matters, on 8 April 1941 a fire broke out in the centre of the West Stand, but was prevented from spreading to the wings and was, it is recorded, put out before black-out time.

While this went on, the team played their war League games at the Pirelli General Works sports ground in Eastleigh, and later at Fratton Park, before returning to The Dell.

After the war attendances rose all around the country, and at Southampton it was decided to raise the ground's capacity by erecting platforms of terracing above the Milton Road End terrace. At first two, then three of these odd-looking platforms were built, and they became affectionately known as the Chocolate Boxes. The existing extra level of terracing is really a modern version of the old boxes, which were quite unique at a football ground for being an upper tier of terracing, but without any cover.

The Dell hit the headlines in 1951 as the first English ground to stage a competitive floodlit match. Southampton had been one of the first clubs to install

The Dell, looking towards the unusual Milton Road End, where the Chocolate Boxes once stood

lights in the modern era, costing only £600 and intended primarily for training purposes. A few practice friendlies were held at first, then the club received permission from the Football Combination to stage a reserve match v. Spurs under the lights on 1 October 1951 (see Floodlights).

Since then, the ground seems to have changed little, but there have been substantial alterations, most of them since the introduction of the Safety of Sports Grounds Act. Viewing at The Dell has always been a major problem, one of which the club are acutely aware, but they were certainly unprepared for the large number of changes called for by the local authority safety inspectors. Since 1978 the club have spent up to £1 million on safety measures, using up their entire grant from the Football Grounds Improvement Trust (FGIT) (see Safety). Among the improvements was the complete renewal of barriers in the ground, which worked out cheaper than spending £2000 a year on just testing the old ones.

The Chocolate Boxes came down, but in their place was built a more solid upper tier of terracing, slightly overhanging the back wall on Milton Road. The club wanted to build a similar addition to the Archers Road End terrace, but this was denied planning permission, as the authorities felt that just the slight overhang would be enough to make drivers of high-sided vehicles move towards the middle of the narrow, busy road.

At one stage the club nearly decided to build a new cantilever West Stand estimated to cost £880 000, and there was another suggestion that they should sell up completely for £3 million and rebuild elsewhere, in less confined surroundings. But a new stadium would have cost at least £9 million to build,

and the club are now relieved that they stayed at The Dell.

The Dell's highest ever attendance was 31 044, for a Divison One match v. Manchester United on 8 October 1969. Since 1978 the ground's capacity has been reduced to 25 000, probably enough to satisfy current demands. Now bench seats have been installed in both stand paddocks, making a total of 9000 seats.

Ground Description

The Dell's real essence lies in its confinement, pressed between two roads which cut across the ground to form a parallelogram, so that each end terrace is like an elongated triangle. From the road to the goal-line is a matter of a few yards at either end. The two stands, facing each other like mirror images in a poor man's Highbury, increase the cloister-like feeling of the ground.

The West Stand is a double-decker, characterized by the lines of green floodlight gantries along the grey pitched roof. These are linked by a steel walkway along the front. There is simply no room to erect corner pylons, so these original gantries have never been replaced. In the centre of the roof is a white canopy housing the television camera platform, and to support it the two central pillars in the stand have been doubled in thickness. This platform alone cost £36 000 to construct, divided between the club and the two television companies.

An unusual feature of The Dell, seen in both stands, is the arrangement of bench seats in the paddock. The supporters wanted some standing space in these sections, so the paddocks have been divided in half. But to avoid awkward sight lines, seats and terracing have been spliced together at an angle, with a diagonal gangway in between. This method allows the seated spectators to gain a view past the standing ones into the far corner.

There is no players' tunnel in this stand. The dressing rooms are up some stairs at the south end of the stand, so that losing teams have to suffer not only a long trudge to the end of the ground, but then a short climb up to the privacy of their quarters.

The West Stand paddock has one unusual feature. Each dug-out is covered by a curving, clear plastic roof. Directly behind them, where viewing is difficult, the club have a section where the visually handicapped can sit and listen to match commentaries – and presumably overhear some choice words from the managers too.

The East Stand opposite is almost identical to the West, but has no space under the upper tier, and has aluminium rather than wooden bench seats.

To the left is the open Archers Road End, a narrow strip of terracing with St Mark's church and some student flats visible behind. The back of the goal is inches from the perimeter wall, so that fans can almost whisper to the goalkeeper. In fact the pitch is not the shortest length possible, measuring 72 yards, a yard longer than Highbury's, which seems huge in comparison.

To the right is the Milton Road End with two tiers of terracing. This section alone cost just under £500 000 to build in 1981. From the triangular-shaped top tier, which rises quite steeply, is gained a magnificent view of the ground, and to the left, Southampton docks and the distant New Forest.

From here it is evident how much attention has been paid to the ground's safety requirements, for although at first glance The Dell seems quite un-developed for a First Division venue, every barrier and step is new, every piece of steelwork repainted. The club has made an enormous effort on a difficult site, not as limited as Kenilworth Road perhaps but nevertheless extremely expensive to modernize in proportion to its size.

It is unquestionably a Southern ground, in at-mosphere and hue, yet however small and basic it may seem compared with its fellow stadiums in Division One, The Dell has one major asset – an administration which cares for its surroundings. Like Watford, Oxford, Luton, and Ipswich a decade ago, Southampton is a club with advanced ideas living in a small, old ground. In view of football's receding audiences, it is probably happy to stay that way.

◆PORTSMOUTH◆

Fratton Park

When the town's leading football club, Royal Artillery, was suspended by the FA for breaching amateur regulations, it was decided to form a professional club called Portsmouth. A limited company was set up in 1898, and for £4950 it purchased a market garden near Fratton railway station. As we learn from Pompey's history, written by Messrs Neasom, Cooper and Robinson (Milestone, 1984), a further £16 000 was spent on laying a pitch and building two wooden stands; a short South Stand with seats and a full length North Cover for standing.

After success in the Southern League, in 1905 a grand pavilion was built on Frogmore Road, with The Pompey public house behind. On the pavilion roof was a clock tower (now gone), a gift from Sir John Brickwood, brewer and co-founder of the club. The buildings' mock-Tudor style was extremely popular in vernacular architecture at the turn of the century.

Portsmouth joined the League in 1920 and while on their way up in Division Two they commissioned Archibald Leitch to design a new Main Stand on the south side of the ground next to the pavilion. A brass plate inside the stand shows that the first steel column went up on 17 June 1925, another indicates that J. McKenna, President of the Football League, officially opened the South Stand on 29 August 1925. The stand was one of the grandest in the country at the time and cost £20,000 to build.

Having lost the 1929 Cup Final, Portsmouth failed a second time at Wembley in 1934, but their Cup-run netted profits of over £10 000, as did the sale of Jimmy Allen to Villa. With this money in hand the club erected the existing North Stand during the 1934–35 season. For a while it was even called the Jimmy Allen Stand.

In February 1949 with Portsmouth going for the Double, Fratton Park saw its highest crowd of 51 385 for a 6th Round Cup tie v. Derby. The ground's lights were first switched on in 1953, but their most famous use was on 22 February 1956, the very first Football League match played under floodlights (see Floodlights).

The team was declining by 1957 when the club built the Fratton End Stand, providing covered standing accommodation for 10 000 spectators. It was an early example of prefabricated concrete design and merited a short study in the technical magazine, *Prefabrication* (April 1957, p. 254).

In 1962 the original floodlights were replaced by the existing pylons, a gift from the supporters' club in October of that year. The ground has changed little in appearance since then but has improved consider-ably in substance. In 1985 fire escapes were added to both the pavilion end of the South Stand and to the North Stand, in a general programme of improve-

Familiar Leitch steelwork at Fratton

ments which cost £200 000 and reduced Fratton Park's capacity marginally to 36 000, including 7000 seats.

Ground Description

Fratton Park is in the middle of Portsea Island, which is really a peninsular, and is a few hundred yards east of Fratton Station, on the line from Portsmouth to Waterloo. The best approach is along Frogmore Road, from Goldsmith Avenue, to the ground's magnificent main entrance which occupies the end of the cul-de-sac. A small, mock-Tudor cottage, half-timbered gable window in the centre, is placed over a large gate which leads straight onto the terraces. To the left are the club offices. Just in front is The Pompey, the club's public house, with a sign depicting a player who resembles the Scottish winger, John Robertson, after a gruelling 90 minutes.

Through the large blue gates we come into the south east corner of the ground, with the South Stand to our right. Underneath, it has a system of corridors and stairs like a small business warehouse, a little cramped but well lit from the roof. From inside the ground, however, the South Stand is perfection: Leitch at his best. His trademark is especially prominent, the balcony wall criss-crossed with blue steel supports, apparently deeper than its younger sisters at Roker, Ibrox or Goodison, but actually the same dimensions, just lower down. Imagine the Bullens Road Stand at Goodison sunk a few feet into its foundations, moved nearer the pitch and you have Fratton Park's South Stand. (The Everton stand was 1926, Roker Park's 1929 and Ibrox's 1929, so perhaps in 1925 Leitch was just practising at Portsmouth!)

Notice how the skylights along the back of the roof help avoid the gloominess often found in older stands, even if they show up a rather unfortunate combination of blue and purple seats side by side. You will also see that instead of dug-outs, awkward wooden huts have been put onto the terracing on one side of the tunnel, which seems to disappear into the paddock. The television camera gantry in front of the

balcony wall was once moved across to the North Stand because it was thought to be too close to the pitch. In its new position, however, after all the advertisements had been moved to face the cameras, the gantry was found to be looking directly into the sun and was too far from the pitch! Now it is back where it started.

To the right of the South Stand is the uncovered Milton End. In the north east corner of this terrace where the floodlight pylon stands, is a section often referred to as the 'Boilermakers' Hump', apparently once a favourite spot for local shipyard workers.

To the left is the covered Fratton End; an unusual feature of this terrace is its division into two tiers, with a white wall between top from bottom. Anyone who has stood on the terraces will appreciate the benefit of grabbing a barrier just above such a wall, for the best possible view. Another detail is a clock, set in the centre of the roof fascia, common on side stands but rarely seen on an end roof. The Fratton End Stand itself is plain, but nicely boxed in against the elements. Behind are railway goods' yards. Commendably the club have opted to build a small moat and only a low security fence at this end, thus allowing unhampered vision.

Opposite the South Stand is a deep bank of terracing, on top of which sits a long, low blue stand, angled slightly inwards. The North Stand looks much older than its counterpart, although ten years younger, being mainly wooden. The terrace rear walls, all blue, are particularly high. From the South Side the pitch appears to slope quite badly, but on closer inspection it is the North Side terracing which slopes. The North Stand is built on stilts behind the banking and with much wasted space underneath. Milton Lane runs behind.

Fratton Park for years had a dowdy sort of appeal; a sort of Northern dourness which strangers might have been surprised to find in such dull surroundings on the South coast. Fortunately Pompey's return from the depths of the Fourth Division in 1980 enlightened the ground's atmosphere and saved it from becoming a dusty relic, so that the unique half-timbered entrance, which once appeared to symbolize the club's decline, now appears as a picturesque gateway to potential glory – a perfect example of how success on the pitch can alter entirely one's perception of a football ground.

BRIGHTON & HOVE ·ALBION·

Previous Grounds

A team called Brighton United played on Sussex County Cricket Ground in 1898, but the ground lacked any cover, gates were poor, and the club was wound up two years later. In their place Brighton and Hove Rangers formed, at Home Farm, Withdean. Their players were so keen to establish the club that they would help collect the gate money before kick-off. From August 1901, as Brighton and Hove Albion, they were back at the cricket ground.

Meanwhile, another team, Hove FC had moved from Hove Park the previous April to a site known as Goldstone Bottom, paying rent of £100 a year. The town was clearly not big enough to sustain both clubs, so the following February Albion moved in with Hove, who soon after went back to Hove Park, having sold Albion the ground lease for £40.

Goldstone Ground

How Goldstone Bottom got its name is told in a history of the club by John Vinicombe. Apparently it is derived from a stone reputed to have belonged to Druids and which stood on a local farmer's land. He became so tired of visiting archaeologists that he buried it in 1834. The stone was recovered in 1900 and put up in Hove Park, just across the road from the ground.

When Albion first played at the Goldstone Ground in February 1902, the pitch was overlooked by Goldstone House, home of Alderman Clark, who owned the land on a lease from the Standford Estate. On the north side was a large pond into which players were known to deliberately kick the ball to soften the leather. In the south east corner was a ladies' section. In 1904 a small, white stand with lattice-work decoration was put up on the West Side. In keeping with the town's genteel image, the stand had been bought from Preston Park where it was used for a horse show. Many years later it was hoisted up and plonked on a raised terrace. During the summer in those halcyon days sheep would graze on the pitch, but although Brighton's reserve team is nicknamed The Lambs there is no apparent connection!

When the First World War broke out soliders were drilled on the pitch, and they practised their marksmanship by potting at crows, but by 1918 the Goldstone was nearly derelict. Extensive redevelopment was necessary and the pond was drained to make way for the North Bank. In 1926 Brighton council bought the ground for £8000 – to Alderman Clark's annoyance since his lease was not expired – but with the important condition that in deference to the view and value of the houses along the rise, no structure higher than 50 feet above pitch level should be built.

The North and South Ends were covered, and then in 1957, to celebrate promotion after 37 years in Division Three, the old West Stand was replaced after over 50 years' service with the present structure, for a sum of around £30 000. While in Division Two Brighton's highest crowd, 36 747, watched a League match v. Fulham in December 1958.

The Goldstone Ground, with the now dismantled West Stand extension on the right

Drenchlighting – Scottish style, pictured at Brighton

The first floodlit game was v. Frem, a Danish team, on 10 April 1961. Promotion to Division One in 1979 brought increased demand for seating, so at a cost of £150 000 Brighton built a temporary 974-capacity free-standing structure known sarcastically as the Lego Stand, scheduled to remain for five years. It was not the first of its kind on the West Side, for in 1933 a similar sized extension was built for a cup tie v. West Ham. Even with the extension, the Goldstone was still about the worst in the top division, lacking parking facilities, restricted by the lease of 1926, and with insufficient seats and standing cover. The chairman wanted to move to a new site on the outskirts of town, but the money was simply not available. To improve matters a little, when a fire gutted the South Stand in May 1980, it was extremely well converted to a seated enclosure.

At the same time, however, the North Stand roof had to be taken down in compliance with the Safety of Sports Grounds Act, leaving the ground with no standing cover apart from the West Stand paddock. But then with Brighton back in the Second Division, as the temporary stand was removed in 1985, a replacement cover was built over the North Stand at a cost of £150 000. This more or less restored the ground to its pre-1979 appearance, but safety work since 1975 has cost Brighton more than £500 000, a figure topped by only a handful of other clubs.

The result however is a relatively high capacity, reduced from 38 000 to 29 026, with 5000 seats.

Ground Description

Although it is next to a large park, the Goldstone Ground is actually hemmed in by narrow roads, small factories and the natural incline along the East Side. One notices the floodlights first, more in keeping with Brechin than Brighton, with their distinctly Scottish pylons, lamp holders angled down towards the pitch as if bowed in prayer. The system was called 'Drenchliting' by the Edinburgh manufacturers.

The three-quarter length West Stand is externally drab though bright inside, and now appears rather awkwardly next to flat ground where the Lego Stand once stood. A police unit fills part of the space (Brighton have closed-circuit television).

To the left is the newly covered North Stand. The roof is plain and high but provides much needed terracing cover. Behind is a small area of land sold by the club for office development in 1986 on Old Shoreham Road. Hove Park is across the road.

The terraces curl round and rise up the open East Side, behind which stand the rows of houses overlooking the ground. All the crush barriers are painted, not in the usual gloss but in matt blue, which stands out most effectively against the light brown concrete.

As it nears the South Stand, the banking falls away rapidly to only a handful of steps by the corner flag. From here you can see how the pitch slopes 4 feet from the North to the South Stand, with its old roof and bright new seats in light and dark blue, which closes off the ground from the less attractive landscape beyond.

Car drivers find the Goldstone Ground a nuisance. Handicapped spectators appreciate the covered enclosure built for them in the south west corner. Players for their part enjoy the excellent pitch while everyone else should congratulate Brighton on really making the very best out of an unpromising, unwieldy site.

·BRISTOL ROVERS·

Previous Grounds

On 26 April 1986 a crowd of 3576 turned up at Eastville to see Bristol Rovers' final home match of the season v. Chesterfield. Rumours circulated that this might be the very last game at the ground, but then the supporters had heard this before a few years previously, and nothing had transpired then. So there was little emotion when the players left the pitch after an uneventful 1-1 draw.

Some weeks later it was announced that Rovers had decided to quit Eastville for good and for the immediate future would be based at Twerton Park, home of Bath City. It was the end of a long and often uncertain relationship, and in truth, came as no surprise.

Rovers formed under the evocative title of Black Arabs in 1883 at Purdown. A year later as Eastville Rovers they were at Ashley Hill, before moving to the Ridgeway, Upper Eastville. Eastville Stadium was then home to the Harlequin Rugby Club, but in 1896 a syndicate bought the ground for Rovers, whose first game there was a 5-0 defeat by Aston Villa on 3 April 1897. Later that year Rovers bought the 16-acre site for just £150. To buy the ground now would cost between £1·5 and £4 million.

For two decades all went well. The ground expanded to hold 30 000, and in 1924 Rovers built a large South Stand. Further prosperity was envisaged in 1931 when Eastville was adapted to stage greyhound racing, run by a separate company which became tenants of the football club.

By 1939 Rovers were in trouble; £16 000 in debt and having to seek re-election. Even so, when the chairman Fred Ashmead agreed to sell Eastville to the greyhound company in 1940 for £12 000 his fellow directors refused to sanction the deal. Had their will been enforced, who knows what might have been?

After the War, life seemed rosy again as the supporters raised money for a new North Stand in 1958 and floodlights, first switched on in September 1959 v. Ipswich. Both the stand and lights automatically became part of the stadium company's property, but this hardly seemed important when a new 21-year lease was signed later that year 'on favourable terms' and soon after, in January 1960, Eastville's record crowd of 38 472 watched a Cup match v. Preston.

Apart from the brief introduction of speedway to Eastville in 1977 little changed until the lease came up for renewal on 31 December 1979. From this point Rovers' relationship with their landlords changed, because after failing to agree new terms the club took their dispute to the High Court. A hearing was set for 30 November 1981.

The club was determined to stay at Eastville, for tradition's sake and because they and their supporters (with whom they did not always see eye to eye) had invested so much in the ground, including £70 000 on safety improvements since 1975. But their world fell apart on 16 August 1980 when the South Stand, housing their offices and dressing rooms, was destroyed by fire. Forced to make hurried arrangements, Rovers played their next five home games at Ashton Gate, and for a time it was thought a ground-sharing scheme – the first in Britain – would be feasible.

Anxious then to avoid possible legal costs of at least £50 000 in the High Court, Rovers met with the Bristol Stadium Company a week before the scheduled hearing. They expected a compromise but instead received an almighty shock. They were given notice to quit.

Compensation of £280 000 was offered in return for Rovers' giving up their rights under the Landlord and Tenant Act and they were allowed to use Eastville rent free until 15 May 1982. After that they would have to move. To make matters worse Rovers had just been relegated to Division Three.

But their torment was still not over. Rovers managed to negotiate a £40 000 per annum ground-sharing scheme with City (much to the dismay of supporters in both camps), to start in August 1982, but when City folded and were reconstituted that year the new board at Ashton Gate doubled the rent previously agreed. It was too much for Rovers, who were thus given no choice but to reopen negotiations with the Bristol Stadium Company and accept a five-year licence at £50 000 per year. City meanwhile plummeted past them down to Division Four.

Eastville in happier days, before the fire destroyed the South Stand on the left

With offices now at their Hambrook training ground, apart from match days Rovers' only presence at Eastville was the groundsman. It was a tenuous existence and in May 1986, a year before the licence was due to expire, Rovers finally called it a day. The reason was simple. Eastville was costing around £2000 per home game, which with falling gates resulted in a loss for almost every match.

The stadium company was unperturbed. Before Rover's departure, Eastville was already used three times a week for greyhound racing. Once Rovers were gone a fourth meeting was added, making Eastville the busiest greyhound track in Britain, with forty races a week. This was worth at least £500 000 per annum to the stadium company, ten times the income derived from Rovers.

Rovers had a number of options. Buying Eastville was clearly beyond them, even presuming it was up for sale, but two years earlier they had, in conjunction with the Bristol Stadium Company and other parties, drawn up plans for a sports centre and stadium to be built by the motorway in Stoke Gifford, a mile from Hambrook. Planning permission was refused on that occasion, but there is always a chance that if Rovers could attract the necessary finance a new plan could be drawn up in collaboration with the stadium company. That is a long-term possibility.

The second, much quicker option was sharing with Bristol City, who were by then back in the Third Division and in better shape. But City asked for a rent of over £60 000, more than Rovers paid at Eastville, and it was apparent that there was no real desire to accommodate their homeless neighbours.

Two other options, closer to Eastville, were the Gloucestershire County Cricket Ground at Ashley Hill and the Memorial Ground, home of Bristol Rugby Football Club. Neither organisation wanted Rovers (which in the latter case was unfortunate because the Memorial Ground is a charming enclosure). Gloucester City, who were building a new

stadium 34 miles away, were also mentioned as a possible destination.

Finally Rovers approached Bath City, 13 miles away. They had already considered a ground-sharing scheme in 1982 and found Bath's directors willing to agree on a seven-year lease to be reviewed after four years. Rovers would pay £20 000 per season plus a percentage of gate receipts, half the costs of laying a new pitch and, with FGIT grants, £80 000 towards improvements in order to bring Twerton Park up to designated standards.

Meanwhile, the Bristol Bombers American Football team played a few exhibition matches at Eastville in front of disappointing crowds and Rovers issued leaflets to supporters explaining the reasons for their move. Twerton Park, it was stressed, was the only possible venue Rovers could use while the club investigated sites for a new stadium in Bristol, a long-term project which would take a minimum of five years and £1 million to realize.

(No easy task for, as Watford, Oxford and Luton have each discovered, however much support exists for a new stadium, when it comes to planning permission no one wants a football ground on their doorstep.)

Eastville in 1986 was a dispiriting sight. Safety restrictions in Rovers' last season had cut the capacity from 38 500 to 12 500, and it still needed further work – all of which Rovers would have had to finance.

Hemmed in by a motorway, markets, a new hi-tech supermarket and new retail units to the west, Eastville thus awaits its fate, to be decided no doubt in London among property dealers. It may well be profitable and busy as a greyhound track, but the fate of tracks like Shawfield and White City suggest that Eastville surely cannot survive in its present state for more than a decade.

It is all a far cry from the stadium's hey-day, when flowerbeds grew behind each goal and the high banks

165

of terracing at each end were often packed to capacity. In latter years sometimes dozens of spectators risked arrest by viewing from the hard shoulder of the M32 motorway which runs within yards of the south side. That side, where the stand once stood, has lain bare since the fire.

There should be no doubt at all that Eastville is finished as a League venue; there will be no Rovers' return. Bought for £150, sold for £12 000 and now worth a fortune, all that Rovers fans have left of Eastville are memories. They at least are priceless.

Twerton Park

Sceptism, anxiety and fear haunted both sets of supporters as Rovers moved in with Bath City, a senior non-League side who have played at Twerton Park since 1932, when the present Main Stand was built. The ground's record attendance was 18 020 for a Cup tie v. Brighton in January 1960, and in the days when Malcolm Allison was Bath's manager and Tony Book one of the players the floodlights were switched on for a game v. Arsenal in the 1963–64 season. The current capacity is reduced from 21 000 to 5100 (in season 1985–86 Bath's average gate was about 700).

Before Rovers' arrival the ground was neither better nor worse than several in the Fourth Division. It needed a face-lift but had already been passed by the League when Bath twice applied for membership in recent years.

A few miles east of Bath's enchanting Georgian centre, Twerton Park is built into the side of a hill so that, like Albion Rovers, the 40-yard long Main Stand seems disproportionately tall from the entrance. It is a simple, 600 seater, all-wooden construction with a blue corrugated façade, green sides, yellow interior walls and a black balcony wall with white facings; enough colours to make most teams feel at home. A clock is attached to one of the roof supports and there is flat ground on either side.

Behind here the Lansdown heights stretch out on the horizon, with Beckford's Tower a prominent landmark on the summit, near Bath racecourse. To the left is the narrow, open Bath End, a few steps of terracing with a mesh fence protecting the modern houses immediately behind.

Opposite is the Covered Enclosure, which like the pitch slopes down about 5 feet towards the Bath End. Behind this undulating terrace are more modern houses, whose upper windows have a fine view over the pitch. The rising grassland of Innox Park is beyond.

To the right is the open Bristol End, a modern terrace with white barriers. It presses up to the goal stanchions with barely an inch to spare. These goals, ten turnstiles and the groundsman are, incidentally, all that Rovers brought with them from Eastville.

Will ground sharing at Bath succeed? At worst Rovers will have to manage until they find a suitable site in Bristol. Twerton Park is 40 minutes from

Twerton Park – now home to Bath and Bristol Rovers

Eastville and though hardly ideal, compared with the journey Charlton supporters must make to Selhurst Park it is a gentle drive.

But if all goes smoothly perhaps more non-League clubs will be eyeing their beleaguered League neighbours with a view to sharing. The League will then be in danger of unwittingly sanctioning a quasi-franchise system, whereby any club could relocate to a town with a non-League ground and thus take it over by stealth.

If Bath deserve a League place they should have it, as Bath. If Bristol can support two League clubs then both must be in Bristol. I therefore make no apology for repeating once more that given the recent histories of Rovers and City, Ashton Gate is big enough and good enough for both clubs. If their long-suffering fans want the level of success a city of Bristol's size easily merits, they must surely be prepared to compromise, one day.

·BRISTOL CITY·

Previous Grounds

Formed as Bristol South End in 1894, their first ground was at St John's Lane, Bedminster, still in use today as a sports ground. South End became Bristol City in 1897 and simultaneously one of several professional teams in the city. Apart from Eastville Rovers, there was Warmley, whose ground held 9000, St George FC and a club called Bedminster, who played at Ashton Gate. As rationalization inevitably occurred, City amalgamated with but soon absorbed Bedminster, beginning in 1900. Both grounds were used alternately, but as Ashton Gate had an iron stand and a better pitch, it was the site chosen when Bedminster was absorbed completely and City settled permanently in 1904.

Ashton Gate

Ashton Gate's beginnings are well detailed in the club's history by Peter Godsiff. In the early years there were two stands on either side of the pitch, No. 1 and No. 2 Stands, but the first development as we know it today was at the Winterstoke Road End. This covered terrace was built in the late 1920s after the sale of two players, Keating and Bourton, for £3000. For a time it was called the Keating Stand. While in Division Three, City's record crowd of 43 335 assembled for a Cup match v. Preston in February 1935. Yet such were the club's financial problems during this period that they offered to sell Ashton Gate to Bristol Corporation for £16 000, in return for a long lease with a rental of £640 a year. The Corporation declined.

In February 1941 half of the No. 1 Stand was destroyed by an unexploded bomb and the other half was bombed the following night. City received £16 500 from the War Damages Commission towards the rebuilding costs of £18 000, but by the time the existing Grand Stand was completed in the 1950s, the cost had escalated to £30 000. The supporters' club, who wanted accommodation underneath the stand, contributed £3000 for steelwork City could not afford.

At this time, the club chairman was Harry Dolman, who designed the club's first floodlights. Set on removable poles along each touchline, they had to be switched on individually. Their first use was in a friendly v. Wolves in January 1953. Floodlit rugby was also staged. The existing pylons cost £25 000 and were also switched on for a game v. Wolves in December 1965.

Opposite the Grand Stand, behind the old wooden cover, arose a new council block called Southbow House, from whose roof the view was so good that the caretaker would charge people to watch games, a practice which ended with the building of the new stand, named after Harry Dolman. As before costs

Ashton Gate from the Open End. The Dolman Stand is on the left. Notice the Scottish style floodlights

rose faster than the structure. The first estimate was for £50 000, but by the time it was opened in 1970, and an indoor bowling green installed underneath, the cost was £235 000. The debt incurred was enormous for a Second Division club, and City had to sell all 16 of its club houses and obtain pledges of £3000 each from the FA, various companies and individuals. Yet one cannot blame the Dolman Stand for City's subsequent decline, because six years after its completion, the club won promotion to Division One, after a 54-year absence. City's record descent to the Fourth Division thereafter was due to other causes, although the drop in average gates from 19 000 to around 4000 made any repayments of debts impossible, and led to the winding up of the original 1897 Limited Company. Bristol City can at least claim to have had the best ground of any club ever to have occupied 92nd place in the League. By 1986 City's fortunes had improved and it was a mark of their efforts that when further safety checks were made in 1985 Ashton Gate's capacity remained unchanged at 30 868 with 7628 seats, and the club had to spend only £2000 on minor details.

Ground Description

Whatever City's ranking in the League, Ashton Gate's pedigree is unquestionable. It is the trimmest ground in the South West. The Grand Stand sits on a bank of terracing, not quite running the length of the pitch. The white terrace rear wall stands out, and unusually is castellated at the centre. Of note are the two advertisement hoardings suspended from the roof, an unusual feature, and the unique mesh tunnel cover on wheels which is retracted when the teams have run out or returned to their dressing rooms. From the seats you can see a famous Bristol landmark, Cabot Tower, which stands on a hill due north across the River Avon, to the left of the Dolman Stand opposite.

City's pride is this modern, full-length stand whose roof is suspended from a cross girder mounted on two uprights outside the screen walls, as at Ibrox. Like a cantilever, the view from the stand is totally unimpaired by any uprights. In order to create sufficient height needed for the facilities beneath, the stand is fronted by a high plain brick wall, which even with the very narrow terrace in front rather isolates it from the rest of the ground (as at Chester and Swindon). The wall, despite its array of large advertisements, really needs a bit more colour, as does the bare, ribbed roof fascia. Once again, my plea is for a club crest, a signboard, a flag or two to liven up the stand and reinforce the ground's sense of identity.

In defence of Ashton Gate, however, it has to be said that every inch of steelwork is neatly painted a glossy scarlet. No slap dash work here at all. It also has to be said that the view from the Dolman Stand is superb, not only of the pitch but of Wills' Bonded warehouses to the left beyond the Winterstoke Road End, of the green expanse of Ashton Park straight ahead, and to the right of the hills beyond the Avon Bridge and Clifton Suspension Bridge. Behind the Dolman Stand is Southbow House, and the Bristol Bowling Club.

Harry Dolman was a keen bowler, hence the long, low hall underneath the stand, having two artificial flat greens, which alone cost £20 000 to lay. The bowling club pays City a £20 000 annual rent, and has a thousand members, who can play quite undisturbed even during a football match.

The Winterstoke Road End, or Covered End, but no longer the Keating Stand, is in fine condition for one so old, although it suffers in design from some awkward pillars at the front. The roof extends notably, and perhaps unnecessarily some 30 yards beyond the sidelines. Notice how gangways are marked out on the terracing in red paint, and how each pillar at the front is numbered. This is to help the police, who have a new surveillance unit in the corner next to the Grand Stand.

Opposite is the red-fenced Open End, backed by houses along Ashton Road. The floodlight pylons, which mark out the ground for miles around, are of the Scottish design.

Ashton Gate's facilities would have been perfect for the two Bristol clubs to share when Rovers decided to leave Eastville in 1986. They had already played here five times when their stand burned down in 1980, and a year later were almost agreed on a permanent move. But in 1986 Rovers could not have afforded City's asking price and it was felt that neither set of supporters would have been happy with the arrangement. Given Ashton Gate's advantages this must count as an appalling waste of an opportunity for ground sharing. Ashton Gate is a ground of which all Bristol should, in theory, be proud, and even more so after 1986 when it became the city's only League venue.

·SWINDON TOWN·

Previous Grounds

Swindon did not stay long at their first ground in 1881. It was a field in the Old Town area, next to a quarry, now part of Bradford Road and Avenue Road. After a small boy fell into the quarry during a match the club moved to Globe Field, now Brunswick Street and Lansdowne Road, then in 1884 to the Croft, home of Swindon Rangers Rugby Club. Swindon switched to the County Ground in 1895 but began playing on where the cricket pitch is now.

County Ground

The club's early years at the County Ground were successful enough for them to move away from the cricket pitch and establish a separate enclosure beyond the boundary. The terraces were laid out and a full-length grandstand built by 1911. In 1920 Swindon joined the League.

The Shrivenham Road Side was first covered in 1932, and in August 1938 the Town End covered terrace, then called the Hotel End, was opened. The supporters' club met the cost of £4300. During the Second World War, the County Ground became a prisoner-of-war camp, with huts placed on the pitch.

The ground staged one of the first floodlit games in modern times, an exhibition match v. Bristol City in April 1951. There were just eight lamps behind each goal. In February 1956 Swindon were also one of the first clubs to host a League fixture under lights, by then improved from the originals. The present pylons date from 1960.

A new stand for the Shrivenham Road Side was bought in 1958 from the grounds of the Aldershot Tattoo, but there is no record of how long it had stood there. Thirty years would be a fair estimate. The stand was one of two at Aldershot's military grounds, the other went to Accrington Stanley. The original Main Stand made way for the present North Stand in 1971. Similar to one at Chester, it cost £264 000, and is the only stand in Britain to have a bookmaker's shop underneath. Next to this was a squash club which has since been converted into headquarters for the Swindon Athletic Club, who use a new running track opposite the stand. The local council own the ground and rent the space independently.

Perhaps because of the council's tenure, when designation under the Safety of Sports Grounds Act was imposed in 1985 the County Ground became subject to one of the most stringent safety checks in the country. Indeed, Swindon's experience shows only too well how the Act has continued to be applied unevenly throughout the country.

Firstly, the upper tier of the Shrivenham Road Stand was closed, because although the framework is steel the remainder is wooden, and its narrow exits

Swindon's County Ground, with the remains of the old Main Stand still in front of the North Stand

lead down only from the rearmost seats. Secondly, the club were ordered to resurface parts of the terracing, build new turnstiles behind the Stratton Bank and put up new security fencing around the pitch.

But thirdly, and most surprisingly of all, the recently built North Stand had to be fitted with four new exits from the front rows down onto the pitch. This, and the fact that virtually every wooden structure had to be removed, came as a shock. How was it that a modern concrete and steel construction needed so much work when up and down the country at places like Torquay and Blackpool predominantly wooden stands still remain? Of course Swindon could not complain – safety considerations brook no compromise – but their costs of over £100 000 were ill-afforded.

While work was being carried out the County Ground's capacity was reduced from 26 000 to 12 500. Once complete however the limit rose to 22 000, of which 5245 are seated.

Ground Description

From certain approach roads, because the County Ground stands on such flat land and is surrounded by low buildings and open space, it is visible from a long way off. On arrival you will notice that only one end of the ground does not border on open land. Since the land belongs to the council, it has been suggested that the council should have built a leisure centre at the County Ground, at the same time as the North Stand was built, instead of at another site called the Oasis. Certainly the ground's central location makes the surrounding land ripe for development.

The North Stand is not only similar in design to Chester's Main Stand, it also has a wide patch of ground between a high front wall and the touchline. The gaps exist because the new stands were constructed directly behind the old ones, in order to minimize disruption during building.

Swindon had hoped to cover this grass patch with terracing but safety work has taken a higher priority. Four new exits lead down to the pitch from the seats, but otherwise the high brick frontage is unadorned and plain. Brightness is, however, not a problem inside the stand, where a sickly mix of blue, orange, lemon and green plastic seats makes one long for higher attendances! In contrast, behind the stand and across the cricket pitch where Wiltshire County Cricket team play, is a delightful wooden cricket pavilion, tastefully painted but probably extremely uncomfortable.

To the left is the open Stratton Bank, named after a nearby district, with a distinctive, if dated, clock at the back. To the right is the covered Town End for standing, with security fencing going right up behind the goal to the roof.

But the best feature of the County Ground is opposite the North Stand. Approached from Shrivenham Road, the South Stand, with its large green corrugated back, appears to have grown out of the parkland on which it rests. There are no fences or walls to separate it from the passing pedestrians.

Sadly, the future of this unique, green and cream coloured stand must be in jeopardy. It is a narrow double-decker, slightly cranked in the centre with only a shallow tier of wooden seating on the upper tier, now closed. Behind the stand are several snake-like stairways leading up to the seats and these were also deemed unsafe.

Although hardly in prime condition the stand still has a great deal of charm, not least for having so much steelwork for only 1423 seats. But improving its access and renovating the upper tier would have been an expensive business and the most likely solution would seem to be its replacement with a lower roof over the standing area, which in 1986 was confined to members only.

The possible demise of this finely proportioned structure is just one consequence of the designation of Third and Fourth Division grounds, which, one cannot help but feel, has been applied with varying degrees of strictness. The County Ground, a pleasing mixture of modern and traditional, will miss the old Tattoo Stand if it has to go.

·PLYMOUTH ARGYLE·

Home Park

Plymouth formed in 1886 as the Argyle Athletic Club, a group of amateurs willing to play whatever sport they fancied, be it cricket, football, rugby or athletics. They had no settled home of their own, playing instead on their opponents' grounds, and then on various pitches in the Plymouth area. But in 1901 they were fortunate in securing a long and inexpensive lease on a ground called Home Park. The owners were only too happy to let Argyle move in, for it had originally been built for the Devonport Rugby Club, but since the club had departed after a rent dispute, the ground had lain deserted for three years.

Argyle took over on Whit Monday 1901, and immediately held a series of popular events. Even so, the leaseholder, Clarence Spooner decided that amateur sport did not yield sufficient revenue to maintain such a large ground. Since cities such as Bristol, Southampton and Portsmouth had their own senior football clubs, and the entire county of Devon had not one, it was decided that the successful amateur Argyle Athletic team should join the ranks of the professionals.

To test public reaction, Spooner invited some of the top clubs in the country to play Argyle in exhibition matches at Home Park. Aston Villa came first and beat Argyle 7-0 in front of an encouraging 16 000 crowd. Others followed, and on 24 April 1903 Home Park staged a game between The Wednesday and Notts County, both First Division clubs, to give the public a truer example of League standards.

The success of these matches persuaded Argyle to concentrate on professional football and take on a new lease of the ground. On 5 September 1903 Home Park staged its first senior competitive game, v. Northampton Town in the Southern League, watched by 4438.

Home Park then was surrounded by farms. One end of the ground is still known as Barn Park. The approaches to Home Park were along country paths, the main one leading from Pennycomequick between hedges and over a stile just before the ground. There was always considerable congestion at this point on match days. Inside the ground had two stands. On the Popular Side was a small cover known either as the 'Flowerpot Stand' or Spooner Stand, since Mr Spooner's department store was advertised on the roof. A fire once broke out in this stand during a match causing a minor panic. A second fire resulted in a section being dismantled.

The Main Stand was more substantial. Roughly 40 yards long, it was a simple wooden post and beam construction with the then common pointed gable in the centre. In 1914 a prominent triangular bay was added to the gable for the local newspaper reporter

Leitch's spirit lives on at Home Park. The old Directors' Stand in the far corner was built after the disruption caused by German bombs

and his new-fangled telephone.

In 1920 the club joined its fellow Southern Leaguers in a mass exodus to the Football League. To celebrate promotion to Division Two in 1930 an £11 000 grandstand was built in place of the old wooden one which was sold off for timber. At the same time the supporters' club paid £1511 for the erection of a roof, giving shelter for 6000 spectators at the Devonport or Milehouse End. Two years later this cover was extended towards the Grand Stand, for £400, and concrete terracing laid.

Home Park's record attendance of 43 596 came to see Plymouth play Aston Villa, in that club's first ever season out of Division One, on 10 October 1936. Also in 1936 the entrance to Home Park was rebuilt, again paid for by the supporters' club.

During the Second World War, as an important naval base, Plymouth became a natural target for the German bombers. Home Park was closed between 1940–45 but did not escape the air raids. The pitch was covered in bomb craters, but more distressing, the Grand Stand was completely destroyed by high explosives and fire, set off by incendiaries and made worse by piles of furniture people had stored in the stand during the raids. But Home Park also played its part in the war effort. Soldiers returning from Dunkirk camped behind the Barn Park End and, as at Tranmere, the car park was used for smoke generators (to screen air defences). Behind the ruins of the Main Stand the US Navy built a warehouse and its

men played baseball on the ruined pitch.

For four years the ground lay in a heap of rubble and devastation, the grass became overgrown, twisted steelwork littered the craters, and nothing could be done until 1945. Fortunately for the club, a new board of directors under the chairmanship of Sir Clifford Tozer dedicated themselves to the enormous task of rebuilding both the club and its ground. Tons of rubble from the ruins of the town centre were dumped in the craters and on the banking around the pitch. Old tramcars were used as offices, army huts became dressing rooms, railway sleepers were laid on the terraces. The wrecked stand was cleared and temporary uncovered seating installed in its place. In the corner of the pitch a wooden pavilion was built for the directors. Home Park was back in use by the beginning of the 1946–47 season.

Two years later Argyle won the Third Division, and on their return to Division Two opened the present Grand Stand, an impressive double-decker in the pre-war style of Archibald Leitch, almost as if the club had simply followed the late architect's plans from the mid-1930s (see Design). It was certainly the last of this type ever built. On 26 October 1953 the club officially switched on their floodlights at Home Park for a friendly v. Exeter City. Unfortunately only 2000 attended the game, played in poor weather, whereas a total of 12 000 had seen two earlier reserve matches under the new lights.

In 1963–64 a large cover was erected over the

Popular or Lyndhurst Side, so that Home Park was now open at only one end. In 1969 extra seats were installed in the Grand Stand, giving a total number of 4100 seats, in a capacity of 40 000.

The Devonport End roof was deemed to be unsafe in 1977. It would have cost £50 000 to repair, or £70 000 to dismantle and restore. For £100 000 Plymouth could have replaced it completely. But they had neither £50 000 nor £100 000, so the roof came down. At least something was saved. The roof sheeting was used as fencing round the ground.

As at Brighton, the loss of this terrace roof proved only temporary. In 1984 a smaller cover costing only £40 000 was erected, thus restoring the ground's former appearance.

Safety considerations halved Home Park's capacity in 1985 from 38 000 to 19 000 (including 2933 seats) and the club had to spend over £300 000 on improvements. The former director's cabin was refurbished for use as the police's surveillance unit. Outside the ground temporary offices had to be moved from the main entrance to behind the Lyndhurst Side, in order to avoid congestion in the event of an emergency. Because this work was not technically inside the ground it was not eligible for FGIT aid.

But the work was not all safety orientated. At the rear of the Mayflower Stand, a seated section of the Main Stand paddock, 16 executive boxes were built and opened on February 1986, as Plymouth were en route for promotion to Division Two.

Home Park has two additional points of interest in its history. In 1960 the ground became the centre of a test case, between the club and the authorities. The Lands Tribunal assessed Home Park's rateable value at £2250 a year. Argyle appealed against this amount, arguing that a football club was the only possible tenant of such a site. They also invoked pleas of tradition and limited finances, with the result that the rates were lowered by a Court of Appeal.

Secondly, in 1977 Home Park staged a European Cup Winners Cup match (although Argyle had never progressed further than the 5th Round of the FA Cup). This was because Manchester United supporters had rioted in France and the club was ordered to play its tie v. St Etienne at least 200 miles from Old Trafford (Manchester is 280 miles from Plymouth).

Ground Description

It is apt that Plymouth Argyle should play in green, because the overwhelming impression of Home Park and the surrounding area is of greenery. There is not a prouder, more open location for a League ground than that enjoyed at Plymouth.

The main approach to Home Park leads into a vast car park with room for 2000 vehicles. The ground stands on a slight, grass-covered rise, surrounded by trees and meandering pathways.

Behind the Grand Stand is an open plain, on which stands the Mayflower Sports Centre, a swimming pool and municipal football pitches. Argyle have two training pitches nearby, known as Harper's Field, named after a famous Scottish international who joined the club from Arsenal in the early 1930s and served thereafter as player, trainer and groundsman. On the other sides of the ground are Central Park and the ground of Plymouth Cricket Club.

We pass through the main entrance, above which is a plaque recording its construction in 1936 and the name of A. C. Ballard, president of the supporters' club at the time. The detached offices are on the right.

The Main Stand, though substantial, manages to seem quite light and airy, with a green and white balcony wall, in typical Leitch style (as for example on White Hart Lane's East Stand). A large uncovered paddock with silver crush barriers stands in front. Even the details seem delicate. There are flower boxes over the players' tunnel. The lower tier of seats behind the paddock is named the Mayflower Stand. Lining the rear are the new executive boxes. The upper tier is illuminated by glass panels along the rear wall, creating the impression of an enormous greenhouse. There it is again, that word green!

From here to the right is a small pavilion in the corner, once for directors but now used by the police. This terrace is called Barn Park and has been completely resurfaced. Needless to say, neat green fencing lines the rear. Sadly at the front and all around the terracing is a new security fence. Even the homeliest of grounds need protecting these days. Tree-lined steps on the far side lead down into the public park and have prominent signs above each section, as on end-of-the-line tube stations on the outskirts of London, except that this one is called '10 STEPS START HERE', and Ongar is over 200 miles away.

Opposite the Main Stand, backed by yet more trees and more greenery, is the Popular or Lyndhurst Side. This is another pleasant section, with wide terracing and silver barriers, covered by a well-lit roof. The steelwork is green and cream with black trimming, like a Southern Counties' bus station.

To the left is the Devonport End, with its new, but plain cover at the rear. It is of course clad in green. The terrace is divided into two sections by a wide gap on one side of the goal. This is to facilitate the entrance of marching bands, tattoos and such like; Home Park is rented from the local council, and the club therefore have obligations to fulfil.

Plymouth is the second largest city in England never to have had a First Division club (Hull is the biggest), and it shows at Home Park. Rather like the city centre itself, there is plenty of space to breathe, and to cast a wide view over the surroundings. There is orderliness, not dull but reassuring.

But Home Park is no quaint outpost. Recent years have seen the ground improve in substance and appearance, so that it has both the charm of a gentle giant – a green giant that is – and also a scale and potential to match any aspiring First Division club.

·EXETER CITY·

St James' Park

Though much less famous and imposing than its namesake in Newcastle, St James' Park, Exeter has a history as old and as colourful dating back to at least 1894. For some years a team called Exeter United used the ground, sharing it with a farmer who grazed his pigs there before slaughter. Such 'ground-sharing' schemes were then quite common (see for example Brighton).

In 1904 Exeter City were formed at St James' Park from the successful St Sidwell's Old Boys team, and when in 1908 they turned professional and joined the Southern League, the first grandstand was built. Opposite, the terrace was nicknamed the 'flower-pot'.

In 1910–11 first Nelson, then Burnley refused to play City in the FA Cup unless another venue was chosen, because the St James' Park pitch was not long enough to meet FA requirements. This was a source of considerable annoyance to Exeter, badly in need of the revenue, but the owner of the land adjoining the far end of the pitch refused to sell them part of his land. City therefore began negotiating for the purchase of the St Thomas's County Rugby Ground on the other side of the city, until in 1911 the local MP, H. E. Duke, came to their rescue. He persuaded the landlord to part with some of his land, and Exeter were able to extend the pitch, first used on 14 October 1911. Before the game v. West Ham, H. E. Duke's daughter cut a red and white ribbon stretched across the new section of the pitch and then hoisted the new Exeter City flag. Among the attendance of 7000 people were the Archdeacon, several councillors, and the architect Archibald Lucas. In recognition of H. E. Duke's invaluable assistance, for some years that end of the ground was called the Duke Bank.

On 24 June 1921, at the end of their first season in the League, City purchased the 3·7-acre site for just over £5000, most of which came from the sale of goalkeeper Dick Pym to Bolton.

In 1925 the wooden cover now called the Cowshed was built, and a few months later on 17 November, fire destroyed the original Main Stand, together with all the players' kit, except for defender Bob Pollard's boots which were being repaired in Northampton. The present Main Stand was built during the following summer, after delays caused by the General Strike. The early 1930s were happy years at St James' Park. City enjoyed their best ever run in the FA Cup, which ended with the visit of Sunderland for a 6th Round replay on 4 March 1931. The game attracted City's highest gate, 20 984. The Cowshed was extended to its present length the following year, then in 1933 the club achieved their highest ever placing in the League, runners-up in Division Three South. St James' Park has changed little since. Dur-

St James' Park

ing the Second World War, US Army troops moved into the ground, using the pitch for training and the stand for cooking and sleeping.

Floodlights were installed relatively early at Exeter, as at several smaller southern clubs. The first game was v. Plymouth in 1953. The lights were primitive indeed, but have been updated twice since, although they are still fairly basic.

Designation under the Safety of Sports Grounds Act in 1985 reduced St James' Park to a capacity of 8000, including 1300 seats. But work costing over £100 000 during 1986 helped to raise this limit to approximately 12 000, with 1742 seats. Gangways and exits in the Main Stand were improved while the Cowshed was reroofed and its wooden sleepers replaced by new concrete terracing.

Ground Description

Like the town of Exeter itself, St James' Park is a rather sleepy, old-fashioned but appealing ground, caught in the midst of narrow, meandering streets. It was said that supporters would forecast match results by the relative positions of gulls which habitually settled on the crossbars at each end. The ground also has its own railway station, a few yards from the main entrance. The railway line, which links Exmouth with Exeter, runs directly behind the north east corner of the Main Stand, its grass-covered cutting providing a pedestal for the club's buildings above.

In the other corner of this side is the Grecian Gate (City are nicknamed the Grecians), which despite its romantic title, is hardly inspiring. It was paid for by the supporters' club after the War. The Main Stand runs three-quarters of the pitch's length and is the standard pre-war small club construction – sloping roof, dark wooden interior, glass screen walls – but with the players' tunnel, over which hangs the club crest, at the south end of the stand. Along the front of the roof and at either side are 13 floodlight poles barely 2 yards higher than the gutters. They must be the lowest in the League, and make it hard to spot the ground from a distance.

From this side you can see the St James' Road open terrace to the right, just 13 steps deep, behind which the houses opposite command an uninterrupted view of the pitch. The turnstiles at this end of the ground are open, an unusual feature. Note that the two telegraph poles at either end of the ground, in the middle of the terraces, were part of the original floodlighting system.

To the left is the old Duke Bank, now known as the Big Bank. Between this rather irregular open mound and the Main Stand, where the railway cutting is within yards of the corner flag, there is no terracing, and the groundsman has planted a row of lime trees to help stop the ball going onto the line below.

Opposite is the Cowshed, a long, low cover which used to have some rather ramshackle wooden terracing but is now completely refurbished. As shown at so many other grounds, concrete may be safer and stronger but worn creosoted wood used to be so much warmer, friendlier and with a wonderfully rumbling acoustic effect. Of course it had to go, such is progress, but the atmosphere of places like the Cowshed will hardly be the same again.

One unusual feature is that the terracing starts about 4 feet above pitch level, with a grass slope running from the touchline up to the Cowshed's perimeter wall. In the centre of the grass slope is a cut-away section which the players used to use for shooting practice against the wall. Behind the stand, clearly visible because there is only a low back fence along one half, is the Bishop Blackhall School. On the roof are another 13 floodlight poles.

Although much improved in substance St James' Park retains much of its rather makeshift appearance, as if it were held together by poles, wire and a coat of paint. But on a big match day the atmosphere is as vibrant as anywhere. Stepping through the Grecian Gate, you find a lovely football ground, quite unlike any other; a picture of warm red and green virtually untouched by the worst excesses of modernity, as quaintly southern as its namesake is so ruggedly northern.

◆ TORQUAY UNITED ◆

Previous Grounds

The club began in 1898 at Teignmouth Road, moving two years later to the Torquay Recreation Ground. In 1905 they were at Cricket Field Road, followed by the Torquay Cricket Ground in 1907. It is said that they should never have left this ground, now used by Torquay Athletic Rugby Club, because it is close to the station, on the sea front and situated in a natural bowl. But Plainmoor offered greater working-class support, so as Torquay Town, they moved in 1910.

Plainmoor

Plainmoor is rented at a nominal rent from the council, which was bequeathed the land by the Cary Estate, on the condition that it would always be open for public recreation. In theory, therefore, anyone can walk across the pitch at any time.

Torquay became United in 1921, after merging with Babbacombe FC, and joined the League six years later. The all-wooden Main Stand, which still occupies two-thirds of the South Side, was just finished in time for their first League fixture. It came from the now defunct Buckfastleigh racecourse, 10 miles east (where from the main road you can see the remains of another grandstand, forlorn in the midst of an open field).

In the early 1950s the Popular Side opposite was partly covered, as the team began a successful run. The visit of Huddersfield in the 4th Round of the FA Cup attracted Plainmoor's largest attendance, 21 908 in January 1955. A new end section was added to the Main Stand at this time, and floodlights on poles were installed for a friendly v. Birmingham in November 1954. They were not good enough for competitive games and had to be replaced later in the decade. The existing corner pylons date from the mid-1960s.

A few years later, the concrete cantilever 'Mini-Stand' went up on the Ellacombe End in place of the 'Cowshed' and would have covered the whole end had funds not run out.

On 17 May 1985, just six days after the appalling events at Bradford, an overnight fire destroyed the Main Stand's end bay. This had to be demolished, and safety officers ordered the rest of the stand to be closed as a further precaution. Only the dressing rooms underneath were allowed to be used until the 1986 fireproofing and structural improvements enabled the stand to reopen. Bench seats have also been added to the former narrow paddock area.

Meanwhile United cleared sections of old timber terracing at either end of the ground and flattened the ground in preparation for rebuilding concrete terracing. Bench seats holding over 400 spectators were installed in the Mini Stand, now used as a family enclosure.

Plainmoor's Main Stand before the 1985 fire. Once at a racecourse, it apparently doubles here as drying space for the playing strip

These measures and safety restrictions have led to Plainmoor's capacity being cut from 20 000 to only 4999, including 1400 seats. This low limit meant that in 1986 Torquay was the only League club whose ground was not designated under the Safety of Sports Grounds Act (which licences only grounds with a capacity above 5000).

In 1987 Torquay emulated Luton and Colchester by making Plainmoor a members-only ground. This was partly precipitated by the appalling behaviour of some visiting Wolves fans earlier in the year, yet another sign of how just a tiny minority has robbed the rest of us of some of our pleasures. The loss of a trip to Plainmoor is to be regretted most deeply.

Ground Description
Long before nearing Plainmoor you see signs pointing the way, almost pleading for your interest. The council obviously sees the value of a League club in its midst.

The ground is edged by neat avenues of daintily gabled guest houses and homes, all faced in light granite. Entering through the main gate you pass a white, detached chalet with porch, the club offices, and further along is the back of the Main Stand, lined by small windows. The stand is low, built entirely in dark wood, with blue and yellow pointed boards lining the gutters, like bunting. It is a showground stand, crafted and creaky, and it as much a reflection of its age as the 1950s' extension next to it; drab and metallic. The stanchions on the roof were for the old floodlights.

Left is the Ellacombe End, named after the district, in the centre of which stands the grey Mini-Stand, like an overgrown bus shelter. Formerly for standing only, it is now rather awkwardly flanked by two areas of flat ground.

The Popular Side on Marnham Road has a flat section in front of a 40-yard covered terrace and the open Babbacombe End on the right has a small patch of new terracing holding 300 fans, also flanked by flat ground where once lay timber terracing. Behind are immaculate gardens with granite walls. Even the floodlights, squat and low, do not intrude upon this very English scene. They are like cartoon floodlights in a Roy of the Rovers comic.

More seriously, Torquay must take credit for spending over £20 000 on safety work long before it was demanded and at a time when attendances hardly encouraged further outlay. Plainmoor nevertheless remains pleasantly underdeveloped, if somewhat ill-equipped to host a visit from a big club. It is 'plain' in an unspoilt sense. A real 'home' ground, now in reality as much as in appearance.

·14·
SOUTH WALES AND BORDER

·HEREFORD UNITED·

Edgar Street

Edgar Street was originally the home of the town's senior club, Hereford City, who let United share the ground when they were formed in 1924. City were almost defunct by the time United joined the Southern League in 1939; and United went on to establish themselves as a consistent force in the early rounds of the FA Cup. They were one of the very first clubs in the country to have floodlights, given to them by a local firm which had constructed the Skylon for the 1951 Festival of Britain Exhibition. The first flood-lit game was against Walsall in the Birmingham League in March 1953. Hereford's record crowd, 18 114, came for one of their many Cup matches with League opposition, in January 1958 v. Sheffield Wednesday.

In 1968 the cantilevered Main Stand was built, no doubt a further factor in their successful application to join the League in 1972, in place of Barrow. A wave of optimism following quick progress to Division Two, led to the erection of another cantilever stand in 1974. The Len Weston Stand was named after the club president who had died just before seeing his dream of League football at Hereford come true. Edgar Street thus became the only non-First Division ground to have two cantilevered stands, albeit comparatively small ones. Their modernity ensured that when the ground became designated in 1985 only a few alterations were needed, reducing the capacity from 17 500 to around 15 000 with 2100 seats.

Ground Description

Edgar Street is on very flat land, with a light-industrial estate and a vast parking area on two sides.

The Main Stand is characterized by deep overhanging roof fascia, and at its front, at pitch level, by a box-like vice-president's club resembling a modern house extension overlooking a garden lawn. The large windows, only 10 feet from the touchline, had to

The narrow, prefabricated Len Weston cantilever stand at Edgar Street

be boarded up in 1985 when legislation prohibited the consumption of alcohol within sight of the pitch. This at least saved players from what must have been a tempting view of the bar. Further along, the secretary's office window also looks out onto the pitch.

Next to the Main Stand on the right, the terrace has been removed and foundations for a stand extension laid. From here the terrace curves round in a big semi-circle behind the right hand or northern goal at the Merton Meadow End. The whole site occupies what used to be Merton Meadow. There was once a thin running track all round the perimeter, but the stands on both sides now cover the straights, and the semi-circles at each end are walled in.

A simple rectangular cover sits on the rounded terracing, from where you can see the medieval tower of Hereford Cathedral straight ahead.

Both ends of the ground are the same shape, although the Blackfriars Street End opposite has a wider roof. In the main reception area is a plaque which records the names of those who donated 250 or more bricks to the Blackfriars Street Brick Wall Fund in 1976.

The Len Weston Stand, made out of pre-cast concrete for just £30 000, is most unusual. Firstly, it covers a thin side of the ground hemmed in by Edgar Street, so by necessity is tall and narrow. The steep upper tier of 1200 seats, covered by the cantilever roof, is divided into only six rows, supported underneath by concrete pillars on a standing terrace. A double-decker stand in such a confined space is remarkable for such a small outlay.

Secondly, the stand follows not the line of the pitch but Edgar Street, and so the ends are further from the pitch than the centre, the exact opposite of many stands which are angled from the middle inwards.

Another visual curiosity is the floodlighting system. The four gantries are proportionately large and almost half the height of the pylons they rest on. The awkward proportions are accentuated by having only eight tiny lamps mounted on each gantry.

Most noticeable of all however is the pitch, the widest in the League. Measuring 80 yards across it is a full 30 feet wider than the smallest in England.

This width, despite two such modern stands, combined with the distance from each end terrace to the goal-lines and the lack of anything taller than a tree all round the ground, gives Edgar Street an exposed, even rather unspoilt appearance.

· SWANSEA CITY ·

Vetch Field

Swansea Town was one of several teams in South Wales to begin their professional life just before the First World War, encouraged by the Southern League in its attempts to keep pace with the Football League. A tithe map of 1843 shows the ground as 'cae vetches', a field for growing vetch or tare. Commonly known however as the Old Town Ditch Field, it was opened as a sports ground on Whit Monday 1891, complete with cinder running track and a turf track for horses. An amateur team Swansea AFC played there from 1892–99, reforming in 1900 and becoming Swansea Town. A professional team with the same name moved back to the Vetch in 1912 and became a limited company. David Farmer's history of the club (Swansea City 1912–82, Pelham Books, 1982) tells us that the first building at Vetch Field occurred in 1913, when the present Main Stand was built on Glamorgan Street, just after Town had won their first Welsh Cup Final. But for the first season the pitch was cinders only, and until turf was laid the players had to wear knee pads!

The 1920s were a period of excitement and success, resulting at Vetch Field in the erection of the present West Stand, a large double-decker, in the summer of 1927. Such large stands behind the goal were then a rarity.

In order to build the open North Bank terracing in 1925, the Vetch Field Infants School had to be demolished and the pupils transferred. Perhaps some of them were among those supporters who in 1959 helped raise £16 000 to reshape and cover the North Bank. In September 1960 Swansea's floodlights were first used for a friendly v. Hibernian.

By 1967 the club had slipped into the Fourth Division, but still managed to record its highest attendance, 32 796, for the visit of Arsenal in the FA Cup 4th Round in February 1968.

Exactly two years later Swansea became City instead of Town, but found the change of little help to their ailing fortunes. Desperate for money the club sold Vetch Field to the local council in December 1974 for £50 000, plus an additional grant of £150 000 to keep the club in business. A year later City reached their lowest point, having to seek re-election for the first time.

However, under John Toshack's management, Swansea rose from the Fourth to the First Division in just three seasons. For Vetch Field, considerable changes to the ground's facilities and more importantly its safety had to take place to keep pace with this galloping success.

There was one major piece of construction, the East Stand, completed in January 1981 at a cost of just under £800 000. Seating 1841 the stand includes new

View from the West Stand at Vetch Field overlooking the original stand and its new neighbour (with the prison behind)

offices and was intended to continue round the south east corner and replace the already antiquated Main Stand.

Although City received planning permission to continue the stand along the South Side, capital was simply not available. Apart from concentrating funds on building a team, City had also to spend a further £700 000 on safety improvements, almost stretching their grant from the Football Grounds Improvement Trust to the £360 000 limit. New terracing had to be laid, barriers replaced, access improved and steelwork in the West Stand strengthened. Having spent all this money on achieving First Division standards, the club promptly dropped back into the Fourth Division in four seasons, and at one stage during the 1985–86 season came within a hair's-breadth of extinction. Fortunately Swansea survived several winding-up orders in the High Court as supporters and saviours rallied round, but for a few days the story of the club's fateful rise and fall captured the nation's attention.

Meanwhile, local safety inspectors had already ordered the closure of the West Stand and the wing section of the Main Stand, reducing the number of seats to 2900 in an overall capacity of 23 830.

Seldom had a ground witnessed so much pain and glory in the same decade.

Ground Description

It is hard to believe that the seafront is only 300 yards away, because there is not an inch to expand on any side. To illustrate this, two corners of the ground are actually cut across by the back gardens of neighbouring houses, divided from the crowds by just a brick wall.

There are two entrances on Glamorgan Street, one for players and officials – through a gate tucked in between two houses, if you do not look hard you will miss it – and a larger entrance leading to the new offices in the East Stand. The Centre or Main Stand is not visible from outside the ground, hiding behind a row of terraced houses.

It is all seated only as far as the West End 18-yard line, after which there are terraces, but all under the same low, sloping roof, supported by a line of pillars along the touchline. The little white gable has a flagpole at each of its three points. One bay to the west, a flat, window-lined box on the roof houses the press.

Behind here are the taller buildings of a Territorial Army Drill Hall, with windows overlooking the pitch. The high walls of Swansea prison also overshadow the stand.

From the Main Stand you can see the tall West Stand to the left, now closed for safety reasons. Large enough to be a main stand, it is actually extremely basic, the top tier having long, worn bench seats only, the passageways and corridors being dark and cramped. The high screen ends are made of rusting, green-coloured corrugated iron. Underneath the balcony are terraces. For years this was a depressing, neglected stand, and its closure is a shame if only because from the top of the upper section one had the best possible overall view of Vetch Field, especially the cramped borders to the left, immediately next to the disused stand. Here the terraces give way to an angled wall, behind which are the gardens of City's long-suffering neighbours.

Looking opposite, the North Bank runs the length of the pitch, and is a large covered terrace built on earth banking at the front and steel supports at the back. Before this was built there was a clear view of the Swansea suburbs rising up the distant hills.

To the right is the new East Stand, painfully modern and efficient in comparison with its ageing neighbours. But again, this has an odd appearance, because it fills only three-quarters of the pitch's width. More gardens abut on the thin section of open terrace in the north corner. And rather than finish at right angles to the pitch, the East Stand begins to curve temptingly around the corner before coming to a dead halt next to the old stand.

However quaint the Main Stand may be, that it should stop this graceful sweep of the cantilever is visually most irritating. To confound matters, the new floodlight pylon in that corner is just about the oddest in existence, leaning over the back of the stand and hanging suspended above the roof at an angle completely at variance with the rest of the ground, like a crane waiting to lower its load onto a ship's deck.

Otherwise the stand is clean and simple, finished in white concrete – to blend with the predominantly white neighbouring houses – and open at either end to keep the view unhindered.

The Vetch Field has four totally different stands, each with its own character, notably the two older constructions. These may not be wholly satisfactory, but they are unpredictable, and placed next to that odd pylon and the streamlined East Stand they make the Vetch Field seem an apparently disjointed venue, in which the only predictable feature is the pitch. For the traveller who thinks all football grounds are the same and cannot possibly divert one's attention from the field of play, this one is therefore an unexpected, but welcome curiosity.

·CARDIFF CITY·

Previous Grounds

Although club football in Cardiff was recorded as early as 1884, Cardiff City's clearest origins date back to 1899. That year Riverside Cricket Club formed a football team and in 1902–03 played on a stony pitch at Roath before disbanding, only to re-emerge in November 1905 at Sophia Gardens, a public park belonging to the Marquis of Bute on the west bank of the River Taff. In 1906 the team tried to change its name to Cardiff City, in recognition of the borough's new status, but had to wait until 1908, when the local FA decided that the name would only be granted to the first team in the city to turn professional.

The comprehensive study, *Football in Cardiff* by Derrick Jenkins (1983), from which much of the following derives, relates how the club decided to gauge public opinion before risking professionalism, by staging a series of friendlies against first-class opposition. The first two such games were staged at Cardiff Arms Park, the national home of Welsh Rugby, City drawing with Southern League Crystal Palace and losing to First Division Bristol City in October and November 1909. In March 1910 Cardiff invited Middlesbrough, also of the First Division, for a friendly at the then Harlequins RFC ground. Satisfied with the public's reaction the club decided to turn professional and find a permanent home.

Of their previous grounds, only Sophia Gardens exists as a sporting ground, now the home of Glamorgan County Cricket Club and also the site of the National Sports Centre, between Cathedral Road and the River Taff.

Ninian Park

In February 1910 Cardiff Corporation's Parks Committee agreed to grant the club a seven-year lease of a 5-acre site, the former rubbish tip on the fringes of Leckwith Common, between Sloper Road in Grangetown and the Taff Vale railway line. City had to guarantee their ability to pay annual rent of £90. All augured well until one of the guarantors withdrew his support, but after a short period of uncertainty, Lord Ninian Crichton Stuart, second son of the third Marquis of Bute, came to the rescue. Until then, the ground was going to be called Sloper Park, but since his intervention secured the lease, his name was adopted in appreciation.

Cardiff City turned professional and joined the Southern League Second Division, but they decided to open Ninian Park with an attractive friendly against Aston Villa, the current League Champions, on 1 September 1910. Among the new professional players' first tasks was clearing the pitch of broken glass and debris, left over from the rubbish tip, start-

Ninian Park in 1947 before the Grand Stand was extended. The Grangetown End roof (left) is now gone

ing at dawn on the opening day. The ground was prepared with a small wooden grandstand, low banks, and a dressing room built on the corner of the pitch on Sloper Road. A photograph taken on the first day shows the railway signal box clearly visible behind the then very low Bob Bank, opposite the stand.

A crowd of 7000 came to the match, which was scheduled at the unusual time of 5 o'clock on a Thursday afternoon (Villa presumably having League commitments at that time of the year). Lord Ninian kicked off for Cardiff, who did well to lose only 1-2. Lord Ninian thereafter became a firm supporter of the club and became an MP for Cardiff in December 1910 (he died only five years later in action during the First World War).

The first international match at Ninian Park was in March 1911 v. Scotland. City were elected to the Football League, Division Two in 1920 and won promotion in their first season, the beginning of a successful run.

Ninian Park advanced with the team. In 1920 the Canton Stand, named after the district, was built behind the north goal, a covered bank with bench seats. To have seats arranged like this was unusual

at the time, if not unique, for it is only in recent years that clubs have started installing seats on their standing terraces. The Bob Bank was covered with a simple flat roof supported on columns, with an exposed girder along the front, as at the Racecourse Ground.

In the summer of 1928 a much larger roof was erected over the Grangetown End, also named after a district, for standing spectators only. But its presence did the players no good at all, for Cardiff were relegated the following season, and only two seasons later found themselves in Division Three South. During this miserable run it was reported that for the game v. QPR on 14 November 1931, not a single person was standing on the Bob Bank, out of an attendance of only 2000. Cardiff were still in Division Three, struggling still, when on 18 January 1937 the wooden Main Stand burnt down, apparently the result of thieves trying to blast open the club's safe which they wrongly believed to contain the gate money from City's Cup tie two days before. In place of the old stand was built a brick and steel construction some 60 yards long on the half-way line.

The visit of League leaders and eventual Champions Arsenal, on 22 April 1953, attracted City's biggest home gate of 57 800. Cardiff were relegated in 1957, but in 1958 the Bob Bank was doubled in height and depth and a new roof built over the back section. Two years later the first floodlights were switched on for a League match v. Sheffield Wednesday at the opening of the 1960–61 season, when Cardiff were yet again back in Division One. Ninian Park's biggest ever crowd came for an international match v. England on 14 October 1961. The 61 566 attendance is the highest also for a Welsh international match played in Wales.

Since the Second World War, Ninian Park had become almost the permanent home of the Welsh team, with 51 games played here between 1946–77 compared with 16 at the Racecourse Ground and 7 at the Vetch Field. But the ground's facilities were still far behind those at Wembley or Hampden, although in 1973 the Main Stand or Grand Stand was extended on both sides to run the whole length of the pitch. But as an international venue, as well as the fact that City were then a Division Two club, when the Safety of Sports Grounds Act was brought into effect in 1977, Ninian Park was severely affected by the findings of the safety inspectors.

Despite the number of ambiguities and the implied need for reasonable interpretation when implementing the Act, it seemed that the South Glamorgan authorities chose to follow the book, and they reduced Ninian Park's capacity to just 10 000 until repairs were made. Such zeal cost Cardiff City £600 000, of which £200 000 came from the Football Grounds Improvement Trust, and in view of Ninian Park's national status, £27 000 was granted by the Welsh FA.

One of the most significant changes brought about by the Safety Act was the demolition of the Grangetown End roof in 1977, and the cutting back of the banking, thus reducing its capacity by half, and palpably affecting the whole ground's appearance and atmosphere. Identical measures were taken at Home Park and Bloomfield Road, with similar results. As already noted, Ninian Park staged two-thirds of all Wales' home fixtures between 1946–77. Having spent so much money on restoring the ground's capacity in order that it would be able to continue to host such matches, it was reasonable for Cardiff to believe that once the safety requirements were met the Welsh FA would return to the status quo existing before 1977.

Throughout 1977, Wales played at Wrexham, plus one 'home' game at Anfield v. Scotland in the World Cup. With much of the repairs effected, the national team returned to Cardiff in 1978. Between then and Wales' final unsuccessful World Cup qualifying match v. USSR in May 1981, Swansea staged two games, Wrexham six but Cardiff only five.

The club felt cheated. They had a large capacity ground which they were unlikely to fill for League matches, but which was now liable only for one or two internationals a year. This situation was made worse when the annual home internationals were abandoned and the Welsh FA decided to allow Cardiff only 15 per cent of gate receipts from internationals as opposed to 20 per cent of gross income (which included television rights and so on). In addition, Cardiff argued that all internationals should be staged in the capital, as in rugby, and that the FA headquarters be situated there rather than in Wrexham.

This debate will no doubt continue for many years, leaving Cardiff in 1986 with a capacity of 40 000, including 5550 seats, but with average League gates of below 5000.

Ground Description

Although very close to the centre of Cardiff and the main railway station, Ninian Park stands on the edge of a large expanse of flat, open ground, with playing fields, Ely River, woods and the large Trelai Park to the west, and a huge web of railway shunting yards to the east. Beyond lies the district of Riverside, where the club originally formed (Cardiff Arms Park, three-quarters of a mile to the east, is in contrast completely submerged in a built-up area on the banks of the Taff).

From certain approaches, therefore, one can see Ninian Park from a considerable distance, and it is an imposing sight with the city skyline in the background. Close to, however, Ninian Park holds no surprises. The Grand Stand is a very plain unembellished design, with a slight, pitched roof, white terrace rear wall and an open paddock in front. The roof fascia bears the club crest and name, and one can see quite clearly from the roof where the new wings were added in 1973. It is a neat stand, but colourless also. It holds 3500 seats.

From here, to the left is the Canton Stand, its low pitched roof so brightly covered with a large advertisement that it almost overpowers the ground. At the back of the stand, under the original roof, the club started to build a restaurant (still unfinished), the best alternative Cardiff could find when the safety inspectors determined that the rear section was unsafe. This has reduced the number of seats to 2050, while the view from the very front is poor anyway, being too low for seated spectators. The stand is also much closer to the Grand Stand than to the opposite side, giving the impression that the pitch was either shifted or widened when the Bob Bank was redeveloped.

The extremely large Bob Bank, so called because it cost a shilling to stand there, is opposite the Main Stand. There are taller sides in the League, at St Andrew's for example, but none are quite so deep as this one. From the very back in the centre, it is about 50 yards to the nearest touchline. The terracing is only half-covered, and rises in shallow steps, divided by wide gangways. It has been said the safety inspectors ordered so many crush barriers to be built here in 1977 that there's hardly any room left to stand!

From the back of the bank, looking behind the cover, one can see the signal box, the shunting yards, the docks and all of Cardiff city centre stretching ahead, including Cardiff Arms Park.

Finally, to the right is the now open Grangetown End. Its roof is missed no less than the one taken down at Blackpool, for it was the largest cover at the ground, dark and low, and without it the ground seems far more exposed. There is naturally a tendency for spectators to seek cover under the Bob Bank roof in wet weather, leaving just a handful of individuals on the Grangetown End. Ninian Park's atmosphere has suffered accordingly.

Behind the terrace a wide gangway has been built, floodlit by pylons at the top of the terrace, providing access from Sloper Road to the Bob Bank. Each of the main floodlight pylons is wrapped in barbed wire. In recent years the ground has staged two other sports. An attempt to introduce Rugby League to Cardiff failed – predictably in view of Rugby Union's hold on the city – and in 1986 the Cardiff Tigers American football team played at Ninian Park during the summer, with marginally more success.

But as with football, small crowds tend to become lost in such a large stadium. Cardiff are toying with the possibility of laying artificial grass in order to gain more community involvement, but that would of course signal the end of its role as an international venue.

Ninian Park thus falls uneasily between the demands of the national team and the more modest needs of Cardiff City. It is doubly ironic therefore that nearby lies Cardiff Arms Park, so cleverly and neatly built, side by side to the smaller, but very adequate ground of Cardiff RFC. If only the soccer authorities could have been so clever.

·NEWPORT COUNTY·

Somerton Park

Newport have played at Somerton Park since forming in 1912, since when ownership of the ground has changed hands no less than eight times. County were formed by workers of the Lysaght's iron and steelworks, and rented Somerton Park from a private concern. During the First World War the property was sold, but the new owners demanded a higher rent from County. Not wishing to waste what progress had already been made the Lysaght company decided to buy Somerton Park in 1919, at a cost of £2200, and handed it over to a committee of employees to use as they thought fit. They were naturally determined that County should remain at the ground.

During the 1931–32 season when the club were out of League action, after years of depression, significant changes occurred at Somerton Park. In order to save the club from extinction the workers' committee which leased the ground to County sold it to a bookmaker. They gave Lysaght back the £2200 invested in 1919, settled the rest of the club's debts, and then discovered the bookmaker had sold it to the Cardiff Arms Park Greyhound Racing Company at a vast profit. The company set about transforming Somerton Park, which had only a small main stand opposite where the Main Stand is now, and a cover over the Cromwell Road End dating from 1922. To accommodate the dog track the pitch was moved, the banking reshaped and the present Main Stand built. County's original Main Stand was converted into a social and viewing area and a gable on the roof added to house the starter and timing devices needed for greyhound racing. So although County were again tenants of an outside company, they at least had a better equipped ground for their return to the League.

For a Third Division derby v. Cardiff City on 16 October 1937, Somerton Park's highest gate of 24 268 was recorded. The team won the Third Division South Championship in 1939 and were just beginning the following season when war broke out. Blackout was imposed and the greyhound company was forbidden to hold Saturday evening meetings at Somerton Park, so they switched to Saturday afternoons and forced County to play elsewhere. For a time the club played at Rexville, the ground of a works' team on the other side of Newport, Lovell's Athletic. Somerton Park was then taken over by the Civil Defence, and County played on at the Rodney Parade Rugby Ground.

Floodlights were installed in 1957, and first used on 21 October for an exhibition game v. an All Star FA XI.

In 1963, after years of fading interest, the Cardiff Arms Park Greyhound Racing Company decided to

Somerton Park, showing the 'Social Side'

leave Newport (it vacated the rugby stadium in the 1970s) and sold Somerton Park to the local council for £30 000. Now down in the Fourth Division, County found themselves sharing the ground with a speed-way team. Then in 1978 the team began to improve culminating in 1980 with their winning promotion to Division Three and the Welsh Cup. At last they had the resources to buy Somerton Park, and in April 1980, for a sum of at least £100 000, negotiations were concluded with the council.

The ground then had a capacity of 18 000, but was in such a poor state that frankly Newport could barely have afforded promotion to Division Two – which they came close to – because it would have meant bringing the ground up to the standards required by the Safety of Sports Grounds Act.

In the event promotion was not achieved and in 1986, struggling again, Newport were forced to sell Somerton Park back to the council for £220 000. During their brief, six-year tenure County had given the ground something of a face-lift but little else of substance, and when designation of Third and Fourth Division clubs was ordered in 1985 Somerton Park's capacity was reduced to 8000, of which 1200 are seated.

Ground Description

This is another ground difficut to find, with low stands and floodlights hidden amid railway lines, pylons and gantries. Once spotted there can be no mistake about whose ground it is; Somerton Park is a splash of amber and black on the landscape.

Passing through the courtyard, lined by sundry offices and social facilities, the Main Stand is seen on the Somerton Road Side of the ground, some 50 yards long. It has a gently pitched black roof supported at the front, with plain white fascia and amber paint-work. Now all seated, the original paddock is divided by the tunnel, distinctively covered in red and black sheeting, with the warning that the paint is of the variety that stays wet.

From here, to the right but on the same touchline, is an awkward standing cover in the top corner. It is

close to the Main Stand, but set several yards back, so that the view from underneath is rather impeded. Perhaps it was built before the Main Stand.

To the far right is the Railway End, a shallow earth and cinder bank curving round the old track, which is fenced off by a wall topped by wire mesh. It is a miserable end indeed, with no concrete terraces, no crush barriers, made grimmer by the railway line from Cardiff to London and the West Country run-ning directly behind. One suspects it was no great loss to local supporters when the authorities ordered this end to be fenced off as a safety measure in 1985.

To the left is the Cromwell Road End. (Newport are known as the Ironsides because the link with Lysaght's ironworks and the proximity of Cromwell Road made this the most popular submission when the local newspaper held a competition to find a nickname.) This end of the ground is oddly square next to the curved ends of the pitch and old track, because it predated the arrival of the greyhound company. There is a flat roof at the back of some extremely shallow terracing, with an open set of flat concrete in front, bounded by a curved wall around the track. To make viewing worse, the front level is a couple of feet below the pitch level, and in the middle of the covered section is a large gateway where there is no terracing, and a toilet block jutting out, taking up valuable covered standing space. Almost in recog-nition of this, between the toilets and the gate is a section of concrete terracing just 1 foot wide!

The roof continues round the far corner at a right-angle, and because of the track's curvature, the cor-ner is some way from the pitch. It meets up on the far side with the 'Social Side'. This is a stand covering thick wooden terraces, backed by a social club whose windows look out on the pitch. On the roof is a little covered platform for cameras. Another stretch of flat concrete divides the stand from the perimeter track. To the right of the Social Side, meeting up with the Railway End is a 20-yard length of open terracing.

For standing spectators, Somerton Park is most unsatisfactory. One is either too low down, too far back, blocked by fences and pillars, or just out in the open on a rough bank. Of all the grounds once used or still used by greyhounds or speedway, Newport's is the most awkwardly adapted. And although the am-ber paint helps to liven up a rather jumbled collection of old stands and covers, there is no escaping the fact that until one owner, any owner, is prepared to hang on long enough to be able to modernize Somerton Park properly, the ground will simply rot, rust and waste away. Unless the Council have some hard cash and bright ideas, Somerton Park, sad to relate, does not appear to have much of a future.

·15·

WEST MIDLANDS, SALOP AND STAFFORDSHIRE

·COVENTRY CITY·

Previous Grounds

Coventry City began life as Singers FC, a bicycle factory's works team. From 1883 they played on Dowells Field, between where St George's Road and the railway line now lie off Binley Road, moving to their first enclosed ground, called Stoke Road, in 1887. The pitch was between Wren Street and Swan Lane, just south of the current ground. Ten years later the pitch was moved 40 yards east to allow for new building, but in 1899, having been renamed Coventry City, the club had to leave for an adjacent piece of land now known as Highfield Road, owned at the time by the Craven Cricket Club. For this information I am indebted to the club history, *Singers to Sky Blues*, by Messrs Brassington, Dean and Chalk.

Highfield Road

In recent years Coventry City have been something of a trendsetter, whose innovations have been studied and copied by clubs all over the country. Some of Coventry's ideas have been sound and some controversial, but they have succeeded in transforming the ground from an ordinary, small town's enclosure to one of the best in the League.

Highfield Road began humbly. City spent £100 on clearing elm trees (which stood more or less along the present half-way line) and building the 2000-seater John Bull Stand on the south side. Rent cost £60 a year but City were able to earn this by sub-letting the pitch to a junior team.

In 1910 a barrel roof stand with a large open paddock in front was built on the Thackhall Street side and in 1922 the open Spion Kop was built up with rubble cleared from laying tramlines in the city. The opposite West Terrace was covered five years later by a roof bought for £2000 from Twickenham RFC, but once erected it became apparent that the pitch sloped 7 feet from north to south.

To celebrate Coventry's first really promising run of form the John Bull Stand was replaced in 1936 with a new pitched-roof Main Stand costing £14 000 (Arsenal's Main Stand built during the same summer cost almost ten times as much). An extended canopy over the paddock area was added three years later, by which time City had taken out a loan of £20 000 to purchase the freehold of Highfield Road.

In 1940 Highfield Road took its share of the Blitz which devastated so much of the city. Three direct hits put the ground out of action for eighteen months.

The first floodlit match at Highfield Road was on 21 October 1955 v. Queen of the South, attended by 17 000. The city was then in the awesome process of recovering from the destruction of the war, and appeared to be an important symbol of Britain's future prosperity. But the team still had to hit the bottom before it could reach the top. In 1958 City went down to the newly constituted Division Four, escaped at the first attempt and then welcomed James W. T. Hill as their new manager, recently retired from playing. From that moment on, Highfield Road was never the same.

Hill did not just build a team, he created an image; one which was to mould the corporate development of the club on the Sky Blue theme. Without a decent team this might have seemed like empty gimmickry but Hill took City out of the Third Division and into the First within six years.

The crowds loved it. Hill's image building coincided with exciting developments in the city, for example, the building of a new shopping precinct.

To begin Highfield Road's development the Thackhall Street Stand was replaced, section by section with a revolutionary type of prefabricated construction. There had been one such stand built before, at Fratton Park, but City's Sky Blue Stand – as it was inevitably dubbed – was larger and more sophisticated. Built by a firm called Banbury Grandstands it was claimed to be 'a future concept' in stand design, could be made to fit any size, and at Highfield Road was built at a cost of £120 000 between 1963–64. Suddenly Coventry became the focus of other clubs' attention.

The next improvement came in September 1964, when the *Coventry Evening Telegraph* gave City a £3000 electric scoreboard. Compared with today's

Newly-seated Highfield Road, with the distinctive, vaulted Main Stand roof. The seats nearest the camera were replaced by terracing in 1985

computer-operated data boards it was a primitive collection of bulbs and wires, but again, in 1964 it was yet another demonstration of Sky Blue razzmatazz. In the same year the League's first real executive club was set up in the Main Stand (costing members 100 guineas a year) while the Kent and England cricketer Godfrey Evans introduced Radio Sky Blue to keep fans entertained before matches. There were netball matches, dog handling displays, even pop groups on the pitch.

Other clubs' officials were now visiting Highfield Road to pick up ideas and advice on pepping up their own outdated images. In 1965 came another innovation, which although it proved to be just a novelty was nevertheless a bold scheme. Coventry filmed their away match at Cardiff on closed-circuit television, and screened it live at Highfield Road, on four huge boards placed on the pitch, on 6 October 1965. For a while it seemed as if fog might ruin the whole event. But fortunately the weather cleared and a crowd of 10 295 at Highfield Road watched in wonderment as their team won 2-1 at Ninian Park, where the live attendance was 12 600. Such a system was made even more potentially viable by the fact that Coventry were then staging their reserve games in mid-week – another innovation – and gates were sometimes as high as 12 000.

There was only one more closed-circuit broadcast at the ground; Coventry's match at The Valley later in the season. The attendance was a healthy 11 321 at Highfield Road, but the experiment was dropped thereafter. The two Liverpool clubs tried it with great success in March 1967, but by then televised football was becoming established and the idea was never revived. Naturally, the 'away' clubs objected because

closed-circuit television reduced their potential gates.

Coventry were certain of promotion on 29 April 1967 when Wolves were the visitors for a match which would help decide which of the two would win the Second Division Championship, attracting Highfield Road's largest ever attendance, 51 455.

City became Champions and looked forward almost incredulously to life in Division One. During the close season a double-decker West Stand was built at the relatively low cost of £85 000, with seats for 3200. A new idea for match programmes was launched; the Sky Blue match day magazine, a fore-runner of many of today's more successful publications, and all boded well, until at the beginning of the new season, Jimmy Hill resigned as manager.

Suddenly the dream was shattered and with relegation looking increasingly likely, disaster struck on 6 March 1968. The Main Stand was destroyed by fire and with it the Second Division Championship Trophy.

City rebuilt the stand immediately, a larger version of the Sky Blue Stand, with a restaurant on the first floor – a rare feature then – thereby raising the seating capacity to 12 000. If the team did not always seem of First Division standard, Highfield Road certainly was.

In 1970 the original roof of the Sky Blue Stand, which like the new Main Stand was a series of light-weight aluminium vaulted sections, was found to have structural defects and was replaced with a plain, flat roof. (Even this new roof was to have problems, when a gale blew part of it down in 1983.)

But the greatest transformation came during the summer of 1981. City took the momentous decision to

185

turn Highfield Road into the first all-seater stadium in England (Scotland had two: Aberdeen and Clydebank). Again the ground became the centre of widespread attention. The conversion required an extra 8000 seats and cost £400 000 to complete, reducing the overall capacity from 38 500 to 20 616. City's main motive was to reduce hooliganism, which they felt had deprived the ground of its 'family' atmosphere. After almost annual destruction of certain sections of the ground, especially the toilets, vandal-proof fixtures were installed wherever possible. Every game was made all-ticket, with only a small number of tickets available on match days, at £5 each, again in an attempt to dissuade the casual away fan.

It did not succeed entirely, for hooligans still managed to destroy seating. But the all-seating arrangement did at least allow outbursts of violence to be quelled from the outset. Attendances flopped disastrously however. In 1979–80 they were over 19 000 on average. By 1986 the average was below 13 000. Yet the recession hit Coventry harder than many cities in England and it would be unwise to attribute City's declining support solely to the concept of an all-seated stadium.

Certainly Coventry were quickly forced to reconsider, for example, the match day ticketing arrangements. Then in 1983 they reopened a small section of the East terracing for 2000 standing fans only. At the same time Jimmy Hill resigned from the board, thus ending an eventful association of twenty-five years.

'Something which is revered in Aberdeen,' said Hill, 'is almost spat upon in Coventry.' But a survey indicated that the hurried, tactless manner in which Highfield Road had been converted had alienated supporters almost as much as the concept itself. At Pittodrie the process had been more gradual, and crucially, in my opinion, utilized bench seating in certain areas (see Aberdeen).

Pitch invasions in 1984 led to the reintroduction of perimeter security fences – a sad admission that seated areas were as vulnerable to hooligans as others – and in 1985 the East Terrace had all its seats removed to allow room for approximately 9000 standing spectators in an overall enlarged capacity of 28 000. The all-seater experiment was over, in Coventry at least. (For details of a specialized analysis of the experiment see Bibliography.)

Ground Description

For anyone unused to watching football in an all-seated stadium, Highfield Road used to be an unsettling place to visit. Even now, the remaining 19 000 seats are light blue of course, and unless a large crowd is in attendance, this colour combined with a bright terracotta track and an excellent playing surface, makes the ground seem almost synthetic, almost too bright.

The Main Stand is the most interesting construction, largely because of its vaulted roof, like a huge section of corrugated iron. The wavy lines protrude far beyond the slanting pillars and from below resemble the underbelly of a fantasy spaceship. There are two lines of private boxes, 12 at the front uncomfortably close to the touchline, and 17 at the very back, and in addition several other small boxes dotted about the stand. Even the dug-outs are covered huts moulded into the stand above the tunnel. All the facings are in dark, polished wood. Further evidence of the club's ambition and foresight is the existence of a high-quality restaurant in the stand. Many clubs have now built restaurants but none have carried the approval of Egon Ronay, as at Coventry.

To the left from here is the West Stand, a simple but efficient double-decker, similar to its contemporary at the Baseball Ground. It is the same height as the Main Stand, but has a flat roof and vertical pillars. The balcony wall also has polished wood panelling, much of it obscured by advertising.

Opposite is the Sky Blue Stand, on Thackhall Street. Now looking faded from the road, it has had a new lease of life inside since seats were added to the large paddock. When this also had a vaulted aluminium roof the two side stands were in perfect harmony. Now the Main Stand steals the show.

None of the new seats have simply been attached to the old terracing. Experience at grounds like Villa Park and St Andrew's made Coventry realize that for the best view, new steps would have to be laid with higher risers. But since the pitch level had once been so distorted, the original terracing sloped at all the wrong angles. Indeed between 1963–81 the pitch was surrounded by a concrete white wall, which to compensate for the varying heights rose from nearly 8 feet high in one corner to just a few inches in the opposite corner. All this had to be corrected to create acceptable sight-lines for the new seats.

To the right, from the Main Stand, is the open East Terrace, now restored to all-standing. At the rear is an electronic scoreboard, installed in 1985. Unlike those using small bulbs, this one operates like the indicator boards at railway stations, with thousands of tiny flip-over sections.

When Highfield Road was all-seated both the club and players insisted that the atmosphere had not changed. Spectators have other memories; of cold, sullen fans dotted around the seats, occasionally uprooted by rival hooligans rampaging through the aisles. If this was the stadium of the future the prospects for football were chilling indeed.

And yet the experiment might have worked elsewhere, and might still, with better public relations. Highfield Road is undoubtedly a better ground for the experience; neater, cleaner and with better overall facilities. Just as QPR were bold enough to try an artificial pitch, enabling others to learn from their mistakes, so will Coventry's pioneering work also serve as a valuable lesson.

Meanwhile, those die-hards who refused to sit down can now stand up and be counted.

BIRMINGHAM CITY

Previous Grounds

City's first ground in 1875 was on a piece of waste ground in Arthur Street, near St Andrew's, as Small Heath Alliance. To gain some revenue they rented an enclosed pitch on Ladypool Road, Sparkbrook for a short time, but as interest grew they moved back to Small Heath in 1877 to Muntz Street. Although it had a fine, ornate, white wooden stand at one end, with a pointed gable and flagpoles, the pitch was notoriously full of pot-holes. To avoid playing there, Wednesbury Old Athletic offered Small Heath £5 to reverse the venue of a cup-tie, which Small Heath then won. By 1891 the asking price was £200, paid by The Wednesday to play their cup-tie at Olive Grove. To the annoyance of their fans, Small Heath lost.

The rent at Muntz Street began as £5 a year, but in 1905 with the club established in the League it rose to £300, for a ground already too small for Small Heath's growing support. The largest gate was for a First Division derby v. Villa in 1902–03 when 29 000 attended. While at Muntz Street the club became Small Heath FC Limited, the first limited liability company in football, and in 1905, just before moving to St Andrew's they adopted the title Birmingham.

St Andrew's

St Andrew's was typical industrial wasteland, a desolate valley with a railway line along one bank, but director Harry Morris convinced the board that the site had potential and a 21-year lease was secured. A year of hard work followed, in which the Kop was raised to a height of 47 feet on rubbish dumped by anyone who cared to pay for the privilege. The ground plans were drawn up by a young carpenter, Harry Pumfrey, whose only credentials were that he had once studied at the School of Art, and that he gave his services cheaply. A huge main stand was built, reputedly the second largest in the land, and St Andrew's was opened on a snowy Boxing Day in 1906 by Sir John Holder, with a goalless draw v. Middlesbrough.

By 1939 there was a small roof at the back of the Tilton Road End and a low cover at the Railway End with two angled wings, one of which survives in part. Often this end would be obscured by smoke as passing engine drivers let off steam during matches. In this year the highest attendance at St Andrew's, 66 844, watched on FA Cup-tie v. Everton.

If Old Trafford suffered the costliest damage in the Second World War, St Andrew's had the worst luck. Weeks after the war began the local Chief Constable closed the ground in fear of air-raids. MPs raised the matter in Parliament, and although the Home Secretary refused to overrule the decision, because St Andrew's was the only ground in the country to be shut the ban was lifted by March 1940. The Chief Constable did have a point, however, for the ground was subsequently hit by no less than 20 bombs during the Blitz.

More was to follow, for in January 1942 the Main Stand was destroyed by fire, not from bombs but by a member of the National Fire Service! The stand had become an auxiliary fire station, and one of the men tried to put out a brazier with what he thought was water but turned out to be petrol.

With St Andrew's now a sorry wreck of twisted steelwork and cratered terraces, Birmingham sought refuge at Leamington and at unscathed Villa Park, until 1943. After the war, now called Birmingham City, the process of rebuilding began once funds and materials were available. The new Main Stand was begun in the early 1950s, with a rather advanced

Muntz Street at the turn of the century. It is hard to believe that all trace of this apparently substantial ground has disappeared. Notice how crooked some of the wooden barriers were

St Andrew's. Notice the remnant of the old Railway End cover in the bottom corner

propped cantilever roof. In October 1956 the flood-lights were switched on for a game v. Borussia Dortmund. Although each pylon is 114 feet high, the Tilton Road End pair is sited appreciably higher.

As the club prospered after successful runs in the early years of the European Fairs Cup, the Tilton Road End and the Kop were both covered and in the mid-1960s the Railway End gave way to the City Stand, a carbon copy of the Main Stand. There are now 9291 seats in a capacity of 43 204. Percy Young was perhaps right in 1958 when he wrote of St Andrew's, 'Here was the quintessential Second Division atmosphere', and although much improved since, there is no noisier ground than Birmingham's when the team are in the throes of yet another promotion battle.

Ground Description

There is a utilitarian 1950s' drabness about both the stands, which cry out for some uplifting feature – a crest on the roof fascia perhaps, or a clock. Flagpoles along both roofs help slightly. Now the paddocks in front of each stand are seated, with 26 boxes added rather awkwardly to the Main Stand, similar to the Hawthorns and Portman Road. In the corner between the stands, where once the players used to leave the pitch through a gate, there is a token remnant of the old Railway End cover. This odd little enclosure was

converted into an excellent viewing area for the disabled in 1983.

On the other corner of the City Stand is a 90-minute clock, brought back by a club chairman after a Swiss tour. Next to it is the Jeff Hall Memorial half-time scoreboard. Hall was only 30 when he died of polio in 1959, after 227 appearances as a right-back for City. (He played a record 17 successive games for England in partnership with Manchester United's left-back, Roger Byrne, who also died tragically in the Munich air crash.)

The Kop, with its vast roof, was for some years the centre of a political wrangle in Birmingham. Asda Supermarket wanted to develop the large open space behind it, sharing the cost of a new stand with the club – as has happened at Selhurst Park and Boothferry park. But one of the councillors approving the plan was a City director, and the Co-op also had a plan for a superstore nearby. Accusations flew as councillors and planners battled over the rival schemes. In 1986 however the open space behind the Kop was still undeveloped and City used it for car parking. (St Andrew's, incidentally, has the only side terrace, as opposed to an end terrace, named the Kop.)

Opposite the City Stand is the Tilton Road End, formed by a natural rise which is surmounted by the former works of T. Williams, drop forgers. A small

section of terracing between the roof and the Main
Stand has been closed for safety reasons, although
part of that corner suffered from a restricted view
anyway. It was a wall behind here which collapsed in
May 1985, causing the death of an innocent spectator
after a riot caused by Leeds supporters had left 96
policemen injured. This occurred on the same afternoon as the Bradford fire and resulted in the events at
St Andrew's being made part of Justice Popplewell's
inquiry (see Safety). Birmingham have since taken
the temporary precaution of closing off the seated
paddock areas on two sides of the ground.

In recent years City's neighbourhood has become
almost unrecognizable. Gone are the slums and dingy
streets, but gone too is much of the identity and
character which made St Andrew's, perched on a hill
overlooking the city, such a landmark. But like most
other inner city clubs, Birmingham find that all too
many of the faithful no longer come to the mountain,
in which case the mountain may well have to go to
them.

An unexpected opportunity to make such a move
came by virtue of Birmingham's bid to stage the 1992
Olympics. An Olympic Stadium was to be built next
to the National Exhibition Centre, which has perfect
road and rail links and is conveniently close to the
heartland of City's support in south west Birmingham. Unfortunately, in October 1986 Barcelona won
the bid for the Games, leaving Birmingham City as
well as the City of Birmingham to reflect on what
might have been.

WEST BROMWICH ·ALBION·

Previous Grounds

Albion began life as the West Bromwich Strollers in
1879, the last of Birmingham's three League clubs to
form. Thanks to research by Peter Morris and Tony
Matthews, there is a detailed account of the club's
grounds, beginning with a field on Cooper's Hill
in September 1879, where a bowling green is now
situated next to The Expressway.

In order to save wear and tear on the pitch, West
Bromwich played some games at the newly opened
Dartmouth Park. The players carried a pair of port-
able goalposts with them, since they were never quite
sure if they would be playing at Dartmouth Park or
Cooper's Hill. Hence the name Strollers. Dartmouth
Park still exists, also next to The Expressway.

In 1881 the club moved to Bunn's Field, on the
corner of Walsall and Alfred Streets, and adopted the
title Albion. Although it was their first properly
enclosed ground, it was very primitive and the
players had to change at the nearby Roebuck Inn.

At this time Albion's main local rivals were West
Bromwich Dartmouth FC, who played at a well
known sporting arena called Four Acres. As Albion
began to dominate the local football scene, Dartmouth decided to concentrate on cricket, so in
September 1882 Albion took a lease on Four Acres,
on condition they played there on Saturdays and
Mondays only. The ground had been dedicated to the
citizens of West Bromwich by William, fourth
Earl of Dartmouth. Albion's first game there was v.
Stourbridge Standard on 7 October.

In July 1883 Dartmouth agreed to let Four Acres to
Albion for a further two years at £15 a year, and to
pay a third of the cost towards a new ticket office and
pavilion.

The biggest crowd at this ground came in February
1885, when Albion played Blackburn Rovers in the
quarter-finals of the FA Cup. A crowd of 16 393
packed into Four Acres, according to a report in The
Athlete, filling all the stands, both temporary and
permanent, as well as 'the walls and house-tops,
everywhere, in fact where a footing could be
obtained . . .'.

Aware of the ground's limitations, Albion were
even then looking for a new ground, and on 6 April
1885 played their last game there v. Wednesbury Old
Athletic. Four Acres is to be found today off Seagar
Street.

The next move took the club to a field at the back of
the Sandwell Brewery in Stoney Lane, conveniently
close to the club's headquarters at the Plough and
Harrow public house. The site belonged to an under-
taker, Mr Webb, who gave Albion a seven-year lease

The original Main Stand at The Hawthorns. Oxo advertisements were prominent at almost every League ground

at an annual rent of £28.

The pitch had to be returfed and a wooden grandstand was built on the Sandwell Road Side. Holding 600 people on bench seats, the stand became known affectionately as 'Noah's Ark'. The cost of preparing Stoney Lane amounted to £370, and the first game was a friendly v. Third Lanark Rifle Volunteers on 5 September 1885.

Despite the improvements, viewing was still a problem, and Albion allowed vehicles to park behind the banking to allow extra vantage points. During one match, v. Blackburn, the iron railings broke and sent 20 fans hurtling into the next field. Furthermore, the pitch suffered from a pronounced slope. As one reporter wrote: 'What a terrible set the Albion forwards were when they came sweeping over the brow of that hill and down the incline, carrying everything before them.'

An interesting feature at Stoney Lane was that admission was by ticket only. Having found the pay boxes unsuitable, the club sold tickets from small openings around the walls, and in the Plough and Harrow.

By 1899 the club faced a financial crisis, and although some £2500 had been spent on the ground, the directors were loath to spend more on a rented property. By the end of the century, therefore, Stoney Lane had deteriorated quite badly, and was probably the worst in Division One. Another move was planned in the hope of finding a ground closer to the expanding populated areas, nearer Birmingham, and with a cheaper annual rent. Albion's average gate at Stoney Lane had been around 6000, reaching a peak of about 12 000. These figures, and the state of the ground, despite Albion's Cup successes, made the club very much the poor neighbours of Aston Villa and Wolves, each boasting large new grounds and growing support.

The site of Stoney Lane is now covered by the aptly named Albion Field Drive, off Sandwell Road and Stoney Lane itself.

The Hawthorns

The Hawthorns site was an attractive proposition because rent was lower than Stoney Lane, and it was situated on the border between three boroughs, West Bromwich, Smethwick and Handsworth. The tram fare from the densely populated suburb of Handsworth had just been reduced to one penny, and although the new ground was over a mile south east of West Bromwich town centre, the directors felt that the Birmingham side offered greater potential support.

The land belonged to Sandwell Park Colliery, and on 14 May 1900 Albion signed a lease giving them the option to buy within 14 years. There were two farms and two large public houses adjacent to the field. On the Handsworth Side stood the Woodman Inn, and on the Halford's Lane corner was the Hawthorns Hotel, from which the ground's name was derived. On the Smethwick End of the field stood a large private house, Oaklands.

The field itself presented enormous difficulties. It measured 10½ acres, sloped quite badly and worst of all had a brook running diagonally across. It took 120 men to build a culvert, lay 1600 yards of drains and shift tons of soil to level the surface. Once this was done, 300 loads of ashes, new top soil and 12 000 square yards of turf were laid. The original pitch was a massive 127 × 87 yards with a 9-feet wide cinder track around.

The Handsworth Side was covered by Noah's Ark, from Stoney Lane, while opposite was built the 5000-seater Halford's Lane Stand, designed by Enoch Wood. A month before the big kick-off, The Hawthorns had been just an open meadow. Now it was ready, Albion having spent some £6000 on preparations, twice as much as their first estimate. The Hawthorns had to be a quick success, or the club would fold.

The grand opening took place on 3 September 1900, Albion playing Derby in front of 20 000 people. Present were William McGregor, an official of Aston

Villa and founder of the Football League, and the League president, John Bentley. The following week 35 000 came to the ground to see Albion v. Villa. Receipts were high, much to the directors' relief, but the team were in such terrible form that the season ended with a crowd of just 1050 to see Albion play Sheffield United, one of the lowest attendances ever recorded at a First Division match. Albion were relegated for the first time in their League career.

On Guy Fawkes night 1904 Noah's Ark burnt down. Two years later the first part of the Smethwick End roof was put up, in a style known as a 'Belfast' roof, with lattice work wooden planks curved over in a barrel shape. An identical construction was used for Preston North End's West Stand, also built in 1906.

In 1911 Albion managed to win promotion back to Division One, and during the close season the Main Stand on Halford's Lane was overhauled and the opposite embankment increased in size. A year later they reached their sixth FA Cup Final, and their share of the receipts enabled them to purchase the ground's freehold in 1913, at a price of £5350. The Main Stand was extended at a cost of £2860.

After the First World War, West Bromwich won their first League Championship, made a dazzling profit of £7432 and during the summer of 1920 a concrete wall was built around the pitch and the first concrete terracing laid.

Despite the team's subsequent decline, The Hawthorns continued to develop. The Handsworth Side embankment was extended still further and the roof heightened, and the club's offices were improved in the Main Stand, at a total cost of £25 000. The ground staged its first full international in October 1922 and on 8 December 1924 staged England v. Belgium, only the second time a foreign international team had played against England on English soil.

The ground at this time had a capacity of 70 000, which was never to be tested. In 1931 Albion became the first club to win both the FA Cup and be promoted to Division One, and again the profits were put back into the ground, with the concrete terracing being completed and tip-up seats (as opposed to the then almost universal bench seats) installed in the Main Stand wings. The Hawthorns was visited by the Prince of Wales that year, and on Christmas Day the Great Western Railway officially opened the Hawthorns Halt, Albion's very own railway station. In 1934 a corner stand, seating 750, was added to the Main Stand, at the Smethwick End corner. The club reached their eighth FA Cup Final in 1935, and in the 6th Round v. Arsenal on 6 March 1937 recorded the highest attendance at The Hawthorns, 64 815. Yet two years later, after Albion had slipped into Division Two, only 3109 watched Albion's last home game v. Norwich in 1938–39.

The summer before the outbreak of war was taken up with the replacement of the original wooden roof of the Main Stand with a new steel and asbestos sheeting cover.

In the late 1940s the original wooden terracing in front of the Main Stand was replaced by seating, for an additional 750 people, and The Hawthorns became the first British ground to have electronic turnstile counters installed.

The first floodlights cost £18 000 and were switched on for a Division One game v. Chelsea on 18 September 1957, but officially inaugurated in a game v. CSKA, the Russian Red Army Club, on 29 October in front of 52 800 people. (The lights have been updated twice since.)

In 1958 the Birmingham Road End corner stand was added to the Main Stand, and in 1964 a new 4300-seater stand replaced the Handsworth Side embankment. The cover that had stood on this side was re-erected over the Birmingham Road End terrace. Albion had spent a total of £250 000 on ground improvements between 1945–65, including laying out car parks. So convenient had the ground become for parking and road access that in April 1968, a few weeks before Albion's fifth FA Cup triumph, the Hawthorns Halt station closed. The ground was now a few hundred yards from the M5 and only three miles from the M6.

Since then executive boxes have been added to the Handsworth Side Stand, now called the Rainbow Stand because of its multi-coloured seats, and in November 1980 the first stage of rebuilding the Main Stand began. When completed in August 1981 it had a full-length cantilever roof with 4150 seats and 27 private boxes. The contractors were Norwest Holst, builders of new stands at Molineux and the City Ground.

Soon after, a further improvement was made with the reconstruction and re-roofing of the Birmingham Road End, and in 1985 the roof of the Halford's Lane Stand was continued round, over the south west corner and behind the Smethwick End goal, to replace the Belfast roof which had served so well since 1906. Not so reliable was an erratic electronic scoreboard which had been mounted on the old roof but was not reinstated.

These extra touches, plus safety work which alone cost £158 000 in 1985–86, gave The Hawthorns a capacity reduced from 38 600 to 33 565, of which 12 500 are seated.

Ground Description

The Hawthorns is situated on the border of Sandwell Borough, in which West Bromwich lies, and Birmingham. Furthermore, between the ground and West Bromwich is the M5 motorway. So Albion live in a sort of no-man's land between two centres of population, and it could be argued that the adjacent suburbs of Handsworth and Smethwick are as much Aston Villa's territory as Albion's. In one sense Albion can look down on all their neighbours, because at 550 feet above sea level The Hawthorns is thought to be the highest ground in England.

Since its reconstruction, the main entrance on

Halford's Lane is much improved, with a long, clean white façade along the pavement. Inside, the new stand is as impressive, but on a quite modest scale. It has one tier of blue seats, from the boxes at the back down to the touchline. Unusually, the television camera position is in a gap between the centre boxes, rather than on a special gantry. Called variously the Halford's Lane, the West or the Main Stand, it is a remarkably compact construction, imposing its character on the ground not through its size so much as its glossy brightness.

At both ends are corner stands, each holding about 400 seats. In front of the north corner is an excellent section for the disabled.

From the new stand, to the right, is the Smethwick End terrace. Now neatly reroofed at the rear – although the dog-tooth boards of the old Belfast roof did have an irreplaceable charm – this end is divided into three sections for visiting supporters. It was, in 1982, the scene of one of the most calculated acts of vandalism ever witnessed at a football ground, when Leeds fans managed, after 20 minutes of rocking back and forth, to twist and break down a length of the steel perimeter fence. Their determinedly destructive efforts cost Albion over £10 000.

Opposite the Main Stand is the Rainbow, or East Stand, on the Handsworth Side, behind which runs the border of Sandwell and Birmingham. The stand is typical of the mid-1960s, being rather plain in style but has been considerably smartened by the addition of new seats, executive boxes at the back of the paddock (as at St Andrew's and Portman Road, with sloping roofs), and additional seats now in the paddock.

To the left of this in the north east corner is the uncovered Woodman Paddock, named after the Woodman Inn directly behind. A half-time scoreboard stands at the back of the terrace, topped by the Golden Throstle, an emblem which derives from the days when the club's headquarters were at the Plough and Harrow. The landlady kept a small thrush, or throstle in a cage, and this was adopted by the team as its mascot. For some years there was a bird in a cage inside the Main Stand. It was claimed that when the bird was 'on song' so was the team.

The Birmingham Road covered terrace fills the North End, and holds 10 000 standing. Albion have never quite managed to level The Hawthorns pitch. It slopes about 3 feet from the Main Stand down to the Rainbow Stand, and about 6 feet from north to south, clearly visible along the walls of the new stand.

Although now just over half its original capacity, the ground seems perfectly proportioned for the current demands of first-class football. It is one of several middle-range grounds – very neat but not quite imposing, yet better equipped than the average ground in the Second Division: as Woody Allen might have put it, a good ground but not a great ground.

·ASTON VILLA·

Previous Grounds

The site on which Villa Park is built was the mid-Victorian Aston Lower Grounds amusement park, with facilities almost as varied as those at Crystal Palace in London. It was thus the natural venue for the newly-formed Aston Villa to play in 1874, although their first pitch was actually across the road in what is now Aston Park. The Lower Grounds park was the scene of much illustrious sport, as Gibson and Pickford's 1906 *Book of Football* describes:

'There George and Snook, the great pedestrians, put up their records; there H. L. Cortis rode his 60 inch "ordinary" bicycle in a way which (relatively) no living wheelman could parallel; there Iroquois Indians played lacrosse, the national game of Canada; there the Australian cricketers won their match v. an England XI in 4½ hours; there W. G. Grace drew the Midland multitude which was privileged to watch him when he was at the zenith of his powers, and there was founded the Birmingham Cricket and Football Club, the first club of importance which played the Association game in Birmingham.'

With so much competition in the district, and because the club needed a properly enclosed ground, Villa moved in 1876 to a field in Wellington Road in the adjacent suburb of Perry Barr. There was a hayrick in the middle of the pitch which had to be shifted before each game, a hump near one goal and a line of trees along one touchline. The land was sub-let to Villa by a butcher, for £5 a year. Just behind the pitch was Birmingham's first steam tram depot, now a bus garage. The players changed in a blacksmith's hut.

Despite the poor facilities the club enjoyed great success at Perry Barr, which also hosted several important games, including an amateur international v. Ireland in February 1893. It was at Perry Barr that one of the most serious incidents in early football occurred, when part of a 27 000 crowd twice invaded the pitch during a Cup game v. Preston. Although the cause was overcrowding rather than violence, Hussars had to be called in to restore order, and Villa, the Cup-holders, were subsequently disqualified from the competition for failing to maintain order at their ground.

By the mid-1890s less successful First Division clubs like Blackburn, Wolves and Everton had moved to fine new grounds, and with Villa's annual rent raised to £200 the club looked elsewhere. The choice fell, not surprisingly, on the Lower Grounds, which

Blackburn's fine, oak-panelled boardroom at Ewood Park in Leitch's Main Stand, built in 1906. On match days the huge table is laden with tea and cakes for admiring visitors

Leitch's South Stand at Ibrox Park, built in 1929 and the focal point of the ground's redevelopment. The castellated press box on the roof is nowadays less ornate. English football followers will recognise the Leitch style of balcony wall from his stands at Goodison, Roker and Fratton Parks

Newcastle's cantilever stand dominates the sky-line. But it had to get on with its venerable Georgian neighbours

Nottingham Forest's Executive Stand illustrates the development of cantilever design and luxury boxes. Such stands allow for extension. The use of coloured seats to pick out the club's name is now very common

Chelsea's famous East Stand towers above the now-demolished North Stand, (which itself was twice the height of the original Main Stand). It is unlikely that such a large, expensive stand as this will be built again in Britain

Brilliant colours brighten up Roker Park. Leitch's criss-cross steelwork is just visible on the right hand balcony. Predominantly red grounds always seem warmer than those decked in blue

White Hart Lane before the new West Stand was built. Two generations of Leitch's stands face each other; they were built 25 years apart

The familiar television image of Wembley disguises the enclosed greenhouse effect seen from the terraces, while the perimeter track exaggerates the apparent size of the pitch

Gay Meadow has one of the most idyllic settings in League football, with the River Severn running behind the trees on the left. The castle tower is visible behind the far end. It would be possible to fit the entire population of Shrewsbury into Wembley Stadium (above)

The mock-Tudor gateway to **Fratton Park,** with The Pompey pub on the right

Highbury's main entrance reflects the prestige of the club and the orderliness of the stadium. Notice the symmetry, the use of emblems and colour, and the lamps flanking the doorway. The marble hall lies within

Capturing the spirit of the 1950s is Elland Road's entrance, now joined by a massive floodlight pylon

The Bill Shankly Gate at Anfield, a fitting tribute to the man who largely created the ground's aura of invincibility

A rare surviving Leitch gable, at Hillsborough

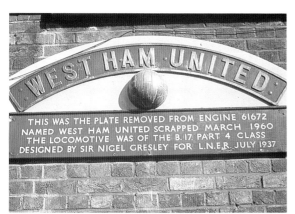

Several grounds display engine plates such as this one at Upton Park (above left)

The famous ball and cockerel at White Hart Lane, proudly displayed on Leitch's stand (above)

A Charlton faithful takes a last Souvenir of The Valley (left)

No two grounds in Scotland have changed so dramatically as Pittodrie (above) and Ibrox (below). Pittodrie is now all seated while Ibrox retains a standing area in Leitch's beautifully preserved South Stand. Before 1979 Ibrox was the same oval shape as Celtic Park or Hampden. Compare the new layout with the photo in the section on Rangers

Villa Park in 1907. Notice the use of the cycle track for extra spectators and the boards on Trinity Road (top right) to deter people from watching on the slopes of Aston Park

had in the meantime staged various big matches, such as Cup semi-finals in 1884 and 1890. Work began on preparing part of the amusement park for a stadium in 1895, and on Good Friday 1897 Villa played their last game at Perry Barr, a reserve game v. Shrewsbury. The old ground was soon swallowed up by houses, on what are now Willmore and Leslie Roads. There was talk in the 1970s of the club returning to Perry Barr, to the athletics stadium of Birchfield Harriers, near the old ground, but the plan thankfully stayed on the drawing board. Otherwise football would have lost one of its prized possessions.

Villa Park

The return of Villa to Aston signalled the end of the amusement park as an open leisure centre. The surrounding land was already being bought up for redevelopment into housing and the park's popularity had been waning. Football was the new mass spectator sport, and Villa were the most powerful team in the country. Just one week before their first match at the new ground, a friendly v. Blackburn on 17 April 1897, the club equalled Preston's feat of winning both the League Championship and the FA Cup.

The transformation of Aston Lower Grounds, not called Villa Park until later, was swift, total and in view of the club's success, fully justifiable. The land belonged at the time to Flowers and Company, brewers in Stratford upon Avon, who charged Villa £250 a year rent, with the option to buy the land at 5 shillings a square yard within 21 years.

For a while the ground was unfinished – most spectators were soaked at that first match – but gradually, under the astute direction of Frederick Rinder, a committee member and surveyor, all trace of the amusement facilities were removed or adapted. The old aquarium, skating rink and restaurant became Villa's new offices and gymnasium. The ground's maintenance man took charge of the rifle range. At the rear, a practice pitch and car park was laid on the site of a theatre and concert hall, and on the far side of Witton Lane, housing was built where once had been a boating lake with ornamental island. The Witton Lane Stand covered what had been a sub-tropical garden. Another lake became, as at Crystal Palace, the site of the new pitch. Until 1914 a 24-foot wide concrete cycle track around the pitch was used for major events.

However grand Villa Park appeared, it was in fact a cramped ground for the 40 000 spectators who would often attend, so before the First World War Rinder and an architect E. B. Holmes made bold plans for a redeveloped stadium holding 130 000. The first stage was in 1911, when Villa purchased the land for £8250 and the office buildings and car-park area for £1500. The carriage drive and a bowling green, which remained a unique feature of the ground until 1966, were also bought for £2000.

In the summer of 1914 the cycle track was re-

193

Villa Park in 1951. Notice how much of the original Victorian buildings survive to the right of the Main Stand. Only a wall or two remains today

moved, the Witton Lane Stand extended, and the banking at both ends built higher. An observer welcomed the fact that there was now 'no track to terrorize visiting players', and that the crowds were now closer, but not close enough 'to whisper to the players'.

Had not the war interrupted development, Rinder and Holmes might have gone further to create the largest stadium in England, although with post-war average gates of 30 000 it was probably just as well.

The most important post-war development was the building of the Trinity Road Stand in 1922. Its use was delayed by a series of disputes among the builders until 26 August, for a match v. their old rivals Blackburn Rovers. The stand, which was and still is unique, was officially opened two years later by the Duke of York, later King George VI. It is believed that the original design was drawn up by Archibald Leitch in 1914 – hence the gable – but Leitch's drawings did not include the distinctive central staircase (featured on the front cover).

Much later than planned, because the 1930s saw Villa's fortunes flag for the first time since their formation, the Holte End banking was built up just as the Second World War broke out. The work was finished in February 1940, the only example of any ground development being effected during hostilities. By that time the Trinity Road Stand had been refitted as an air-raid shelter and the home team's dressing room occupied by a rifle company of the 9th Battalion of the Royal Warwickshire Regiment.

Soon after the War, the extended Villa Park had its highest attendance of 76 588 for a Cup match v. Derby County, in March 1946.

Floodlights were installed relatively late at the ground, and first used in a friendly v. Hearts in November 1958. In 1962 the Holte End was covered at a cost of £40 000, and two years later, down came the wonderful Witton Lane roof, one of the landmarks of English football. It was replaced with a plain sloping roof.

The decision to stage World Cup matches at Villa Park brought further changes. The Witton Lane Stand became all seated, the players' tunnel covered by a grill, the pitch widened 3 yards, 6250 temporary seats were put on the then uncovered Witton End banking and most drastic of all, the bowling green in front of the Trinity Road Stand was built over with a new social club. Thus was lost yet another link with the Aston Lower Grounds.

Altogether Villa spent £99 000 on improvements for the competition of which £45 000 was a government grant. From 1966 the club went into decline, but once safely re-established back in the top ranks, prepared for another major development; one which was not only to change the appearance of the stadium but also shake the entire club to its Victorian foundations.

The eruption was caused not by the erection of the towering new North Stand, which replaced the old, uncovered Witton End in the late 1970s, but by the installation of offices under the stand. After various allegations about inflated building costs, two independent reports were commissioned in 1982, the second of which found that Villa had paid ten per cent more than they need have done on the work and that normal building procedures had not been followed.

That was unfortunate enough, but then a police investigation, begun originally to look into the installation of closed-circuit television cameras at Villa Park, found other suspicious transactions. The investigations branched out to three other League grounds and led eventually to the stand's architect and the former stadium manager being given suspended sentences in March 1985. The late Villa chairman was also implicated in attempts to obtain money by deception from the Football Trust and FGIT.

From this book's point of view one of the saddest side-effects of this 'seabed of corruption', as the judge described it, was that the Victorian buildings which used to house Villa's offices were demolished, and thus the last link with the old pleasure gardens was lost. Decaying though the buildings were, and expensive though they would have been to restore, they could have made a fine museum or restaurant block and a splendid counterpart to the clean, modern lines of the North Stand.

Unfortunate though the scandal was, no one can deny that Villa Park has been considerably improved by the North Stand. Certainly the club's offices are the most spacious in the League. Car parking is now also much improved, and behind the stand Villa were able to buy extra land for future development as an indoor cricket school. This scheme, together with the Aston Villa Sports Centre, built a few hundred yards from the ground on the former car park, in conjunction with a supermarket chain, restored to this part of Aston its role as a focus for leisure.

Villa Park's current capacity is 48 000, of which 19 900 are seated.

Ground Description

In true Parliamentary tradition, I should first 'declare an interest' for it was at Villa Park that I saw my first football match at the age of seven, sitting in the Trinity Road Stand. My description of Villa Park is therefore coloured by long familiarity.

Approaching the ground from the city centre or from nearby Spaghetti Junction, you pass under the Aston Expressway and see the floodlights ahead. On the right is the tall spire of the Victorian Aston church, and on the left, high on a hill in Aston Park is the red-brick Jacobean mansion, Aston Hall, built in 1618 by Sir Thomas Holte, from whom the name Holte End is derived. The Holte public house stands directly ahead, where Witton Lane and Trinity Road fork apart, gripping Villa Park like a pair of open tweezers.

Would anyone argue against the assertion that the Trinity Road entrance of Villa Park has more pomp and style than that of any other ground? In the 1930s Arsenal came close but does not enjoy the benefit of an open space in front of the entrance, and recently Bramall Lane has created equal scale and effect but significantly less grace with its new South Stand.

In a wider context, the Trinity Road façade is only as grand as any good municipal building of the period, a library or town hall perhaps. The twin towers are relatively simple, topped by pediments, the balcony balustrade is not too ornate, and the circular windows along the front are of a type which might easily be found at public swimming baths. The imposing features are the sweeping central steps, leading up to the upper seating tier, like those of a Palladian villa, and the central, also Italianate, pediment. A flagpole and some gold flourishes, with the words Aston Villa marked out on the towers, enlivens the red-brick walls. Football grounds, as stated earlier, are hardly resplendent with examples of worthwhile architecture, but here at Villa Park is one example that merits some critical attention. Yet Pevsner did not give it even a cursory glance. From here, we pass along Trinity Road to the main drive, where the social club covers the old bowling green, and enter the grounds by the car park. Apart from a wall or two, any trace of the former Aston Lower Grounds buildings has disappeared.

Inside the Trinity Road Stand is a typical 1920s' construction, with a sloping roof supported by a maze of steelwork and several pillars. There are now seats in the paddock, with a line of private boxes at the back. Above is the distinctive balcony wall which is gracefully curved to accommodate the steelwork underneath (compare with the balcony walls at Ibrox, Goodison or Roker Parks, where the steelwork is exposed), and painted in light blue with thin claret stripes. Sad to relate, this unique balcony wall is now almost entirely concealed behind advertisement boards. Thus a little bit more of football's grandeur is lost to commercial interests. How long, one wonders, till the Royal Box at Wembley is decked out with greetings from the sponsors?

At either end of the stand, angled screen ends, at the Holte End flush with Trinity Road, are lit by round windows with patterned glass, a detail typical of this stand. Crowning the roof is a wide, flat-topped gable, with the club's motto 'Prepared' and the lion crest featured in the centre, flanked by vertical bordering. The gable used to have short iron railings, but even without these it is quite splendid, and unmatched by any other gable.

To the right is the tall Holte End, able to hold 22 600 and therefore marginally the largest Kop in the country (although Molineux's South Bank could hold up to 30 000 until the introduction of safety laws). Notice that the barriers on the Holte End run the width of each section, to comply with the 1975 Act's guidelines. The roof is plain and covers half the terracing.

Opposite is the Witton Lane Stand, also plain and

simple, badly in need of a more compelling focal point than the present square clock. Along the front perimeter wall, behind the advertising hoardings, is a rolled up plastic pitch cover, which unfurls under mechanical power.

After the North Stand was built, the pitch suffered badly from lack of ventilation. A new pitch was laid, but this too had problems. The new cover has improved matters very little and is now used mainly during heavy rain. (For the failure of such covers in general, see Pitches.)

To the left is the North Stand, as tall as the Holte End, with 4000 seats, two lines of private boxes and standing room for 5500 in front. It is built with a roof suspended from a huge crossbar, whose posts stand outside the screen walls, as at Ibrox and Carrow Road. Villa was the first club to experiment with perspex shields as a means of segregating fans on the terraces in the North Stand.

The outside walls and facings are in rippled concrete, the support beams are dark brown. The only claret and blue is the seats, which pick out the initials A.V. in huge letters, visible even from the motorway.

The floodlights are also arranged in the shape of A.V., the outside walls have the name painted everywhere, and even the two clocks inside the ground have the letters of Aston Villa arranged around the face instead of numerals.

These details apart, Villa Park has actually very little unity. Each stand is a separate entity, totally different from its neighbour in size, shape and design. It will never, therefore, achieve the enclosed atmosphere found at Anfield or Old Trafford. But it shares with Hillsborough, Highbury and Goodison Park that aura of tradition and class, which regardless of executive facilities, makes Villa Park a sporting institution and a perfect stage for football. More people go there than to Aston Hall, which makes Pevsner's omission all the more surprising, since both structures represent the wealth and prestige of their respective owners.

Villa Park's North Stand

WOLVERHAMPTON ·WANDERERS·

Previous Grounds

Wolverhampton Wanderers were formed by the amalgamation of two clubs, St Luke's, Blakenhall, and The Wanderers (not the famous team of the 1870s). Their early grounds were at Goldthorn Hill, from 1877–84, then a nearby field on Dudley Road, south of the town centre. But accompanying the town's growth were property developers, and during the summer of 1889 Wolves moved a mile north to the Molineux Grounds. Dudley Road was rapidly built over with terraced villas, but when the club won their first Cup Final in 1893, the developer decided to name a street on the new estate Wanderers Avenue, and some of the houses Fallowfield Terrace, after the Cup Final venue. In addition, small stone replicas of the trophy were placed in front of each house. Some remain to this day, somewhat weatherworn and masked with paint.

Molineux

The Molineux Grounds were a famous sporting venue long before Wolves arrived. Like the Aston Lower Grounds, on which Villa Park was built, the site accommodated pleasure gardens, a boating lake, and most important of all, a cycle and athletics track, where many major events had been staged. Indeed Molineux was the home of a professional cycle racing team. Above the grounds stood the Molineux Hotel, once the home of the Molineux family and in the 1890s a venue for League committee meetings.

In common with many clubs of that period, Wolves were helped in their attempts to settle by brewers, the Northampton Brewery Company, which built dressing rooms, an office, a stand seating 300 people and shelter for an additional 4000 on cinder banking, for only £50 a year rental. At roughly the same time Villa were paying up to £200 for their much less developed ground in Perry Barr. The first game at Molineux was v. Villa on 2 September 1889.

In 1923 disaster struck as Wolves crept down into the Third Division. But out of failure came renewed hope, for a new limited company was formed which immediately bought Molineux from the brewery for £5607, a very reasonable price for such a large site.

Promotion to Division Two came a year later, and in 1925 the first major stand was built at the ground, on the Waterloo Road Side, with seats for 2600 and standing room for 4000. Around the same time a 'cowshed' cover was put over the North End.

To celebrate the club's return to Division One in 1932, the Molineux Street Stand was built, in place of an old cover blown down in a gale. This distinctive structure held 3400 seated and 4500 standing, under a multi-span roof, with a clock mounted in the centre gable. (The only major stands of a similar design were at Old Trafford, built in 1909, Highbury, 1913, at Orient's Homerton ground and The Valley. None survive, mainly because the roofs were so heavy and costly to maintain.)

During the 1930s Wolves were dominated by the autocratic figure of their manager, Major Frank Buckley. One of his most controversial ploys was to water the Molineux pitch just before home games, because he knew the team preferred playing on heavy pitches and wished to gain maximum advantage. The League soon ruled there should be no artificial irrigation carried out between the months of November and February.

During the successful years up to the Second World War, the present North and South Bank roofs were built, and Molineux housed its highest attendance. A crowd of 61 315 saw Wolves v. Liverpool in the FA Cup 4th Round on 11 February 1939.

The team reached their pinnacle during the 1950s, and Molineux saw one major development, the installation of floodlights. Between 1953 and 1956 Molineux was almost synonymous with floodlighting, as top European clubs visited Wolves to play friendlies and later European Cup ties. Indeed it was games like the Wolves v. Honved match in December 1954 which gave the European Cup much of its impetus, as all Europe considered the possibilities created by both air travel and floodlit mid-week matches (see Floodlights).

The first game under lights at Molineux was on 30 September 1953 against a South African XI (a fixture not allowable today under FIFA rules). Other visitors included Moscow Spartak and Moscow Dynamo. The present pylons were installed only a few years after the original set, which were sold to a non-League team in the area.

Molineux changed little until the introduction of the Safety of Sports Grounds Act, when in 1978, it was felt the Molineux Street Stand – by then all-seated – would not pass the required standards. At the same time a plan was drawn up involving re-development of that side of the ground but allowing room for expansion on the cramped Waterloo Road Side. So the Molineux Street Stand was demolished – farewell the gold-gabled-roof – and the club purchased 71 terraced houses on Molineux Street and demolished them also. Where the stand once stood the pitch was extended; where the houses once stood the new stand was built. The architects were Atherden and Nutter, who had designed the cantilever stands at Old Trafford.

It was quite a revolutionary design, the first of a new generation later to be copied at the City Ground and improved on by Atherden and Nutter at White Hart Lane; a sweeping, curved cantilever stand with two tiers of seating divided by a single row of private boxes. The new stand had 9500 seats, with 42 boxes, and cost Wolves £2 million. But in real terms it cost a great deal more, because Wolves were never quite able to cope with the resultant debt. In 1982 at the eleventh hour they were rescued from extinction by a consortium led by former player Derek Dougan and for one season, although no money was available to update the rest of the ground, all seemed rosy as Wolves sprang back to the First Division.

Four seasons later they were in the Fourth Division, £1·8 million in debt and continually plagued by intrigue surrounding the Bhatti brothers, who had

Molineux in the 1970s. Notice the multi-span roof, now demolished together with the houses behind, to make room for the extended pitch and new stand. The Molineux Hotel is top right

been part of the initial rescue package but were later regarded as shadowy figures who were allowing Wolves to die. Never had such a once-proud club fallen into disarray so rapidly or lost so substantially the sympathies of its supporters.

And just to rub salt into Wolves' growing number of wounds, in 1985 Molineux was shaken by stricter safety checks made shortly after the Bradford fire, despite the fact that it had been among the first grounds to be designated. It showed how easily a ground could deteriorate in such a short space of time.

The 50-year-old Waterloo Road Stand was closed to spectators, although the dressing rooms and offices remained in use, and the North Bank, which had all wooden terracing at the back, was also closed. Thus an already awkward Molineux was rendered even less atmospheric, although this was hardly alleviated by the fact that despite a reduction from 41 000 to 25 000, Wolves only managed to attract an average gate of 4016 during the 1985–86 season.

By July 1986 the situation looked graver even than four years previously. Not only did the club go into receivership but the local authorities ordered the additional closure of the enormous South Bank, leaving only the 9500 all-seated new stand available for match days. Could the Wolves be possibly hounded any further?

August brought a reprieve, again at the very last moment, but with a greater promise of long-term redemption than at any time since 1982. Molineux, its large adjacent social club and the club's training ground were bought by Wolverhampton Council for £1·1 million, while the club's £1·8 million debt was paid off by ASDA supermarket in conjunction with a developer.

Did this signal the construction of some vast superstore on Molineux's wide open acres? Fortunately not. Asda wanted to develop wasteland which lies behind the North Stand.

But Molineux could well change radically itself, if the council proves able to gain sufficient grants from the Sports Council, Urban Aid and the EEC, for redeveloping the ground into a multi-purpose sports centre.

The plan involves demolishing the condemned Waterloo Stand (which would cost £250 000 to fireproof and make safe, hardly a worthwhile proposition), and laying a running track in front of the new stand opposite, which would then house the club office and dressing rooms. The track, to be used by the local Wolverhampton and Bilston Athletic Club, would entail losing part of the South Bank, but then there is so much room on this terrace that the ground's capacity would barely suffer.

In place of the Waterloo Road Stand a new terrace, closer to the pitch, would be built, and the two adjoining floodlight pylons moved also. Finally, on the North Bank there are plans to build a leisure pool (modern jargon for a swimming pool where people can muck around without being shouted at) with a social facility incorporated, perhaps overlooking the pitch.

All that is in the long term. For the immediate future the council was keen to get Molineux's three closed sections reopened. The last time Wolves slipped into the lower divisions in 1923 it was the spur they needed to rise up again and redevelop their ground. Could the late 1980s see a similar surge of energy?

Ground Description

You have to be very sharp to spot Molineux from Wolverhampton town centre. The roads take you endlessly around the town, giving you teasing glimpses of the solid floodlights, yet you always seem to be higher than the stadium.

The Molineux Hotel, a listed building, is on the heights of the main ring road. In 1986 it was almost derelict. The old signs on the wrought iron gates were broken and not a window was intact. It was like a memorial to the decline of Wolves. Passing to the left of this building, is a narrow alleyway which runs adjacent to the South Bank. Both its length and slope give an indication of the massive size of the South Terrace. Molineux Alley is a public right of way, but part of the 15-acre site once owned by Wolves. Eventually you emerge into Waterloo Road, a gentler slope now, with the main entrance right up against the pavement of this narrow, busy road.

This entrance, if it survives beyond publication date, is another indication of how the ground has been neglected. The design tried hard to emulate Villa Park's impressive facade, but on a smaller and cheaper scale. Two 'Italianate' towers flank the central stairs, but where Villa Park has decorated brickwork, Molineux has fading yellow corrugated sheeting. The foyer is even gloomier with low ceilings, uneven floors and glass-fronted cupboards packed with silverware.

Inside the ground, the Waterloo Road Stand continues to show its ageing character, but rather than seeming forlorn actually looks quite cosy and appealing. In plan the stand is cranked with the wings nearest the pitch. Every bit of wood is yellow or ochre, even the television camera gantry on the roof. At one end of the paddock is a half-time scoreboard, at the other a section for the disabled, complete with its own little roof. Close to, the stand is obviously patched and ailing, but from a distance it appears quite charming. The safety inspectors obviously took the closer view because they condemned it in 1985.

But once the new stand was completed and the pitch moved away, the Main Stand was in a real sense already slipping away from the main action. The near touchline, for example, is about 15 yards from the perimeter wall, and the pitch is 174 yards wide, so football could be played the other way, from east to west, and a game of cricket or baseball would be quite acceptable. But for viewing football, the distance can

Molineux's new cantilever became, in 1986, the only usable part of this once-proud venue

be irritating. To add to the visual imbalance, the two end terraces finish well within the new touchlines. If you look hard, you can see the crown of each of the original goalmouths, some 12 yards wide of the present posts.

To the left is the North Bank, with a light brown, weathered pitched roof with solid screen ends. The rear terracing is constructed in wood, providing excellent acoustics. A tiny camera gantry sits on the roof in curious isolation. This end was also closed in 1985.

Where the pitch continues but the North Bank ceases, a tall yellow fence carries round towards the new stand, behind a rather awkwardly isolated scoreboard which barely fills the void in the corner.

Dominating Molineux, yet also somehow distant from its heart, is the new stand, named after the former club president, John Ireland. It does not have streamlined glass screen ends as at Forest or Spurs, nor are there any words spelt out in coloured seats. But the effect is no less impressive. The red seats contrast richly with gold fascia, and a line of flags along the roof adds a touch of glamour. But its chief value, which marginally eases the club's financial burden, is the office complex incorporated in the rear section, rented by the nearby Polytechnic's Faculty of Art and Design. Next to these offices is space which could house new club offices and dressing rooms.

It seems hard to believe that as recently as September 1979 Andy Gray posed in front of this swish new stand having signed for the club at a record fee of roughly £1.1 million, the amount Molineux was worth when sold in 1986.

If Molineux then derived new-found confidence from the John Ireland Stand, it gains a sense of scale from the South Bank. As tall, if not taller than the

Holte End at Villa Park, the sheer enormity of the concrete terracing, climbing up the natural slope towards the hotel, makes Molineux seem quite massive. Before it was closed for repairs in 1986, the South Bank was actually a fraction smaller than the Holte End, holding 22 000, but before 1977 it held 30 000. The roof sits back from the rest of the stands, and from its sheltered terraces one can see, far beyond the North Bank, a panoramic view of South Staffordshire.

One can also see the roof construction of the new stand. At Molineux the roof is suspended from the top girders (as at White Hart Lane), whereas at the City Ground the girders support the roof and are therefore visible from below. Behind the South Bank some old air-raid shelters are buried. The signs pointing to them are still visible.

But from here the most notable feature is the distended nature of the ground, for between the terrace and the new stand is a bare slope of earth, fenced off but quite destroying the sense of enclosure which is so important to football grounds.

It is, however, too easy to criticize Molineux for being in a state of flux. It must be remembered that the building of the new stand, accompanied by poor management and bad luck, very nearly put an end to Wolverhampton Wanderers. In 1983 it really did seem as though Wolves' new regime would restore the team to its former glory, if not find the immediate resources to realign the ground on a more normal, rectangular four-sided plan. By 1986 the regime had changed again, the hope was the same and the need was even greater, if Wolves were to avoid joining the likes of Burnley, deep in depression but with a bright modern stand to show for it. The old gold ground has never seen more testing days.

·WALSALL·

Previous Grounds

Two teams, Walsall Swifts and Walsall Town amalgamated in 1888 to form Walsall Town Swifts, a convenient merger since they used adjacent pitches on a sports ground at Chuckery (a district near the famous Walsall Arboretum). It was here that the club played their first League match, in September 1892, but residents in Sutton Road complained about the noise. The club found a new ground on West Bromwich Road for the following season, although it was not ready in time for the first two games, played instead at the Wednesbury Oval. The first game at the new ground was on 23 September 1893. In 1895, Town Swifts failed to be re-elected to the League, and the club's name was changed to plain Walsall. The following year their return to the League was marked by the opening of the present ground in Hillary Street.

Fellows Park

Walsall played their first game at the ground in September 1896, a friendly v. Glossop North End, but within a few years were in financial trouble. On 8 December 1900 the club had to return to West Bromwich Road for a short spell, unable to pay the rent at Hillary Street, even though the owner was also the club president. Agreement on leasing Hillary Street was finally reached in September 1903.

After rejoining the League in 1921, it was decided around 1930 to rename the ground Fellows Park. The suggestion came from the *Walsall Observer*'s correspondent Bill Rowlinson, pen-name 'Philistine', who thought the club should honour the chairman H. L. Fellows, the key man to Walsall's survival. Fellows Park is one of only three Football League grounds to be named after an individual, the others being Bournemouth's Dean Court and Cardiff's Ninian Park.

The first section of the Main Stand was built on the south east side and a roof was provided over the Popular Side opposite, in time to witness Walsall's finest hour, the famous 2-0 victory over Arsenal on 14 January 1933.

During the next two decades, Walsall flitted between the Northern and Southern sections of Division Three; their location made it easy for the League to swap them about to balance numbers. In December 1955, Fellows Park held its first floodlit game, a friendly v. Falkirk. In 1961 Walsall won promotion back to Division Two, after a 60-year absence, and built a new dressing room block next to the Main Stand. A record crowd of 25 453 attended their opening home fixture v. Newcastle United, just relegated from Division One, in August 1961. In the same period the northern end of the ground, until then almost wholly occupied by laundry buildings, was cleared for spectators' use, although it remained a very narrow terrace.

The Main Stand at Fellows Park, with a small roof extension covering the paddock

In 1965 the Hillary Street End was covered. Ten years later, with funds raised by a Cup run, an extension was added to the Main Stand, and the dressing rooms moved back into this section of the ground. The extra stand accommodation gave Fellows Park a total of 1500 seats, in an overall capacity of 24 100. This was reduced in 1985 to 12 000, with only 844 seats, but the ground was changed very little in appearance, apart from the removal of open wooden terracing next to the Main Stand.

Ground Description

With respect, Fellows Park is not one of League football's more attractive enclosures.

The Main Stand runs the length of the touchline between each penalty area, with open terracing on each wing. Nearer Hillary Street is the original section, mainly wooden, with a black, gently sloping roof. Built onto this is the more recent addition, constructed to the same pattern but with a plainer, glass-panelled screen end and a brick paddock rear wall. The join is clearly visible on the roof. A narrow roof extension gives shelter to those in the small paddock. Red walls and white facings give the stand a modicum of unity. From here, to the left is an open stretch of earth upon which wooden terracing stood until 1985. Its removal was no loss; it commanded a hopeless view. Just behind are the old dressing rooms.

To the far left you can see the covered Hillary Street End, which continues round the corner terracing until level with the penalty area. Its roof steps up to form three levels, like Kenilworth Road's Oak Road End, and is most modern nearer the Main Stand. Underneath, some of the barriers are like those once built at bus-stops, among newer, more sturdy brown barriers.

Opposite the Main stand is the Popular Side, its roof covering only the rear half of the terracing. A large advertisement tries hard to brighten the dark roof, and at the end of the terrace, stands a scoreboard.

Finally, the Railway End to the right is just a few steps of terracing with a brick wall behind. Behind this is a patch of unused land once occupied by the laundry, backing onto the Wallsall to Birmingham railway line. In the corner nearest the Main Stand is an enclosure for the disabled.

As unappealing as Fellows Park may seem to the visitor, with its lack of focus and rather drab surrounds, to Walsall supporters it is a popular, homely enclosure. But it has also become almost a symbol of defiance, like the terraced slum with an outside toilet which the owner clings on to rather than move to a modern high-rise flat in an alien environment.

Fellows Park's future has always been uncertain, and never more so than in the summer of 1986. There have been two plans to sell the site to a supermarket developer and move to a new stadium half a mile away at Bescot. At one stage in the 1980s rumours had it that Walsall were going to move to Molineux, then when Wolves' fortunes declined they were going to move into Fellows Park. Ground-sharing speculation reached ridiculous heights when it was suggested that Walsall, Wolves AND Birmingham City were all going to share Fellows Park!

But the most preposterous and controversial plan came in mid-1986 when the ex-chairman of Walsall, Ken Wheldon, announced from his new desk at St Andrew's that Walsall were going to transfer to Birmingham's ground, ten miles distant but on the far side of the city. This came very soon after a plan for the two clubs to share Birmingham's training facilities (even further from Fellows Park) and a reassurance given to Walsall's shareholders that no ground sharing was being contemplated.

Had the scheme been approved it would have been akin to Brentford playing at Upton Park, or Oldham playing at Old Trafford, and would have stripped Walsall of any possible vestiges of identity. It was also apparent that City needed Walsall more than vice versa because while they were heavily in debt, Walsall had been running for the previous decade on an even keel.

Furthermore, because the Birmingham chairman had retained a major shareholding in his old club, contrary to League rules, Walsall were hardly in a position to act independently.

Protests from the Save Walsall Action Group were so strong that the League eventually rejected the plan and, to the delight of the supporters, a London businessman called Terry Ramsden – whom they had approached – landed in his helicopter on the Fellows Park pitch like an angel from above and bought up the club, including Mr Wheldon's shares.

Walsall's rescue does not necessarily mean a final reprieve for Fellows Park, which still might attract a supermarket developer, being close to the motorway and Walsall town centre. It should not be forgotten that Mr Ramsden held a sizeable stake in the property developers Marler Estates, who already owned Stamford Bridge and Craven Cottage. But the important principle of retaining League football with an independent identity in Walsall had been preserved after a fight, and once again it was largely due to the efforts of supporters. They are the jolly good fellows of Fellows Park today.

SHREWSBURY ·TOWN·

Previous Grounds

Shrewsbury's origins date back to 1886. The club used two grounds, at Sutton Lake and Copthorne, before moving to the Old Racecourse Ground on the Mount. The site is now covered over by a council housing estate. Town made their final move to Gay Meadow in 1910.

Gay Meadow

In a town so steeped in history, it is inevitable that Gay Meadow had a story of its own long before the football club arrived. The field acquired its name because it was a favourite spot for fun and games. Adjacent to the Abbey Church it is pleasantly situated on the banks of the River Severn, overlooked by the town and castle.

One of the first recorded events on Gay Meadow took place in 1581 when Sir Henry Sidney (whose son Philip was studying at the grammar school in Shrewsbury) paid a visit to the town. A group of 360 schoolboys gathered on the meadow and several addressed speeches to Sir Henry, who was President of Wales and Lord Deputy of Ireland. He arrived at the field by barge to a wooden jetty just behind where the present Riverside Terrace is situated.

One of the most spectacular but tragic events to

take place at the field was in 1739. A young steeplejack, Thomas Cadman, made a bold attempt to walk along a tightrope stretched from the spire of St Mary's Church, over the ice-bound River Severn down to Gay Meadow. The memorial plaque on the wall of St Mary's tells the tale:

Let this small Monument record the name
Of CADMAN and to future times proclaim
How by'n attempt to fly from this high spire
Across the Sabrine stream he did acquire
His fatal end. 'Twas not for want of skill
Or courage to perform the task he fell:
No, no, a faulty Cord being drawn too tight
Hurried his Soul on high to take her flight
Which bid the Body here beneath good Night.
Feb. 2nd 1739 aged 28

One of the last public events at the ground took place in 1903, when to celebrate the 500th anniversary of the Battle of Shrewsbury a grand fête was held. Miss Kathleen Penn, who lived in Merevale House, on the site of the Wakeman School, recalled how the Meadow was used to stage a series of Shakespeare plays performed by the well-respected company of Sir Frank Benson. The proceeds were spent on the repair of the Abbey church roof. Miss Penn also remembers how her family used Gay Meadow as their own playground and for haymaking parties.

When Shrewsbury Town moved to Gay Meadow, they therefore found a well-used, much loved venue, barely changed over the centuries except for a rail-

The riverside enclosure at Gay Meadow. Notice there is no running track

way embankment along the eastern side of the field, carrying the line from mid-Wales and Hereford into Shrewsbury station. Railway and football clubs were close associates during that period before motorways developed. Shrewsbury built a small wooden grandstand on this east side, with some huts under the embankment for dressing rooms. In 1921 new dressing rooms took their place next to the stand, and it is recorded how a year later the club trainer, a jack of all trades, installed electric lights. On 28 October 1922 the new Centre Stand, built around these dressing rooms, was officially opened by the Lord Mayor.

The 1930s brought many improvements to Gay Meadow. The Station End cover was built in stages between 1932–37, followed by the centre section of the Riverside cover between 1936–39. Also during this decade the terracing was concreted over, and in 1938–39, just after Shrewsbury had joined the Midland League, a new wing was added to the Centre Stand at the Station End, at a cost of only £1500.

All these improvements were paid for by the supporters' club, formed in 1922, and were a sign of the club's growing stature in a part of the country remote from the hustle and bustle of League football.

A development outside the ground between 1936–38 was the building of the Wakeman Technical School, on the site of the old Merevale House. The southern terrace, which backs onto the school, was named thereafter the Wakeman End. Shrewsbury were renting the ground from the council at this time, for £125 a year (they have since bought the site).

After the War Shrewsbury's success continued to make them firm candidates for League membership. They won their second Midland League Championship and staged an amateur international between Wales and England, both in 1948, and finally achieved League status two years later when the Third Divisions were extended by four clubs.

Gay Meadow in those years was a remarkably open ground. It was quite possible to view matches from high vantage points on the other side of the river. Apart from the Castle Tower, the infirmary opposite had a splendid view, at least before the Riverside cover was completed and tall trees planted. It was apparently quite common to see invalids being wheeled out onto the balconies and grass slopes for a glimpse of the action.

The first floodlights at Gay Meadow were switched on for a Third Division match v. QPR on 21 November 1959, although their official inauguration took place four days later for a friendly v. Second Division Stoke City.

It was a Third Division match which attracted Gay Meadow's highest attendance, 18 917, on 26 April 1961, the crowd no doubt boosted by travelling Walsall supporters anxious to see their team win promotion to Division Two (Walsall's next match, on the opening day of the following season, also attracted the record crowd at Fellows Park).

In 1965–66 Town enjoyed their best ever run to date in the FA Cup, reaching the 5th Round before succumbing to Chelsea. With the profits gained, the club built new offices behind the Centre Stand and at the same time extended the roof over the open terracing on the east side. Previously this terrace had had a 'pigeon-loft' press-box perched at the back. The whole development was officially opened at the start of the 1966–67 season by the Minister of Sport, Denis Howell.

Since then the stand has been converted into one full-length stand with the adaptation of the paddock and the Wakeman End section to seating, giving Gay Meadow a total of 4000 seats in an overall capacity of 16 000.

One of the ground's appealing qualities has also been one of its major drawbacks in past years; the closeness of the river and not surprisingly Gay Meadow has suffered from serious flooding over the years. The worst in modern times occurred in 1948 and 1967, when the water level reached as high as the top of the Abbey doors and Town's playing gear had to be stored at the top of the stand. The problem has been alleviated by the building of dams, but excess water may still seep up through the drains.

But of course the most famous consequence of this proximity to the river were the antics of Fred Davies, the former official ball retriever. His job was to jump into his coracle, tied up behind the Riverside terrace, and fetch the balls as they were kicked over, once a game on average, at 25p a ball. It could be a hazardous job, for 500 yards down river is a treacherous weir. Once, by mistake, Fred picked out a swan from the river! He retired in 1986.

Gay Meadow's tranquillity and that of the riverbank was jeopardized in the early 1980s when the council drew up plans for a relief road to pass behind the Main Stand and Station End, to carry traffic over a new bridge to a multi-storey car park planned next to the station. The authorities tried to put a compulsory purchase order on parts of Shrewsbury's land, and the matter was even discussed in Parliament. Town wrote to every MP in the House of Commons asking for support, and ultimately the controversial scheme was dropped.

Only too aware of the ground's limitations however – and its potential attractions for developers – Shrewsbury may well seek a new site in the coming years.

Ground Description

Grounds like those at Chester and Cambridge do not reflect at all the towns they are in. Gay Meadow not only reflects the town of Shrewsbury but is an inescapable part of it. It has no special architectural merit. Rather, it derives its appeal from the riverside setting.

From the climbing, winding streets of the town centre (the old medieval stronghold is almost encircled by the river as it doubles back on itself), you approach Gay Meadow across the English Bridge,

Cast-iron Victorian turnstiles at Gay Meadow's Station End

built in 1774 and reconstructed in 1927. At the far end there used to be a portcullis and drawbridge. Ahead is the Benedictine Abbey Church. An unlikely location for a football ground.

A private road between the Wakeman School and the railway embankment leads to the ground. The Main Stand, theoretically three stands joined into one, is by no means outstanding but is a neat modernization. It has become less interesting from inside the ground since the central gable was removed in the mid-1960s. Some years before the Bradford fire highlighted the need for escape routes onto the pitch, Shrewsbury were one of the first clubs to see the value of having aisles running straight down to gaps in the perimeter wall. There is no track around the pitch, which adds to the field-like appearance of the ground.

From here, to the left is the uncovered and fairly narrow terrace named after the Wakeman School. The school's windows look down onto the ground and are used as a vantage point for the club's video camera. Behind this terrace is the Abbey Garden into which many a ball is kicked (and often lost). From the ground one can see the white stone head of a statue only feet away from the terrace rear wall. This is Viscount Hill (1800–75), a local dignitary whose devoted tenants and friends erected the statue after his death.

On the far side of the terrace is a lovely old half-time scoreboard, built in 1936 and adorned with a disproportionately large loudspeaker. The club will never be able to cover this end because of the school's proximity.

Opposite the Main Stand is the Riverside, an equally narrow stretch of terracing covered by a quaint, slightly curving low cover. It is a simple corrugated roof over the rear section, supported by a closely spaced line of pillars. To compare it with a bicycle shed would not be unkind, yet this is one of the most charming sides of any football ground. Above it is a thick range of trees along the river bank, hiding most of the view of the far bank. Running behind the back of the stand is a narrow and overgrown pathway by the river, leading from the car park to the Abbey Gardens, but there's hardly a crack or a hole in the wall for any potential peeping toms. Finally, to the right is the Station End, also covered with a simple roof. This is the visitors' end, and Shrewsbury, perhaps because of the narrowness of their terraces, were one of the first clubs to segregate properly rival supporters. Behind this end you can see Laura's Tower on the hill, a small red, sandstone tower, standing out above the trees, built in the Castle grounds in 1790 by Thomas Telford. (See colour section.)

Immediately behind the Station End is the club's floodlit practice pitch and car park, both once threatened by the road scheme. The station is a few hundred yards from here, spanning the river. The other large building, just visible, is HM Prison.

There is one feature at the Station End of particular note. One of the turnstiles dates back to 1885 and was made by Stevens and Sons, Southwark (London). It is suggested that this superbly intricate piece of metalwork may have arrived at Gay Meadow via the old Crystal Palace ground, where the Cup Final was staged between 1895–1914.

There are certainly grounds with more intrinsic merit and certainly more old-fashioned charm than Gay Meadow. Far from seeming outdated or run down, everything at this compact ground is quite fresh and neat. Gay Meadow's appeal lies in its location, which like Sincil Bank or Valley Parade lends it a firm identity. All around are definitive sights that could only belong to Shrewsbury. As at Blundell Park, a visit to Gay Meadow is itself a visit to the town, tempting one to venture back across the bridge for a stroll.

·STOKE CITY·

Victoria Ground

Stoke is not only the second oldest club in the League, but has been in continuous occupation of its present ground longer than any other British League club. In Scotland, Dumbarton have been at Boghead Park since 1879, but in England, Stoke have kept the same address since 1878.

The club was formed by clerks of the North Staffordshire Railway Company in 1863, but did not settle until 1875 at a ground called Sweeting's Field. This was opposite the present ground and is now covered by the Victoria Hotel. In September 1878 Stoke amalgamated with the Stoke Victoria Club and moved to the new athletic ground across the road, which soon assumed its present title because of the Victoria Hotel.

As an athletics venue, the ground was originally an oval shape to accommodate a track. Both ends were open banking, with one small wooden stand on the East Side, on Boothen Road. Although Stoke were founder members of the Football League, their early years were fraught with difficulties. They dropped out of the League in 1890, to be replaced by Sunderland, rejoined it in 1891 with Darwen, thanks to an expansion of the competition, then after being relegated to the Second Division resigned their place on 17 June 1908. The board, perhaps for financial reasons, sponsored Tottenham's application to join the League in Stoke's place, then realized their folly in resigning and tried to rejoin. But it was too late. Spurs were in and Stoke were doomed to play non-League football until 1919. By strange coincidence, neighbours Port Vale were also out of the League

from 1907–19, so Stoke at least did not lose its seniority in the area.

When Stoke returned to Division Two in 1919, followed in October by Port Vale (in place of Leeds City), the Victoria Ground had two stands, another small wooden stand seating 1000 having been built opposite the Main Stand. In the south west corner, between where the Boothen Stand and Boothen End are now, was a small hut for the players' dressing rooms, remembered especially for an old stove in the centre, around which players would huddle after winter games. Above the hut was the directors' box, rather like a primitive version of the Craven Cottage.

During the 1920s, a new but still mainly wooden Main Stand was built alongside this hut, with seating for 2000 spectators, and in 1925, with the joining together of the towns of the Potteries to form the new corporation of Stoke-on-Trent, the club added 'City' to their title.

In 1930 the Boothen End of the ground was terraced and later covered, and thus the original oval shape of the ground was lost. In 1935, with Stoke now back in Division One and a young winger called Stanley Matthews beginning to make news, the Butler Street Stand was built. This had 5000 seats with a small paddock in front, and at each end the barrel roof curled slightly round the corners. The stand was no doubt full when the Victoria Ground's highest crowd, 51 380, saw Stoke v. Arsenal in March 1937, in the First Division. During the Second World War, the Butler Street Stand was used as an army camp.

The Victoria Ground's first floodlights were switched on in October 1956 for a match v. Port Vale, when both clubs were in Division Two. The Main Stand and dressing room facilities had long been outdated, and in 1960 the club at last began the process of modernizing that side of the ground. The new stand was built in three stages, the last one coinciding with Stoke's

The Victoria Ground before one roof fell down and another went up

return to Division One in 1963. During the summer months, the players were offered one shilling an hour to help lay the concrete terracing in the paddock!

The 1970s were bright years for Stoke, seeing them reach two FA Cup semi-finals and winning their first major honour, the League Cup, in 1972, in their 109th year of existence. They had even begun to compete in Europe, and almost as a reminder not to get too carried away with success, a gale carried away the roof of the Butler Street Stand. The club had to play one home game at Vale Park, but soon replaced the roof with a smart, new white cover. Only the south west corner of the old roof survived. To replace it would have entailed costly engineering work because this corner of the ground runs closest to the River Trent, a few yards behind, and the foundations were sunk deep into the river bed.

In October 1979 the Stoke End Stand was opened. A simple two-tiered stand, with 4000 seats behind a paddock, its erection dictated a change of the floodlighting system, since the original pylons had stood on the open banking. In their place were installed two smaller, more compact pylons, and so the Victoria Ground now has two different pairs of lights, as at Carrow Road. This new stand completed all-round cover at the Victoria Ground, pleasant for the fans, but difficult for drying the pitch. It had always been a muddy surface, because of the proximity of the River Trent, and had been returfed in 1965. Now it had to be sand-injected, and at the same time a proper track was laid around the perimeter.

Eventually the surviving corner of the old Butler Street roof had to come down in 1983, leaving that corner exposed. This was sad, because it was a quaint contrast to the adjacent new roof, like a bird cage next to a steel box.

But behind this corner even greater changes were planned. The Victoria Ground occupies a massive 18-acre site valued at £2 million, the extra land on two sides of the ground being used for car parks and training, although the team now trains mostly at nearby Keele University. Naturally the site was a great temptation to a supermarket chain, and after planning permission for a superstore was turned down in 1985 the scheme's future rested upon an appeal in 1986. This too was unsuccessful.

At the same time there was talk of Stoke and Port Vale selling their grounds and, with various grants, building a new stadium on part of the Etruria grounds used by the 1986 Stoke Garden Festival. The idea was sound in theory but considering the Victoria Ground's excellent road links and its acres of space one wonders why anyone need look further for a major sporting venue.

The Victoria Ground's current capacity is 35 000, including 12 338 seats.

Ground Description

With or without a superstore, there are no parking problems at the Victoria Ground, for behind the Butler Street Stand between the Trent and the motorway link road is space for about 2000 cars. This facility alone makes the ground a pleasure to visit.

The main entrance is on Boothen Road, in a narrow street dominated by the back of the Boothen Stand. No doubt when first built this was an exciting, modern piece of architecture. Britain abounds with such buildings; 1960s' blocks dressed in coloured panelling. But they faded quickly and already look dated.

Inside the Boothen Stand – I recommend you have a peep at an enormous and grotesquely executed oil painting in the foyer – the 'modern' design continues throughout like an exhibit from the 1951 Festival of Britain, although of course once into the ground all is forgiven. The stand appears quite ordinary, faced in red with a plain sloping roof, a paddock in front of the seating tier. To the right is the Boothen End, named after a nearby district. In the corner between here and the Boothen Stand, on the site of the old dressing rooms, is a block comprising various social facilities, and a unique feature – a place for players' wives to view the match. The Boothen End itself is a sloping bank, covered at the back and joined at either side to the adjacent stands. It holds 11 000 standing.

In the corner is the now exposed section next to its smart neighbour. All that is new about the Butler Street Stand, however, is the roof, terracing and fencing. Otherwise the seats, floors and walls are all original. What a difference a modern white, flat roof can make to an old stand! Almost like a hairpiece, you cannot see the join.

The River Trent flows past this corner somewhat narrower here than when it passed by Nottingham Forest, because its source is just a few miles north, east of Vale Park, three miles away.

The new roof links up in the north east corner with the Stoke End Stand, a plain construction again but brightened by red seats and a white roof. The roof fascia of both these two new sides of the ground are left plain, and might well suit a crest or clock.

The Victoria Ground has never been highly praised; always classified as one of those 'quintessentially Second Division grounds'. Since the addition of the Stoke End Stand, I consider it to be one of the best in the League, small but with good seating providing clear vision all round. The new stand also adds a more enclosed atmosphere, so that taking into account the splendid access and parking, the Victoria Ground would seem perfectly equipped to face soccer in the late twentieth century. All that it lacks now is a tradition. The least altered part of the ground is the trophy cupboard, and of course great football grounds depend not only on their outward appearance but also on their atmosphere. As yet the Victoria Ground does not have one. It is not yet a place to fear.

·PORT VALE·

Previous Grounds

Port Vale were formed in a house of that name in Longport, Burslem, one of the six towns of the Potteries, in 1876. Their first ground on Limekiln Lane, near Alexandra Road, has since been built over. From 1881–84, Vale played on a pitch by Westport Lake, then for two years used some waste ground on Moorland Road, Burslem, adjacent to the present ground. Here they adopted the title Burslem Port Vale, but had to move in 1886 when the ground was bought by the corporation. It now forms part of Burslem Park. Vale moved south, to the Cobridge Athletic Ground on Waterloo Road. When the Cobridge Ground began to subside, and their support decline, Vale moved to Hanley.

The club's new home, the Old Recreation Ground was in the centre of Hanley, so Vale dropped the prefix Burslem from their name. A crowd of 13 000 came to their opening Central League match v. Blackburn Rovers in September 1913.

The players at Hanley had to change in a room over some stables and walk between the houses to enter the pitch, until a new stand was built for £12 000 along what was called Swan Passage. In their first season back in the League, Vale had their highest attendance at the ground when 22 993 saw them play neighbours Stoke in Division Two on 6 March 1920. This match had particular significance because both clubs had been out of the League for some time. After limited success in the Division until 1927, the club bought the Old Recreation Ground from the corporation.

In 1943, despite advice to the contrary and much protest, the board decided to ease their financial burdens by selling the ground back to the corporation for £13 000, and play there on a short lease. They then bought another site in November 1944, next to Burslem Park, although Vale's final game at the Old

Recreation Ground was not until the end of the 1949–50 season, when the lease ran out. For thirty-five years, Swan Passage and parts of the banking survived as part of a car park on Bryan Street and Quadrant Road, until in 1986 the Hanley by-pass swallowed up every last reminder.

Vale Park

Two other clubs have moved to new grounds since the Second World War, Hull City in 1946 and Southend United in 1955, but neither had such ambitions as Port Vale in 1950. The club had no money after the War, was living in the shadows of First Division Stoke City, and yet it planned to build a super-stadium holding 70 000 spectators! This was to be the 'Wembley of the North', the envy of every League club and the pride of the Potteries.

The prime-mover behind this ambitious, and even foolhardy scheme was Vale's chairman, Alderman Holdcroft. In 1944 when work began, the 14-acre site (later expanded to 18½ acres) was an old marl pit, a common feature in the Potteries, excavated for deposits of lime clay. Levelling the surface required the shifting of 30 000 cubic yards of earth, but finding building materials during those austere, post-war years of rationing was far more difficult. Somehow, however, Holdcroft managed to obtain the necessary steel, timber and concrete.

When Vale's lease at Hanley ran out, the new ground was just about ready for football. The turf was large enough for a huge pitch measuring 115 × 83 yards, and a running track around the perimeter. At the North End was placed the steel-framed stand taken from Hanley, and on either side of the ground were to be two identical stands each seating 4000, with large paddocks in front. Behind the East Stand ran the loop line from Stoke to Kidsgrove, and it was intended to build a station there, just like Wembley.

That Vale Park did not become a super-stadium was largely due to the state of both the club and the country. Holdcroft could not make Vale a wealthy club, nor could he divert sufficient materials from post-war rebuilding efforts. Despite initial expenditure of £50 000, the ground on its opening day was almost entirely open. A crowd of 28 000 saw Vale play Newport County, and heard it announced that the ground was to be called Vale Park. Temporary dressing rooms had been built at the rear of the Lorne Street Side, and around them laid the foundations of the planned Main Stand. The opposite Railway Stand was begun, but not completed until 1953. Not that despondency had set in. Dreams take time to come true, and the team was at least helping to raise the extra funds needed to complete the stadium. In 1954, they enjoyed their best season to date, winning promotion to Division Two and becoming only the second Third Division team to reach the FA Cup semi-final. The average gate at Vale Park in that memorable season was 20 801.

Floodlights were installed at a cost of £15 000 and

An artist's impression of Vale Park as planned in 1950, the Wembley of the North

Vale Park. The Main Stand was never built, but the tunnel (right) indicates its intended scale. Notice how open the ground is on all four sides

first used for a friendly v. WBA on 24 September 1958, and two years later Vale Park witnessed its highest gate of 50 000, for the visit of Villa in the FA Cup Fifth Round on 20 February 1960. But by then, Vale were back in the lower Divisions and the dream for a super-stadium was no longer in cold storage, it was over.

Inevitably, the ground has declined. The Railway Stand has begun to rot, the old Hanley Stand on the Bycars Lane End had to be replaced after a fire, and the covered corner between the two roofs was fenced off as a safety measure. By 1982 the capacity had been limited to 35 000, half the figure projected in 1950, and when Vale Park became designated in 1985, the limit was further cut to 16 500, including 3500 seats.

Ground Description

If you were not aware of Vale Park's short history, it would seem at first sight an odd sort of ground, built the wrong way round. The offices, changing rooms and directors' box are housed in a tiny structure, opposite a much larger stand, rather like The Shay.

The administrative centre looks like a sea-side promenade restaurant. It is a low but quietly dignified building, the now permanent 'temporary' structure erected when the ground was opened. Some 50 yards long, it has a small covered enclosure for the directors and their guests, seating 200, and lies above an open terrace, divided down the middle by a grand player's entrance, lined in white concrete. This was intended to be the centre piece of the Main Stand, and you can see some of the original foundations behind the terracing. Placed over this tunnel is a large clock. If completed, it would have been quite a stand.

From here, to the left is the Hamil Road open terrace, behind which is the market place, a vital source of revenue. To the right is the Bycars Lane End, covered at the back.

The Bycars Lane End roof continues round the corner to meet up with the Railway Stand, the largest structure. To imagine the stadium as it should have been: each end was to have been covered, joining up with the side stands in each corner to create an all-enclosed stadium.

If the Railway Stand looks impressive from a distance, at close quarters it is sad indeed. The seating tier is dark and gloomy, the seats are dilapidated, and the railway line behind is now disused. No station was ever built.

Vale Park thus has a strange lop-sided feeling; terraces exposed to winds which whip across the open surrounds, dark little corners, rickety fences, all overlooked by a cosy little directors' box.

The site still has possibilities. For example, the playing surface is still large, with plenty of turf to spare beyond the touchlines. And since the ground is a perfect bowl with space behind all four sides, the scope for expansion and modernization is enormous. There are car parks on either side of the ground, a thriving market place and two social clubs, so that if Port Vale did achieve success – and local support has been forthcoming whenever this was promised – they could, with help, transform Vale Park into something approaching Holdcroft's dream. Not Wembley of course, but certainly a multi-sport stadium, perhaps all-seated. Holdcroft and his fellow board members might have bitten off more than they could chew in 1944, but for comparatively little outlay they did endow the club with a ground of enviable potential.

MERSEYSIDE, CHESHIRE AND NORTH WALES

· LIVERPOOL ·

Anfield

Liverpool's birth as a football club is quite unique in the history of the English game. There were to be cases where a club utilized an already existing ground, as at Chelsea and Plymouth, but none where that ground had previously been the home of an established First Division side. If Everton had not rowed with their landlord and most ardent sponsor, John Houlding, Anfield today would be decked in blue, Goodison Park would never have existed, and perhaps a club like Bootle might have become the second most important team in the city.

Everton made the decision to move to Mere Green in January 1892, half-way through the season. On 15 March Houlding established his own club, Liverpool FC. He had wanted to keep the name Everton, but the Football League ruled against this. The title Liverpool FC was then challenged by a local rugby union team of the same name, so the soccer team adopted Liverpool AFC as their name. Houlding's investment was £500. By the end of the season Everton had gone and the Reds moved in. Their first year's rent at Anfield was £100; one of the reasons for Everton's argument with Houlding was that he had raised their annual rent to £250. There is a tiny road named after Houlding very near Anfield, off Walton Breck Road.

Liverpool were an instant creation; professional players, a limited company and a ground all at the same time. Just one season later they were elected to Division Two, and one season after that, in 1894, had their first taste of First Division football. But Anfield was still much less advanced than its new neighbour across the park. Liverpool's first League game attracted 5000, far fewer than Everton were used to. By the turn of the century, however, the two clubs were at least on a par in footballing terms, Liverpool winning their first Championship in 1901.

The first change at the ground had come in 1895, after Liverpool won the Second Division for the second time in three seasons. A Main Stand seating 3000 was built on the site of the present Main Stand and for the next 75 years was something of a landmark in English football. It resembled Newcastle's West Stand (built in 1906), with a semi-circular gable in the centre of a barrelled roof. The gable was red and white mock-Tudor style, topped by ornate ironwork.

In 1903 the first stand on Anfield Road was constructed, mainly from timber and corrugated iron, also with a barrel roof, and in 1906 when Liverpool won their second Championship the first 'Kop' was built. It was by no means the first tall section of banking at a football ground, but possibly the first to be christened Spion Kop, on the suggestion of a journalist, Ernest Edwards, sports editor of the local *Post and Echo* (but see Arsenal and Appendix also). On Kemlyn Road was built a third barrel-roofed stand, with an uncovered paddock in front.

During the 1920s Anfield was a busy place. In 1921 George V and Queen Mary attended the ground. Having watched the Grand National at Aintree the day before (the race used to be held on Fridays), they saw a Cup semi-final replay between Wolves and Cardiff. The 1920s began for Liverpool with two Championship wins in a row, there was a fire in the Main Stand during a game in 1922, and a few years later the ground became the finishing point for the annual Liverpool Civic Marathon. Apparently the runners would enter the stadium during the closing stages of the annual pre-season practice match (Reds v. Whites) and had to complete one lap of the pitch before finishing. The race was held until at least 1951. World Championship boxing matches were another regular attraction, as was exhibition tennis, played on boards in the middle of the pitch during the 1930s. Anfield also staged an exhibition basketball match in 1958 featuring the Harlem Globetrotters.

A major ground development occurred in 1928, with the extension and covering of the Kop in its present form. Designed at the time to hold 30 000, it was without question the largest covered Kop in the country. On the Kemlyn Road corner of this new structure was installed another landmark, a tall white flagpole with a history of its own. Originally it

Just in case the players forget . . . the tunnel

had been the top mast of the *Great Eastern*, one of the first iron ships in the world, whose maiden voyage was in 1860. By 1888 she lay broken up in the Mersey docks, having served in latter years as a floating advertisement for Lewis's, the department store, and as a fun-fair in the Liverpool Exhibition of 1887. When the Kop was completed, the surviving top mast was floated across the Mersey and hauled up to Anfield by a team of horses.

On the day the Kop was opened, for a game v. Bury, Liverpool's programme displayed an artist's impression of a double-decker stand to be built at the Anfield Road End. The picture suggests that Archibald Leitch was to be the designer – his familiar criss-cross balcony wall was portrayed – but the stand was never built.

The ground's biggest crowd came after the Second World War, for Liverpool's 4th Round FA Cup tie v. Wolves, in February 1952. The attendance was 61 905. Liverpool's first floodlights, which cost £12 000 and were on four quite small pylons in each corner, were installed in 1957. To celebrate the 75th anniversary of the Liverpool County FA, the first floodlit game at Goodison Park had taken place on 9 October, Everton beating Liverpool 2–0. The Anfield lights were switched on three weeks later, this time Liverpool beating Everton 3–2.

At that time Liverpool were in the Second Division, but once they were promoted in 1962 life at Anfield changed dramatically. The old Kemlyn Road Stand came down in 1963 and the present cantilevered stand was erected at the then enormous cost of £350 000 (Hillsborough had paid about £100 000 a few years earlier). The new stand was an all-seater

with room for 6700 spectators, and has remained one of the most unusual constructions at any British ground. It was given a national airing on 22 August 1964 when Anfield was the venue of the very first broadcast of BBC's *Match of the Day*, then on BBC 2. A television audience of only 75 000 saw Champions Liverpool beat Arsenal 3–2.

The following season Liverpool won the FA Cup for the first time and with the profits the club built a new stand on the Anfield Road End, a covered standing enclosure.

Another television event at the ground came in March 1967, when a crowd of 40 149 saw Liverpool's FA Cup 5th Round match v. Everton on closed-circuit television, beamed onto huge screens direct from Goodison Park, where a further 64 851 watched 'live' as Everton won 1–0. That game would have been seen in black and white, but on 15 November 1969 the first colour transmission of *Match of the Day* took place from Anfield, for a game v. West Ham.

Liverpool's most consistent run of success began in 1971, after losing their fourth FA Cup Final. Between then and 1982 the club won the Championship six times, the FA Cup once, the UEFA Cup twice, the European Cup three times and the League or Milk Cup twice. There were really only two aspects of the ground that they could improve with the revenue left after buying players, namely the old Main Stand and the floodlights.

The new Main Stand was opened officially by HRH the Duke of Kent on 10 March 1973, during Liverpool's eighth Championship-winning season. At the same time the present floodlighting system, along the roofs of both side stands (as at Goodison Park) was installed at a cost of £100 000. Anfield's present capacity is 46 000, including 21 700 seats.

Ground Description

Anfield has the reputation of an opera house, dental surgery and casino all rolled into one. You visit the ground expecting to see finesse and hear fine tunes, but if an away fan you go in fear of pain, and never expect to come away with a win. What makes Anfield most daunting of all is the team, and although the stadium is enclosed and cavernous, and the atmosphere can at times be electric, for partisanship, vehemence and noise level I consider Old Trafford or Celtic Park to be more oppressive for visiting teams and supporters. Despite the reputation Liverpool's more unruly fans gained for their appalling behaviour at the Heysel Stadium in 1985, Anfield is still a relatively hospitable ground, often made welcoming by the general good humour which prevails. Of course with such a strong team the home crowd can afford to be generous towards visiting teams.

The Anfield experience begins, perhaps more than at most grounds, in the approach roads. Gradually all the houses and shops seem to be decked in red and white, or red and yellow. There are road signs directing you to Anfield and Liverpool FC (yet

The old Main Stand, demolished in the early 1970s

The white roofs of Anfield, with the Kop on the left

very few pointing to Goodison Park), though you barely see the ground until you reach the doors. Particularly disorienting is the approach along Walton Breck Road, from where you can see the hump-back shape of the Kop and the odd floodlight gantries on the Kemlyn Road Stand roof. It is hard to work out what the back of the Kop is, so strange are the angles of its roof.

The entrance to the Main Stand on Anfield Road should be seen by every visiting spectator, because it has a magnificent set of wrought-iron gates dedicated to the memory of Liverpool's late manager, Bill Shankly. Above the gates is the inscription, 'You'll never walk alone'.

The Main Stand is very plain at the back and has an unimaginative entrance hall. Considering the unparalleled success of the club in recent years, it is a shame that it did not try to emulate those grand entrances found at Highbury or Ibrox, or at least build a small façade on the impressive lines of Elland Road or Bramall Lane. Nevertheless, Liverpool's success does tend to speak for itself.

The Main Stand seats 8600 in the upper section, 2150 in the paddock. The roof is enormous, supported by two thin central uprights, with a large suspended television camera gantry. Otherwise this is a very plain structure; clean, modern and better to sit in than to look at. As the players emerge from the tunnel in this stand, they see a sign above, proclaiming: 'This is Anfield'.

To the left is the smallest section of the ground, the Anfield Road Stand. Constructed mainly in plain brick and concrete, it has a slight roof, pointing upwards and supported by columns near the back. It used to be all-standing, until seats were installed

over all but the Kemlyn Road corner section in the summer of 1982. The rest of Anfield has a pleasant sort of dignity created by the colour combinations of red, grey and white, so the new seats in this stand come as a particularly glaring shock. They are from left to right, orange, ochre, violet, red, emerald green and cream. These colours were partly chosen because when the Main Stand paddock was seated in the summer of 1980, the Liverpool manager Bob Paisley watched a reserve match at Anfield and was irritated that the red shirts of his team seemed to get lost against the new red background of seats. There is no danger whatsoever of this happening with the new Anfield Road seats.

Opposite the Main Stand on Kemlyn Road is one of the most unusual constructions at any League ground. It is an early example of a cantilever roof, but one never copied since because it has not been a success. The space was confined by a row of houses directly behind the stand, and the roof therefore had to be angled in such a way as not to cut out what little light the houses enjoyed. Massive wedges of steel necessary to support the ungainly roof meant that fewer seats could be installed at the back, with the result that more had to be crammed in at the front. The result was an expensive stand which did not fulfil its potential. It cost more than the United Road cantilever stand built at Old Trafford, yet held over 3000 fewer people. Visually, however, it is quite remarkable. From the top of the back wall the roof leans forward at an angle of 45 degrees, reaching a peak about half-way over the seating tier. It then dips down at a sharp angle, ending above the perimeter track. This front section, unsupported at the edge almost looks precarious enough to fall onto the pitch.

And to confuse the design further, the floodlight gantries protrude high above the back of the roof while the front slopes down.

Mather and Nutter, the architects who designed the new stands at Molineux, Old Trafford and White Hart Lane have drawn up plans for a redeveloped Kemlyn Road Stand which would alleviate its current problems. Making use of space created by the demolition of houses in Kemlyn Road, the plan is to take off the existing roof and add a rear section of seats with 36 private boxes and an impressive frontage. Liverpool however are not a club to take risks and despite their success on the pitch the redevelopment seems certain to stay on the drawing board for some years.

Finally, we come to the Kop, the southern end of the ground whose patrons – Heysel notwithstanding – have made Anfield famous with their passion, wit and sportsmanship. The capacity of this enclosure is now reduced to 21 500, and although it seems physically much smaller than for example, Villa Park's Holte End (capacity 22 600), because the terracing is covered right up to the front, it has a darker, more ominous presence. It is the Kop, more than any other part of the ground, which makes a visit to Anfield such a potentially daunting experience. As mentioned earlier, the roof looks rather odd from the outside. It is predominantly grey topping a high, well-fenestrated wall of cream concrete and red brick. The famous flag-pole is on the corner with Kemlyn Road.

Inside, the Kop appears surprisingly bright because of the windows and sky-lights. The barriers are all white. Apart from the corners, where there are dividing fences, the view is very good, despite security fencing at the front. In August 1987 the Kop was closed for the start of the season after the collapse of a sewer underneath the terracing. It must have been all that jumping up and down after each Liverpool goal. Since the other three sides are now all seated they have low perimeter walls only, which has the effect of bringing one closer to the players. It is said that Liverpool's men always seem that much taller as they emerge from the tunnel, and this lack of barriers is one of the reasons. In addition the pitch is the minimum length, none of the stands is very tall and their roofs pitch relatively low on each side; factors which combine to create an almost claustrophobic atmosphere. It is hard to say whether this effect was intentional, but the psychological advantage it has given Liverpool either through fact, illusion or merely by suggestion is indisputable.

Anfield on a big match day is probably the most exhilarating, and at the same time, unnerving experience one could sample in English football. The design of the ground helps this, as does the temper of the crowd. But the club, and especially the late Bill Shankly, have deliberately created a fearsome reputation for the place. Anfield would not seem half so imposing if it were not for the formidable team who call it home.

◆EVERTON◆

Previous Grounds

It is seldom remembered outside Merseyside, but never forgotten in Liverpool, that Everton played at Anfield for eight years between 1884–92, and it was only their departure from the ground that prompted the formation of rivals Liverpool. Furthermore, Everton even won their first Championship at Anfield in 1891. For a fuller account of Everton's early years, see John Roberts' excellent centenary history of the club.

The club began life as St Domingo's FC in 1878 and found a pitch in Stanley Park, which had just been laid out for the public and still stands between Anfield and Goodison Park. They played opposite the house of local Alderman and Conservative MP, John Houlding, who was soon to become known as 'King John' of Everton. (Everton is the name of the district just west of the park.) By 1882 unofficial attendances for Everton's matches had risen to 2000 and so it was decided that a properly enclosed ground where the club could charge admission would be advisable.

At a meeting in the Sandon Hotel, owned by Houlding's brewery, in March 1882, a Mr Cruitt of Coney Green offered Everton a fenced and gated field in Priory Road opposite the park. Enough funds were found to move in the following year and changing rooms and a small stand were built. The first match, a representative game between Liverpool and Walsall, raised gate receipts of only 13 shillings. The ground was inconvenient for public transport and the noise from Everton's growing number of followers 'disturbed the pastoral serenity of Mr Cruitt's environment'.

Instead, in 1884, Houlding secured them a field which he partly owned in Anfield Road. He also acted as agent on behalf of the landlord of the other part, a Mr Orell. The Sandon Hotel became the club's headquarters, and fences and hoardings were erected by members. Match receipts rose immediately from £45 at Priory Road to £200 at Anfield by 1885. In Everton's last season before joining the new Football League in 1888, they paid Houlding a rent of £100, but after finishing as runners-up in their second League season their rent increased to £250 a year. Houlding also had the sole right to sell refreshments at Anfield.

Unhappy with this situation, the committee met in May 1889 and decided to look for another ground. Some of them objected to having the club's affairs run from a licensed hotel, while others were reluctant to lose the money invested in fixtures and fittings at Anfield. The ground was quite suitable after all, and in March of that year had been host to an international match between England and Ireland. They offered Houlding a compromise rent of £180 for the next season, but received no reply. In fact Houlding was incensed. He had already tried to buy out Orell, who planned to make alterations to his part of the field, and offered to sell Everton the entire plot for £6000. When the club refused, Houlding served them notice to quit, and attempted to form his own Everton FC and Athletic Grounds Limited at Anfield. (He succeeded, but the new club became known as Liverpool, since the League ruled that Everton should take their name with them.)

In response to Houlding's wrath, Everton held a special meeting in January 1892, by which time they had consolidated their position by winning the Championship in 1891, making a profit of £1700. A committee member, George Mahon, the organist at St Domingo's church, revealed that he had an option on a field on the north side of Stanley Park, called Mere Green. Gibson and Pickford's *Book of Football* in 1906 described the field as having, 'degenerated from a nursery into a howling desert', rather similar to the site on which White Hart Lane was built.

Everton formed a limited company and with considerable help from another committee member, Dr James Baxter, bought the 30 000-square yard site for £8090, a high price even in those days. At last they had a home of their own, and were free of Houlding's tyranny! Houlding even tried to stop Everton officials as they attempted to take away the turnstiles and fittings from Anfield.

Goodison Park

Goodison Park was the first major football stadium in England. Molineux had been opened three years earlier but was still relatively undeveloped. St James' Park, Newcastle, opened in 1892, was little more than a field. Only Scotland had more advanced grounds. Rangers opened Ibrox in 1887, while Celtic Park was officially inaugurated at the same time as Goodison Park. Everton performed a miraculous transformation at Mere Green, spending up to £3000 on laying out the ground and erecting stands on three sides. For £552 Mr Barton prepared the land at 4½d a

Goodison Park in the late 1930s. Notice how the church cuts into the terracing and the houses, bottom left, cut into the back of the Park End Stand

square yard. Kelly Brothers of Walton built two uncovered stands each for 4000 people, and a covered stand seating 3000, at a total cost of £1640. Outside, hoardings cost a further £150, gates and sheds cost £132 10s and 12 turnstiles added another £7 15s to the bill.

The ground was immediately renamed Goodison Park and proudly opened on 24 August 1892, by Lord Kinnaird and Frederick Wall of the FA. But instead of a match the 12 000 crowd saw a short athletics meeting followed by a selection of music and a fireworks display. Everton's first game there was on 2 September when they beat Bolton 4-2.

The following description comes from *Out of Doors*, October 1892:

> Behold Goodison Park! . . . 'no single picture could take in the entire scene the ground presents, it is so magnificently large, for it rivals the greater American baseball pitches. On three sides of the field of play there are tall covered stands, and on the fourth side the ground has been so well banked up with thousands of loads of cinders that a complete view of the game can be had from any portion.
>
> The spectators are divided from the playing piece by a neat, low hoarding, and the touch-line is far enough from it to prevent those accidents which used to be predicted at Anfield Road, but never happened . . . Taking it altogether, it appears to be one of the finest and most complete grounds in the kingdom, and it is to be hoped that the public will liberally support the promoters.

A year after moving, Everton were FA Cup finalists in 1893, then runners-up again in the First Division in 1895. The ground was honoured in 1894 when Notts County beat Bolton in the FA Cup Final, watched by a disappointing crowd of 37 000, but Everton were still the richest club in the country, and League gates such as the 30 000 which attended in February 1893 were still regarded as enormous.

Despite the initial developments, it was not long before Goodison Park was improved even further. A new Bullens Road Stand was built in 1895 at a cost of £3407 (although the original construction seems to have been more than adequate, unless the work involved only spectator facilities) and the open Goodison Road Side was covered for £403.

Meanwhile competition in the city was reaching peak levels. Everton were yet again runners-up in both the League and FA Cup, while across Stanley Park, Liverpool won their first Championship in 1901.

The Goodison of today really began to take shape after the turn of the century, beginning in 1907 with the building of the Park End double-decker stand, at a cost of £13 000. In 1909 the large Main Stand on

Main Stand number three at Goodison Park, the first triple-decker in Britain, built in 1971

Goodison Road was built. Costing £28 000 it housed all the offices and players' facilities, and survived until 1971.

At the same time another £12 000 was spent on concreting over the terracing and replacing the cinder running track. The *Athletic News'* correspondent wrote in the summer of 1909, 'Visitors to Goodison Park will be astonished at the immensity of the new double-decker stand'. The architect was Archibald Leitch, and the front balcony wall bore his criss-cross trademark, which can still be seen on the Bullens Road Stand opposite and on the Main Stands at Ibrox and Roker Parks.

In recognition of the fact that the ground was by far the best equipped in England, Everton hosted the 1910 Cup Final replay between Newcastle and Barnsley. On this occasion 69 000 attended. Then on 13 July 1913 Goodison Park became the first League venue to be visited by a ruling monarch, when George V and Queen Mary came to inspect local schoolchildren at the ground.

During the First World War Goodison was used by the Territorial Army for drill practice. Soon after, the US baseball teams Chicago White Sox and New York Giants played an exhibition match at the ground. One player managed to hit a ball right over the Main Stand.

The next major development followed in 1926, when at a cost of £30 000 another double-decker, similar to the Main Stand, was built on the Bullens Road Side opposite. Again, Leitch was the architect.

In the 1930s, Everton borrowed an idea from Aberdeen FC, who they had visited for a friendly. At Pittodrie in 1931, trainer Donald Colman had built the first ever dug-outs in the country, and probably the world. Not only did Colman want shelter on the touchline, but also a worm's eye view of his players' footwork. From Pittodrie and Goodison Park the idea soon spread, and now the covered dug-out is a feature of almost every ground. (Quite how managers and coaches can command a decent view of the game from this level is beyond the average fan, and in recent years several managers have taken up vantage points higher in the stands, with telephones linking them to the bench. This seems much more sensible, but does rather isolate them from the centre of the action.)

Another Royal visit occurred in 1938. George VI and Queen Elizabeth, the present Queen Mother, came to Everton and saw the new Gwladys Street Stand, just completed for £50 000. Notice how costs had escalated over the years. Goodison Park thereby became the only ground in Britain to have four double-decker stands and was newly affirmed as the most advanced stadium in Britain. Some writers referred to it as 'Toffeeopolis', after the club's nickname.

Goodison Park suffered quite badly during the Second World War, because it lies so near the Liverpool docks, and the club received £5000 for repair work from the War Damage Commission. Shortly after the work was completed Everton enjoyed their highest-ever attendance, 78 299, for the visit of Liverpool in Division One, on 18 September 1948.

Floodlights came to both Liverpool clubs in October 1957. The Goodison Park set, which were originally mounted on four extremely tall pylons, were switched on for an Everton v. Liverpool friendly on 9 October.

A year later the club spent £16 000 on installing 20 miles of electric wire underneath the pitch. The system melted ice and frost most effectively, but the drains could not handle the extra load, so in 1960 the pitch was dug up again and new drainage pipes laid.

The 1960s, like the 1930s, saw Everton win the Championship twice and the FA Cup once, and in 1966 Goodison Park staged five games in the World Cup, including that memorable quarter-final between Portugal and North Korea. No other English venue apart from Wembley staged so many World Cup games. In preparation for the World Cup, the club had bought and demolished some of the Victorian terraced houses which stood behind the Park End Stand, in order to make the present entrance way from Stanley Park. The houses had originally been built by the club for players, and Dixie Dean lived in one of them.

The final and perhaps most spectacular development was in 1971, when the 1909 double-decker Main Stand on Goodison Road was demolished to make way for a massive new three-tiered Main Stand. The old stand had cost £28 000 and was then considered immense. The new stand cost £1 million, was nearly twice the size, and was the largest in Britain until 1974, when Chelsea opened their mammoth East Stand, which cost twice as much.

Because the Goodison Road Stand is so tall, the floodlight pylons were taken down and lamps put on gantries along the roof. The Bullens Road roof was replaced by a modern roof and similar gantries installed there also. Anfield's lights followed the same pattern a year later.

When the Safety of Sports Grounds Act came into effect in 1977, Goodison Park's capacity was greatly reduced from 56 000 to 35 000, mainly due to outdated entrances and exits. So Everton had to spend £250 000, in order to reach a capacity of 52 800. The 1986 figure stood at 53 419, of which 24 419 were seated.

Ground Description

Anfield, at the top of Stanley Park, is a solid mass on the skyline while Goodison Park, at the foot of the gentle slope, is a gaunt cathedral among low terraced houses. Two such important clubs, so close, yet seemingly turning their backs on each other across the green expanse.

Goodison Park is difficult to see from street level, not merely because it has no floodlight pylons. The tall Main Stand does not at first look like a football stand, but part of a factory or brewery perhaps. The main entrance is on Goodison Road, where on one side is an unbroken line of terraced houses, on the other the high wall of the stand. There is no room for a gate or a courtyard. Above the doors and windows are a succession of signs, pointing here and there, telling you where you are or how you can get to where you should be; one of those admirable grounds that likes to keep its public informed and does not assume that everyone is a regular.

Inside, the stand seems titanic. The front section is for standing, and in part is backed by a line of executive boxes, later and clumsy additions similar to those at St Andrews or Portman Road. When the stand was built, the club either saw no demand for this kind of accommodation or were unable to afford them – Manchester United had built boxes years earlier – so they have had to add boxes in a way which detracts from the original design. The middle tier houses, among others, the directors, sponsors and their like, above which is the upper tier.

Unfortunately, because of the angle of Goodison Road, at the end closest to the Park End the back wall angles in towards the pitch, and creates the illusion that the stand is somehow falling down, because the top tier of seats falls away, row by row, into the corner in a most alarming way. At this corner, between the Main Stand and the Park End Stand, is a tall rectangular block, clad in blue. It houses stairways vital for safety in such a large stand, but has the additional and detrimental effect of closing off that corner in darkness. The opposite end is much more impressive. A large expanse of glass panelling is dramatically cut in half by the sloping rake of the upper seating tier, apparently suspended in air. Notice at the front the very compact dug-outs, and the barely visible players' tunnel in between.

This dominating, but scarcely attractive structure holds a total of 15 055, more than the total capacity of several grounds in the lower divisions. It has 10 155 seats, standing room for 4900, plus 12 private boxes.

From here, look down to the left where there is a clock in front of Goodison Park's most famous landmark, the church of St Luke the Evangelist. The church presses into the corner of the ground so far that its walls are just feet from the stands. Everton once tried to pay for its removal in order to gain extra space, but had they succeeded a familiar landmark would surely have been sorely missed. As it is, this corner is the most open of all. On the left is the Gwladys Street End, similar to the two ends at White Hart Lane, with a balcony wall distinguished by thin blue vertical lines along white facings. There is standing room for 14 200 in the lower section, which at one stage had the front terracing nearest the goal cut away to prevent missile throwing incidents. The original corrugated roofing of this stand, which links up in the corner with the Bullens Road side, was replaced in the early 1980s by blue cladding, which gave the roof a rich, colourful hue. However in 1987 it is intended to remove the pitched roof and replace it with an upturned sloping roof on the same lines as the Bullens Street Stand.

The Bullens Road Side, opposite the Main Stand, is now in three tiers, the terracing having had its rear section converted to seating, as at Highbury. There are 8067 seats on two levels, with space for 5900 standing. Notice particularly the distinctive balcony wall, criss-crossed with blue steelwork on a facing of white wooden boards. The seating in the upper tier, now much less gloomy with the new upturned roof, has the name Everton picked out in white seats among the blue. Between this stand and the Park End Stand, to the right, is another clock, with another blue wall closing in the corner.

The Park End Stand, the oldest surviving part of the ground, is lower than its fellows, and has been considerably modernized. The front standing section, for example, which holds 4000, now stops at the wall which runs directly under the seating balcony wall. There are 2340 seats above. Along this back wall is an electronic scoreboard, which must frustrate the people sitting above who cannot see it. Sadly, because of the high security fencing, the view from these terraces is rather obstructed, and demands much straining from those who stand there.

Goodison Park still has the hallmarks of a fine stadium, and although it can no longer claim to be the most advanced in the country, it does offer seating and standing on every side of the pitch, a feature much appreciated by spectators and found elsewhere only at Old Trafford. It has none of the grandeur or impression of space experienced at Hillsborough or Highbury, neither do any of the stands have the individual appeal of those at Villa Park or White Hart Lane. The site also suffers from being hemmed in. Nevertheless, perhaps because of its crucial place in the history of football grounds, and the atmosphere which prevails here on special occasions, Goodison Park is still one of the best grounds in Britain. 'Toffeeopolis' lives on!

TRANMERE ·ROVERS·

Previous Grounds

Tranmere's roots go back to a club called Belmont FC, formed in 1881 by the members of two Birkenhead cricket clubs. The name Tranmere Rovers was adopted in 1882. Their first home was Steele's Field, from where they moved in 1883 to a ground in South Road, Devonshire Park, not a hundred yards from the present ground but now built over with houses. Rovers played on Ravenshaw Field, also close, from 1886–96, when they opened a new ground called Prenton Park. This ground was on the site of a school which now stands on Prenton Park Road, opposite the main entrance to the present ground, also called Prenton Park.

Prenton Park

When Rovers finally settled at Prenton Park (the second), Prenton had lost most of its identity as a village in Birkenhead. The area derived its strength from the nearby docks and shipyards of Cammell Lairds, and Goodison Park and Anfield were then just too far to draw away all the local support. Nevertheless, Prenton Park has been developed on a shoe-string since the first game there in March 1912. The club joined the League in 1921 and brought over an old wooden stand from the nearby Oval sports ground (referred to below). Known as the Weekend Stand, it was basically a showground building with a few seats and no dressing rooms. Opposite this stand, on Borough Road, was a cover similar to the existing one.

During the War, Birkenhead suffered considerably from bombing raids because of the important shipping in the dock areas, and the Prenton Park car park was used as a base for sending up black smoke screens to confuse German aircraft. There were huge tank traps in Borough Road and the cover on this side was destroyed during a raid.

After the war Rovers struck a bargain with the local council. In return for giving up 6 feet of land behind the Borough Road Side, which the authorities wanted for bus-loading bays and pavement widening, Rovers would have the tank traps lifted over to the Kop End in order to provide a base on which to raise the banking. Since each one weighed 10 hundred-weight, they needed the council's help.

The cover on Borough Road was replaced, and in 1956 the Cowshed on Prenton Road West built. Floodlights were first switched on at Prenton Park in September 1958 before a game v. Rochdale. The supporters' association raised the £15 000 cost of the new lights.

On promotion to Division Three, Rovers began

Prenton Park

building a new Main Stand in place of the old wooden structure. The Sports Minister and ex-football referee, Denis Howell, opened it in December 1968. Although the club had insufficient capital to build dressing rooms under the stand for a while, it was still at the time one of the best new stands outside the First Division, and had cost only £80 000.

In February 1972, Prenton Park's highest crowd, 24 424, attended an FA Cup tie v. Stoke City, a match which also brought Rovers record receipts of nearly £9000.

Developments since then have centred largely beyond the stands. With aid from the Sports Council, Tranmere built a sports centre at the back of the Kop, including squash courts and one of the first indoor crown bowling greens in the world. But the club's own costs escalated during construction, they were unable to run it properly, and so in November 1981 the centre was sold to private interests.

Rovers also had their own social club, now sold, and have since parted company with three-quarters of their large car park behind the Main Stand. This used to be the site of a brick works but is now covered by the Mersey Clipper public house, built in 1984, and a small all-weather sports area built by Tranmere in conjunction with the council.

At one stage, just before the club came perilously close to extinction in December 1982, finances were so limited that the club could afford only a part-time groundsman assisted by a youth on a YOP scheme. Since then the situation has improved somewhat and the pitch is now under full-time care. To save wear and tear of the pitch, the club trains at the Oval, in Bebington. (Just south of Prenton Park, the Oval, part of a large sports complex now owned by Wirral Council, was built in 1888 for the workers at the Port Sunlight Soap Works. The Lever family once offered to buy up Rovers, move the whole club to the Oval and change its name to Port Sunlight.) The Oval retains a splendid grandstand which was used on location in the film *Chariots of Fire*.

In 1983 Rovers were one of the first clubs to apply, unsuccessfully, for permission to install an artificial pitch, but by the time such pitches were more widely accepted in 1986 the situation at Prenton Park had changed considerably.

Designation under the Safety of Sports Grounds Act in 1985 had cut the capacity from 18 000 to 8000. The entire Kop End was closed, mainly because there were insufficient access points, and in the Main Stand, Tranmere were told they could only use 1000 of the 4000 seats, until more exits were provided. Overall, Rovers had to spend £50 000 on safety work just to maintain this level, part of the work being to smooth off the edges of several crush barriers.

No further improvements were carried out because in 1986 Rovers applied for planning permission to build a superstore on the site. If their appeal against a first refusal proved successful, Prenton Park's days would be numbered.

Ground Description

Despite the club's recent financial plight and its long-standing struggle for support on Merseyside, Prenton Park does not externally bear many scars. It stands in a post-war housing area, on ground so flat and in air so fresh that although you cannot see it, you know the sea must be close. In fact it is five miles north, and five miles west. A short distance east takes you to the River Mersey.

From Borough Road the back of the stands are entirely green. Even the floodlight pylons are green. A couple of flags fluttering in the wind add some style and already Prenton Park looks orderly and respectable.

The main entrance on Prenton Park West takes you into the car park, behind the large Main Stand frontage. With more money this could have been made quite grand, but it is still impressive for a small club.

The plain roof pitches upwards, and has just two central supports. The seating tier stops at a brick wall which forms the rear of the terracing in front, and although slightly drab is compensated by the liberal use of blue paint all over the stand. Underneath it is quite spartan, but dressing rooms must come before refreshment rooms in order of priority. Even so, it was said that Rovers had the best toilets and turnstiles in the Fourth Division, but one of the worst teams. From the back rows of the Main Stand one has a panoramic view of the land between Devonshire Park and the Mersey.

To the left of the stand is the much lower, multispan cover called the Cowshed, with Prenton Road West behind. Since being reroofed after a gale in the 1970s, and more recently repainted with advertising, this stand looks quite dapper. The terracing underneath is shallow, without barriers, and has at the back a section marked out with a court for training.

Opposite the Main Stand is the Borough Road Side. recently reclad in smart green sheeting. Quite a shallow terrace, its perimeter fence is pressed up against the touchline. Flagpoles along the roof brighten it up considerably.

To the right is the open Kop End, the banking built up on the old tank traps. For some reason the crush barriers here are very low. Behind this bank you can see the Shaftsbury Boy's Club's headquarters and the old social club, and nearer the Main Stand the sports centre.

The Kop End was closed in 1985, a measure which seemed to be just one more nail in the ground's coffin. Having lost the sports centre, most of the car park and now the Kop (unless sufficient funds were miraculously found to refurbish it), Prenton Park appears to be a rapidly diminishing asset, obviously prey to the advances of developers. The ground remains one with a certain tidy character, but with average gates of around 1500 it is possible Rovers would be better off elsewhere. Their best bet, a Scouse wit might say, would be a site blocking up the Mersey Tunnel, thereby stopping the weekly exodus towards Stanley Park. And so it goes on; the rich get richer, and the poorer go to supermarkets.

·CHESTER CITY·

Previous Grounds

Chester were formed in 1884 and first played at Faulkner Street, in the district of Hoole, just east of their present ground. Soon after, they switched to Chester's Old Show Ground on Lightfoot Street also in Hoole, then in 1904 used a ground on Whipcord Lane, near Sealand Road. All three of their previous grounds have been built over, although the roads still exist. Chester moved to Sealand Road in 1906.

Sealand Road

When Chester were elected to the Football League in place of Nelson in 1931, Sealand Road and its environs were very different from the ground we know today. There were fields all around which are now covered by light industry and the ground was covered on two sides only. The Main Stand, which survived until 1979 was a small, wooden construction, made distinctive by vertical blue and white stripes on the paddock rear wall, and along Sealand Road was the standing cover known as The Barn, still in existence.

It has been claimed that Sealand Road was one of the first League grounds to have a public address system installed, at least as far back as August 1931 when the club began their League programme. For many years the announcer would begin with the words 'Hello Spion Kop, hello Albert!' apparently addressing a long-standing supporter in the crowd.

Like Brunton Park, one of Sealand Road's major problems in those early years was flooding from the nearby River Dee, which flows through the town centre at every high spring tide. This was solved in 1936 when the club installed proper drainage at a cost of £400.

One of the most unusual events at the ground came on 5 January 1935, when the FA organized an experimental game using two referees for a match between two amateur international trial teams. A similar experiment was tried at The Hawthorns in March of that year, before the idea was dropped.

Sealand Road's highest attendance, 20 500, came in January 1952 for Chester's replayed 3rd Round Cup tie v. Chelsea, won by the visitors. The club's first floodlit game at the ground was on 12 October 1960; a League Cup match v. Leyton Orient. The lights were later updated in 1974.

In 1968 the Popular Side opposite the Main Stand was covered, then in December 1979 the old wooden stand was replaced by the present Main Stand at a cost of £556 000. Like Swindon's new stand, it had been built directly behind the old one, and in consequence there is now an awkward flat space between the front wall and the touchline. This development raised the number of seats at Sealand Road to 2874, in a total capacity of 20 000. Designation in 1985, however, brought a reduction in the terracing ca-

Sealand Road has interesting details but is spoilt by the plain, high facing of the Main Stand

pacity, bringing the overall limit down to 9500. But the Main Stand presented no safety problems and Chester's main expenditure of £5000 was on a new perimeter fence.

Ground Description

Sealand Road and its surrounds have changed immeasurably in recent years, from a drab, soulless environment on the edges of a beautiful Roman and Georgian city to a landscaped area sanitised by new roads and massive retail outlets. The ground has perked up slightly too.

The entrance leads you from Sealand Road to the Main Stand, behind which lies the site of the former Chester Greyhound Stadium. The stand has been pepped up with bright blue paint on its roof and the addition of several advertisement hoardings along the fascia. The most prominent feature however is the high, breeze-block wall at the front, broken only by staircases leading up to the seats and a few advertisement boards. If there was a terrace in front, as at Wrexham, even a token terrace, as at Ashton Gate, the stand might look quite smart. As it is the wall is bare, and in front is a 30-feet gap before reaching the touchline. And where Swindon have at least turf, Chester have only a flat expanse of tarmac. To make matters worse, instead of a perimeter wall or a few low advertisement hoardings, there is a chicken-wire fence with concrete posts dividing the pitch from the patch of earth. Miserable enough to look at, this arrangement has an inevitably detrimental effect on the atmosphere at the ground.

To the left from the Main Stand, which at least provides a reasonable view, is the open Spion Kop. Although overgrown at the top, it has good terracing, formed unusually out of paving stones. The barriers are extremely thin. To the right is The Barn, a decaying barrel-roofed cover over the Sealand Road End terrace, with 16 uprights along the front. At the back are some uneven, but quite solid wooden terraces, with an ancient sign above from the Liverpool, London and Globe Insurance Company Limited warning that dropping lighted matches is dangerous. Between here and the Main Stand is a modern block overlooking the pitch housing social facilities.

Opposite the Main Stand is the all-covered Popular Side, a simple cover over terracing. An unusual feature is the floodlighting, which is on the classic Scottish pattern with gantries leaning down towards the pitch, as if eager to be closer to the action. The system was built by the same Edinburgh company which supplied, among others, Hearts, Hibernian and Brighton.

Such curiosities still barely elevate The Stadium above the tedium, for the ground remains in need of a focal point. However, Sealand Road may well have a limited future. The site is wanted by retail developers and Chester, with debts of their own, are keen to sell up and move on. One site they had in mind was just across the Welsh border but the plan was turned down by the local council in 1986. Yet with Sealand Road's improved access, non-residential setting and ample parking space nearby, it is difficult to envisage how the club would be better off elsewhere.

219

· CREWE · ALEXANDRA

Previous Grounds

Crewe's first home in 1877 was Earl Street Cricket Ground, which they soon vacated in favour of Nantwich Road, a comparatively well-developed ground. It was chosen as the venue for a Wales v. England international in 1880, and for an FA Cup semi-final between Aston Villa and Glasgow Rangers in 1887, the last year Scottish teams entered the English competition. Perhaps inspired by the occasion, Crewe went on to the semi-finals themselves the following year, their greatest achievement. Nantwich Road was also witness to one of the very earliest floodlit games in November 1878 but was finally swallowed up by the rapidly expanding railway industry. In 1896 the club moved to Edleston Road, then to Old Sheds Field, now the Royal Hotel car park. Crewe returned to Earl Street, used nowadays for stock-car racing, and from there to Gresty Road. All five grounds were within a stone's throw of each other.

Gresty Road

Although Crewe Alexandra is a romantic name for a football club, Gresty Road sounds anything but mysterious. The first point of reference is during the early 1930s, when the original Main Stand burned down. The present structure was opened by Sir Francis Joseph, ironically on Guy Fawkes Day 1932.

The ground was first floodlit in October 1958, by lights on telegraph poles bought second-hand from Coventry City for a game v. an All Star XI. The club were in the new Fourth Division in January 1960 when all-conquering Tottenham came to Gresty Road for an FA Cup 4th Round tie, and were held to a draw in front of Crewe's record gate of 20 000. In the early 1970s Crewe came second in the Ford Sporting League for good behaviour. Their £30 000 prize money was spent on rebuilding the Popular Side.

Designation under the Safety of Sports Grounds Act in 1985 brought great changes to Gresty Road. The capacity was reduced from 17 000 to 5000, and only 640 of the stand's 1700 seats were allowed to remain in use. The biggest upheaval was at the visitors' end where the Gresty Road retaining wall, a long, uneven, red corrugated iron fence, had to come down and four wooden steps at the rear of the cover, built in the 1930s, were removed. In the corner of this end was an example of the primitive conditions the 1975 Safety Act aimed to eradicate – a urinal dug into a bank, whose design might easily have been based on that of a First World War trench. All this antiquated muddle was demolished, bringing the Gresty Road End up to the standard of the two other terraces. In addition, Crewe made improvements to the Main Stand and laid a five-a-side training area on the car park.

Ground Description

It is easy, when approaching the ground for the first time, to mistake the proliferation of lighting gantries around Crewe station for the club's floodlights. In fact they are still mounted on the original telegraph

Gresty Road – railway lines to the right, British Rail headquarters in the background and a British Rail helicopter providing the aerial view

poles, linked by a web of smaller poles, gantries and wires, so that Gresty Road appears to be held up like a marionette. The old dressing rooms stood near where the main entrance is now.

The Main Stand, plain but neat in its scarlet coat, with an ordinary house door in the centre marking the players' tunnel, looks rather impromptu from the narrow alleyway behind, where more poles and wires perform a delicate balancing act.

To the left is the Gresty Road enclosure, greatly changed since 1986. It had been a dark, ramshackle enclosure until remodelled and brought into line with the Popular Side.

Opposite the Main Stand, this terrace is the neatest part of the ground. The roof is plain but light, the terraces spacious. Looming behind is the office block of the town's *raison d'être*, British Rail. At such an open ground as Crewe's, a tall building so near has a barrier effect on the wind, causing swirling currents to whip up the ball.

Behind the open small Railway End to the right – five steps below a cinder bank – is the main goods line to Chester and the North.

Comparison with a railway sidings yard is tempting, but not fair. The yards all around Crewe are none so appealing as Gresty Road's unpretentious red and green enclosure. The club may never have reached the First Division, but has survived commendably well in the guard's van of the League. And in common with the likes of Rochdale and Halifax, it is what goes on in the adjacent social club which has often more significance than events on the field of play.

Gresty Road before 1985. These were the kind of outdated conditions swept away when the Safety Act was extended after the Bradford fire

·WREXHAM·

Previous Grounds

Although most sources give the date of Wrexham's formation as 1873, as Anthony Jones reports in his history, the present club dates from 1875. But the first ground, Acton Park, had certainly been used by a Wrexham team of sorts since 1873. Nevertheless, Wrexham is the oldest Association football club in Wales. Acton Park is now part of a council estate, but there was once a hall there, standing in substantial grounds, of which the lake still survives. The present day Acton Park is not the same location of Wrexham's first ground.

The town was also the birthplace of the Welsh FA, so Acton Park had the honour of staging Wales' first home international, v. Scotland in March 1877.

Racecourse Ground

Wrexham had used the Racecourse Ground on a few occasions before moving there permanently in 1905. But many years before the site had been typical of nineteenth century sporting venues, described in 1850 as 'a place where drunkardness and vice were encouraged to a terrible extent'. Later the Racecourse became more respectably occupied by fêtes and charity shows.

On the Mold Road Side of the ground was and still is the Turf Hotel, which Wrexham used initially as a dressing room. The players stepped down a wooden staircase and across the paddock to the pitch. The Turf Hotel belongs to Border Breweries, which owns the Racecourse Ground.

Perhaps soon after moving, Wrexham built the first stand in the corner of the pitch along the touchline from the Turf. Called the Plas Coch Stand (Red Hall), the stand had bench seats for a few hundred, and new dressing rooms below. The only entrance to the ground was between this and the Turf, where the club installed a turnstile on wheels.

Wrexham joined the League in 1921, and were helped considerably by the formation of a supporters' club in 1926. This immediately raised £300 to pay for the erection of a cover behind the Plas Coch goal, which was extended round the far side at a cost of £2000 in the late 1930s. Also during the inter-war period, a stand was built between the Turf and the original stand, parallel with Mold Road. In front of the stands, supporters laid terracing. The standing covers were low, and characterized by large girders along the front, parts of them lined with advertisements. They made the Racecourse seem small and cramped on two sides, whereas the rest of the ground was fairly well set back from the pitch. Advertising in the club's programme in 1937 the builders of these covers, W. H. Smith of Whitchurch, described themselves as 'specialists in cowsheds' and other farm buildings.

The Racecourse in the mid-1970s with the new Yale Stand on the far side and the old 'Pigeon Loft' Stand on the right

After the Second World War the supporters laid down concrete terracing over the Kop. In January 1957 the Racecourse Ground had its highest crowd, when 34 445 came to see a Cup tie v. Manchester United, the eventual losing finalists, and two years later in September 1959 the floodlights were switched on for the first time, in a game v. Swindon Town.

Wrexham won promotion, also for the first time, in 1962, and in order to increase the seating capacity at the Racecourse, then only just 1000, the club erected one of the oddest stands ever to grace a football ground. Its steel frame and seats came from the Majestic Cinema in Wrexham, and when covered it provided accommodation for 1000 spectators. The stand was dubbed 'The Pigeon Loft' and stood on top of the Kop. Its origins were obvious since it had a curved balcony wall such as one would see at any cinema. Underneath the seating tier was a little refreshment stall amid the open steel supports. Incredibly the stand lasted until 1978, when it was deemed unsafe, but it won a third chance when sold to Wrexham Rugby Club.

European football was staged at Wrexham in the early 1970s, as the club was a regular winner of the Welsh Cup and thus eligible for the European Cup Winners Cup. The revenue from these games helped finance a substantial building programme which changed the ground completely. First, a new stand was built along the Popular Side. Called the Yale Stand, because Yale Further Education College is behind, this became the Main Stand and was completed in 1972. Three years later the dressing rooms were transferred here from the Plas Coch Stand. In December 1978 another new stand, the Border Stand, was opened behind the Plas Coch goal. The two new structures cost nearly £900 000 to complete and provided a further 6000 seats. Finally in 1980, in place of the Pigeon Loft, a new cover was erected at the top of the Kop.

One of the most important effects of this rebuilding was the return of regular Welsh international football to the Racecourse. Before and after the Second World War, Cardiff had taken over from Wrexham as the established home of Wales, acting as host for 51 international matches between 1946–77, compared with a total of only 16 at the Racecourse, and 7 at Vetch Field. Since 1977 Wrexham has enjoyed the greater share of Welsh international fixtures, undoubtedly due to the better facilities, but also partly because with smaller crowds attending games, the Racecourse can provide a better atmosphere than a half-empty Ninian Park.

Townspeople also claim that they are the more passionate patriots, and that as the birthplace of the Welsh FA as well as the location of its headquarters, Wrexham is the natural choice. So where were they all when Wales played Northern Ireland on 27 May 1982 at the Racecourse Ground? The attendance of 2315 was the lowest for any international match in Great Britain since 1892.

Although the ground was already designated, following the more stringent checks made after the Bradford fire in 1985, both the Plas Coch and Mold Road Stands, plus the terracing in front were closed. This reduced Wrexham's capacity from 28 500 to 23 250, of which 5250 are seated. The club estimated that it would cost about £20 000 to reopen those parts of the ground, but having spent £360 000 on safety work in recent years, and with gates averaging 2500 in 1985–86, the further expenditure was not deemed worthwhile (unless Wrexham managed to draw a major European club side in the Cup Winners Cup).

Yet the safety authorities were not entirely consistent in their ruling, apparently, for when Uruguay played at Wrexham just before the 1986 World Cup, the closed sections of the ground were allowed to open again. So were the stands safe or not safe, or were they only safe when foreign teams with few supporters were visiting? An anomalous situation indeed.

Ground Description

The ground is conveniently situated north west of the town centre, a two-minute walk from the main railway station. From Mold Road one sees only the older stands next to the Turf Hotel, where the official entrance used to be. It looks an unlikely international venue. Yale College and its playing fields provide a pleasant, green background to the modern Main Stand, which although very similar to the one I have been so unkind about at Chester, is a busy looking construction brightened by liberal amounts of red paint.

Inside, it is dominated by cross-beam girders supporting the roof, just as the old covers on this side were. The seating tier seems quite small, sandwiched between girders and the high brick terrace rear wall. But far from seeming bare and exposed, as at Swindon or Chester, this wall is relatively hidden by its stairways and by the spectators in the front paddock. Both this and the similar Border Stand, to its right, are very simple, plain and economically constructed. Wrexham have opted, rather like QPR, for cheap stands providing seats and standing accommodation, and have maintained them well. But if once they start to fade they would be miserable indeed, as only modern buildings can be.

From the Yale Stand to the left you can see the tall Kop, known as the Town End, behind which lies Crispin Lane and the railway station. Again, the application of red and white paint to the barriers smartens up the banking, as does the new roof over the rear half. This section of the ground holds 13 000 standing spectators.

But the most interesting part of the Racecourse Ground is opposite the Yale Stand, along Mold Road. From the Town End corner we see first the Turf Hotel, standing behind the paddock. Built in the nineteenth century, it is not a particularly distinguished piece of architecture, but with its balcony overlooking the pitch the hotel forms an apposite link between the ground when used as a racecourse in Victorian times and its sporting activities now.

Between here and the Mold Road Stand is an awkward gap, forming an entrance to the paddock and backyard to the hotel. The Mold Road Stand, closed in 1985, runs along a third of the length of the touchline, but still is set some way back with the paddock in between. From here the pitch looks wide enough to kick the other way, or stage cricket. In fact the width is not more than 78 yards. Touching the end of the Mold Road Stand is the corner Plas Coch Stand, also closed, but since they seem like one long stand together they are referred to by either name. On the roof of what I shall term the Mold Road Stand, the younger of the pair, is a small viewing box.

Although now closed, the Plas Coch Stand is in good condition for its age, with rows of bench seats visibly smoothed with age. Each bench has curious little handgrips for every spectator. The view from here across the pitch, wooden pillars and all, is like that from an old pavilion. Underneath, nearest the corner, the paddock stops and there is a flat section by the pitch. The players used to enter from here, from the old dressing rooms under the stand.

Notice how many lights the floodlight pylon holds, over 40 on each, in differing sizes. New lamps were installed in 1978, but the very smallest ones are used only for European and international games.

If the Mold Road Side is a little disjointed, this is only a reflection of the ground's previous life as a racecourse, and it by no means detracts from the modernity of the other three sides. The Racecourse Ground has a comforting scale, cluttered in places yet apparently wide open in others. No doubt visiting international players and officials, accustomed to vast concrete stadiums, look at the old Plas Coch Stand and have a quiet scoff, without realizing how much the ground has advanced in recent years, or indeed that when it comes to building football grounds the British are quite different from the rest of the world. The Racecourse Ground is a perfect illustration of haphazard development compensated by restrained modernization. Safe for one match, but not, apparently for others.

17

BEDS, HERTS, WEST, NORTH AND EAST LONDON

· LUTON TOWN ·

Previous Grounds

The club formed in 1885 at the Excelsior Ground in Dallow Lane, where in 1890 Luton became a pioneer of professional football in the south. According to *The Luton Town Story* by Timothy Collings, Dallow Lane, often called Town Meadow, was situated between Dunstable Road School and the Dunstable to Luton railway line, which was close enough for a player to claim that he missed one good scoring opportunity by being blinded by smoke from a passing locomotive (that same railway line irritates the club to this very day). The ground's only stand remained on the site for some fifty years after Dallow Lane was taken over by Brown's timber yard.

Just before being elected to the Football League Luton moved a short distance to a ground on Dunstable Road, sometimes referred to as Bury Park. It was opened on 3 April 1897 by the Duke of Bedford for a game v. Loughborough. After three seasons Luton dropped out of the League and in 1905, on re-election, moved a short distance to their present home. The Dunstable Road ground was on the site of the Odeon Cinema, now a bingo hall.

Kenilworth Road

The new ground was opened on 4 September 1905 with a match Timothy Collings refers to as the 'Green game', because Town's opponents were Plymouth Argyle, who play in green; a local brewer Mr Green kicked-off, and both Town's secretary at the time and the referee were also called Green.

In 1920 Luton joined the mass exodus from the Southern to the Football League but a season later suffered the misfortune of having their stand burnt down. In its place was built the centre section of the existing Main Stand, the structure having been brought from Kempton Racetrack.

By the beginning of the 1930s the team began to look more promising. The ground was purchased and after the formation of a supporters' club in 1931 the Bobbers Stand, a narrow cover opposite the Main Stand, was opened in September 1933. Naturally it cost a bob to stand there. A cafe in the Bobbers Club underneath served lunches and no doubt witnessed a celebration or two when Luton won promotion to Division Two in 1937. To cater for the larger crowds the Kenilworth Road terrace was raised to its present height and the opposite Oak Road terrace covered. At the same time the Main Stand was extended to join up with the Oak Road roof in the north west corner.

Floodlights were installed in 1953, and first used on 7 October for a friendly v. Fenerbahce of Turkey. The lights were individually mounted on short poles on each stand roof, but even when the system was updated several years later there was insufficient room to erect corner pylons, so four narrow pylons were placed along the front of each stand.

The late 1950s brought great excitement to Kenilworth Road after Luton reached Division One in 1955. As crowds grew there was only one way to expand the ground – to steal a few yards from the houses behind the Oak Road terrace and build a few extra steps. Luton were able to do this because they owned the houses until 1974.

The record attendance for the ground occurred on 4 March 1959, for an FA Cup 6th Round replay v. Blackpool. A crowd of 30 069 saw a win for Town.

Between then and 1974 the club slipped down to the Fourth Division, then rose back up to Division One, and it was as a Second Division club in 1977 that their ground came under the jurisdiction of the Safety of Sports Grounds Act. The club had done little to improve the ground, simply because the site was so inadequate that they always hoped to resite further away. To bring the ground into line with the safety recommendations £350 000 had to be spent, mainly on improved access points and barriers, and the capacity dropped from 30 000 to 22 601. That included 4506 seats, of which 1539 were installed in the Bobbers Stand on the original terracing.

Steam trains may no longer cloud the view of Luton forwards but the same railway line continues to rattle the club. For over twenty years Town engaged in a struggle with Bedfordshire County Council over plans to move the railway line even nearer the

Kenilworth Road; the controversial railway line, to the left, cuts across the ground. There is not even room for corner floodlight pylons

ground and build in its place a new relief road from Dunstable to Luton (the existing route is Bedfordshire's busiest trunk road).

Luton were resigned to moving but from 1979, when the first legal moves were made to instigate the road plan, every site they put forward for a new stadium was rejected on planning grounds by the Borough Council (shades of Watford and Oxford). Luton spent £200 000 in legal fees alone arguing their case over the next three y' ars and finally, after receiving no positive indications from the Borough Council, decided to investigate a move to the new town of Milton Keynes, twenty miles north. Luton estimated that only half their supporters actually lived in Luton, while the possibility of a futuristic indoor stadium seemed the club's best option.

A sufficiently vocal element of the Luton-based fans thought otherwise, and with Kenilworth Road's days becoming fewer, the club changed tack. Now under a new chairman, it was decided to set up a working party, including supporters' representatives and local councillors, to look for alternative sites.

The urgency of this committee's task was made clear in November 1985 when the County Council intimated that work on the relief road would commence in March 1987. Given that the club would lose half their car-parking space and their access behind the Main Stand, it was apparent that once the work began Kenilworth Road would cease to be a viable First Division ground. The sooner they found a new home the better.

Stadiums are not built in a day, however, and for the interim period Luton embraced a radical notion, regarded outside Luton at least as one of the most controversial ever conceived in football.

In short, Kenilworth Road was to become a members-only ground, open to bona fide, card-carrying Luton Town supporters, each of whom could admit three guests each by booking tickets in advance. No one else would be admitted, except bona fide card-carrying journalists and broadcasters, who thus formed the only possible link between visiting teams and their frustrated supporters.

Membership schemes are discussed earlier in this book (see History), but Luton's reasoning has to be considered in the context of their need to move.

Firstly, changes in the League rules have meant that clubs now keep all the receipts of a home game. Therefore banning away supporters would not penalise visiting clubs financially.

Secondly, in the summer of 1985 Luton became the second League club to install an artificial pitch. Superior in many ways to QPR's pitch, Luton's surface, laid by En-tout-cas (see Pitches) converted Kenilworth Road overnight into a major community asset. Obviously Luton's community profile improved enormously, as inevitably did the Borough Council's attitude towards the club. Only in such an atmosphere could Luton hope to win council backing for a new ground.

But Luton had other reasons for wanting to concentrate their efforts on home supporters. No one who attended Luton's Cup tie v. Millwall in March 1985 will forget the scenes of violence which visited the ground that evening. Apart from the wanton damage caused in the town by so-called Millwall supporters en route from the railway station, the Bobbers Stand was invaded, plastic seats were torn up as if they were merely cardboard, and innocent spectators and the police were subjected to a hail of missiles from youths who at one stage seemed uncontainable.

It has to be said that there were mitigating circumstances which led to a pitch invasion before the match – Luton admitted that the Kenilworth Road End had been overfilled – but there could be no excuse for the violence which followed.

Luton certainly could not brush the issue away, especially after the events at Brussels two months later, and in December 1985 they finally decided upon their radical course of action: no more away fans.

There was a fourth reason for the members-only policy. Luton reckon that they will have to leave Kenilworth Road between 1989 and 1991 if they are to maintain the standards expected of a top club.

A new ground would cost several million pounds. Of that, approximately £2 million was due in compensation from the County Council (because of the road scheme) but the rest would have to come from grants and the club itself. In its pre-1986 state Kenilworth Road could only earn a limited income, but with changes that income could rise substantially in the ground's few remaining seasons.

A membership scheme alone would make no profit, because the £1 joining fee covered only administration charges. But extra seating would increase revenue, as would private boxes. Town could hardly squeeze in boxes behind the Main Stand – there is little enough room without railway lines and new roads – so there was only one place to put them, in the Bobbers Stand.

But the Bobbers Stand is too narrow for anything but private boxes, so all the seats there had to be moved to the covered Oak Road End. This in turn displaced the home standing supporters, who had to be rehoused on the Kenilworth Road terrace, which then had to be covered to give the Town faithful decent accommodation. And since it would have been impossible to segregate properly home and away fans on the one terrace, only one solution offered itself. Whichever priority Luton advanced – improving local relations, anti-hooliganism or increasing revenue – the answer was the same. Members only.

During the summer of 1986 Luton began issuing computerized cards to those living in recognized catchment areas and others who could prove they were genuine supporters. (A grey area this. One imagines an interrogation in the depths of the Bobbers Stand; 'When did you last see a Luton match?' Luton claim they had to reject very few obviously invalid applications.)

By the start of the 1986–87 season the number of cards issued more or less doubled the 1985–86 average gate of 11 000. Luton reckoned, therefore, that gates would actually rise, since most households purchased only one card and with each member bringing three guests this represented a potential support of over 80 000 (although alterations to the ground had meanwhile reduced the capacity to approximately 14 000). Hardly a word of dissent was sounded . . . in Luton, although many recognized how unfair the scheme was to genuine visiting fans.

But life is seldom fair, and not all clubs are about to have a railway line and major road thrust upon their backyard, so we must judge Luton's decision fairly.

Above all it is important to consider how Luton is different from other grounds in human terms. The surrounding streets, for example, are populated largely by Asians for whom Saturday afternoons were a complete misery. Windows were frequently broken, shops vandalized and individuals harassed by racists among the visiting supporters.

Luton fans themselves were often terrorized in the narrow streets and alleys around the ground. It is a fact recorded by a survey of the members-only scheme, conducted by Leicester University (see Bibliography), that whereas for example, Leeds fans have a bad reputation but Elland Road itself sees little trouble, Luton's more troublesome fans fought most of their battles on home ground. Peaceable Luton fans therefore had enough experience of violence to support the members-only scheme.

In short, Luton's situation was acute, and it is important not to confuse their solution with the very different needs and demands of other clubs.

The attractions of the scheme are, however, con-siderable; potentially lower policing costs, an encouragement for the 'ordinary' fan to return, a more relaxed atmosphere both inside and around the ground on match days and, not least of all, a totally partisan crowd which is in no danger of being out-shouted. Anyone with experience of American sport-ing events, where away fans rarely attend, will know that atmosphere does not necessarily suffer.

Indeed, with the onset of cable television British football supporters may well become accustomed to watching their team's away matches live on tele-vision. Of course it would not be the same, but then football can never be the same again anyway, if it is to thrive beyond a few venues in the major cities.

That was the theory. But what actually happened when the scheme began to operate?

Apart from a few minor delays the computerized card-reading equipment worked well. If any non-Luton fans did obtain cards or admission then at least they behaved themselves.

Attendances were disappointing initially, being about 500 down per game on average. But policing levels were also down.

Perhaps most difficult of all to adjust to was the more subdued atmosphere at matches. Visiting play-ers quite naturally disliked the lack of noise which accompanied their better moments. But the atmos-phere in the town itself and among Luton's neigh-bours was greatly enhanced. For the first time in years shops were able to open on Saturday after-noons, and the once-familiar sight of youngsters sporting club colours returned to the streets.

The League's first public reaction was much de-layed. In May 1986 the Management Committee had approved the members-only policy for League match-es, only to see their newly-elected successors over-turn the endorsement when it came to Littlewoods Cup matches, on the grounds that the exclusion of visiting fans broke the competition's rules. The com-mittee then put it to a vote among the 92 clubs and Luton lost. They were barred from the Cup and their executive director John Smith had no choice but to resign from the Management Committee.

Meanwhile the FA backed Luton, as did the Gov-ernment, who reacted by giving the League an ulti-matum to formulate a plan for the introduction of membership schemes. But since Luton's chairman was a prospective parliamentary candidate for the Conservatives, the issue became more than a simple one of controlling football supporters. Indeed it could be argued that this issue cut right across traditional right-wing opinion. If free trade was to be main-tained, how could the banning of customers be up-held? Which was more important, law and order or the rights of the individual away supporter?

Public opinion, if the press was to be believed, was largely in sympathy with Luton, especially after Leeds and Cardiff fans had behaved so appallingly on their travels at the time of the controversy.

But in all this debate two factors were ignored.

First, Luton's policy was an experiment forced upon them by the circumstances of their ground. In view of this, to have rejected Luton on the pretext of a minor infringement of a competition's rules showed that the problem was not so much the issue of Luton's ground itself as the continued inability of Football League clubs to put wider issues above their own short-term needs.

The second issue largely ignored by other clubs was a moral one. Luton believed that if the only way in which visiting supporters could attend an opponent's ground was by frog-marching them from station to turnstile, confining them in caged enclosures and separating them from their rivals by lines of police, then perhaps it was time to call a halt. Football, in that situation, ceases to be a game or mere entertainment.

Better, said Luton, to free the town from this fortnightly tyranny. Opposing club chairmen may object, but have they ever wandered around their town in the few hours preceding kick-off? Arriving in a luxury coach or a Rolls-Royce is no way to assess the effect visiting fans have upon the locality.

One may question Luton's motivations endlessly, but until and unless the basic moral questions underlying their decision were addressed, the debate remained essentially worthless.

Ground Description

Whenever the state of modern British football grounds is discussed, one of the most popular points to be raised invariably concerns how cramped many grounds are by their surroundings. Until you have been to Kenilworth Road you cannot appreciate how cramped is 'cramped'.

Behind the Oak Road End the car park – to be dissected by the new road – leads to a narrow drive behind the Main Stand, where various offices, social clubs and hospitality suites appear to cling to the ground as if in fear of passing trains. The railway line runs parallel with the stand and conveys a profitable cargo of oil and cement.

The first surprise once inside Kenilworth Road is the artificial pitch, laid in 1985. Glossy, smooth, and with the sponsor's name embossed on the touchline, it lends the surrounding stands a totally different hue.

The Main Stand appears quite tall, but this is an optical illusion created by the ground's narrowness. Viewing from here was improved considerably in 1986 by the removal of the narrow floodlight pylons which rose from pitch level in front of the stand. The lights are now mounted on the roof, but there are still numerous uprights to contend with. Inside, the stand is mainly wooden, with creaky floors and wide gangways. It runs only threequarters of the length of the touchline, with a paddock in front. The most unusual feature is a long players' tunnel.

To the left of the Main Stand is the Oak Road terrace, covered by an unusual roof built in three sections, climbing from the far corner to the Main Stand roof. In 1986 this end had 2000 seats placed upon the terracing and, to ensure some sort of continuity, a new Bobbers Club was built here. An electronic scoreboard adorns the front. Perhaps here more than in any other part of the ground one is reminded of how little space Luton possess.

To enter this stand supporters pass through gateways underneath the first floors of the terraced houses on Oak Road, under bedrooms and bathrooms, then through a pathway and up some stairs which look down on the gardens below. In times gone by visiting fans would throw litter and urinate on these gardens. Residents here will not miss the fortnightly stamp of visiting feet one iota.

Opposite the Main Stand is the new North Stand, which in 1986 replaced the lovable Bobbers Stand. This side of the ground is quite unique in British football, since it comprises nothing but private boxes. But they are not the usual glass-fronted variety which transform the outside world into a muffled unreality.

Luton saw at Lord's cricket ground that by putting in sliding glass doors and installing a few seats outside on a private balcony, box-holders can have the best of both worlds. Inside or out, depending on the weather and their own inclinations. Watford took up the idea as soon as they saw it, and no doubt more clubs will follow.

Convenient though these boxes are, there can be no doubt that they alter that side of the ground entirely. The only visual reminder of the Bobbers Stand are lines of advertisements above and below the windows (the old stand appeared to be held up by little more than hoardings, which in turn helped stop the ball flying over into the back yards beyond).

Finally, to the right is the now covered Kenilworth Road End, which holds 8000 standing spectators and has its own electronic scoreboard on the roof. Hoping for good behaviour from their own fans, Luton were able to put a lower security fence at the perimeter with a dry moat in front for stewards and police.

The conversion of Kenilworth Road, including the addition of new toilets, refreshment bars and so on, cost £1 million, half of which was financed by private box rental fees. The expenditure will have proved worthwhile if Luton stay in the First Division and can raise sufficient cash to help build a nice new stadium miles from any railway line, back garden or narrow street.

Whatever the team's fortunes, the members-only policy may one day be eased. But if Luton do admit opposing fans after 1986–87 it will not be on the old terms. There will be no more segregation, for example. Luton's message in 1986 was that fans have to learn to behave en route to the ground and then sit or stand next to their rivals without fighting. It seems a reasonable enough requirement for our so-called civilized society.

·WATFORD·

Previous Grounds

Two clubs joined forces in 1898 to form Watford FC: Watford St Mary's, who played at Wiggenhall Road, near Vicarage Road and West Herts, who played at the West Herts Sports Ground on Cassio Road, in the centre of Watford. It became apparent that the town was not large enough for two professional clubs, and as the ground in Cassio Road was better suited, this became the newly-formed club's permanent headquarters.

In 1909 a limited company was formed and Watford became tenants of West Herts Sports Club, at an annual rent of £50. The ground was an enormous circular bowl, large enough for two football pitches. Other attractions at Cassio Road were athletics fêtes and concerts, as well as cricket during the summer. The only covered accommodation was on either side of the pavilion, the opposite touchline being open.

The team struggled in the Southern League, and were continually in need of financial aid from benefactors, whose faith was rewarded in 1915 when Watford won their first honour, the Southern League Championship. Unfortunately, war-time football was hardly a major attraction and despite their success, Watford's gates were so low that West Herts decided to end the club's lease of Cassio Road. In 1916 therefore Watford had no ground, no players, £3 in the bank and assets of £30 only, consisting of a stand and some turnstiles.

The board of directors began looking elsewhere, and settled on the Recreation Ground, Vicarage Road as the likeliest venue. Watford Urban District Council was happy to give its approval for the move, but the Local Government Board refused permission. It was the first of many tangles with the local authorities.

Benskins Breweries offered to buy Cassio Road for them from its owner, the Dowager Lady Essex. She turned out to be an opponent of professional sport, and had actually told West Herts Sports Club that they were not to continue sub-letting the ground to Watford, although this had not been revealed when the lease ended in 1916. Benskins' persuasion worked, however, and the 1919 season began with renewed confidence.

Several makeshift stands were made from brewery drays and hay wagons and even a press-box was built. Attendances in the immediate post-war era rose to unprecedented levels at Watford, and as the team became more successful it became apparent that Cassio Road would not, after all, be such a suitable home. Apart from the lack of facilities for spectators, the players' baths had to be heated in two large copper containers and carried up six steps to the pavilion in buckets. Then in 1920 Watford were one of the leading Southern League clubs absorbed into the Football League's newly formed Division Three. A new ground was therefore a priority.

Cassio Road's highest gate was 13 000, recorded for the League derby match v. rivals Luton Town.

Shortly after this, as we learn from Oliver Phillips' comprehensive history of the club, to which I am indebted for much of this section, a local character called Joey Goodchild performed his usual trick of climbing onto the stand roof to perform a tap dance for the delight of the crowd. But on this occasion someone asked him to stop, he fell off the roof and landed on a gentleman, whose glasses were broken, and an unfortunate lady. She received £25 compensation from the club, and Joey's dancing had to come to an end. The last Watford match at Cassio Road was v. Gillingham, attended by 5000 spectators. The ground is still open land today, used for hockey, tennis, cricket and squash.

Vicarage Road

Vicarage Road was an obvious choice for Watford's new ground. It was large enough in 1919 to have two junior pitches running side by side and was a natural bowl shape; perfect for redevelopment and expansion. On one side of the recreation ground was a cart track, on the other stood the old Union Work House on the site of what is now Watford General Hospital, formerly Shrodells Hospital.

On the South Side were the old buildings of the Rookery silk mill, in 1922 occupied by the Watford Steam Laundry. The present terrace end of Vicarage Road is still known as the Rookery.

Watford had wanted to move to Vicarage Road as early as 1916 but were prevented by the Local Government Board. When negotiations reopened in 1921, the authorities were still not wholly in favour. Benskins offered to buy the Recreation Ground for £2300, but Watford Urban Development Council wanted compensation for the three remaining years which the site still had to run on its lease. The problem even became an issue in the local elections of that year. Eventually Benskins agreed to pay £450 compensation, and Vicarage Road was handed over to Watford on a 21-year lease.

The club had little money to invest in the new ground so Benskins loaned Watford a further £12 000 for improvements, in return for 10 per cent of the club's gate receipts. Half of this was to pay interest on the loan, the other half to pay off the capital sum. The brewery also insisted on having three directors on the seven-man board, all of whom had to be in agreement before any Watford player could be sold. But in the end, Benskins managed to have not just three, but five of their men on the board, and as Oliver Phillips writes, 'Not surprisingly Watford became known as the Brewers'.

The main work to prepare the ground was carried out under the direction of architect S. E. Gomme, his most notable contribution being the design of the 3500-seater East Stand, built by the firm of Harbrow

Vicarage Road before the erection of the new West Stand on the nearside touchline

Limited. Costing £8000 it was considered at the time to be among the best and most modern in the country.

Vicarage Road was opened on 30 August 1922, by Charles Healey of Benskins; a crowd of 8000 then saw Watford and Millwall Athletic play out a goalless draw. Money was very limited for a long time after this, with Watford having to hand over a tenth of their receipts and attendances affected by rival attractions, such as the rugby at Cassio Road. To raise more cash the club staged a horse show, coaches and carriages included, during the summer of 1923, with inevitable consequences to the turf.

The club's financial problems reached crisis point in 1926, with Benskins considering putting in an official receiver, the Football League issuing an ultimatum that Watford must pay its way and Harbrow Limited about to sue for non-payment of £5800 worth of building work to the rest of the ground, plus £1000 interest charges.

In despair, Watford sought help from the people of the town. Harbrow had settled behind the scenes for a sum of only £3500, and at the public meeting other creditors were asked to take a similarly indulgent line. Again Benskins came to the rescue, and again Watford lived to fight another day.

During the 1930s Vicarage Road developed gradually while the club remained in the Third Division South. Towards the Second World War, they finished just behind the promotion contenders three seasons running. During this period concrete terraces were

laid by the players during the close seasons, and a West Stand was built on the Shrodells Side, to replace an old wooden stand brought over from Cassio Road in 1922.

In 1934, Vicarage Road was first used for the newly popular dog-racing, organized by the Dutch family twice a week. The track was not the right shape for top-class greyhound events, and was used for 'flapper' racing instead, that is, one class above whippets.

Vicarage Road's first floodlights were switched on in October 1953 for a friendly v. Luton Town. They were then on poles along the touchlines, until being updated on the present pylons in 1960. Shortly before then one of the more unusual features of the ground was removed, the trees which stood on top of the Vicarage Road Terrace. Also in 1959 the supporters' club raised the money to build a roof over the Rookery End Terrace.

In 1967 Watford were granted security at Vicarage Road when Benskins gave the club a 150-year lease, due to expire in March 2118. But for the time being, Watford were more concerned about the immediate future. Having slipped into Division Four for two seasons, the club was promoted the following year, and in 1968–69 at last escaped Division Three by winning the Championship. During that eventful season Vicarage Road's highest ever crowd, 34 099, watched Watford's 4th Round Cup tie v. Manchester United on 3 February 1969. Though they failed to surmount this hurdle, to celebrate promotion the club spent £45 000 on an extension to the Main Stand, adding a further 1700 seats. It was intended to replace completely the old stand, but sufficient funds were not available. Also in 1969 the Dutch family stopped holding dog-racing at Vicarage Road. For three years the track was unused, until in 1972 the Greyhound Racing Association began staging meetings. They installed modern equipment and built new kennels and outbuildings behind the Rookery.

If Watford thought promotion in 1969 was to signal the start of a new era, they were mistaken. Only six seasons later the club was back in Division Four. A new era did not begin until 1977, when the partnership of Graham Taylor as manager and Elton John, the rock singer, as chairman began. As the team started to rise up the Divisions, so Vicarage Road began to change, almost imperceptibly.

In 1978, after winning Division Four Watford installed one of the first American-style electric scoreboards, at a cost of £40 000. In December 1979, by which time Watford were in the Second Division, the greyhound company's lease ran out and the track was removed.

Meanwhile, unseen but vital improvements were being made in line with the recommendations of the Safety of Sports Grounds Act, under whose jurisdiction Vicarage Road fell once Watford were promoted. Every metal fitting in the ground had to be replaced, the cinder banking in the south west corner was terraced for the first time and access points were redesigned at a total cost of £750 000. Watford therefore used up almost their entire allotted grant available from the Football Grounds Improvement Trust. But the money was well spent, for in 1982 Watford realized their dream of First Division football.

Vicarage Road now had a capacity of 30 000, perfectly adequate for future demands, although the total number of seats was still too few for first-class fixtures. The West Stand paddock had 2200 seats added in 1979, and a small section of open terracing next to the Main Stand was converted with an extra 250 seats in 1982 (all sold immediately). But the obvious area for improvement was the West Stand, and when hospital buildings immediately behind were demolished it provided just enough space to give Watford the access they needed to develop this side. In 1986 work began on a completely new West Stand to fill the entire length of the pitch.

Original plans for this side entailed a steel-framed stand costing £3·5 million, but in December 1985, with attendances dropping after Bradford and Brussels and the Government clamping down on the sale of alcohol at football grounds, Elton John announced on television that the scheme was having to be shelved. Watford, in common with several leading clubs, could not afford the financial risk.

Watching the press conference were members of a Norwich firm, Anglian Building Products, who had already built stands at Twickenham rugby ground and Goodwood and Cheltenham racecourses.

Anglian approached Watford with designs for a pre-cast concrete stand costing £2·2 million, and this proved to be within the club's budget.

These events demonstrate Elton John's value to Watford. Not only did his presence at the press conference render it newsworthy, but he was also able to donate £1 million towards the stand's costs.

Opened officially on 18 October 1986 by Elton John, the West Stand was named after Sir Stanley Rous, who had died only a few months earlier. Building was in two phases. First the main body of the stand and upper tier, seating 2124 with 34 private boxes, was completed during the close season, a remarkable feat made possible by using pre-cast concrete sections. A month later 1050 temporary seats were added to the front. When funds become available those seats will make way for a permanent lower tier – another example of how Watford take each step with care, seldom allowing their ambitions to stretch beyond their resources.

The Rous Stand brought Vicarage Road's seating total to 6906 in a total capacity of 25 000.

Ground Description

Access to Vicarage Road has never been easy, which is one reason why the club has tried for years to find an alternative site. The East Stand is reached from a narrow private track called Occupation Road. This was the former cart track. At its south end the road leads to the club's new offices, on the site of former dog-racing kennels. Above this block are three executive boxes, opened in 1985, with an enclosure for the disabled behind the corner flag.

The immediate impression is one of bittiness, yet Vicarage Road does have some sense of unity, largely due to colour coding and graphics. Every sign and every building is marked in some way with the red, yellow and black of Watford. The oldest part of the ground is the East Stand. No doubt it was quite modern in 1922, but in design it is now quite ordinary, especially since the original striped paddock rear wall has been painted over (as it has at most grounds). But nevertheless it looks as smart as possible, with all the woodwork yellow and all steelwork and the roof black. The upper tier seats are orange, the paddock seats are red.

Next to this central stand is the more recent extension, a rather uncomfortable neighbour, but then even in 1969 £45 000 bought very little. Here the roof slopes upwards, at variance with the pitched roof of the older stand, and has a solid screen wall at the Rookery End. The old stand has a glass screen wall. No unity but everything is quite spruce.

To the left is the covered Rookery. The cover itself is satisfactory, like an open-fronted box, with a clock in the fascia. But the terracing it shelters is surprisingly shallow, rising only 8 feet in about 60 feet of steps from front to back. If these were close to the pitch it would be acceptable, but because of the old greyhound track there is a flat section in front of the terrace with a high wall dividing it from the pitch. Therefore the view from the back of the Rookery is not ideal in a packed crowd. It also seems curious that the back wall of the stand should be so high when the back steps are so low.

To the right of the East Stand, where the terracing curves round to the North End, is the small section of red backless seats. Uncovered seating is always a risk, but here they are very popular. On each side of these seats are enclosures reserved for families, one seated, one for standing. Watford were among the pioneers of family involvement in football.

From there the terracing continues round to the Vicarage Road End. The old elliptical shape of the ground from the greyhound days is still in evidence behind each goal, where there is a semi-circle of extra turf. The open terrace is dominated by the large scoreboard at the back, behind which you can see the row of houses on the opposite side of the road.

The new Rous Stand is typical of a new generation of pre-fabricated, medium-sized stands: neat, quick to build and adaptable for today's requirements. It is characterized by its cantilevered roof, formed of twelve barrel-vaulted, translucent sections (as seen at Twickenham and Maine Road) and by a line of 34 executive boxes at the rear. These boxes are of a new type for football (the idea came from Lord's cricket ground) because they each have sliding glass doors leading onto a private balcony with eight seats – a simple, but quite ingenius innovation which allows the box-holders and their guests to escape from their cubby hole and experience the true joys of watching football on a cold, windy afternoon in mid-winter. Luton have similar boxes at Kenilworth Road.

Until a lower tier of seats could be added, the front of the stand was characterized by a line of black panels, like lock-up garages, but the use of red and yellow seats and the rather pleasant greyish-pink light cast by the p.v.c. roof shells gave the upper section a most unusual outlook for a football stand. Notice that the lines of the stand show how the pitch slopes down from the Vicarage Road End. Also, at each end are protruding beams of bare concrete, suggesting that if Watford ever had the funds they could extend the structure.

The Rous Stand adds First Division style to this otherwise adapted ground, but its construction had other consequences.

First, the roof obstructed the two nearest floodlight pylons. These had to be repositioned. Second, the pitch had to be moved towards the East Stand and completely resurfaced to allow for a shift in the camber. The new dimensions were those set by international standards of 115 × 75 yards, slightly bigger than the former pitch.

The third problem is more long term. For years Watford's supporters have lacked a roof over the Vicarage Road End Terrace. Planning permission was refused initially but now the main obstacle is money. Watford calculated that even though they

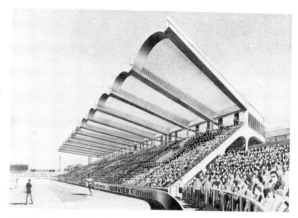

Watford's new Sir Stanley Rous Stand as it will look when completed. The upper section was opened in 1986

were getting higher gates than several other First Division clubs, their revenue was lower because of the lack of seats. They had to rebuild the West Stand, therefore, in order to earn the extra income needed for a terrace cover. At the same time, lack of access to the site meant that the West Stand had to be built first. Watford estimate it would cost £800 000 to cover the terrace, of which 50 per cent might come from FGIT. In the meantime the standing supporters might note that Vicarage Road is probably the only ground in the League not to have covered dug-outs for the managers. Former manager Graham Taylor once said that he would be prepared to sit out in the open as long as the fans on the Vicarage Road End had to do the same.

His attitude typified the fact that Watford possess one of the most aware, talented and dedicated administrations in the Football League. It is no accident that the club has risen from the Fourth to the First Division, and no accident that, unlike Northampton and Swansea, they have held their status.

Vicarage Road was never the ideal First Division venue and perhaps never will be, but it has retained its friendly spirit throughout. Violence is rare, while the staff and stewards all seem to have attended charm schools. Whether it is staging a football match or the now annual community fireworks display (a sell-out success) the ground is proof of what astute planning and imagination can achieve in the most adverse of circumstances.

TOTTENHAM ·HOTSPUR·

Previous Grounds

In common with so many football clubs, Tottenham's origins go back to a group of cricketers. They formed Hotspur FC in 1882 and played on public pitches at Tottenham Marshes until 1887. (The club's name was chosen because of the fiery reputation of Shakespeare's Harry Hotspur, a character based on a fourteenth century ancestor of the Northumberland family, landowners in the Tottenham area in the 1880s.) It is widely recorded that the early Hotspur team had no headquarters of their own until 1886 and so the committee had to meet under a gas-light lamp-post on Tottenham High Road, very close to the present ground. It is also suggested that they built their own goalposts and touchline posts (in the days before pitch markings at public parks) and 'bitterly regretted not being able to make their own footballs'.

During the week the blue and white striped Hotspur goalposts were stored at Northumberland Park railway station, and the players had to cross the Great Eastern railway line to reach the Marshes. In 1885 Tottenham was added to their title, and a year later they set up headquarters at the Red House, 748 High Road, in the building later to become the offices of White Hart Lane. As the team improved it became apparent that they would need a ground of their own. Crowds of up to 4000 had been assembling on the Marshes to watch them, but of course no gate money could ever be collected.

In 1888 Tottenham moved to their first enclosed ground at Northumberland Park. This was a playing field behind the Northumberland Arms public house on Trulock Road, on the other side of the railway line from the Marshes and only a hundred yards from the present ground. Rent was fixed at £17 a year and Tottenham's first game there was in September 1888, a reserve match v. Stratford St Johns. Yet even then, as Phil Soar writes in his history of the club, *And the Spurs go marching on . . .* , there were still some people who thought the club was overreaching itself by hiring a ground. But the club was cautious, for the first stand was not built until 1894 and it was not until 1895 that professionalism was adopted. The stand cannot have been terribly substantial because it blew down in a gale soon after.

The crowds soon began to outgrow even this ground, as southern professional football became more and more competitive. Northumberland Park was closed down once, in 1898, when Spurs' fans invaded the pitch and assaulted three Luton Town players. The ground's highest recorded attendance was 14 000, for a match v. Woolwich Arsenal in April 1899. During that game the roof of a refreshment stall, on which many spectators were perched, collapsed causing several minor injuries.

It was clear that Tottenham would have to move again if their ambitions were to be realized. The surrounding districts were expanding so rapidly that they were sure to attract even larger gates in the future. The answer to their problems was almost on their doorstep.

White Hart Lane

Tottenham may have been comparatively late in developing as a top professional club, but once moved into their present ground their ambition was given full rein. The site of their new home could not have been better placed; close to White Hart Lane railway station, on the main thoroughfare in Tottenham, and in the midst of an expanding North London suburb with no professional club for miles around. Nevertheless, the beginnings were still relatively cautious. White Hart Lane was not developed as rapidly as The Dell, Hillsborough or Roker Park, opened in the same period.

The site was a neglected nursery which the brewers Charrington had bought from a firm called Beckwiths. There were still greenhouses and sheds on the land, but the brewery intended to build houses there. Charringtons also owned the nearby White Hart Inn. The landlord, however, was quite keen on having a football club on his doorstep, for his previous hostelry had been close to Millwall Athletic's ground and he knew the profits large crowds could bring. The Tottenham directors came to hear of his preference and approached Charrington. Agreement was reached whereby Spurs could rent the ground on condition they guaranteed attendances of 1000 for first team matches and 500 for reserve games.

An added convenience of the ground was that the club's headquarters were already at 748 High Road, next to the public house. The only stands to begin with were those brought from Northumberland Park, providing cover for 2500 spectators.

Tottenham's first game there was a friendly v. First Division Notts County. A crowd of 5000 saw the Southern Leaguers win 4-1. By the end of that season Tottenham were Southern League Champions. As a result of their success, Tottenham were able to purchase the freehold of the ground for £8900 and with the help of Charringtons were able to find another £2600 to buy land and houses behind the northern end, then known as the Edmonton goal, now Paxton Road.

Photographs taken in the early years of the twentieth century show the pitch surrounded by a white wooden fence. Until 1904 there had been extra seats inside the perimeter fence, such as there were at many other grounds, given to people on a first come, first served basis for the same price as entry to the terracing. But on 20 February 1904 the ground was packed to overflowing, and those on the touchlines led a pitch invasion at half-time, when visitors Aston

The West Stand at White Hart Lane, the most expensive ever built in Britain, largely due to the two tiers of executive boxes. Notice the awkward link with the old roof (right)

Villa were one goal up in an FA Cup match. Spurs were heavily fined.

The East Side was partially covered by a simple cover, lined with advertisements, and on the West was a small wooden stand from their previous ground.

In 1908 Tottenham were elected to the Second Division of the Football League, thanks mainly to the resignation of Stoke; Spurs had resigned from the Southern League in a fit of frustration because of the organization's over-conservative approach. It took Tottenham only one season to gain promotion to Division One and to celebrate this momentous event they officially opened their new West Stand in September 1909. The designer was Archibald Leitch. It was a larger version of his stands at Craven Cottage and Stamford Bridge, both 1905, seating 5000 with room for 4000 in the covered paddock in front. A large, mock-Tudor gable displayed the words 'Tottenham Hotspur F. & A. Co Ltd' in ornate lettering, and there were flag poles at both ends of the pitched roof.

In 1910, added to the top of the gable was the famous ball and cockerel symbol, which became synonymous with Tottenham thereafter. As Phil Soar suggests, its origins are obscure but probably have a connection with Harry Hotspur, so-called for often pricking his horse with his spurs. Spurs were attached to the legs of fighting cocks, so perhaps the two symbols were linked – the cockerel on a ball – to signify the football club. Unconfirmed rumours suggest that the copper ball which supports the cockerel may be a time capsule, filled with mementoes from the period. Among the objects reputed to be inside are documents relating to Spurs' acceptance into the League in 1908 – these would make fascinating reading – coins and some newspapers of the period. Perhaps it is time to investigate the secrets within, and discover if, for example, Hillsborough's copper ball contains similar mysteries?

Also in 1910 both open end banks were doubled in size and soon after the East Side cover taken down so that the terraces there could also be expanded. The ground now had a capacity of 40 000, and appeared to be the archetypal Leitch ground – one grandstand and three large open sides, almost identical to his other designs in London, at Leeds Road and later at Selhurst Park.

When the First World War broke out the ground was taken over for use as a rifle range, opened by the founder of the Scout movement, Baden-Powell.

Until then, Tottenham's home had usually been called the High Road Ground. Several other names had been suggested but eventually White Hart Lane was popularly adopted, even though the lane itself is a few hundred yards from the ground. The fact that the nearest station was called White Hart Lane was probably the most important factor, because it meant Tottenham were on the map.

The first season after the war found Tottenham in Division Two, in completely new circumstances. Before the war they had been the senior club in North London, their nearest neighbours being Clapton Orient, five miles to the south east. But now they had The Arsenal only three miles to the south west. Their position was considerably worsened by the scandalous events in 1919 which saw the new arrivals take Tottenham's place in Division One. Briefly, Spurs finished bottom of Division One in 1915, just behind Chelsea. In 1919 it was decided to expand Division One to 22 clubs, but instead of keeping both Chelsea and Spurs in the division, Chelsea were retained, the two promoted Division Two clubs admitted, and instead of Spurs, The Arsenal were voted to move up, despite the fact that in 1915 they had finished only fifth in Division Two. In addition to this insult, there was the scandal of a fixed match involving Manchester United, whose win v. Liverpool in 1915 kept them above Spurs at the foot of the table. Players were suspended, but United were not penalized. So Tottenham were justifiably bitter when peace-time football resumed in 1919. (For the full story of this scandal and its consequences see the author's *Soccer in the Dock*, Collins Willow, 1985.)

It took Spurs only one season to get back to Division One, and they soon overtook their new neighbours. During the first few years after the war they also effected major changes at White Hart Lane. The Paxton Road End was covered, paid for by the profits of Tottenham's victorious Cup run in 1921, and then in 1923 an almost identical stand was built at the Park Lane End. Together these two new double-tier all standing structures raised the ground's covered accommodation to 30 000 spectators, a figure exceeded only by Goodison Park. They were both designed by Leitch, who was again commissioned when Spurs decided to build a stand on the uncovered East Side in 1936.

This project was in many ways a terrible risk. Spurs had spent the years 1928–33 in Division Two, at exactly the time Arsenal were beginning to impose their almost total dominance over English football, and had also started to redevelop Highbury into the most modern and fashionable ground in the League. Tottenham were in danger of being totally eclipsed.

Leitch's huge new East Stand cost £60 000; potentially crippling for a club just relegated. Fortunately Barclays Bank was willing to finance the deal. In addition, a row of houses had to be demolished and the tenants rehoused.

In design it appeared to be one of the largest stands in the country, although it was essentially a standard Leitch design placed on an extra pedestal of terracing. The gable housed the press-box and was similar to one Leitch had designed for Ibrox in 1929. There were 5100 seats and covered standing for 10 000,

with extra uncovered terracing in the front paddock. It was one of Leitch's last major works before he died in 1939 (see Design).

But even at the proud moment of opening the new stand, Spurs were again eclipsed by events at Highbury, for only a month later in October 1936 Arsenal's new East Stand was opened. It had cost more than twice the one at White Hart Lane. The architectural press gave coverage to Highbury's and none to Tottenham's.

It was in this otherwise gloomy spell that Tottenham's highest attendance was recorded at White Hart Lane, when 75 038 saw Spurs lose 0-1 to Sunderland in the FA Cup 6th Round on 5 March 1938. Spurs were still in Division Two when the Second World War broke out, and in 1941 the club gave Arsenal use of White Hart Lane while bomb damage at Highbury was repaired. Tottenham's ground was untouched by the Blitz, unlike the surrounding areas and for a time the top part of the East Stand was used as a mortuary for victims of the raids. Another section of the ground was used as a gas-mask factory.

For many years the White Hart Lane pitch had drained poorly and was consequently very muddy in winter. During the summer of 1952 it was completely reconstructed; 3500 tons of soil were dug up and dumped on nearby Hackney Marshes. Underneath the pitch the old foundations of the Beckwith Nursery greenhouses were found. These were removed and a new filter bed system installed, with one and a half miles of drains and a 9-inch layer of ash, covered over by 2000 tons of specially imported topsoil and 25 000 squares of turf. It was claimed that the heavier pitches had been a factor preventing Tottenham's famous 'push and run' side winning their second Championship in 1952 (they finished runners-up), but it can also be said that there have been many other Champions with pitches as poor. The system Tottenham installed was one of the most advanced ever laid.

Floodlights came to the ground in September 1953 and were switched on for a friendly v. Racing Club de Paris. The system was mounted on four corner poles (not pylons) each a few feet lower than the East Stand, with additional gantries on the two stand gables. It was because of these extra lamps that the ball and cockerel was moved to the East Stand gable, where it remains today, flanked by the lights. About the same time, the West Stand gable was repainted with a new motif in which the letters THFC were intermingled in light blue on a white background.

Spurs won the Double in 1961, the FA Cup in 1962 and 1967, the League Cup in 1971 and 1973, the European Cup Winners Cup in 1963 and the UEFA Cup in 1972. Throughout these decades of success the only major change at White Hart Lane came between 1962–65 with the conversion of the rear half of both end stands to hold 3000 seats each. The ground therefore held 60 000, including 16 000 seats, had two-tier stands on all four sides, an excellent pitch and adequate floodlights (updated in the late 1950s). What else could be done?

The answer came in 1979, when it was decided to rebuild completely the West Stand. The stand was getting old and also had been designed at a time when a football ground was used only for football. Tottenham could no longer afford this luxury, so they decided to invest in a new structure which would give White Hart Lane the potential for every day usage. The architects chosen were Mather and Nutter, the designers of Old Trafford's and Molineux's cantilever stands, and consultant architects at Anfield.

In the autumn of 1980 demolition of the old stand began, and slowly in its place arose the most spectacular modern stand built in England.

Officially opened for a game v. Wolves on 6 February 1982 by Sir Stanley Rous, the new West Stand has seats for 6500, 72 executive boxes in two tiers, costing £10 000 each for a three-year lease, and two very large reception areas called the Bill Nicholson Suite and the Centenary Club. There are four main office areas and of course facilities for the players. Furthermore, this was to be just the first stage in a complete redevelopment of the ground.

The controversial decision to go ahead with the project was made even though the chairman knew that the projected expenditure of £3·5 million could either make or break the club, which had an annual turnover in 1980–81 of £2·8 million. It was hoped the new stand would bring in two to three times more revenue per seat than the old one. It was an enormous gamble.

On paper, all seemed well, Tottenham's average gate in 1981–82 was 35 099 (compared with Arsenal's 25 493), the club won the FA Cup two years running again in 1981 and 1982, and were losing semi-finalists in the European Cup Winners Cup also in 1982.

But the cost of finishing the stand in 13 months had taken the total expenditure to over £4·2 million (the stand at Molineux had cost £2·8 million), and inevitably, there were repercussions. During the autumn of 1982 there were major changes at board level, forced to a certain extent by the fact that the stand was not financing itself as planned. Only two-thirds of the executive boxes had been sold and no sponsors agreed on. Tottenham's new administration rescued the situation and were helped by further success in 1984 when Spurs won the UEFA Cup a second time. One indication of their change in approach was the opening up of Tottenham's two indoor ball-courts, just behind the West Stand. These had lain redundant for hours every week until artificial surfaces were installed and the community allowed in.

Plans to continue White Hart Lane's development were delayed in 1985 by legislation controlling the sale of alcohol at football grounds. Like every club Tottenham depend to an extent on the profit from drinks sales, but more importantly on the £750 000 income they receive from letting out their 72 private boxes, which with alcohol restrictions are less attractive to lessees. Until the legislation was revoked or altered Spurs expected to lose as much as 75 per cent of their executive box income and so, like Watford, announced the shelving of their plan to build a new £3 million stand.

Spurs' plan, which involves continuing the West Stand round to the Paxton Road End, was also put back because applying the finishing touches to the West Stand cost a further £1·8 million, putting the final bill at around £6 million, more than any other football stand has ever cost in Britain. Not surprisingly it costs £12 to sit in the stand's best seats (compared with £5·20 for Old Trafford's best ones).

Tottenham spent another £450 000 on safety work at the ground, including the installation of thirteen closed-circuit television cameras. It is interesting to

White Hart Lane in 1966. The playing field behind, part of Tottenham's previous ground, is now a sports centre. Notice how the Park Lane End (right) is angled away from the pitch

note that only two of those cameras actually focus upon events within the ground. Finally, in 1986 Spurs replaced their undersoil heating system, at a further cost of £100 000. It is all a million miles away from the struggles of clubs like Halifax, and the gap gets wider ever year.

White Hart Lane's current capacity is 48 200, including 17 000 seats.

Ground Description

White Hart Lane is not just a football ground, it is part of a small kingdom. The block in which Tottenham are based is owned almost entirely by the club; the houses, the majority of the shops, and the Chanticlear night-club. In rents alone Spurs receive at least £50 000 a year.

On the High Road between Paxton Road and Park Lane is the Spurs souvenir shop, supporters' club headquarters and even a Spurs travel agent. Gateway to the kingdom is the Red House, with its large clock on the wall surmounted by a proud cockerel. On the other side of the house is the White Hart Inn, now part of the Bass Charrington group.

Entrance from here to the main courtyard is through tall, wrought-iron gates, threatened with removal when the new stand was built but happily since preserved. Through these we come to a small open space, on the left of which are the drab ball-courts which consist of two indoor courts, large and small. To the right of the courtyard is an engineering factory.

And so into the plush new West Stand, a wall of tinted glass forming the façade. The stand itself is typical of the new generation of cantilever stands, curving slightly round the touchline, with textured concrete facings, a vast roof supported from above so that no steelwork is visible, and sleek, glass screens at each end. It is the logical successor to the Hillsborough cantilever, built 20 years before, but with greatly more sophisticated facilities underneath. The architects described it as 'a hotel with seats on top'.

Overall it seems enormous, both tall and deep, and indeed there are stands with larger seating capacities that still have less visual impact. Nevertheless, there is still somehow a lack of focus; nothing has replaced the old gable in drawing one's attention to the stand. It is a large mass, bereft of detail.

One effect of the West Stand, hardly the architects' fault, is that the two corners of the end roofs which used to link up with the old stand, now appear to jut out in awkward suspense. In addition, many of the seats under these corners have been rendered useless because the larger dimensions of the new stand obscure the view. Had the club not ordered two tiers of boxes but one, the upper tier of seating could have been less steep and the roof lower.

These end stands are in comparison homely little structures. Each has a grey, pitched roof supported by white pillars, with a seating tier tucked away behind the standing paddock in front. Barely perceptible is the fact that both of them are built at an angle to the pitch, moving slightly away from the touchlines towards the East Side. This is because they follow the lines of Paxton Road and Park Lane respectively, rather than the right-angle of the terracing. This is most pronounced at the Park Lane End, to the right of the West Stand. The broken line of roofing just above the goal shows where the stand begins to bend away from the pitch.

Both stands have Leitch-type balcony facings, painted with light-blue steelwork and white walls. The barriers are coloured silver.

If the West Stand represents the mood of the new era, the East Stand represents a pinnacle of the old. It is built in three tiers: an ordinary open paddock at the front, with a double-decker placed above, each section a little further back than the one below, and there is a quite magnificent gable in the centre. Along the front of this is a line of windows, of what used to be the press-box before the new stand was built. Above appears the club crest, and surmounting this, standing against the sky is the ball and cockerel.

This single gable alone has everything that the West Stand lacks. It proves that scale and uniformity are not enough, that there has to be a touch of grandeur, however self-conscious or unnecessarily pompous, to give a grandstand any sort of visual merit. On the East Stand the gable not only provides this, it also makes the stand appear deceptively larger.

Looking more closely one sees the Leitch trademark along the balcony wall, not as intricate as those at Roker or Goodison Parks, but the steel supports fulfil the same function of tying the construction together. The standing area below is called 'the shelf' and is most popular with Spurs supporters. It is fenced off from the lower paddock by a white, wooden wall.

It is a wedding cake stand, shining with whiteness; the light-blue trimmings like icing, the gable like the top tier and the floodlights and cockerel like candles. It is a joy to behold, at once perfectly proportioned yet apparently extraordinary. But sadly, as dramatic as the stand is from the inside, from the street it appears massively drab and ugly. As Alan Ross wrote in 1950, 'Huge grey walls surround the ground, a barrier to revolution. They might have enclosed a prison or a mental home'. In both corners of the East Stand are short rows of terraced houses. On Paxton Road next to the night-club is a Salvation Army building. Every palace has a back yard and every empire its uglier face. But inside, the heart of the kingdom is vast and empty, until homage time on Saturdays.

·ARSENAL·

Previous Grounds

Between 1886 and 1913, Arsenal was just another small club playing without much success in South London. They were like Newton Heath before the coming of J. H. Davies, like Watford before Elton John. In 1913 the club was transported far from its roots, transformed into a new organization, until in the 1930s it transcended all opposition. Highbury Stadium stands as monument to this achievement, and as such has crucial significance to the study of football grounds.

The beginnings were humble. The workers of the Royal Arsenal put together a scratch team and played impromptu games near the workshops where they were based, as Dial Square FC. In 1886, reorganized under the name of Royal Arsenal, the team began playing on Plumstead Common, which still exists, before moving a year later to the Sportsman Ground, a former pig farm next to Plumstead Marshes. When this pitch became waterlogged one afternoon the club were forced to play at the adjacent Manor Field, where they moved in 1888 for two seasons. The players changed in the nearby Railway Tavern, or the Green Man pub.

Royal Arsenal's first substantial ground was a few hundred yards away at the Invicta Ground, also in Plumstead. It belonged to George Weaver, of the Weaver Mineral Water Company, and stood at the rear of Plumstead High Street, where Mineral Street is now. This was a ready-made ground with a stand, dressing room and terracing. There are still traces of the old terracing in some of the gardens in Hector Street (see History). Royal Arsenal played there between 1890–93, crucial years in which they turned professional – the first London club to do so – and changed their name to Woolwich Arsenal. At first Weaver charged a rent of £200 a year, extremely high in view of the club's status, but in 1893 when he heard they had been elected to League Division Two this amount rose extortionately to £350 plus tax. Only a few years earlier Everton had thought their rent increase to £250 sufficiently extreme to look for a ground elsewhere.

Woolwich Arsenal decided to seek alternative accommodation, having unsuccessfully offered the landlord a compromise of £300 including tax. Immediately the supporters rallied round and decided to try and buy the Manor Field, where the club had played before moving to the Invicta Ground. A limited company was formed and £4000 raised to purchase the site. At first conditions were fairly basic. There was one iron stand, and until banking could be raised, military wagons were brought in as viewing platforms.

When Arsenal began their League career at the Manor Ground they were the only members south of Birmingham. All the other southern professional clubs were in the Southern League. So for northern teams travelling down to play Arsenal, the visit was something of a novelty, and soon became linked with exhibition games and friendlies played at other London and southern grounds.

Woolwich's first success came in 1904 with promotion to Division One, but by then the club's whole complexion had changed. Until the turn of the century it had been run essentially by exiled northern working men, still closely connected with the Woolwich Arsenal. But the outbreak of the Boer War in 1899 meant more overtime for the men, and less time spent on the football club, which soon ran into debt. The organizers had never wanted it to become 'a proprietory or capitalist club' but now they were helpless to prevent capitalists moving in. The team was not the problem, they were solid middle-of-the-road performers, but the ground was a non-starter. As we discover from Phil Soar's and Martin Tyler's *The Official Centenary History of Arsenal Football Club 1866–1986* (Hamlyn, 1986), the Manor Ground offered a free view to many spectators from the top of a large, overground sewage pipe. When Arsenal won promotion in 1904 they built in front of the pipe a high bank of terracing which was soon nicknamed Spion Kop by many of the Boer War veterans who supported the club (Arsenal had a strong military following because of its origins and location). The suggestion that the Manor Ground and not Anfield was therefore home to the first so-called Kop might not go down too well in Liverpool (see Appendix).

This apart, the mortgage payments were too high, and gates were too low, mainly because it was in an awkward location for public transport. By 1910, when the team just escaped relegation, Woolwich Arsenal were £3000 in debt and went into liquidation.

But for the intervention of Henry Norris, Arsenal may have remained yet another struggling club. Norris was a director of Fulham, Mayor of Fulham, a wealthy estate agent and property developer, responsible for building over 2000 houses in the Fulham and Wimbledon areas. And yet for some reason he felt that Fulham FC were not champion material. They had just developed Craven Cottage into one of the best grounds in the country and joined the Football League, but still Norris was not happy. He wanted to mastermind the best. And he chose Arsenal, at the point when they were most vulnerable, and therefore most malleable.

At first Norris proposed a merger between Arsenal and Fulham, but the FA and League refused permission, saying that two clubs could not play on the same ground (Norris had suggested Craven Cottage) with the same name. So Arsenal stayed at Plumstead, and Norris started to plan a move.

The Plumstead area was simply unable to or uninterested in supporting League football, even though a few miles west Millwall Athletic had recently opened their new ground, The Den, and an amateur team Charlton Athletic were just becoming successful almost on Arsenal's doorstep.

The club's last season at the Manor Ground, 1912–13 was an unmitigated disaster from every point of view. The team were relegated while off the pitch financial matters went from bad to worse. The last game played at the Manor Ground was on 28 April 1913, and of this unloved little enclosure opposite Plumstead Station there is now no trace.

Highbury

Highbury Stadium as it is known today is not the ground that Norris built. He was responsible for the move to North London, for the purchase of the site and for the establishment of Arsenal's potential as a leading club. But Highbury itself did not become a major stadium until the 1930s, by which time Norris's involvement with football had come to an end. Nevertheless, as Bob Wall wrote, Norris's action in taking Arsenal to Highbury 'was the most astute single decision ever taken by the club'. Understandably, it caused a barrage of reaction.

Firstly, Tottenham and Clapton Orient did not want a third professional club in North London. Survival was hard enough without more competition. Furthermore, the whole concept of physically transporting a football club from one place to another seemed quite preposterous. Until then about the most adventurous move any club had taken had been Newton Heath's relocation to the other side of Manchester, but if clubs were going to be allowed to resettle on someone else's patch the moment life started to get tough, the whole fabric of professional football would be damaged irreparably.

Secondly, Islington Borough Council did not want Arsenal. So much so they gathered a petition to protest against the granting of the lease at Highbury, claiming that football clubs exploited footballers for dividend purposes and that a popular football ground in the area would decrease property values (that was more honest at least). In short, they mounted a campaign described variously as one of: 'calumny, misrepresentation and jealousy' and 'unscrupulous agitation'.

Thirdly, the local residents around the proposed ground did not want Arsenal, fearing the 'undesirable elements of professional football'. Arsenal were taking a huge gamble and had no way of knowing if there would be sufficient surplus spectators.

The new ground was to be situated on playing fields belonging to the St John's College of Divinity. It cost Arsenal £20 000 for only a 21-year lease, negotiated with the Ecclesiastical Commissioners on condition that the club were not to play home games on Good Friday or Christmas Day. Signing the agreement for the church was no less a figure than the Archbishop of Canterbury.

The site had two main advantages. It was in the centre of a densely populated area which although only four miles from White Hart Lane and even less

Highbury's original East Stand in 1925. The last bay (under 'C') was all standing. Such roofs were very heavy and costly to maintain

from Clapton's Millfields Road Ground, was closer to the inner city areas of London. But most importantly, next to the site was Gillespie Road underground station, opened in 1906. No other ground in London had such an advantage.

Archibald Leitch was asked to design the new stadium, which was to have one main stand on the East Side and three large banks of open terracing – the usual Leitch format (see Design). But Highbury's stand was to be quite different from any of his previous designs, and became the largest in London. It was a two-tier stand, with 9000 seats. The roof was also unusual. It was a multi-span roof, with the individual letters of the word 'Arsenal' painted on each gable front. Another stand of a similar construction was built at Molineux, ironically just a few years before this East Stand was demolished to make way for the present one. The banking was raised using excavations from the underground railway, and the West Bank called the Spion Kop.

On the opening day, 6 September 1913, the ground was not nearly complete and the stand least of all. The pitch was not up to standard, having been raised 11 feet at the North End and lowered 5 feet at the South, and the players had to wash in bowls of cold water. When a player was injured in the first game, v. Leicester Fosse, he had to be carried away on a milk cart. According to one observer, the match was played in the atmosphere of a builder's yard.

However, The Arsenal, as the club was now called, did win the game, and by December the seats were completed and conditions improved. That it had taken so long was mainly due to Arsenal's cash shortage, and work only continued after the builder agreed to take a share of gate receipts. Even so, the stand was still not entirely finished by February and tarpaulins had to be hung at the rear to keep out wind and rain. It was hardly an auspicious start, but the team at least managed a creditable third place in Division Two.

The First World War was a disaster for Norris. He had invested the then enormous sum of £125 000 in the club, but especially the ground, and there was no way of recouping it during hostilities. By 1919 The

Arsenal were £60 000 in debt, paying 10 per cent interest on their overdraft, and perhaps even more ominously, support was no more than lukewarm. The problems that had beset the club in Plumstead had not only persisted but had become magnified. Sir Henry (he had been knighted in 1917 and elected as Member of Parliament for Fulham in 1918) desperately needed a miracle. But rather than wait for one, he made his own.

The Arsenal had finished in fifth position in 1915. In 1919 it was decided to expand Division One by two clubs. The bottom two clubs in Division One in 1915 had been Chelsea and Tottenham, the top two clubs in Division Two were Derby and Preston. Norris bargained behind the scenes and when Chelsea, Derby and Preston joined the new-sized First Division, The Arsenal went in place of Tottenham.

This was quite scandalous. The whole affair had obviously been a complete fix, leaving Spurs quite understandably fuming at their new neighbours. But for Arsenal, and especially Norris, the vote to promote them was a lifeline. They have not left the First Division since, the only club in continuous membership since 1919, and they are the only League club not to have been promoted on playing merit to their present status.

Highbury soon became a focal point in the capital, if only because it was so large. In March 1920 the ground staged its first international (before White Hart Lane, even though Tottenham's ground had more cover and better facilities) and in 1923 Highbury became the first English ground ever to play host to the national team of a foreign country, when Belgium played England on 19 March.

The Arsenal, however, failed to make much of an impression in Division One, and finished the 1924–25 season in twentieth place. Norris needed another miracle to save his plan from financial ruin, and yet again, he found one. Herbert Chapman was appointed manager in May 1925. A new chapter began. The 10-acre ground was purchased outright for £64 000 and Norris even persuaded the Ecclesiastical Commissioners to drop their prohibition of games on Good Friday or Christmas Day. It was to be one of Norris's last acts for the club, because in 1925 he was suspended by the FA for illegal use of funds, for among other things, hiring a chauffeur. But having lured Chapman away from Leeds Road he had most certainly assured the realization of his dream.

Although the team's success enabled the club to rebuild completely the stadium, without Chapman's progressive thinking and the support of the board, its development might have been quite different.

In the 1930s Arsenal ruled almost supremely. It was during their third Championship-winning season in a row in 1934–35 that Highbury witnessed its largest crowd, 73 295, v. fellow title challengers Sunderland, on 9 March 1935.

The redevelopment of Highbury began in 1931. In order to increase the banking, Arsenal (they dropped the 'The' from their title in 1927) asked local inhabitants to bring in their rubbish. One coal merchant duly responded to the call, backed up too near the hole dug for the North Bank, and in fell both his horse and cart. The animal sustained so many injuries it had to be put down. The body was buried there and then, and remains under the North Bank to this day.

The following summer work began on the new West Stand. Until then this side had been uncovered banking, but in its place arose the most advanced, the most architecturally dazzling grandstand ever seen in Britain. The difference between this and Leitch's work of the same era was that whereas Leitch was a fine structural engineer, the West Stand at Highbury was designed by an acclaimed architect, Claude Waterlow Ferrier.

Ferrier worked in partnership with Major W. B. Binnie, and had already designed important works such as Trafalgar House, in London's Waterloo Place, the Army and Navy Club in Pall Mall, the National Institute for the Blind and the Western Synagogue, off Edgware Road. Ferrier's acceptance says a great deal for the importance of Highbury and for the club's prestige and taste, not to mention resources. The West Stand was completed six weeks before schedule in December 1932, and cost £45 000, making it the most expensive stand of its time. It needed 700 tons of steel for the frame, had three flats built into the façade on Highbury Hill, and most unusual of all had an electric lift. There were seats for 4100, plus standing room for 17 000, in a simple double-decker arrangement but in a totally new style.

As if to mark its pedigree, Chapman arranged the best possible publicity coup by inviting the Prince of Wales (he who abdicated) to open the stand on 10 December 1932.

The team's success had already earmarked Arsenal. Now Highbury too had to be special, and the inspiration came not from well-tried ideas dating from the beginning of the century, as did most of Leitch's work, but from bold statements of modern style. The West Stand was unquestionably a child of the 1930s.

There were other changes at Highbury at the same time and in the same spirit. Most important was Chapman's success in persuading London Transport to rename Gillespie Road underground station after the club. The authorities took several weeks to agree to the suggestion, feeling that a station named Arsenal would be tantamount to subliminal advertising, which of course was exactly what Chapman intended. The official change of title occurred on 5 November 1932, just in time for the opening of the West Stand. Another change of name was the ground's, from Highbury to 'Arsenal Stadium'. This change has not survived the test of popular usage.

Still Chapman did not relent. His next innovation was to place a 12-feet diameter, 45-minute clock on top of the North Bank. The FA objected on the grounds that it would impinge on the referee's au-

Typical of 1930s' design, Highbury's East Stand, already blackened by London smog. Notice the mouldings on the balcony wall below the streamlined glass screen-end

thority. That it might be of value to spectators, only Chapman had the foresight to realize.

His other ideas included numbering players' shirts, a cause taken up by many progressive people in the game, the use of a white ball – the dark leather ball was often hard for the crowd to follow (although after a trial he gave up the idea) – and the adoption in 1933 of red shirts with white sleeves as Arsenal's new strip, because so many teams played in all-red shirts.

Finally, the Arsenal manager was an early exponent of floodlit football. He put on a public demonstration of floodlights at Highbury in November 1932, on the eve of a London conference at the Great Eastern Hotel on the future of floodlit football, but despite the game's success, the FA heartily disapproved and Arsenal had to wait until 1951 to use lights (see Floodlights).

It was Chapman who suggested in 1929 that the 10-yard penalty arc be introduced to this country, as used abroad. Again the FA refused, and the marking was not introduced until 1937. He was the first manager to try out rubber studs, to suggest 'all-weather' pitches, and even the idea of roofed sports' stadiums. He was not in search of gimmicks, but of new methods to maintain professional football as a popular spectator sport. Highbury was in many ways only the first ground to benefit from his foresight, and long after his death in January 1934, Chapman's spirit lived on. (In fact the late Arsenal secretary, Bob Wall, even claimed that Chapman's ghost used to haunt the corridors of Highbury.)

In 1935 the North Bank was covered by a roof identical to the one seen today, while the clock was moved to the opposite end, called thereafter the Clock End.

In 1936 work began on a new East Stand on Avenell Road. The club had not intended to start building another stand until 1941 – the West Stand and North Bank had left them short of resources – but as had occurred with other multi-gabled roof stands Arsenal found that the fabric was too costly to maintain (the roof was over elaborate and top heavy). Demolition began in April and the tip-up seats were sold to Ipswich, who had just turned professional.

This new stand was to be almost identical to the West Stand, but would house all the offices, players' and executive facilities, and unlike its counterpart would actually have a façade visible to the road. It therefore became the grand entrance to the new Highbury.

Claude Waterlow Ferrier had died in 1935 but his partner William Binnie carried on their work, so that apart from a few structural changes the two stands are virtually indistinguishable. The East Stand had five floors, held 4000 seated on the top tier and 4000 on a lower tier, with a narrower paddock in front. Without question it was the finest grandstand of the era, but then it cost £130 000 to build, more than twice as much as Leitch's East Stand at White Hart Lane, also completed in 1936.

The East Stand at Highbury was opened before a match v. Grimsby Town on 24 October 1936. The programme for that match modestly described the new stand as 'a noble thing, a building of wonder and unparalleled in football'. Arsenal's debt as a result of their noble aspirations was also unparalleled. Within a few months of the East Stand's opening they were £200 000 in the red. But the development stood them in good stead, because in outward appearance Highbury has barely changed at all since 1936.

There was one other major occurrence at Highbury during the Chapman era, the arrival of broadcasting. This was not merely Chapman's influence; the proximity of Arsenal to the BBC's unit at Alexandra Palace was decisive. Highbury was the scene of the first radio broadcast of football match on 22 January 1927, H. B. T. Wakelam providing the commentary of Arsenal's game v. Sheffield United. The ground also featured in the first television transmission of a game, a practice match at Highbury between Arsenal and Arsenal Reserves on 16 September 1937.

From the small screen to the big screen, in 1939 Highbury became a star in its own right when Leonard Gribble's rather tame novel *The Arsenal Stadium Mystery* was made into a film starring Leslie Banks, Greta Gynt and Esmond Knight. The film featured Arsenal v. Brentford, Arsenal's final first-class game before the Second World War. That Highbury, a 1930s ground par excellence, should end the decade on celluloid seemed entirely fitting.

When the Second World War began the ground became a first aid post and an air raid patrol centre, with a barrage balloon flown from the practice pitch by the college. The dressing rooms became clearing stations for casualties, all windows were boarded over, and a blast wall was built inside the main entrance, in that famed marble hall. A 1000-pound bomb fell on the training pitch, while five incendiary bombs destroyed the North Bank roof and burnt the set of goalposts to the ground. Arsenal had no choice but to vacate Highbury and accept refuge at White Hart Lane. Then just as hostilities were ending, in 1945 the college behind the Clock End was also destroyed by fire, and so the last remaining link was lost with the ground's previous owners. A housing estate now occupies the site.

Although post-war developments at Highbury have hardly changed the ground's outward appearance, they have had a substantial effect. In September 1951 the first official game was played under floodlights, v. Hapoel Tel Aviv of Israel, in front of 40 000 spectators. The lights were mounted on gantries along the stand roofs, so that unlike lights on four corner pylons there were no awkward shadows on the pitch. Unfortunately these gantries replaced the original roof fascia, although these have now been restored with the updating of the lamps.

Also in the early 1950s the Highbury pitch was relaid, with turf specially brought from Sussex. In 1954 the North Bank roof was rebuilt, an exact copy of the pre-war construction, with money granted by the War Damages Commission.

Arsenal were one of the first clubs in Britain to try undersoil heating, when in 1964 an electric wiring system costing £15 000 was installed. Five years later an extra 5500 seats were put into the West Stand paddock, at a cost of £80 000. At the same time Arsenal also reconsidered Chapman's idea of erecting a roof over the pitch, to slide over from either stand. The estimated cost was £750 000 (when the country's most expensive player, Allan Clarke, had cost a mere £150 000), but if contemplated nowadays the price would be, at the very least, ten times that amount. In 1970 the present undersoil heating system was installed, for £30 000 and in 1986 overhauled at a cost of £100 000, an indication of how costs had risen.

If a fan of the late 1930s was to return to Highbury today he would see little difference. More barriers perhaps, since the Safety of Sports Grounds Act, a better pitch certainly, advertising even, but essentially Highbury as it stood before the War. The only visible changes are the replacement of the pitch-level half-time scoreboards in each corner with advertisement hoardings (no loss, they were almost impossible to read anyway) and the installation of toilets and a refreshment bar on the North Bank. A measure of Highbury's modernity, despite its dated appearance, is that it was this last improvement rather than safety considerations which reduced the capacity from 60 000 to 57 000 with 17 200 seats. Highbury is still the second largest club ground in Britain, after Celtic Park.

One possible development will alter the ground, if sufficient funds become available. Arsenal have received, after an appeal, planning permission to build a cover over the Clock End, incorporating at the rear a double line of executive boxes. It is one of several schemes devised for that terrace over the years, including one for an electronic scoreboard for which planning permission was refused. If carried out, the planned cover will provide long-awaited shelter for visiting fans on the terracing, and, perhaps more importantly, it will avoid disturbing the symmetry of the two opposing stands.

Ground Description

If you were to leave the underground station without knowing the stadium's location you might easily fail to spot it between the houses. The lack of floodlight pylons is one reason, the other being that the ground is tucked into the side of Highbury Hill, surrounded on three sides by tall houses.

The main entrance is in the East Stand on Avenell Road and it immediately sets the tone. There are few really impressive façades at football grounds, the most notable being at Villa and Ibrox Parks, Bramall Lane and here at Arsenal, where despite the narrowness of the road one can still appreciate the clean, unfussy, frontage dependent on understated detail rather than intricate mouldings.

Like the rest of the stadium, the walls are cream, the metalwork is grey or green. Above the main doors is the AFC motif, and above that the Gunners' emblem, framed in a moulded recess flanked by tall windows. The words Arsenal Stadium adorn the top, where there are two flagpoles.

When writers refer to the marble halls of Highbury, they mean the main foyer of the East Stand; a tall, almost spartan hall, rightly focusing on a bust of Herbert Chapman by Jacob Epstein, lit reverently in a niche.

We make no excuses for making a brief description of the stand's interior, for more than any in England (though Ibrox is similar in Scotland) this stand is in itself full of history. From the foyer, the offices are on the left, with the club's very own red post box in the corridor. On the right are the dressing rooms. Up the curving stairway we enter the board room and guest rooms. On view is Herbert Chapman's carved chapel seat, presented by his Yorkshire church in Easter 1931. Glass cases bulge with silverware and memorabilia, such as many clubs have, but these are presented in quite a different atmosphere. At Highbury it is like being at an exhibition.

Inside the boardroom are two small cannons. One of them was reputed to have been fired before each game in the Woolwich Arsenal days. There is also a most unusual five-legged chair, specially designed for a gout-suffering director who had the habit of suddenly rising from his seat and knocking it backwards.

On the opposite side of the stairway are the reception rooms, including one specially for the directors' wives and lady friends, with flowers laid out for each game in red and white, and the colours of the opposition. The press room beyond is equally impressive, equipped by the sponsors with a video playback of the game for journalists to watch at half-time and after the match. Highbury has the capacity for 300 outgoing telephone lines at any one time.

But now we must enter the stand side, and emerging into the daylight the first impression is of the ground's symmetry, for directly opposite is a mirror image of the East Stand. Red seats in the directors' box face red seats in the executive box. Crest faces crest.

One should think of these two stands as belonging to the same era as bakelite encased wireless sets, early airliners at Croydon airport, Odeon cinemas and Ovaltine. In architecture it was an age of rationality, of linear designs and metal frame windows. Highbury embodies the spirit of this age.

Each stand is in three tiers: an upper tier, each with 4000 light green seats. The lower tier is divided in two, a rear section of seats, a front section for standing. The West Stand lower tier holds more, being further back from the pitch and having no offices or other ground floor rooms.

Along the roof, wrapped round the sides, is an awning, or 'marquise' hiding the very slightly pitched grey roof. The awnings were originally intended to shield spectators from bad weather, but it was found that installing glass screen ends was more effective. Only at Mansfield's ground can a design remotely similar to this be found.

The roof or awning fascias are covered in an ornamental frieze, embellished with the club's crest and name at intervals. On each side of the stand is the Gunners' emblem in red on cream backgrounds. The balcony walls are also cream, apparently plain until close up one sees scrolled stonework lining the ledge. Again the understated detail allows the overall form to dominate.

There are, however, some differences between East and West. The East for example has side towers at each end, and houses all the touchline facilities. The tunnel is flanked by two sections of bench seating, reserved for the club reserves and juniors, and the managers' shelters (they are not dug-outs), encased in glass, like small greenhouses.

To the left of the tunnel in the paddock is a square section of green covers, beneath which is found the undersoil heating mechanism. The system can either blow steam or suck in water, according to conditions, but on one occasion it got mixed up and blew water everywhere in thousands of fountains. Next to the heating system is an area for the handicapped, part of which used to be reserved for a brass band and opera singer who provided pre-match entertainment. It would be nice to say their music is missed, but in truth they were usually inaudible above the general pre-match hubbub.

One feature which most observers would hope to be preserved at Highbury is the structural integrity of the two stands. Highbury might have been behind Tottenham in the provision of private boxes but they do have excellent catering facilities on the top floors of the West Stand. In one of these areas is another bust, this one of Claude Waterlow Ferrier, the main architect of the stand. Some stands, as at West Ham, have a plaque commemorating the architect, but only Arsenal have a bust.

Back in the ground, the Clock End forms the South or what used to be the College End. The clock itself is large, round and white, with black markings, and is virtually unchanged since its installation in the 1930s. As important as the clock is the high grey corrugated fence lining the back of the terrace, sealing it off from the buildings behind. These are the flats of Aubert Park Estate, and the Arsenal indoor training hall, built on their old practice pitch in 1963. In past years the indoor surface was shale and acted as a car park on match days. Now there is an artificial surface, well used by the club and the local community.

The North Bank is covered by a simple, pitched black roof, but far from seeming plain it has a white rippled fascia all round, with red and white corners and two Arsenal crests at the front. Here, exemplified, is the attention to detail which I have cried out for at so many other grounds.

Indeed the entire stadium is enhanced by such detail: by four flag poles along the front of each stand roof, by the Gunners' emblem on the side of the stands, by the careful balance of cream and green.

Despite the scale of the ground, the pitch is actually the smallest in London, measuring 110 × 71 yards, even smaller than West Ham's apparently tiny playing surface. There is a slight slope of 2 feet, from the Clock End penalty area down to the East Stand.

Arsenal's apparent obsession with preserving the ground's visual integrity has been scoffed at by many, who see Highbury as a cold, outdated, dusty mausoleum of long-lost glory. Others would perhaps rightly point out how few improvements standing spectators have been given in recent years, how although the club had sufficient funds, the Clock End remains uncovered, and the dark North Bank roof was not updated.

Now of course the money is not available and Highbury is a very expensive stadium to maintain. But the critics have a point. Highbury does seem lost in the past, caught in a time trap. I believe, however, that Arsenal have a responsibility to preserve Highbury, as a symbol of a bygone age and as an example of fine architecture. Pevsner ignored the stadium on his perambulation around Islington, perhaps he did not notice it. I cannot believe that if he had ever set foot inside the stadium he would have failed to give it a mention, for quite simply it is the most balanced and orderly ground in the country. There is not a line out of place; all is in total harmony. Perhaps the ground is best summed up by the fact that in his obituary, the architect Claude Waterlow Ferrier was described as a man to whom 'untidiness was anathema'. May his vision and that of Arsenal be preserved.

QUEEN'S PARK ·RANGERS·

Previous Grounds

If any club is worthy of the name Wanderers, it is this one. QPR have had more home grounds than any other League club – 12 altogether – and have played individual home matches at two further venues. They were formed in 1885 when two West London teams merged into one, St Jude's and Christchurch Rangers. Queen's Park was the district most of the players inhabited, and there is still a park of that name today.

The marathon succession of grounds began on a piece of waste ground near Kensal Rise Athletic Ground, before moving to nearby Welford's Fields for a rent of £8 a year. Both these grounds were in the vicinity of present day Harvist Road, Queen's Park. Next came the London Scottish ground in Brondesbury, rented between 1887–89 for £20 a year. Here the club began to collect gate money for the first time, although at times they might not have bothered, so few were the spectators. Eventually the pitch became so waterlogged QPR had to move again.

Between 1890–92 the club used four grounds: Home Park; back to Kensal Rise Green; across the Grand Union Canal to the ground of the Gun Club, on Wormwood Scrubs, then back to their roots at the Kilburn Cricket Ground on Harvist Road. Here they settled until 1896. This was the club's first properly enclosed ground, and their reasons for leaving in 1896 were most encouraging. Gates were rising, so they moved to the Kensal Rise Athletic Ground, with a ten-year lease at £100 a year. It was here that Rangers turned professional in December 1898 and joined the Southern League the following summer.

The first years of professional football did not bring prosperity, and the club was forced to give up the ground and move to one at the rear of St Quintin's Avenue, on Latimer Road in North Kensington. The players had to change in the Latimer Arms and run down the road to reach the pitch, hardly ideal for professional sportsmen, and apparently not for the local residents either. They felt QPR's presence lowered the tone of the area and in 1902 took the matter to court, which ruled against the club. It was time to pack their bags once more, this time back to the Kensal Rise Athletic Ground, where their old landlord gave them a two-year lease, but at £240 a year, more than twice their previous rent.

Even worse was to come, however, for at the end of the lease in 1904 the landlord offered them a five-year lease for £2000 (£400 a year), expensive even for a top club, and though QPR tried to bring down the annual rent to £300, they failed. This time they moved further west to Park Royal, two miles south of

Loftus Road, a model development

the site of Watkin's Tower, later to become Wembley Stadium.

They played at the Royal Agricultural Society's ground in Park Royal, reputed to hold up to 40 000 spectators, between 1904–07, before moving a few hundred yards to a new ground which had been built by the Great Western Railway Company. This stadium held 60 000, including 9000 under cover and 4000 seated, and was opened on 2 November 1907. With time and prosperity it may well have become one of the leading grounds in London.

Certainly QPR enjoyed their most successful spell at Park Royal, winning the Southern League Championship in 1908 and in anticipation of election to the Football League they even resigned from the Southern League. When their application failed they found that their former competition would only read-mit the club if it played all its games in mid-week, since the fixtures had already been arranged. Un-daunted, the team continued to improve. During the 1912 season they played a few games at White City (opened in 1908) when a coal strike prevented any trains from reaching Park Royal.

After the outbreak of the First World War, the Army took over Park Royal in February 1915. Rangers were homeless yet again, and finished off their home fixtures at Stamford Bridge and their previous ground on Harvist Road, Kensal Rise. And just in case the club seemed to be establishing roots, the Kensal Rise site was taken over in 1917 for use as allotments, and QPR were home hunting once more! This time they found Loftus Road, but as subsequent events showed, even this was never a totally perma-nent base for the apparently restless wanderers, until very recently.

It is almost impossible to trace the location of the club's previous grounds, because although almost most of the roads still exist, the open ground has long been built over by housing, or as at Park Royal, by industrial units.

Loftus Road

QPR's move in 1917 took them to within a few hun-dred yards south west of White City. Their new home had belonged to Shepherd's Bush FC, an amateur club disbanded during the War, and although it be-came known as Loftus Road, that was only one of four roads bordering the ground. It was however the nearest to Shepherd's Bush underground station.

QPR took one stand with them, originally built at Park Royal, and this became the Main Stand, hous-ing the offices and dressing rooms on Ellerslie Road. The other three sides were open, and an almost unobstructed view could be had from blocks of flats built all around the ground between the wars.

Loftus Road was closed in 1930 after crowd disturb-ances, so Rangers yet again played a home fixture at another ground, this time, Highbury. By then their playing fortunes had improved, crowds had risen, and in 1931 the board decided to play first team matches at White City, at that time one of the major greyhound racing circuits in London. They may have thought a bigger stadium would increase public interest or inspire the team. But although White City was only a minute's walk from their ground, once inside it was another world – an ex-Olympic stadium designed to hold 60 000 spectators. Their first game there was v. Bournemouth on 5 September 1931, a crowd of 18 000 seeing Rangers lose 3–0. The team continued to lose, yet by the end of the season even though the team finished in only thirteenth place, gates averaged a respectable 17 000.

On 4 January 1933 two London representative teams met at White City for a floodlit game, played with the FA's approval. Also at White City Queen's Park enjoyed their highest ever attendance recorded at any of their many grounds, when 41 097 saw them beat Leeds United in the FA Cup 3rd Round on 9 January 1932. But the following season White City started to turn sour for Rangers. Gates fell, and crowds of under 10 000 in a huge stadium seemed completely lost. They struggled on at White City until the end of the season, which saw them finish even lower than before, and they returned to Loftus

Road with a huge loss of £7000.

Once home, life began to improve almost immediately. The team achieved fourth place in Division Three in 1933–34, and in 1938 the supporters' club collected £1500 to build a cover over the Loftus Road End terrace, providing shelter for 6000 spectators.

The club's commitment to Loftus Road increased when they won promotion to Division Two for the first time, in 1948, and bought the ground's freehold plus 39 houses adjoining Ellerslie Road and Loftus Road for the sum of £26 250. At the same time the terraces were concreted and plans discussed for a double-decker stand on the Popular Side, along South Africa Road, although these were not realized for many years.

A further improvement came in 1953 when floodlights costing £5000 were first switched on for a friendly v. Arsenal on 5 October. By then Rangers were back in Division Three, where they stayed until 1967. During that time Loftus Road hardly changed.

For just a few months of the 1962–63 season the club tried out White City once again, on the suggestion of the manager Alec Stock. He felt that although some £300 000 had been spent on Loftus Road in ten years, the effect seemed negligible. It remained an underdeveloped, even somewhat ramshackle ground. If Rangers used White City, argued Stock, they might perhaps share it with another League club, perhaps Fulham. But as in the 1930s, small attendances in the large stadium were too distant from the players, whose form was affected by the huge surroundings.

In 1966 Rangers won promotion again, and this time they decided to improve Loftus Road. An architect, Michael Newberry, drew up a plan for the complete redevelopment of the ground, to cost £340 000 and to provide a circle of stands in two phases, due for completion in 1969. In fact the plan was used by Rangers only to get planning permission from the local authorities for their subsequent intention, which was to build a new stand on the Popular Side. This was the South Africa Road Stand, a two-tier construction, built quickly and at low cost, £162 000, to celebrate Rangers' promotion to Division One. The new stand and the new status made Loftus Road a proud ground, and even though the team was relegated in its first season at the top, the plans for the ground continued.

In 1972 the old Main Stand came down and in its place was built another very cheap, but remarkably cost-effective 5000-seater single-tier stand, also designed by Newberry. Quoted in *Design*, Newberry described the QPR board as 'very hard-headed, very successful businessmen who know the value of money very well'.

The importance of their attitude may easily be seen when contrasted with that of their neighbours at Stamford Bridge, who at the same time opted for a much larger, more prestigious rebuilding programme which was to cost over £2 million and plunge Chelsea into deep financial trouble. Loftus Road was being developed bit by bit, with simple, almost spartan stands which could be improved in time. Certainly the shock to both players and spectators was minimal. Loftus Road seemed to grow, rather than sprout up suddenly. It was intended to be used, not to be admired.

Rangers reached a peak in the mid-1970s. On 28 April 1974 Loftus Road's highest attendance was recorded for a match v. Leeds United, that season's League Champions. The crowd of 35 353 was nevertheless smaller than their best gate at White City, coincidentally also for a game v. Leeds. Two years later Rangers achieved their highest ever placing in the League, runners-up to Liverpool, then in 1979 found themselves back in Division Two.

At that time the School End sported a very impressive new-style electric scoreboard, and the opposite Loftus Road End cover was taken down to make way in 1980 for a double-decker stand. Again, nothing grand, but cheap and utilitarian, although as described below by no means unattractive.

It was joined by an almost identical stand opposite, at the School End, a year later, and executive boxes were installed in the South Africa Stand, which had now taken over as the club's administrative centre.

Loftus Road is now covered on all four sides, with a capacity of 27 500 of which 17 000 are seated.

In the summer of 1981 QPR became the first British League club to install artificial turf at their ground. The system they chose was called Omniturf and cost £350 000 to lay, in place of a pitch which for years had been notoriously compacted and threadbare. (For a full account see Pitches.) Rangers' decision was one of the most controversial ever taken in the entire history of British football. Not only was the whole future of natural grass questioned, but the essence of what a football ground should be: an expensive enclosure in use for perhaps two or three hours a week, or a community centre for leisure and spectator events.

Rangers opted for the latter, and inevitably there were many who criticized the new pitch. These criticisms were hardly allayed when extra sand was injected to soften the notoriously high bounce. Yet when advances in synthetic grass soon made the Omniturf obsolete, the Loftus Road pitch was still cited in arguments against the whole concept.

That will no longer be the case after 1988, for in February 1987 Rangers were bought up for £5.5 million by David Bulstrode, the chairman of Marler Estates (a property company which also owns Stamford Bridge and Craven Cottage), and he announced that the Omniturf would be dug up and replaced, not by a new synthetic pitch but by grass, probably a Cellsystem pitch as used at Fulham. The prototype experiment was over, although other clubs continue to reap the benefit of Rangers' experience.

In other respects however Loftus Road is still a model ground. It is probably the least costly yet most rapidly completed, and also one of the most capable grounds in Britain of catering for current spectator demands. It was significant that in the summer of 1982, the club actually took out seating from the main stand paddock, because supporters had expressed a preference for standing in that part of the ground.

Perhaps the most ambitious scheme for Loftus Road is to install a retractable roof over the stadium, thereby allowing it to be used for concerts, meetings and other sporting events. The idea is not a new one. Arsenal investigated the possibility of roofing Highbury in the 1970s, as did QPR in the early 1980s, but the projected bill then of £6 million was beyond Rangers or indeed any club in Britain.

However, with developments in new materials and construction methods Rangers carried out another feasibility study in 1987, the result of which is awaited with great interest.

But one factor Rangers cannot change and that is their location. Loftus Road is so hemmed in by housing that even if the ground were booked six or seven days a week for sporting events, it would be very difficult to get permission to stage them all, because of residents' objections. After Rangers' experience with the residents of Latimer Road back in 1902, they would not wish to cause antagonism again.

Ground Description
Officially of course it should be called South Africa Road, or at least the Rangers' Stadium, but old habits die hard. Loftus Road is a short walk from Shepherd's Bush underground station, in an area made famous not only by the now demolished White City but by the BBC television centre on Wood Lane, just behind the ground.

The main entrance is on South Africa Road, where the stand is fronted by a three-storey section of offices leased out to the BBC.

Inside, the ground is quite unlike any other. There are grounds such as the Baseball Ground which are as enclosed, but none quite as boxed in as this. It appears that every stand has been built in kit form, not because they are primitive, but because they are each so simple. That is their virtue.

The Main Stand is the tallest, with blue fascia, and blue steelwork standing in marked contrast with the bright shiny green of the turf, which reflects and enhances all the colours around. There are private boxes under the top tier, with dark reflective glass making it impossible to see from the outside how luxurious they are within. The stand is not a cantilever, but simply a modern, plain post and beam construction, with a paddock in front.

Pressed up on either side are the two double-decker end stands, Loftus Road to the left, the School End to the right (the road behind this stand is Bloemfontein Road – far too long for the average supporter to fit into a chant: 'We are the Bloemfontein Road End'). Each stand is like a shoe box cut-out, again with all

blue facings and steelwork, and with a standing terrace under the seating tier.

The Ellerslie Road Stand is different, being one tier of seats and with less bright blue appeal. Along its deep, plain roof fascia is the club crest. But it too is of simple design, post and beam.

Loftus Road always had a reputation for being a cramped ground where players and fans could exchange banter, and even though the ground has been rebuilt entirely within the space of 14 years, that atmosphere still prevails. The pitch comes right up to the perimeter, and even the rear sections of seating are comparatively close to the touchlines. Economy of space is emphasized by the new floodlight system, four thin poles with small gantries at the top. Very continental. Why don't other grounds have such attractive installations?

Loftus Road is a theatre, an arena to perform in, in which you expect fans to clap rather than chant obscenities; eat choc-ices rather than chips, drink coffee, not bovril.

Loftus Road is quite unique among British grounds, and one can pay no higher tribute to the ground's planners than to say it should serve as a model to any club of the size or status of QPR.

Perhaps Rangers did make a mistake in laying their artificial pitch before the technology was fully developed, but one could also argue that someone had to take the plunge so that everyone else could make up their minds. Rangers have now decided that they don't want their Omniturf, and nor do they want a more advanced synthetic surface. So in 1988 it's back to grass roots at Loftus Road, and, who knows, in 1998 we might be there debating the advantages or disadvantages of playing football under a roof.

· FULHAM ·

Previous Grounds

When formed in 1879 Fulham St Andrew's Cricket and Football Club was one newcomer in an already established soccer scene in a part of West London thriving with sporting activity, at a time when most open spaces were being steadily bought up and developed. Fulham's early grounds were all within a mile of their present home. They began at Star Road, near where Earl's Court is now, then moved to the Ranelagh Club, changing in rooms above the Eight Bells on Fulham High Street. The Ranelagh Club had to move in 1884 so Fulham St Andrew's moved to a ground on Lillie Road at Fulham Cross. This was close to the Queen's Club and also to Lillie Bridge, West Brompton, where the 1873 FA Cup Final was staged.

In 1886 Fulham moved across the River Thames to the new home of the Ranelagh Club, at Barn Elms, Barnes. This is still a sporting ground and is exactly opposite Craven Cottage on the west bank of the Thames. Here they dropped St Andrew's from their title in 1888. The club moved back to the Fulham side, to a ground by Purser's Cross, on Fulham Road, near the present Parsons Green underground station. From here it moved to Eelbrook Common, which still exists on the junction of Kings Road and Wandsworth Bridge Road, very near Stamford Bridge.

But Fulham's first properly enclosed ground was back across the river, off Putney High Street, behind the Half Moon. They shared this with Wasps Rugby FC until the ground was closed in 1894. The club was by this stage anxious to have a home of its own, and so it was the present ground was purchased in 1894. We learn this and more from club histories written by Dennis Turner and Morgan D. Phillips.

Craven Cottage

The site Fulham bought was a wilderness, overgrown and neglected, and the original Craven Cottage no longer existed, having burnt down in May 1888. Built in 1780 by the sixth Baron Craven, the Cottage stood on land once part of Anne Boleyn's hunting grounds. George IV used it as a hunting lodge after which it became the home of a money lender, Charles King, Sir Ralph Howard, and an author, Edward Bulwer-Lytton. The latter wrote *The Last Days of Pompeii* during his sojourn at the Cottage, and therefore provided later writers with a useful tit-bit to pad out reports of less scintillating matches. Of course the present Cottage is an entirely different structure.

The land partly belonged to the Church and partly to the Dean family, who have been closely involved with Fulham since 1894, and it was prepared for play by the building firm of Mears, which was to build Stamford Bridge and found Chelsea FC a decade

later. The original Cottage stood in the centre of what is now the pitch, which had to be levelled with excavations from the nearby Shepherds Bush underground railway. The workers found a secret underground tunnel linking the old Cottage site to a wharf on the Thames. Banking was raised on three sides with road sweepings, courtesy of the Borough Council, while on the Stevenage Road side a most distinctive stand was erected nick-named the 'Rabbit Hutch'. Seating 300 in four distinct blocks, it was about 40 yards in length, very tall and narrow, covered by four separate gabled roofs with two canopies added to cover the standing area in front. But trade disputes and problems with the site meant that Fulham were unable to play at the new Craven Cottage ground until 10 October 1896, having spent the two previous seasons wandering around West London from ground to ground.

Now at last the club was able to progress. In 1898 they turned professional and joined the Southern League, and in 1905 hired Archibald Leitch to re-model the ground. It is possible that Craven Cottage was Leitch's first major commission at a football ground south of the border. His work at Fulham certainly coincided with other work at Ewood Park and Stamford Bridge, and only just predated his efforts at White Hart Lane (see Design).

Leitch designed banks of terracing on three sides, with an impressive new full-length stand on Stevenage Road, costing £15 000. The format was one he used at virtually every other ground he worked on, up to the mid-1920s at Selhurst Park. But Fulham's ground was to have one significant difference. In the south east corner on Stevenage Road, Leitch built the present day Craven Cottage, in the same red brick of all his stands but in a more familiar residential style. Indeed the Cottage did have a small apartment for a player to occupy, as well as a boardroom, offices and a dressing room. It is reputed, however, that there was no electricity connected to the building until 1933!

The new stand was opened on 2 September 1905, and no doubt inspired the team to win the Southern League Championship in the next two seasons. During the club's last season before joining the League, Craven Cottage was chosen as the venue for England v. Wales in March 1907. This was the first time the ground of a professional London club had been used for an international, apart from the stadium at Crystal Palace.

Fulham's chairman at this time was Henry Norris, who three years later decided to leave Fulham and sponsor Arsenal. He was convinced that Fulham did not have the potential to match the great clubs of the day, and indeed between 1907 and the Second World War Fulham were an almost permanent resident at the middle of Division Two, broken only by a four-season spell in Division Three. Not that the club lacked ambition; in 1935 there was a proposal to build a stand on the river side of the ground and Leitch was again called in.

Craven Cottage's curious set of stands on the Stevenage Road Side pre-1905

It is not clear whether the proposed stand's designer was Leitch or his son Archibald Kent Leitch, who followed in his father's footsteps and continued to liaise with Fulham until after the Second World War. Whoever it was, Fulham could not afford the projected cost of £11 000, and though the idea was revived in 1950, when Fulham were in Division One for the first time, estimates had risen to £40 000. It was another 20 years before the matter was raised again.

When Craven Cottage's record attendance of 49 335 came for Fulham's derby game v. Millwall in Division Two, on 8 October 1938, they found therefore a ground unchanged since 1907. From the top of the Riverside banking one had a clear view of the river, and especially of the annual Oxford and Cambridge Boat Race. Often the ground was opened early, to let the crowd see the boats negotiate the stretch between Hammersmith and Putney Bridges. At the top of the Riverside terrace was a line of advertisement hoardings in the centre of which was a clock. The central gable of the Main Stand announced the words: 'Fulham Football and Athletic Co. Ltd. Craven Cottage'.

Fulham were back in Division One in the 1960s and the first major changes were made to the ground. Firstly, a cover was erected over the Hammersmith End, the tallest bank of terracing at Craven Cottage. Then in September 1962, Fulham became the last Division One club to install floodlights, first used in a League match v. Sheffield Wednesday. One reason given for this tardiness was the club's worry that

being so close to the river, the pylon's foundations would not be sufficiently firm, which would explain why the City Ground was also late in having its lights installed. But Fulham really wanted to use their available capital to buy back Bobby Robson (later to become the England manager) in August 1962. As at so many clubs, it was the supporters who rallied together to pay for the floodlights.

Other changes at the ground during that summer included the construction of an electic scoreboard on the terracing, which according to one observer no one could understand, and the replacement of the familiar advertisement hoardings with a smart set of flagpoles, each carrying the flag of a First Division club. But at the cost of £1500 a set, when Fulham found themselves relegated twice in successive years, there was hardly time or money to buy replacement flags from all the different clubs they had to face, and sadly the idea was allowed to drop. After returning to Division Two the Riverside terracing was built over with a fine new stand, opened in February 1972 with a friendly v. Benfica. The Riverside Stand cost £334 000 to complete, of which £250 000 was still claimed by the builders five years later. It was named the Eric Miller Stand to commemorate the Fulham director who died in the aftermath of a financial and political scandal, revealed in 1977.

Recent years have seen Fulham involved in financial and political wrangles of their own. Until 1985 Fulham had a 125-year lease from the Church Commissioners, at a token rent of £2000 per annum. When it became known that the Commissioners were prepared to sell the freehold (they could not sell to an outside party because of Fulham's long lease), Fulham decided that in view of Craven Cottage's high property value it would be in the club's best interest to negotiate a deal. The club's chairman Ernie Clay chose not to finance the £940 000 purchase himself, as he was already owed about £1·6 million by the club.

Rather, he borrowed the money from a Manchester-based property company called Kilroe Enterprises, who themselves had to borrow much of the money from a bank. Kilroe's interest was not in football (although one of their directors was Matt Busby) but in building flats on 2 acres of the 6½-acre site. The sale of such flats could raise as much as £26 million, which would be more than enough to pay off the bank, settle Fulham's debt to Mr Clay, still provide Kilroe with a healthy profit and leave Fulham in the black, with the freehold of their beloved Craven Cottage, which would be much improved in the process.

But attractive though all this was, Kilroe's scheme was controversial in several ways. Nothing of this nature had ever been contemplated for a football ground, and it was only Craven Cottage's location – in West London, on the river – that made it in any way viable.

Kilroe originally submitted plans in November 1985 for an L-shaped block, comprising 179 luxury flats, to be built on the site of the Putney End terrace and the adjacent Eric Miller Stand, both of which would be completely demolished, as would Leitch's famous Cottage. To reduce the disruption caused by dismantling the Eric Miller Stand, barges would transport the rubble and scrap metal down the River Thames. The stand would thus become the shortest-lived grandstand in modern times.

This first submission, designed by the Culpin Partnership, was rejected by the Council's planning committee in March 1986 partly because of its height (eight storeys in one corner), partly because it came in the sensitive run-up to a local parliamentary by-election. (Ironically the very same committee meeting approved plans to develop Stamford Bridge which would effectively mean Chelsea's departure by 1988. See Chelsea.)

Kilroe submitted a modified version of the plans, for 175 flats with a 30 per cent height reduction, a few months later, by which time the Borough Council had reverted to Labour's control. The new Council pledged itself to keeping all three of its League clubs (Fulham, QPR and Chelsea) at their present grounds, which suggested that they would have to give Fulham some sort of a lifeline. Kilroe's plan was that lifeline.

But how would the flats affect the football ground? Two new sides, with integrated cantilever roofs from the back of the flats, would provide 4500 seats, plus executive boxes, a restaurant and new club offices. This would give Craven Cottage a maximum capacity of 22 000 including 7000 seats. For a club just relegated to the Third Division with average gates under 5000 this was more than adequate, although with two sides all-seated it would make segregation of visiting fans difficult on big occasions.

But, and this became the biggest 'but' in West London, would these potential segregation problems and the limit of 22 000 enable Chelsea to stage First Division football at Craven Cottage?

Why bring Chelsea into it, you may well ask? At this point you must cease to think as a football lover and transport yourself into the mind of a property developer.

Briefly, the effective owners of Stamford Bridge, Marler Estates (through their subsidiary SB Property) have plans to redevelop Chelsea's ground (see Chelsea). Unless Chelsea can afford the probable asking price of £25 million when their current lease is up in 1989, under the terms of that lease Marler must find Chelsea a suitable, alternative ground within a radius of 15 miles.

Sharing Craven Cottage would be Marler's perfect solution, but, if the Council had already agreed to Kilroe's development, would the ground still be viable for First Division football? Would residents resist the prospect of Chelsea fans moving into their quiet neighbourhood once a fortnight (remembering the fact that several influential politicians live in the area)?

This already complicated scenario was further entangled in May 1986, when completely out of the blue Ernie Clay agreed to sell his 75 per cent shareholding in Fulham to . . . Marler Estates.

Clay became Fulham's chairman in 1977. In 1986 Marler paid £9 million for Fulham, of which approximately £4·5 million was for Clay's 11 250 shares. After various additional debts and expenses had been settled, this allegedly gave the former chairman a profit of about £2 million. Not bad for ten years with a team left dangling in the Third Division.

Marler's surprise involvement at Craven Cottage raised several new issues.

Kilroe's contract to carry out the flats development was with Fulham FC, not with Ernie Clay. Kilroe contended therefore that whoever owned the club, their contract still held good. This gave rise to the prospect of one property developer developing a section of the property of another property developer. Kilroe were determined to proceed.

Had Marler been able to buy Kilroe out, would Marler have considered a similar development at Craven Cottage? Not if, as was being widely conjectured, it harmed their overall plan to move in Chelsea by 1989. But Marler later insisted they had no plans to move Chelsea to the Cottage.

In February 1987 Fulham's dwindling band of supporters learned to their horror of Marler's real intentions, when it was announced out of the blue that Marler and Fulham's chairman, David Bulstrode, had bought up QPR lock, stock and barrel and intended to merge Fulham with Rangers at Loftus Road. Supporters everywhere knew what that meant – it meant killing off Fulham – and in a remarkable display of solidarity, fans from all over the capital rallied round Fulham at a public meeting at the Hammersmith and Fulham Town Hall. Marler soon found out what a hornet's nest they had upturned.

Plans were made by a consortium led by former Fulham player Jimmy Hill to save Fulham as a separate entity, even if the ground couldn't be saved. Then the League refused to sanction the merger and Craven Cottage itself was reprieved when both Archibald Leitch's Stevenage Road brick frontage and the actual Cottage were given Listed Building Grade Two status, thus helping (though not guaranteeing) to limit the developers' ambitions.

The situation in 1987–88 therefore was that Fulham survive as occupiers of the ground under a three-year license from Marler, but must be prepared to move out at some stage temporarily while Marler carry out partial redevelopment to earn some return on their massive outlay.

This is of course better than extinction, but it still leaves one question to be answered. No matter who owns Fulham, no matter how well the team performs, can the club, whose support lies predominantly beyond the borough boundaries, really justify their existence in this crowded, outrageously overpriced part of London?

Football lovers will respond without hesitation in the affirmative. Fulham without the Cottage, as Ernie Clay himself once declared, would be like Laurel without Hardy. As a *Guardian* leader comment also stated, 'Football is more than balance sheet inevitabilities'. If Fulham were to move to Stamford Bridge, or Chelsea to the Cottage, Fulham as the smaller club would inevitably be swamped. Try telling that to a property developer.

Amid all these uncertainties, back at the Cottage there were other problems. Rugby League had come and gone within the space of a few years, at the eventual cost to Fulham of £600 000. Ground sharing had been no problem. Lack of interest in expensive players was the real killer.

Meanwhile, the capacity of Craven Cottage, designated under the Safety of Sports Grounds Act in 1979, was reduced from 39 518 to 19 830. This was not so much due to deficiencies on the terracing as to the lack of access. The Hammersmith End, for example, was cut from 14 750 to 6600. In May 1985 further safety checks made after the Bradford fire resulted in the Stevenage Road Stand (which would, thankfully, survive the planned development) being closed. It was reopened in November 1985 after a £30 000 interior sprinkler system was installed. Additional barriers and exists also enabled the Hammersmith End's capacity to be increased to 12 600. Craven Cottage therefore held 26 013, with seats for 6610.

Ground Description

The first sight on entering the ground is Leitch's red-brick façade, nicely understated with a faint trace of decorative mouldings along the top. Notice the line of windows, shaped like classical thermal openings; a semi-circle divided by two vertical mullions, one of Leitch's favourite early features. But before entering the Main Stand, remember this is not the power house of Fulham. That is in the Cottage. Entering the Cottage up a flight of stairs, there is a reception office like that of a run down insurance broker's. But through the offices, onto the balcony overlooking the pitch, and all is forgiven.

The Cottage is a landmark of football; there is no other building quite like it. Underneath the balcony is a high white wall, behind which is the entrance to the dressing rooms, so that the players enter the field at the corner. Just like a cricket pavilion, the Cottage has benches overlooking the pitch and that homely atmosphere which lends itself to tea and cucumber sandwiches. But it is also the vantage point for chairman and manager, who can look out upon their domain. And it is, from here, a pleasant view indeed.

To the right is the Main Stand, with its familiar gable in the centre, now bearing the title 'Fulham Football Club'. The stand is almost the same design as Tottenham's old West Stand, but on a slightly smaller scale, as it does not house any dressing rooms or offices. From the pitch it seems to be all roof, dark and sloping, but closer to, the plain brick facings are also distinctive. You can see where Leitch's thermal windows have been bricked in at the back of the paddock, though the top ones at the back of the stand are still prominent. Each section of seating is divided by wooden slatted fencing, giving the stand the look of a well-tended railway station. Notice also how at each end of the stand, the sides of the roof above the paddock curve in a slight arch. This was typical of Leitch's work.

The far covered terracing is the Hammersmith End, named after the district nearby. Under the roof are sections of the old electric scoreboard, barely discernible in the shadows, and still hard to fathom.

Opposite the Main Stand is the Eric Miller Stand, tall and efficient, its hard lines and metallic and concrete finish in stark contrast with the stand opposite. It seats 4216, although not all these can be used, because access is so limited. The river bank is a few yards behind and you can see clearly over the water, to the trees and green spaces of Barnes. How nice it would be to look over the river from the top of this stand, like spectators used to do when there was an open terrace here. But the builders installed frosted glass along the top corridor behind the seats, unlike Chelsea's West Stand which has clear glass at the top giving a superb view.

At the back of the Eric Miller Stand is a line of private boxes. They look like waiting rooms at a DHSS office. But in the stand's favour, it has a clean grey roof fascia, bearing the crest of the Borough of Fulham and Hammersmith, and so looks modestly dignified.

It seems hard to believe that this, the most modern part of the ground, may well be demolished while Leitch's old stand survives. No doubt the Scottish engineer would raise a smile over that. But he would have to confess that the stand's riverside location, and its splendid view over Barnes (where Fulham once played) is a natural temptation for developers.

Finally, the south open terrace is called the Putney End, and is attractively lined at the back with tall trees in Bishop's Park. Underneath the terracing you can see old air raid shelters half buried in the earth. The pitch was cratered by bombs during the war.

If the projected development of the ground does go ahead, the Putney End may well become a narrow, covered all-seated end, with flats, new club offices, dressing rooms and so on behind. The Cottage itself might still make way for an access road. This would not raise a smile with Leitch, nor indeed with the majority of Fulham supporters, for whom the Cottage is the very symbol of Fulham's unconventional identity.

The ground certainly has an unconventional pitch. In 1983 Fulham became the first club to install a Cell System pitch, a revolutionary system described in the chapter on pitches. Its installation was financed by the Greater London Council, thus giving rise to the glorious irony of Ken Livingstone authorizing the payment of about £160 000 to a company whose chairman was Denis Thatcher.

Since its early teething problems, Fulham's pitch has comfortably withstood 150 hours a year extra use by local schools. In two seasons only three games were postponed, because of frost or snow rather than the old pitch's perennial problem of flooding.

Furthermore, the pitch can be tended by just one man. Fulham reckon, therefore, that although expensive in fertilizers, the new pitch saves them the salaries of two extra groundstaff. If it had undersoil heating as well, estimated to cost about £80 000, the pitch would be well nigh perfect. (Craven Cottage's facilities are used for about 500 hours a year by the community – one reason why the Council are happy to keep the club at the ground.)

The proximity of the water and of Bishop's Park makes the environment particularly pleasant at Craven Cottage, while the ground itself has an intriguing balance of styles, old and new, large and small. But on gates of less than 5000 the club cannot realistically expect to cling on to this charming riverside spot without some major concessions to a developer. It would seem, therefore, that whatever transpires, whoever owns the ground, a present-day Bulwer-Lytton may yet be able to sit in a penthouse suite, overlooking both the river and the ground, and write *The Last Days of the Cottage*. All football winces at the thought, but if it keeps the club alive it is a small price to pay.

·CHELSEA·

Stamford Bridge

Stamford Bridge is unique in the history of English football grounds as the only ground to have been built before the creation of the team whose home it became. Stamford Bridge was bought and developed even when it was not clear if it would be used by an existing club, a new club or for Cup Finals and internationals.

The story begins in 1896, when two brothers, H. A. and J. T. Mears tried to buy the leasehold of Stamford Bridge, then the headquarters of the London Athletic Club who had taken the site over in 1876, when it had been a market garden. H. A. or 'Gus' Mears intended to turn the ground into the biggest and best football stadium in London – hardly a difficult task considering that of the leading London clubs at the time, only nearby Fulham had moved into their present ground and all the other club grounds were highly primitive compared with some northern or Scottish grounds. That London should have only one large venue at Crystal Palace, and that hardly adequate, seemed ridiculous to the Mears, who foresaw how the game would capture the metropolitan imagination.

But they were unable to take over Stamford Bridge until the owner, a Mr Stunt, relinquished control. Even when he died in 1902, the Mears had to wait because a clause in the lease gave the London Athletic Club tenure of the ground for two years after the owner's death. Finally they took possession on 29 September 1904, eight years after their original idea.

Several options were available to them. Should they develop Stamford Bridge and then rent it out to another club, perhaps nearby Fulham, or should they start their own club? Or even more sensibly, should they accept an attractive offer made to them by the Great Western Railway, which wanted to turn the site into a coal dumping yard?

Gus Mears was very tempted by the railway offer and the prospect of a quick profit, and it was only the influence of his friend, Frederick Parker, that saved Stamford Bridge from the railway company. Parker tried to persuade Mears that the ground would be viable for football and that it could be rented out for Cup Finals (Crystal Palace was already almost obsolete) for a potential profit of £3000 a game. But Mears was unconvinced. At that point, Mear's dog bit Parker's leg! The story goes that as Parker reacted in such a cool manner, Mears decided that maybe Parker's judgement was to be trusted! On such a small incident rested the fate of Chelsea FC.

Parker and Mears' first step was to visit Glasgow, home of three of the biggest football grounds in the world, and the man who had been responsible for their design, Archibald Leitch.

Suitably impressed, the pair returned to London

and by early 1905 the work at Stamford Bridge was well under way. Like Leitch's Glasgow designs, the London ground was to be a large bowl with one main stand, on the East Side. That stand to hold 5000 seated, with a covered paddock in front, and was virtually identical to those Leitch built for Fulham and Tottenham at the same time (and Huddersfield a few years later) with that distinctive central gable.

The other three sides were open banking, built up with thousands of tons of soil and clay excavated during the construction of the nearby underground line. Gradually, the earth was raised up to form the now familiar bowl shape, and extra cinders were brought in from a local sewer.

Stamford Bridge, it was claimed, 'will stagger humanity', with a capacity of 95 000, a figure tested only once. It was the second largest stadium in England, behind Crystal Palace, which had its own professional club installed.

Mears offered Fulham the chance to rent the ground for £1500 a year, but they chose to develop their own home at Craven Cottage in 1905, so he had no alternative but to form his own team. The story is well told elsewhere, so suffice to say here that Chelsea was born in April 1905, without players but with a very determined board of directors.

Stamford Bridge was closer to the centre of London than any other ground and in the midst of one of the most fashionable and wealthiest parts of the city. It was little wonder therefore that one of the names considered for the new club was London FC. But in the end Chelsea was the preferred choice, although even this was something of a pose, for Stamford Bridge actually stood almost opposite Fulham Town Hall and close to Fulham Broadway. (In fact many of Fulham FC's previous grounds had been within a very short distance of the Stamford Bridge site.) Chelsea were charged £2000 for the use of Stamford Bridge by Mears, who also ran the ground's catering facilities.

The new club began to make some impressive signings, but incredibly were refused admittance to the Southern League. Chelsea therefore applied to the Football League, whose membership included only two clubs south of Birmingham, Bristol City and Woolwich Arsenal. They had a strong case, for not only was their ground superb but they had £3000 in the bank. It needed only one ballot for them to be elected, and after a friendly v. Liverpool, Stamford Bridge staged its first League competitive match when Chelsea beat Hull City in Division Two 5-1, on 11 September 1905.

One of the new team was the famous 6 feet 3 inches tall, 20-stone plus goalkeeper Willie Foulke, the club's first captain. It is said that Stamford Bridge was the first ground ever to employ ball-boys, because manager John Tait Robertson thought that if two small boys stood behind Foulke's goal it would emphasize his enormous frame. It seems more likely that the boys were there because there was so much

room behind the goal that Foulke did not want to have to keep retrieving loose balls.

A bright start in the League saw Chelsea enjoy healthy gates, including one over 60 000, and win promotion in their second League season. In 1911 a record crowd of 77 952 packed into Stamford Bridge for a 4th Round match v. Swindon Town. Parker had been right, the ground was a success.

A weather-vane became one of the landmarks of the new stadium at about this time and it has a history of its own. Originally placed on the apex of the Main Stand gable, the vane had a silhouette of a football on one side, a ball on the other. The figure was said to have been modelled on one of Chelsea's greatest players, George 'Gatling-Gun' Hilsdon, an England international who played for the club before the First World War but was sadly crippled by mustard gas in 1918.

The weather-vane and Hilsdon became legendary at Stamford Bridge. It was reckoned that if ever the vane came down, so would Chelsea's luck. Such a prediction was to prove correct.

Meanwhile the ground continued to improve. Chelsea became popular very quickly, and their arrival on the local scene may even have had some bearing on Henry Norris's decision to quit Fulham and take over ailing Arsenal (see Fulham and Arsenal). In 1909 extra banking was raised behind the goals, adding room for a further 10 000 spectators, and in 1913 Stamford Bridge staged its first international fixture, England v. Scotland. Stamford Bridge did not become a regular home for England games (it has staged only four in total), but it did take over from Crystal Palace as home of the FA Cup Final in 1920. There had been one Final between the takeover, played at Old Trafford.

Stamford Bridge did not really develop sufficiently to maintain its status. It had a marvellous chance when it staged the Cup Final, but the crowd of 50 018 was a great disappointment and well below pre-war gates at Crystal Palace. The following year was better, but the 1922 Final fell to only 53 000, and by then another venue had been decided on. Wembley took away the Cup Final from 1923 onwards, while Highbury became the favourite choice for internationals in London. Quite simply, the Chelsea ground had too few seats, too little cover and suffered from limited access from Fulham Road (two sides were hemmed in by railways).

The 1930s began with Chelsea in debt – some £12 000 by 1933. Stamford Bridge therefore became a centre for the new craze, greyhound racing, so popular at nearby Wembley and White City. The ground also had a speedway team between the wars.

The first major piece of construction at Stamford Bridge since 1905 was the building of the so-called Shed, at the South End, although it did not acquire the nickname until after the War, and its unwholesome reputation not until the 1960s. It was a plain cover at the back of the terracing, at an angle which

Chelsea built a special platform in order that Charles Cundall could paint this picture of a match v. Arsenal in the 1930s

suggested it was only half finished and had been intended to continue round towards the Main Stand. In 1935 Stamford Bridge's official record attendance, 82 905, came for the First Division game against Champions Arsenal on 12 October. This is the second highest club attendance record after Manchester City's 84 569, recorded in March 1934. There is an oil painting of this match, painted by Charles Cundall, from a platform specially erected by the club in the north west corner. The club has always had a good relationship with local artists, and it was significant that of 130 works exhibited in 1953 to show Football through Fine Art, ten depicted Stamford Bridge.

The odd looking North Stand was built in the summer of 1939, a double-decker stand seating about 1000, built on stilts above the terracing, immediately next to the Main Stand. It sat rather awkwardly in the corner, slightly angled but giving the impression that the roof was sagging. It had a large pitched roof, with two large glass screen walls at either end, one of which, because the stand was taller than the Main Stand, looked down on its roof. The two buildings looked quite uneasy next to each other.

Although the Arsenal fixture in 1935 was the official attendance record, this was broken when immediately after the Second World War Moscow Dynamo visited Stamford Bridge for the first in a series of friendlies against British clubs, in November 1945. A total of 74 496 people actually went through the turnstiles, but so vast was the crowd that gates and fences were torn down and the final total numbered anything from 90 000 to 100 000, with several thousand spilling onto the greyhound track and the touchlines.

Floodlights were first used on 19 March 1957 for a friendly v. Sparta of Prague. There might have been more improvements had the club not adopted such a high and mighty attitude towards the supporters, who had attempted to form a supporters' club in the late 1940s but were rebuffed by the parent club. When one sees how many grounds all over Britain were transformed by the fund-raising efforts of supporters' clubs, Chelsea's attitude at that time seems quite foolhardy.

The Bridge was shaken up during the 1960s, and especially by the efforts of manager Tommy Docherty, and at last in 1965 a new stand was built on the West Side of the ground. Costing £150 000, with seats for 6300, it was a relatively plain construction, essentially a roof over the reshaped banking. Incorporated at the back were some of the country's first, though not luxurious, private boxes – a significant sign of future developments. (Old Trafford had the first boxes in 1964.)

The stand was designed by an architect called Skeels, who had great visions of 'the stand of the future'. Among his plans was the provision for cars to drive onto the roof and for their occupants to watch the game from there!

But the important fact from the club's point of view was that the stand was soon paid for, by runs in the FA Cup and European Fairs Cup, and by continuing good form in Division One. 'Chelsea' during the 1960s did not merely suggest football but was associated with the swinging image of the surrounding areas and the Kings Road.

Sadly, Chelsea were the first club to erect security fences at their ground, 8-foot high barriers being put up behind each goal in October 1972.

Between 1963–72, the club finished lower than the top seven only once and the directors decided to give Stamford Bridge a face lift. There are many cases of a club building a new stand and suffering the consequences – Wolves are the best known victims of their own ambition in recent years. But Chelsea were probably the first to have almost planned their own extinction, even though they had no reason to suspect that their winning streak would come to an end so abruptly. But they must have forgotten that warning about the weather-vane. Once it came down, nothing seemed to go right.

The club planned a new look stadium which would not only cater for football, but would include a swimming pool, gymnasiums, squash courts, and an open piazza for the public's enjoyment. The ground was to become a huge leisure centre.

The decision to commission a new stand came in 1970, and resulted in March 1971 with preliminary discussions with a firm of architects called Darbourne and Darke. Although this firm had no previous experience of stadium design the plans drawn up seemed most impressive. Their clients were keen to portray image and status in the designs.

Furthermore, an attempt by another design company to urge restraint on Chelsea failed miserably. A consortium of companies put together a strategy which argued that Chelsea had to take into account falling gates and the comparative value of their land. Stamford Bridge, they said, was worth about £7 million in land value, yet was hopelessly under-used. To make a profit the club would have to attract at least 30 000 people each home game. The consortium argued that Chelsea should diversify before building a new stand. Their proposals included the staging of pop concerts, exhibitions, restaurants, night clubs, and so on, allied to an intensive marketing of Chelsea FC as a product like any other.

Either the club could build bit by bit, or they could do it all at once, but with artificial turf and a community sports centre. Alternatively they could sell the site and build a new ground on the profits at their training ground in Tooting.

Chelsea opted for Darbourne and Darke's much more prestigious plan for a £1·6 million stand, to be built as part of an overall £5·5 million scheme to enclose Stamford Bridge completely and create a 60 000 all-seater stadium. (As reported in *Design*, March 1975, the unsuccessful consortium went on to advise Leeds and Arsenal, again without joy.)

Work began in June 1972. Down came Leitch's stand, and the weather-vane was stored in a shed. Chelsea had finished that season in seventh place, but by the time the new stand was ready in August 1974, they were down among the bottom clubs.

For two years the East Side of the ground had been taken up by the building work, and it was surely more than coincidence that in such an unsettling atmosphere for both players and supporters,

Chelsea's fortunes plummeted. By the end of the stand's first season in use, they were relegated.

Ominously, gates began to drop alarmingly. Who would pay for the stand now? Chelsea spent two seasons in Division Two, and by May 1976 their debt stood at £3·4 million, most of it caused by the East Stand – tall, massive, imposing, but ruinous.

Danny Blanchflower, manager of the club for a short spell, wrote in his *Sunday Express* column, shortly after the resignation of the chairman Brian Mears: 'They had to do something about the old stand. It would fall down if they did not. So they spent a lot of time planning a new one to match their winning desires and ambitions. They spent too long thinking about it. And the stand they planned was too grand.'

The disaster had occurred at Chelsea primarily because for two years the club had no income from seats on the East Side and because the stand was designed for a top, successful club, not an ailing one with small gates.

After the East Stand came the Safety of Sports Grounds Act. By now any intention of carrying on the Darbourne and Darke plan had been frozen and the ground's capacity of 52 000 was reduced to 41 500. The North Stand had to come down, after less than 30 years of use, and benches were put in on the West Stand paddock.

From this period onwards the history of Stamford Bridge becomes complicated. Saddled with debts amounting to £1·5 million, mainly from the East Stand, Chelsea formed SB Property, as a holding company to own the ground, while the club itself could be run separately. This distinction between ownership of the club and ground was to have disastrous consequences.

Ken Bates, a former Wigan director, purchased Chelsea in April 1982 for a nominal amount. But SB Property's value was quoted at £1 million (plus debts of £1.75 million), and although Bates got as far as agreeing on a price for a 40 per cent share of the company, he was foiled when the club's former vice-chairman, David Mears, decided to sell elsewhere, as soon became apparent.

Several months after Bates's takeover, a 70 per cent share of SB Property was bought up by a small property company called Marler Estates, whose chairman David Bulstrode also became chairman of SB Property. Chelsea retained 24 per cent of SB Property's shares, but there was no doubt who benefited most from the control of Stamford Bridge. Marler's shares rose appreciably in value as a result of the deal.

Chelsea have a seven-year lease for Stamford Bridge, paying SB Property a 10 per cent share of gate receipts. Whether the club can remain at the ground when the lease expires in August 1989 depends on several factors.

Firstly, Marler have gained outline planning permission for a massive redevelopment of the site. This would include 99 houses, 128 flats, and 16 000 square feet of industrial and office space. In order to carry out the industrial and office development alone, for which detailed planning permission was received in March 1986, Marler would have to build over Chelsea's car park, thus raising the kind of access questions which eventually forced Charlton to leave The Valley.

If Marler decided to initiate the entire plan, Chelsea would definitely have to move. According to the lease, however, Marler would have to find Chelsea suitable alternative accommodation within a 15-mile radius and pay Chelsea's expenses. To that end Selhurst Park was considered, until Charlton nipped in. One venue nearer Chelsea is Craven Cottage.

So it was that in May 1986, to everyone's surprise Marler Estates raised the funds which enabled them to buy Fulham FC from the Clay family for £9 million.

This move clearly suggested that their overall plan was to prepare Craven Cottage for ground-sharing with Chelsea. Or was it to move Chelsea in with QPR, which Marler bought up in February 1987?

Another option existed. If Chelsea wanted to stay at Stamford Bridge – and this was the club's stated aim – Marler could sell them the site at the current market value. The price might be anything from £15–30 million.

How can a ground worth an estimated £3–4 million in 1982 suddenly be worth so much only a few years later? The key to this is planning permission. As a sports ground alone the current value would still be under £4–5 million, but once Marler received outline planning permission for their residential and office scheme, the value shot up. A few pieces of paper, that is all it took. No wonder so many football fans feel disillusioned and helpless.

Chelsea alone are unlikely to generate such a massive sum. So in April 1987 Bates announced the formation of the Chelsea Community Trust, whose aim was to raise the cash needed to buy out Marler's interest in Stamford Bridge. Among the trustees are athlete Sebastian Coe (a dyed-in-the-wool Chelsea fan), the film director Sir Richard Attenborough (a former Chelsea director) and various other local MPs and councillors.

'It is not a question of if we do it, but how we do it,' declared Bates defiantly.

Part of his plan is to raise money by building a community recreation centre and an underground car park for 120 vehicles where the Shed is now, which would mean a great loss in terms of tradition but none whatsoever in architectural terms. Above this centre would be a 160-room hotel. Perhaps it could be named the 'Shed Inn' as a tribute.

Extra money would also be raised from selling off Chelsea's 24 per cent shareholding in SB Property and disposing of about five acres of the 11-acre site for further commercial development.

Even all that might not be enough, so Bates also launched a 'Save the Bridge' appeal for fans to raise money to help buy off Marler. And to allay fears that the money would be raised, then squandered (especially if Marler's asking price wasn't met), independent auditors and scrutineers were appointed.

The final element of this bold plan is to remodel Stamford Bridge into a 40 000 all-covered stadium with a Cellsystem pitch, the only surviving structure being that towering East Stand.

Chelsea have to start negotiating with Marler in August 1988. But what if they cannot raise the money?

The chances of Marler agreeing to extend the seven-year lease are hard to assess. Some observers reckon they will undoubtedly go ahead with developing the site. Others suggest they will have a battle to fulfil their side of the lease and therefore have to sell Stamford Bridge to Chelsea. So the situation is extremely fraught, more so since Marler took over neighbours Fulham and QPR.

In such circumstances it seems almost superfluous to add that Stamford Bridge's present capacity is 43 900, including 20 264 seats.

How different footballing history would have been had Fulham accepted Gus Mears's invitation to use Stamford Bridge in 1905. There would have been no Chelsea and perhaps no Craven Cottage.

How different too would be the conclusion of this sad, unsettled tale of Stamford Bridge had the Chelsea directors not opted to rebuild the East Stand in such a spectacularly expensive manner. Almost everything that went wrong thereafter can be traced back to the debt incurred by that one stand.

Ground Description

The ground is on Fulham Road, and has three gates only. The main one leads onto a courtyard next to a line of tall houses behind the South Terrace. The East Stand appears before you like a space rocket on the launching pad, quite isolated. Such high-tec, and yet the club offices are in an unsophisticated little block next to the main entrance, almost like a converted stable.

Walking past the offices we reach the south east corner of the ground, and may turn either left, onto the open terracing, or go straight ahead into the concourse under the new stand. To the right, behind the stand, is a railway line in a cutting, with the large Brompton Cemetery behind.

The East Stand is quite the largest single free-standing construction at any League ground, or at least seems so in its isolation. It has three tiers, each quite visibly separated by distinctive balcony walls. The top tier has 5019 blue seats, the middle tier 2108 brown seats and 26 boxes, and the lower tier, much of it uncovered, has 3382 khaki-coloured seats.

Surrounding all this is a gigantic frame, completely exposed to view, and finished in brown cor-ten steel with sides of semi-transparent plastic, hung several feet from the ends of the tiers. The cantilever roof, suspended from yet more exposed steel frames, is 140 feet long, and at the front can sway up to 18 inches in high winds.

If you look through the clear glass windows at the back you can see right across London as far as St Paul's Cathedral and the Houses of Parliament. Straight ahead, Craven Cottage's floodlights are visible.

Some credit is due to the designers, because even at the very back one is still relatively close to the touchline, although the ground seems a long way below. There are only 22 seats in the stand with an impaired view, these being the ones next to the rear cantilever supports at the very back of the stand. But one of the main problems of this stand, apart from its horrendous cost, is the lack of protection it offers against the elements, especially for those seated in the lowest tier.

Beneath each seat is a 10-centimetre hole, or at least a litter-filled 10-centimetre hole. These were originally intended to convey warm air which when mixed with cold air would provide a mean temperature of 70 degrees Fahrenheit around the ankles. The system was never installed.

From a purely aesthetic point of view there is no doubt that the stand is quite startling. Above all, it is quite disproportionately massive. Everton have a three-tier stand of the same scale, but because it has two double-decker neighbours it is not overwhelming. Chelsea's East Stand hovers over Stamford Bridge, making the surrounding terraces appear like neolithic ruins next to a twenty-first century intruder. It is over twice as high as Leitch's old stand.

The East Stand has been built over the length of the greyhound track which used to surround the pitch, but now is visible only on the three other sides. The last races took place in August 1968, and the surviving track is now bare and untidy. The elliptical shape of the ground has been kept, however, so each end terrace is curved around a semi-circle of turf behind each goal.

To the left is the South End, covered by the Shed. In the near corner are the remains of a concrete base for an old floodlight pylon, taken down because the East Stand has lights mounted in the roof. There is a fenced-off section of terracing in front of it, found to be unsafe. To refurbish this and other unsafe areas would cost Chelsea at least £250 000. The actual Shed cover sits at a strange angle, far back from the pitch, as if it does not want to be part of the action.

Despite the many changes in the ground, it is quite remarkable how similar the view over this side of the ground is to that in 1905. Many of the buildings in the vicinity have survived, with the Lots Road gas works and a power station's chimneys still visible, as in Cundall's painting of 1935.

The West Stand is hugely plain is contrast; a typically dour 1960s' construction brightened only by recent coats of blue paint. It has a deep, flat roof, with six boxes at the rear. The front paddock is now lined by concrete benches, so narrow and cold that it would take a dedicated thin man to perch there on a wet day.

Along the perimeter is the high security fencing upon which Ken Bates once installed electric wires, until ordered to remove them by the safety authorities.

Suspended from the roof of the West Stand is a camera gantry and press-box (the press were sent there under some duress from the East Stand, where they were taking up expensive seats). On the stand roof is the traditional weather-vane. A copy it may be, but since being restored Chelsea's League form has looked up considerably. To the right of the stand is another fenced-off portion of terracing, another sign of how the ground has decayed through lack of funds. Along this side are the three remaining floodlights, each as tall as Nelson's Column.

To the right is the open North Terrace, behind which, in a cutting runs an open section of the District Line, between West Brompton and Fulham Broadway stations. The massive building visible behind is Earl's Court Exhibition Hall. The foundations of the old North Stand, which stood in the eastern corner, are partly visible beyond the embankment, where there is an expanse of flat ground used for parking. An electric scoreboard now crowns the terrace.

Stamford Bridge in the 1980s is in a state of limbo. Trees and bushes at the back of crumbling terracing; concrete and steel walkways and glass-fronted bars and restaurants; plush new executive boxes; decaying wooden steps leading to archaic offices, all in acres of space leaving plenty of room for speculation. The biggest question, of course, is whether Chelsea will be able to stay here. Looking around this huge elliptical stadium one is compelled to ask, how on earth could any developer clear this site for development without vast expenditure?

The exits lead out onto a busy, narrow high street, and yet some 80 000 cubic metres of banking would have to be removed and the gigantic steel framework of the East Stand dismantled. Marler estimate the steelwork's scrap value to be £800 000, but how much would it cost to transport, even using the adjacent railway line as a convenient route for disposal?

One small detail might reduce the costs of clearing the site. When the banks were raised in 1905 it was said that part of the rubble came from Lord Phillimore's house, which was being pulled down by the Mears demolition firm. Workmen dislodged a hidden store of old coins, but for some reason they were considered worthless at the time. The rubble, coins and all, was then dumped at Stamford Bridge.

So if Chelsea do have to leave the ground, and the terracing is cleared, the workmen should look out for some rare spade guineas, believed to be some 30 feet under the West Stand.

· BRENTFORD ·

Previous Grounds

There is a popular belief that the game of football began when Julius Caesar crossed the Brent, kicking the skull of a defeated Briton. It was some 1800 years later that the sport caught on in the area, when Brentford FC were formed in 1889. They began playing on a field behind the Wesleyan Chapel in Clifden Road, just by Braemar Road. Two years later they moved north to Benns Field, Little Ealing, then in 1895 to Shotters Field in Windmill Road, now a main road. From 1898–1900 Brentford played at the Cross Roads, South Ealing, followed by four years in Boston Park, a mile west of Griffin Park, their new home in 1904.

Griffin Park

The first major development was the Main Stand's erection in 1927. Perhaps inspired by its presence, Brentford won every match at home in 1929–30 and by 1935 rose to Division One. During this period of prosperity covers over the extended Brook Road and New Road terraces were built, and angled corners of seating added to the Main Stand in 1935. The players helped with the work to earn extra cash during the close season. Brentford's record attendance of 39 626 is for a quarter-final Cup match against Preston in 1938.

Back in Division Three, Brentford's floodlights were first used for a friendly v. Chelsea in October 1954.

Speculation has often surrounded Griffin Park's future. In 1967 QPR wanted to develop the ground, then a year later Brentford announced they would move to Hillingdon Borough. In February 1983 fire destroyed two-thirds of the original wooden Main Stand and it took 18 months and £800 000 to build a replacement alongside the surviving remnant.

That confirmed the club's commitment to the ground but did not help the finances, so in January 1986 the Brook Road terrace was demolished to make way for a smaller modern stand with room for 2000 standing and 600 seating, behind which construction began on 48 private flats on the old car park and training area. The sale of these was aimed at restoring the club's viability and resembled similar schemes at Hull and Crystal Palace.

After the Bradford fire, Griffin Park's capacity was reduced from 37 000 to 9500, rising to 20 000 when the new Brook Road Stand was opened in December 1986.

Ground Description

Between the Thames and M4 Motorway, Griffin Park is tucked in on all sides by small terraced houses and cottages. From Braemar Road the Main Stand's entrance appears as a sudden splash of red, white and

Griffin Park – on the flightpath to Heathrow. The old Brook Road Stand is to the left

grey amid the low roofs. To the left is the modern section, neatly finished with grey cladding and red tubular steel fittings. The roof is plain with a deep grey fascia board. Immediately to the right, in stark contrast, is the now disused remains of the old stand with its sloping roof, wooden steps and distinctive red and white striped paddock wall. Sadly the stripes have not been repeated on the new section.

From here, to the left is the small but neat, newly developed Brook Road End, once a spacious, covered terrace. The new stand is an admirable example of how football clubs have learnt to adjust to smaller gates and lower expectations. With its 600 red and white seats and paddock in front, the clean-cut stand encloses that section of ground neatly and complements the modernity of the Main Stand's new section. Opposite, the New Road terrace has a fenced off section at the rear with an extended sloping roof over the front. To the right is the uncovered Ealing Road or Clock End terraces. Back gardens abut both terraces, with an occasional washing line tied up to the steel uprights.

Having remained unchanged for so long Griffin Park is now a homely mix of old and new; there are still no high perimeter fences, while the realities of modern football finance are evident not only in the Brook Road development but in the roof advertising. Because the ground lies under the flight path to Heathrow Airport, the three roof adverts yield up to £30 000 a season. 'Next time . . . fly KLM' proclaims the New Road roof in blue and white, while the Main Stand carries the name of Forward Air Cargo. In area this is reputedly the largest advertisement in the world. As far as some fans are concerned, however, Griffin Park's biggest asset is that it is the only League ground with a pub on each of its four corners.

·WEST HAM UNITED·

Previous Grounds

Contrary to common belief, West Ham are not called 'The Hammers' because they come from West Ham. Rather, the hammers symbolize the tools of a shipyard worker, for it was in London's East End docks that the club originated. The idea for a football team came from Arnold F. Hills, the owner of the largest surviving shipyard, the Thames Ironworks.

From 1895 to October 1896 the team, known as Thames Ironworks, played at Hermit Road, Canning Town, where in March 1896 they staged two floodlight games against Woolwich Arsenal and WBA. In December 1896 the Hammers moved to Browning Road, East Ham, a mile north east of the present ground. But Hills was an ardent sponsor, a Victorian capitalist who appreciated the efficacy of physical recreation for the welfare of his men, and in March 1897 he announced in the *Thames Ironwork Gazette* that he had found a suitable site for a new and magnificent stadium. It would be opened on the sixtieth anniversary of Queen Victoria's accession, and have facilities for football, cricket, tennis and 'a cycle track equal to any in London'. The ground became known as the Memorial Recreation Ground and was reputed to have a capacity of 120 000, 'good enough to hold the English Cup Final'. (In fact in 1901 the ground was scheduled to stage a Cup semi-final replay between Spurs and WBA, but in the event no replay was necessary.)

Fine though the setting no doubt was, the football club was anxious to improve and since professionalism was abhorrent to Hills, he asked the team to leave so his amateurs could use the ground. So four years after adopting the name West Ham United and forming a limited company, the new professional team looked elsewhere and found the site of their present ground in 1904. The rift between Hills and West Ham widened when United's directors heard that the then amateur Clapton Orient were hoping to play at the Memorial Ground; they threatened to publish Hills' letter to them which stated that he had reserved the stadium for his Thames Ironworks' team and no other.

The Memorial Recreation Ground still exists as a public park, part of which is used by the East London Rugby Club. It can be seen from a tube train on the right as you emerge from West Ham station en route for Plaistow. United played on the area now covered by children's swings.

Upton Park

Although most people refer to West Ham's home as Upton Park, it is strictly speaking only the name of the district. The ground's exact title is the Boleyn Ground. The name derives from a house which stood until the 1950s next to the ground, on Green Street.

It was built in 1544, but had two prominent turrets added soon after and thenceforward was traditionally known as Boleyn Castle after Anne Boleyn. The house served many purposes over the centuries, including a reformatory, a Priory and a bowling club's headquarters.

When United left the Memorial Grounds in Canning Town in May 1904, the site they chose was just a cabbage patch next to Boleyn Castle, then being used as a Catholic School. The club rented the land from the Catholic ecclesiastical authorities and at the same time merged with a local side called Boleyn Castle FC. It took two months to prepare the ground, in time for United's Southern League games the following season.

The Boleyn Ground, as it was inevitably called, then had a small grandstand on the West Side, a covered bank opposite; on the south west corner stood a directors' box with press facilities (rather like the Cottage at Fulham's ground), and on the north west corner a hut for changing rooms. A more substantial West Stand with dressing rooms was erected in 1913 as part of a general improvement scheme which cost United £4000.

In 1919 West Ham were admitted to League Division Two, played in the first Wembley Cup Final and gained promotion, both in 1923. This quick success enabled them to build a large new West Stand with a terraced enclosure in front in 1925. The stand, which has since been enlarged, was designed by Sir E. O. Williams and D. J. Moss. At the same time the old West Stand roofing was transferred to the South Bank.

Opposite the West Stand was the cover known for years as the Chicken Run, a primitive construction of corrugated iron and timber. The terraces were simply wooden bleachers, under which accumulated vast amounts of litter. Miraculously it did not burn down.

The Boleyn Ground's record gate probably came for United's Division Two match v. Charlton Athletic on 18 April 1936; 43 528 were reported to have attended, but this cannot be officially confirmed because during the Second World War the ground suffered considerably during the Blitz and records were lost. The West Stand had to be evacuated, so the club set up offices in Green Street House, the so-called Boleyn Castle. The worst destruction befell the South Bank.

It needed until the 1950s to repair the bomb damage, during which time the ground's floodlights had been installed. They were used first for a friendly v. Tottenham on 16 April 1953.

When United returned to the First Division in 1958, after a 26-year absence, a new main entrance on Green Street was built. Sadly this necessitated the demolition of the last remaining turret of the Boleyn Castle. The house had been in an advanced state of dilapidation, but one cannot help feeling it would have been appropriate to preserve just one feature. The site of the house is now occupied by the school behind the South Bank, on Castle Street.

The Boleyn Ground looking towards the original West Stand and the directors' pavilion *c.* 1905

The 1960s brought considerable changes to the Boleyn Ground, beginning in 1961 with the covering of the North Bank. In 1965 an extra block was built onto the West Stand, which had always been a bit lop-sided, then in May 1968 to the consternation, if not surprise, of the club's followers, the Chicken Run was demolished. In place of this venerable shack was built, at a cost of £170 000, the East Stand, opened in January 1969 with a standing enclosure in front.

West Ham's official record attendance, 42 322, was in October 1970 for a Division One game v. Tottenham. Since the introduction of the Safety of Sports Grounds Act, the capacity has been reduced to 35 500. There are now seats on the West Stand's front terracing, but a corner of the North Bank has had to be fenced off as a safety precaution. The total number of seats is 11 600.

Ground Description

As I have mentioned, the ground is in Upton Park, not West Ham. The underground station nearest the district of West Ham is called Plaistow. Visitors to West Ham United must alight at Upton Park, a couple of miles east of West Ham station, which is actually on the doorstep of United's first ground in Canning Town. Students of early football history should not confuse West Ham with the famous London amateur club, Upton Park, who apparently played in Epping. Nor should one think that the short-lived East End club Thames FC, who played at somewhere called the West Ham Stadium, had anything to do with West Ham United. There!

The main entrance to the Boleyn Ground is on Green Street, but before you enter it is worthwhile making a quick perambulation. Just past the entrance is the narrow Castle Street, with a small, nicely proportioned chapel on the corner, the sole reminder that this was once all church land. On the next corner, on Barking Road, is the large Boleyn Tavern. Down Castle Street next to the West Stand is the Roman Catholic primary school which occupies the site of the old house. Notice that the surrounding streets are all named with the Tudor connection in mind.

Back at the main entrance, you pass through a pair of wrought-iron gates and along a short driveway, which opens out on the right where there is a school playground. The back of the West Stand is less imposing than it might be, having several bare concrete uprights forming open bays, clutterd with outbuildings and stairways. It cries out for a much bolder sign announcing the club's name, especially since the façade is so clearly visible from Green Street. Inside, the stand is spacious without being particularly attractive, but has some awkwardly arranged offices squeezed into the southern end. This is behind the A block, seating 750, added in 1965. Previously the stand ended at right angles to the pitch. Because the rest of the stands are much lower, the West Stand dominates the pitch quite considerably. Notice the prominent ventilation grilles built into the apex of the roof, and how far the roof extends beyond the seating tier (an almost identical stand, but in shorter form, exists at Filbert Street).

To the right is the South Bank, a covered terrace with room for about 9000. It is a simple, low construction, backing directly onto Castle Street. To the left is the North Bank, a larger terrace not quite fully covered, but still cavernous, dark and ominous at the back. In the north western corner is an awkward section of terracing which actually runs parallel to the west touchline and thus almost faces the North Bank. This is the fenced-off portion. Facing it on the east corner of the terracing is another section, raised above the corner flag, which has steps leading up to a refreshment bar. It may be suitable for children, since the viewpoint is higher, but prolonged patronage might lead to a stiff neck, as the terracing here also faces the North Bank. The eastern corner of the South Bank is at a similarly awkward angle.

At the back of the north terracing are signs warning fans to 'Remember Ibrox, please leave slowly'. Above them is a white line. The paint above this line is of the non-drying variety, put there to deter enthusiasts climbing the roof girders. I have some sympathy for such people, having stood at this end and developed all kinds of muscular strain trying to see goal-mouth incidents, mainly due to the fact that the

The Boleyn Ground is considerably less hemmed in today owing to slum clearance

♦ LEYTON ORIENT ♦

Previous Grounds

Orient are relative late-comers to their present ground on Brisbane Road. The club was formed by members of the Glyn Cricket Club, for the usual reason of keeping together during the winter months, and first played football on waste ground near Glyn Road in 1884. The road still exists, in Homerton. In 1888, on the suggestion of a player who worked for the Orient Shipping Line, the club adopted the current name, apt indeed since it plays in East London.

Four years later the club moved a short way up the road to the Whittles Athletic Ground, Pond Lane Bridge. Next door was the Whittles Whippet Ground, so spectators could watch either sport over the fence. When the borough took over Orient's pitch to build a power station, the club simply moved next door. Meanwhile, in 1898 they added the prefix Clapton to their name in the hope that since Clapton was a desirable suburb they could gain some respectability.

Orient moved once again in 1900, also not far away to Millfields Road, Homerton, a ground which had belonged to the Bailey Fireworks Company. It was at the time one of the best venues in the South, holding 12 000 spectators, with terracing built on top of slag from the nearby power station. The players had to change in horse-drawn tram cars.

Admission to the Football League came in 1905, but the expense of running a professional club proved hard for the club to bear. A new company was formed in 1906 to replace the one set up a year earlier, and among various fund-raising activities at Millfields were boxing matches, and baseball. A crowd of 3500 saw Orient beat Fulham in 1908 to win the 'British Baseball Cup Final'. There were even plans to increase the ground's capacity to 40 000.

During the First World War, when Orient players formed the largest single contingent of the Footballers' Battalion, Millfields Road was taken over by the Army. In recognition of the club's patriotism, the Prince of Wales visited the club soon after the war, and a year later was followed by the Duke of York. A new multi-span stand (similar to Highbury's) costing the enormous sum of £30 000 was opened at the ground in 1923, and in the late 1920s crowds of up to 30 000 flocked to see Orient's FA Cup exploits against First Division opposition. But the record gate was for the visit of Second division Tottenham in 1928–29: 38 219 attended, the highest at any of Orient's three League grounds.

During the Easter of 1927, the syndicate which owned the Millfields Road Ground spent £80 000 on installing greyhound-racing facilities and inevitably a few years later Clapton Orient were asked to move. To exacerbate matters, the club had just been rel-

goal-line is only two yards from the front terrace. The fans there can almost breathe down the goalkeeper's neck, but from the back, clear vision is the prerogative of the fittest.

Opposite the West Stand is of course the East Stand, quite clearly the most modern part of the Boleyn Ground. The light grey roof is cantilevered and extends over the touchline. There are seats for 3500, and although the enclosure has room for 3300 standing there are no crush barriers, because the steps have an 8-inch rise and the section is supposedly narrow enough not to suffer from crushing. I have felt differently when standing there. Behind the East Stand are a range of tower blocks, part of a large new estate set in parkland. The back of the East Stand is covered in grafitti making it look distinctly seedy despite its young age. From within the ground however it is clean, obviously efficient, but looks narrower than it is.

Other odd visual details are the floodlights; notice that the pylons just sit on the terrace roofs, with no strengthening support underneath, and the pitch, which looks deceptively small because the ground is so enclosed, the touchlines so close to the spectators. Standing on the corner one feels eminently capable of knocking over a far-post cross. In fact, although the pitch is the minimum length, in width it is a fraction wider than Highbury's, such is the optical effect of the surrounds.

West Ham are fortunate to attract sufficient support to create a daunting atmosphere even when the ground is two-thirds full. Players cannot fail to see, hear, even smell the crowd and sense their delight or their derision. This is surely in keeping with the cramped nature of London, echoed most strongly at Loftus Road, but rarely encountered at top grounds in the North. The dimensions make the greatest player seem human but his greatest acts that much more breathtaking. Unlike Highbury or White Hart Lane, pride and glory do not exude from every stand. Instead the Boleyn Ground is a hideaway, a place to jostle and cheer and not worry too much about the final score.

egated to Division Three South. The Clapton dog track no longer exists, it was built over with homes for the aged in the mid-1970s.

Orient's new ground was only half a mile away, at the large but rather bleak Lea Bridge Speedway Stadium. They managed to take with them a few fittings from Millfields Road, but soon encountered problems. After beating Torquay United at Lea Bridge in one of their first games there in 1930–31, complaints were made that the perimeter fences were too close to the touchlines. The League ordered Orient to lay extra turf within a fortnight, since the lines could not be moved inwards as the pitch was already the minimum width. The speedway company refused to sanction this alteration, so Orient had to make hurried arrangements to find another venue for their home games. Neighbours Leyton FC and Walthamstow Avenue were approached unsuccessfully, then incredibly, Wembley Stadium agreed to host Orient's next fixture v. Brentford. Wembley's officials had already been considering leasing the stadium to a League club in order to increase its usage, and were therefore pleasantly surprised when a crowd of 10 300 watched Orient's 3-0 win on 22 November 1930. (Although Wembley is a long way from Clapton, it is very near Brentford.) The *Daily Herald* correspondent 'Syrian' noted, 'I question if Brentford will ever play at Wembley again' and also reported that the sacred turf had been a quagmire and might need relaying.

At this point the speedway company agreed to add the turf at Lea Bridge, but Orient, flushed with victory in nobler surroundings went to Highbury for their next home fixture, a Cup replay v. Luton on 4 December. But after their second game at Wembley two days later against Southend – the attendance was only 2500 and receipts of £100 were insufficient to cover Wembley Stadium's guarantee – they returned to Lea Bridge, poorer but wiser. Wembley also decided to drop the idea of staging League football.

The 1930s continued to be difficult years for Clapton. There was talk of a merger with Thames FC, another East London club in the Third Division, and of moving to Hackney Wick Stadium where the rent would be less. Nevertheless, Lea Bridge gates averaged 7000, and in 1936–37 Orient's match v. Millwall attracted the ground's highest attendance, 20 400. But the club was never happy at the Speedway Stadium, and in 1937 made their final move to Brisbane Road, a mile away in Leyton. The Stadium has gone since, the site having been taken up for industrial use.

Brisbane Road

Orient's present ground was the home of Leyton Amateurs in 1937, who were having some difficulty paying their rent to the council. Wasting no time, Orient stepped in and took over the ground during the summer. There was one stand seating 475 people, scathingly referred to as 'the orange box', and a cover

on the West Side for standing spectators. All the banking was cinder. The club's first game there was on 28 August 1937 v. Cardiff City, watched by 14 598.

At last it looked as if Clapton Orient had a permanent home, but the club's financial problems had not disappeared. After the Second World War, when the club changed its name yet again, to Leyton Orient, a fighting fund was needed to save the club. This, and the appointment of a new chairman and manager, paved the way for a successful period ahead.

In 1951 a new perimeter wall was built in place of the rather quaint white wooden fence left over from the pre-war years, and in the summer of 1956 after celebrating promotion, a new Main Stand was erected on the East Side. The stand was bought from Mitcham Greyhound Stadium in South London, but initially Orient rebuilt only two-thirds of the structure, storing the remainder elsewhere.

The East Stand was opened for a game v. Nottingham Forest in October 1956, and very nearly ruined the same day by a fire, thankfully spotted in time. The late chairman, Harry Zussman, quoted in Neil Kaufman's and Harry Ravenhills' history of the club, said afterwards, 'For years we hoped the old stand would catch fire to collect the insurance, and now the new one nearly goes up on its first day of use!'

Brisbane Road's floodlights were first used for a game v. Brighton in August 1960, and cost £15 000.

The club reached its zenith in 1962, winning promotion to Division One for the first time. To accommodate extra seats, the remaining section of the East Stand, at the southern end, was completed, and the west terracing opposite improved. But their joy was shortlived, for one season later Orient were back in Division Two, their financial struggles returning as gates dropped. By 1966 Orient (they dropped the prefix Leyton that year since the area had been absorbed into the new Borough of Waltham Forest) had to pass a bucket around to help raise cash needed to keep the club afloat. More mergers were mooted, with Romford FC and with Basildon.

By 1970 Orient were back in Division Two, and so in 1977 came under the jurisdiction of the Safety of Sports Grounds Act. It is interesting that the club found it cheaper to put seats onto the West Terrace, rather than pay for new crush barriers, even though this reduced the capacity of that section from 11 000 to 3700.

Brisbane Road's highest gate had been in January 1964 for the Cup visit of neighbours West Ham: 34 345 attended. The capacity is now 26 500, including 7171 seats.

Ground Description

Brisbane Road, Osborne Road, Leyton Stadium, call it what you will, lies between Leyton High Road and Hackney Marshes. The main entrance, now much improved and faced in red and white, is on Brisbane Road, although some of the club offices are above the souvenir shop on the corner of Osborne Road.

Bad weather and bare terraces at Brisbane Road in 1985

The East Stand runs the length of the pitch, with the common arrangement of a paddock in front of the seating tier. The corrugated roof is noticeably clean and light, with a central gable, believed once to have housed the photo-finish equipment used at the greyhound stadium.

To the left is the open South Terrace, behind which are neat, municipal gardens on Buckingham Road. The terrace is slightly smaller than the open North Terrace to the right of the East Stand. Behind this is a typical suburban London street of small terraced villas.

In the north east corner of the ground is the Bowater Scott enclosure for disabled spectators, sponsored by that company since it discovered that one of its disabled staff was an Orient fanatic. This is an excellent feature, with room for 20 people.

Opposite the East Stand is the West Stand, which dates back to the 1930s but has been modernized since. It incorporates throughout the new type of backless plastic seats which many other clubs have also begun using. Underneath the roof is the tele-vision camera platform.

The pitch, once troublesome and muddy, is now much improved since being resewn in 1978 (see Ipswich Town). Notice how it slopes a couple of feet from north to south. Since the ground is still rented from the council, but on favourable terms, the pitch is often used for important schoolboy and junior matches.

Overlooking Brisbane Road are tall blocks of flats behind the North Terrace, and the disused chimney of the sewage works behind the West Stand. Behind these works stretch the vast open fields of Hackney Marshes, the site of reputedly the largest number of municipal pitches in Britain.

Brisbane Road is such a bright and uncluttered ground, and Orient such an hospitable club, that visiting it is always a pleasure. But this is also partly owing to the fact that small gates, in an area torn between Upton Park and White Hart Lane, make access and parking almost trouble-free. Small wonder the club have struggled, but full credit for their maintenance of such a friendly enclosure.

18

SOUTH LONDON AND KENT

·MILLWALL·

Previous Grounds

Formed in 1885 as Millwall Rovers, the club began life in the docklands of Millwall, which form the southern district of the Isle of Dogs. In 1886 they switched to a 3-acre ground behind the Lord Nelson pub on East Ferry Road, now a park by Manchester Grove, but in 1889 were told to leave because a newly-formed company had plans – never realized – for a switchback railway and recreation area on the site. Now called Millwall Athletic, the club moved a short distance in 1890 to another ground on East Ferry Road, opposite Millwall Docks which, although later one of the finer venues in London, was known initially for its unseemly surroundings. A visiting Corinthian player, Frederick Pelly, remarked that he did not mind playing there but objected to falling on the pitch because 'the smell wouldn't come off for weeks'. Conditions improved, as did the team, and the ground was also used for cycling, athletics, tennis and cricket practice. The East Ferry Road ground became a timber yard and is now covered by a supermarket. Millwall's next ground from 1901–10 was close by in Millwall Park. Although within yards of the other former grounds this one was rather confusingly referred to as North Greenwich. It proved to be Millwall's last home north of the River Thames.

The Den

The new ground in Cold Blow Lane was immediately named The Den, since it was home of 'The Lions', and although hemmed in considerably by railways and narrow lanes, had the advantage of being within walking distance of three railway stations and in the midst of a rapidly growing residential area.

Volunteer labour raised the banking on this former vegetable patch, using up to 400 cart-loads of rubble per day, and a main stand was designed by Archibald Leitch (see Design). In common with most London grounds, the contractors were Humphreys of Knightsbridge. Costing £10 000 in total, The Den was opened in 1910 by FA President Lord Kinnaird, and

although Millwall were then a Southern League team, such was the club's stature that the ground staged an England v. Wales match on 13 March 1911.

Millwall joined the League in 1920 and in 1925 dropped the title Athletic. The ground developed in the next decade along lines similar to today's appearance and saw its highest ever crowd of 48 672 for the club's 5th Round tie v. Derby County on 20 February 1937. Like most of south east London and the dock areas, New Cross suffered badly during the Blitz. The Den's Main Stand was damaged, as were sections of the terracing. Millwall sent their first team to play at The Valley, while Charlton's reserves used the bomb-scarred Den. But even when the seniors returned, they found the directors sitting on two wooden benches by the track and the press similarly accommodated behind one of the goals.

With compensation from the War Damages Commission, Millwall set about restoring the ground and in 1947 began covering the Ilderton Road End terrace. By the mid-1950s there were covers on the remaining two sides of terracing. Floodlights were first used for a friendly v. Manchester United on 5 October 1953. Little has changed within the ground since, apart from the addition of a wing to the Main Stand, bringing it up to the Ilderton Road End, and the installation of seats in the paddock.

Outside the ground much has changed. Formerly, one of the railway lines close to The Den used to run within yards of the back of the Main Stand, as at Bloomfield Road. Once the line became disused the club were able to buy the land, make a narrow car park and improve access. Also, the New Cross Speedway and Greyhound Stadium was once behind the Ilderton Road End. This too became disused, in the late 1970s, and is now open parkland. The only railway line still in use runs across Cold Blow Lane, from London Bridge to Croydon. In bygone days, engine drivers would stop to watch from their footplates, as at Bolton.

The Den's major problem has always been access, as described below, and since British Rail owns much of the surrounding land but has proved unwilling to sell, Millwall have no room to expand. There would be little point in developing the ground further un-

The Den, rebuilt after the War without Leitch's gable

called it Cold Blow Lane.

The main entrance is unexpected as the narrow lane bends, only just wide enough for a coach, with just enough space for a crowd to gather in the forecourt before the banking rises up sharply to the Cold Blow Lane terrace. Stairs half way up the bank lead to the offices, squeezed in behind the stand. Underneath are all the players' facilities, The Den being one of only four grounds to have its tunnel behind one of the goals. The Main Stand runs up the left, and you can see where one railway bridge across Cold Blow Lane has been taken away, leaving the embankment to form the new car park. Still, there is little room.

Behind the bank are more embankments, yards, tunnels, dark brick houses, the hum of traffic and tall tower blocks in the distance.

The Main Stand is dark with a low roof lightened only by the retention of the white paddock rear wall and the addition of orange seats. Unusually, those seats have been put on metal frames placed on top of the terrace, to provide a better view than is normal from such conversions. On the top of the roof in the centre is a sign with the club's name, in place of Leitch's original gable, destroyed during the war.

To the left is the Ilderton Road End, whose roof joins the Main Stand in the corner, where netting protects the seats from the terracing. Everywhere are signs warning spectators not to throw missiles. In the front section of this terrace, a large cut-away section gives groundstaff access to the pitch from behind the stand. The old greyhound stadium was just a few yards beyond this end.

Notice that the two end roofs are identical, supported by attractively splayed pillars. Also, each floodlight pylon is on a white concrete base on the terracing, with a blue lion painted on each facing side. A nice touch.

Opposite the Main Stand is the large open North Side banking, with a cover at the back, in the same style as the other roofs, grey with blue steelwork. To its right a high wall cuts across the terracing at an angle towards Cold Blow Lane. On top of this grey concrete wall is a clock and a police observation hut.

To the right is the Cold Blow Lane End terrace, into which is buried the well-protected tunnel, on the right of the goal. All three terraced sides are fronted by security fences built on a light blue perimeter wall, and the goals have especially close-mesh nets. All are reminder of The Den's past.

The Den is a tight enclosure, dominated by the drab, weathered tones of its uniform roofs and terracing. Because the approaches are so twisted and awkward, one feels it is an island of order in a sea of confusion. But the walls, the police hut, the dark stand and the low roofs also make it resemble a huge trap. It is no surprise that Millwall established a record of 59 successive League matches here without defeat. Not every team can be as cool as Daniel in the Lion's Den.

less access, especially by car, was improved. One supermarket chain offered to help the club rebuild the site into a sports complex, perhaps using part of the land occupied by the old stadium, but then withdrew its offer.

The Den holds two distinctions it would prefer not to have. It has been closed by the FA following crowd disturbances more frequently than any other ground, in 1920 (their first League season), 1934, 1947, 1950 and 1978. It is also the only League venue in London never to have staged First Division football. But it was certainly the first League ground to host a League match on a Sunday, when Millwall played Fulham on 20 January 1974. In 1985 The Den was designated under the Safety of Sports Grounds Act and had its capacity reduced from 32 000 to 19 000, with 3200 seats, reserved for members only. But in order to maintain that capacity Millwall had to spend £400 000.

Ground Description

Many factors make The Den probably the hardest ground of all for strangers to find. Firstly, you must not make the mistake of going to Millwall. Millwall FC play in New Cross, south of the river. Secondly, if approaching the ground by car, only one road actually touches the ground, Cold Blow Lane, which meanders away from the ground and disappears under railway tunnels before emerging in a sprawling new housing estate.

But worst of all, The Den is shielded behind New Cross Hospital and various railway embankments. Its floodlights are so low and inconsequential against the skyline as to be almost worthless homing guides, and even if you can spot them, can you get through the maze of roads to find the ground? Cold Blow Lane on a dark, wet night might be a perfect setting for a *Jack the Ripper* horror film; dry ice wafting about the cobbled streets and under the low tunnels. There are mysterious yards full of scrap, malodorous goings-on behind high fences, tower blocks looming in the distance, even old tram lines still embedded in the roads. They knew what they were dealing with when they

CHARLTON ·ATHLETIC·

Previous Grounds

This is one of the sadder chapters in the book; sad not only because Charlton have had to leave The Valley but because, as this story shows, they left in an atmosphere of bitterness, recrimination and concealment. There was an argument, but no one seemed to speak. There were questions aplenty, but no one prepared to answer. If the fans felt hard done by it was because no one made the effort to explain. And if they felt swindled, it was because the protagonists' own actions were hard to comprehend. The story was bound to end in tears, although there may yet be a happy twist at the end.

When Charlton Athletic formed in 1905, they were just one of many amateur teams in South London, but in an area dominated by rugby enthusiasts. A mile or two east was Plumstead, home of First Division Woolwich Arsenal who eventually moved away because gates were so poor. To the east, also a mile or so away, another professional club, Millwall Athletic, played in the Southern League. Being sandwiched between two senior clubs was reason enough for Charlton to remain amateurs, as they did until 1920.

Their first ground was Siemens Meadow, almost on the banks of the River Thames next to the Royal Dockyard, Woolwich. Siemens Road still exists a few hundred yards from The Valley across Woolwich Road. In 1907 Charlton moved south to Woolwich Common, which is still on Shooters Hill Road, a mile south east of The Valley. Two years later found them playing in Pound Park, almost next door to The Valley by Maryon Park, and in 1913 Charlton moved east to Horn Lane. Their ground was next to Greenwich Marshes, also on the banks of the Thames, and the land can still be seen next to the approaches to the Blackwall Tunnel.

Charlton decided in 1919 to find a permanent home, no doubt prompted by the fact that the club had only 2s 3d in the kitty and needed an enclosed ground to raise revenue. With the help of Colin Cameron, the club's historian, I shall relate how Charlton have been plagued either by big ideas but limited resources, or limited ideas and no lack of capital.

Charlton were playng in the Kent, London and South Suburban Leagues when they chose to set up home in the centre of Charlton Village. The site was then a derelict chalk pit with a well; a natural bowl but one hardly big enough to accommodate a minimum-size pitch. An army of volunteers helped dig the pit into shape, forming the vast banking which was to dominate the ground on three sides. Some of the extra gravel and earth brought onto the

site came from a nearby hospital excavation, and was said to have been full of old bones! A boost came from the MP, Sir Ion Hamilton Benn, who promised to act as guarantor on behalf of the club for a sum of £700. But in the event, such was the enthusiasm of all concerned that the money was raised independently.

Charlton called their new home, aptly enough, The Valley, and first played there in a match v. Summerstown on 13 September 1919. There were no stands and no fences, so a collecting box was sent around the crowd. The players had to change in a house in Ransom Road. This was at the time when Highbury was getting ready to host its first international, Goodison Park was fully developed as the finest ground in England and, just a few miles down the road, the country's most illustrious venue, Crystal Palace, still lay unused after war-time use as a munitions dump. Yet within a few years The Valley had become the biggest ground in England, and even a possible successor to Crystal Palace as a Cup Final venue. But if you expect a fairy tale story of rags to riches, remember also why Arsenal had left the area only a few years before.

Charlton turned professional in 1920 and joined the Southern League. The first professional match at The Valley was on 4 September 1920, v. Brighton and Hove Albion (whose first team had just started playing in the League's Third Division).

The Valley was still without a stand when Charlton were elected into the Football League in 1921, to join the Third Division South in its first season. The engineering firm of Humphreys Limited was contracted to build a grandstand on the flat, West Side of the ground, and add dressing rooms, terracing and all the necessary turnstiles and fittings. For a club so new to senior football the £14 000 estimated cost of this work seemed enormous, particularly when the final bill came to £21 314, nearly £20 000 of which was for the Grand Stand alone. Although only some 60 yards long, the Grand Stand was tall and distinguished, with a multi-span roof that was for years to become the endearing trademark of The Valley. It was in fact an almost exact copy of the main East Stand erected at Highbury (replaced in 1936), but only four spans long. Charlton however had to begin their League career without it, since the work was delayed and not fully completed until 1922.

Nevertheless, The Valley was taking the shape of a magnificent new stadium, prompting the *Athletic News'* correspondent to state that here was a: 'prospective Venue for future FA Cup Finals', and representative matches. The Valley, it was claimed, would make a suitable site for the FA to construct 'a national home' (work was soon to begin on Wembley Stadium). Yet despite this apparent promise, in 1923 Charlton's directors made a quite startling decision to leave The Valley, after only four seasons in residence! Support, they said, was not sufficiently forthcoming in the area. The summer of 1923 was spent preparing a new ground called The Mount, on Late

The Valley in 1939. The distinctive roof was replaced in 1979

ham Road, home of Catford FC, four miles south west of The Valley and slightly south of The Den. A further, enormous sum of £17 330 was spent preparing the new ground, which was not ready until 22 December 1923, for Charlton's game v. Northampton. Even then, Charlton had to seek special permission to stage an FA Cup match v. Wolves in February 1924, because the Catford ground lacked adequate seating accommodation. Meanwhile Charlton's reserves played on at The Valley, which Millwall were said to have been interested in taking over.

The move was an unmitigated disaster, both financially and in terms of attracting extra support. Although some games had attracted capacity crowds of 10 000, by the last match of the 1923–24 season only 1000 people attended. So poorer but wiser Charlton Athletic returned to The Valley after only half a season away. The Mount is still open ground, now called Mountsfield Park. There can have been fewer decisions more unwise than that taken by the Charlton board to leave in the first place, but as subsequent years were to prove, no administration at the club was ever able to really develop the ground to its full potential.

In his autobiography, the ex-Sunderland, Tottenham and Sheffield Wednesday player, Jimmy Seed, who managed Charlton during their finest years in the 1930s, wrote of the possibilities which never materialized:

'. . . if Charlton had built a second stand and had improved the accommodation, not only for fans but also for visiting directors and officials, they may well have staged international games which would have put the club on the map, like Arsenal and Tottenham. Members of the FA visited the ground on international selection duty, but quite clearly the club could never cope with an important international occasion.'

That The Valley was inadequate is borne out by the fact that although so close to the old Crystal Palace stadium, no major games were staged here, and that although Highbury, Stamford Bridge, White Hart Lane, even The Den and Craven Cottage had been or were being used for England matches more than Wembley up until the Second World War, The Valley was never chosen. Even Selhurst Park staged one international in 1926.

The only development seen at The Valley was the construction, in 1934, of a cover for standing spectators at the northern end. Costing about £3000 it was officially opened on Good Friday, March 1934. In the following years, under Jimmy Seed's beguiling control, the team's fortunes began to rise. They were higher than mighty Arsenal and they had the largest club ground in Britain, proved when on 12 February 1938, 75 031 attended Charlton's 5th Round Cup tie v. Aston Villa. Although six clubs have recorded higher attendances at their grounds, the important fact was that at The Valley there had still been more room! It is probable that its capacity was around 80 000 at this time, but it was never filled. However, the money collected by Charlton during this incredible spell of success was not used to improve facilities at The Valley.

During the Second World War there was slight damage caused to the North Stand, but not as much as their neighbours at The Den suffered, so for the 1943–1944 season Charlton shared The Valley with Millwall.

After the war, Charlton ceased to be such a force in the First Division but The Valley became the first venue ever to have an FA Cup match other than the Final itself broadcast live on television, when Charlton met Blackburn Rovers in the 5th Round on 8 February 1947. But still, incredibly, the money from these successes was not used to develop the ground. Charlton's First Division career came to an end in 1957, and with it, apparently, any chance of The Valley realizing its potential. Floodlights, for example, were installed relatively late at The Valley, on 20 September 1961 v. Rotherham United.

Finally, in 1979 the club began a series of developments at The Valley which were to radically alter the ground's character and capacity. When the Safety of Sports Grounds Act came into effect in 1977, The Valley's capacity dropped more than any other League ground, from 66 000 to 20 000, and then in January 1981 to only 13 000. Vast open stretches of decaying terracing were the main problem, as were the lack of entrances and exits to handle any larger crowds. So the directors rightly opted for a smaller stadium with more cover and seats, just as their predecessors might have done 30 years earlier.

Between 1979–81, three major alterations were effected with the eventual aim of making the ground all-seated. The total cost of £350 000 was raised by an extremely successful lottery. The charming but by then infirm roof of the West Stand was replaced with a square, modern cover. Seats were installed on the covered North Stand, and on the South Bank a completely new stand was erected, all-seated and appropriately named the Jimmy Seed Stand, when officially opened on 18 August 1981.

The extra seats gave The Valley a total of 10 000 seats, in an overall capacity of 20 000. But by 1984–85, after years of uncertainty and disruption at boardroom level, average gates were down to only 5039 and having been rescued from receivership the previous season, survival alone was something of a bonus.

Fate had not finished with Charlton, however, for in the summer of 1985 it dealt the club two further almighty swipes. Had each come separately Charlton might still be playing at The Valley. When they arrived simultaneously the directors found themselves boxed into a corner, with the ropes taken away, the referee deaf to their appeals and the promoter turning out the lights.

That it ever got to such a fight is in itself a painful story. For nearly fifty years Charlton were run by the Gliksten family, but in 1982 they sold out to a company called Marman Ltd. Under the chairmanship of Mark Hulyer The Valley began to buzz again, until eventually the club went into receivership, from which it was rescued by new owners, Sunley Construction, just 25 minutes before the deadline set by the Football League.

Sunley now owned the club, but (as at Chelsea) the former chairman, Michael Gliksten, retained ownership of the ground, plus Charlton's training ground at New Eltham. Charlton's new board tried to buy The Valley but Mr Gliksten turned down their reported offer of approximately £1·25 million.

Unable to buy the ground, Charlton '84 therefore had to accept being tenants on a seven-year lease costing £70 000 per season. Demanding though this was, at least Charlton had some security, since no member of the Gliksten family would surely ever turn Charlton out of their home. After all, Charlton was the Glikstens, for half a century at least.

The first tremors at The Valley came shortly after the Bradford fire in May 1985. Although the ground was already designated, the Greater London Council (since disbanded) ordered the ground's main standing accommodation, the East Terrace, to be closed completely.

The East Terrace had been a problem for some years. Originally built over a large sewer, the banking had been continually sinking and shifting in such a way as to make the terracing subside, crack and become dangerously distorted.

To complicate repair work, the sewer ran at an awkward angle underneath the terrace, making it almost impossible to rebuild even the front section without excavating the entire bank. This would have cost in the region of £2 million, certainly beyond Charlton's limited resources and apparently beyond Mr Gliksten.

When The Valley had first been designated in 1979 the GLC wanted to limit the East Terrace to only 3000 spectators. Eventually however the GLC agreed with Mr Gliksten that they could allow 10 000 on the East Terrace on the understanding that substantial repairs would be effected.

They were not, and in May 1985 the GLC decided to get tough. They determined that even 3000 on the East Terrace would be unsafe and ordered it to be closed completely, a decision which Charlton's lengthy appeal in the courts failed to reverse.

Without the East Terrace it would have been hard, though by no means impossible, to keep fans segregated, and hard, though not impossible, to retain a reasonable atmosphere at the ground with only three sides in use. And on gates of only 5000 there were still plenty of good seats available.

Charlton could have coped, even with a reduced capacity of 10 000 and standing accommodation for less than 2000 on either side of the West Stand. Ironically the seated sections of the ground were in better condition than ever before.

Repairing the East Terrace was never really an option. Having already put £2 million into saving the club, for Sunley, as tenants, to have invested a further £2 million on the terrace would have been an act of faith which surely no Charlton fan had the right to expect.

The East Terrace was closed the day before a pre-season friendly v. Liverpool, never to reopen. Meanwhile, a second blow to the Charlton chin was on its way.

At about the same time as the GLC's decision, completely out of the blue Michael Gliksten decided to take over 2 acres of The Valley behind the West Stand, an area used for car parking, toilets and turnstiles. As owner of the land, through his company Adelong Ltd, it was his prerogative because the 2 acres were not included in Charlton's 1984 lease. The club were aware that the former chairman could occupy this land at any time, but believed they would be able to use it right up to the point when builders moved in.

Mr Gliksten did not order any builders in. He did not even apply for planning permission to build on the site. He simply ordered the area to be fenced off. One may speculate as to his motives for doing this, but one can have no doubt about its effect. Charlton were out. For the count.

Even had they wanted to stage a match, it is highly unlikely that the police, fire or safety authorities would have allowed them. A ground without its most important turnstiles, without a car park, without substantial access and with segregation and crowd control rendered impossible, simply could not stage League Football.

Months after these events Charlton fans still ask, could the directors have fought more than they did? Their answer is this; against the GLC they did fight, and lost. Against Michael Gliksten they claim to

Last rites at The Valley, looking down from the heights of the woebegone East Terrace during the final game

have had no legal case to argue. The land belonged to Gliksten. He could do with it as he pleased, and he did. He caught them on the hop.

Did Michael Gliksten want Charlton out? A year after Charlton left, neither he nor his company Adelong Ltd had made any planning applications for the controversial 2-acre site. The rest of The Valley was designated by Greenwich Borough Council for public recreational use, so one might speculate that he would be unlikely to obtain permission for a supermarket or hotel on the actual stadium site.

Perhaps he intended to sell the land? If it could only be used as a sports ground it was hardly worth much, in which case he might yet be persuaded to sell to Charlton or Greenwich Borough Council. But if it could be used for housing, the land would be worth much more. So what did he plan for the site? By August 1986 no-one knew and Adelong Ltd were refusing to comment.

(One might also speculate that as a construction company, Sunley's interest in Charlton Athletic was also linked to potential development of The Valley, but if this ever was the case the site's limited prospects must have become apparent fairly soon.)

Charlton in the meantime had to face the agonizing choice of where to play. There were several options. In the short term, Greenwich Borough Council had no suitable venues to offer for senior football and no surplus cash to pay for one. But they did pledge to support Charlton's return to the borough at the earliest possible opportunity.

The fans' reluctant choice would have been The Den. Though Millwall and Charlton were hardly bosom pals, at least the ground was only four miles away, and the two clubs had mucked in together during the war. Reports suggested that Charlton's directors had approached Millwall, but Millwall officials said no such approach had been made. Once again the fans asked, what is the truth? (Millwall

later commented that in view of the fact that The Den required £400 000 to be spent on safety work, perhaps Charlton were best off elsewhere.)

Charlton did approach West Ham, who turned them down, and Arsenal were said to be considering the matter when a deal was finally struck with Crystal Palace.

Selhurst Park had three advantages. Firstly, it was a modern ground with a good capacity, private boxes and a profit-earning social club – attractive to executive supporters and sponsors but hardly important to the average fan. Secondly, Palace needed the money, so they would be welcoming landlords, and finally Charlton would not be overshadowed by Palace, since both teams were then in the Second Division. (Cynics would also point out that Selhurst Park is only two miles west of Sunley's head office.)

The disadvantages however were many. Charlton and Crystal Palace were long-standing rivals; again, not important from the comfort of an executive box but deeply felt on the terraces.

Public transport from the Charlton area to Selhurst Park is appalling. Although only seven miles away as the crow flies, as the London bus weaves it takes a full hour. As for rail, the bus would be quicker.

But the distance was more than just time or effort. Selhurst Park was in another world, as different from Charlton as Darlington is to Middlesbrough or Dumbarton to Glasgow. David Lacey expressed it succinctly in *The Guardian*. 'Charlton Athletic,' he wrote, 'are the Woolwich Ferry, the Greenwich loop line and the Blackwall Tunnel Approach; Crystal Palace are Norwood Junction and Thornton Heath Pond. Charlton are Thames Estuary and North Kent; Palace are Croydon and the A23.' In short, ground sharing was a rational step, but it was the wrong choice of ground for Charlton.

Perhaps the most disturbing element of this sorry

tale is that the first the Charlton fans heard of the move was on 7 September 1985 when they arrived at The Valley, ironically on the afternoon of their home game against Crystal Palace, to be handed a leaflet which began 'It is with regret that we must announce . . .'

There had been no public meeting. No face-to-face discussion between the supporters and the directors. As an exercise in public relations the Charlton board had made the Bhatti brothers at Wolverhampton look positively effusive.

And what made it all the worse was that just at a time when Charlton seemed to have, at last, a team capable of reaching Division One, most Charlton fans would have preferred to see Fourth Division football at The Valley rather than promotion battles at Selhurst Park. Some said they would rather see Charlton die than go to Palace.

And still no-one talked to them directly. No-one explained anything. They were left to work it out from the newspapers.

Over at Palace an action group fought the move, as commentators and fans alike feared that ground sharing would inevitably lead to amalgamation. One report had it that Sunley planned to buy up Selhurst Park in order to merge the two clubs, although as long as Palace were in charge a merger was unlikely since it would have negated the financial advantages of two clubs sharing one ground. Charlton's arrival cut Palace's bills virtually in half overnight.

Meanwhile Michael Gliksten, now regarded by Charlton fans as the *bête noire* who had stabbed his family's heritage in the back, told the press, 'It will be the saddest day for me if Charlton Athletic abandon their traditional home at The Valley.' His comments were not well received, especially when some of the ramifications of Charlton's move became apparent.

Firstly, Gliksten claimed that Charlton owed him the remaining five-and-half-years' rental of £70 000 per annum, as agreed in 1984. This was a matter for the courts to settle, but it could result in Charlton having to pay nearly £400 000 to Gliksten on top of their rental at the Palace. Charlton agreed a seven-year lease for Selhurst, paying 10 per cent of gate receipts.

Secondly, Greenwich Borough Council, in which The Valley is situated, had a five-year sponsorship agreement with Charlton, worth some £250 000. Since Charlton were no longer playing in the borough the deal was eventually cancelled.

Saturday 21 September 1985 – almost exactly 66 years after the first game – saw The Valley's final act, a sombre crowd of 8858 seeing Charlton beat Stoke 2-0 to maintain their challenge at the top of the Second Division.

A half-time demonstration on the pitch held up the restart, and at the end a few fans ripped up patches of turf. Tears were shed, in the directors' box as well as on the terraces, and suddenly it was all over. Maurice Banham, the groundsman, was pressed into early

retirement, a few regulars sent back their season tickets in disgust, and North Kent, one of the most populous regions in the South East, lost its one and only League club.

The Valley has lain redundant ever since. Vandals have made their mark, while on one occasion the former Charlton player and manager, Mike Bailey, who in 1986 was running the still popular Valley Club, nipped onto the pitch and mowed one of the goalmouths. Maurice Banham meanwhile was chased off the ground by guard dogs.

So what do we see as we walk up Sam Bartram Close and look down over The Valley from the heights of Valiant Tower? The Main Stand creaks a bit, the almost-new Jimmy Seed Stand gathers dust and weeds, goes to seed, and an overbearing silence hangs over the East Terrace, as if it were desperate for nature to shield it from the harsh world of bureaucrats and squabbling businessmen.

Who was to blame for this senseless waste? Was it Michael Gliksten, whose family had saved the club once and who had himself kept it going for so long? Was it the GLC for their harsh attitude? Might they have been more tolerant had it not been for the incidents at Bradford, Birmingham and Brussels? Was it the new board of directors, who might have pushed harder and might have kept the fans better informed? Or was it the fans themselves, for being lukewarm in their protests and passive in their relationship with the directors? After Charlton had moved to Palace they booed chairman John Fryer. At the end of the season they chaired him off the pitch at Carlisle when Charlton won promotion.

There is hope yet for the old Valiants. Greenwich Borough Council want them back, and have a perfect site on Greenwich peninsula, where Charlton played between 1913–19. But it will take pressure, protest and determination. The kind of concerted action which Walsall fans mounted to keep their team at Fellows Park. A 10 000-signature petition collected in autumn 1986 was the first indication of any mass support for The Valley, but it may well have come too late, especially in view of Charlton's paltry attendances in the First Division during the 1986–87 season.

The alternative is clear. Seven years at the Palace and Charlton's fans will have forgotten The Valley. There will be new fans who have no idea of Charlton's origins. And one day someone will say, 'Enough is enough, let's merge both clubs and call it the Croydon Crunchers or the Selhurst Smashers'.

And The Valley will become like Cathkin Park in Glasgow – a nice schools' pitch with some strange echoes from the surrounding banks.

Selhurst Park

Take the number 75 bus, some sandwiches for the journey, turn to the following section on Crystal Palace and put on a brave face.

· CRYSTAL PALACE ·

Previous Grounds

As the name suggests, Crystal Palace's early history is bound up with the famous glass and iron palace built by Joseph Paxton in 1851 for the Great Exhibition of Hyde Park, but soon after moved to Upper Sydenham heights in South London (see Big Match Venues). A football club called Crystal Palace was formed as early as 1861 by members of the exhibition groundstaff, and played in the park grounds. It entered the very first FA Cup in 1871 and reached the semi-final. Roy Peskett's club history tells us much about those early years.

The idea for a professional club at Crystal Palace first came in 1904, when the ground's owners tried to form a team to enter the Southern League, only to find the FA thought it unwise for the Final's hosts to have their own team in the FA Cup. So the following year a separate company was formed, and became tenants of Crystal Palace. If ever there was a big match at the ground, such as a rugby international, Palace had to switch to other venues, but in 1915 they had to vacate the ground altogether when it was taken over by the Army.

Keeping the same name (for they were not to know that they would never return to Crystal Palace), the football club moved to Herne Hill, a few miles north to where the athletics ground is now, a short distance from The Den.

In 1919, Palace moved again, further south to the district of Selhurst, to a ground called The Nest. This had been the home of an old Southern League team, Croydon Common, and it was here in 1920 Palace began their League career.

But the ground was not entirely suitable for a club with ambition, and was about to be submerged by railway developments, so Palace rented it out to Tramway FC, for 10 per cent of their gate receipts, and secured the freehold of a site nearby.

Selhurst Park

Selhurst Park cost the club only £2570 in January 1922, but needed considerable preparation. The site was a brickfield belonging to the London Brighton and South Coast Railway Company. Two chimney stacks stood where the pitch is now. But the advantages were apparent, for it covered 15 acres and was within walking distance of three suburban railway stations, Thornton Heath, Selhurst and Norwood Junction.

Palace commissioned Archibald Leitch to design their new ground. He predicted that Selhurst Park would be the largest ground in London, the most modern in the country, but could do little to prevent industrial disputes holding up the work. The official opening by the Lord Mayor of London, on 30 August 1924, took place in a still unfinished stand. The contractors at Selhurst Park were Humphreys of Knightsbridge, a firm which built, among other grounds, The Valley. Leitch's Main Stand was virtually identical to his designs of 20 years before at Fulham, Huddersfield and Stamford Bridge, but without the triangular roof gable. The rest of the ground was open banking, although terracing only covered the lower reaches of each bank, the tops being covered in grass.

At the end of the first season Palace were relegated. But the club was honoured on 1 March 1926 when Selhurst staged England v. Wales.

In those early years at Selhurst there was a ditch running in front of the Main Stand along the touchline. To save players having to retrieve the ball from its murky waters, Palace covered it over in 1935 and relaid the pitch. They also installed a tap by the trainer's bench, for wetting the magic sponge. The ground was used for Army internationals and like most London grounds, by Millwall, when their own ground had been closed because of crowd disturbances. But it remained completely unchanged during the club's long sojourn in Divisions Three and Four; a large, but increasingly unkempt ground with cover only on one side, holding 55 000 spectators.

Floodlights were first installed in September 1953, when Palace played a friendly v. Chelsea, and were updated in December 1955. Also in that year a new entrance hall and boardroom were opened by Sir Stanley Rous. The floodlights were still rather too primitive however, being mounted on four poles on the open side, four gantries on the stand roof, all apparently linked by wires draped around the ground, so in 1962 Palace spent £18 000 erecting a new set on four corner pylons. They then effected a major footballing scoop by persuading Real Madrid to visit Selhurst Park to play in the first game under the new lights, watched by 25 000.

Palace's fortunes in the League began to improve during the 1960s, and in 1966 work began on a new stand on the uncovered side. It was named after the club's long-serving chairman, Arthur Wait, who was a builder by trade and was occasionally to be seen working on the construction himself. Seating 5000, the stand was fully finished in 1969 when Palace won promotion to Division One.

The last major improvement at the ground took place in the early 1980s when the Whitehorse Lane End, an open bank of terracing, and the large car park behind, were leased to a supermarket chain in a £2 million deal. The supermarket built their store on the car park, but also had to refit the terraces along its back wall. There is now a more modern, but truncated bank holding 5000 standing spectators, but designed in such a way as to make possible the provision of a roof, or even a stand above the shop behind the terracing. It is identical to the project undertaken at Boothferry Park.

The Main Stand has also been adapted, into an

Selhurst Park in the 1970s. Notice the two floodlight systems

all-seated stand holding 5000. There are therefore 10 000 seats in a total capacity of 38 266. So Leitch was wrong in predicting that Selhurst Park would be the biggest ground in London, although before the Whitehorse Lane End was cut down, the ground did at least come close to that distinction. When Palace were again chasing promotion to Division One in May 1979, a record attendance of 51 482 saw them win the Second Division Championship after a game v. Burnley.

First Division football returned to Selhurst Park in 1986, although not with Crystal Palace. The previous September, Palace and their South London neighbours Charlton became the first League clubs in Britain to agree upon a ground-sharing scheme, when The Valley was rendered unviable.

The controversial aspects of this move are discussed elsewhere (see Charlton), but for Palace it proved a welcome bonus. Charlton have a seven-year agreement to share Selhurst Park, paying 10 per cent of gate receipts to Palace (with a minimum set figure) plus half all the running costs.

For example, during the summer of 1986, while Charlton were preparing for the First Division and Palace faced another season in Division Two, £100 000 had to be spent on new barriers. Each club shared 25 per cent of the costs, FGIT paying the remainder.

If all goes well – and what could be better than both clubs in Division One? – the projected cover at the Whitehorse Lane End might be built, at an estimated cost of £500 000, and the Arthur Wait Stand made all-seated.

Charlton's only weekday presence at Selhurst Park is in the form of temporary offices next to the Kop, and on match days a few token signs for Charlton at various strategic points.

But no matter how sensible the concept of ground sharing, Charlton's longing for home, be it The Valley or anywhere in Greenwich, will surely not abate for many a year to come.

Ground Description

Selhurst and its neighbouring districts all seem to lie at the foot of the hill on which the Crystal Palace stood until destroyed by fire in 1936. The ground merges into its surrounds, tucked in between the rising slopes of South Norwood and the flatter land of Selhurst. Entrance is from Whitehorse Lane, a thoroughfare made busier by the arrival of the new supermarket. The Main Stand is entered via a private road between the ground and Lady Edridge School, but instead of finding the normal foyer, one finds the entrance to a rather seedy-looking nightclub, its presence under the stand seeming rather incongruous.

Otherwise, the stand looks very sombre indeed. All the steelwork and seats are black, and the once so familiar and homely claret and light blue striped paddock rear wall disappeared when the terracing was seated. The stand facings are now dark blue with touches of white and red along the centre and exits. In the left-hand corner remains just a short section of the old striped wall. Quite why Palace opted for such a dark colour scheme is difficult to understand, for although Leitch's stand was never so distinctive as its forebears at Craven Cottage or Leeds Road, it was bright.

One unusual feature of the stand is the lack of any front perimeter wall. As the stand is old and mainly wooden, the club considered the best fire escape to be straight onto the pitch. Hence anyone in the stand can simply walk down to the front, and enter the pitch past a few low advertisement hoardings on the touchline. If anyone does, he might notice that the dug-outs have polished pine benches inside. Very fashionable. As a further precaution in the event of fire, two extra staircases have been built behind the stand, like twin towers.

At the back of the stand is a line of executive boxes, which on closer inspection resemble slightly outdated small hotel rooms with intricate light fittings. The directors are less fussy: their seats are just like those in the rest of the stand. Very egalitarian.

From here, to the left is the Whitehorse Lane End with the supermarket directly behind. It used to be twice as high and hold 12 000 standing. The terrace stops within a few yards of each corner, allowing room for the floodlight pylons which face the pitch square on, staring at their opposites on the other side like totem poles guarding Selhurst Park from evil spirits. Each pylon has 48 large lamps.

The new terracing is sturdy, with thick-set steel barriers. Opposite here is the taller and original banking, the Holmesdale Road End, or the Kop. Palace tried to persuade the home fans to move over to the new terracing, but they held firm on these exposed slopes. Here the barriers are red and blue, rising up to a grass-topped bank, which then subsides towards the road. At the front, Palace have borrowed an idea from Newcastle, using not tall security fencing but a low angled fence divided from the pitch by a slight moat. I cannot understand why this excellent device is not used more often, for it not only works as an anti-hooligan measure but also prevents that caged-in effect. Most important, the view from the lower terraces is not in any way impeded. This end holds 17 000.

Opposite the Main Stand is the Arthur Wait Stand. It follows the traditional pattern, combining seats and a paddock, with a large, propped flat roof, whose fascia is marked with claret and light blue stripes. It should sparkle, it should sport the club's name in big letters, it should have a flagpole or two to lessen the monotonous lines, but all it has is a small square clock in the centre. Behind the white concrete paddock rear wall are 5000 seats, but unfortunately placed on very shallow raked steps. Altogether it is rather a dull stand, like the loading bay of a warehouse. Finally, notice how many different colours are used at Selhurst Park, from the garish tones inside the foyer to the blue stanchions and orange nets on each set of goals. Consequently, there is no unity, no indication of who plays here and in what colours. It would be preferable if parts of the colour scheme indicated Charlton's presence, although it has to be said that claret and blue might clash rather badly with scarlet and white.

Both Charlton and Palace fans fear that one day the two clubs will merge, but that would be to negate the main advantages of ground sharing; that is, two clubs providing income for the maintenance of one ground. Perhaps one of the biggest fears they should have is for the pitch. Ultimately Selhurst Park may have to install an artificial pitch to withstand the extra use.

Ground sharing is not perfect, but it can work. The Milan and Turin teams manage and in South America several teams often share the same stadium. This is, of course, no consolation whatsoever to either Palace or Charlton devotees, but it had to happen somewhere. It's just that no-one wanted to be the first.

·WIMBLEDON·

Plough Lane

Wimbledon were for 75 years among the top amateur clubs in London. They formed in 1889 and under the name Wimbledon Old Centrals played on Wimbledon Common until moving to Plough Lane in 1912. As a successful South London club, they were able to attract gates of up to 10 000 during the 1930s.

At that time the ground had two stands. The Main Stand was a small, all-wooden affair with separate dressing rooms. Opposite, the club installed the South Stand in 1923, purchased from Clapton Orient who were then playing at Millfields Road. The South Stand is still on the Plough Lane Side. A particularly unusual feature of the ground was a privet hedge which grew between the Main Stand and the touchline. The ground's highest attendance, 18 000, was at an Amateur Cup match v. HMS Victory in 1935.

Plough Lane really developed in the late 1950s and early 1960s, under the chairmanship of the late Sidney Black, a generous, forward-thinking man to whom in many ways the club owe their present status. The Sportsman public house was built at the ground on Durnsford Road in 1958. In 1959 Wimbledon bought the site from the council for a sum of £9000, but only on the condition that if the ground were to be sold, it would have to go back to the authorities at the same price. As a result, Wimbledon were never able to borrow much money because the ground was worth so little as security. (In recent years the situation has been resolved; the club bought out the limiting clause and therefore now own a valuable piece of land. Wimbledon also bought extra land in front of the ground and by the car park.)

Also in 1959, the rear section of the present Main Stand was built, and instead of the privet hedge, shrubs were grown along the front railings. The following year saw the construction of the slight cantilevered cover at the West Terrace end, and all the concrete terracing. In October 1960 Arsenal visited Plough Lane, to play in the first floodlit game at the ground. The existing lights are more recent installations.

This transformation of the ground would have been impossible without Black's financial help. In their third Final and their only appearance at Wembley Stadium, Wimbledon beat Sutton United to win the Amateur Cup in 1963. They were then in the Isthmian League. A year later they turned semi-professional, formed a limited company, and within a comparatively short time became candidates for League membership. This they achieved in 1977.

Extra facilities were soon added; an extension over the small paddock in front of the Main Stand in 1979 and the building of bars, a lounge and a multi-gym behind the stand.

The Main Stand at Plough Lane

By 1984 Wimbledon had reached the Second Division. A year later, as a result of the Bradford fire, they were ordered to close the mainly wooden South Stand, so that during their historic 1985–86 season they were confined to only 1700 seats, the lowest in the Second Division.

Incredibly the team won promotion to Division One, in just their ninth League campaign, and immediately there was talk of a Wimbledon move. Sharing with Fulham (4½ miles north) would have been the nearest option. Chelsea was also mentioned, while Charlton's move put Selhurst Park out of the question (Palace is 5½ miles away as the crow flies, but a lengthier distance by road).

There were also tentative plans for an all-seater stadium to be built half a mile south of Plough Lane at Colliers Wood, on the site of a disused sewage works. That might have had the players kicking up a stink, but in fact Wimbledon sensibly decided to remain at Plough Lane for the time being, knowing their First Division career might not last long and that Plough Lane's scale and atmosphere might prove to be one of their best assets against the bigger clubs.

The summer of 1986 therefore saw £350 000 worth of improvements at Plough Lane. Happily the South Stand was saved, albeit with only 900 seats, after being completely fire-proofed and underpinned. Crush barriers were replaced and new turnstiles and security fencing installed. This allowed Wimbledon to raise their capacity from 13 500 to 19 000, of which 2600 are seated. This work notwithstanding, and even taking into account Oxford's ground, in 1986–87 Plough Lane was the most basic ground to have staged First Division football since Northampton's brief elevation in 1965–66. Space was so limited that Wimbledon felt justified in charging from £7–£13 for seats, with variations made depending on the opposition.

Ground Description

Anyone expecting tranquillity such as one might expect to find in the neighbourhood of the All England Tennis Club will be very disappointed by Plough Lane. Because Plough Lane's stands and terraces are so low, the constant sound and smell of traffic is never far away.

To find the ground simply follow a line of electricity pylons. One such pylon towers over the ground, making the floodlight pylons look distinctly insignificant. Although called Plough Lane, the main entrance is on Durnsford Road next to the Sportsman pub.

The Main Stand is about 60 yards long on the half-way line, a miniature version of Doncaster's at Belle Vue, with an older rear section and a newer extended roof over the paddock, which has now been fully seated. It is too small and unevenly built to have any impact on its surroundings, especially as the pylon behind is over twice its height. Behind the Main Stand is a busy courtyard with detached offices, just enough room for a few Rolls-Royces, and on match days sufficient hubbub in such cramped quarters to make every game seem like a major Cup tie. Journalists might not feel so enthusiastic, however, for at the rear of the Main Stand is perhaps the most cramped press-box in the League. By all appearances the birds seem to like it up there during the week anyway.

From the Main Stand, to the left is the open East Terrace, with the River Wandle behind, and to the right, the West Terrace with its cover at the back, behind which is Durnsford Road, forever shaking under lorries and buses.

Opposite the Main Stand, also sitting on the half-way line, is the very narrow South Stand. It presumably dates back to the turn of the century, and has just a few rows of narrow bench seating behind a wooden terrace rear wall. After it was brought here from Clapton Orient, a nearby bomb explosion during the Second World War was thought to have made it unsafe, but it survived until 1985, when it was closed for a season. Recent safety work has given it a new lease of life. Plough Lane is directly behind.

Though lacking sophistication or aesthetic value, Plough Lane does have the neat and homely atmosphere which is more often the mark of non-League grounds. The perimeter fence on either side of the Main Stand is, for example, the old curled iron railing type, once found at better grounds but now replaced by ugly concrete and steel security fencing. The colour scheme is tastefully uniform; yellow railings, yellow, royal blue and white steelwork and barriers, black seats.

Wimbledon have crammed a respectable array of facilities into their ground and if it still looks slightly unprofessional from the terraces, you should not decry their efforts. Something of the spirit of their amateur days still lives on. The ground's major drawback is that in its underdeveloped state it is unable to shut out from view the overwhelmingly uninteresting bits of South London in which it finds itself absorbed.

· GILLINGHAM ·

Priestfield Stadium

The Medway towns were home to one of the most formidable of early teams, a team of officers, the Royal Engineers. But the best local side was Excelsior, who played on a ground called the Great Lines (still used today), known for its downward slope and proximity to a manure heap. This team was so successful that it was decided to put their activities on a more formal basis and look for a properly enclosed ground of their own.

Thanks to the excellent research of the club's historian, Tony Conway, this is one of the few surviving accounts of how such choices were made in those early years. No doubt the process was similar at many other clubs. From the *Chatham and Rochester News*, 13 May 1893, came this report of a meeting at the Napier Arms:

> 'Is it possible and practicable that the New Brompton football enthusiasts shall have a ground of their own to centralise and encourage local players and to run the club on democratic lines as well as make it pay? That question – not a slight one by the way – is at present occupying intense attention at New Brompton, and has been the object of many meetings. Time will show . . .'

One of the committee reported to the assembled he had been unable to agree terms with a Mr Webb for his land. Another member produced a plan of ground on the Beacon Court estate, 6½ acres in all, and informed the meeting of its cost. A third committee member came with another plan of land which had the advantage of being almost flat, 'the fall being only one foot in 190'. He thought the land might be had at a reasonable price, but thought it would be wiser to buy it outright. Again costs were mentioned, prompting Mr Croneen to remind the meeting that if it were made public that they were keen on a particular plot, they would 'have to pay through the nose for it'. From then on, it was agreed, no figures were to be mentioned. The reporter notes, however, that sums of between £600 and £1200 were discussed.

Mr Croneen now stood up with his plan, of land near the level crossing, on Gillingham Road. It was large enough for football and even a cycle track, and was hedged on two sides, so that less fencing would have to be erected. The chairman, Dr Warren, then asked the assembled if the club intended entering for the All England Cup, meaning the FA Cup. This drew forth a unanimous "yes"' from all concerned, and Dr Warren had to remind them, therefore, that hedges would not be sufficient to satisfy the Association. The FA 'would insist on having the ground

properly enclosed', he said.

The discussion then turned to the matter of using a future ground for cricket as well as football, but it was concluded that after the rough wear of winter, the pitch would not be suitable for cricket but might make a splendid tennis ground. It was also asked how long a pitch would need to be prepared, followed by an inconclusive exchange on 'the properties of lucerne, grass-seed, etcetera'.

Mr Winch spoke next, in a clear and practical speech on how to go about obtaining the ground; whether to secure 'a site on a lease' with 'a number of gentlemen to guarantee a sum of money to defray initial expenses', or perhaps to 'float a company to secure the ground and then let it to the Football Club'. He made the following calculation; the population of Gillingham was 30 000, of whom one-fifth were adult men. Only about half of them could be expected to attend regularly, giving a potential gate of 3000. Mr Winch 'did not wish to throw cold water on the idea' but wanted to raise the 'question of preliminary costs, future expenses and probable returns' (cheers).

The first plan brought to the meeting had not been properly explained, said one. Some favoured another plan. Dr Warren said they must get a ground, or where would all these famous clubs they wanted to invite play? Another speaker hoped that if a company was formed, some of the 'bunce' would go to the players. Finally, Mr Thompson proposed: 'a limited liability company be formed with £1 shares'. The motion was seconded, and after a lengthy discussion, carried. A provisional committee to investigate setting up a company was formed and the meeting adjourned.

A week later the company was formed, then a name decided on – New Brompton Football Club Company Limited – and finally Mr Croneen's suggestion of adopting 'a section of land in Gillingham Road close to the level crossing' was agreed on. This was the present ground, and the land cost £600. £10 was paid for a turnstile, and then an argument ensued. The committee argued over what type of goalposts to buy with their Brodies Patented Goal Nets, and whether a 16- or 24-inch lawnmower be purchased. Also from Mr Conway's history we learn that a flagstaff was presented to the new company to add some dignity to the ground.

This is a report of the opening day:

> 'Here everything was of the newest, even the grass, in fact there had not been time to indulge in the luxury of paint; but a little powder there may have been, as ladies mustered a strong force, and they do sometimes use "just a little" you know [so much for Mr Winch's calculation on male attendance at that opening meeting!]. Finishing touches were being put here and there and "Mein Host" of the "Napier Arms" was making

Until condemned in 1985, the Gordon Road Stand at Gillingham was the oldest in use at any League ground

ready for his share in the day's proceedings – not inconsiderable as events turned out, and Mr Chairman H. G. Croneen, at last triumphantly exclaimed, "Now we are ready for them." Spectators dropped in by twos and threes until some 500 were present to witness the first match.'

New Brompton soon discovered the financial burdens of running a football team, so the Priestfield Ground was used for all manner of fund raising events, including smoking concerts, fêtes, athletics meetings, and even a ladies' football match. In common with many other grounds, sheep were allowed to graze on the pitch during the week. But still the club struggled and had to sell part of the land for £2500, where Gordon Road is now. They even had to rent out their turnstiles for other events. But the aforementioned hedges around the ground remained for some time.

It is hard to say what stands and terraces were built in those early years, though photographs taken at the turn of the century show a stand identical to one which was in use on the Gordon Road Side of the ground until 1985. Hence we may suppose that this was at the time the oldest surviving structure at any League ground, dating back to the middle or late 1890s. Dockyard workers were responsible for its erection.

In 1913 New Brompton changed their name to Gillingham and in 1920 joined the newly formed Division Three. By 1938, the Main Stand on Redfern Avenue had been built, and pictures show it to have been characterized by a slatted wooden wall at the rear of the paddock. A white wooden fence surrounded the pitch, but even in the 1920s the hedge around the ground survived.

As Gillingham struggled to get back their League status after the War, huge gates in the Cup and Southern League allowed the club to level the pitch, concrete the terracing and build proper turnstiles. A record gate of 23 002 saw Gillingham's 3rd Round

Cup tie v. QPR on 10 January 1948, when the club was still in the Southern League, and such success (though they lost that particular match) no doubt helped them in their return to the Third Division, when the League was expanded in 1950.

Developments since have been the erection of a roof over the Rainham terracing and floodlights in 1963. Priestfield was one of the very last League grounds to be lit up, and the club's highest gate for years, 17 500, came to see the first game v. Bury in August of that year. On promotion from Division Four in 1964, in a series of further improvements, the Main Stand was completely refurbished and reroofed and a floodlit pitch built behind the Rainham End. In more recent years this area behind the ground has been enhanced by a £350 000 sports centre.

Priestfield Stadium was probably the only Third or Fourth Division ground to have its capacity increased following the extension of the Safety of Sports Grounds Act in 1985. Further checks showed a need to spend some £80 000 on safety work but they also determined that rather than its previous capacity of 16 000, the ground was in fact capable of holding nearer 19 000 (according to the police) or even 21 000 (according to the fire authorities). But Gillingham did have to lose some seats because of the need for improved fire precautions. The number dropped from 1500 to 1089, and sadly this included the loss of about 300 seats in the delightful Gordon Road Stand, the oldest stand still in use in the League (this distinction now belongs to a section of Grimsby's Main Stand). The Gordon Road Stand, lovingly preserved by the club, was apparently too much of a fire hazard. There was a void underneath the bench seats and the rake was too steep.

Considering those other wooden structures (at Blackpool and Colchester, for example) which survived the increased checks made in 1985, the decision to close the stand seemed harsh, but after the Bradford fire no club would dream of arguing.

Ground Description

Priestfield Stadium is a bitty ground, in five sections. The Main Stand is some 60 yards long astride the half-way line, flanked by open terracing to the right, and a smaller patch of newer terracing to the left, behind which are the modern club offices. The original Main Stand is enveloped by a more recent roof, covering the paddock, now seated. The roof slopes upwards from the road, then pitches sharply down to the gutter, and has awkward cross struts at either end to increase its strength. In effect, Gillingham have done what Charlton were to do many years later, giving an otherwise obsolete stand a new lease of life. Notice that the front row of seats is open to the touchline, with no perimeter wall.

To the right is the uncovered Gillingham End, which despite its name is reserved for visiting supporters. Behind here, at right angles to the ground, is Priestfield Road, a cul-de-sac. An interesting feature of this end is the way the terracing was obviously laid in line with the old slope of the pitch. Now that this has been levelled, the steps themselves slope down about 3 feet from Gordon Road towards Redfern Avenue. Adding to the weird sightlines is the fact that the front terraces are a couple of feet above the perimeter track.

The open terracing continues around the pitch until 25 yards down the touchline we come to the now disused Gordon Road Stand. A narrow, 30-yard long stand with nine yellow uprights supporting a roof over simple blue and white bench seats, it looks remarkably neat. Regrettably its days are numbered.

Almost touching the stand is a slightly taller cover over the terracing which extends to the corner flag, and rather awkwardly turns a few yards into the Rainham End. Next to this simple, sloping roof, along the rest of the Rainham End, and in turn going round the corner to where it meets up with the terracing next to the Main Stand, is a clean, light-grey, barrel roof cover, curling slightly upwards at the gutter. Behind this end is the sports centre, built jointly by the club and the Sports Council. It incorporates a squash club, a sports hall and three tennis courts.

Even before the demise of the Victorian stand built by dockers, Gillingham were planning to build a new stand along the Gordon Road side. But their plans have been twice rejected by the local authority, despite the fact that the projected roof was to be lower than the existing ones.

Until this impasse can be overcome, the Priestfield Stadium is unlikely to change substantially and it will remain something of a hodge-podge of styles.

But with its ample capacity and now much improved infrastructure, it is nevertheless more than able, on Mr Winch's calculation, to accommodate one tenth of Gillingham's current adult male population and still have room for 'a strong force' of ladies to muster with 'just a little' powder.

·19·
WEST OF SCOTLAND

QUEEN OF THE ·SOUTH·

Palmerston Park

Fifteen miles from the border and closer to Carlisle than to any Scottish ground, Palmerston Park, Dumfries, has been Queen of the South's home since the club's formation in 1919. (Technically the ground is in Maxwelltown, which merged with Dumfries in 1929.) A small wooden stand was erected and in 1927 the sloping pitch levelled, the surplus soil being used to bank up the Terregles Street End.

W. Jardine's club history relates how promotion to the First Division in 1933 (under the chairmanship of one Jimmy Jolly) brought improvements; a cover over the King Street Side in 1934 and the purchase of grassland behind the new stand. The small wooden grandstand was enlarged two years later. German prisoners of war helped restore Palmerston Park after the Second World War and on 23 February 1952 a record gate of 24 500 attended the visit of Hearts in the Scottish Cup 3rd Round.

Queen of the South were the first Scottish club to have floodlights on pylons, costing £10 000 and switched on for a friendly v. Preston in October 1958 (in 1983 it cost £26 000 to update them). In the same year the present cover on the Glasgow Street End was erected. A fire in the Main Stand in March 1964 led to the construction of the existing stand, built in stages behind the old one to minimize disruption.

Following safety work, Palmerston Park's capacity has been reduced from 20 850 to approximately 18 000, including 1300 seats.

The ground's greatest asset however is its 7 acres. With a large car park in front of the Main Stand and extra land on the opposite side, Palmerston Park was always ripe for development. Plans drawn up in 1986 involve the leasing to a supermarket of part of the car park while in place of the decaying terrace cover – known locally as the Bull Shed – Nithsdale Council drew up plans to erect a £5 million leisure centre, incorporating indoor bowling, an ice rink, a con-

Palmerston Park, with Jimmy Jolly's Bull Shed on the right

ference hall, and, of note to ground designers, an integral roof to cover that side of the ground. Since the land would only be leased the club stands to gain all round: facilities enhanced and annual income increased.

Ground Description

Calling the club Queen of the South – a title ascribed to the town of Dumfries itself – was a shrewd move, for despite occasional attempts to change it the name attracts visitors from all over the world, lured by romance and curiosity.

Palmerston Park is hardly romantic, however. A very down-to-earth ground it is, owned entirely by the club and brimming with potential. A vast open car park leads to the Grandstand, a plain brick and steel construction not unlike Oxford United's. Some 70 yards long with a small paddock in front, the stand has one sturdy central roof support and blue facings, with a hand-painted crest over the tunnel, above a horse-shoe. The crest refers to the club's nickname, Doonhamers (literally 'down homers').

From here there are short, open terraces on either side of the stand, and to the right an open bank at the Terregles Street End. As is common at Scottish grounds, the terracing is angled to improve viewing from the sides.

To the left is the covered Glasgow Street End, which used to be capped by a tall half-time scoreboard. The cover is unusual, with brick walls on three sides and, like the Grandstand, one trunk-like steel roof support. Though simple in design the cover has the solidity and presence of a much more substantial ground.

Opposite the Grandstand is the now almost dilapidated but intimate Bull Shed, with old timber and ash terracing worn smooth by time and a rotting corrugated roof whose chief value is its overhanging front which carries advertising. The building of the new leisure centre will sweep away this small stand and confirm the club's wisdom in buying land when money was available and then refusing to sell it for short-term gain.

Together with the supermarket development, this new centre will ensure that Palmerston Park lives up well to the club's name; a modest palace for the Queen which the citizenry of the South can enjoy for a long time to come. Long will they reign as a result.

·STRANRAER·

Previous Grounds

Third oldest club in the Scottish League, Stranraer started in 1870 at Rephad before moving to Ladies Walk, where crowds would sneak a view from the road. In 1896 the club moved to the Bowling Green, then to Sandmill and on to the Trotting Track, now King George V Park. Their wanderings continued to the Recreation Ground and back to the Bowling Green, where again there were so many onlookers from the road it was suggested they be photographed to shame them. Stranraer returned to Rephad before a final move in 1907.

Stair Park

As the park had been bequeathed to the town by the Earl of Stair in 1905 the council opposed Stranraer enclosing their pitch. A Pavilion was built in 1909 (a prerequisite for SFA membership) and the council finally relented a year later, although there were still protests when the fence went up. In 1911 the pitch was moved nearer the railway and the Pavilion shifted bodily into position.

Uncertain times ensued; the ground was closed after a pitch invasion and for a while Stranraer shared the ground with a village side, Kirkcolm.

Stair Park's development began in the early 1930s. Banking was raised and the present Grandstand built by the council at a cost of £3000. While work was in progress Stranraer played across the London Road at the Transit Camp, also known as Westwood, where now there are rugby pitches. Poor accommodation almost jeopardized their SFA membership until a canny official persuaded the authorities that there was adequate changing room in Stair Park's tennis pavilion. Judge for yourself.

Stair Park was reopened in June 1932 with a friendly v. Ayr, and as the team's fortunes fluctuated gates went from 100 to the record 6673 who saw Rangers' visit in the Scottish Cup 1st Round on 24 January 1948. League football arrived in 1955 and although gates rose to 3000 there was talk of returning to Westwood. The building of a terrace cover indicated their resolve to stay.

Stair Park staged an amateur international in 1970 and in August 1981 became the last British League ground to switch on floodlights, in a League Cup tie v. Albion Rovers. Before 1985 its capacity of 5500, including 500 seats, made it the smallest League venue in Britain. The current limit is 4250 pending safety work.

Ground Description

Nearer to Belfast than Glasgow, Stair Park is a veritable outpost of the League, in a town where most traffic heads for the Larne ferry. Approach to the ground is through a public park, an iron bandstand

Stair Park, a veritable outpost

marking the entrance. The 20-yard long wooden Grandstand is surrounded by grass, and with blue facings and blue bench seats – for directors too – is basic but homely. A few feet behind runs the main Glasgow line bearing Sealink passengers past a forlorn collection of derelict railway sheds.

From the stand, to the left is the open Town End, a narrow cinder path lined by a brick wall. Behind is a training pitch. Opposite is the 30-yard long terrace cover called the Shed, or Wee Stand, with the park behind, and to the right is the open Rephad End, a grass bank lined by trees. Four floodlight poles line each side of the pitch, which is surrounded by a black cinder track and undulates as if in harmony with the low hills on the horizon.

The only barriers on view surround the perimeter, but these could hardly stop regular incursions by a grey rabbit which became quite a favourite during games in 1986. Perhaps it embodied the Earl of Stair's spirit, making sure the ground was still open to all.

·AYR UNITED·

Previous Grounds

Ayr FC started at Beresford Park, which though central had the disadvantage of being requisitioned for an annual cattle show. When an important friendly v. Aston Villa clashed with the show in 1888 Ayr moved to Somerset Park. From 1903–04 and 1906–10 the town had two Second Division teams; the more successful Ayr at Somerset Park and amateurs Ayr Parkhouse at Beresford Park, until in 1910 the two amalgamated as Ayr United with Somerset Park as home. Being closer to the station, however, when travel restrictions and early kick-offs were introduced during the First World War, Beresford Park was used. It was finally taken over in 1926 by the railway company who owned it. The site later became an ice rink and is now covered by a supermarket. Parkhouse Street and Beresford Terrace mark its location.

Somerset Park

When Ayr FC arrived in 1888 the park was described as 'the ungrazed lands of Hawkhill' in 'a remote corner of the globe'. The pitch was laid on a north to south axis and one report tells of how a stand collapsed, without serious injury, mainly because it was regularly dismantled for use at the cattle show.

In 1896 the club shifted the pitch 45 degrees and built a tarmac cycle track, and in 1919 there was an attempt to negotiate a lease on the Oval in Dam Park. Only when this failed did United begin to develop Somerset Park (in August 1972 United played two League Cup matches at the Oval, which has a small stand and an athletics track, when Somerset Park's new pitch was not yet ready).

In 1920 they bought the ground for £2500 and in 1924, after a good Cup run, revamped it entirely. The cycle track was removed, the pitch shifted a second time to its present east–west axis, the north side terraced to accommodate 10 000 and the present Main Stand built. While work was in progress United returned to Beresford Park for a few matches. New Somerset Park was opened on 13 September 1924 with great pomp, the chairman's wife cutting the ribbon.

In 1929 the newly formed supporters' club started to raise money for a roof over the Railway End, and as Carrick Hill relates in his *Ayr United Story* (to which I am indebted) the club divided into sections for men and women. The newly-covered terrace was opened in October 1933 by the SFA President; the women had donated £130 and the men £230. Two years later on their 25th Anniversary four leaded windows depicting local scenes were installed in the boardroom (an idea which perhaps led to Preston following suit a few months later).

So favourable is the Ayrshire climate that the first

Somerset Park – an honest enclosure

match postponed because of pitch conditions was not until 1939. On one occasion in 1958 Somerset Park was the only ground playable in Scotland, and for a short time after the Second World War Morton used the ground while Cappielow Park's pitch was being restored.

United's highest gate came forty-five years to the day after the ground was reopened, on 13 September 1969, when 25 225 saw a League match v. Rangers. But despite First Division status Ayr still had no floodlights. These, costing £20 000, were belatedly switched on for a friendly v. Newcastle on 18 November 1970, after careful consultation because of the ground's proximity to Prestwick Airport. Ten months later the Somerset Road End cover, which cost £12 000, was opened.

Somerset Park was among the first of the Scottish grounds to be designated under the 1975 Safety of Sports Grounds Act and now has a reduced capacity of 18 500, including 1200 seats.

Ground Description

In a coastal resort surrounded by stunning scenery, the football ground almost inevitably finds itself amid grimy railway sidings and factories. A background rumble of diesel engines is thus enjoined by the calls of seagulls and the roar of an occasional jet approaching Prestwick.

Somerset Park itself is a spotless, compact enclosure. The 70-yard long Main Stand, which backs onto a car park, is clad in red corrugated iron and, unusually, has a chimney in the centre of the frontage. Inside it is as intimate and unfussy as the day it was opened, with a high black balcony wall in front of a narrow paddock and bench seating flanking a block of red and black plastic seats. Externally the pitched roof is weathered like old corduroy but inside is, unusually, panelled red and grey.

From here, to the left is the covered Railway End. Its simple white roof and perimeter wall stand in pleasing contrast to the darker tones around. A gasometer peeps over the end, which is backed by railway sidings.

Opposite is the open North Terrace, higher to its right and topped by an old-fashioned half-time scoreboard. The cinders on the slopes behind this terrace are as black as the players' shorts. A disused foundry backs onto the terrace.

To the right is the covered Somerset Road End, an exceptionally neat terrace with new black and white barriers and clean black steelwork. Each barrier at the ground has a number, a useful aid when it comes to testing 10 per cent of the total each year, as required by the Safety of Sports Grounds Act.

Only three grounds share Somerset Park's layout of three covers with one open side (Brighton, Peterborough and Lincoln). Otherwise the ground is exactly as one might expect for a team nicknamed 'the Honest Men'; nicely self-contained, a touch old-fashioned but extremely trim.

·KILMARNOCK·

Previous Grounds

Originally formed as a cricket club, Kilmarnock started playing rugby in 1869 and football in 1873 (as founder members of the SFA). Their first soccer matches were at Wards Park, where Dundonald Road and South Hamilton Street are now situated, near the present ground. Months later they moved to the Grange, by Irvine Road, rental consisting of one bag of meal to the farmer, who apparently told the players that his grass would be all the better for being trampled down a bit. But for the second game he demanded £8, a huge sum considering their previous ground cost only £3 for six months. After three years the footballers moved to Holm Quarry, behind the present Electricity Board offices, but a dispute with cricketers soon had them back near Dundonald Road, on a site now occupied by Charles Street. Also called Rugby Park, one of the earliest and least successful floodlit games was staged there on 8 November 1878 (see Floodlights). Better remembered was Scotland's 5-2 win over Wales at the ground in March 1894.

Rugby Park

The ground Kilmarnock built on their election to Division One was on the same open site as the first Rugby Park but with the pitch moved slightly. A new barrel-roofed stand with semi-circular gable was erected and the first match on 26 August 1899 v. Celtic attracted 11 000.

A second international v. Wales took place in 1910 and in 1914 Kilmarnock spent £1600 on extending the stand and increasing the capacity to 20 000. By 1935 that figure had risen to 32 000 and a cover, since dubbed the Johnny Walker cover (after the roof advertisement), was built over one half of the South Terrace.

The Second World War brought mayhem when the army converted Rugby Park into an oil and coal storage depot, because of its proximity to a railway line. Large storage tanks on concrete bases were sunk into the pitch, with fire trenches dug around them.

After the war the pitch had to be relaid twice to restore the damage but Kilmarnock never gained compensation. They did however receive help from Italian POWs, who built up the North Terrace. Floodlights arrived in October 1953, when 16 000 saw one of the first appearances of Manchester United's Busby Babes.

The period of Kilmarnock's full-time professionalism between 1959–71 brought the club its greatest success. The East Enclosure roof had been built in 1958 and four years later work on the present Main Stand began, its structure being formed over the old stand. The existing floodlight gantries also date from

this period, which featured Rugby Park's highest gate of 34 246 for a League Cup tie v. Rangers in August 1963.

Four times Kilmarnock finished as runners-up in those years, until in 1965 the club won its first Championship. But a year later signalled the end of another era at Rugby Park with the death of the ground's most unusual inhabitant.

Wilma was the third and last sheep Kilmarnock had nurtured as a mascot and, although locked up during games, she and her predecessors, Ruby and Angus (who had a predilection for nibbling filter tips and fences), enjoyed the freedom of Rugby Park's extensive 13 acres.

Despite its scale Rugby Park's capacity has been almost halved to 17 500, including 4090 seats but alas, not one sheep.

Ground Description

With its curious floodlight gantries hidden amid the low rooves of genteel suburbia, Rugby Park is no easy ground to find. Yet it is one of the few really expansive grounds still in use.

Open space greets the visitor at each entrance, with several acres of grass and a car park lying behind the South Terrace. Lesser Rugby Park, as the training area is known, backs onto the Kilmarnock to Ayr railway line and a large open area formerly covered in sidings. Close scrutiny of the car park shows up some of the concrete bases surviving from the war.

The Main Stand is typical of its period, with grey roof sheeting, solid screen ends, brick facings and blue steelwork. Spotless inside and out, it has two sets of ornamental gate posts on either side of the narrow tunnel. On the slightly pitched roof four tripods, almost as tall as the stand itself, support gantries with four large lamps on each.

These unusual lights are mirrored opposite on the East Enclosure, whose roof stands high over the terracing, which though large has relatively few

Wide-open spaces at Rugby Park, with the curious Johnny Walker cover far left

A rare example of the traditional half-time scoreboard at Rugby Park

barriers. A high security mesh at one end makes viewing particularly irksome.

To the left of this enclosure is the curved open North Terrace, which has even fewer barriers. A traditional half-time scoreboard with a flagpole on one side and a bottle-shaped whisky advertisement on the other, sits on top of the terrace (whisky is Kilmarnock's best known product).

To the right is the half-covered South Terrace. Had sufficient funds been available no doubt the Johnny Walker roof would have covered the entire terrace, instead of which it stops abruptly in line with the penalty spot; a most disconcerting sight.

The sum of these parts would hardly draw one's breath were it not for the scale of Rugby Park. An oval-shaped running track around the pitch is a major factor, but so too is the accessibility of the pitch from the terraces. The perimeter railing seems more suited to a village ground than a major footballing venue. This, and the open nature of the surrounds is Rugby Park's great appeal, for although shaped for greatness the ground does not quite assert itself and barely intrudes upon the tranquility of its suburban confines.

·MORTON·

Previous Grounds

Morton formed in 1874 on a rough field now covered by Octavia Cottages on Grant Street, Greenock. Taking their name from Morton Terrace, where early members lived, in 1875 they found a better pitch at Garvel Park. Construction of the James Watt Dock (Watt was born in Greenock) forced another move in 1879 to Cappielow Park where, apart from the 1882–83 season which they spent at Ladyburn (later the site of a tram depot), they have remained ever since.

Cappielow Park

As Tom Robertson's informative history of the club relates, Cappielow Park was a busy place in its early years. The first clubhouse was well-used, its attractions including lectures by one Dr Cluckie (a quack doctor perhaps?). The ground hosted cycling, athletics and even women's football.

Together with neighbours Port Glasgow Athletic, Morton joined the League in 1893 and in 1896 became the first Scottish club to form a limited company (Small Heath were the first English club in 1888). In 1900 on election to Division One, a new pavilion and members' enclosure were opened, with the Provost kicking off a celebratory match, passing straight to Morton's opponents.

In March 1902 a capacity 12 000 crowd watched Scotland v. Wales. In August 1906 rather fewer were on hand to see the new pavilion burn down. It cost £195 to replace.

As at Kilmarnock, for a time Cappielow had ovine occupants when a local butcher offered lambs to every Morton goalscorer. Several used to graze on the pitch and one, Toby, became mascot until, in Robertson's words, he came 'to a sad and untimely end in the players' bath . . .'

Crowd violence, which had dogged the club over the years, returned to Morton during a Championship decider against Celtic in 1922, when Cappielow recorded its highest attendance of 23 500. Gates were broken down and a pitch invasion plus widespread gang fighting left the ground, parts of Greenock, several trains and dozens of participants badly scarred. Another outbreak closed the ground for two weeks in 1930.

On a more positive note, Cappielow became the first British ground to offer commentaries for the blind in 1923, while a year later the Scottish runner Eric Liddell, fresh from his Paris Olympics triumph, joined in an athletics meeting at the ground.

The present Main Stand was built in 1931 at a cost of £10 000 but by the late 1940s Cappielow was in a poor state. Drainage was so bad that midway through 1948–49 the pitch had to be dug up and Morton played their remaining home games at Ayr and St Mirren.

Cappielow Park, with the all-seated West Terrace overlooked by one of Greenock's shipbuilders' cranes

Floodlights were switched on for a match v. Third Lanark on 4 November 1958. They were mounted partly on a newly constructed roof over the Enclosure. Promotion to the Premier Division in 1978 enforced expenditure of around £500 000 on improvements, which included installing bench seats on the open West Terrace. This gave Cappielow a capacity of 16 600, including 6250 seats.

Ground Description

Tightly sandwiched between both the railway line and main road leading from Glasgow to Gourock, Cappielow Park has barely an inch to breathe. Whichever way one looks the surroundings intrude; rolling hills and tower blocks to the south and east, daunting ship yards and chimneys to the north. Seagulls flit over from the nearby Clyde while trains, cranes and lorries clank and trundle all around.

Inside, Cappielow is so tight and trim one wonders how it was ever possible to squeeze in an oval running track.

Backing onto a railway embankment which gives passengers an unobstructed glimpse of the pitch, the cosily enclosed Main Stand is all-seated and inexplicably, since Morton's colours are blue and white, decked entirely in claret and light blue. A busy section around the tunnel has two small canopies over the managers' benches, although in place of benches there are old cinema seats. Rather like The Dell, four upright banks of floodlights line the roof.

From here, to the right is the uncovered Sinclair Street End, behind which runs the only road access to Cappielow. Of note, apart from the half-time scoreboard and clock, are some robust, tubular barriers. Opposite is the covered Enclosure, which has a plain roof with three floodlight gantries. A slim pylon alongside bears the remaining lights.

To the left is the West Terrace, which with its neat rows of pale blue bench seating gives Cappielow a distinctly Continental air. To cover it would cost over £250 000 but in good weather it provides an excellent view of the ground and its surrounds. Locals dub this the Wee Dublin End, because in the late nineteenth century the area behind was filled with prefabricated bungalows used by Irish immigrants. A huge shipbuilder's crane towering behind helps explain why so many flocked to Greenock.

For compactness and atmosphere Cappielow can hardly be faulted; it is the archetypal British enclosure, tucked in among the very railways, roads and industries which gave the town life. Similar circumstances often make for grim stadiums. Cappielow however has a cheery air. Shipyards, seagulls and soccer are old acquaintances in Scotland.

·DUMBARTON·

Dumbarton's 'Postage Box' just before demolition – surely the smallest main stand at any League ground

Previous Grounds

Formed in 1872, Dumbarton began on Broadmeadow, now an industrial estate, before moving in 1873 to a field near Boghead Park, their home since 1879.

Boghead Park

One of three major clubs from the west in Scottish football's early days, along with Renton and Vale of Leven, Dumbarton's best spell came between 1881–97 when they won the League twice and the Cup once. Boghead's pitch, which really was a quagmire at first, then lay at a right-angle to the present pitch until 1913, when the first proper stand was built. Only 25 feet long, it housed dressing rooms and offices with 80 seats above. Dubbed the 'Hen House' or 'Postage Box' there has surely never been a smaller Main Stand at any League ground.

Another small stand was built opposite but this was destroyed by fire during a game in the 1930s, without injury, when a cigarette set alight straw stored underneath (the straw was used for greyhound racing, introduced, ironically, in an attempt to save the ailing club).

A brick-based stand took its place and no further developments took place until floodlights were switched on for a friendly v. Celtic on 23 January 1957. Five weeks later Boghead recorded its largest gate, 18 000, for a Scottish Cup tie v. Raith. Shortly after the club chose an unusual way to cover the Overwood Drive End. The supporters re-erected a disused railway platform roof from Turnberry station in Ayrshire. A few years later the larger Boghead End cover was put up.

With promotion in 1972 the Postage Box's days were numbered. With some regret it was finally demolished in May 1979, almost exactly 100 years after Dumbarton arrived at the ground, and in February 1980 the Secretary General of the Football League, Alan Hardaker, opened a new 300-seater stand in its place. Although still small the £300 000 cantilever stand incorporated every modern facility for players and spectators alike.

Promotion again to the Premier Division in 1984 brought designated status and a reduction in Boghead's capacity to 10 700, including 800 seats.

Ground Description

In contrast with Cappielow Park which lies immediately across the Clyde, Boghead Park is surrounded by scenic rural views. Indeed the loudest sound, apart from on match days of course, comes from cocks crowing at nearby Boghead Farm, whose former land the ground occupies.

The new Main Stand is short, square, modern and neatly turned out in brown cladding. It is a miniature cantilever with glass screen ends and an open paddock in front. To its immediate left is a smaller, basic white corrugated cover once known as the Bookies Stand, as this was their favourite spot in greyhound racing days.

To the far left is the Overwood Drive End. Unusually intricate steelwork gives a clue as to the roof's railway origins, especially the columns with ornate capitals and deep concrete plinths. Tall in the distance are the Kilpatrick Hills, dotted with firs and white houses like a Bavarian landscape.

Opposite the Main Stand is the Old Stand: a short, traditional construction with red corrugated sides, a white balcony wall and glass screen ends. In 1986 it was sorely in need of refurbishment to erase the work of both time and vandals. Again, behind this stand is a marvellous view, of the old Dumbuck basalt quarry, jutting out against the sky.

To the right is the curving Boghead End, the largest terrace at the ground, covered in the centre by a deep corrugated roof on white steel supports. Behind here one can see over the Clyde to the Renfrewshire hills beyond.

And if this panorama fails to raise the spirits a glimpse behind the Main Stand reveals the Luss Hills with Ben Lomond a hazy peak yonder. In such pleasant surrounds who needs a super stadium?

·CLYDEBANK·

Previous Grounds

Two clubs with the same name predate Clydebank. One played in Rutherglen. Another, better known, played in the League from 1914–31 at Clydeholm Park, Yoker, which was also a dog track (now a car park, it should not be confused with Holm Park where the junior side Yoker play).

The current Clydebank originate from Clydebank Juniors, formed in 1899. Until 1939 they played at Kilbowie Park on Livingstone Street. Players changed in Russell's Bake House nearby until in 1912 a Pavilion was opened in front of 3000 spectators for a game v. Celtic. The ground was on land now occupied by Clydebank's shopping centre.

New Kilbowie Park

Called 'their venture up the hill', New Kilbowie Park was bought by the junior club in 1937 for just £900. J. & R. Stutt of Paisley laid the pitch at a cost of £1000, although the turf was donated by Clydebank Town Council who were obviously keen to help since the town's former League club folded in 1931. A novelty at the new ground, in Scotland at least, was the installation of round goalposts.

Further help came from McAlpine's the builders, who provided 28 000 tons of rubble for the banking and built the fencing and a Pavilion for £2500, while the local Singer manufacturing company gave ash for a running track. Volunteers did the rest, and after considerable effort New Kilbowie Park was opened with great ceremony in 1939.

Two years later Clydebank was devastated. Its important shipyards were bombed over two nights by the Germans and although the football ground largely survived, its surroundings were irredeemably altered (stories that a huge bomb crater on the New Kilbowie pitch was later filled in with a double decker bus are not true, although this possibly happened at nearby Glenhead).

After the war, the Pavilion Stand went up in the mid 1950s and the banking was terraced but not until the Steedman brothers, Jack and Charles, became directors in 1965 did Clydebank Juniors progress to League membership. (The full story of how this was achieved after a 12-month merger with East Stirlingshire FC is told in my book *Soccer in the Dock, A History of British Football Scandals 1960–65*, Collins Willow 1985.)

Amid great controversy and a prolonged legal battle, East Stirling's floodlights and enclosure cover were transported to New Kilbowie, and, as E. S. Clydebank, the club played in the League during 1964–65. In February 1965 Sunderland came for the first floodlit match and in the same month New Kilbowie recorded its largest gate of 14 900 for a Cup tie v. Hibernian.

A few months later Clydebank lost the court case brought against them by East Stirling, who thus won back their separate identity, and the following season saw Clydebank return to junior football. The club finally entered the League in its own right in 1966.

New Kilbowie developed rapidly. The Bankies Social Club, overlooking the pitch, was opened in December 1966. Next to it, a few years later, a small stand was erected and remarkably, in 1977, the team reached the Premier Division. At this point another stand – dubbed the Davie Cooper Stand, since his transfer to Rangers raised the money – was built next to the Pavilion Stand and Clydebank took the major step of converting New Kilbowie into an all-seated ground.

At that time Premier Division grounds had to be designated under the Safety of Sports Grounds Act only if their capacity was over 10 000 (the rules have changed since). By installing bench seats, which was in any case cheaper than revamping the terraces, the capacity dropped to 9950 and further expenditure was avoided. Even so these and other safety improvements have cost £350 000 and although the ground has since been designated anyway, there is no doubt that the conversion has been successful.

Ground Description

In a town so dislocated by bombs, planners and declining industry, New Kilbowie Park provides a welcome point of focus. Tucked into the side of a slight rise it is bordered by a railway line to the south, a main road to the east and a council housing estate to the north.

Ironically these houses replaced the dark, brooding tenements which once overshadowed the ground, prompting Jack Steedman to say during the 1965 court case, 'You need black tenements for football supporters, not delightful houses . . .'

Starting at the ground's main entrance, the Bankies Social Club, a square unattractive two-storey block, sits in a corner behind the west goal. Although the pitch is clearly visible from here, by law the club must draw the curtains two hours before and after kick-off to prevent spectators drinking during games.

To the immediate right, also behind the goal is a 30-yard long stand with a distinctive yellow roof and yellow bucket seats. The goalposts, incidentally, are the old-fashioned square variety. Perhaps the new-fangled round ones in 1939 went towards the war effort.

Along the touchline to the right is the so-called Davie Cooper Stand, about 25 yards long with a plain roof and red and yellow seats. Next to this, on the half-way line is the Pavilion Stand, a box-like structure which houses changing rooms and a seated enclosure for club officials.

Behind, trains from Glasgow gain a perfect view of the ground. In the distance Clydebank's surviving

Cranes and pylons fill the skyline at Clydebank, where bench seats now fill the terracing

shipbuilders' cranes point up at a steady flow of aircraft descending towards Glasgow Airport two miles away.

Opposite the Bankies Club is the open Montrose Road End. A short stretch of this road offers a clear view of the pitch. Not surprisingly, on match days a policeman is usually on hand to move on lingering pedestrians.

This end and the covered Kilbowie Road side to the left is lined by bench seats. When the ground was converted to all-seating there was no protest at all from fans and this may well be due to the fact that, unlike tip-up seating as installed at Highfield Road, bench seating allows the hardy to continue standing; it also allows relatively free movement (see Aberdeen). The Kilbowie Road roof, bought from East Stirling in 1964, covers the rear half of the seats and its sloping fascia is lined with colourful advertisements.

With six floodlight pylons, each with the archetypal Scottish leaning gantries, Kilbowie Park has a pleasing compactness. Indeed the pitch is only 68 yards wide. Rather like Oxford, Clydebank have come a long way in a short time, building piecemeal as they progressed. In doing so they have also, however motivated originally, proved that a small ground can be all-seated without detracting from the vital relationship between the players and the spectators. Other clubs might well take note.

·ST MIRREN·

Previous Grounds

St Mirren's cricket and rugby players first tried football in 1877 at Shortroods, a field just north of the current ground. It is hard to pinpoint their movements for the next two seasons, but by 1881 they were based at Thistle Park, Greenhill (which may also have been called Abingdon Park) until in 1883 they moved to a nearby field at Westmarch. This new ground had a racing and cycling track, staged a military tournament and, according to Willie Hunter's club history, an early display of parachute jumping by one Prof. Higgins. Until 1888 however the players had to change at the nearby public baths. In 1890 St Mirren and their Paisley neighbours Abercorn were founder members of the League and in 1895, with Westmarch's facilities proving unsatisfactory, the club moved a few hundred yards east to Love Street.

Love Street

The new ground was far from ideal. Next door was a slaughterhouse – the club earned £5 a year for grazing rights – the ground was too small, had poor access, a high rent and, perhaps most oddly of all, a cottage actually inside the ground. At one point the Scottish goalkeeper John Patrick lived there.

St Mirren considered buying Shortroods but with only £500 in the bank the asking price of £4500 was beyond them. The club finally bought Love Street for £3900 and after effecting some improvements reopened the ground in August 1905, an event marred somewhat by St Mirren losing and a wall collapsing.

Over the following years terracing was raised by the usual method; inviting the public to dump rubbish, although a board meeting in 1921 heard that only 'clean rubbish' was to be allowed in future. On the growing banks, railway sleepers costing only 6d each were laid and in 1911 work began on a new Main Stand to replace the Pavilion. The stand took ten years to complete at a cost, together with a new pitch, of £30 000. It was opened in 1921, when the ground was announced as 'Greater Love Street' with a reported capacity of 70 000, a figure never tested – the record attendance is actually 47 438 for a League Cup match v. Celtic on 20 August 1949.

Life in Paisley was seldom easy, and in 1932 to raise cash greyhound-racing equipment was installed. A dog called St Mirren won on the first night but the experiment failed because of poor equipment and strong competition (an attempt to popularize

Love Street – plenty of good potting turf here

speedway at the ground also failed in the 1970s).

By 1933 the club were even trying to sell off bits of the pitch. 'Good potting turf' was advertised at 4s per cart.

In the more prosperous post-war era, a cover was built over the Enclosure in 1957 and, ignoring superstition, on Friday 13 February 1959 the club first switched on its floodlights during a Cup tie v. Peebles Rovers. (A 10-0 win set them on the road to victory at Hampden.) Little changed until 1977, when the ground was designated under the Safety of Sports Grounds Act.

St Mirren felt that the local authority's safety requirements had been too strict and they became the first club to appeal successfully against some of the conditions (see Safety). Neverthless roughly £1 million has been spent, with St Mirren being one of the first clubs to have used their entire allocation of FGIT grants.

Love Street's current capacity is 25 250, including only 1340 seats.

Ground Description

Rather like Hampden Park, at first glance it seems hard to appreciate how Love Street or, as it is known officially, St Mirren Park remains so basic after so much expenditure. For a premier club the ground particularly lacks sufficient seated accommodation.

The Main Stand, trim inside but drab outwardly, is 60 yards long astride the half-way line. A tall, traditional two-tier construction, it has an extended grey roof over the sides and front paddock, with glass screen ends and a high balcony wall covered by advertisements. Red, blue and grey seats, with grey criss-cross steel roof columns, contrast with the comparative simplicity of the black, white and grey interior.

To the immediate left is flat ground, to the immediate right is a disused section of terracing. This used to be known as Cairter's Corner, a favourite gathering spot for Paisley carters, who were apparently both noisy and noisome. A white flagpole stands behind the corner flag.

Beyond here is the open East Terrace, which has been levelled, reshaped parallel to the pitch and completely refurbished. As at Hampden, red brick walls and turnstiles line the rear, behind which a modernized concourse and car park lead to Love Street. The black and white barriers are numbered for safety testing.

A measure of the costs involved in improving terracing can be seen by contrasting this section with the disused section by the flagpole. Standards have improved enormously. One day it is hoped this end will be seated and covered.

Opposite the Main Stand is the Covered Enclosure with a corrugated pitched roof, high and light enough to make this side pleasantly airy. Again, a new brick wall and toilet block at the rear add to the new sense of orderliness.

To the left is the expansive, open West Terrace, whose curve shows how the ground was originally oval shaped. The terracing is cinder infill with concrete footings, backed by a large grass embankment.

There is, it has to be said, little to capture the eye. Love Street's pitch, if official statistics are to be believed, is a gigantic 120 × 80 yards, making it easily the largest of any League ground (see Pitches). But the ground is open without being impressive, old-fashioned in parts without retaining much character. Hardly lovable, Love Street is however typical of several once large grounds, trying to find new shape and purpose in a shrinking market. Greater Love Street, like Greater Hampden, has had to slim down and wise up.

·20·
GLASGOW

·PARTICK THISTLE·

Previous Grounds

Partick's first games in 1876 were at Kelvingrove, on a pitch behind the present art gallery. In 1881 the club moved to Jordanvale Park, which later became the Whiteinch tramway terminus. Two years later Muir Park, near Hamilton Crescent (venue of the first football international), was used until in 1885 the club returned to Whiteinch, to Inchview Park, former home of rivals Partick FC. Thistle's fifth home from 1891–1908 was Meadowside, on the banks of the Clyde, a ground initially intended to rival those of Rangers, Celtic and Queen's Park. A 750-seat Grandstand with integral dressing rooms was built for £200 (most Scottish grounds then had separate pavilions and stands) but as at Shrewsbury a boat had always to be on hand to fish out stray balls from the river.

Bigger boats were Glasgow's business, however, and in 1908 Partick were forced to leave Meadowside to make way for Henderson's Shipyard. As Ian Archer wrote in his affectionate centenary history *The Jags*, the parting shot on 1 May 1908 was an emotional affair:

'A small group of spectators gathered around the flagpole and, as the Union Jack was being hauled down for the last time, one of the band pulled it away from the steward and wrapped it around his body. He then started singing *Will Ye No Come Back Again*, and the rest of the group took up the chorus.'

In vain Thistle sought a new ground in their native Partick, until with their future in doubt Rangers offered the use of Ibrox. In fact during a disastrous 1908–09 the club played 'home' games on all Glasgow's League grounds, finishing bottom of the First Division with only 8 points from 34 games.

Firhill Park

No ground suffered such a disastrous inauguration as Firhill. After an appalling season and heavy financial losses, miserable months of searching ended at some 'riggy waste-ground' in Maryhill, owned by the Caledonian Railway Company. But Partick's problems were not quite over.

The new ground was due to open on 21 August 1909, but when thousands arrived for the first match, v. Queen's Park, they found the gates closed and guarded by police. The words 'Match Off' had been hastily daubed in red paint on the doors and while most disgruntled fans left in search of other matches in the city (never a problem in Glasgow), hundreds hung around outside voicing their anger.

Inside the ground, according to *The Weekly News*, 'an amazed and indignant crowd of players, officials and friends' gathered. 'The refreshments, which were liberally provided in a large marquee, were consumed by the guests, who protested instead of congratulated.'

The butt of their anger was the Chief Inspector of the Office of Public Works, whose decision that the ground was unsuitable for the public reached Firhill only two hours before kick-off. Although the Grandstand was apparently still a mere skeleton, his main objection had been the state of the banking, for which no planning warrant had been applied.

One publication, the *Scottish Referee*, called the debacle 'unparalleled in the history of British sport', and it took a further month's work before Firhill was fit for the public.

After this unfortunate beginning, the 1920s were busy years at the ground. Apart from success in the Cup, Partick's record crowd of 49 838 attended a League match v. Rangers in February 1922 and on 13 August 1927 the club opened a new 6000-seat Main Stand. Its erection, together with terrace improvements, cost Partick £60 000, a considerable sum for the period.

This time there were no delays and in February 1928, to celebrate Firhill's transformation, Partick hosted an international v. Ireland, attended by 54 728, the ground's largest ever crowd.

Firhill's Main Stand – in the style of Leitch

A few years later greyhound racing was introduced, while on the footballing side further success waited until the 1950s. Three League Cup Final appearances helped towards the cost of a cover on the Enclosure and the installation of floodlights, first switched on for a friendly v. Spurs in November 1955.

Since then there has been much talk of revamping Firhill, including plans in 1977 for a £2 million sports centre based at the ground and the adjacent Firhill canal basin. But the only major change came with the announcement that from 1986–87 Clyde FC, who had been forced to vacate Shawfield, would share Firhill.

Thus Partick, who had once depended on the likes of Clyde for hospitality during the 1908–09 season, became the first Scottish club in modern times to implement a ground-sharing scheme. Firhill's current capacity is considerably reduced from its original 50 000 capacity with 6000 seats to 20 500 including 2900 seats.

Ground Description

That Firhill has survived while so much of its surrounds have been demolished is in itself remarkable. It was said that the best view of the pitch used to be from neighbouring tenements; few survive today. Facing the ground's main entrance is wasteground, echoed by the fading browns and greys of Firhill's façade. A decorative pediment above the main door gives the date 1927. Inside the stand is the £5500 cheque which the club handed over to buy the ground some seventy years ago.

The two-tier Main Stand built on rising ground with a pointed gable was the work of D. Mills Duncan, a Glasgow architect who designed Celtic's South Stand two years later and was obviously familiar with Leitch's work. It quite dominates the ground but has lost something of its original purity; the South End has a blocked off section on stilts, formerly a club (destroyed by fire in 1975), while

seven floodlight gantries along the roof rather detract from the gable.

From here, to the left is the North Park Street End, an open curved terrace cut into the rising ground. This end used to be covered. Worth noting is a large mural, painted in Partick's colours, visible from this end on a nearby house.

Opposite the Main Stand is the Covered Enclosure, also built into the hillside. The pitch is actually 8 feet below the foot of this terrace. A high, grey perimeter wall is divided from the pitch on this side by a track whereas, unusually, the semi-circles of turf at both ends extend right up to the perimeter wall. The pitch is only 106 yards long, making it one of the shortest in Scotland.

Beyond the Enclosure is Firhill Basin, a section of the Forth and Clyde Canal, once an industrial lifeline, now used for pleasure. Drab housing and grassland rise up from the basin. To the right is the Town End, an open terrace behind which more distinctive high-rise blocks with blue and red facings tower in the distance.

Almost stripped of the community in which it grew, Firhill can seem a soulless environment. It lacks colour, is far too big for most club requirements and needs to be modernized in a similar fashion to Love Street. There was renewed hope when Clyde moved to Firhill in 1986 and Partick applied for permission to lay an artificial pitch, in an attempt to transform the ground into the inner-city sports and leisure centre which seemed to represent its best bet for the future. But permission was withheld and then in 1987 Clyde announced that they would be moving back to Shawfield the following year. Firhill was back where it started.

·CLYDE·

Previous Grounds

Barrowfield Park, near the banks of the Clyde, provided the club's first home and thus probably its name in 1877. The site of Barrowfield is thought to be on French Street, near Rutherglen Bridge. After joining the League in 1891 facilities there proved inadequate so in 1898 Clyde moved just south of the river to Shawfield.

Shawfield

A trotting track with vast potential, Shawfield was equidistant between Hampden and Celtic, on the main road from Rutherglen to Glasgow. A 1500-seater stand was built and thousands of tiles were put down to aid pitch drainage, but when 10 000 spectators came to the opening match v. Celtic, according to Tom Greig's history of the club, they saw bare turf and no roof on the stand. Plans to create a 100 000-capacity stadium at Shawfield were forgotten when within
a few years Ibrox, then Third Hampden were developed.

Shawfield was always a multi-purpose venue, staging football, athletics and boxing. One World flyweight bout in the 1930s attracted 36 000 spectators. There is however some doubt as to Clyde's record gate, which is given as either 52 000 v. Rangers in November 1908 or 48 500 v. Celtic in February 1914.

Financial problems were a constant burden to Clyde and, in common with Bristol Rovers, greyhound racing saved the stadium but ended up being the cause of the club's departure.

The story begins in 1926 when Britain's first greyhound racing company from Belle Vue, Manchester offered Clyde £2000 a year plus a share of receipts in return for the right to stage this new sport. The club wanted to accept but a clause in the original lease specifically excluded dog racing.

Clyde spent the next six years trying to buy Shawfield while the chairman, having toured some of England's new greyhound stadiums, persuaded his fellow directors to set up an independent greyhound racing company. Shawfield was the perfect venue; close to areas of dense population but with no immediate residential neighbours to complain about night-time meetings (this was before regular floodlit matches).

A small crowd watched the first races in November 1932 but a shrewd move by the chairman increased support soon after. He made Shawfield appear more respectable to wealthier punters by parking extra cars outside on greyhound nights.

Shawfield quickly assumed all the trappings of a greyhound stadium; a massive Tote board dominated one end, lights and a track separated the terraces from the football pitch, while betting booths, social clubs and restaurants sprang up within viewing distance of the track. So successful was the venture that in 1935 the Shawfield Greyhound Racing Company took over the stadium's ownership and from then on Clyde were tenants again.

Still they had their moments. Two Cup wins in the 1950s helped popularize a club already well-known for the exploits of its jocular trainer Mattha Gemmell. And Shawfield was certainly well-appointed. Two sides of paved terracing were covered, a third side had a Main Stand, built after a fire had destroyed the original in 1917. Shawfield's floodlights were switched on for a friendly v. Huddersfield on 30 March 1954 and although safety measures limited the stand to only 900 seats (excluding restaurant facilities), the ground had a capacity of 22 000 in later years.

Clyde always knew they might have to move. They

Shawfield: gone to the dogs but now back in harness

considered East Kilbride in 1966, and four years later came very close to taking over Douglas Park (see Hamilton).

But in 1971 the Greyhound Racing Association bought Shawfield and in November 1984, after years of running at a loss, the GRA decided to sell up to developers. Clyde, unable to afford the asking price of £750 000, were given 18-months' notice. Like Charlton, the supporters simply had no choice.

Clyde looked seriously at two options. The first was Lesser Hampden. With negotiations apparently advanced, Queen's Park finally felt the ground was already used to its capacity by their junior and local teams. They may have been swayed by the possible sale of Lesser Hampden for a shopping development, or by the threat to their amateur status which Clyde's arrival might have represented.

After Lesser Hampden, Clyde looked at Rosebury Park, a small undeveloped ground near Shawfield on Toryglen Street. This belongs to Glasgow's Education Department and is used for schools' matches (Frank McLintock played here as a boy). To bring it up to League standards would probably have cost no less than £500 000 (although FGIT grants would have helped), and although it was in many respects a perfect venue – a good pitch nicely enclosed with evenly banked turf terracing – the council proved unwilling to lose the facility.

In the meantime Clyde made tentative arrangements to share Partick Thistle's ground should work on Rosebury Park begin. So when the move fell through it was decided to make a lengthier arrangement at Firhill. Thus Clyde and Partick became the first clubs in Scotland to agree on ground sharing.

It was as controversial an agreement as Charlton's move to Palace in 1985. Clyde and Partick were fierce rivals, and Clyde's support came from south of the river, whereas Firhill, some five miles distant by road, was north. Still, Clyde had no choice.

Shawfield in 1986 was for the most part a forlorn prospect, with overgrown terraces, crumbling roofs and antiquated stands. Since they were only tenants Clyde had asked for no grants from FGIT (Meadowbank are the only other club not to have received such aid) and ultimately their biggest asset was the floodlight pylons, which were sold for community use.

What was thought to be Clyde's final match at Shawfield was on 28 April 1986, when a crowd of 1200 saw Alloa beaten 4-2. Then the final greyhound race was run the following October and 88 years of history seemed to be at an end. But the Bully Wee weren't finished yet, because when the GRA couldn't get planning permission for their own redevelopment scheme they sold the site to a consortium in 1987 for £750 000. The new owners applied a coat of paint or two, brought the dogs back in June 1987 and Clyde were due back from Firhill in August 1988, after a two-year absence. Against all the odds, Bully Wee had beaten off the Big Bully developers. Who other than Mattha Gemmell would have bet on that?

⬦RANGERS⬦

Previous Grounds

Rangers predate rivals Celtic by sixteen years. Beginning on Glasgow Green in 1872, where they had to hire small boys to guard their pitch on match day mornings, they moved to Burnbank in 1875 and to Kinning Park, south of the River Clyde, a year later. There it was amidst the shipyards that Rangers began to attract the largest support of any Glasgow team. Kinning Park is mainly remembered for being the first ground to have its gates locked before a match. A crowd of 10 000 squeezed in to watch the 1881 Cup Final between Queen's Park and Dumbarton, but after losing 2-1 Dumbarton protested that spectators had obstructed the touchlines. The gates were locked again before the replay and this time with only 7000 watching Dumbarton lost 3-1.

Forced to leave in 1887 Rangers soon found another ground a mile to the west. This ground, next door to the site of the present one, was named Ibrox Park after the district, and was opened on 20 August 1887 with a friendly v. Preston North End.

A cake and wine banquet was held for a large number of important guests and, as Bill Murray writes in his study of Rangers and Celtic (*The Old Firm*, John Donald 1984), such was the demand for a sketch of the new ground that the *Scottish Umpire* magazine had to print an extra 3000 copies. Matters became less than cordial when a disgruntled minority among the 15 000 crowd, which included a 'large sprinkling of ladies from the fashionable suburbs of Ibrox', launched the first of many recorded pitch invasions after the Old Invincibles had gone 8-1 up.

First Ibrox was largely the work of Fred Braby and Co. of Petershill Road, Glasgow (near where Cowlairs played). It had an open stand with 1200 seats and an ornate one-storey Pavilion rather like a small chapel or railway station. Braby's corrugated iron fences were advertised as being 'unclimbable' but at that first match a railing proved to be breakable, causing a spillage of spectators onto the pitch.

Ibrox established itself rapidly. Three internationals were staged and in February 1890 the ground hosted the Scottish Cup Final and replay between Queen's Park and Vale of Leven.

But First Ibrox proved too small for Rangers' growing popularity and in 1899, after the unprecedented feat of winning the League without dropping a point, Rangers became a limited liability company and developed their new ground on the adjacent site. Gradually the new ground started to dwarf First Ibrox, whose stands were already partially dismantled by the time the last match was played there, on 9 December 1899. 'A playing field,' commented the *Scottish Umpire* stoically, 'becomes like a friend, and the wrench at parting is a bit stiff.'

Ibrox Park before redevelopment. The notorious Stairway 13 is bottom right. Compare this with the picture in the colour section

Ibrox Park

The Ibrox which Rangers developed between 1899 and 1978 bears no resemblance to the ground today. When first opened the ground held 40 000 and had a two-storey Pavilion and a substantial stand with semi-circular central gable alongside (pictorial evidence suggests that perhaps the roof of this stand might have been re-erected from First Ibrox).

The inaugural match was v. Hearts in Division One on 30 December 1899. There was a drizzle, but Rangers were top of the League, unbeaten and apparently well-prepared for the new century.

Yet the ground's early days were marked by tragedy. In an attempt to match Celtic, who staged most of Scotland's internationals between 1893 and 1901, in 1902 Rangers expanded Ibrox by erecting wooden terracing at the West End, built up on a tall iron and wood framework.

When this gave way with disastrous results during the Scotland v. England match on 5 April 1902 (see Safety), it was chilling proof that the contribution of companies like Braby and Co. with their simplistic designs and materials were over and that it was time for experienced engineers to introduce more solid methods of construction. Archibald Leitch, who had already worked with Celtic and was currently engaged at Hampden Park, was such an engineer.

Leitch became closely involved with Ibrox after the disaster. It was apparent that solid earth banking was the only safe way to expand and so, having risen to a capacity of 68 000 for the ill-fated international, Ibrox was rebuilt on safer lines by 1905 to hold 25 000. Within five years further work enlarged the limit to 63 000, as Ibrox took on the shape it was to have until 1978.

This was, in common with Leitch's designs at Parkhead, Hampden and Stamford Bridge, elliptical in plan with three open sides. Ibrox gradually took over from Celtic as a venue for athletics and cycling, and in September 1917 the ground staged a Royal Investiture attended by George V.

In 1928 Rangers achieved their first League and Cup double and began building the grandest stand in Britain. With both money and space in abundance Rangers were able to give Leitch the chance to surpass himself, and the end result, opened on 1 January 1929, probably represented the pinnacle of his career. Although superficially similar to his previous stands at Goodison Park and Fratton Park, the 10 000-seat construction for Rangers was the most luxurious of them all (described below).

Ibrox continued to expand until on 2 January 1939 it proved able to hold 118 567 spectators for the annual New Year duel with Celtic, a record for any League match held in Britain. Thus Ibrox had outgrown Parkhead by some 26 000 and was second only to Hampden as the biggest ground in Britain. It was also the first Glasgow ground to have floodlights, switched on officially for the then annual friendly v. Arsenal on 8 December 1953. The lights were also used during a League match v. St Mirren but because the authorities had not yet sanctioned the use of floodlights, the referee ordered them to be switched off immediately. Ibrox still had the honour of officially staging the first Scottish League match under lights when they played Queen of the South on 7 March 1956. The visitors were obviously dazzled because they lost 8-0.

By the late 1960s Ibrox had two covers over the terracing. On the North Side a smaller barrel roof cover had been expanded and then doubled in depth to create a double-pitched roof. In 1966 the East End was also covered, so that Ibrox really did look remarkably similar to Parkhead, although its lights were mounted along the stand roofs rather than on pylons.

Ibrox's safety record however was worse than any other ground in Britain. In September 1961 two spectators died when a barrier collapsed on the notorious Stairway 13 in the north east corner. Two further incidents on the stairway in 1967 and 1969 led to 32 further injuries, and on 2 January 1971 the second Ibrox disaster resulted in the deaths of 66 people, making it the worst in British football history. For a while even the intense rivalry of Old Firm fans was shelved as they collectively mourned the dead.

Whatever the causes of the tragedy and its later consequences nationally (see Safety), Ibrox would never be the same again. An enquiry found that in view of the previous accidents Rangers had been lax over safety matters, while the club claimed that it had spent large sums on improvements.

Studies after the event led to a few changes on the Stairway itself, and in 1973 at a cost of £70 000, 9000 bench seats were installed on the North Enclosure, which was then renamed the Centenary Stand (even though that anniversary should have been celebrated a year before). But in 1977, when the ground's capacity was cut from 100 000 to 65 000, the club finally embarked on a complete redesign of the ground. The spectre of Stairway 13 was to be eradicated, once and for all.

Rangers rejected piecemeal development such as had plagued other grounds. They refused to compromise in size or materials. Ibrox was to have a new shape, three new stands and enough office and showroom space to create an income independent of football. And instead of luxury accommodation for a minority, Rangers opted for maximum comfort and an unimpeded view for all.

First revealed in November 1977, the remodelling was said to have been based on the Dortmund Stadium in West Germany. Costs were estimated at £6 million, and the work was to be planned so meticulously that players and fans would suffer a minimum of disruption. A vital link with the past was the retention of Leitch's South Stand as the centrepiece

of the ground, and a portion of terracing in its Enclosure was retained for those supporters who preferred to stand.

No other club in Britain could have afforded such a massive redevelopment. The income from Rangers' pools however, the most extensive in Britain, was sufficient to risk what turned out to be a staggering outlay of £10 million over a three-year period. At the same time British Steel, who supplied the new stands' infrastructure, saw the project as a prestige development.

Phase one of the mammoth operation began in August 1978 with the removal of the east and west terracing, including all vestiges of Stairway 13. Perhaps the removal of this, more than any other section of the ground, was the most symbolic departure from the past.

Rangers bought a disused railway cutting in which to dump the surplus material and on the flattened land built two identical stands each seating 7500, parallel with the touchlines. Thus the ground's elliptical shape disappeared.

The method of stand construction was similar to that used at Villa Park and Carrow Road, with a goalpost frame 78 metres wide supporting the roof. The area behind each stand, once taken up by the banking, now became flat concourse areas for parking and pedestrians.

Phase Two began in August 1980 and involved the demolition of the Centenary Stand and its replacement by a longer version of the two end stands. This new North Stand holds 10 300 with a double-thick girder 110 metres long supporting the roof. This girder alone cost more than the entire roof built on Tottenham's new West Stand two years later.

Once finished with undersoil heating in 1981, the new Ibrox had a capacity of 45 000, of which only 9000 were standing.

Since then there have been a few additions. After years of resistance Ibrox finally succumbed to the lure of ground advertisements – Arsenal were among the last to give in south of the border – and, to help the flow of spectators before games, each turnstile has been linked to a central monitor. When each section of the ground is filled alarms sound and the public are advised to proceed to different turnstiles.

Rangers have even taken computer readings to determine which kind of supporter goes to which part of the stadium, in order to tailor their catering and ticketing policies accordingly. Closed-circuit television and computerized ticketing complete the ultra-modern set-up at the new Ibrox.

No ground in Britain has ever been transformed so comprehensively in such a short space of time. But painful as this was no doubt to many Ibrox regulars, it was certainly no more painful than the stigma which two major disasters had already attached to the ground. There simply had to be change, and Rangers were rich enough to make that change almost total.

Ground Description

Were an old-time Rangers fan to find himself at the main entrance on Edmiston Drive, he would find little change. Leitch's imposing red-brick façade, in mock neo-classical style with arched windows on upper and lower floors, square windows in between and pedimented windows at either end, still exudes prestige and power. On each corner is the club crest, in blue and gold mosaic, with the motto 'Ready' (echoing the Lion crest on the side of Aston Villa's Trinity Road Stand) and at each end is a large wrought-iron gateway in blue and white. The whole façade is due to become listed, such is its grandeur.

The old-time Rangers fan might still be oblivious to the changes within, even as he steps into the famous foyer to be greeted by the uniformed commissionaire – an Englishman by the name of Stanley Holloway. Decorated with potted plants, Art-Deco lamps, trophies and a huge oil painting of the Wee Blue Devil, Alan Morton (a Rangers hero of the 1920s), this entrance hall is one of the most imposing in football; as redolent of Leitch's era as Highbury's Marble Hall is of the 1930s.

The staircase, cleaned twice a day, leads up through dark, wood-panelled corridors to a stately boardroom, vast offices and a trophy room glinting with silverware. Like Highbury, this is not just a football stand but a small museum, a symbol of prestige.

Each dressing room is the size of a small gym with polished wooden benches and clothes hooks which had to be lowered some time ago because the club disliked so many players standing on the benches. The referee and linesmen have a changing room as large as that provided for whole teams at most grounds, and the route to the pitch passes a long shale practice area under the stand where players can train in bad weather and warm up before kick-off. It is a unique feature.

The rest of the South Stand is equally impressive. Despite strict safety precautions there are still 10 000 seats on the upper tier, with standing room for 8910 in the front enclosure. On the refurbished cream clad roof is a large press-box, flagpole in the centre and floodlights on each side. Similar to the now unused press-box on Tottenham's East Stand (both are pictured in the colour section), it used to be ornately castellated. Leitch was obviously fond of this Scottish motif because he also used it at Hampden.

But the feature which really marks this stand out as Leitch's work is the criss-cross balcony wall, as repeated at Fratton, Roker and Goodison Parks.

So far all this will have been familiar to our old Rangers fan. But once he turns his back and looks out onto the pitch he is in for a shock. To the left, to the right and straight ahead are three, awesome new stands. Gone is the oval track, gone are the high banks of terracing. These new stands are free-standing, with gaps in all four corners. Apparently

the cost of building round these corners would have been prohibitive, while the free flow of air helps dry the pitch, which is otherwise totally enclosed.

Rather than being left flat, each corner has been landscaped by shrub covered earth-banks around the stairways. Each new stand is faced in red brick, echoing the materials used by Leitch, and one is reminded of Aberdeen's tentative hope; better surroundings might lead to better behaviour.

Clean white facings line the three stands, each of them two-tiered with rows of red, yellow, orange, brown and blue seating. These colours can seem intrusive when there is a small attendance, but otherwise the stands cannot be faulted. They allow every one of their patrons an unimpeded view of the pitch within the recommended 90 metres optimum viewing distance (see Design).

From the South Stand, to the left is the Broomloan Stand on the site of the west terracing (where the first disaster occurred). Opposite is the North or Govan Stand, and to the right, where Stairway 13 used to be, is the Copland Road Stand, with the large Rangers social club behind.

Ibrox is not just a football ground. It has staged concerts and boxing matches. It has 24 000 square feet of office space rented out, and a 2000-square feet exhibition suite. Excluding the football club staff, approximately 300 people work at Ibrox during the week.

In common with most Rangers fans our old-timer would be shaken by this transformation, but in one way Ibrox has hardly changed at all. The lovingly preserved Edmiston Drive façade is still a mark of Rangers' mystique as a club, an organization and as a symbol of Scottish football. It still represents, whether true or not, a bastion of sectarianism in a changing world. Above all, Ibrox Park remains a ground founded upon wealth and conviction. Few grounds in Europe match its facilities, and few bear such distinction.

·QUEEN'S PARK·

Previous Grounds

Scotland's oldest club, Queen's Park, formed in July 1867, five years after England's oldest League club, Notts County. For the first six years the Queen's Park Recreation Ground, from which the club took its name, provided a home pitch. Here it was that the amateurs of Queen's Park pioneered the passing game and formed the basis of Scotland's first international teams.

In 1873 the club moved a few hundred yards to a pitch overlooked by Hampden Terrace, named after John Hampden, an English Parliamentarian in the Civil War.

The first Hampden Park was basic and, at £20 a year rent, cheap enough for such a consistently successful outfit. Queen's Park spent a further £21 on a clubhouse, although water was not laid on for the first year, and in 1876 built a Grandstand for £306. Two years later the club bought a Pavilion from the Caledonian Cricket Club.

But their tenure was short-lived. The rent rose to £100, and when work began in 1883 on the railway line between Mount Florida and Crosshill, Queen's Park decided to move. All that remains of First Hampden is a bowling club by the railway on Queen's Drive and Cathcart Road.

For one season Queen's Park played at Titwood Park, Clydesdale Cricket Club's ground (still used, off Titwood Road) until in October 1884, the Second Hampden Park on Mount Florida was ready. Only a few hundred yards from the first, this new ground had proper banking, a two-storey brick Pavilion, two open stands and a cinder track. One innovation was a wooden perimeter railing, in place of the usual but unreliable rope.

Although Queen's Park gradually lost their dominance of Scottish football, Second Hampden became the preferred venue for Cup Finals and staged the first ever all-ticket match, when 10 000 saw the ground's opening international fixture between Scotland and England on 15 March 1884.

Still on a short lease, Queen's Park hardly developed the ground further. Yet so concerned were they that Celtic's new ground had won the right to stage the profitable Scotland v. England fixture that in 1894 they offered Hampden free of charge. The offer was refused and, recognizing that their facilities were outdated, a few years later Queen's Park sought and found a permanent home, again only a short distance away.

Overlooked by the houses of Somerville Drive, the 12½-acre site was on offer at £850 an acre. A condition of sale was that streets and sewers had to be laid and Mall's Myre Burn be culverted. There was also a problem with old mine workings in the area.

In view of these difficulties Queen's Park offered £750 an acre and on 3 April 1900 settled at £800, even though they had less than £5000 in the bank at the time.

For a professional club such an outlay would have been a struggle; that Queen's Park could even contemplate such a purchase showed not only their status but also their desire not to fall behind the likes of Rangers and Celtic.

The Second Hampden Park was vacated at the end of the 1902–03 season, after which it was renamed New Cathkin Park and became home to Third Lanark (see Lost But Not Forgotten). Its layout is still clearly visible despite that club's demise in 1967.

Third Hampden Park c. 1904. Note the corrugated pay-boxes in the foreground and the two main stands, still to be linked by a central pavilion

Hampden Park

Completion of the Third Hampden Park in 1903 meant that Glasgow possessed the three finest football grounds in the world. Each was the work of Archibald Leitch, who repeated at the new Hampden the design and general oval-shaped format he executed at Ibrox and Celtic Park (and several other grounds subsequently – see Design).

One different feature at Hampden was the building of two separate stands along the south side to allow a Pavilion to be built in between. Vast open terraces on the three remaining sides were lined by barriers with one-inch thick wire ropes slung between uprights. Hampden Park number three held 40 000 standing, 4000 seated and 530 in the Pavilion but, incredibly, one feature of a modern ground was apparently omitted. When the pitch was dug up in 1971 it was found that no proper drains had been laid.

Opening day was 31 October 1903, when the honours were performed by the Lord Provost of Glasgow, Sir John Ure Primrose. Queen's Park beat Celtic 1-0 in a Division One match. Celtic returned to the new ground in April 1904 for the first Cup Final at Third Hampden, which they won v. Rangers in front of 65 000 spectators, the competition's largest ever gate.

Fire destroyed the first Pavilion in 1905, but a 1908 photograph shows the two side stands to be linked by a lower-roofed Pavilion with three uprights and a gable. This in turn was replaced in 1914 at a cost of £4700 by a four-storey structure which tied the two stands into one and which essentially survives today.

(The main difference from the present stand is the roof-mounted press-box, which originally had vertical facings with a clock and two pointed white gables, each bearing a flagpole. This was destroyed by fire in 1945 and replaced with the present, plainer press-box.)

Inside, the new centre section boasted a swimming pool for players, while externally its twin-tower entrance was the most grandiose piece of architecture yet seen at a British football ground. Was it coincidence that the twin-tower motif was to reappear south of the border a decade later at Wembley?

While the once proud amateur team slipped into mediocrity, large attendances at finals and internationals allowed Queen's Park to invest further in their prestigious headquarters. In 1923 additional land was purchased – the club now owned over 33 acres – new streets were built nearby and Lesser Hampden, a practice pitch behind the west goal, was laid for the club's junior teams. In 1927 extra terracing added a further 25 000 places and in 1928 rigid crush barriers replaced the 'wire-rope' variety which Queen's Park had so strongly recommended only four years earlier at the 1924 Committee on Ground Safety (see Safety).

Another improvement was the erection of a red-brick castellated entrance-way on Somerville Drive, in place of some corrugated turnstiles which had lent

that corner the appearance of a US Cavalry Fort. Indeed the turnstiles had seen a battle of sorts. In April 1909 they were set alight by fans rioting because no extra-time had been allowed after the Cup Final replay between Rangers and Celtic (critics of modern hooligans might note that apart from burning the goalposts, these Edwardian rioters cut firemen's hose-pipes, injured several policemen and were not fully subdued until two hours after the match. Another riot in 1980 saw little damage to the ground, as the new breed of hooligans concentrated on damaging each other).

Hampden reached its peak in 1937 when the North Stand was built at the back of the enormous terracing opposite the Main Stand. Built from drawings by Leitch, who had long since removed to London and was now almost retired, this added a further 4500 seats in a total capacity of 150 000. The North Stand was to be Leitch's last work at a football ground. He died in 1939. It was also his shortest-lived stand, surviving only forty-five years.

From 1937 onwards Hampden began to register almost every British attendance record possible.

Scotland v. England on 17 April 1937 attracted the highest official attendance ever recorded in Britain – 149 415 (sometimes given as 149 547), although at least another 10 000 were said to have entered after smashing down gates.

Aberdeen v. Celtic's Cup Final a week later attracted the highest gate ever recorded between two club sides, given as either 144 303 or 147 365. Some reports reckon there was a further 20 000 locked out.

Hampden can claim the record attendance for a club game other than a final – the semi-final Rangers v. Hibernian, 27 March 1948, watched by 143 570, and also for a European club game, when Celtic played Leeds in the European Cup semi-final on 15 April 1970, in front of 136 505. This figure is higher than for any European Cup tie, including finals, yet it was played mid-week.

Hampden's other attendance record is for a friendly match staged in Britain, when 104 494 watched Eintracht Frankfurt play Rangers on 17 October 1961. This was also the first time Hampden's floodlights were used.

By comparison Queen's Park's usual gates were paltry, and yet their own attendance record at Hampden of 97 000 for a Cup-tie v. Rangers on 18 February 1933, still outnumbers any English club's record.

In 1949 Hampden began to shrink. For safety reasons the crowd limit was reduced to a mere 135 000, and when the 200 000-capacity Maracana Stadium in Brazil opened the following year, Hampden lost its title as the world's largest football venue.

It was also becoming rapidly outdated. The terracing was in poor condition and 90 per cent of spectators had no cover. This was greatly alleviated in 1967 when, to celebrate Queen's Park's centenary, a large roof was built over the West Terrace. The architects were Thompson, McCrae and Sanders, who were later to be entrusted with the planning of Hampden's complete redevelopment.

This scheme came not a moment too soon. By the late 1960s Hampden was a national disgrace. The relatively young North Stand in particular was dark, dilapidated and graffiti-ridden and the cinder terracing appeared to be shored up more by thousands of discarded beer can ring-pulls than by its rotting timber footings. The barriers themselves were merely bolted on to wooden risers, an arrangement long since swept away south of the border at even smaller League grounds. It was therefore no surprise when after the passing of the Safety of Sports Grounds Act, Hampden's capacity was reduced once more to 81 000.

Hampden's transformation began in 1981, but only after years of protracted and often highly charged campaigning which alone would take a book to recount fully.

Briefly, the debate began in 1968 when a fire destroyed 1400 seats in the central section of the Main Stand (there was a similar fire 24 hours later at Ibrox, which immediately aroused suspicions of arson). A Glasgow politician then raised the idea of making Hampden an all-purpose stadium under public ownership. Queen's Park were not amused, but neither could they claim to have enough funds to improve Hampden further; building the West Terrace roof had put them heavily into debt.

Talks between the club, the SFA and Government representatives began in 1971 and over the next decade Hampden's future became a political football, with a glorious goal in prospect one moment and a humiliating own goal likely the next. Questions were asked in Parliament and among various multi-million pound schemes put forward were ones to make Hampden fit for the Commonwealth Games and even the World Cup Finals. Meanwhile Queen's Park failed in 1972 to sell off part of their land for a supermarket.

By 1978, it was thought that Hampden's future had been secured. The SFA had won full backing from other League clubs for rebuilding Hampden. The two local councils offered support, as did the Scottish Sports Council. For their part, the Labour Government had in August 1978 promised to provide half the estimated £11 million bill on condition that the other interested parties paid their share.

Thereafter, Glasgow City Council and the Strathclyde Regional Council fell in and out of love with Hampden, depending on their budgets and their willingness to co-operate with the newly elected Conservative Government in 1979. The Government for their part stunned everyone with a complete U-turn in the days when the Prime Minister, Margaret Thatcher, pledged that she was not for turning.

A few hectic weeks in 1980 almost sounded the death knell for Hampden.

By then the estimated bill had gone up. Glasgow Council withdrew their offer and there were rumblings on the Conservative back-benches, especially when, after seven years of debate, Rangers registered their objections at the eleventh hour. They insisted their opposition to Hampden's renewal had nothing to do with Ibrox Park's credentials. Rangers felt, suddenly it seemed, that the money was better invested elsewhere.

The League and SFA replied by insisting they had already won unanimous support among League clubs, and for a while Rangers' late intervention was viewed with some hostility. Nevertheless an announcement was made on 16 June that work would go ahead.

But as the bull-dozers prepared to move in, at Westminster one Scottish Tory MP urged Mrs Thatcher to withdraw the offer of Government money, and only two weeks after allegedly giving written assurances that a £5·5 million grant would be paid, the Government suddenly changed its mind.

'An unbelievable U-turn', wrote Ian Paul in *The Glasgow Herald*. Others called it 'a spineless decision', 'an act of betrayal' and 'another example of Thatcher's indifference'. One writer even went so far as to call it 'ineptitude exceeding even Scotland's dismal performance in Argentina two years ago'. It was that bad!

On the other hand, several commentators criticized the original concept of a revived national stadium. They argued that Hampden was not worth the massive sums needed to make it into a modern stadium, that the money would be better spent on community sporting facilities and improving other League grounds. Their arguments were strengthened by the fact that Old Firm supporters had rioted at Hampden only a few weeks earlier.

With the scheme in tatters, Queen's Park went so far as to consider selling the site. But its scrap value was estimated at a mere £7000 and the land valued at around £30 000 an acre; not enough for the club to rebuild anew elsewhere in the city. Even without any wholesale changes it was still estimated that £1 million had to be spent on safety measures alone.

Finally, the SFA and Queen's Park launched their own appeal, and a national fund-raising campaign began. Lord Wheatley, whose report on ground safety had formed the basis of the 1975 legislation (see Safety), became chairman of the appeal, which aimed to raise £2·2 million for the first phase.

With the help of lotteries and private and public money, the appeal succeeded. In October 1981 the bulldozers finally moved in and Hampden was saved for Scotland.

Phase One, which took until 1986, involved demolishing the North Stand, removing the top layers of the East Terrace, and concreting all the terracing and installing new barriers, refreshment bars and toilets. New red-brick turnstiles were built around the upper curve of the East Terrace.

The work cost £3 million (36 per cent above the original estimate) of which £586 000 was received from the Football Grounds Improvement Trust and a further £800 000 in grants from the Football Trust (Wembley received a similar amount).

The next phase, due to start in 1988 and estimated to cost approximately £4 million, includes plans for a roof over the remaining two uncovered terraces and the installation of more seats.

Hampden's current capacity is 74 370, including 10 000 seats, which oddly enough is almost exactly half the figure of that record gate in 1937. But few Scots will worry too much about that – Hampden, the mecca of every Scottish supporter and player, has survived.

Ground Description
Watching Queen's Park play in front of a few hundred spectators in the enormous empty bowl of Hampden is one of football's eeriest experiences. It is hard to believe that this ill-supported amateur club is master of such an overwhelming stadium.

Almost as difficult to grasp is the fact that even after such vast expenditure, Hampden remains extremely basic. That alone gives an indication of how deeply the stadium had slipped into disrepair.

Now considerably neater, Hampden fortunately retains much of its scale and charm. From Somerville Drive the castellated turnstiles are a foretaste of the grand entrance to the Main Stand, whose two brick towers are typical examples of the Victorian and Edwardian Scots' apparent fascination with medieval castle motifs.

The rest of the two-tier stand is large but essentially characterless apart from its extraordinary press-box. This two-layered protrusion leans forward on the sloping roof so precariously that one feels uncomfortable for the occupants, who must surely be about to slip over the edge and onto the pitch. One journalist, David Lacey of *The Guardian*, once described that from here Hampden Park was the only ground in the world that looked the same in colour as it does in black and white.

Tonal qualities apart, from this odd vantage point, to the left is the covered West Terrace, whose roof is identical to that over the East End at Celtic Park. From outside Hampden the West Terrace appears to be quite low; inside it seems cavernous because the pitch is actually several feet below street level. Hampden sits at the foot of a steep incline, allowing for a dramatic approach from the north.

Opposite the Main Stand and to the right are huge expanses of open terracing which await more work in the second phase. At the top of the North Terrace and from Somerville Drive the grim surviving foundations of the short-lived North Stand, which sat over the back of the terrace, are still visible.

At the rear of the East Terrace is a curving concourse with new turnstiles. Rather than pay at street level before climbing up to the terracing, this new arrangement allows spectators to step freely up the embankment to a high level concourse and then gain

Hampden 1986, back from the brink

direct access from the turnstiles onto the terracing; an unusual arrangement which avoids congestion in the surrounding streets.

Lesser Hampden behind the West Terrace is overshadowed by the tenements of Somerville Drive. Apart from its new surrounding wall it is barely developed, with grass slopes and a few patches of wooden terracing. The small dilapidated Pavilion was once a farmworker's cottage.

Yet the pitch is actually larger than Hampden's and the floodlighting makes it a compact enclosure full of potential as, perhaps, a 3000-capacity all-seated ground. One or two first-team matches apart, it is the well-used home of Queen's Park's reserves, known as 'the Strollers', the third team, known as 'the Victoria eleven', their Under-16 side and numerous other schoolboy teams.

In 1986 Lesser Hampden's future was uncertain. Clyde, who were forced to leave nearby Shawfield that year, tried negotiating a ground-sharing scheme at Lesser Hampden. The cost then of bringing the ground up to League standards was estimated at £500 000, 75 per cent of which would have come from FGIT. But with Lesser Hampden already in use much of the season Queen's Park rejected the idea and Clyde turned instead to Partick Thistle. Meanwhile there was a distant possibility of the ground being sold for property development.

Hampden itself has an assured future as the centrepiece of Scottish football. The famous Hampden Roar, a phenomenon created not only by numbers but also by the swirling winds which cross the stadium, can still be an awesome experience despite smaller crowds. And there is no doubt that, once completely updated, Hampden will be capable of staging games of the highest stature, perhaps even the European Championship Finals. Several other Scottish grounds could well support such an event, but the Final itself would be the perfect way to celebrate the rebirth of one of the greatest footballing venues in the world. Scotland's passionate fans deserve no less.

·CELTIC·

Previous Grounds

Impressed by the popularity of Scotland's two main Irish Catholic clubs, Hibernian (formed 1875) and Dundee Harp (1879), Celtic were established in 1887 as a charitable trust to serve the poorer Catholic communities in Glasgow's East End. The first Celtic Park, rented at £50 a year and built by volunteers, was opened on 8 May 1888 with an exhibition match between Hibs and Cowlairs. Celtic's first match at the ground was appropriately enough v. Rangers on 28 May, although few of the 2000 spectators could have imagined how the two clubs would soon become such rivals.

Having become founder members of the Scottish League in 1890, Celtic were, as Willie Maley wrote in his history of the club, forced to leave 'in true Irish fashion' as victims of rack-renting. Their landlord, mindful of the club's stature, had raised Celtic's rent to £450. The site of this ground is now wasteground between the Eastern Necropolis and Springfield Road, 200 yards from the existing ground.

Celtic Park

For many years Celtic Park, sometimes known by the district Parkhead, was called Paradise, after one observer described Celtic's move as 'like leaving the graveyard to enter Paradise'. The new ground was a quarry hole next to Janefield Cemetery. It was leased initially and then purchased in 1897 from Sir William Hozier for the extremely high sum of £10 000. A mile away was Barrowfield, home of Clyde.

Summer 1892 saw the construction of the two most advanced football grounds in Britain: Goodison Park in Liverpool and Celtic Park in Glasgow. As the Irish patriot Michael Davitt laid Celtic Park's first turf,

with Irish shamrocks of course, he recited a verse: 'On alien soil like yourself I am here, I'll take root and flourish, of that never fear.' (As it happened, that first turf had no chance of taking root. It was stolen soon after, causing one poet to write the words, 'blast the hand that stole the sod that Michael cut'.)

For the period 1892–1914 the ground became one of Scotland's prime sporting venues; athletics meetings were staged every summer and in 1897 Celtic hosted the first and only World Cycling Championship to be held in Scotland. Extensive wooden terracing was built for this event, a measure which Rangers copied with disastrous results at Ibrox in 1902 (see Safety).

Celtic were possibly the first club to consider permanent floodlighting, soon after the ground's opening. With lamps on poles around the ground and others suspended on wires above the pitch, a match v. Clyde was played on Christmas Day 1893, but although quite successful it was not repeated (see Floodlights), partly because the ball kept hitting the overhead lamps!

Celtic Park also became Scotland's main venue for internationals, until in 1906 Hampden took over (from then until the ground's last international in 1933, it was mainly used for Scotland v. Ireland fixtures).

Other events in the ground's early years included a Coronation parade in 1911 and, during the First World War in front of a huge crowd, a demonstration with the aid of mock bombs and explosions of trench warfare methods. Celtic Park has also been used to hold open-air masses. One, in May 1949, was attended by 27 000 people. Finally, the ground has a special place in the history of speedway. The first official meeting took place at Celtic Park in April 1928 after it was realized that the intended venue – West Ham stadium in London (not Upton Park) – would not be ready in time.

Celtic Park in 1900, with the ill-conceived Grant Stand on the right. Note the typical Scottish layout of pavilion with stand alongside

A picture of the ground in 1898 shows both a running track and concrete cycle track, and a two-storey Pavilion with a central gable next to a two-tier wooden stand on the North Side along Janefield Street. It was a familiar format, found at Ibrox, Pittodrie and several other Scottish venues.

But Celtic Park possessed one stand quite unlike anything built before or since. James Grant, an Irish director of the club, decided in 1898 to set up a separate company to build a grandstand on the South Side, opposite the Pavilion and stand. The so-called Grant Stand was built behind the terracing on stilts, with a pointed central gable, padded tip-up seats inside and large, sliding windows along the front and sides which offered, as one advertisement claimed, 'freedom from atmospheric inconvenience'.

It looked remarkable but was a complete failure and Grant lost all his investment. Patrons had to climb four flights of stairs to reach the seats and the designers had not allowed for condensation, so that even when the stand was only half-full the windows soon steamed up.

The glass was removed when, in 1904, a fire destroyed the Pavilion and Main Stand – arson was suspected – and the Grant Stand had to take over as the only seated accommodation at Celtic Park. A new Pavilion, with a cover, for standing only was built soon after (on the site of the present North Terrace).

The ground's next major development took place in 1929. As the Grant Stand was being demolished on the south side of the pitch, fire broke out in the Pavilion opposite and destroyed it within an hour. Celtic Park would never be the same again. In place of Grant's folly arose a new 'noble' South Stand, designed by Messrs Duncan and Kerr, who had also worked on Partick's new stand (some references attribute the South Stand to Leitch – it is possible he may have been involved in an advisory capacity). Costing £35 000, it was smaller and less grandiose than Rangers' new stand, opened the same year, and had the unusual arrangement of pointed central gable over a rectangular, glass-fronted press-box. Accommodation for 4800 spectators was provided with a paddock in front.

Celtic Park by then was actually smaller than Ibrox and Hampden, though still larger than any club ground in England or Wales. Even so, the oft-quoted record attendance of 92 000, for the traditional New Year derby v. Rangers on 1 January 1938, is probably false. Contemporary accounts put the attendance at around 83 500.

The modern era saw Celtic Park change further. In 1957 a cover was built at the very back of the East Terrace, known as the Celtic End, and on 12 October 1959 floodlights, described at the time as being the best in Britain, were first used for a match v. Wolves, the kings of floodlit football.

In 1966, to replace the rusting old roof built in 1904, the north terracing or 'Jungle' was covered by a surprisingly traditional double-pitched roof cover.

After Celtic's triumph in the European Cup in 1967 the club borrowed the more up-to-date design of Hampden Park's newly-covered West End and for £300 000 built an almost exact replica over their East Terrace, thus providing cover on all four sides.

(Because the East Terrace, traditionally known as the Rangers End, now offered better cover than the Celtic End, it was suggested that Celtic fans switch their allegiance to the opposite end, but old habits die hard and they stayed out.)

The most startling development came in April 1971 when Celtic removed the South Stand roof and replaced it with a most unusual angular white canopy. Costing £250 000, the work was done in such a way as not to disturb the facilities below (Maine Road underwent a similar process in 1982).

The canopy was supported on a massive goalpost-like framework, the 'crossbar' of which was one of the biggest tubular-steel girders ever constructed, measuring 97·5 metres long and 5·3 metres deep, transported to Glasgow all the way from Chichester. It was a novel, and expensive, method of redeveloping a stand, and it quite transformed the original base, which was then converted to an all-seater with room for 8686 spectators.

But it proved to be a regular source of irritation to Celtic, who six years after completion sought damages from the architects, consulting engineers and British Steel. All three denied liability in a prolonged and complicated court hearing. The club argued that it had needed to make a series of repairs, had lost income while these were carried out, and had found basic design faults in the roof, particularly during the wind and snow. Even when solved the stand had its problems, as we shall discuss later.

With the passing of the Safety of Sports Grounds Act, Celtic Park's capacity was reduced from 80 000 to 56 500. Yet even though this still meant Celtic Park was one of the biggest club grounds in Britain, the club invested further sums in increasing the capacity a year later to 67 000.

Celtic Park is one of the most basic of the big grounds, having relatively few seats and no private boxes. There was therefore some surprise when in 1986 the club opted to spend roughly £1 million on a cover to replace the old West End roof.

Similar in design to the East End cover, it obviously improved the standing spectators' lot but hardly seemed to enhance the ground's overall facilities. Certainly no other club has spent so much in recent years on completely rebuilding a standing terrace. On the other hand, its construction did raise the possibility of the two end roofs being linked over a new North Enclosure roof. Perhaps Celtic had a long-term plan after all.

Instead, it was announced in July 1986 that Celtic were considering building a seated stand above the 'Jungle', a curious idea indeed. But then considering the ground's hitherto piecemeal development anything seemed possible.

Ground Description

Celtic Park is, with Hampden and Wembley, the last of the truly big British football grounds. But whereas Ibrox is a stately home, Parkhead is a down-to-earth people's palace. Even the brick façade is restrained, as if Celtic disapproved of the sort of pomp displayed at Ibrox (in fact they were just less wealthy when it was built).

Although the South Stand is familiar from the rear, inside it is wholly unrecognizable. The new roof hangs over the multi-coloured seats like the top of a kitchen bin waiting to flip shut. In the middle, suspended from the roof girder, is a large, green, glass-fronted press-box, which when lit at night adds drama to Parkhead as it seems to hover above the action.

Impressive though the roof's vast white cleanliness and sharp, pointed angles may appear, as a means of protecting spectators from the elements it fails somewhat, especially for those sitting on the shallow rake of front seats, almost all of which are exposed to any wind or rain (those seats on the former paddock are, incidentally, coloured orange, which may or may not indicate an easing of sectarian sensibilities).

Several architects have tried to find an alternative to the traditional form of grandstand roof but this attempt, brave though it is, will not I fear win too many imitators, especially in light of its earlier technical problems.

From here, to the right is the covered East End, a twin to Hampden's West End, even down to the design of floodlight pylons, poking through the roof. Celtic's pylons are, however, painted matt black, making them stand out even more against the Glasgow sky. This vast curving terrace, immaculate with unusual barriers consisting of concrete uprights and solid wooden horizontals in green, is also known as the Rangers End, since this is where away fans congregate for meetings of the Old Firm. The semi-circle of turf behind the goal at this end was removed to allow players a training area in the wet.

Opposite is the covered North Enclosure, known as the Jungle: a title supposed to reflect the steamy, animalistic nature of its patrons. Perhaps their instinct for survival is heightened by the proximity of the Eastern Necropolis, a few yards behind on Janefield Street. In fact, the terrace is large, airy, with green steelwork supporting a double pitched roof, lined by flagpoles and a grey ribbed fascia which cries out for a club crest or signboard.

One of the flagpoles carries the Irish tricolour, a source of considerable controversy since the 1950s because of the sectarian rivalry between Celtic and Rangers.

To the left is the newly covered West or Celtic End,

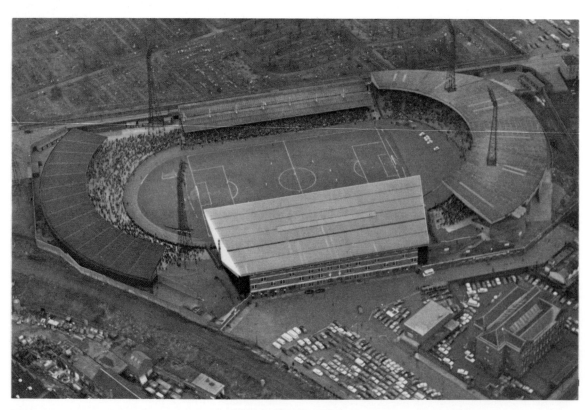

Celtic Park in 1980, the biggest club ground in Britain, before the West Terrace was redeveloped

Celtic's unusual South Stand roof with suspended press-box. The far East End and floodlight pylon are identical to Hampden

a mirror of its opposite. No other ground except Wembley possesses two such large, covered end terraces.

Despite the reputation of Old Firm supporters, there is only a low, barely obstructive perimeter fence at Celtic Park, and this open quality, allied to the wide elliptical shale track, makes the ground seem vast, yet somehow underdeveloped. One Celtic fan called it 'the best nineteenth-century ground in Britain'.

While other big clubs have dispensed with or intruded upon their running tracks, invested in seating and cut down their terraces, Celtic have kept faith with both the elliptical plan and the standing spectator. They claim to have done this after a poll among fans on the terraces, few of whom wanted more seating.

Wisely or not, therefore, Celtic Park thus runs against the trend followed at most other club grounds and is the complete and absolute antithesis of Ibrox Park.

But does this indicate that Celtic are a populist club who have stayed faithful to their roots, or does it suggest they are ultra-conservative and too shortsighted in their planning?

Only time will tell. Until then, Celtic Park remains one of the greatest enigmas in British football; a modern ground built on traditional principles which may prove to be either brilliantly successful or disastrously misguided.

·21·
LANARKSHIRE

HAMILTON ·ACADEMICAL·

Previous Grounds

Originating from Hamilton Academy, the club began in 1875 at Bent Farm, now Bent Recreation Ground. Apart from 1885–86, spent at South Avenue, Hamilton played from 1883–88 at South Haugh, after which they moved another short distance to Douglas Park.

Douglas Park

Two years after Hamilton's first Cup Final appearance the first major construction took place at

Douglas Park. Built from plans prepared by Archibald Leitch (see Design), it was a low, 90-yard long stand with 1221 seats. This was Leitch's smallest known and possibly his only 'Belfast' roofed stand (that is, with a shallow wooden barrel roof). Opened on 30 August 1913 by Provost Smellie before a game v. Rangers, it was joined in 1919 by another stand across the pitch. This survived only five years before being destroyed by fire.

Hamilton's record gate is 28 690, for a Cup tie v. Hearts in March 1937 and it must have been a profitable crush because shortly after new terracing was laid. In 1949 a cover was erected opposite the Main Stand and thus the ground remained until the belated introduction of floodlights in March 1971. Gwardia Warsaw of Poland provided the first floodlit opposition.

That the match was played at all was a minor

Hamilton's Main Stand, one of Leitch's more modest efforts

miracle in itself, for in 1970 Hamilton almost ceased to exist. Beset with debts after finishing bottom of the Second Division, in August 1970 the club resigned from the League and failed to fulfil their two opening fixtures. Reports of Clyde moving to Douglas Park (under the dreadful title of Strathclyde Academical) were finally scotched when four rebel Hamilton directors won control and reclaimed membership of the League.

Their efforts were certainly not in vain because in 1986 the team attained Premier Division status. With it, of course, came designation under the Safety of Sports Grounds Act. Still short of funds, Hamilton spent £75 000 in 1986, improving terracing and facilities for visitors, extending the Main Stand and putting seats in the paddock. It is hoped eventually to re-roof and extend the stand further. Until then it has 1650 seats in a total capacity of 10 000.

Ground Description

Situated on the west side of this former coal-mining town a couple of miles from Motherwell, Douglas Park in 1986 seemed an unlikely venue for Premier Division football. Its crumbling terracing and a single band, in parts disintegrated, of red and white barriers hardly reflected success.

The Main Stand, with its plain façade backing onto a rough car park and railway line, is intimate but basic. Tucked into one end are the red walls of the club offices. Advertisements line the perimeter and fascia boards, which since improvements in 1975 only retain the original dog-tooth boarding at the screen-ends. As far as can be ascertained no other Leitch stands of a similar design survive, nor do many examples of Belfast roofs at football grounds. The roof is formed by an intricate web of dark wooden joists over which a slightly arched wooden skin is tied. Clearly distinct at the South End is the new extension.

To the right is the South Terrace, an open end backed by grass and overlooked by a Social Security office block. Opposite is the Covered Enclosure which, with neat red steelwork and three thin floodlight pylons protruding through its roof, is the neatest part of the ground. To the left a scoreboard fills the corner next to the open North Terrace, lined at the rear by a brick wall.

Hamilton devotees will argue, with some justification, that success on the pitch (which slopes incidentally 9 feet from south to north) take precedence over ground improvements. Until extra money is available, therefore, given its essentially drab surrounds, Douglas Park still lacks a certain touch of style, be it a large welcoming sign along the façade or a few fluttering flags behind the terraces. Having eluded extinction so narrowly once before, a celebratory flourish here and there would be most welcome, and highly deserved.

·MOTHERWELL·

Previous Grounds

Motherwell owe their origins in May 1886 to a merger between the town's strongest teams, Alpha and Glencairn. The club based itself at Alpha's ground on Roman Road, just off Merry Street, before moving to another pitch by Airbles Street. Named Dalziel Park, this ground opened in March 1889 with a game v. Rangers. We know a stand was built because according to John Swinburne's affectionate *History of the Steelmen* (MFAC 1985), to which I am most indebted, during a 16–1 rout the bored Motherwell goalkeeper stood under it to shelter from the rain. Apart from a narrow pitch, which on one occasion obliged Motherwell to replay a Cup tie, election to the League in 1893 raised further questions about Dalziel Park. Although a scheme to lease land from the Duke of Hamilton fell through because it was too near the County Hospital, the Duke leased Motherwell another piece of ground on the edge of Fir Park.

Fir Park

Opened in 1895 in front of 6000 spectators with an 8-1 defeat by Celtic, Fir Park, set in wooded parkland, was practically a rural retreat from the smoke and clatter of Motherwell's coal mines and steelworks. But although the capacity expanded to 15 000, gates were sometimes lower than a local junior side, and in 1900 there were reports of Hibernian taking over the ground. By 1905 however Motherwell had fulfilled their potential and were elected to Division One.

Various minutes from board meetings selected by John Swinburne tell us more about the ground. For example, in 1910 the board opted not to insure spectators against accidents at the ground – a disturbing ommission perhaps common at that time. In 1912 they ordered posters urging fans not to swear, misbehave or interfere with players and officials, and in 1929 they resolved not to allow advertising inside Fir Park (a resolve shared by few other clubs then and certainly none currently).

For years the only stand at Fir Park was a 70-yard long two-tier construction, from whose tunnel emerged in 1932 the only team able to break the Old Firm's stifling hold on the Championship between 1904 and 1948. Fir Park's record gate however came in March 1952 as 35 632 squeezed in for a replay against Rangers during Motherwell's successful Cup run. Unofficial estimates put the crowd nearer 42 000.

Two years later an Enclosure roof was built at a cost of £6500 and shortly after individual lamps on slender poles were placed at regular intervals along each stand roof. Initially used only for training, the first floodlit game was against Preston in February 1956 but, after a gale tore through the Enclosure roof,

The steel framework of Fir Park's Main Stand rises up in 1962 behind the existing stand, but not as far as Motherwell would have wished. The girders on the left remain curiously exposed

in 1959 the present pylons were installed.

In 1960 the Knowetop End was concreted and in 1962 construction of a new Main Stand begun. To minimize disruption its steel frame was erected behind and above the existing stand. Although the cost, some £92 000, was relatively inexpensive for such a substantial stand, supporters were nevertheless disgruntled that two bright young stars, Ian St John and Pat Quinn had just been transferred for healthy fees. The real curiosity about this new stand is explained later.

In 1977 when Fir Park became designated, standards were high enough to require only routine expenditure. The current capacity is 22 500, including 3500 seats.

Ground Description

Some of the trees which once made Fir Park a haven survive, otherwise the area is now largely built up. One thing is certain: it would be impossible to mistake this for any other ground, if only for the sheer number of signs telling you that this is indeed the home of Motherwell. Approaching the main entrance on Fir Park Street, the first indication is a delightful block of turnstiles bearing the club's full title above tiled roundel windows reminiscent of an inter-war municipal lido or Odeon cinema.

The main entrance is pure 1960s-plain brick alleviated by coloured panelling, with of course the club's name generously displayed in Motherwell's colours, claret and amber (originally the racing colours of Lord Hamilton of Dalziel).

Having established without doubt that this is Motherwell's ground we are then faced, on entry, with a curious sight. Although this tall, imposing stand extends to the Knowetop End in the left corner, it stops abruptly some 30 yards short of the bye-line on the right. Yet the steel roof girder does not halt. It pierces the screen end and juts out 30 yards, supported in the corner by a skeletal steel support

rising from flat ground below.

One's immediate reaction is that Motherwell must have run out of funds in mid-construction. The truth is that the club wanted a full-length stand but were prevented by the owner of a house immediately behind this corner of the ground. His garden abutted directly onto the ground and quite justifiably he argued that a hulking great stand would inhibit both the growth of his plants and the value of his property. He won, and the stand had to stop short.

By the time he had sold up and departed, money really had run out and in the end the steel frame was left – it still supports the stand after all – and the club moved their offices into the house. With gates in decline it is unlikely an extension will ever be built.

The stand itself is constructed on the goalpost principle (see Glossary) with two narrow columns for extra support. Its presence is both large and colourful; the club's name is written on the TV gantry, along the press-box and on the balcony wall. Almost every surface is yellow or red, although for contrast the perimeter wall is white and the roof fascia and balcony wall are both corrugated grey. The stand has one problem; because of its length the south screen-end creates a blind spot which prevents a triangle of seats being used.

From better placed seats, to the right is the curved open South Terrace, a high bank with, of course, yellow and red barriers. Two archetypal Scottish pylons rise up from the sides, their gantries bowing reverentially to the pitch. Opposite is the Covered Enclosure, with red steelwork and a yellow interior ceiling. The external roof is lined with advertisements. Behind this terrace is a school set in leafy grounds.

To the left is the Knowetop End, another uncovered terrace, beyond which the town centre and the unmistakable buildings of the Ravenscraig Steelworks are clearly visible. How ironic that the town's major industry, which in recent years has proved so vulnerable, should be represented at Fir Park in those exposed girders of the Main Stand – constructed in hope but now surplus to requirements.

·AIRDRIEONIANS·

Previous Grounds
Formed as Excelsior FC in 1878 – the present name was adopted in 1881 – the club's first ground was Old Mavisbank, a cricket field later the site of Airdrie Academy. In 1886 this ground staged the first recorded schoolboy football competition in the world.

Broomfield Park
Opened in 1892 with a match v. Queen's Park (who had in 1871 been persuaded of the efficacy of goal-tapes during a match in Airdrie), Broomfield Park belonged to the North British Railway Company. The existing Pavilion was built in 1907 and has barely altered since.

The 1920s were Airdrie's best years, allowing them to buy the ground in 1922, and after winning the Cup in 1924, build the Main Stand a year later. Comparative success after the Second World War brought enlargement to the terracing, material from an old coal pit being brought in. Broomfield was used during this period for military tattoos and on 8 March 1952 recorded its highest attendance, 24 000 for a Cup tie v. Hearts.

Floodlights were first switched on for a friendly v. Blackburn Rovers on 15 October 1956 and three years later a roof over the Enclosure went up. The final piece in Broomfield's jigsaw was the opening of a social club behind the Main Stand in 1969.

After safety work in 1985, when the ground was designated, Broomfield's capacity was reduced to 11 430, including 950 seats.

Ground Description
Almost within the town centre itself, Broomfield Park nestles in a hollow between Graham Street and a railway cutting, its low floodlight gantries barely visible on the skyline.

Entrance from the main road, past the Social Club, takes one along the back of the Main Stand to the ground's pride and joy, its Pavilion in the west corner. Apart from Fulham's Craven Cottage, this is the only surviving pavilion at a British League ground since the demolition of Bradford Park Avenue's former ground (see Lost But Not Forgotten), and although it lacks the intricacies of the average cricket pavilion, in footballing terms it is a little gem.

Three pointed gables, the central one bearing a flagpole and Union Jack, crown the upper tier which holds about 100 spectators. Like cricketers, the players emerge from their dressing rooms through a central gate onto the pitch. Old photographs show that, apart from the loss of the mock-Tudor decoration on the gables, the white and red balcony, the wood panelled offices and staircase are barely altered from 1907.

Raise the flag for Broomfield Park's pavilion – the sole survivor of a long tradition in Scotland

From this cosy vantage point, to the immediate right is the open West or Gartlea Road Terrace. The telegraph pole here and a pair at the opposite end are remnants of the original floodlight system. Airdrie town centre lies behind.

Across the narrow, 67-yards wide pitch, to the right is the Covered Enclosure, which has all concrete terracing and simple red barriers at regular intervals. On the roof sits a rather odd covered box used for television cameras, with two stubby little floodlight gantries on either side.

Opposite is the East or South Nimmo Street Terrace, shaped like an hourglass, with a curved wall at the rear. To the left is the Main Stand which, though basic with bench seats and a plain corrugated roof, is brightened up by its red fittings and red screen-ends. Of note are the exceptionally low dug-outs, which explain why most managers prefer using the red benches provided on the perimeter, and four floodlight gantries with distinctive red steelwork. These lights lean forward as if anxious not be excluded from the action.

The juxtaposition of so many red fittings around the green of the turf is always warmly satisfying to the eye, and, given the charming presence of Airdrie's Pavilion, Broomfield Park has a scale and charm which modern grounds never quite capture. It is to be hoped that whatever improvements are effected these qualities will remain.

·ALBION ROVERS·

Previous Grounds

Starting in 1882 at Cowheath Park, later a greyhound stadium and now ASDA's car park, Rovers moved out to Meadow Park, Whifflet, in 1883 where, according to Robin Marwick's history of the club, *The Boys from the Brig*, strong winds managed to blow down the Grandstand twice. Gales apart, the location proved inconvenient so in April 1919 work began on the current ground. Meadow Park's site is marked by a sub-station on Calder Street.

Cliftonhill Park

While building progressed in the grounds of the then derelict Cliftonhill House, Rovers played home games at Airdrie, two miles away. The ground was eventually opened on Christmas Eve 1919 v. St Mirren, the only structure being the old Pavilion brought over from Meadow Park. The current Main Stand was opened in August 1920, just after Rovers' one and only Cup Final appearance.

The ground was larger then, with a bank extending up to where Cliftonhill House once stood and where council houses now line Albion Street. Before a record 27 381 watched a Cup tie v. Rangers on 8 February 1936, those houses were in mid-construction and the club borrowed the builders' tools to improve the banking.

In 1954 a roof was built over the Coatbridge End. Five years later it was rebuilt opposite the Main Stand, where it remained until more strong winds felled it in January 1968. The present Enclosure roof went up the following summer, by which time the terracing had been sliced in half and a new boundary wall built, cutting off the bank behind (since landscaped into a recreation area).

Cliftonhill's floodlights were switched on with a match v. Airdrie in October 1968, but track-side lights have long been used since greyhound racing began at Cliftonhill in 1931. Stock cars took over in 1964, superceded by speedway in 1968, until in 1977 greyhounds returned.

Of all the grounds affected by safety checks made after the 1985 Bradford fire, Cliftonhill suffered the worst. So dilapidated was the terracing that a 9000-capacity was reduced to a mere 850, confined to the Main Stand and paddock. Even the floodlights were unusable for a season, thus sending Rovers to Airdrie for a second time in their history, for games during 1985–86.

Cliftonhill Park – vast, crumbling and forlorn

Ground Description

Rumours of Cliftonhill's demise are hard to believe as one passes by landscaped shrubberies and under a wrought-iron archway on Main Street. Because the ground sits on a rise some 20 feet above the road, the 35-yard long Main Stand, whose entrance is also at street level, appears disproportionately tall at the rear. Its height is accentuated by bright new cladding in black, red and yellow horizontal stripes, resembling an enormous West German flag.

Begun in 1985, this refurbishment – some would call it merely window dressing – was paid for largely by the Coatbridge Project, a local initiative designed to help the depressed town. Once inside the ground, the illusion evaporates instantly.

The Main Stand is worn, wooden and basic. Red and yellow paintwork barely conceals its patched upper tier. The paddock leads onto the track, half sand, half grass, beyond which is a chicken-wire fence and two free-standing dug-outs.

Beyond the stand Cliftonhill stretches out like a forgotten hinterland, even though the pitch, measuring 100 × 70 yards, is deceptively small. To the right is the flat, open Airdrie End. Opposite, the Covered Enclosure has a tidy roof but the cinder terracing and barriers are badly neglected. To the left is the curved Coatbridge End, with the greyhounds' starting traps in the near corner.

In the far corner a grass mound beyond the boundary wall affords an unencumbered view of the pitch. Paying fans call it 'Aberdeen Gate'. In Scotland Aberdonians are held to be parsimonious, but with Coatbridge suffering an unemployment rate twice the national average, who would judge the onlookers?

There are plans to rescue the ground from its pitiable state, but on average gates of a few hundred, money and commitment is limited to those few loyalists who every week must witness dozens of well-filled buses leaving Coatbridge for their regular destinations, Ibrox and Celtic. It is a scene repeated all over lowland Scotland, but one whose consequences are no better judged than at Cliftonhill.

·22·
CENTRAL SCOTLAND

·FALKIRK·

Previous Grounds

Brockville Park, a farmer's field, was Falkirk's original ground in 1876. Three years later the Bairns (after the old motto 'Better meddle wi' the Devil than the Bairns o' Falkirk') moved to Randyford, off Grangemouth Road, then in 1881 to Blinkbonny, a ground memorable in name only. Finally, in 1882, Falkirk returned to their first home.

Brockville Park

Back near the town centre, Falkirk did not join neighbours East Stirling in the League until 1902, but thereafter they achieved pre-eminence. Despite a controversial fire which had just destroyed their first Grandstand, they were runners-up in Division One in 1908 and Cup winners in 1913.

The 1920s were prosperous for Falkirk. Having purchased Brockville they then considered a larger site at Bell's Meadows. This fell through, but the record-breaking transfer of Syd Puddefoot from West Ham did not. He cost £5500. Another site, now Graeme High School, was also considered before Falkirk finally invested £7600 in the construction of a large Main Stand at Brockville in 1928.

The ground changed little until the erection of the Watson Street cover in the early 1950s, followed by the installation of floodlights, first used for a friendly v. Newcastle in October 1953. Earlier that year on 21 February, Brockville's record crowd of 23 100 attended a Cup match v. Celtic.

Safety improvements came early to Brockville. In fact the 1972 Wheatley Report, which presaged the Safety of Sports Grounds Act (see Safety), cited Brockville as an example of what measures could be taken. Falkirk's solid concrete terracing and sturdy barriers were particularly commended.

As a result, Brockville's current capacity is barely altered at 22 550, of which 2750 are seated, and apart from renewing the floodlights and the Enclosure roof

Brockville Park – the smallest pitch in Scotland but one of the safest grounds the Wheatley Report came across

in 1986, very little has had to be spent on safety work since 1975.

Ground Description

Only 100 yards from Falkirk's main Grahamston Station, Brockville Park is quintessentially British, hemmed in on all four sides by cuttings, industry and terraced housing, but without seeming at all gloomy and with plenty of unusual details for the grounds' connoisseur.

A narrow, bending lane leads one alongside the railway line to behind the Main Stand, whose dark frontage faces the grim, grey walls of a refuse disposal unit. No doubt many an unhappy fan has commented on this juxtaposition over the years.

The two-tier Main Stand runs the length of the pitch and is lined by unobtrusive lights along the plain pitched roof. It has an entrance hall resplendent with coloured glass, polished wood and lino, and from the ground is neatly turned out with red steelwork and blue fittings. A gate at the tunnel, designed by former player and manager John Prentice, displays the club crest, with the Falkirk steeple clock reading three o'clock. The motto, 'Touch 'ane, touch a'' warns opponents that the Bairns stick together as a team. Also worth noting is the press-box, which has its own sash windows – a most unusual feature.

From here to the left is the slightly cranked, open Watson Street End with a car park behind and the Ochil Hills visible in the distance. All Brockville's barriers and perimeter fences have silver-coloured horizontals supported by posts with rounded humps on the square top, like rooftops in Marrekesh. Three wooden floodlight poles are set into the concrete terracing.

Opposite is the Covered Enclosure, with its low roof and floodlight gantries. Tall spectators might have to stoop at the back to avoid bashing their heads on the steelwork. One spectator who cannot complain, however, is the owner of the house on Meeks Road, whose side wall actually forms part of the ground. From one tiny window the pitch is clearly visible, although it is not known if he incurs extra rates for the privilege or has them deducted for the inconvenience. Or if he can see to the far end of the pitch, which happens to be the smallest in League football, only 100 yards long × 70 yards wide.

To the right is the open Hope Street End, in the corner of which is another Brockville curiosity, a cute little covered enclosure for schoolboys. Legend has it that a ball kicked over the Hope Street Terrace landed in a passing goods truck and was eventually discovered at Perth, 43 miles up the line. Mighty long kickers, those Bairns.

EAST ·STIRLINGSHIRE·

Ground Description

Formed as Bainsford Britannia in 1880, the club's first home was Randyford Park, once home to East Stirlingshire cricket club whose name Britannia adopted in 1881, and also recently vacated by neighbours Falkirk. Within months the club moved to Merchiston Park, where they remained until a foundry swallowed it up in 1921.

Firs Park

After searching for a ground in their familiar Bainsford, East Stirling were eventually forced closer to Falkirk town centre, to Firs Park, which was officially opened in August 1921 with a friendly v. Hearts. As Falkirk's poorer relations, life has never been easy for East Stirling. Gates have fluctuated between the record 11 500 which attended a Cup tie v. Hibernian in February 1968 to occasional crowds of less than 50.

Relocation has been considered. Nearby Grangemouth was one possibility, and in 1964 directors tried to relocate the club to Clydebank. But after one season playing as E. S. Clydebank at New Kilbowie Park, Shire's shareholders won a twelve-month legal battle to bring the club back to Falkirk (see Clydebank).

During 1964–65, Firs Park lay idle. Clydebank had taken possession of the floodlights and Enclosure cover, while vandals helped to make this one of the saddest sights in sport – the neglected football ground.

After the club's triumphant return in 1965, the Enclosure roof was rebuilt and new floodlights installed, but the bare facts had not altered. Support has remained so poor that Firs Park is barely modernized at all. The current capacity is given as 11 500, with 450 seats.

Ground Description

Though hard to find, Firs Park is a welcome oasis of green in an otherwise drab part of Falkirk. The main entrance at Firs Street leads to a sign on the perimeter gate warning 'Hampers Only'. Thus players and officials must walk around the track to the small Main Stand on the far side.

Two immediate impressions. First, the ground is lovingly maintained. Though small, compact and hemmed in, every border is neat, every bit of metalwork painted in the club colours, black and white. Second, this sense of order is enhanced by distinct lines of terracing, which are in fact made up of worn timber footings pegged into dark cinders.

All terracing used to be like this, but to add to the

Firs Park – barrel-roof and benches, all in black and white

·STENHOUSEMUIR·

Previous Grounds

Stenhousemuir's village team played first in 1884 at the Tryst – flat expansive ground which for many years was the site of a famous cattle and livestock fair. As Peter Moulds' detailed history *The Warriors* informs us, the pitch was located around the eleventh fairway of the golf course which now occupies part of the Tryst ground next to Ochilview. In 1886 the club moved to Goschen Park, now partly a school playing field on Church Street.

Ochilview Park

Opened in 1890, Ochilview is one of the least developed grounds in the Scottish League. The exact site of the original ground may have differed from the present one, which really took shape after Stenhousemuir joined the League in 1921. A small Main Stand was built and after a fire, replaced in 1928, but the club achieved few headlines until 1951 when, as every schoolboy used to know, Ochilview was the unlikely setting for the first modern floodlit match in Scotland, a friendly v. Hibernian on 7 November 1951 (in England Southampton had been first a month earlier – see Floodlights).

Ochilview's lights were apparently not much better than street lamps – they had been installed a few years earlier for training purposes – but as in England it was often the smaller clubs who made the first pioneering efforts.

Ochilview's record gate is 12 500 for a Cup tie v. East Fife on 11 March 1950, but the current capacity is a maximum 10 500, of which 500 are seated.

Ground Description

With a population of only 10 000, Stenhousemuir and its neighbouring parish of Larbert are actually outer suburbs of Falkirk, which has two other League clubs within minutes of Ochilview.

That so open, barely developed ground should host League football is, to a Sassenach at least, something of a surprise. The Main Stand is 25 yards long with a high balcony wall and bench seats in white and steelwork in maroon. Staircases on either side are not so much the result of safety improvements as an absent-minded architect who forgot to provide for internal stairs.

From the stand's rear windows an excellent view, naturally, of the Ochil mountains can be had. In the foreground, over the boundary wall is the Tryst ground, which still stages an annual fair and is partly occupied by golf and cricket clubs.

To the immediate right is the Warriors Social Club, opened in 1968, a prefab block overlooking the pitch. It is reached by a tarmac drive which runs between the pitch and the low, concrete South Terrace. Behind

ground's dated appearance there is not one crush barrier in the entire ground.

The Main Stand is a short, barrel-roofed construction with white bench seats and black trimmings, primitive but spotless. Each team emerges from a separate door at the base. Visual impact is enhanced by a long barrel-roofed building whose black corrugated side forms the rear wall of the ground and matches perfectly the style of the stand, as if the two structures were built simultaneously.

A peep through the many holes in the corrugated sheeting reveals a treasure trove of dusty, decaying railway engines and carriages, some almost as old as the football club. This is the shed of the Railway Preservation Society.

From the Main Stand, there is open terracing at the Bainsford End to the left, backed by gardens, and also at the Bison End to the right, overlooked by the modern offices of Bison Concrete. Opposite is the Covered Enclosure with floodlight gantries along the roof.

The future of Firs Park may rest with the railway shed. Shire has first option on its purchase, and if money was available it could become a sports centre linked to the ground.

But even then, logic still dictates that Falkirk is far too small to support two League clubs, however much a visit to this tight, trim little ground may soften the heart. Of course other Scottish grounds are as basic as this and almost as ill-attended, but none of them lie within half a mile of another, far superior League venue. Firs Park is an anachronism which no amount of emotion can deny.

Ochilview Park, with its two flanking staircases, an embarrassing afterthought

this open terrace are gardens offering their owners easy access to Ochilview.

To the left is the open North End, merely a grass bank divided from the pitch by a red rail on white posts. Behind, a brick wall cuts the ground off from a field. In the north east corner just beyond the boundary wall runs Jenny's Burn.

Opposite the Main Stand is the Covered Enclosure, a sloping roof over basic concrete and cinder terracing. Behind is a toffee factory.

Ochilview's pitch is large, measuring 112 × 78 yards, with at least 15 feet of spare turf on each wing. Apart from the floodlights and a nearby church spire all else seems flat until the Ochils rise dramatically in the north, beyond the River Forth. In fact, leaning on Ochilview's perimeter rail, turf underfoot, it is hard to shake off a sense that man and football have barely infringed upon this natural domain.

·STIRLING ALBION·

Annfield Park

Stirling's previous League club, King's Park, ceased to operate during the Second World War after some unfortunate experiences (see Lost But Not Forgotten). As Allan Grieve's club history relates, rather than resurrect the club, in 1945 amid some controversy the former chairman, coal merchant Tom Fergusson, led a group of businessmen in the formation of a new club and organized the purchase of the Annfield estate for £5000.

Against opposition from conservationists, oak trees were cleared to lay a pitch, and because there were no stands at first, officials sat on chairs placed in the back of scrubbed-out lorries. These were Albion trucks, from which the new club derived its name. Annfield House, the adjacent mid-eighteenth century mansion, was used for offices and dressing rooms.

The East Stand, built in 1946, was rebuilt in 1949, and a walled but uncovered walkway for players led from Annfield House to the stand. The West Stand was built a few years later and the North Terrace roof went up soon after Annfield's record gate of 26 400, for a Cup tie v. Celtic on 14 March 1959. Floodlights were switched on for a friendly v. Birmingham in November 1961.

Annfield House continued to serve the club until 1974, when a new block comprising offices, social club and dressing rooms was opened behind the East Stand. To ease their financial problems in 1983 Stirling sold Annfield to the council for £250 000, and now lease it back at £3000 per annum. But April 1984 brought a considerable shock when after safety checks the council condemned parts of the East Stand.

The council would only invest more money in Annfield if it could be more widely used by the community, and that meant installing an artificial pitch. Permission for this was finally granted by the Scottish League in 1987 and an En-tout-cas surface similar to Luton, Preston and Oldham's was laid during the summer at a cost of around £450 000, the first in senior Scottish football. (It was more expensive at Annfield because the sloping pitch needed levelling first.)

The ground has thus been transformed in recent years, starting with £100 000 spent on new floodlights, barriers and gates in 1986, followed in 1987 by the new pitch and the installation of 600 plastic seats in the West Stand. Eventually it is hoped to rebuild the East Stand, which was almost completely demolished in 1987. Annfield's current capacity is 14 000 with 600 seats.

Annfield Park, looking over the West Stand towards Stirling Castle

Ground Description

Emerging from Stirling's historic centre, Annfield's more mundane pleasures are found in the midst of comfortable suburbia. A track from St Ninians Road leads to the club's main entrance, with the now derelict Annfield House, a listed building, creating a forlorn presence by the car park. The players' walk-way once dissected the car park, cutting off access to the rest of the ground from this route – a very odd arrangement.

In contrast to Annfield House, the club's new block behind the stand has little aesthetic value but is quite immaculate, and it comes as rather a shock to see the adjoining East Stand in a derelict state. It resembles a toy building with compartments deline-ated by white brick walls. About 30 yards in length, between its two players' tunnels (one was linked to Annfield House) is a small section with a low roof for directors, behind which and on either side are disused sections covered by another low roof. Although un-usual, it seems far too modern to have been con-demned.

Since we cannot sit in this section we will cross the immaculate new pitch, which is bordered by a wide new tarmac track, and go over to the South Terrace.

From the South Terrace, a rising open bank lined by silver-coloured barriers, is gained the best view of Annfield's scenic surrounds. Looking forward to the right are the Ochil Hills, with the Wallace Monu-ment (built in 1869 to honour the thirteenth-century Scot who defied the English) clearly visible.

To the left on the half-way line is the small West Stand. A basic cover with a slightly pitched roof but no screen-ends, there are now 600 new seats where before there used to be a standing section at the back and a line of old cinema seats at the front; rusting, threadbare but where the springs weren't exposed, rather comfortable. Since the demolition of the East Stand, the West Stand is now the only seated area.

Opposite is the North Terrace, with a roof over the centre rear section. Before Albion bought the estate a tennis court stood here. Behind the tree-lined ter-race, the rising silhouette of Stirling Castle is prom-inent on the skyline. Part of the castle is called Ladies Rock, from where ladies of the court would watch games being played in the valley below. Had they owned binoculars they might just have been able to catch Annfield in their sights. Anfield it may not be, but at least it's home to many a stirling performance!

The first Scottish League match to be played on an artificial pitch was on 5 September 1987 against Ayr United.

·ALLOA ATHLETIC·

Previous Grounds
Starting on a public park in 1880, in 1882 the club adopted its present name and moved to Gaberston Park, now a brewery car park, then a season later to Bellevue Park, on the banks of the Forth, where it was hoped to attract greater support. When the move failed Alloa found their current ground in 1895.

Recreation Park
Alloa first made footballing headlines in 1922, becoming the first Scottish club to be promoted when the previous system of election to Division One was abandoned. That this happened in their first ever League season was also noteworthy (a neighbouring village team, Clackmannan, fared rather worse by finishing bottom in their first and last League season). The present Main Stand dates from this period and was completed in time to see the club go straight back into the Second Division a year later.

Alloa's fortunes have been changeable ever since,
although the Recreation Park or Ground has altered little. A roof was added to the Enclosure about 1950 and floodlights were first used at the start of the 1979–80 season, making Alloa the second last Scottish club to have lights. The ground's record attendance was 15 467 for a Cup tie v. Celtic on 2 February 1955.

Ground Description
Once known as a brewery town in the midst of a thirsty mining area, Alloa is one of the smaller Scottish towns whose credentials for a League club are questionable, whose ground is primitive, but whose team flits up and down between divisions while bigger clubs stay put.

The Recreation Ground is as wide open and basic as one would imagine major grounds were at the turn of the century. There is not a barrier in site, only a few steps of terracing here and there, and the surroundings are so flat that the tallest building in view is the nearby fire station practice tower.

The Main Stand, 40 yards long, is reached from a gate on Clackmannan Road. With a low uneven wooden roof, a brick base and no paddock, its structure is simple but brightened by white, yellow and

Recreation Park's Main Stand

315

ture is simple but brightened by white, yellow and black paintwork. Bordering the pitch is a wide ashlar track with four thin grey floodlight pylons like motorway lampposts behind yellow and white railings.

From here, to the left is open Railway End Terrace, a grassy cinder bank with a section of old timber terracing in the corner. Two yards beyond the corrugated boundary fence is the old Perth to Alloa line. Several thousand yards beyond are the Ochil Hills, which seem to peer down on so many football grounds in this region. The tallest peak to the north is Ben Cleuch.

Opposite is the Hilton Road Side, a sloping cinder bank with a simple black and yellow cover at the rear and terracing at the front. To the right is the open Clackmannan Road End, another unadorned, undeveloped cinder bank.

Recreation Park is too open to feel homely, too basic to seem grand; just like the team in recent years really, it is in between.

·23·
NORTH EAST AND TAYSIDE

·ABERDEEN·

Previous Grounds

Aberdeen were formed in 1903 by the amalgamation of three senior clubs: Orion, who played at Cattofield, Victoria United, based at Central Park, and Aberdeen. This third club, set up by teachers in 1881, played on the Links before moving to Holburn Cricket Ground and in 1885 to an enchanting enclosure in Old Aberdeen called the Chanonry. Set amid woodland this site was eventually taken over by King's College for botanical research. For a decade Aberdeen played in the district of Kittybrewster until making a final move to Pittodrie in 1899.

Pittodrie Stadium

Aberdeen's new ground had a curious name. The first, more prosaic explanation is that the ground's owner was called Mr Knight Erskine of Pittodrie, a village 20 miles north west of Aberdeen in Garioch.

But a second, far more endearing possibility is that the word Pittodrie can be interpreted as Celtic for 'place of manure', a most apt description since the ground was formerly a dung heap used by the local police. Horse dung then was valuable currency, being sold for manure (Pittodrie can also mean 'place of bleaching' but this is much less appealing).

Before its dung days, maps show the site to have been used as an army rifle range and, before then, it was known as Gallows Marsh. This was hardly just a name, because a certain Rope Walk was in the vicinity too. Certainly after executions and effluvium a football ground must have been quite welcome among the area's inhabitants.

Aberdeen took over this endearing spot in February 1899 on condition that they restored the agricultural state of the land, repaired a cart road and cleared a rubbish dump. They must have done a good job because only six months after the grand opening Pittodrie staged its first international, in February 1900 v. Wales (in this and four subsequent inter-

nationals at the ground Scotland have never lost).

Jack Webster's entertaining history *The Dons* (Stanley Paul 1978) tells us that amalgamation of Aberdeen's three senior clubs in April 1903 was motivated, as in Dundee, by a desire for League status. Although Orion and Victoria had better teams, it was Aberdeen's name and ground which prevailed. Orion's stand was transported from Cattofield and a limited company formed at Pittodrie to promote – modestly – football, cricket, lacrosse, tennis, hockey, bowling, cycling, athletics and 'the physical training and development of the human frame'.

Pittodrie Park – the title Stadium was adopted in the 1960s – was reopened officially on 15 August 1903 for a Northern League fixture v. Stenhousemuir. A year later Aberdeen won a Second Division place. The club then bought the ground for £5668 and after election to Division One (Aberdeen have never been relegated), a Pavilion was built in the north east corner and the banking improved. In the same period the Burgh surveyor condemned the old Cattofield stand and in 1908 Pittodrie became the last ground in Britain to drop free admission for women.

Pittodrie began to develop during the 1920s, beginning with the erection of a small stand on the South Side in 1920 and the present Main Stand in 1925 after the sale of Alec Jackson to Huddersfield for £4500. The stand filled the North Side and in the manner of Leitch had a central gable, echoed by a small gable on the adjacent Pavilion roof. Once completed, in 1928 the club bought land on Pittodrie Street, now a car park and training pitch, and erected the ornamental granite entrances which still adorn the Merkland Road turnstiles. Aberdeen is after all the Granite City. That end of the ground was also covered in the period leading up to the Second World War, when Pittodrie became an air-raid patrol post.

But the most unusual innovation at Pittodrie came in the early 1920s when Aberdeen trainer Donald Colman invented the 'dug-out'. According to Jack Webster, Colman was a boxing and dancing enthusiast obsessed with his players' footwork. Because he also made meticulous notes during each game and

Mist enshrouds the gasometer which peeps over Pittodrie's bold cantilever stand

therefore needed a dry notebook, he had built at Pittodrie a sunken, covered area, soon termed a 'dug-out'.

A few years later Everton visited, liked the idea and built one at Goodison. The dug-out soon spread, leaving fans to ponder how any manager could reasonably assess his team from such a disadvantageous position. Dug-outs do have one advantage though – being so low the inhabitants rarely obstruct the spectators' view.

Aberdeen's growing success in the 1950s brought further change to Pittodrie. As Cup finalists the year before, Aberdeen recorded their largest gate, 45 061, for a Cup tie v. Hearts on 13 March 1954. In the summer of 1959 a cover was built at the Beach End and on 21 October floodlights were first used for a match v. Luton (like Aberdeen, losing Cup finalists that year). These original lamps were later sold to Arbroath.

During the 1960s, with the Pavilion demolished, the Main Stand was lengthened to increase the seating to 6000, a trend followed in 1968 when 1400 seats were installed in the Main Stand paddock. Although no long term plan existed at this stage to make Pittodrie all-seated, the ground's gradual conversion started before the Safety of Sports Grounds Act took effect in 1976. In other words, Aberdeen were not solely motivated by the desire to save money by simply replacing expensive crush barriers with inexpensive bench seats, as was the case at Clydebank, Scotland's other all-seated ground.

Before this, however, Aberdeen faced a crisis when fire following an explosion devastated half the Main Stand, towards the Beach End, on 6 February 1971.

Of greatest concern to many was the Scottish Cup, on display in the stand after Aberdeen won it in 1970. Fortunately it survived, but the club had to spend £140 000 to restore the stand.

At the same time the Merkland Road End was converted to hold bench seats, followed a season later by the Beach End. The final area to be seated was the uncovered South Side in 1978, thus making Pittodrie the first all-seated stadium in Britain. By that stage the ground's capacity had dropped from 45 000 in 1970 to 24 000.

More improvements followed as Aberdeen's fortunes improved on the pitch. In 1980 a dramatic hanging cantilevered roof costing £750 000 was built over the South Side, whose open bench seats had understandably been unpopular in bad weather, and in 1983–84 the bench seats on that side were replaced by plastic tip-up seats.

Executive boxes, a novelty in Scotland, were also installed in the Main Stand. All were sold immediately, thus making them completely self-financing. Lastly, in 1985 it was felt the Merkland Road roof was too old and a new cover costing £500 000 was erected.

By 1986 Aberdeen had spent more on safety work and improvements on their ground than any Scottish club outside Glasgow without ever going into debt, thanks largely to their European exploits. More significantly, with a capacity of 22 568 they had proved that an all-seated stadium can be viable, popular and not prey to the same criticisms which beset Coventry when they tried the same idea three years after Aberdeen in 1981.

Aberdeen have achieved this in simple ways.

Firstly, Pittodrie's conversion was gradual, allowing supporters to grow accustomed to the idea rather than have it suddenly thrust upon them as at Coventry. Secondly, while Highfield Road's conversion coincided with a period of recession in the city, Aberdeen, thanks to the oil industry, was something of a boom town during the transformation period. It is not insignificant that Pittodrie has more private boxes than any other Scottish ground.

Thirdly, it has to be said that while demand for Coventry's matches was limited, Aberdeen's exploits at home and abroad attracted wide interest. Fans wanted to watch, sitting or standing.

But I contend that the single most important reason for Pittodrie's relative success is the fact that bench seating, rather than tip-up seating, has been installed at the two popular ends of the ground.

Individual plastic seats are fodder to hooligans. Bench seats are solid, immoveable, and most important of all, in times of sudden commotion they allow much freer movement. This permits innocent spectators to evade unrest more easily, and also allows unruly elements to fight among themselves with little damage to the fabric of the ground. Furthermore, if fans wish to stand they invariably do so on the bench seats anyway. The club reports that a majority of spectators sit down most of the time however.

At Pittodrie rival sets of supporters are at opposite ends of the ground, and Aberdeen have made the pragmatic decision to leave the visitor's Beach End comparatively basic while improving the home supporters' lot, thus heightening the pride they feel for the ground.

Whether owing to pride or simply better general behaviour Aberdeen have experienced very little vandalism at Pittodrie.

For example, for years one set of light bulbs in the South Stand had no protective covering. In normal circumstances these would have been an open invitation to vandals, but at Pittodrie there were no breakages. Tentatively the club would claim that improved conditions have led to improved behaviour. It is a theory which works well on the Continent and in the United States but has seldom been tested in Britain.

Cynics might argue that Pittodrie suffers less from invading hooligans because it is so distant. Aberdeen is the northernmost League ground in Britain, closer to Norway or Denmark than it is to London.

Pittodrie is also, as any visitor will soon appreciate, only 300 yards from the North Sea. So cold can the ground be that when alcohol and bottles were banned from the ground, most complaints came from fans whose thermos flasks of tea and soup were also prohibited because of their glass content. Warm rugs are often as important as club scarves in Aberdeen.

Ground Description

Pittodrie has aesthetic as well as technical qualities,

but these are least evident outside the ground. The Main Stand on Pittodrie Street has only a plain brick façade looking onto an all-weather training area cum car park.

Inside it is a traditional post and beam construction with a front tier of red and a rear section of black and red seats. Along the back are 24 executive boxes, along the front are the two historic dugouts.

The roof is in two sections, a front addition with skylights being supported by girders tied from behind, above the older roof – an unusual arrangement designed to provide better shelter. The facings are in grey, and this combined with red seats reminds one of another famous ground – Anfield.

From here, to the right is the Merkland Road or King Street End. The new roof, which is clad in blue sheeting, is quite low but because of yellow tinted skylights the home fans at this end have a distinctly sunny (or is it jaundiced?) view of proceedings. The stand has simple grey bench seats, grey steelwork and quite immaculate toilets, almost completely unsullied by graffiti artists. Behind is the ornamental stone entrance and a timber yard.

Opposite is the breathtaking sweep of the South Stand. On each side are corners of uncovered seats – inevitable in a converted ground – but to allow these sections good sightlines the new roof has no screenends. This may enhance viewing but it does little to keep out cold winds.

The South Stand was originally a large bank of terracing, over which the propped cantilever roof is suspended quite magnificently. Red and yellow seats, red facings and grey steelwork add colour (more echoes of Anfield) and behind the stand a gasometer peeks over the roof. Aberdeen have bought a section of the Gas Board land behind for improved access to the banking.

To the left of the South Stand, beyond the other uncovered corner, one can just see the wild, grassy heights of Broad Hill and a nearby cemetery on Golf Road, which lies between the Links golf course and the cold, brooding sea.

The Beach End, an optimistic title one feels, is to the left, its tall roof actually overshadowing a corner of the Main Stand roof. Angled around the curving pitch, this visitors' end has grey bench seats and cavernous dimensions. Its sloping rear banks, visible from Golf Road, have been valiantly landscaped against the bracing winds (see colour section).

Pittodrie is a unique ground. Though unified by its seating and colouring, it remains a ground of four completely different sides; different in dimensions, shape and design. And large though it is, there is a definite sense of it being a barrier against the sea, a place to huddle, as well as a place to demonstrate that Glasgow and Edinburgh do not have the monopoly of good ideas or fine players. Pittodrie, the outpost, the former dung heap, is now one of the best grounds in Britain; a gem amidst the granite.

·MONTROSE·

Links Park – its former Highland Games stand still watching the action

Previous Grounds

Montrose first played in November 1879 on the Links, on a pitch known as 'Metally' because it was by the Metal Bridge. Amalgamation with Montrose United was followed by a short move to a pitch next to Dorward House, whose walls formed one side of the ground and provided a useful vantage point for spectators. Canvas sheeting was rigged up around the other sides. Called Links Park, the ground shared changing facilities with the adjacent curling club and was opened with a match v. Arbroath on 12 August 1885. This first Links Park was on the north side of what is now Dorward Road.

Links Park

Rented from Montrose Old Church, the second Links Park was opened in 1887 with a match v. Caledonia Rangers of Perth. To keep up with demands of professionalism over the next few decades, Links Park was often hired out for other uses, including a circus, women's football and grazing livestock. Less welcome was the army during the First World War, who, after prolonged arguments, finally paid Montrose compensation of £50 in 1920.

Links Park had no proper changing facilities or perimeter fencing until 1919 and for one Cup tie benches had to be borrowed from the King's Playhouse. Indeed Montrose were so impecunious they borrowed a junior club's goalnets until they could afford their own in 1920.

That year fund raising for a grandstand began, raising the not-so-grand sum of £7 in one season. When a stand costing £150 did arrive it was second-hand from the Montrose Highland Games. Even then players still had to change in a hut on the car park until Montrose joined the Second Division in 1929 and formal dressing rooms were built behind the stand. This arrangement essentially survives today.

Also in 1929 the directors had to complain about poultry wandering into the ground from Wellington Street and damaging the pitch!

No further changes were made until a Development Association formed in 1960 (although fund raising for a terrace roof had begun way back in 1936). Two terrace covers were erected over the next decade and training lights, put up in the 1960s, were upgraded to League standard during the 1970s, although there was no official inaugural game.

Links Park also recorded its record gate in this period, 8983 for a Cup tie v. Dundee on 17 March 1973. Since then safety work has reduced the capacity to 6500, including 324 seats.

Ground Description

Tucked among the quiet sea-front streets by the Links, the ground's unobtrusive gateway is approached down a small backstreet. Few grounds are so hidden.

Squeezed in behind some gardens the all-wooden stand, one of the smallest in the League, has a low corrugated roof decorated by a blue dog-tooth fascia board, and just four rows of blue and grey seats behind a low wooden fence, fronted by two such sunken dug-outs that visiting managers might wish to bring a periscope. Access to the stand is from a thin tarmac path between the fence and the touchline. The boardroom, like a scout hut, stands behind with an adjacent hut acting as the home dressing room.

From here, to the left is the open Beach End (being closest to the sea). Opposite is the covered Union Street Side with blue and red steelwork, behind which is a flat training area and more houses.

To the right is the covered Wellington Street End whose roof is angled in the corner towards the Main Stand. The terracing here as in the rest of the ground is newly concreted and has low red barriers. A blue and white rail surrounds the pitch, which has no track, and the goalposts are of the traditional Scottish square variety.

Links Park possesses a cosy simplicity, rather like a suburban bowling club – well tended and private. It is a back yard of a ground, in the nicest possible sense.

·BRECHIN CITY·

Glebe Park

Formed by the amalgamation of two Brechin teams, Hearts and Harp, City first played at Glebe Park in August 1906. On joining Division Two in 1929 the small stand, a portable one from the Perth Show, was supplemented with a Pavilion built alongside. A cover at the Cemetery End was also built during this period.

Glebe Park barely changed until the 1970s. In February 1973 the record gate of 8123 attended a Cup tie v. Aberdeen, and in August 1977 floodlights were switched on for a League Cup tie v. Hibernian. Brechin were the third last Scottish League club to have lights (Stranraer were the last).

But the greatest change came when half the famous hedge which runs down the North Side of Glebe Park became so easily penetrable that a wall was built in its place. The surviving half is, nevertheless, the only one at any League ground in Britain.

The old stand was finally replaced in 1981 by a modern single-tier construction costing £60 000. Since then the capacity has been reduced from 7300 to 3000, including 291 seats, until more safety work is completed.

Ground Description

It is not just the hedge which lends such appeal to Glebe Park. It is the setting amid spires and rolling lawns, and the inescapable irony that although Brechin, population 6500, is the smallest place in Great Britain to have its own League team, that very team rejoices in the name of City.

Of course Brechin is a city by right, however small, and lest we deride the club's pretensions we should note that when Glebe Park has a gate of 1000, the proportional equivalent would be, for example, 77 000 at Leeds or 24 000 at Northampton.

Statistics apart, Glebe Park is a treasure. Entrance is via a large car park surrounded by wooden garages, through a gate which emerges behind a low terrace. This a ground without barriers, one can walk about freely.

The new Main Stand, a tall, 30-yard long construction has a plaque displaying the names of those who sponsored its opening on 4 August 1981. The club crest adorns the centre, the front wall is white, the safety railings scarlet and the roof matt black, with a floodlight gantry in the centre. Only one feature mars the stand – small panes of glass on each screen-end make viewing towards the corners quite irksome.

We shall manage however. Behind the stand is a market garden, divided from the ground by a tall hedge. Immediately to the right is a low hut which used to house dressing rooms and has a small verandah for club officials.

Glebe Park – the famous hedge on the far left

To the left is an uncovered open cinder bank with a few steps of terracing at the front. With no track intervening, grass runs down to the pitch, which is only 67 yards wide and slopes down to the near right hand corner.

To the right is the covered Cemetery End, with an angled roof covering an unterraced slope. Grassland and a cemetery lie behind.

But the real character of the ground derives from the tall hedge opposite, which runs from the top left corner to just past the half-way line. There is just enough room between hedge and touchline for three thin floodlight poles and a narrow path, making it the narrowest side at any League venue. The hedge is patched up with wire in places, but the club well knows that to replace it would be to provoke immeasurable discontent, among home and away supporters alike.

Beyond the hedge is grassland used for training and on a rise the buildings of the Glencadam distillery.

The russet-coloured hedge, the green of the turf and the ease of movement around this unspoilt enclosure, combine to create a warmth rarely found at football grounds and certainly never in the midst of a real city.

·FORFAR ATHLETIC·

Station Park

Having played as Angus Athletic's second eleven, Forfar established a separate identity in May 1885. After using Manor Park occasionally, the club first developed Station Park in 1888, improving the pitch and building a 400-seater stand. But as Douglas Souter and David McGregor relate in the club's centenary history, before it could be used strong winds blew off the corrugated roof. Five years after this inauspicious start the whole caboodle came down in a gale.

That same year, 1893, could have been Forfar's last at Station Park. The neighbouring auction company wanted tenancy of the ground, so Athletic considered moving to Lilybank. They stayed put, however, and have lived in harmony with the auctioneers since.

With a new, more compact Grandstand in place, Forfar slowly developed, but when Celtic arrived for a Cup match just before the First World War, Station Park's changing facilities were deemed inadequate so the teams used the newly-opened public baths. Expansion of the banking allowed a 6000 crowd to pack the small ground.

Greater profits enabled Forfar to open their first substantial stand, seating 400 in 1919. Not so substantial, however, that it could resist another gale which destroyed the stand roof a third time just before Athletic joined the League in 1921.

Station Park had one up on its neighbours at this time when the future King George VI and Queen Mother sat in the stand with their host from nearby Glamis, the Earl of Strathmore, himself a Forfar fan. Another event at the ground was the staging of the Forfar Games.

This period also saw the erection of a low, narrow shelter along the South Side Terrace and in time-honoured tradition this too was damaged by gales in the early 1950s.

Forfar finally purchased Station Park in 1956 and in February 1957 suffered yet another bout of wind.

Station Park's Main Stand, no problems in the wind now

Not before time, therefore, the club launched a fund-raising campaign – which included the sale of the world's largest bridie (a meat and onion pie) – to build a stand that would surely defy the elements. Yet even as the money came in, the east wing of the old stand was terminally wrecked by more gusts, so construction work had to be stepped up. Three months before schedule on 31 January 1959 the new stand was opened, for a match v. Rangers.

Perhaps they should have taken a bit more time, however, because from the moment it was first used patrons complained that the sight angles were wrong. This, it has been said, was because it was designed by the architects of the Royal Show-grounds who were accustomed to different viewing requirements.

Station Park's record gate, 10 780, was for a Cup tie v. Rangers in February 1970 and the first official floodlit match was v. Aberdeen on 11 October 1971.

Since then Station Park has much improved. Beginning in 1976 each terrace has been completely resurfaced and new barriers installed at a cost of around £500 000, and in 1985–86 a cantilevered cover was built behind the South Side Terrace. Once complete the old terrace was removed and the pitch now has room to move away from the Main Stand and thus improve all-round vision. For a small club, the work was ambitious and far-sighted, giving Station Park a capacity of 9800, including 800 seats.

Ground Description

The name Station Park conjures up an image of urban gloom, and as one approaches the ground under a railway arch that impression is reinforced. But the reality is quite different. Forfar's station buildings are derelict, the last passenger train having passed through in 1967. Thanks to Dr Beeching, the nearest working station is in Dundee.

The box-like Main Stand is 30 yards long astride the half-way line, with a high brick balcony wall and blue and yellow bench seats. Grass screen-ends and the stand's position make viewing a real problem. Behind the stand is a rough track and the open fields of North Mains Farm.

From here, to the right, also backed by fields, is the neat West End Terrace with silver barriers. Opposite is the cantilevered cover with blue fascia and a high breeze-block wall. One doubts if it will keep the weather off spectators, but if it withstands the gales, the £132 000 investment will be worth every penny. Behind here is the auction mart.

Finally to the left is narrow, open East Terrace which has no barriers. Behind is the old station site, to be used for housing, and an unused gasometer.

Station Park may be bleak at times, it may seem exposed, but for such a small club it is in prime condition. Though the trains have long gone, at least Forfar have established a firm platform for their future development. And, dare one say it, the ground now seems to be totally windproof.

·ARBROATH·

Previous Grounds

Arbroath's first ground from 1878–80 was the Hospital Field Estate on a pitch opposite the Faces, between the sea and railway line.

Gayfield

Originally a seaside rubbish dump, Old Gayfield was opened with a match v. Rob Roy in 1880. It was, according to *The Red Lichties* by Malcolm Gray and Stephen Mylles, a tight little ground with a narrow pitch. Photographs show that along the Dundee Road Side, there was not even room for spectators between the wall and the touchline.

Rangers, once defeated on what they called this 'back green', complained about the pitch dimensions and won the replay 8-1. Another team had less cause for complaint. Their record 36-0 defeat in September 1885 was fair and square. They were, of course, the hapless Bon Accord.

To improve the ground, Arbroath bought up part of the seashore belonging to the Aberdeen and Dundee Railway and extended the pitch eastwards, towards what locals called the Tuttie's Neuk End.

After joining the League in 1921, rumours that the ground was to be partly sold by the Dundee and Arbroath Railway Company persuaded the club to raise £1050 by subscription in order to purchase Gayfield, on condition that if Arbroath ever folded the ground would revert to public use.

Old Gayfield's last match was on 28 March 1925, v. King's Park. The pitch was then moved 60 yards south west so that the original half-way line became the new goal-line. More fund raising enabled Arbroath to build a stand on the Dundee Road Side (Old Gayfield's stand was on the sea-side).

Greater Gayfield, as it was called, was opened v. East Fife in front of 7000 spectators on 29 August 1925 by the sports-loving Earl of Strathmore, father of the Queen Mother, whose home was at Glamis Castle 18 miles away.

In 1949 a boundary wall was built after special dispensation (because of post-war shortages) and Gayfield's record attendance came in February 1952 when 13 510 saw a Cup tie v. Rangers, who this time made no complaint about the pitch.

Temporary floodlights were erected in October 1955 and in their second inaugural match v. Dundee United, it was reported that the match's high-spot came when an Arbroath player smashed one of the lamps with a hefty clearance! (The lamps were replaced in 1970 with ones bought from Aberdeen, and these were in turn sold in 1986 to English non-League club Eastwood.)

In September 1958 fire caused £7000-worth of damage to the Main Stand after a match v. Partick, whose players saw the flames from their hotel across the road. While a replacement all-concrete and brick stand went up, the players changed in a nearby boys' club.

By this time there were small covers on three sides of terracing, all since replaced; at each end in 1979 and on the sea-side a year later. A new adminis-

Gay Field, funfair and sea-shore

trative area and boardroom was added to the back of the stand in 1975 at a cost of £10 000, and in the 1980s the terracing was completely rebuilt, giving bright new Gayfield a capacity of 10 000, including 896 seats.

Ground Description

Shrewsbury's Gay Meadow may be closer to water but Arbroath's Gayfield is closer to the sea than any other League ground in Britain. Although one cannot feel any spray from the terracing, the waves are only a matter of yards away. This proximity means that the pitch drains easily while the sea air fends off any frost.

From Dundee Road, the ground is as spruce as a private beach club, with a clean white frontage leading to the 70-yard long Main Stand. Here the white facings and maroon steelwork set the tone for the whole ground. The roof is low, barely pitched with glass screen-ends. Inside are maroon bench seats.

From here, to the left is the Ladyloan End, named after the nearby school which stands beyond the grassland where Old Gayfield lay. The new concrete terracing with simple maroon barriers and a short cover over the centre is identical to the right hand Seaforth End Terrace, named after the nearby hotel. An amusement arcade stands directly behind.

Opposite is the Covered Enclosure, 70 yards long, behind which is a low brick wall, once demolished by the waves in 1962, a road which was once the railway line, and beyond that the North Sea – cold, murky and not in the slightest bit inviting. Indeed, as winds and waves pound the shore in mid-winter, Gayfield can be one of the most bracing grounds in the land.

·DUNDEE·

Previous Grounds

As in Edinburgh, the story of Dundee's football grounds can be likened to a game of musical chairs, further complicated by mergers, splits and name changes. I am indebted, therefore, to Jim Wilkie's study *Across the Great Divide* (Mainstream Publishing 1984) for unravelling this footballing web.

Dundee's formation in 1893 resulted from the amalgamation of two of the city's four top clubs, Our Boys and East End, each formed in 1877. (For future clarity it is worth noting that a third club, Dundee Harp, was the precursor of Dundee Hibernian, later Dundee United. The fourth was Johnstone Wanderers, an offshoot of Our Boys.)

Our Boys had played at West Craigie Park since 1882 while East End used Clepington Park (the present Tannadice) until 1891, Pitkerro Park briefly and finally Carolina Port, a ground reckoned to be the best in Dundee. Situated by the harbour, it had a capacity of 12 500, including 1500 seats plus running and cycle tracks.

West Craigie Park was less developed and had lost its Grandstand in a fire, so that when East End and Our Boys amalgamated on the strength of winning League membership in June 1893, it came as a shock that the new club kicked off here rather than Carolina Port. In fact Carolina Port had been surprisingly taken over by another local team Strathmore.

West Craigie was far from ideal, however, and a few months after the first League match in August 1893, Dundee bought control of the company which owned Carolina Port.

(Strathmore then amalgamated with Johnstone Wanderers at Clepington Park to form the Wanderers, who then gained a League place, moved to Harp's former ground at East Dock Street, returned to Clepington and were later ousted by Dundee Hibernian – see Dundee United. To complicate matters further, West Craigie was then taken over by Dundee Harp who between 1894–95 were renamed Dundee Hibs!)

Carolina Port is remembered for two reasons. First, overlooking the ground was a mound or 'bing' of shale known commonly as the 'Burning Mountain', because it always smouldered. Secondly, the ground staged Dundee's first international, against Wales, in March 1896 attended by 11 700. Financial ills led to reorganization of the club in 1898 and this in turn led to Dundee's final move a few months later to farmland on Dens Road.

The remains of West Craigie Park are now bordered by Morgan Place, Park Avenue, Baxter Park Terrace and the Tayside Works. Carolina Port was built over and is now occupied by the works of J.

Dundee's duo, with Dens Park in the foreground

T. Inglis (no relation) and potato merchants Pattullo Barr, between Camperdown Street and Eastern Wharf.

Dens Park

Inaugurated by Lord Provost McGrady on 19 August 1899 v. St Bernard's (within the same few weeks as Rugby Park, Pittodrie, Owlerton and Fratton Park were opened), Dens Park's most startling attribute was that next door was Clepington Park, home of Dundee's second best club, the Wanderers.

League football was however a greater attraction than the Northern League and within a short time Dens Park became the city's best ground. On the Dens Road side Dundee placed the stand from Carolina Port and shortly after a new Main Stand was built opposite on Tannadice Street.

The present lay-out took shape when Dundee purchased the ground for £5000 in 1919, after hearing that the neighbouring engineering works were also anxious to buy the land. Archibald Leitch supervised the new format (see Design) and his pen and ink drawing is still displayed at Dens Park. It depicts the standard Leitch pattern – an idealized view of a vast bowl, open on three sides around the present Main Stand, adorned as was the fashion with decorative ironwork on the roof.

Opened on 17 September 1921, the new Dens Park cost £60 000 to develop and upstaged Tannadice completely. It may have been a coincidence but the old Carolina Port Stand, which did not appear on Leitch's drawing, rather conveniently burnt down soon after on Christmas Day. One's suspicions are echoed in Jimmy Guthrie's autobiography *Soccer Rebel*. A former Dundee player, Guthrie wrote, 'In one season there were three mysterious fires, all put out thanks to the energetic work and bravery of the groundsman, but instead of a gold watch the hero got the sack. There was another fire early in the following season and with the insurance money the foundations for the present stand were laid . . .' Guthrie was no friend of officialdom and confused the chronology of events, but one suspects a similar story could be told at many a ground.

Dens Park has staged three full internationals, in 1904, 1908 and 1936, all v. Wales, but in 1938 after several years without success Dundee were relegated for the first time and the Scotland team have avoided the city since.

Successive victories in the League Cup after the Second World War brought at least a smile back to Dens Park, which experienced its biggest-ever crowd of 43 024 for a Cup tie v. Rangers in February 1953. But the ground only changed in 1959 when the combined transfers of Davie Sneddon to Preston and goalkeeper Bill Brown to Spurs for £29 500 paid for the erection of a cover on the South Side Terrace and floodlights, first switched on v. Liverpool in March 1960 (Dundee, managed by Bob Shankly, were Champions a year later while Liverpool, managed by his brother Bill, won the Second Division).

European football came to Dens Park in 1962–63 but few of the profits from this or several big transfer deals went into ground improvements, apart from the erection of a cover at the West End Terrace in the mid-1960s.

With the Safety of Sports Grounds Act in 1975, however, Dens Park was forced to adapt. In common with several Scottish clubs, Dundee chose to install bench seating rather than upgrade crush barriers, and in 1982–83 some £350 000 was spent on seating the South and West Terraces.

Thus the capacity was reduced over a period of fifteen years from 45 000 including 5000 seats to 22 381 including 12 130 seats.

Ground Description

Despite its post-war additions, Dens Park remains an Archibald Leitch ground through and through. The large cranked Main Stand, beautifully maintained, is the chief element and, though similar to others at Hibernian and Blackburn, Dundee's stand, with its red pillars, deep blue balcony wall and light blue screen-ends, has a special presence.

Much of this is due to the wide, angled track and paddock in front. Two semi-circular concrete bays in front of the dug-outs lead the eye toward the centre, but the players actually emerge from the wing. Just behind one dug-out is surely the narrowest crush barrier in Britain. Numbered seven, it is less then 3-feet wide. Also unusual, for a two-tier stand (as opposed to a double-decker), is the opening under the balcony wall allowing spectators to walk into a concourse under the upper tier, as used to be the case for example at Tottenham.

From this stand, behind which runs Tannadice Street, to the right is the West or Provost Road End, with a deep pitched roof covering the near side only. Again the steelwork is red, but the real colour derives from the red and blue stripes of the bench seats.

These seats continue round to the South Side, whose roof starts level with the penalty area. Behind here, something of the scale Leitch intended can be seen from the massive landscaped banking which leads down from the terrace to Dens Road, 50 feet below. The waste ground beyond here was once a jute factory, the industry which shaped Dundee's destiny and whose captains dominated the club's boardroom for decades.

Further in the distance are two high-rise tower blocks, from which an excellent view of both Dundee grounds can be had, and the 571-feet high Dundee Law, a hill crowned by a war memorial.

To the left is the open East Terrace, a narrow undulating terrace with red and white barriers curving around the pitch. Some locals call it the T. C. Keay End after the engineering works behind. These works continue down Tannadice Street to Dundee United's ground, a hundred yards away.

The proximity of these two grounds, discussed in the next section, is perplexing enough, but Dens Park has a character far removed from that of Tannadice. It was once said that Tannadice was for thrills, Dens Park for skills. Perhaps this had something to do with the restrained tones and flowing unity of Dens Park and its peculiarly old-fashioned air, which, thanks to careful maintenance, borders almost on the stately.

· DUNDEE UNITED ·

Tannadice Park

From the entangled roots of Dundee's footballing family tree, Dundee United began life in 1909 as Dundee Hibernian. Although unconnected with previous clubs of the same name, Hibernian were the natural inheritors of an Irish Catholic tradition borne for many years by the once great Dundee Harp (although as it happened Hibs did not adopt a sectarian policy). For their first ground Hibernian considered Carolina Port, Dundee's ground until 1899, before honing in on Clepington Park, now called Tannadice.

As home to East End and Johnstone Wanderers, Clepington had been a focus of local football for some twenty years before the opening of Dens Park (see Dundee). In 1909 it was the home of a modest but established Northern League club, Dundee Wanderers, who had moved there in 1891 and as brief members of the Second Division played a few League games at the ground between August and December 1894.

Hibernian's choice of ground raised two problems; first they had to oust the Wanderers, second they had to cope with the proximity of Dens Park, whose incumbents Dundee were then one of Scotland's top clubs.

Liverpool and Everton have some historical excuse for being so close, while Notts County's ground is at least separated from Forest's by the width of a river. But why Dundee Hibernian, given these two obstacles and the rest of the city to search in, still chose Clepington Park must remain one of the enigmas of British sport.

Three explanations offer themselves. Clepington Park had a long-standing tradition as a football ground and, although basic, it was ready-made. Hibs also must have genuinely felt that potential support among the 35 000-strong Irish community would be sufficient to establish the club wherever it was based.

Or perhaps it was just sheer bravado on their part. A correspondent of the *People's Journal*, quoted by Jim Wilkie (see Dundee), argued that Wanderer's stagnation had been due in no small part to the arrival of Dundee on their doorstep. Hibernian, the correspondent added, 'have made a very big initial blunder in going to Clepington Park which has been a starvation hole from first to last'.

Apparently unmoved, Hibernian proceeded to arouse more publicity by conniving with Clepington Park's owner over Wanderers' departure. Understandably aggrieved, Wanderers took their revenge by ignoring legal advice and ordering a 'wrecker' to remove every possible fixture and fitting from the ground, including even the goalposts and fences.

Hibs thus found themselves leasing a large, vacant

Like a set of jaws waiting to snap shut – Tannadice Park's unique cantilever stand

expanse of grass, described by one Dundee player as being 'bare as a bald head'. For years the press had urged the formation of a senior club to rival Dundee. Now those hopes seemed to have faltered before a ball was even kicked.

But as Mike Watson's admirable history of the club *Rags to Riches* (David Winter 1985) relates, Hibs appeared to have ample reserves of money and determination. Within months at a cost of £3000 they had enclosed the ground once more, built up banking to hold roughly 15 000, and finished a two-storey Pavilion with a 1200-seater stand alongside. As is the case now, the stand extended only to the half-way line, as at Raith. Clepington was also renamed Tannadice Park, after the street which links it to Dens Park.

Amid doubt and speculation as to the new club's chances of survival, Tannadice Park was opened on 18 August 1909 with a match against another club who knew well the anxieties of starting afresh, Hibernian of Edinburgh.

After former Harp stalwart Paddy Rock raised the green flag, the Lord Provost kicked off amid a carnival atmosphere and the new boys did well to earn a 1-1 draw. Officials of neighbouring Dundee were also invited to this carefully stage-managed inauguration, watched by a 7000 crowd.

Ironically the second match was a Northern League fixture against Dundee Wanderers, who were still homeless and had to wait another year before setting up at St Margaret's Park. To ease their resentment Wanderers won the match but a year later Hibs left them behind (they survived only four more seasons) by winning a Second Division place, ahead of established clubs like Dunfermline and St Johnstone. No other club in the history of the game had achieved so much in such a short time in such apparently unfavourable circumstances.

As the team wavered in Division Two, Tannadice barely developed. For a cup match in 1913 v. Forfar, rather than use the larger Dens Park, the banking at

Tannadice was built up to hold around 20 000, but by 1922 the ground was still quite undeveloped.

That year almost saw the end of Dundee Hibs. They lost League status and were only hauled back from the brink by a consortium of businessmen who worked hard to gain re-election a season later. The new board changed the club's name to Dundee United and a progression to full-time professionalism also brought a change in rank in 1925, to the First Division.

This new status encouraged United to buy Tannadice for £2500 and initiate wholesale improvements. Although a new share issue failed to raise sufficient cash to carry out all their plans, which included a 3000-seater stand, with the £7000 raised they were at least able to complete two major tasks – partially reducing the pitch's steep slope, which involved dynamiting sections of solid rock under the surface before new drains could be laid, and terracing the three embankments with railway sleepers. This work increased Tannadice's capacity to roughly 30 000.

Over the next seven seasons United bounced up and down between the divisions. Each promotion brought with it a ground inspection, and in 1931 the League ordered the Pavilion to be improved and, surprisingly, the pitch to be widened from 65 yards to 70 yards, which meant a perimeter wall had to come down. It seems odd that the width of the pitch was not spotted earlier.

But then Tannadice in the 1930s was always a venue for the unexpected, as a series of disasters and revivals made them one of Britain's most idiosyncratic clubs. These surprises continued during war-time, when Tannadice played host to an Empire bantam-weight title fight (won by local boy Jim Brady). After the War, in 1956 they became the first Scottish club to operate their own pools competition, a pioneering step which was to prove the club's making over the following decade.

First came the construction of a cover over the Dens Park End during the 1957–58 season and the concreting of the Arklay Street End. Tannadice's Pavilion and Stand were now woefully outdated and after one season back in Division One, they were finally demolished in 1961.

Not that conditions improved, because while the new stand struggled towards completion the players had to train in public parks and on match days change at a ground on Kingsway and be ferried by bus to Tannadice. Half-time was spent across Tannadice Street in the Jute Industries canteen. Then the pitch had to be moved to accommodate the new stand and wooden changing huts were belatedly installed until finally, in August 1962, the new Stand was opened. United had muddled through again, in a manner quite unlike that of any other club.

'Greater Tannadice' cost around £250 000 to create; this included enlarging the North Terrace to give an overall capacity of 28 500 and erecting only the third cantilevered stand built in Britain (after Scunthorpe and Sheffield Wednesday). United's however was L-shaped and was therefore unique. All that remained was for floodlights to be switched on, an event which followed during a League match v. Rangers on 10 November.

Tannadice's new capacity was tested only once, when a record 28 000 all-ticket crowd saw the visit of Barcelona in the Fairs Cup on 16 November 1966.

In 1971 Tannadice was the first Scottish venue to have a glass-fronted lounge in the stand for sponsors, and after the sale of Ray Stewart to West Ham in 1979 for £400 000, the ground improved further with the erection of a cover over the large North Side terracing. As Watson writes, its cost, according to manager Jim McLean, equated roughly with Ray Stewart's left leg.

Against most established principles, Tannadice had been transformed into a modern stadium without one single success in a major tournament. This came belatedly with victory in the League Cup in 1980, since when United have become established as one of Scotland and Europe's premier clubs.

This late development has meant a relatively low expenditure on safety improvements, resulting in a current capacity of 22 310, of which 2252 are seated.

Ground Description

A basic grasp of Dundee United's early history can only add to the inevitable puzzlement any visitor experiences on entering Tannadice Street for the first time. From United's main entrance Dens Park is but a couple of kicks away on the other side of the road.

Like St Pancras and King's Cross railway stations in London, the grounds stand together as monuments of private endeavour coupled with unwavering pride. Their juxtaposition can be explained but never entirely justified.

Tannadice, the older ground now regarded as the upstart, is an angular ground, dominated by the L-shaped cantilever whose ends resemble a grey, open jaw, poised to clamp shut. Its rear leans out over Tannadice Street in order to gain a few precious extra rows of seating.

With its plain corrugated fascia, silver railings, brick facings and polished wooden seats it is drab but efficient, the only relief being a splash of orange seating behind the goal.

But every seat offers an excellent view. There are duckboards for the feet – to stave off damp and cold (other clubs please note) – and a wide concourse along the balcony. In the corner, above the player's entrance is a line of executive boxes while along the touchline is another set of lounges and boxes, topped by brown cladding.

This stand stops openly and abruptly at the halfway line, as if the money ran out. From here, to the left along the touchline is uncovered terracing arranged in sections, two of them raised.

Tannadice Street, with its low-rise factories, runs

behind and the Main Stand and floodlights of Dens Park are clearly visible. Indeed from the top right-hand corner of the Main Stand, one can even see the far goalposts at Dens Park. It is hard not to stare incredulously.

To the right is the uncovered Arklay Street End which sinks down from the Main Stand towards the far corner, where because of the pitch's pronounced slope there is a high compensating wall down to the pitch in front of the floodlight pylon. In the distance, beyond the allotments and greenhouses behind this terrace is the River Tay.

Opposite is the Covered Enclosure, almost identical to Easter Road's but with unadorned orange fascia. The plain though high roof with silver steelwork is considerably lightened by numerous skylights, and the terracing both here and on the Arklay Street End has relatively high 8-inch risers with silver-coloured barriers. Before the North Terrace was raised and covered the upper tenements on Sandeman Street had an unrestricted view of the pitch.

Finally, to the left is the covered Dens Park End more commonly known as the Shed. Its dark pitched roof is brightened up by a large orange advertisement. Behind here a triangle of grass leads to Dundee's main entrance.

United have invested too much on Tannadice to even consider becoming truly united with their neighbours. But although the few hundred feet that separates the grounds might so easily have become a hate-infested divide, apart from natural jealousy when either team does better, familiarity in this case seems to have bred little discontent. Both sets of players occasionally share the same training facilities and it is not uncommon to see staff from Tannadice trot up the road for a chat with their Dens Park counterparts. Hard to fathom it may be, but in the context of Dundee's tangled footballing history, very little seems surprising at all.

·ST JOHNSTONE·

Previous Grounds

When St Johnstone cricket club formed a football team in 1884 they joined a handful of Perth teams (one with the delightful name of Fair City Athletic) playing on South Inch, where there are still pitches. In 1885 the club rented an adjacent piece of land known as Craigie Haugh from Sir Robert Moncrieffe. Opened in August with a game v. Queen's Park, the ground was called thereafter St Johnstone Park or the Recreation Ground. Once the club achieved League status in 1911, however, its facilities were deemed inadequate and in 1924 when St Johnstone won promotion they moved to their present home.

Muirton Park

Although normally a working day in Perth, there was such excitement on Christmas Day 1924 when the ground was inaugurated that a public holiday was declared. Over 11 000 attended in fine weather to see the Lord Provost declare Muirton Park open before a League match, coincidentally also against Queen's Park.

The present Main Stand was the centrepiece of the ground, which barely altered until the early 1950s when a cover was erected over the east terracing. Around this time, in February 1952, Muirton Park's record gate of 29 972 attended a Cup tie v. neighbours Dundee. FA Cup winners West Ham came for the club's first floodlit match on 16 December 1964.

Financial difficulties have brought about a number of plans for Muirton Park; in 1973 a scheme to introduce pony trotting was considered – it had proved an attraction at Motherwell – and in 1977 plans for a sports and leisure complex at the ground were announced.

Neither came to fruition, and in 1983 when St Johnstone rose to the Premier Division the ground became designated under the Safety of Sports Grounds Act. Top status lasted only a year but the designation remained valid, and as the club fell straight down to the Second Division fewer funds were available to carry out the work required. As a result the capacity is reduced to 11 500, of which only 500 are seated, in a stand actually containing 2185 seats.

Ground Description

Without peering too closely, Muirton Park retains a definite aura of scale and efficiency. From Dunkeld Road the white and blue façade is plain though orderly, and the Main Stand appears to have changed little from the day it was opened. It is a simple two-tier construction with bench seats at either end and a blue balcony wall and perimeter fence enclosing a terraced paddock. Blue screen-ends and a blue roof

Muirton Park – once the pride of the Fair City

create a unified whole. A large advertisement which once distinguished the roof – 'Dryborough's beer for the discriminating man' – is regrettably no more.

From here, to the right is an open terrace curving around the pitch, continuing under the large Covered Enclosure until it reaches the open north terracing on the left. There is no track at this end, the extra semi-circle of turf being useful for training.

Given its surroundings, mainly utilitarian council housing, the ground is dominated by a stark concrete structure behind the North End. Capped by a large

pale green sloping roof this is the Perth Ice Rink, a famous venue for curling built in 1936. A bowling ring stands adjacent. Intentionally or not, the twin ventilator cupolas of the ice rink are mirrored by similar features on a school behind the south terracing.

Too big for current demands, Muirton Park's sweeping moss-covered terraces with their few scattered barriers tell only too clearly of the cold winds of reality which even this fair city has been forced to weather, leaving a ground with a modicum of colour and uniformity, but no real zest.

·EAST FIFE·

Bayview Park

Known originally as East of Fife, the club was formed in 1903 by footballers from the three adjoining towns of Buckhaven, Leven and Methil. Bayview Park, originally part of Kirklandhill Farm, is in Methil and was opened with a match v. Hearts in August 1903. The first stand, seating 400, was built in 1906 and superseded by the present Main Stand, which was built opposite and opened on 7 October 1922 in East Fife's second League season.

The club's best years came in the decade following the Second World War. Bayview's record crowd of 22 515 was v. Raith on 2 January 1950, the first derby match between these two in Division One. Three League Cup wins (East Fife were already the first Second Division club to win the Scottish Cup, in

1938) added to their prosperity and helped towards erecting floodlights, first switched on for a match v. Leeds on 7 March 1954. On 8 February 1956 Bayview enjoyed with Easter Road the distinction of being the first ground to stage a floodlit Scottish Cup match, when, appropriately, lighting pioneers Stenhouse-muir were visitors.

In September 1967 a cover was built on the Enclosure and four years later a separate block added to the Main Stand for directors. Bayview's terracing and barriers have been completely modernized in recent years while the floodlighting gantries, of which there were five different varieties around the ground at one stage, were replaced in 1986 at a cost of £50 000. These improvements have meant that although small in scale, Bayview has retained a comparatively large capacity of 15 000, of which 800 are seats.

Ground Description

Rather like Kent's Medway towns, the three coastal towns of Buckhaven, Methil and Leven are hard for

Bayview Park with not a drop of seawater in sight

the stranger to differentiate between. Bayview is in the centre of Methil, a few hundred yards from the Firth of Forth, but the only clear view of the water is from the East Terrace. The bay in Bayview is Largo Bay, a few miles up the coast.

The ground itself is a tight, compact enclosure whose greyness is alleviated only by trim yellow barriers and a yellow and red perimeter fence, hard by the touchlines.

The Main Stand is a grey post and beam construction, livened up by red seats. A very low press-box in the paddock area resembles a machine gun post. To the immediate left, sandwiched between the stand and a social club, is a glass-fronted box for the directors, built over the dressing rooms.

From this side, with the sea breezes whipping in from behind, to the left is the open West Terrace on Kirkland Road. A neat, low embankment, it is lined by telegraph poles and wires which continue round to encircle the whole ground. Beyond the houses it is also possible to see the hulking great steel skeletons of oil platforms being built for the North Sea.

Opposite is the Covered Enclosure, another tidy terrace with a black and yellow steelwork roof. A disused railway line is behind, leading towards the open East Terrace. A large grey grain-storage tank dominates the skyline behind this terrace, which is also backed by a primary school.

Like the town of Methil itself, Bayview is orderly but hardly exciting. The club have settled for substance rather than style, sound terracing rather than smart stands. Even so, in a minor resort and port bypassed by railways and motorways, it could just be that the ground is the only site stopping sports lovers from carrying straight on up the road to St Andrews.

·RAITH ROVERS·

Previous Grounds

Raith started in 1883 on Sands Brae, now the Esplanade area between Hendry's Wynd and Buchanan Street (where every April the longest market in Europe is held). Their first enclosed ground was an old claypit where the High School now stands, next to Stark's Park. Not long after they moved to Robbie's Park, a few hundred yards to the north, leased from the Laird of Raith and Novar (Rovers originally derived their name from the Lairdship). In 1891 they were forced to leave when the corporation decided to extend Beveridge Park, which is still a public park (famous for an annual motorbike race).

Stark's Park

Used originally by various Kirkaldy teams, including the Wanderers, Union and Rangers, the ground was named after its owner, Councillor Robert Stark, a rope manufacturer and licensee at West Bridge.

John Litster's loving centenary history of the club, to which I am much indebted, tells an intriguing tale of how in 1887 during a local Cup-tie Councillor Stark cleared the pitch of rival fans by letting loose a bull he kept in a byre at the top of the ground. Modern clubs might take up the idea as an alternative to ugly security fences.

When Rovers moved here from Robbie's Park in 1891 they transported their Pavilion down Pratt Street but managed to dislodge sections of it as it passed under the railway bridge. The opening match was in August 1891, the first Grandstand being built five years later.

In 1902 Rovers became the first Fife club to join the League, at which point Stark's Park held up to 12 000, but when Hearts visited for a Cup-tie in 1907 the club rented a section of the railway embankment and squeezed in 17 000. That year a limited company was formed and the Grandstand extended, followed by the erection of turnstiles and the relaying of the pitch.

But although the ground was ready for their first season in Division One in 1910 the stand was not. In 1911 part of it blew down and in October 1918 it was destroyed by fire.

In 1922, therefore, after the club's best-ever League season, the Raith Rovers Grand Stand Company was formed with £10 000 capital, resulting in the construction of a 2500-seater L-shaped stand in the south east corner. Because of the site's limitations it was an intricate little stand, like a miniature Leitch stand with a small gable on the roof. A more basic seated tin stand was also built opposite on the railway side.

Relegation in 1929 brought hard times to Kirkaldy. Plans to introduce greyhound racing fell

All angles and gables at Raith's intriguing Stark's Park

through and by 1948 the only way to clear the debt was to sell Jackie Stewart to Birmingham. With his £6000 transfer both the 1907 company and the Grand Stand Company were dissolved and a new one floated. The reorganization obviously helped because Raith returned immediately to the First Division and enjoyed a decade of success. After a record gate of 31 036 for a Cup-tie v. Hearts on 7 February 1953, the supporters helped build a cover at the Links Street End, and when Rovers reached their second Cup semi-final in 1956, another cover was built at the Beveridge Park End.

Floodlights came to Kirkcaldy in August 1960, the first of three celebratory games being v. Israeli champions Petach Tikva. The next change came in 1981 with the promise of promotion to the Premier Division. The old Railway Stand was replaced with a 50-yard long cantilevered roof, but by the time it was finished Raith had finished fourth. Since then the capacity has been reduced to 10 000, including 3000 seats.

Ground Description

Commentators often talk about games of two halves, but Stark's Park is the only ground of two halves. Unpredictable, eccentric and in an intriguing location by the North Sea, this ground should lift the spirits of the most blasé traveller just as once, perhaps, it inspired Raith starlets like Alex James and Jimmy Baxter to perfect their own idiosyncratic brands of football.

From the foot of Pratt Street the Main Stand sits high on a rise above, with the club name proudly displayed on a brick façade. But as one climbs the hill

the stand stops abruptly. From inside the ground this interruption is even more surprising.

The two-tier stand, with its gable reading RRFC in blue with a red border, appears to have been cut off in its prime at the half-way line. At one end is an L-shaped corner section, at the other, an oversized gantry on the narrowly pitched roof supports just eight small lamps, used for training sessions only. Other details include blue and red seats with a white balcony wall, and two blue and red half-pediments at each screen-end, with a curious canopy over the half-way line end. The rest of this side is a narrow open terrace.

But while we delight in the stand's peculiarity, the structure itself suffers from exposure. Easterly winds have caused its concrete supports to decay, requiring studies by experts from Heriot-Watt University. Those winds whip in from the sea, where oil platforms can be seen dotting the coastal waters.

From the stand, to the left, the corner section is separated from the Links Street End cover by one of four traditional Scottish floodlight pylons, bowing towards the pitch. The simple post and beam roof, about 35 yards long, covers concrete terracing at the front with irregular timber and ash terracing at the back and sides. And just to avert any sense of symmetry, the cover is placed just off-centre.

Behind here in the distance is the tall tower of Seafield Colliery, one of the new generation of super-pits. Some of its shafts tunnel deep under the sea.

Opposite the Main Stand, but again reaching only up to the half-way line, is the new Railway Stand with a simple blue, cantilevered roof, open ends and bright blue bucket seats on a concrete base. A full-length stand of this type would enclose the ground handsomely. As it is, to the right of the cover is open terracing behind which a few yards away runs the Aberdeen to Edinburgh main line. Since up to 18 000 passengers might pass the spot every day, the back of the new stand provides useful advertising revenue. Beyond the line is Balwearie High School, which sounds like a place for tired players but is in fact a provider of some excellent training facilities, used among others by Forfar Athletic's team.

Raith's original ground was on this site. Robbie's Park was to the right, behind the Beveridge Park End. This is a rather wild terrace with chunky sleepers embedded on a cinder slope. A wide track, at this end only, divides the perimeter rail from the narrow pitch – only 67 yards wide with barely a foot of turf to spare – which slopes some 9 feet down from the railway corner towards the players' tunnel.

The tunnel, like the stands, is also off-centre. In fact nothing is uniform at this ground, except the name. Stark's Park is the only rhyming name of any British League ground – another little quirk of this Kirkaldy delight.

◆COWDENBEATH◆

Previous Grounds
Hardly more than a village team, Cowdenbeath formed in 1881 from three local miners' sides and played at Jubilee Park. In 1888 they moved to North End Park, often called the 'Colliers Den', where whippet racing was also popular. In 1917, after two Second Division Championships, the club moved a few hundred yards to Central Park. North End Park is still open land behind the library.

Central Park
The move heralded Cowdenbeath's best period in the League. Central Park's Main Stand was opened around 1921 and two years later the team reached Division One; quite an achievement for a small community, and possibly owing to increased competition from nearby Lochgelly United (members of the League from 1914–26).

The ground's biggest crowd was in September 1949 for a League Cup quarter-final second leg v. Rangers, when 25 586 – several times Cowdenbeath's population – came to see if Rangers could reverse a shock 3-2 deficit from the first leg. They could. Soon after, a roof was built over the Chapel Street End, and in October 1968, Central Park's floodlights were switched on for a match v. Celtic.

To ease their financial problems, Cowdenbeath have at various times staged dog racing and speedway, followed in the 1970s by stock car racing. The latter has been so successful that Central Park is now a leading venue. In 1985 it staged the World Championships in front of 12 000 spectators.

Football attendances are much lower and for a time the ground declined. The Chapel Street roof was blown down in 1983 and a fire set off by young vandals in November 1985 caused £40 000 worth of damage to the stand. This reduced the seating total from 2700 to 500 in a capacity of 10 000. Some £200 000 has been spent on modernizing the terraces and improving access.

Ground Description
Central Park may have changed only superficially in recent years, but its environment is totally altered. Dominating the ground and the village used to be Number Seven Pit, whose extensive workings were adjacent to Central Park. The area is now landscaped, beautified, and apart from a new swimming pool almost completely open.

The ground is approached from Main Street under a railway bridge and along a private road. Stones mark the entrance of the old pit, which was finally exhausted in 1960. A large car park opens out in front of the ground, with a flat area which was once busy with railway sidings, behind the Main Stand (as at Kilmarnock).

Central Park – big city proportions in a mining village

With its red roof, battered black screen-ends and yellow and blue bench seats, the stand tries hard to belie its age, but decay and fire damage have prevented all but the central section from being used since 1985.

From here Central Park is a large oval ground, dominated by a wide tarmac track, dotted with painted tyres. The areas around the wire-rope perimeter fence are littered with car debris. A few steps of terracing topped by a wide path surround the pitch.

To the left is the curved, open High Street End, with a railway line along the rear as formerly at Burnden Park. Opposite is the much improved open side, with modern terracing and barriers only in the centre, divided unusually by a concrete slope and topped by a welcoming sign. Close by, a hoarding advertises one of the club's former directors, proclaiming him to have been Scotland's Haggis Champion from 1981–84. No small honour.

To the right is the now uncovered Chapel Street End, a high curved bank. A few portions of wooden terracing survive and the ground's origins are clear from the coal black cinders which form the banking. Beath High School (once attended by Jim Baxter) stands proudly on a rise overlooking this end.

So close to Dunfermline and Kirkaldy, Cowdenbeath is hardly more than a village, in which Central Park seems disproportionately large, and ominously, since the death of the coalmine, quieter, cleaner, more alone.

DUNFERMLINE ·ATHLETIC·

East End Park

Dunfermline kicked off in 1885 when the footballing members of a cricket club left their summer friends at Lady's Mill, now McKane Park, and rented East End Park from the North British Railway Company.

Early reports of the ground, recounted in John Hunter's superb centenary history – from which most of this information derives – suggest that although the pitch was often muddy, the Pavilion, opened in 1887, and cinder banking made East End Park one of the best in the region.

Nevertheless senior football eluded this, one of Scotland's most historic provinces, for some time and with an uncertain and occasionally troublesome support, Dunfermline's progress was hardly assured even when the ground was moved slightly east along the railway line and a new Pavilion erected. While smaller neighbouring towns like Cowdenbeath won League status, Dunfermline had to wait until 1912, by which time East End Park was one of the best attended grounds outside Glasgow and Edinburgh.

The time was ripe for improvements, beginning with the opening by Provost Macbeth of a new Pavilion in August 1913. The First World War saw East End Park used by the Army. Dunfermline sought refuge at Blackburn Park, by Milesmark School.

Soon after the war, a limited company was formed and the ground, plus additional land to the east, purchased for £3500. Once again the pitch was moved eastwards, to its present position, and a 50-yard long all-seated stand built in front of the Pavilion. With its low flat roof supported along the front by regular narrow columns, this wooden stand was, even by the standards of the period, a fairly basic construction, yet it was to survive with additions until 1962.

At the same time the banking was extended on the three remaining sides and a new pitch and cinder track laid. But the supporters' behaviour had not entirely improved and after a referee had been barracked, the ground was closed for a month in 1921.

Promotion to the First Division in 1926 brought further improvements, including extending the terraces to accommodate 16 000, but relegation and the Depression forced the introduction of greyhound racing in the early 1930s (so successfully that the rent helped save the club soon after, although the club did complain once that the dogs were damaging the pitch by cutting corners). By 1934 Dunfermline were back in Division One and in the summer erected a simple cover over the North Side terracing. The following summer the East Terrace was improved with wood taken from the liner Mauretania, which was being broken at the nearby Rosyth shipyards, yet still East

Sixties style at East End Park

End Park compared unfavourably with grounds attracting far less support.

The Second World War brought back the Army, who paid £50 a year for parking vehicles – the top of the East Terrace had long been used to park cars and was a favourite vantage point during games – followed in 1940 by the arrival of a Polish transport unit and in 1943 the requisitioning of the Pavilion. To help the Russian war effort East End Park also staged a boxing match.

The Army departed in January 1945, having paid out £329 compensation, while a group of youngsters was paid £10 to weed the terracing. A new car park was also laid. But the Main Stand's inadequacies were still apparent. Even the board admitted it was hardly a comfortable setting for supporters' wives. A few years later local sanitary inspectors found the whole ground badly lacking. A mark of the ground's state is that only after a record 20 000 crowd in 1951 were the first crush barriers installed. Faced with post-war shortages, however, all the club could purchase was three huts to improve the North Terrace cover.

In 1953 wings holding 1000 more seats were added to the wooden stand, some of the new seats coming from an ice-rink. More substantial was a new steel-framed cover built to replace the North Terrace roof in 1953–54 at a cost of £2000. It was only 50 yards long and three years later, despite Dunfermline's relegation, it was moved to the rear of the West End, while a more substantial cover costing £7500 was built over the North Terracing. This structure formed the basis of the present L-shaped roof.

Floodlights costing £12 000 were switched on v. Sheffield United in October 1959 and together with manager Jock Stein these illuminated the club over the next few years. East End Park had finally entered the modern era.

Victory in their first Cup Final in 1961 raised funds for the overdue replacement of the Main Stand at a cost of £60 000. The 3000-seater stand, opened in August 1962, transformed the ground and was a fitting backdrop to Dunfermline's European exploits, which helped fund the extension of both wings of the North Enclosure roof in 1965 and the continuation of this cover round the West Terrace two years later.

By this time East End Park was fully modernized with a capacity of 27 160, although the record gate exceeded this when Cup holders Dunfermline faced Champions Celtic on 30 April 1968. The attendance of 27 816 did include gatecrashers, one of whom, John Hunter writes, later felt such remorse he sent the club a 5s postal order. But while dozens scaled the stand roofs and pylons, one man died from injuries after a fall. It was the last time East End Park was to bulge at the barriers.

By 1986 safety limits had reduced the capacity to 14 000, including 3000 seats, but with crowds above 2000 now regarded as healthy, the stadium which had been built for European glory had to be content with more modest fare.

Ground Description

Even looking down at East End Park's tall floodlights from the town where Robert the Bruce is buried, one gains some impression that, like Motherwell and Kilmarnock, here lies another sleeping giant of the provinces.

From Halbeath Road the Main Stand looms large, box-like and, in true 1960s fashion, utilitarian and plain. It sits behind a narrow steep paddock backed by a high white balcony wall, decorated with a thin red line broken up by three bursts of black and white stripes. Unusually the players emerge from a door in the wall and have to trot down the paddock steps to reach the pitch.

In construction the stand represents a half-way house between the traditional two-tier stands of Leitch and the cantilevered stands of the 1970s – excellent viewing with no concessions to style. A pale green roof and cream-coloured cladding enclose the frame, with solid screen-ends lightened by six rectangular windows. Compared with its predecessor it is vast but artless.

From here, to the right is the open, curved East Terrace which still has concrete footings pegged into cinder infill. Opposite is the North Covered Enclosure, behind which lies the railway and a cemetery. The corrugated roof, supported by cream steelwork and with a refreshment bar at the back hidden by a black and white screen, bends round the corner to cover the West Terrace to the left.

This roof and the black, white and red barriers on three sides give East End Park a unity and sense of purpose which reflect only too well the optimism which European football brought to Dunfermline. How ironic that having realized such potential and brought the ground up to scratch, fate and the times conspired to make the improvements seem over-ambitious in the extreme.

HEART OF ·MIDLOTHIAN·

Previous Grounds

Taking their name from a popular dance club (which was itself named after Edinburgh's former Tolbooth), Heart of Midlothian played from 1873–78 on the East Meadows, along with just about every other Edinburgh club at the time. A year at Powburn (sometimes called Mayfield) in the south east of the city was followed by two seasons in the north east at Powderhall Grounds, which derived its name from a gunpowder manufacturer. All three grounds were used in the same decade by Hibernian, a trend followed over the years by most of Edinburgh's senior teams, who swapped and shared grounds with confusing regularity.

East Meadow is still open ground, Powburn is now Savile Terrace off Mayfield Road, and the Powderhall pitch was built over by the Refuse Department. Being on the banks of the Water of Leith it was susceptible to flooding (the later Powderhall Stadium became popular however – see Lost But Not Forgotten), so in April 1881 Hearts opened a new ground called Tynecastle, where Wardlaw Street and Wardlaw Place are now situated, opposite the present ground.

Since the district of Dalry was then regarded as 'out of town', to attract support Hearts sometimes staged two matches for the price of one, charged 3d compared with Hibernians' 6d and allowed women in free. The final match at Old Tynecastle was on 27 February 1886.

Tynecastle Park

Five weeks later a friendly v. Bolton Wanderers inaugurated this new ground with the old name across Gorgie Road. A modest Pavilion and stand with elevated press-box were completed in 1903, together with a cycle track which was removed to allow more standing room in 1907 (for drawing and photos of Tynecastle in this period see *The Football Industry* by John Hutchinson, Richard Drew 1982).

Two Championships and four Cup Final victories established the new venue and in 1914 work began on the present Main Stand, a 4000-seater designed by Archibald Leitch. By its completion after the First World War the original estimated cost had doubled to £12 000.

Even though Hearts purchased the ground in June 1926 and spent four years expanding the terracing (which resulted in taking down a short barrel-roof iron stand on the Wheatfield Street Side), Tynecastle in the 1930s was often uncomfortably packed – the record was 53 496 for a Cup tie v. Rangers in February 1932. Hemmed in by narrow streets, tenements and a distillery, the only space for expansion,

Tynecastle Park – the tenements offer the best free view in Scotland

behind the McLeod Street End, was occupied by a jealously protected kindergarden. A move to nearby Murrayfield, home of the Scottish rugby team, was one option. Another was to build afresh in Sighthill, further out of town, where the chairman had plans for a 100 000-capacity stadium.

Hitler banished such dreams and the two post-war decades saw further improvements as Hearts won the Championship twice, the League Cup four times and the Scottish Cup once. Tynecastle's terracing was concreted, the first floodlit game staged in October 1957 v. Newcastle and in 1959 a roof was built on the Wheatfield Street Side.

Safety work at Tynecastle has cost nearly £500 000 in recent years. When barriers under the Wheatfield Street cover needed replacing in 1982, it was deemed cheaper to install bench seating. In 1985 half the paddock in front of the Main Stand was also seated, giving Tynecastle a total capacity of 27 500 (reduced from 49 000 in 1981), including 8000 seats.

Ground Description

Many British football grounds are hidden in cramped inner-city locations, but none, surely, are as penned in as Tynecastle. Tenements and a soot-coloured distillery watch over the ground like cell-blocks over a prison yard, while the stands are clothed in a brood-ing, dark maroon; the maroon of old British Railway stations and also of Edinburgh buses. Hearts fans must have once felt very much at home on their travels.

Approaching the ground from McLeod Street, the Main Stand is hidden behind by a modern block on stilts, the former social club, with the club's commercial office housed in an old police station to the left. A few yards away the Tynecastle Arms pub has a jolly football sign, while a plaque on the back of the stand gives its date of construction. (The social club, built in 1969 for £200 000, failed badly and was sold in 1980 to Lothian Regional Council.)

Apart from its modernized lobby, which resembles a new hotel, and a new glass-fronted sponsor's lounge, the two-tier Main Stand retains much of its 70-year-old charm. Splashes of white in the steel-work and fittings help lighten its rather gloomy interior, from which sight of the sky is strictly limited.

To the left, for example, the open Gorgie Road End is backed by a church and a block of tenements whose windows provide an unhindered view of the pitch. No other League ground affords such an excellent free vantage point, and once, when Hearts built a scoreboard on the terrace, some residents actually applied for a rate rebate. They do however pay higher rates than normal, although whether this is because they overlook an open space or because they can watch League football for free has never quite been established.

The terrace itself rises up to the far corner and has silver-coloured barriers with maroon uprights. The floodlight pylons, identical to those at Easter Road, are the familiar Scottish variety with leaning gantries, but one of them, unusually, has its legs splayed wide over a large vomitory.

Opposite is the covered Wheatfield Street Side, with maroon and white bench seating installed on the terracing. This rather gloomy side is lined at the rear by the blackened stone walls of the North British Distillery, whose grim barred and shuttered windows can be seen from the street.

The L-shaped roof follows the distillery wall around the corner of the ground and covers a small portion of the McLeod Street End. This corner is even darker, with old maroon signs creating the distinct impression of a railway station of the steam era. Behind the open part of the McLeod Street Terrace is a school, and a welcome expanse of open skyline.

Maroon boundaries and a perimeter security fence – rare in Scotland – increase Tynecastle's sense of confinement, to which must be added the noise of factories, traffic and railways, and the strong smell of hops and yeast drifting over from the nearby Tennant Caledonian Brewery. It all adds up to an inner-city *mélange* which, however inconvenient or outdated, few would wish to change one little bit. Just as tourists delight in the ramparts and dungeons of Edinburgh Castle, so too do lovers of Scottish football delight in the cloistered intricacies of Tynecastle.

·HIBERNIAN·

Previous Grounds
Formed in 1875, Hibernian's first three grounds were also used by Hearts. Starting on the East Meadows, in 1878, when Hearts went to Powburn, Hibs moved to the Powderhall Grounds, where soon after the ubiquitous Mr Paterson brought his Siemens floodlighting equipment (see Floodlights). In September 1879, Hearts and Hibs switched grounds, Hearts moving to Powderhall, Hibs taking over Powburn (also called Mayfield), which had once been the home of Third Edinburgh Rifle Volunteers. Six months later Hibs moved two miles north to a ground known either as Hibernian Park or First Easter Road. It was sited where Bothwell Street now lies, next to the railway line. John Mackay's comprehensive history *The Hibees* (John Donald 1986) – to which I am beholden for most of this section – explains that although the team won the Cup in 1887 serious problems began when they travelled to Glasgow in May 1888 to open the ground of their fellow Irish Catholic club, Celtic, who then proceeded to sign up Hibs' best players.

Even worse, a split at Celtic gave rise to a club called Glasgow Hibernians who lured even more players from Edinburgh. By 1890 Hibernian were in dire straits. Their ground was threatened by developers, a £300-bid to take over Logie Green (next to Powderhall) from St Bernards failed, and inevitably the team disintegrated. So Hibs gave up the struggle, at a time when Hearts had just won the Scottish Cup.

Easter Road
The first Hibernian Park went to developers and when Hibs were resuscitated two years later they found an adjacent site at Drum Park, 200 yards from Bank Park, the home of League club Leith Athletic. In charge of finding the new site was a Mr McCabe. As John Mackay writes, 'There was one uneasy moment in the negotiations, when the proprietor mentioned a group of wild Irishmen who ran a football team in the neighbourhood a year or two earlier, whose outlandish name he could not remember, but Mr McCabe assured him that he had no idea who that could have been!'

The second Hibernian Park, known better as Easter Road, opened in February 1893, the only access to it being from a path by the Eastern Cemetery. A few months later Hibs joined the League and were strong enough to reach the 1896 Cup Final which, because Hearts were their opponents, was played in Edinburgh at Logie Green, the only Final ever played outside Glasgow.

Hibs were unsettled on their notorious sloping ground. In 1902, despite having lifted the Cup and being on course for their first Championship, they

In the midst of a city, Easter Road looks like a Highland outpost from this angle. Arthur's Seat towers in the distance

apparently considered moving lock, stock and barrel to Aberdeen. Seven years later they drew up plans to build a stadium a mile east in Piershill but were foiled when the North British Railway gained parliamentary approval for their own scheme, which, to rub salt in Hibs' wounds, was never carried out (the site was by Mountcastle Crescent).

Since Easter Road was rented and Edinburgh's city planners had earmarked the site for future development, the club were understandably reluctant to invest in it further. Until the early 1920s it had three banked sides, one small stand nicknamed 'the egg-box' and players had to change in a hut by the touchline. Tynecastle was palatial by comparison.

In 1922, however, the club negotiated a 25-year lease at £250 per annum – a token sum for that period – and redevelopment began immediately. The pitch was moved 40 yards sideways, levelled and a new stand begun on the West Side. This was a time of strikes in the building trade however – Aston Villa's new stand was also affected – and while work was delayed Hibs twice had to use Tynecastle (which was also being shared by St Bernard's, whose Gymnasium Ground was similarly being refurbished).

New Easter Road was finally ready in September 1924. It held 45 000 spectators, including 4200 seats, and cost only £20 000 to redevelop. Success in the immediate post-war period brought further expansion of the East Side terracing, shortly after Easter Road's record gate of 65 840 had squeezed in for a derby v. Hearts on 2 January 1950, but plans to raise each end to a similar height were never realized.

Hibernian were among the first British clubs to investigate floodlighting, which they had experienced on several foreign tours and at that historic first floodlit match at Ochilview. Hibs opted for a 'drenchlighting' system built by the Edinburgh firm Miller and Stables, whose leaning gantries became popular all over Scotland (but only at a few venues in England). Easter Road's first floodlit match was v.

Hearts on 18 October 1954. On 8 February 1956 Hibs, playing Raith, shared with East Fife the honour of staging the first Scottish Cup matches under lights.

A cover on the North Terrace was built in the early 1960s and Easter Road remained unchanged until the advent of the Safety of Sports Grounds Act in 1975, which halved the capacity to 30 000. Bench seats were installed on the North End, because they were cheaper than new crush barriers, and in 1985 Hibs tidied up the once massive East Side by reducing its height and erecting a large cover at a total cost of £412 000. Easter Road's current capacity is 23 416, including 5916 seats.

Ground Description

Approaching from Easter Road itself one might imagine the ground to be as confined as Tyncastle. Indeed the main entrance appears to have been squeezed behind buildings on Albion Road with barely a yard to spare.

Once inside the ground, however, Easter Road unfurls into a wide open stadium, as green as the undulating hills of Holyrood Park half a mile to the South beyond Meadowbank Stadium.

The Main Stand, possibly a Leitch design, is cranked in the centre and large but light on the upper tier. With green corrugated screen-ends, white facings and bench seats on the wings, it remains fairly basic, relying on size and colour to establish its presence.

From here, to the left is the North End, in the centre of which is a heavy concrete roof – comparable with Blackburn's of the same era – with an electric scoreboard mounted on the fascia, the first installed at a Scottish ground. In the near corner of the terrace at pitch level is a boiler house which powers the undersoil heating. Behind the terrace is the Eastern Cemetery (coincidentally or not, Celtic, whose Irish Catholic origins were inspired by Hibs, also chose a ground next to the Eastern Cemetery, in Glasgow).

Opposite is the new Covered Enclosure with a flat roof, grey steelwork, bright green fascia and green and white barriers. This side was formerly almost twice its present height, as can be seen from how much surplus land lies behind. As at Ibrox, the unwanted rubble from here was taken to fill in a disused railway cutting.

To the right is the open, curving South Terrace, guarded by its two rather stubby floodlight pylons. Although backed by a black corrugated fence, when viewed from certain angles this terrace is almost indistinguishable from the rising form of Arthur's Seat in the distance. Meadowbank's floodlights are just visible but the loftier backdrop of ancient rocks and weatherbeaten turf is akin to a Highland League setting. The green of Hibernia thus merges almost imperceptibly into the green of Caledonia.

MEADOWBANK ·THISTLE·

Previous Grounds

Originally formed as Ferranti Thistle works team in 1943, the club graduated from public parks to a base at Crewe Toll. In 1969 the council offered them City Park, nearby on Pilton Drive, the former home of Edinburgh City (one of three defunct League clubs in Edinburgh – see Lost But Not Forgotten). Thistle made great efforts to restore City Park, helped by Hibernian whose reserves also played there for a time. In 1974, amid some controversy and disbelief, Thistle became the first club elected to the Scottish League since Clydebank in 1966 (the numbers had been uneven after Third Lanark's demise in 1967). Two provisos were made – that a better ground be found and that the company name Ferranti be dropped. Both were fulfilled when Edinburgh City Council allowed Thistle to use Meadowbank Stadium and the club adopted the stadium's name.

Meadowbank Stadium

Opened by HRH the Duke of Kent on 2 May 1970, Meadowbank Stadium was built on the site of a speedway stadium at a cost of £2·8 million. Designed to stage the 1970 Commonwealth Games it has since become Scotland's equivalent to the Crystal Palace recreation centre in London, and in 1986 became the only venue to have staged the Commonwealth Games twice.

Thistle are not sole tenants. Matches have to be rescheduled so as not to clash with athletics meetings, and although it holds 16 500, the stadium has never been secure enough for the visit of major football clubs. Meadowbank therefore play important Cup-ties at Tynecastle or Easter Road.

A record gate of 4000 for one of Meadowbank's first games, v. Albion Rovers in the League Cup, August 1974, promised to silence the club's critics, but since then gates have been low, although no lower than several other smaller clubs.

Thistle maintain only a minimal presence at Meadowbank. Their offices are at Ferranti's main factory near Tynecastle, but in the stadium they have converted some outbuildings into dressings rooms. Thistle have a contract to use the stadium until 1995, paying rental plus a percentage of the gate.

In 1983 they became the first League club in modern times to admit women free of charge – a policy, successful in terms of family attendance and good behaviour, which was common in the late nineteenth century (see Appendix B).

Ground Description

Sparsely-attended matches at any ground can be a

Meadowbank Stadium during the 1986 Commonwealth Games. Arthur's Seat dominates as at Easter Road

dispiriting experience, watching football across a running track is never quite satisfactory, but put the two together in an open, modern stadium and even the most committed fan might feel sorely tested. Astonishingly, however, the commitment to Thistle extends to eight branches of the supporters' club, all over the United Kingdom.

For Meadowbank games only the cantilevered Main Stand, overlooked by Arthur's Seat, is used. From its 7500 orange seats, to the left, behind the open seating is a black, monolithic hulk which might have materialized from the film *2001* but is in fact the scoreboard. Its innards are not far removed from Hollywood however. They were bought from the Los Angeles Coliseum after the 1984 Olympics.

To the right is a multi-purpose sports hall, behind which more facilities, including a velodrome and tennis courts, are laid out.

With Easter Road only half-a-mile away such facilities inevitably beg the question, why was Meadowbank not constructed to house at least Hibernian and perhaps Hearts also?

The answer, partially at least, is that big-time football, with its fences, segregation and potential violence would have intruded upon the tree-lined calm enjoyed by so many other sportsmen and women.

Whether or not Thistle should have been admitted to the League is an entirely separate issue, on which the people of Elgin and Inverness have perhaps the strongest views.

·BERWICK RANGERS·

Previous Grounds

Forming in 1881 Berwick played five years at Bull Stob Close, now Lord's Mount Mill, occasionally on Soldier's Flat, also used by the militia, and between 1886–90 on Pier Field. This was so exposed that in 1890 they crossed the River Tweed to Shielfield, a ground belonging to a butcher Mr Shiel Dods. Forced out after an argument, in 1902 Berwick switched to Meadow Field until moving to Union Park, now St Cuthbert's School, where they remained until evicted in 1919. Fortunately Shielfield was available so Berwick returned.

Shielfield Park

After years of competing against Northumberland and Border teams, Berwick were by 1919 firmly in the Scottish camp. Shielfield's pitch was originally next to the current one, but as Tony Langmack's history recalls, apart from a Pavilion opened in September 1932, little work was done on that site.

In 1951 Berwick joined the short-lived C Division and rather than develop their sloping ground they decided to build a new stadium next door.

Constructed almost entirely by volunteers, the new Shielfield Park was set out with a wide track and sea turf from Goswick. The centrepiece was the former Midland Road stand from Valley Parade, dismantled when its foundations were found to be unsafe (see Bradford City) and transported by rail to Berwick at a cost of £400. Rangers spent a further £3000 on refurbishment, with supporters buying sheets of roofing at 10s each. Meanwhile in February 1954 a record 8500 crowd packed Old Shielfield for Berwick's epic Cup victory over Dundee.

A few months later the new stadium was ready. A motorcyclists' stunt team were the first to use the track but the ground's official opening was v. Aston Villa in September 1954.

New Shielfield brought new horizons, for in 1955 the club reached Division Two. A cover was built over the popular side a decade later and on 28 January 1967 Berwick perpetrated one of the greatest shocks in Scottish football by defeating Rangers 1-0 in front of Shielfield's record gate of 13 365. During this period Shielfield also became home to the Berwick Bandits speedway team. The floodlights were first switched on for a game v. St Mirren in October 1972.

To celebrate Rangers' centenary a new £150 000 block was built comprising offices and a boardroom which would put many a big club to shame, but in 1985 a struggling Berwick sold Shielfield Park for £95 000 to the local council. There are plans for an industrial estate on Old Shielfield and long-term hopes of a new training area cum sports centre for the club and community.

Shielfield's current capacity is 10 673, of which 1473 are seated.

Shielfield Park – the Main Stand started life at Valley Parade but is barely recognizable as the intricate stand Leitch created for Bradford City

Ground Description

Neither wholly English nor Scots, Berwick, a few miles south of the border, is actually some 50 miles north of Dumfries in terms of latitude. Had they joined the Football League, Rangers' longest journey would have been 470 miles to Plymouth, whereas in Scotland the furthest club is Aberdeen, 170 miles away.

Shielfield Park is in Tweedmouth, on the south side of the river, set in large recreation space bordered by a housing estate. The Main Stand, opposite a new social club, sits above the main entrance on an embankment.

Only the steelwork originated in Bradford. The flattened barrel-roof and solid screen-ends are black, with plain dog-tooth fascia. Behind yellow and black plastic seats is a glass-fronted directors box. Because of the dark cinder track the stand is set well away from the pitch (the speedway team departed for Berrington during 1980–81 and the track has been unused since).

From here, to the right is the open curving East Bank, without terracing. Houses stand behind. Opposite is a bank of terracing with a 20-yard long roof over the centre. This is known as the Ducket – or dovecote – unfairly, since the terracing is neat, with smart black and yellow barriers. Behind the rear wall is the site of Old Shielfield. Now used by Berwick Reserves and a junior team, there are still traces of the original banking.

Further beyond is a signal box for the London to Edinburgh line, along which 125 m.p.h. trains hurtle past the ground. To the left is the grass-covered West Bank, behind which is a disused railway cutting and an assortment of allotments and real duckets. The huge works of Simpsons Maltings quite dominate the skyline.

New Shielfield is the second youngest venue after Meadowbank and, like Southend's Roots Hall – opened one year after, it represents a community effort, a ground of which, however basic, supporters can justifiably feel proud.

·25·
BIG MATCH VENUES

English Cup Final Venues

Before Wembley the FA Cup Final (known originally as the English Cup Final) was held at seven different venues, with three additional grounds being used for Final replays.

1872–94

The Kennington Oval in south east London was the ground of Surrey County Cricket Club. It was chosen as the first venue simply because the FA secretary at the time, Charles Alcock, was also Secretary of Surrey CCC. Wanderers played the Royal Engineers in that first final on 16 March 1872, watched by 2000 spectators, who paid a minimum entrance fee of one shilling. This was at least double the amount usually charged, which helps to explain why the attendance was so disappointing.

The Cup rules stated that the holders would be exempt until the next Final, and could choose the venue. The Wanderers, having no home at the time, chose to meet their challengers at Lillie Bridge, a ground near the present Stamford Bridge. A crowd of 3000 saw them win again. But this time the rules were changed and the Wanderers had to play in the early rounds of the next competition. Also, The Oval was settled as the venue.

Twenty finals were played at Surrey's ground, but as attendances grew for both Finals and internationals, the cricket club became increasingly worried about their ability to hold so many people, some of them described in London as: 'a Northern horde of uncouth garb and strange oaths'.

By 1892 the Final's attendance had reached 25 000, squeezed into temporary wooden stands and seats inside the ropes. Surrey also worried that their pitch was suffering from rough usage, so in 1892 they asked the FA to look elsewhere.

Of the finals played at The Oval, three needed replays, of which only one was played elsewhere, in 1886. The venue chosen for Blackburn Rovers' replay v. WBA was the Racecourse Ground, Derby, but if the northern venue was expected to yield a higher gate, the reality was otherwise because 15 000 saw the first game in London, and only 12 000 the replay.

Nevertheless, stuck for anywhere else to play the 1893 Final, the FA decided to go north again, at the suggestion of the northern representative J. J. Bentley. He thought the Manchester Athletic Club's ground in Fallowfield would make a very suitable venue, even though it had never been previously used for football.

But the result was chaos. Some 45 000 people paid to get in, but thousands more gained free admittance, preventing ticket holders from reaching their seats and making it hard for even the officials to enter the ground.

Chaotic though the 1893 Final was, the attendance was almost twice that of the previous year and was not matched until 1896. Indeed the large numbers probably took the authorities quite by surprise, as did the record receipts of £2559. But the ground was not chosen again, although it did stage one more major game in 1899, the third semi-final replay between Sheffield United and Liverpool. This time it was a Monday afternoon and only 30 000 attended, but the referee had to abandon the game at half-time, 1 hour and 50 minutes after kick-off, when the crowd yet again spilled onto the pitch. (The ground still exists as an athletics track, on Whitworth Lane, off Moseley Road.)

After the fiasco in 1893, the FA turned its attention to the best League ground in the country, Goodison Park. But only 37 000 watched the 1894 Final there, and the FA decided to take the Final back to London.

1895–1914

The FA thought that London could handle crowds better than any other city. The capital could also give the Final greater national importance. Northerners and Midlanders were far more likely to enjoy a day out in London than in Liverpool or Manchester; it would be a proper occasion. And, the FA's headquarters were in London.

Crystal Palace in 1895 was a natural focal point for recreation, with Paxton's iron and glass palace on a rise overlooking the park. The football pitch was laid on the bed of a bowl, originally created for an artificial lake in the amusement park.

Crystal Palace during the 1911 Cup Final. Notice the ornate multi-span roofs. The crowd on the bottom right and those on the grass between the front and middle slopes at the far end could not see properly

Once inside the grounds, spectators could wander about quite freely, and as William Pickford wrote in A *Few Recollections of Sport*, Crystal Palace 'was more than a venue for a football match; it took on the character of a picnic. Long before the game happy parties sat in groups under the trees, muching sandwiches, and generations of football folk met there to renew acquaintances.' If this sounds idyllic, once the match started the reality was very different.

There were three stands at Crystal Palace, all on the North Side. Two multi-span stands with decorated gables crowned with flags stood on either side of a smaller, pitched roof construction. But the vast majority of spectators were crammed onto sloping grass banks, without any terracing or crush barriers, many of them 50 yards or more from the nearest touchline. Moreover, none of these slopes was particularly high, so that it is probable that when the first six-figure attendance was recorded for the Spurs v. Sheffield United Final in 1901, up to a third had little or no view of the proceedings.

When it was wet, the slopes turned into 'slippery banks of mud', according to the angry *Athletics News'* correspondent, writing after the largest crowd ever to assemble for a football match in the world, 120 081, had struggled to see Villa v. Sunderland. 'It is not pleasant to think,' he wrote, 'that Glasgow has a far better arena for a great match than England, and that arena owned by an amateur club.'

The pitch also came in for criticism. Its rich turf suffered considerable drainage problems, not helped, suggested that same newspaper, 'by galloping horses over the turf'. This was a reference to the other events staged at the ground, among which were rugby internationals.

There is no doubt that the ground had a wonderful setting, especially with the Crystal Palace in the background, and a railway station only a hundred yards from the pitch. And attendances were

consistently high – averaging 73 000 in 20 Finals.

Had the First World War not intervened, it is possible the FA might have invested some money in the ground and turned it into a stadium approaching the standards of several League clubs. Otherwise we can only assume that the FA opted to use the ground because of its scale, because compared with the relative merits of Goodison and Villa Parks, Crystal Palace was undoubtedly third rate.

When hostilities broke out, the ground was quickly taken over as a War Service Depot, and consequently the 1914 Final between Burnley and Liverpool, which was the first to be watched by the King, George V, was also the last at the ground.

After the war it was used by the amateur Corinthians until the Crystal Palace itself was destroyed by a fire in 1936 and the land went into decline.

For a while it was used to stage motor-racing, but in recent years it has become the National Recreation Centre. On the exact site of the football pitch is the magnificent Crystal Palace athletics stadium, with two superb cantilever stands plus additional facilities such as football on artificial turf and indoor sports.

All that is left of the Palace are crumbling foundations, but the rest of the site has new life, with enough of the old park retained to gain an impression of what it must have been like in those early days. It is well worth a visit.

Of the 20 Finals at Crystal Palace, five needed replays. The first, in 1901, was staged at Burnden Park – a disastrous decision which led to only 20 740 officially attending (see Bolton); the second, a year later was replayed at Crystal Palace. The 1910 replay took place at Goodison Park, the 1911 replay at Old Trafford and the 1912 replay at Bramall Lane. After these three in a row, the FA belatedly decided to introduce extra-time into the Final (incredibly extra-time for semi-finals was not allowed until 1981).

1915–22

The only official war-time Cup Final was at Old Trafford in 1915, known as the Khaki Final. After the war, when it became known that Crystal Palace was still not available, the FA switched the game to Stamford Bridge, the obvious choice in London (though Arsenal would not have agreed).

Chelsea, or rather the Mears brothers, had always hoped their ground would become a Final venue, and for three years their dream came true. But in 1921 the FA decided to sign a contract committing them to the new stadium at Wembley.

Had Wembley not been built, might Chelsea have kept the Final? It is impossible to say. Charlton had a much bigger stadium which with proper investment might also have been a contender. Highbury and White Hart Lane were also improving rapidly. But the FA had never been keen on using the ground of one of the Cup entrants, and having suffered the inadequacies of Crystal Palace for 20 years, Wembley was too tempting a prospect.

Wembley

Compared with other modern stadiums around the world, Wembley Stadium is uncomfortable, unsuitable and outdated, yet it remains the mecca of English soccer and the envy of the world. Wembley is an English institution. But it is not, as is sometimes believed, the property of the nation nor even of the FA.

A private company owns the stadium and the surrounding 73-acre complex, and soccer is just one of several sporting activities played there, under contract. If the stadium had to depend on football, rugby or hockey, it would go bankrupt tomorrow. Its most regular income is from thrice-weekly greyhound meetings, attended on average by 1200 to 1500 people. A further 65 000 pass through its doors every year for the guided tours.

The neighbouring indoor 8000-seater Wembley Arena, or Empire Pool was opened in 1934, and is in more frequent use for tennis, table-tennis, skating, horse-shows, five-a-side soccer, ice-hockey, badminton, boxing, basketball, rock concerts and so on. There is also a large new conference centre, with a 2700-seater auditorium, opened in 1977, a hotel and a squash centre. Cup Finals, therefore, play only a small part in the annual events at Wembley. But they are still the most cherished tradition.

The site of the stadium was parkland, in an outer reach of London only connected by the Metropolitan Railway in 1901, when the area's population was recorded as 4519. Where the pitch now lies stood a monument to failure, known as 'Watkin's Folly'. This was the base of a tower which Sir Edward Watkin had intended to reach a height of 1150 feet and therefore dominate the skyline as dramatically as its model, the Eiffel Tower in Paris. But the tower reached a height of only 200 feet before being abandoned, the foundations having proved unstable, despite an in-filling of molten lead and concrete.

After several years of inaction, the tower was finally removed in 1908, leaving four large craters where its legs had stood.

Otherwise Wembley Park remained blissfully rural and unspoilt until 1920, when it was chosen as the site for the British Empire Exhibition, a project which promised to enhance the country's reputation and provide much needed jobs for returning soldiers. Although Lloyd George, King George V and the Prince of Wales each gave the project their support, there was little progress until 1921, when it was announced that the Exhibition's centre-piece would be a national sports stadium, a possible venue for the FA Cup Final itself. Mention of football changed everything. Suddenly the appeal fund was oversubscribed! Among many contributors to Wembley were the people of Glasgow, who sent £105 000. From then until opening day, Wembley Park became the scene

of a minor miracle. Certainly in engineering terms the stadium was the most advanced in Britain, and the architects, John Simpson and Maxwell Ayrton claimed it to be the largest monumental building of reinforced concrete in the world.

The use of ferro-concrete was responsible for Wembley's swift construction in just 300 working days, from January 1922 to April 1923, at a cost of £750 000. Each section was constructed on site (rather than prefabricated), and by placing V-shaped strips of wood inside the concrete the outer walls were given the effect of monumental masonry. This was quick and cheap, and very convincing from a distance. Even now it only begins to look impromptu close-up. A more dramatic effect was created by painting the exterior in brilliant white.

The focal point was the entrance, the now famous twin towers, 126-feet high. The twin-tower motif as a symbol of power and grandeur was nothing new; Leitch had used it at Hampden, borrowed in turn from countless castles and medieval cathedrals all over Europe. But the sheer bulk of each white tower, topped by domes and reinforced concrete flagpoles pronounced a new style, echoed throughout the Empire from London to New Delhi. Wembley was an expression of British confidence in a decade otherwise fraught with problems.

It was a very different stadium to the one we know today. Both ends were open, and the two stands covered only the seated sections, that is 25 000 spectators. The terraces were timber steps with cinder infill on the lower tier, concrete on the upper, providing room for 91 500 standing. In addition, there was provision for 10 000 on bench seats in five rows around the perimeter – giving a total capacity of 126 500.

The pitch was laid with turf cut the same day from the surrounding exhibition grounds (where work was carrying on at a much slower rate).

A last-minute addition to the stadium was a 220-yard long sprint track, a common feature at US stadiums. In order to provide one at Wembley, and the only one in Britain, a 150-foot section of the terracing had to be cut away to allow the extra length for the straight track, in front of the North Stand. This cut-away, where the sprint would begin, still exists but is now used for access of maintenance vehicles.

Also at the western end of the stadium was the players' tunnel, directly opposite where it is now situated. It was just wide enough for the players to enter the pitch side by side.

The FA's president, Sir Charles Clegg, signed a 21-year contract with Wembley's owners, and it was no coincidence that the first event to be held at the stadium, and indeed at the exhibition grounds as a whole, was the fixture which had stirred so many people to invest in the stadium – the FA Cup Final.

It had been quite a risk for the FA, which signed the contract long before the stadium was completed

The site at Wembley in May 1922 when work began; the craters were the foundations of Watkin's Folly. Within a decade the surrounding areas was built up

and with no guarantee that attendances would justify the costs. At the three preceding Cup Finals at Stamford Bridge attendances had been 50 018, 72 805 (when a London team was involved) and 53 000. So no-one knew quite what to expect.

The stadium was completed only four days before the opening Final, and the most rigorous safety test the construction underwent was a battalion of infantrymen stamping in unison on the terraces, while workmen marked time!

But the stadium withstood a much sterner test on 28 April when Wembley was besieged with over 200 000 people, eager to see not only West Ham v. Bolton, but also the King and this new wonder of the Empire. A few important lessons are worth noting. Firstly, the event proved that the Cup Final had the pulling-power to justify the use of Wembley, and that Wembley itself was a popular venue. Secondly, it was realized that from then on Finals should be all-ticket affairs. Although the official gate had been 126 047, an estimated 200 000 actually squeezed into the arena, with thousands more outside (two of whom tried to dig their way under a barrier). The FA had to return nearly £3000 to ticket holders who had not managed to gain admission (out of total receipts of £27 776) while many who had bought seat tickets were forced to stand.

It was a miracle no-one was hurt and that there was little violence despite the crush and the rival supporters who were thrown together. As one observer, Professor A. M. Low commented afterwards, 'It could only have happened in Britain'. (In fact he was not entirely right. Soccer violence was known in Britain, especially in the North East and Scotland, but the occasion, and the presence of the monarch has given Wembley an almost trouble-free reputation over the years.) Nevertheless as a result of that chaotic day a government enquiry was set up to investigate the phenomenon of large crowds (see Safety).

The Bolton v. West Ham match took place a year before the Empire Exhibition was opened on 23 April

1924. Eleven days earlier England played their first international at the stadium, before a very disappointing crowd of 37 250 (the previous year's game at Hampden attracted nearly twice that number). Three days after the Exhibition's opening, the second Wembley Cup Final took place, this time an all-ticket crowd of 91 965 watching Aston Villa v. Newcastle. The next six-figure crowd to watch a Cup Final was in 1950, when Arsenal played Liverpool. Since then every game except mid-week replays has drawn 100 000 crowds (Wembley has a self-imposed crowd limit of 92 000 for evening games).

Once the Exhibition closed in October 1925, after 30 million people had visited it, the organizers wound up their company and the site was put up for auction, but no-one was interested. One reporter described Wembley as: 'A vast white elephant, a rotting sepulchre of hopes and the grave of fortunes.' Not even the lowest price of £350 000 for the entire site was taken.

In the introduction to his history of Wembley, Neil Wilson describes the events which saved the stadium from a premature end. Jimmy White, a renowned speculator who was then close to bankruptcy, bought the site for £300 000 with a £30 000 down payment.

At the same time Arthur Elvin, who had returned from the War penniless and had bought eight kiosks at the Exhibition, realized the potential scrap value of the decaying buildings and was appointed by White to sell them off.

The Palestine building became a Glasgow laundry, the West African building a furniture factory, and some cafes were rebuilt as Bournemouth's new Grandstand. After nine months Elvin had made enough to offer White £122 500 for the Stadium: £12 500 initially and the rest in annual instalments.

No-one else was interested in the investment and the Stadium was even in danger of demolition, when White committed suicide with his creditors pressing, leaving Elvin to face the Official Receiver alone. White's debt on the Stadium was still £270 000.

Wilson writes: 'Elvin was presented with an alternative – find the balance of the £122 500 he had offered White within a fortnight or lose his deposit. Quickly, he persuaded friends and friends of friends to back him, and at 6.30 on the evening of 17 August, 1927, he phoned the Receiver to clinch the deal. A minute later he was on the telephone again, to sell the Stadium to the syndicate he had gathered together for £150 000, a one-minute profit of £27 500.'

Elvin then made himself managing director of this new company, called the Wembley Stadium and Greyhound Racecourse Company Limited, and set about rejuvenating the stadium, while most of the surrounding buildings were cleared. The choice of greyhound racing proved to be the life-saver, for Wembley could not possibly survive on one Cup Final a year and one international every two years. It cost £100 000 to install the necessary facilities, but this was soon earned as 50 000 attended the first race meeting in December 1927. For a while, there were even greyhound meetings after every Cup Final, starting at 8 o'clock.

The dogs were soon joined in 1929 by Rugby League, which although a northern preserve staged its annual Cup Final at Wembley thereafter (apart from 1932). Weekly speedway was also a great success, attracting crowds of up to 70 000 for some meetings and in 1931 an average of over 19 000. It eventually died out in 1956, and after a failed comeback in the 1970s was dropped completely, although Wembley continued to host the World Championships until 1981. (Odsal Stadium, Bradford has since been revamped for the Championships. See Bradford City.)

Wembley's original pitch was replaced in the 1960s by turf from Solway Firth, Cumberland, but this soon deteriorated badly, mainly owing to poor drainage. The final straw was the use of the pitch for two Royal International Horse Shows, culminating in one manager describing it as 'a cabbage patch'. The present pitch was installed under the supervision of the Sports Turf Research Institute, Bingley, at a cost of £30 000 (see Pitches) and the turf comes from Ganton Golf Course, near Scarborough in Yorkshire. At one stage, however, it was suggested that Wembley offered to buy Doncaster Rovers' pitch, which was both large and in good trim. Rovers sensibly turned down the offer (see Doncaster).

There have been many structural changes to Wembley since 1923, beginning with the building of a 250-seater restaurant behind the Royal Box in 1938, designed by Sir Owen Williams, who was also the architect of the Empire Pool. This steel and glass construction was designed to be dismantled for Cup Finals, when extra seating space would be needed, and to have front windows on pulleys, to open up the restaurant in good weather. In fact once built it was never dismantled and the windows are now permanently in place.

After the War the Stadium had a major facelift in order to stage the 1948 Olympics, for which the Stadium Company gave its services free and paid for such improvements as the building of the Olympic Way (now with a ramp) linking the stadium with Wembley Park Station. The present players' tunnel and dressing rooms were built and above was placed the Olympic torch. Bench seats were temporarily installed at both ends.

The entire operation, although a tremendous prestige boost for Wembley, ended in a loss of £200 000, and thereafter the Stadium Company's profits began to fall steadily, as greyhound racing and speedway lost popularity and entertainment tax milked off more each year.

In 1955 the now Sir Arthur Elvin sold a million shares in the company, mostly to Sir Bracewell Smith, then Chairman of Arsenal, and on 4 February 1957 at the age of 57, Elvin died aboard a cruise ship.

The 1950s saw one long-awaited advance at Wem-

View of Wembley Stadium, in its original form, uncovered at both ends

bley, the installation of floodlights in 1955 at a cost of £22 000. The first game was a representative game between London and Frankfurt in the European Fairs Cup in 1955, but the first time lights were used for a major match was at the end of England's match v. Spain on 30 November 1955. That England's national stadium should have waited so long was quite scandalous, but predictable in view of the FA's stance (see Floodlights).

After Elvin's death the new regime restored the Stadium's finances and in 1960 the firm which ran London's weekend commercial television, Associated Rediffusion Limited, bought up most of the Stadium company's share capital. The Stadium became part of the British Electric Traction Company group, and has always been in private hands. Most other countries have state- or municipal-owned national stadiums.

The new owners were responsible for Wembley's most significant facelift, in 1963, when £500 000 was spent completely reroofing the stands and covering both ends for the first time. A major innovation was the use of translucent fibre-glass panels on the inner 36 feet of roofing, giving Wembley that greenhouse feel so familiar now. This gave cover for all 100 000 spectators, of which 44 000 were now seated.

Also at this time the 300-feet long suspended press-box and television gantries were built, and Wembley staged its first ever all-floodlit international, England beating Northern Ireland 8-3 on 20 November 1963. Since then the floodlights have been replaced, in 1973, by metal halide lamps with seven times more power than the original ones, at a further cost of £53 000.

Wembley was by this time known not only for its Cup Finals, both FA and Amateur (since 1949) but also for European Competition Finals. It staged the European Cup in 1963, 1968 (when Manchester United won) and 1971, and the European Cup Winners Cup Final in 1965 (when West Ham won). The height of its international renown came in 1966 with the staging of the World Cup. Wembley is obviously a favourite home for English teams, since none have lost important finals here.

Apart from these important matches, unlike most national stadiums Wembley is not used regularly for football. In the early years there was a plan to base an amateur team at the stadium, called the Argonauts, to play in the League as the Queen's Park of England. But the experience of League matches played at Wembley in 1930 suggested it would not be a suitable venue. Clapton Orient played two Third Division games here when their own ground was out of commission, but the low gates and lack of atmosphere did not augur well (see Orient). One amateur game that did take place at Wembley in those days was between Ipswich Town and the Ealing Association, on 13 October 1928. The Southern Amateur League fixture was scheduled for the nearby ground at Corfton Road, but when the pitch was passed unfit the game was surprisingly switched to Wembley.

The current contract between Wembley Stadium and the FA, signed in 1982 for twenty-one years, is broadly similar to the previous agreement whereby Wembley took a 25 per cent share of gate receipts. The Football League's contract to stage League Cup (now Littlewood's Cup) Finals expires in 1988.

In recent years both the FA and League have contributed further to Wembley Stadium's long-awaited facelift, which saw £5 million spent on completely refurbishing the outside walls, twin towers, steelwork and roofing. Wembley thus wears a much brighter face than ever before, largely thanks to new brands of weather-resistant paints.

But there are plans to revamp the stadium further. In 1984 a consortium called Arena Limited bought 41 per cent of BET's shareholding in the Stadium Company for £25 million and announced ambitious £300-million plans for the whole Wembley complex. Less than two years later Arena sold out to a consortium headed by Brian Wolfson, chairman of Anglo-Nordic engineering group. Wolfson joked that he bought Wembley because he could never get a Cup Final ticket.

The new owners also have big ideas. For the Stadium in particular it is planned to build 72 executive boxes, perhaps suspended from the roof in the manner of the press-box, and install extra seating in place of each rear standing area. Very nice for company directors but hardly fair on the average fan for whom a standing ticket at Wembley is already expensive, that is if he can get one. The new plans would reduce the standing capacity by 15 per cent.

Having witnessed 250 000 visitors for the Pope's visit in 1982 and over 100 000 for the Live Aid concert in 1985, Wembley continues to diversify. The American football showpiece between Dallas Cowboys and Chicago Bears in 1986 was another financial success, indicative of the new owners' intention to utilize the stadium for more than just football and greyhound racing.

They also hope that before and after matches fans will find more to do around Wembley itself; a museum of sport, a £5 million exhibition hall, a shopping mall and leisure complex.

None of the improvements to the Stadium can be carried out without the FA's blessing, because of their lease, and they must also take into account the fact that both the indoor Wembley Arena and the Stadium itself are listed buildings.

But with their 21-year lease and recent heavy investment in the Stadium, the FA will certainly keep the Cup Final and international matches at Wembley for years to come, no matter how reduced the standing capacity or how widespread is the feeling that certain fixtures would be better held at provincial venues, as was the case before 1951 (see International Venues). Want to watch England in Newcastle or Manchester? Turn on your telly then.

Ground Description

The traditional approach to Wembley Stadium is along the famous Olympic Way from Wembley Park underground station, through the grounds of what was the Exhibition site in 1924. Where the car park is now situated were massive pavilions – Australia's to the right, Canada's to the left. The rest of the site is now an apparently random collection of buildings: hotels, the Empire Pool, the Conference Centre, squash centre, light industrial units and disused structures.

At the end of the Olympic Way, appropriately, are two plaques commemorating the Olympic Champions of 1948, on either side of the enormous arched blue doorway which serves as the Royal entrance. It looks more like the entrance to one of Her Majesty's Prisons.

Above the door is another plaque, to commemorate the 1966 World Cup, or as the memorial puts it, The World Football Championship. Above this, on the parapet, is a bust of Sir Arthur Elvin. It is said that the ghost of Sir Arthur still haunts the Stadium. On the balcony behind the parapet stands the original Olympic torch from 1948. From here one can see how smartly the concrete facings of Wembley have been restored to their original cream-coloured glory, visible from miles around, after years of being weather-worn and mildewed. The balcony also offers an excellent view of north and west London.

For those who have seen Wembley previously only on television, inside the stadium seems curiously different – smaller, more enclosed, and yet the pitch further away than one might imagine.

Now that the company operates tours one can see Wembley in all its intimate details, from the Royal Box, where the VIP seats are aged wicker armchairs which you would hesitate to buy from a second-hand shop, to the players' enormous baths and toilets. Yet the dressing rooms are tiny by First Division standards.

Like every large building, Wembley revels in statistics: 40 miles of terracing, 14 miles of concrete beams, half a million rivets and so on, but a few facts are worth noting. Somewhere under the pitch, for example, is a train, buried during the construction of the Stadium. The lift shaft of Watkin's Folly is believed to be 60 feet under the Royal entrance.

Under the box, above where the managers sit side by side during games, is a leaded gable window, behind which is the Royal retiring room. From the Royal Box, the tunnel is to the left, below the electric scoreboard. Directly opposite this, to the right, is the much smaller, original tunnel. Offices now occupy the area where the dressing rooms once stood. Also on the right is the cut-away section built for the 220-yard sprint.

Underneath the stands, in the corridors and gangways, one really appreciates how old and outdated is Wembley Stadium; yet the stadium still retains an irresistible aura which has been enhanced by the recent £5 million redevelopment scheme.

Although it is hard to imagine a Cup Final being played anywhere else, the FA might easily have built its own tailor-made stadium at, for example, Ricketts Wood near Watford. A 100-acre site was offered to them in the 1970s for possible sharing with Watford FC, where a soccer school and England's training facilities could have been added. Many administrators within football believe that the decision to stay at Wembley was a great mistake, and that English football suffers as a result. The idea of a new stadium was turned down, mainly for financial reasons – projected running costs were estimated at £200 000 annually – yet the FA pays high rates at Lancaster Gate and has invested higher sums at Lilleshall and in the building of better rail links with Wembley. Having paid the Chancellor something in the order of £230 000 in taxes after the World Cup in 1966, it might seem that a golden opportunity had been lost. The owners of Wembley Stadium would doubtless disagree, as would thousands of other football lovers, to whom Wembley is still mecca; the ultimate goal.

Scottish Cup Final Venues

The venue of early Scottish Cup Finals depended largely on who was playing. Queen's Park, for example, reached twelve of the twenty-seven Finals played between 1874–1900, so their ground was not always suitable (although they did not have to play the 1884 Final at all because Vale of Leven failed to appear).

Nevertheless the first two Finals in 1874 and 1875 did involve Queen's Park and were played at their ground, First Hampden Park. It is worth noting that the attendance at each match was around double that of the corresponding English Cup Finals.

First Hampden was the venue of four of the next eight Finals. Also used was Hamilton Crescent in 1876 (see International Venues), First Cathkin Park in 1880 and 1882 (see Lost But Not Forgotten) and Kinning Park in 1881 (see Rangers). First Cathkin also staged the 1886 Final.

From 1885 to 1899 Second Hampden, which to confuse matters was later called New Cathkin Park,

became the main venue, staging nine of the fifteen Finals. Also used was the First Ibrox Park, on four occasions. The 1896 Final was the only one ever played outside Glasgow, because Hearts and Hibs were in contention. Logie Green, in Edinburgh of course, was the venue.

In 1900 and 1901 the newly-opened Second Ibrox Park hosted the Final, and it might have staged the 1902 match as well had the disaster not occurred three weeks prior to the event (see Safety). Despite the fact that Celtic were due to play in the Final, Parkhead was made the venue (the new Hampden was not yet ready, but Celtic lost the match anyway). Celtic also hosted the next year's Final, which saw a sudden leap in attendance from 16 000 in 1902 to 40 000 in 1903 (by that stage English Cup Final crowds had easily outstripped those in Scotland).

The Third Hampden Park opened in all its glory in 1903, and in 1904 hosted the third Cup Final meeting of the Old Firm. The first in 1894 had attracted only 17 000 spectators (less than previous years), the second in 1899 was watched by 25 000 (still not a record) but the 1904 Final set a new high of 65 000 spectators.

From 1905 to 1924 the match was shared almost equally between Hampden and Ibrox, with Celtic Park getting a look in twice only. As was to prove the case in later years attendances fluctuated considerably depending on who was playing, but it was not always the big Glasgow clubs who drew the largest crowds.

Partick v. Rangers, for example, attracted only 28 294 to Celtic Park in 1921, whereas the unlikely meeting of Kilmarnock v. Albion Rovers drew a record 95 000 to Hampden the year before. Choosy fans, the Scots.

Since 1925 every Scottish Cup Final has been staged at Hampden, with crowds going as high as 147 365 in 1937 to as low as 30 602 for a second replay in 1979.

Since their inception in 1947 only two League Cup Finals (now Skol Cup) have been held outside Glasgow. Both were at Dens Park. In 1980 Dundee United beat Aberdeen in the replay, and in 1981 a local derby saw United win again v. Dundee.

International Venues

England

Nowadays, we are so accustomed to Wembley as the home of English international football that it is hard to imagine England playing anywhere else. Yet Wembley assumed this monopoly only in 1951, and in the years between the Stadium's completion and the Second World War, of 33 full England home games, only 7 were staged at Wembley. Even the much humbler homes of clubs like Burnley, Middlesbrough and West Bromwich were chosen in preference to Wembley during this period.

English international football officially started in London at the Kennington Oval, a year after the ground had staged the first Final of the English Cup (see preceding section). The first game was of course v. Scotland, on 8 March 1873.

The Oval hosted England's first five home games, until in February 1881 the FA decided to broaden its horizons by playing its second game v. Wales at the home of Blackburn Rovers, at Alexandra Meadows, then headquarters also of the East Lancashire Cricket Club. This was partly because Blackburn was closer to the borders, but mainly because in those early days a match v. Wales was very much regarded as a trial, a second-class affair designed to help choose the side to play in the real battle, against Scotland.

Slower travel also meant that games against Ireland, similarly treated as trials, had to be at grounds nearer the west coast. The first game was played at Aigburth Park Cricket Ground, Liverpool, in February 1883. Three weeks later England played at another cricket ground, Bramall Lane, when they met Scotland on 10 March 1883.

For the next home fixture v. Ireland another venue was tried, Whalley Range, South Manchester, close to where Maine Road now stands and a mile from Fallowfield, scene of the 1893 Cup Final.

Bramall Lane staged the next home match v. Ireland in 1887, and two years later the fixture moved to Anfield, then home of Everton. This was the only time Anfield staged a full England international.

Six weeks after this, The Oval saw its last England game, a home defeat by Scotland on 13 April 1889, and London had to wait another four years before seeing another soccer international.

In March 1891, England travelled to Sunderland's Newcastle Road ground and to Wolverhampton's new ground, Molineux, for internationals v. Wales and Ireland, and as had happened once before (on 15 March 1890), two England teams turned out on the same day, beating the Welsh 4-1 at Sunderland and the Irish 6-1 at Wolverhampton on 7 March. A month later at newly-opened Ewood Park, England beat Scotland 2-1. The opening of a new ground was often celebrated by the staging of an international.

The problem of finding a London venue was not solved until 1897. Having been told only a short time before that Surrey CCC did not want soccer played at The Oval, England played their next home match in April 1893 v. Scotland at Richmond Park, the home of a rugby club and the only ground they could find at short notice. The Scots, despite the relative scale of the First Hampden and First Ibrox Parks, thought that other than Richmond, 'they had never played in such spacious and handsome surroundings'. Richmond also staged the 1894 Amateur Cup Final, but never hosted England again, despite the Scots' recommendation.

The next home game in London was at the Queen's Club, Kensington, then used by the famous amateur club, Corinthians. England met Wales there on 18 March 1895 (Corinthians were asked to select the team), but it was obvious that the best available grounds still existed beyond the metropolis, and a month later the game v. Scotland was held at Everton's new ground, Goodison Park.

For the return to London two years later, England found a new and proud home for internationals, Crystal Palace, the Cup Final venue (see previous section) and the largest stadium outside Glasgow.

But promising though the new venue seemed, in fact it only staged four internationals (The Oval held ten), all against Scotland, between 1897 and 1909. The 1899 Scotland match was held at the recently-opened Villa Park, as was the 1902 match, and Bramall Lane and St James' Park took the 1903 and 1907 matches respectively. Large though Crystal Palace was, it was pitifully short of proper spectator facilities, and hardly surprisingly the FA switched its London internationals elsewhere.

Its choice of venue for the Wales match in 1911 must have been controversial, however, for it was The Den, the new home of Southern League Millwall Athletic. Stamford Bridge was the next London venue, in April 1913 v. Scotland. Indeed Chelsea's ground seemed the natural successor to Crystal Palace for both Cup Finals and internationals, because not only was it large, it was also convenient for the West End and the FA's headquarters in Russell Square.

Until the First World War, England played at several other venues around the country, not mentioned above; v. Ireland at Roker Park in 1899, six months after the ground was opened; Aston Villa's Perry Barr Ground (February 1893); Derby's Racecourse Ground (February 1895); Trent Bridge (February 1897); The Dell (March 1901), while Southampton were still in the Southern League but had the best ground south of Birmingham; Ayresome Park (February 1905, soon after the opening and again in February 1914); the Baseball Ground, Derby (February 1911); and perhaps most surprising of all to the present generation, the now defunct Bradford Park Avenue, then one of the finest grounds in the north, where England beat Ireland 4-0 on 13 February 1909.

Venues for matches against Wales, apart from those already mentioned, were Stoke's Victoria Ground, used in 1889 and 1893; Ashton Gate, home of Bedminster (March 1899) then Bristol City (March 1913); Fratton Park (March 1899); Craven Cottage (March 1907); and the City Ground (March 1909). Crewe is often referred to as staging an England v. Wales match in February 1888, but this was in fact a home fixture for the Welsh.

Altogether, therefore, between 1872–1914, England played 56 home games, at a total of 31 venues in 17 different cities and towns. Only 19 of these games (34 per cent of the total) were held in London, and only 18 of the grounds are surviving League venues. In addition, none of these home games was against foreign opponents. All England's matches with continental teams had been abroad.

Between 1920–51 London started to attract a much higher proportion of England's games. Wembley was built in 1923, and substantial redevelopment at Highbury and White Hart Lane provided two more possible venues to rival the provincial grounds. Of 55 England home games played between the First World War and April 1951, a total of 21 different venues were used, and 26 games were played in London (47 per cent). Gradually the provinces were losing their hold.

The first post-World War One international in England was played at London's newest ground, Highbury, which was even closer to the FA headquarters and had excellent travel links with the rest of the city (although the FA chose Stamford Bridge as the successor to Crystal Palace as venue for Cup Finals).

In the 1920–51 period Highbury staged ten England games, more than any other ground, including Wembley which staged nine. The first was v. Wales on 15 March 1920, but one of the most significant was on 19 March 1923, when England played Belgium, the first continental national team to play a full international on English soil. From then on, Highbury staged internationals against foreign opposition only, and indeed it was rare for any provincial ground to hold such matches at all.

The Hawthorns staged England v. Belgium in December 1924; St James' Park staged England v. Norway in November 1938 (because Newcastle is much nearer to Norway than London); and Leeds Road staged England v. Holland in November 1946. All other games against continental teams were played in London; at Highbury (nine matches, including one v. FIFA in 1938); at White Hart Lane (four matches) and at Stamford Bridge (one match). Wembley's nine matches in this period were all v. Scotland.

Home Internationals were staged at several new venues. Hillsborough was first used in March 1920 v. Scotland, The Hawthorns v. Northern Ireland in October 1922, and to celebrate its opening, Selhurst Park, v. Wales in March 1926. Burnley and Black-

pool were awarded matches v. Northern Ireland in 1927 and 1932 respectively. Old Trafford entered the scene in April 1926 with a match v. Scotland (the last time a ground other than Wembley was used for this fixture). Neighbouring Maine Road was used twice after the War, at a time when it was the largest club ground in England, for matches v. Wales in 1946 and Northern Ireland in 1949.

After Wembley's match v. Scotland in April 1951, however, the Empire Stadium began its tenacious hold on the England team. It already had the FA Cup Final firmly under its belt (since 1923), the Scotland match (since 1928) and had recently become the venue of the Amateur Cup Finals (in 1949), so with attendances at a peak level it was inevitable that Wembley should now assume the role of England's home ground.

Of the 58 home games played between April 1951 and May 1966 (just before the World Cup), only nine were staged at grounds other than Wembley (15·5 per cent). These have been at Goodison Park v. Portugal (1951), v. Northern Ireland (1953) and Poland (January 1966); at Highbury v. France (1951) and Luxembourg (1961); at Villa Park v. Northern Ireland (1951) and Wales (1958); at Molineux v. Denmark (a World Cup qualifier in 1956) and Hillsborough v. France (1962). Curiously Wembley did not stage one England game v. foreign opposition until the May 1951 match v. Argentina.

Since the World Cup, England have only played one full international on an English ground other than Wembley, and that was at Goodison Park in May 1973 when the away game v. Northern Ireland was switched because of the unstable situation in Belfast. England is, therefore, now synonymous with Wembley.

Before 1966 the England team had played at a total of 40 different venues apart from Wembley, in 20 different cities and towns. Every League ground's pitch conforms with the minimum international requirements (see Pitches) and many have sufficient facilities to play host to foreign opposition in terms of spectator, media and executive requirements.

Furthermore, in recent years attendances for several Wembley internationals have not justified the use of such a large stadium. Indeed it could be argued very strongly that a capacity crowd at Villa Park or Old Trafford would provide a better atmosphere for the England team than a half-filled Wembley. It would be wrong to suggest that other grounds could or should host a large proportion of the games, because the organizational problems would be immense. But occasionally the FA should go elsewhere, for the mutual benefit of the team, the clubs and also the spectators, most of whom can never afford to see an England game in person. Provincial grounds should be given back their right to play host to the national team, but as long as London dominates and the FA invests in Wembley, there is little hope of this ever happening.

Scotland

Glasgow's hold on the Scottish international scene is of longer standing than London's is on England, for the simple reason that it has always had the biggest stadiums and crowd potential. Furthermore, since Scotland is a much smaller country, with the bulk of League clubs dotted around Glasgow within a 60-mile radius, Glasgow is a natural focus for international games.

The first international, Scotland v. England on 30 November 1872, was also the first recorded international in the world, and like the follow-on game in England 14 weeks later was played on a cricket ground. This was and still is the home of the West of Scotland Cricket Club on Hamilton Crescent, in the Partick district of Glasgow. It can be seen on Fortrose and Peel Streets. The attendance was 3500 compared with 2500 at The Oval game.

After four games at Hamilton Crescent, Scotland switched to Queen's Park ground, since known as the First Hampden Park, for their next six home games. The first was v. England on 2 March 1878. For a short period Queen's Park were based at Titwood Park, so Scotland played their two games v. England and Wales in 1884 at Third Lanark's First Cathkin Park, before following Queen's Park to their new ground, Second Hampden for the match v. England on 15 March 1884.

In March 1888 Scotland played Wales in their first home game outside Glasgow, at Hibernian's first Easter Road ground, the only time the club's ground has been used. Almost exactly a year later on 9 March 1889 Scotland met Ireland at the new home of Rangers, First Ibrox Park. The game v. Wales a year later was played at Underwood Park, the home of Abercorn in Paisley.

Second Hampden's last international was v. England on 5 April 1890 watched by a record crowd for a Scotland home game of 26 379, and between then and the opening of the Third Hampden in 1903 Scotland shared its favours among several different venues.

First came Celtic's ground (not the present Parkhead) v. Ireland on 28 March 1891. The following year's game v. Wales went to Tynecastle Park, the home of Hearts, while Ibrox staged the England game a week later on 2 April 1892. Celtic's new ground, opened in 1892, then became a regular venue, beginning in March 1893 with the game v. Ireland.

Other grounds used as venues for games v. Wales were Rugby Park, Kilmarnock (1894 and 1910); Carolina Port, Dundee (1896); Fir Park, Motherwell, shortly after its opening (1896); Pittodrie, Aberdeen, also soon after its opening (1900); Cappielow Park, Morton (1902); and Dens Park, the new home of Dundee (1904).

Between 1872 and March 1906, therefore, Scotland played 43 home games (excluding the April 1902 fixture v. England at Ibrox, declared unofficial after the disaster (see Safety)) of which ten were held outside Glasgow (23 per cent of the total). Altogether 16 different venues were used, 8 of which survive as League grounds today.

The Third Hampden was opened in 1903, but did not stage its first international until 7 April 1906, v. England, in front of the highest crowd ever recorded for an international, 102 741. Therefore the new Hampden's potential was proven immediately. Although Hampden Park has staged every Scotland and England match since 1906, it was not until after the Second World War that it established an almost total monopoly on all Scottish internationals.

Between 1906–39 Scotland played 46 home games. Of these 17 were at Hampden, of which all but two were against England. Surprisingly, Scotland did not play against any continental opposition at home until Austria's visit to Hampden in November 1933. Of the 46 home games, 12 were played at grounds outside Glasgow (26 per cent of the total). The grounds used apart from Hampden were Parkhead: eight times; Ibrox: eight times; Tynecastle: five times; Dens Park and Pittodrie twice. Rugby Park (1910), St Mirren Park (1923) and Firhill Park (1928), each staged one international during the period 1906–39.

After the Second World War Hampden took over. Indeed since 1946 only two Scottish international home games have been played elsewhere – an unofficial game v. South Africa at Ibrox in 1956, and a European Championship match v. Belgium at Pittodrie on 10 November 1971.

Attendances had boomed so considerably that Hampden became the natural choice. For example, before 1946 the highest crowd ever to have watched a Scotland v. Wales match was 55 000 at Ibrox in 1928. The first post-war match at Hampden attracted 86 582. Similarly the highest for a Scotland v. Northern Ireland match before 1946 had been 54 728 at Firhill Park, also in 1928. The first post-war match at Hampden drew 97 326.

Since then attendances have dropped steadily, even for games v. England, and there is now a case for using other grounds, such as Ibrox or Pittodrie, for games against Wales, Ireland and lesser continental sides. This however is unlikely to happen, because too much money has gone into rejuvenating Hampden in recent years and the income from international matches is crucial to their rebuilding programme (see Queen's Park).

Wales

The situation in Wales shows greater parity than either Scotland or England, with Welsh international matches being spread regularly between the two main centres, Cardiff and Wrexham, with until recently, occasional games held at Swansea.

The first Welsh home game was at Acton Park, Wrexham on 5 March 1877 v. Scotland, attended by 4000 spectators. As the headquarters of the Welsh FA, Wrexham was the main venue until Cardiff began to enter the scene in 1896. The only home games not played at Wrexham before this date were those in February 1888, at Nantwich Road, Crewe; in February 1890, at the Old Racecourse Ground, Shrewsbury; in February 1892, at Penrhyn Park, Bangor; and in February 1894, at the St Helen's Rugby Ground, Swansea.

The first games in Cardiff were also staged at a rugby ground, at Cardiff Arms Park, where Wales played six soccer internationals until Ninian Park was opened in 1910.

While Cardiff Arms Park and Wrexham shared the England and Scotland games, between 1896 and 1910, the Ireland fixture was still moved about. In 1898 and 1900 it was played at Llandudno, in 1904 at Bangor, and in 1908 at the Athletic Ground, Ynis, home then of Aberdare Athletic.

Also at this time the Wrexham venue was changed, from Acton Park to the present Racecourse Ground, from about 1905 onwards (see Wrexham).

The first international at Ninian Park was on 6 March 1911 v. Scotland, attended by 14 000. The Vetch Field staged its first international on 9 April 1921 v. Ireland, and since then with only one excep-

tion, Cardiff, Wrexham and Swansea have been the venues of all Welsh international home games. Between 1911 and May 1984 the approximate proportion of games at each venue has been: Cardiff 60 per cent, Wrexham 32 per cent and Swansea 8 per cent.

But within that period there were variations. For example, between 1911 and 1950 the proportion was respectively 48:46:6. Between 1951–81 the ratio was 67:24:9, showing the tendency to concentrate more games in Cardiff.

There is still tremendous rivalry between Wrexham, as the Welsh FA headquarters, and Cardiff, as the capital. Between 1956–72 Wrexham staged only four internationals and seemed beyond contention, but once the Safety of Sports Grounds Act temporarily ruled out Ninian Park, while the Racecourse Ground was almost completely transformed, Wrexham began to re-establish its claim to international games.

The one match not played at any of these grounds was on 12 October 1977 when Cardiff's ground was limited to only 10 000 capacity, so the Welsh FA switched the World Cup qualifying game v. Scotland to Anfield.

·26·
LOST BUT NOT FORGOTTEN

All who frequent local football clubs can imagine how chilling it must be to see the ground they love reduced to nothing. This chapter records a few such grounds.

We start this unhappy tour at the site of Peel Park, once home of **Accrington Stanley**. Accrington FC were founder members of the Football League in 1888 and played at the Accrington Cricket Club grounds, which still exist. But the Old Reds dropped out of the League in 1893, unable to pay their bills, and finally disbanded in 1896. At about the same time an amateur side named Stanley Villa (whose players lived around Stanley Street) achieved prominence, and in 1919 bought the site of Peel Park for £2500. Stanley joined the League in August 1921, and that year a crowd of over 20 000 was said to have watched a Lancashire Junior Cup Final at the ground.

Peel Park's official record gate was 17 634 v. Blackburn Rovers in a friendly (Blackburn is only five miles away). But undoubtedly one of the proudest moments was on 13 October 1955 when BBC cameras, Kenneth Wolstenholme and all, televised a Third Division North v. South match under Stanley's new floodlights. Peel Park had floodlights and was on television before most current First Division grounds.

The ground was notorious for its sloping, narrow pitch, and also had cramped dressing rooms with only a thin partition between so that team talks were often overheard.

The last League match at Peel Park was on 24 February 1962 v. Rochdale, after which Stanley dropped out, £60 000 in debt. Low gates were one reason, but the club's refusal to accept the setting up

Peel Park, Accrington. Nothing remains now except a hump and a wall

of a supporters' club was more ruinous.

Peel Park soon declined, and despite efforts to restore the ground it eventually reverted to a bare field. Hardly a trace remains today. There is a wall, the hump of the old terracing, now covered with grass, but otherwise no sign at all that the place was once alive with crowds of up to 20 000. One might easily walk past without realising.

Next is **Gateshead**, just south of the River Tyne, in the shadows of St James' Park. The club originated in 1899 as South Shields Adelaide, played at Horsley Hill and joined the League in 1919. Their record attendance at this ground was 21 000 v. Luton, 29 January 1921. In 1930 the club moved about ten miles west to Gateshead. (Horsely Hill Road is now a housing estate.) Their new ground was Redheugh Park, an elliptically-shaped ground also used for greyhound racing. It had cover on three sides and a record gate of 20 752 v. Lincoln, 25 September 1937. When the team finished third from bottom in 1960, they had to apply for re-election for the first time since 1937 but surprisingly were not re-elected, and Peterborough United took their place. Theirs was probably the most unjustified dismissal in League history.

Redheugh Park went down with the team, and now all that remains is a flat expanse of grass overlooked by some tower blocks. You would be hard pressed to make out any signs of the former ground, apart from a slight bump or two. (Gateshead FC, reformed in 1977, now play at one of the best grounds in the North East, the Gateshead International Athletics Stadium, which has a superb 7300-seat cantilever stand – a situation similar to that of Meadowbank in Edinburgh.)

Third on this doleful survey is perhaps the most depressing relic of all, **Bradford Park Avenue**. By rights, Bradford should never have had two senior football clubs at all, being only half the size of Leeds and a rugby stronghold. But the success of Bradford City, formed in 1903, encouraged Bradford Rugby FC to form a soccer team on the pitch next to Park Avenue, Bradford's major cricket ground, in 1907. The new club was so keen it spent its first season in the Southern League, before joining the Football League in 1908. Over £6000 was spent on improving the ground in 1907, under the guidance of Archibald Leitch (see Design). When finished with its new Grandstand the capacity was 37 000. In 1914 Park Avenue reached the First Division for a three-season spell, before slipping into Division Three in 1922. Their best spell came in the early 1930s, when as a very solid Second Division club they recorded their highest gate of 32 429 for a match v. Leeds. Even in the 1950s they were often higher placed than Bradford City, and there can be little doubt that Park Avenue was a better ground than Valley Parade. It had cover for 14 000.

In 1970 Bradford failed in their fifth bid for re-election and after a few seasons in the Northern

The Dolls' House crumbles at Park Avenue. Only the terracing remains

Premier League spent their last, dying season sharing Valley Parade with neighbours City. They finally folded in 1974. That same year the ground was bought for over £100 000 by the council, who intended to turn the whole area into a sports complex. But six years later no progress had been made and Leitch's much-loved stand was demolished. 'Enough to make a strong man cry', wrote a local reporter. The slates (yes, this stand had a slate roof!) were stacked up and returned to Wales, whence they first came in 1907, for recycling. A farmer bought some roof sheeting for his barn.

But the demolition company kept the backs of certain seats, and wherever possible returned them to former season-ticket holders. A passer-by was given the large sign saying BFC which had adorned the stand for 73 years. Ironically the demolition firm responsible was owned by a Bradford City fan.

Nowadays Park Avenue is a naked ruin. The cricket ground next door has even been shut because the pavilion was deemed unsafe, even though the pitch is acknowledged to be one of the best in England. The three football stands have all gone. One of them, the Main Stand, was a quite remarkable structure with three pedimented gables and a small corner pavilion at the end, known as the Dolls' House. At the back of the stand was a small balcony overlooking the cricket pitch. There was a clock in the centre which adventurous batsmen used to aim for, often overpowering their shots and sending the ball onto the football pitch.

Still visible are the perimeter walls, a very bumpy and neglected pitch, and three sides of crumbling, overgrown terraces. The floodlight pylon bases also survive, as do a few old turnstiles, overwhelmed by trees, bushes and scrap.

Standing on the forlorn concrete steps one can easily reconstruct the picture of Park Avenue at its best, for unlike Peel Park and Redheugh Park the basic shape and form still exists. But there is a ghostly presence, almost as if the departed stands still cast a cold shadow over the pitch and warn one not to tread on too many memories.

Last on our heartbreaking tour is Glasgow's Cathkin Park, the former home of **Third Lanark**, who passed away in the courts in 1967. In the mid-1970s this was one of the sorriest sights in football. The stand was gutted, the enclosure roof rotting, the grass knee-high, and yet at that time some of the surviving terracing would have put several League grounds to shame, including Hampden Park, a few hundred yards away over the ridge.

The ground's deterioration was made even more scandalous by the proximity of a school whose own playing facilities were so stretched.

Third Lanark, nicknamed the Hi-Hi's, were the team of the Third Lanarkshire Rifle Volunteers, who first played in 1872 on a pitch next to their parade ground. Called Cathkin Park the ground was between Dixon Road and Allison Road, on land now bordered by Warren Street. It was host to three Cup Finals. In 1903 the Third Lanark moved into the Second Hampden Park (see Queen's Park) and renamed it New Cathkin Park.

Ten years after the Hi-Hi's had been waved bye-bye in the courts, Glasgow's park department took over Cathkin Park and a £350 000 refurbishment made it into an open access ground with small sections of terracing preserved but all the structures removed. Where the stand once stood are now two park benches. On the enclosure side are bushes and trees. But the ground's basic outline and perimeter wall survive and sad though Third Lanark's demise was, at least the ground now benefits the community.

These four grounds had the longest history of any of the now-defunct League venues. The following are, in alphabetical order, the clubs who also played in the Football League or Scottish League. Notice that of the 26 individual clubs who have dropped out of the Football League (this list does not include clubs whose grounds were taken over by later League clubs, such as Wigan Borough and Leeds City), all but one were either Northern or Welsh.

England and Wales

Aberdare Athletic played at the Athletic Ground, Ynis. Record attendance 16 350 v. Bristol City, 2 April 1923. League members 1921–27 (replaced by Torquay).

Ashington played at Portland Park, still used by present club of same name. Record attendance 11 837 v. Aston Villa, 12 January 1924. League members 1912–29 (replaced by York).

Barrow played and still play at Holker Street. Record attendance 16 874 v. Swansea Town, 9 January 1954. League members 1921–72 (replaced by Hereford).

Bootle played at Hawthorne Road, Liverpool and were the first League club to resign membership, after only one season, 1892–93.

Burton Swifts played at Peel Croft. League members 1892–1901.

Burton Wanderers played at Derby Turn. League members 1894–97. In 1901 Swifts and Wanderers amalgamated to form **Burton United**, playing at Peel Croft, now the home of Burton RFC. League members 1901–07. (The present Burton Albion are no relation.)

Darwen played at Barley Bank, League members 1891–99. Soon after dropping out, the ground was built over. The Club now play at the Anchor Ground.

Durham City played at Holiday Park near Frankland Lane, also used as a greyhound stadium, until 1949. It is now built over. League members 1921–28 (replaced by Carlisle).

Gainsborough Trinity played and still play at The Northolme. Record attendance 9760 v. Scunthorpe 1948. League members 1892–1912.

Glossop North End (Glossop after 1903) played at North Road. League members 1898–1915. Glossop is the smallest town (25 000 inhabitants) ever to have supported a First Division team, for one season, 1899–1900.

Loughborough League members 1895–1900, played at the Athletic Ground, behind Nottingham Road, until it was built over in 1908. W. G. Grace once played cricket there.

Merthyr Town played and still play at Penydarren Park (now as Merthyr Tydfil). Record attendance 21 686 v. Millwall, 27 December 1921. League members 1920–30.

Middlesbrough Ironopolis played at the Paradise Ground. League members 1893–94 (see Middlesbrough).

Nelson played at the Seedhill Ground, now covered by a motorway. Record attendance 15 000 v. Bradford PA, 10 April 1926. League members 1921–31 (replaced by Chester).

New Brighton Tower played at the Tower Athletic Grounds, still visible as park. League members 1898–1901.

New Brighton played at Sandheys Park, off Rake Lane and the above named ground after the Second World War. Record attendance 15 173 v. Tranmere, 26 December 1924. League members 1923–51 (replaced by Workington).

Northwich Victoria played and still play at The Drillfield. League members 1892–94.

Southport played and still play at Haig Avenue. Record attendance 20 010 v. Newcastle, 26 January 1932. League members 1921–78 (replaced by Wigan Athletic).

Stalybridge Celtic played and still play at Bower Fold. Record attendance 9753 v. WBA, 17 January 1923. League members 1921–23.

Thames played at the West Ham Greyhound Stadium, which stood on Prince Regent Lane before being built over. Their record low attendance of 469 v. Luton in 1930 is believed to be the lowest for any scheduled Saturday afternoon League fixture.

League members 1930–32 (replaced by Newport).

Workington played and still play at Borough Park. Record attendance 21 000 v. Manchester United, 4 January 1958. League members 1951–77 (replaced by Wimbledon).

Finally, there is one other ground used for League football which deserves a mention: **White City**.

White City was built for the 1908 London Olympic Games, and earned its name because it was the centrepiece of the massive Franco-British exhibition, housed in predominantly white buildings. It was in design a forerunner of Wembley, holding 70 000 spectators, and even had the Olympic swimming pool in the centre.

After the Games it lay unused until the arrival of greyhound racing in 1927 (greyhounds also saved Wembley from demolition).

It was used twice by QPR, whose Loftus Road ground is a few hundred yards away, in 1931–33 and 1962–63 (see QPR), by Pegasus for one season and for sundry representative games and a few fixtures of the Corinthians.

It was also used for speedway, cycling, athletics, rugby, boxing, show-jumping, rodeos, prayer meetings and baseball. Up to 1958, a total of 44 world records had been broken at White City. In 1937 it had the world's biggest Tote. The most important football match to be held there was in July 1966, when because Wembley was holding a greyhound meeting, France played Uruguay in a World Cup Finals match. Ironically, it could have once staged a World Club Championship, in 1930, but the FA vetoed the plan which Brigadier-General Critchley MP had drawn up.

After the 1960s White City became something of a White Elephant, too large to be sustained by greyhounds alone and too old-fashioned to cope with modern athletics meetings. Safety regulations halved the capacity to 35 000, but in its last years the biggest crowds numbered about 20 000 for the annual greyhound derby. With new investment it could have become London's prime athletics venue – even at the end it had twice the capacity of Crystal Palace – but when the Greyhound Racing Association lost their controlling interest in the stadium in the 1970s its days were numbered.

In September 1984 the last race was run at this sad old stadium, which in 1937 once staged cheetah racing. A year later bulldozers moved in. With barely a whimper from the sporting press White City was flattened. The land was bought by the BBC, whose main Wood Lane television studios are adjacent, for £30 million. One hopes the venerable Beeb will do something to preserve the name.

Scotland

I am indebted to Mike Watson for the following information on Scotland's former League clubs. Several of the clubs below were members of the short-lived Division Three and C Division. (For de-

tails of those clubs not mentioned – that is **Ayr, Ayr Parkhouse, Clydebank** and **Dundee Wanderers** – see the chapters on Scotland.)

Abercorn, founder members, survived until 1915, having once been senior to their Paisley neighbours St Mirren. Main grounds were Underwood Park and from 1899 Ralston Park.

Armadale, one of four former West Lothian League clubs, played and still play at Volunteer Park (as Armadale Thistle). Members 1921–32.

Arthurlie played at Dunterlie Park, Barrhead in Renfrewshire. A club of the same name still plays there. League members 1901–15, 1923–29.

Bathgate played at Mill Park, West Lothian. Members 1921–28.

Beith played and still play at Bellsdale Park in Ayrshire. Members 1923–26.

Bo'Ness played and still play (as Bo'Ness United) at Newton Park, used for Junior Internationals. Members 1921–32.

Broxburn United played at Sports Park, West Lothian, since built over, and were unconnected with present junior side Broxburn Athletic. Members 1921–26.

Cambuslang, founder League members, played just south of Glasgow at Whitefield Park, now built over, and survived only two seasons.

Clackmannan played at Chapelhill Park and were members for five seasons during the 1920s. A club of the same name still competes in Fife junior football.

Cowlairs, members 1890–95, played at Springvale Park in Springburn, Glasgow. The ground was next to the present Hillkirk Place.

Dumbarton Harp played just 30 League games from 1923–25 at Meadow Park.

Dykehead came from the Lanarkshire mining town of Shotts. Members 1923–26, their ground was Parkside.

Edinburgh City, formed 1928, tried to become the Queen's Park of the capital. From 1931–36 they shared Marine Gardens with Leith Athletic. This ground was built over by an open-air lido which is now sadly derelict, in the Portobello district. For one season they used Powderhall Stadium (see Hearts) before taking possession of a new ground, City Park, on Pilton Drive. After leaving the League in 1949 City ceased playing in 1955, but City Park remained in use and for a while was home to Ferranti Thistle (see Meadowbank). The ground, with its original main stand, is still used for local football.

Galston, members 1923–25, played at Portland Park near Kilmarnock.

Helensburgh, members 1923–26, played at Ardencaple Park.

Johnstone, not to be confused with St Johnstone, played at Newfield Park, Renfrewshire, during two spells in the League from 1912–1926.

King's Park were Stirling's League side from 1921–39. They folded when their ground, Forthbank

Park, was damaged in 1940 by the only bomb dropped on Stirling during the War, from a lone German plane randomly jettisoning its payload. Rather than resurrect the club, in 1945 amid some controversy, the former chairman of King's Park, coal merchant Tom Fergusson, organized the purchase of the Annfield estate. (According to club historian Allan Grieve, it has been suggested that Fergusson opposed King's Park's revival because he was responsible for the club's still outstanding debts and had been involved in a bribery scandal at Forthbank). The ground was on the site of the current Players cigarette factory.

Leith Athletic, members 1891–1953. Their first ground was Bank Park, 200 yards north of Hibernian's Easter Road. From 1895 they used Beechwood Park, Marine Gardens (see Edinburgh City) and Logie Green, near Powderhall Stadium. Apart from the war years when the ground was requisitioned, from the 1930s until they folded in 1955, Leith played at Old Meadowbank, the site of the current Commonwealth Stadium, which they shared with Edinburgh Monarchs Speedway team.

Linthouse, members 1895–1900, played near Ibrox at Langlands Park and Govandale Park.

Lochgelly United played at the Recreation Ground during their six seasons in the League until 1926. Neighbours of Cowdenbeath.

Mid-Annandale, members 1923–26, played in Lockerbie near Dumfries, but the ground location is uncertain.

Nithsdale Wanderers, from Sanquhar, also near Dumfries, played at Crawick Holm during their four seasons membership from 1923–27.

Northern played just one season, 1893–94 at Hyde Park, very close to Springvale Park, home of Cowlairs. At this time Springburn was a heavily industrialised area.

Peebles Rovers played and still play at Whitestone Park. Members 1923–26.

Port Glasgow Athletic, members 1893–1911, were Morton's neighbours. They played at Clune Park near Clune Brae, not the same ground used by the town's current Junior club.

Renton, one of the greatest clubs in early Scottish football, from the West of Scotland, played at Tontine Park from 1891, as founder members, until their expulsion in 1897. (Their crime had been to play against a professional team, St Bernards.)

Royal Albert, members 1923–26, played and still play at Raploch Park, Larkhall in Lanarkshire.

St Bernards were members 1893–1939. Their first proper ground was the Royal Patent Gymnasium, next to the Water of Leith and Canonmills Bridge. They moved to various pitches in the vicinity; Old Logie Green, New Logie Green (venue of the 1896 Final) and Powderhall Stadium, which became a mecca for athletics (foot-running as it was called) and was also used by Hibs and Hearts. From 1902–17 they used the Royal Gymnasium Ground (which ran from Royal Crescent to Eyre Place), then returned to Old Logie Green, which was immediately adjacent to Powderhall (only a fence separated the two grounds).

Solway Star, members 1923–26, played at Kimmetton Park in Annan, Dumfriesshire.

Thistle, members 1893–94. It is thought they played at either Beechwood Park or Braehead Park, Dalmarnock, just south of Celtic Park.

Vale of Leven, another once powerful West of Scotland club, were members 1890–1926 in two spells. They still use Millburn Park, Alexandria, where they have played since 1890.

Bye-bye to the Hi-Hi's: Cathkin Park ten years after Third Lanark folded. The terraces are now landscaped but the pitch still remains

APPENDICES

Appendix A

The 1946 Bolton Disaster

A brief summary of the events of 9 March 1946 at Burnden Park, as recorded in the report of R. Moelwyn Hughes KC, appointed by the Home Secretary, Chuter Ede (Command Paper 6846).

The disaster was unique in that no structure collapsed and was the first inflicted by a crowd on itself. The use of the East (Burnden) Stand by the Ministry of Food for storage had no bearing on the accident. The accident occurred in the Railway Enclosure, so called because it was formed on the embankment supporting the LMS main Yorkshire to Bolton line. There were 14 turnstiles, all on the West Side of the enclosure (including two for schoolboys and servicemen). The gaps between the barriers on the higher terraces in the north west corner were wider, because of the curvature, than on the lower terraces, and there was a barrier-less gangway leading from the fatal corner up to the top of the terrace, where the bottleneck occurred. Sufficient police were used. Railway policing prevented anyone from crossing the railway line to gain unlawful entry over fence at rear of enclosure.

The events were detailed as follows:

2.20 p.m. pressure builds up outside turnstiles.

2.30 p.m. some people in crush already trying to escape by moving away from turnstiles.

2.35 p.m. already impossible for those coming through the turnstiles to pass along the terraces. PC Lowe calls for turnstiles to be closed but cannot find Head Checker (who supervised the turnstiles). Some people want to leave ground because they cannot reach terraces.

2.40 p.m. Head Checker looks at the situation. Outside the Chief Inspector of Police cannot get through crowd and has to shout instructions. Inside the police are helping people out of north west corner onto the perimeter track. One man is seen trampled on the ground. Invasion begins over railway line fence and at eastern end of enclosure. Police reluctant to release extra men from East Stand, where they are guarding stockpiles of food. Turnstiles eventually shut, but more clamber over walls and force doors

open. These sealed again at 2.50 p.m.

A father and small son want to escape crush inside the ground near turnstiles. Father picks padlock of exit gate next to boys' entrance and they slip out. But open gate lets rush of people into ground.

More spectators pulled out at front, more seen trampled underfoot. Sergeant orders section of crowd to tear down wooden perimeter fence in order to relieve crush. Inspector and sergeant agree that exit doors should be opened to allow more to leave but cannot find keys or officials with keys.

2.50 p.m. most gates closed. Crowd outside begins to disperse, except around boys' entrance, where fence is torn down and approximately 1000 climb over.

The Railway Police cannot cope either. About 2000 to 3000 people on railway line but few can actually see over fence into ground, except when they perch on wagons of a goods train which pauses there for a short time, so most disperse.

A further 200 to 300 rush through gate by boys' entrance, most of them servicemen. Mounted police and two constables manage to seal this gate.

Still pressure increases in north west corner, despite more people passing onto perimeter track.

2.55 p.m. teams come out, crowd swaying. People at top of terrace find themselves forced down into bottom corner. By boys' entrance two barriers are bent. The weight carries down through the bottleneck where there is barrier-less gap. The two barriers nearest the corner flag collapse. Crowd seems to sink, but crush so great that nothing clearly visible. Two, three then four people pile up and are trodden underfoot. A large number are asphyxiated.

3.00 p.m. match begins as hundreds spill out onto track.

3.12 p.m. bodies brought out and referee informed that there have been fatalities. Players leave pitch, 33 bodies found and laid out on pitch before being taken to mortuaries. First aid given to 500. Hardly anyone not in the north west vicinity realizes seriousness of accident. Chief Constable and referee decide it would be advisable to restart match. East Stand opened for 1000 spectators. A further 1000 remain on track.

Seven of the 33 dead were from Bolton. The *Manchester Evening News* commented two days later that this kind of disaster was always likely to happen at one of the older grounds. On the fact that so many broke into the ground, many of them servicemen, it says, 'Possibly the war has left some people with less respect for law than they used to have'.

Appendix B

The 1985 Bradford Fire

A brief summary of the events of 11 May 1985 at Valley Parade, including extracts from the Interim Report of Mr Justice Popplewell (Command Paper 9585).

It was to be a day of celebration, Bradford having just won promotion. Before the game, against Lincoln, Bradford were presented with the Third Division trophy and the manager Trevor Cherry received a further award. In the stand sat local dignitaries and representatives of Bradford's twin-towns from Germany and Belgium. An estimated crowd of 11 000, well above average, attended. There were between 2–3000 in the stand.

Cameras from Yorkshire TV filmed the match, by all accounts a dull game. Just before half-time a glowing light was visible in Block G, nearest the Kop. The first police message was timed at 15.40 and 58 seconds. A witness described seeing, through a small hole, flames underneath the stand roughly between seats 142 and 143 in either row I or J. He saw what appeared to be paper or debris on fire, about 9 inches below the floor boards.

No witness saw anything thrown into the stand which might have caused a fire. A *Daily Star* reporter, sitting in the press-box 100 feet away, was convinced a smoke bomb had been thrown. Popplewell found his evidence 'not reliable'.

The report concluded that the fire was not started by 'any malicious means'. Its likely cause was the dropping of a lighted match, or cigarette or tobacco. Several people in the vicinity were smoking; it would be impossible, and grossly unfair to point the finger at any one person.

The design of the stand was such that the void between the sloping ground and the stand floor was between 9–30 inches. One policeman describes seeing accumulated rubbish, plastic cups and such-like which had slipped through small gaps in the flooring (as also reported in the first edition of this book, 1983). After the fire a newspaper from 1968 and a pre-decimalisation peanut wrapper were found unburnt under the stand. Another witness described losing his scarf through gaps in the flooring and being unable to retrieve it. A ground maintenance man admitted it was impossible to retrieve rubbish from voids unless repair work was in progress. A forensic scientist said the gaps could have been caused by shrinkage of old timbers.

Between the first sighting of flames and total conflagration of the stand, five minutes elapsed. At first spectators in the area of the fire felt their feet getting warm. One rushed to the back of the stand for a fire extinguisher but found none. A policeman thought the fire was only a minor incident. An officer shouted to another on the touchline to fetch an extinguisher. His request was misheard and instead the policeman radioed for the fire brigade.

Those in the immediate area hesitated, others further away thought it was a smoke bomb. The game continued. People were reluctant to move until persuaded by a police officer. By 15.46 and 20 seconds the stand was well ablaze. Now there was a crisis, as the following events show:

Game stops. Fire described as spreading 'faster than a man could run'. Wooden roof covered with tarpaulin, sealed with asphalt, catches fire. It is this rather than flooring which now spreads fire along length of stand, creating impression of a fire ball. Burning timbers and molten roof felt fall onto crowd below. Thick black smoke envelops rear passage, where many spectators now trying to escape. One dashes to get extinguisher from club house but is overtaken by smoke and crowds. Extinguishers not kept in passage for fear of vandalism, but fire so intense it is believed extinguisher would have made no difference.

Six narrow exits at back were boarded up. Exit through locked turnstiles was impossible. Seven exits either forced open or found open. One man described how three burly men smashed down a door and thus saved his life. One door forced open from people outside ground on South Parade.

Three died trying to get out through toilets, where exit was impossible. Twenty-seven bodies found by exit K and turnstiles 6–9 in centre rear of stand. Half were aged over 70 or under 20. Some had been crushed to death trying to crawl under turnstiles in order to escape approaching flames. At least two elderly people died in their seats. The fifty-one bodies found in the stand were too badly charred to be identified without forensic evidence.

Most of those who escaped onto the pitch were saved, but many emerged with their clothes and hair alight. Men literally threw children over the perimeter wall. A retired mill worker was seen wandering about the pitch, apparently oblivious to the fact he was on fire from head to foot, a human torch. People smothered him until the flames were extinguished, but he died later in hospital. Among those who perished was Bradford's oldest supporter, 86-year-old Sam Firth.

An officer said, 'It must have been the survival of the fittest – men first'. One survivor saw policeman shepherding fans towards an exit which turned out to be locked. Another described how he heard the shouts and screams of people being burned alive. Bodies were welded together by the heat. A father was found trying to shield his two sons from the flames. A crippled man was near to escaping before he fell and was consumed by the fire. A policeman tried to drag a woman from the flames but she too fell back.

Much was made of the fact that the TV crews were pelted by stones from people on the pitch, several of whom tried to shake the camera gantry. This 'hooliganism' was later put down to genuine anger that the cameras should have continued filming during the fire. But fans continued chanting 'We love you City' at the height of the fire, while some so-called hooligans joined in the rescue attempts.

Acts of incredible heroism were recorded, among spectators and police officers who risked their lives trying to save others. One man pulled people from the inferno. 'I danced over the seats pursued by flames,' he said. Asians living in houses adjacent to the ground opened their doors to the injured and shocked. Long-standing racial barriers were instantly forgotten.

A national appeal raised £4 million. *The Guardian*'s David Lacey wrote, 'Soccer attracts more hackneyed hyperbole than most sorts. We talk about "tragedy" when we mean "disappointment" and "disaster" when we mean "defeat". When real tragedy and disaster occur, we tend to be stuck for the right words.'

A witness at the Popplewell Inquiry said that in normal circumstances the Bradford stand took a long time to clear. A Chief Inspector said the stand could not have been evacuated in the 2½-minute period recommended by the Green Code (see Safety). Other sections of the code deal with voids under stands, gaps in flooring and the provision of proper exits. Popplewell's report concluded, 'Had the Green Code been complied with this tragedy would not have occurred.'

Appendix C

Admissions

Going to a football match is marginally less expensive, on average, that it was 25 years ago.

For example, the receipts for Stockport v. Liverpool (att. 27 833) in February 1950 were £4312, an average of 15½p per person. The receipts for Stockport v. Arsenal in 1980 (att. 11 635) were £19 382, an average of £1.56 per person.

In relation to the average weekly wage of a manual worker in 1950, admission costs were about 1 per cent of his gross income. The same applied in 1980. But if we take the average admission cost (15½p in 1950 and £1.56 in 1980), we can see that although the cost is ten times higher, average weekly wages during the same period increased approximately by a factor of 12.5. At the same time average retail prices rose eightfold. So average football admission prices fall exactly between the rise in prices and the rise in wages. In 1950 the average admission fee at Stockport represented 1.8 per cent of the average manual worker's wage. In 1980 it represented 1.6 per cent.

The gap between the cost of sitting and standing has been reduced quite dramatically. For example, in 1910 Manchester United charged 6d to stand and 5s for the best seat. In 1982 they charged £1.80 to stand and £3.80 for the best seat. In 1910 therefore the price ratio of standing/seating was 1:10. In 1982 it was 1:2.1. Comparatively it is now more expensive to stand, but much cheaper to sit (although one can argue that the best seats are now in the private boxes, which do not form part of this calculation).

Costs vary enormously. For the price of one season ticket at White Hart Lane in 1986 you could buy two of the best at Old Trafford plus a season ticket for the car park. The best season ticket at Ibrox costs £235, compared with only £15 at Albion Rovers. Yet just one seat for a match at Wimbledon in 1986–87 would have cost £13.

Collecting gate money was, in the early days of football, a difficult business. Before turnstiles and properly enclosed grounds, the most common method was for clubs to pass a hat around. At Perry Barr, when turnstiles were introduced, match takings rose from an average of £75 to £200. The gatemen were, of course, incensed when this became known, since it implied a measure of dishonesty. In June 1895 the Everton chairman and four directors resigned, 'owing to acute administrative difficulties', despite having announced a £6000 profit in the previous three years. The mystery, it is suggested, may well have been connected with a scandal involving gatemen. But the problem did stop when new turnstiles were installed.

Clubs also had a problem when announcing receipts, because no accurate attendance figures were known, the most publicised figures being a guess by a newspaper reporter, which, clubs often complained, was far too high.

The League has always set a minimum price for admission, but there have been some attempts by clubs to reduce admission for the unemployed. An extreme example of this occurred in 1932 when up to 75 per cent of Merthyr's adult male population was unemployed, and gates were down to 500. In August 1932 the football club, who had lost League status in 1930, largely as a result of the Depression, reduced admission for the unemployed from 9d to 2d. Immediately gates rose to 4000. But the club were forced to stop the reduction when neighbouring clubs and the Welsh FA objected. In recent years the practice of charging unemployed people lower admission has been revived, especially in those areas hardest hit by the recession.

Entrance was free at half-time or during the second half at most grounds. Another way of gaining free admission was to help clear the pitch of snow.

Inevitably free admissions affected the reported attendance figures. At Sunderland until October 1907 there was a pass-out system to enable spectators to leave the ground at half-time and sample the wares of local pubs (this was before licensing hours were restricted during the First World War). Abuse of the system meant that second half attendances were invariably larger.

In the early days free viewing was possible at several grounds. When Darwen played Blackburn Rovers, the hills surrounding the Barley Bank Ground were said to be 'black' with people watching. Similarly for Bolton's Cup replay v. Notts County in 1884, 4000 to 5000 watched from the surrounding hills. One farmer charged spectators half the normal admission cost!

Women were allowed in free at most grounds until the mid-1880s. *The Daily Telegraph* noted in 1873 that: 'ladies always turned up in some numbers for matches at Bramall Lane'. At Deepdale on Easter Monday 1885, some 2000 women attended the game without paying, so the club dropped the concession thereafter. But this did not discourage them. In the reserve stand at Aston Villa it was said that there were 'almost as many ladies as men'. Even when free admission was dropped, women could still buy season tickets at half-price.

But as crowds grew and conditions became more cramped, fewer women attended. Aberdeen allowed women in free up till 1908, and in 1982 Meadowbank revived the practice, with great success.

The most remarkable example of free admission was in 1982 when the Kuwait FA allowed 40 000 spectators to watch a World Cup qualifying match, in gratitude for the fans' support at previous games.

Appendix D

The 92 Club

This dedicated group of enthusiasts was set up in 1978 to recognize the achievements of those who have attended every Football League ground for a first team match. By 1986 it had approximately 400 members and 3 Honorary Members.

They are: Alan Durban, who as a player for Cardiff, Derby and Shrewsbury played at his 92nd ground in 1976; Eric Northover, a director of Northampton Town, and Jim Smith, who as former manager of Colchester, Blackburn, Birmingham and Oxford, visited his 92nd ground in a managerial capacity when he took QPR to Hillsborough, ironically in the city of his birth, in 1986.

Details of this elite group can be obtained by sending a stamped addressed envelope to Gordon Pearce, 104 Gilda Crescent, Whitchurch, Bristol BS14 9LD.

Also of interest to football buffs are:

The Association of Football Statisticians
For information send a SAE to Ray Spiller, 22 Bretons, Basildon, Essex SS15 5BY.

Scottish Football Historian
For information send a SAE to John Litster, 14 Raith Crescent, Kirkaldy, Fife KY2 5NN.

Appendix E

Spion Kop

The name most commonly found at British football grounds is the 'Spion Kop'. Spion Kop was a hill in South Africa, which British Army officers tried to capture in January 1900 during the Boer War (the word Spion Kop is Afrikaans for 'look-out'). The bloody action cost 322 British lives and 563 wounded, plus 300 casualties on the victorious Boer side.

Reporters, among them Winston Churchill, described the 'astounding inefficiency' of the British artillery, calling Spion Kop that 'acre of massacre, that complete shambles'. Leading this futile assault on the hill were the 2nd Royal Lancaster Regiment and the 2nd Royal Lancashire Fusiliers.

Afterwards the mounds on which Lancashire men stood at their football grounds became known as Spion Kops in memory of the tragedy. The first recorded use of the name was at Anfield, in 1906, apparently on the suggestion of a journalist, Ernest Edwards. Although recent research by Phil Soar suggests that the first Kop might have been at Arsenal's Manor Ground in 1904 (see Arsenal), the Kop is still most closely associated with Anfield.

GLOSSARY

There is no formal glossary of terms used for describing football ground architecture, but the following simplified terms refer to the main structures.

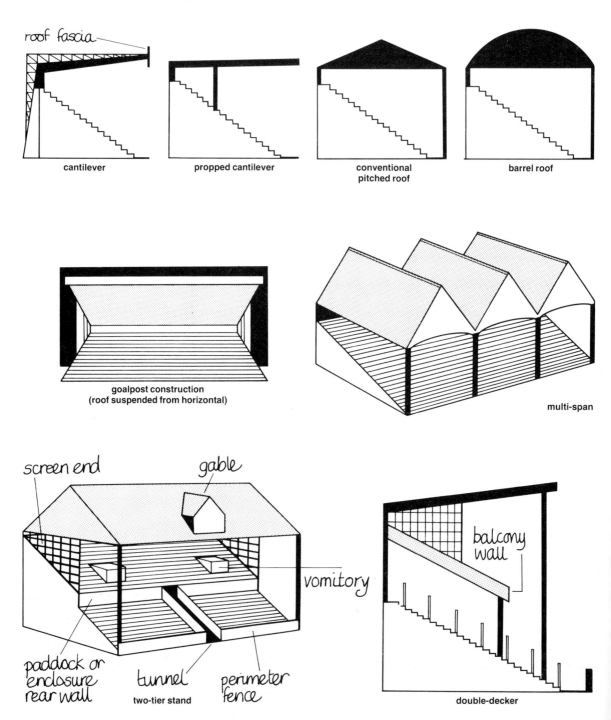

roof fascia

cantilever

propped cantilever

conventional
pitched roof

barrel roof

goalpost construction
(roof suspended from horizontal)

multi-span

screen end

gable

vomitory

paddock or
enclosure
rear wall

tunnel

perimeter
fence

two-tier stand

balcony
wall

double-decker

BIBLIOGRAPHY

GENERAL BACKGROUND

Alcock, A. W., (ed.) **The Book of Football**. London: Carmelite House, 1906.

Appleton, Arthur, **Hotbed of Soccer**.

Douglas, P., **The Football Industry**. London: Allen and Unwin, 1973.

Fabian, A. H., and Green, G. (eds), **Association Football**. London: Caxton, 1960.

Gibson, A., and Pickford, W., **Association Football and the Men Who Made It**. 1906.

Golesworthy, Maurice, **Encyclopedia of Association Football**. London: Robert Hale, 1956–76.

Green, G., **The Official History of the FA Cup**. 1949.

Hutchinson, John, **The Football Industry**. 1982.

Keeton, George W., **Football Revolution: A Study of the Changing Pattern of Association Football**. David & Co., 1972.

MacDonald, Roger, **Soccer: A Pictorial History**. London: Collins, 1977.

McCarra, Kevin, **Scottish Football, a Pictorial History**. Glasgow: Third Eye Centre and Polygon Books, 1984.

Mason Tony, **Association Football and English Society 1863–1915**. Eastbourne: Harvester, 1980.

Morris, Desmond, **The Soccer Tribe**. London: Cape, 1981.

Moynihan, J., **The Soccer Syndrome**. St Albans: Macgibbon & K., 1966.

Murray, Bill, **The Old Firm**. Edinburgh: John Donald, 1984.

Richards, Harold, **How to Get There**.

Strutt, Joseph, **The Sports and Pastimes of the People of England**. 1903.

Studd, Stephen, **Herbert Chapman, Football Emperor: A Study in the Origins of Modern Soccer**. London: Peter Owen, 1981.

Sutcliffe, C. E., **Story of the Football League 1888–1938**. 1938.

Wall, F., Sir., **Fifty Years in Football**. 1935.

Walvin, J., **People's Game: A Social History of British Football**. London: Allen Lane, 1975.

Young, P. M., **History of British Football**. London: Stanley Paul, 1968.

REFERENCE AND STATISTICS

Robertson, Forrest, **Mackinlay's A–Z of Scottish Football**.

Rollin, Jack and Dunk, Peter (ed.), **Rothmans Football Yearbook**. London: Queen Anne Press, 1970–86.

Soar, Phil, **Hamlyn A–Z of British Football Records**. London: Hamlyn, 1984.

Clydesdale Bank, **Scottish League Review 1985–86**.

RESEARCH PAPERS AND GOVERNMENT PUBLICATIONS

Report on Crowd Behaviour at Football Matches, Command Paper 2088, 1924.

Inquiry into Bolton Disaster, Command Paper 6846, 1946.

Wheatley Report, Command Paper 4952, 1975.

Safety of Sports Ground Act, 1975.

Guide to Safety at Sports Grounds, 1976.

Chester, N., **Report of Committee on Football**, 1968.

Lang, **Report on Crowd Behaviour at Football Matches**, 1969.

Economic Trends, CSO, 1982.

Inquiry into Crowd Safety and Control at Sports Grounds; Interim Report 1985, Command Paper 9585, Final Report 1986, Command Paper 9710.

Artificial Grass Surfaces for Association Football, Sports Council, 1986.

All Seated Football Grounds and Hooliganism; the Coventry City Experience 1981–84. Williams, Dunning and Murphy, Leicester University, 1984.

The Luton Home-only Members Plan—a preliminary report. Dept. of Environment and Football Trust, 1986.

CLUBS AND GROUNDS

Wherever possible I have made reference to club histories in the text. The following authors (clubs) have also provided information: Brown, Deryk; Finn, Ralph; Joy, B., and Wall, B. (Arsenal); Morris, P. (Aston Villa); Garrad, John (Birmingham); Francis, Charles (Blackburn); Daniels, Robin (Blackpool); Jackson, Peter (Cardiff); Lawson, Martin and Cowing, Ronald (Carlisle); Sewell, Albert (Chelsea, 1955); Finn, Ralph and Moynihan, John (Chelsea); Foulger, Neville and Henderson, Derek (Coventry); Peskitt, Roy (Crystal Palace); Edwards, George (Derby); Keates, Thomas (Everton); Ekberg, Charles (Grimsby); Conway, Tony (Gillingham); Folliard, Robert (Leicester), Liversege, Stan (Liverpool); Lawson, John (Notts Forest); Kaufmann, Neil and Ravenhill, Alan, (Orient); Signy, Dennis (QPR); Brown, Dennis, Finn, Ralph Holland, John and Soar, Phil (Spurs); Korr, Charles P. and Helliar, Jack (West Ham), Young, P. M., (Wolves); Crampsey, Bob (Queen's Park); Fairgrieve, John (Rangers).

NEWSPAPERS AND PERIODICALS:

Athletic News;
Daily Mirror;
Daily Sketch;
F.A. News;
F.L. Review;
Glasgow Herald;
Manchester Guardian;
Match Weekly;
Pall Mall Gazette;
The Times; Sunday Times;
American Architect (7 May 1924);
The Architects' Journal (24 Feb 1926; Nov 1932; Apr 1936; Aug 1973; Jan 1979);
Architect and Building News (25 Feb 1938);
Architectural Psychology Newsletter (Aug 1972);

Architectural Review (Nov 1932; May 1968; Jan 1973);
Art and Industry (Aug 1945);
British Builder (Jan 1923);
The Builder (Oct 1922; July 1935; Mar 1957; Jan 1962; Apr 1963; Nov 1963);
Building Design (May 1972; Nov 1974; Oct 1976);
Building Materials (Nov 1961);
Design (Feb, Mar 1975; Sept 1978);
Design Methods and Theories (Vol. 2., No. 2);
Journal of Architectural Research (Aug 1979);
Prefabrication (Apr 1957);
Progressive Architecture (Mar 1973);
R.I.B.A. Journal (Vol. 43 No. 9, Vol. 88 No. 4);
Structural Engineer (Feb 1933, Nov 1962, Nov 1974);
Tubular Structures (Nov 1972).

ACKNOWLEDGEMENTS

Since the publication of this book's first edition in 1983 I have been overwhelmed by the response of readers from all over the world. Many have contributed invaluable information which has allowed me to correct, revise and update the entries on each ground. I am particularly indebted to Ray Spiller and members of the Association of Football Historians, whose little-publicised research made my job that much easier. In Scotland, Mike Watson, John Litster and various contributors to the *Scottish Football Historian* have also been of immense help. I would also like to thank Sports Pages Bookshop of Charing Cross Road, London for their invaluable assistance with references.

After visiting 130 League grounds in Britain plus several other football venues, my thanks go also to the many club secretaries and groundsmen who not only withstood my barrage of questions but helped, simply by showing an understanding of my quest, to revive my occasionally flagging spirits.

Once again I am grateful to those friends and relatives who both put me up and put up with me during my travels and travails. Thanks also are due to Jackie Spreckley, without whose hard work, support and affection my task would have been much less bearable.

Additional information was supplied by: Arthur Appleton, Geoff Allman, William Bancroft, Ted Brammer, Randall Butt, Derek Buxton, John Byrne, Richard Cairns, Denis Clarebrough, R. A. Clarke, Peter Cogle, Vic Couling, Jim Creasy, Trevor Denton, John Dewhirst, David Downs, Peter Dunk, H. Ellis Tomlinson, Keith Farnsworth, Harold Finch, Gary Ginsberg, Maurice Golesworthy, Ted Griffith, Alf Hall, Stan Hall, Roy Hewitt, Dave Hillam, Brian Horsnell, Malcolm Huntingdon, Colin Jeffrey, Paul Joannou, Tom Lane, A. J. Brian Lile, Desmond Loughrey, John Lovis, David Markham, Kevin McCarra, Bill Miles, J. C. Morris, Simon Myers, Geoffrey Needler, Paul Plowman, Sam Rendell, David Roberts, Graeme Robertson, Dave Russell, Revd Nigel Sands, Stan Searl, Phil Shaw, Richard Shepherd, R. K. Shoesmith, John Taylor, Paul Taylor, Tony Thwaites, Howard Walker, Roger Walters, Harry Warden, Roger Wash, Stephen Watt, Eric White, Ted Wilding, Andrew Wilkie, Gordon A. E. Williams, Alex Wilson, Mike Wilson, Harold Wolfe, John Woodcock, Ted Woodriff and Pat Woods.

The Football League, The Football Association, Football Grounds Improvement Trust, Football Trust, Institute of Structural Engineers, Scottish League.

Birkenhead News, Bolton Evening News, Bury Times, Chester Chronicle, Crewe Chronicle, Cumbrian Newspapers, Manchester Evening News, Oxford Mail, Portsmouth Evening News, Sheffield Morning Telegraph and *Star, Stoke Evening Sentinel* and *The Architects' Journal.*

The Publishers are grateful to the following individuals and organizations for allowing their photographs to be reproduced in the book. Where more than one picture appears on a page, they are listed additionally in alphabetical order from top left to bottom right.

BLACK AND WHITE SECTION

Aerofilms 58, 73, 75, 80, 82, 85, 88, 96, 97, 98, 112, 113, 116, 124, 134, 137, 141, 143, 157, 169, 173, 188, 194, 197, 205, 208, 211b, 213, 222, 225, 229, 293, 323, 325, 347, 355

BBC Hulton Picture Library 17, 28, 40, 46, 71, 238, 266, 345

Bristol United Press 165

Colorsport 131, 154, 193, 210, 233, 271, 341

Eastern Daily Press 132

FA News 105

Forward Air 257

Adrian Gibson 34b, 34c, 44, 51, 138, 145, 149, 153, 163, 171, 175, 183, 202, 204, 217, 221, 303

Glasgow Herald 359

Grimsby Evening Telegraph 106

Jack Helliar 260

Simon Inglis 14, 19, 22, 36, 37, 55, 77, 78, 84, 93, 104, 133, 156, 159, 161, 166, 167, 176, 178, 196, 200, 214, 273, 275, 277, 279, 280, 281, 282, 283, 286, 287, 290, 291, 299, 303, 304, 307, 308, 310, 312, 313, 314, 320, 321, 322, 327, 330, 331, 333, 335, 338, 340, 342

Ipswich Town Football Club 128

Lancashire Picture Agency Ltd 69

Liverpool Daily Post and Echo 211a

Jim McAusland 315

Manchester United Supporters' Club 60

Mitchell & Averell 284

Tom Morris 268

Ged Murray 34a, 42, 65, 66, 68

Jack Murray 63, 248, 296, 302

Norval Photographers Ltd 336

Martin Parr 86, 123, 356

The Photo Source 39, 180

Picture House 118

Popperfoto 12a, 30

Port Vale Football Club 207

Press Association 64

Sheffield Wednesday Football Club 20

Phil Soar 12b

Sport and General 16, 240, 244, 262, 348

Sporting Pictures(UK) Ltd 99, 101, 110, 115, 126, 146, 151, 162, 185, 199, 219, 264

Stan Plus Stan Two Photography 103

Stewarts and Lloyds Ltd 306

Syndication International 11, 31, 32, 50, 91

D. C. Thompson 319

Waller and Partners 121

Watford Football Club 231

Horace Wetton 220

COLOUR SECTION

Colorsport iib, ivb, va, via, vib, vic, viic, viid, viie

Adrian Gibson i

Oldham's Press iia

Peebles Publications viiib

Sport and General iiib

Sporting Pictures(UK) Ltd iiia, iva, vb, viia, viib

Taylor Industrial Photography viiia